BENEATH THE MASK

Beneath the Mask

AN INTRODUCTION TO THEORIES OF PERSONALITY

Christopher F. Monte
Elizabeth Seton College

Praeger Publishers · New York

© 1977 by Christopher F. Monte
All rights reserved

Library of Congress Cataloging in Publication Data

Monte, Christopher F
    Beneath the mask.

    Bibliography: p. 6.41
    Includes index.
    1. Personalities. I. Title.
BF698.M64   155.2   73–15177
ISBN 0–03–033696–1

Printed in the United States of America
789   074   9 8 7 6 5 4 3 2

COPYRIGHT ACKNOWLEDGMENTS

From *Studies on Hysteria* by Joseph Breuer and Sigmund Freud, translated and edited by James Strachey, published in the United States by Basic Books, Inc., by arrangement with The Hogarth Press. From *The Interpretation of Dreams* by Sigmund Freud, translated and edited by James Strachey, published in the United States by Basic Books, Inc., by arrangement with George Allen and Unwin, Ltd. From "Mourning and Melancholia," in *Collected Papers* by Sigmund Freud, Volume IV, authorized translation under the supervision of Joan Riviere, published by Basic Books, Inc., by arrangement with The Hogarth Press, Ltd. and The Institute of Psycho-Analysis, London. From "On Beginning the Treatment," in *Collected Papers* by Sigmund Freud, Volume II, authorized translation under the supervision of Joan Riviere, published by Basic Books, Inc., by arrangement with The Hogarth Press, Ltd. and The Institute of Psycho-Analysis, London. From *The Origins of Psycho-Analysis: Letters to Wilhelm Fliess, Drafts and Notes, 1887–1902* by Sigmund Freud, edited by Marie Bonaparte, Anna Freud and Ernst Kris, copyright 1954 by Basic Books, Inc., Publishers, New York. From *The Life and Work of Sigmund Freud,* Volume 1, by Ernest Jones, M.D., copyright 1953 by Ernest Jones, Basic Books, Inc., Publishers, New York. From *Three Essays on the Theory of Sexuality* by Sigmund Freud, translated and newly edited by James Strachey, © 1962 by Sigmund Freud Copyrights, Ltd. Reprinted by permission of Basic Books, Inc., Publishers, New York. From "Further Remarks on the Defence of Neuro-Psychoses," in *Collected Papers* by Sigmund Freud, Volume I, authorized translation under the supervision of Joan Riviere, published by Basic Books, Inc., Publishers, New York, by arrangement with The Hogarth Press, Ltd. and The Institute of Psycho-Analysis, London. From *New*

For my mother and father

PREFACE

For most practical purposes, psychological theories of personality may just as well be called theories of human nature. The psychologist, like the philosophers who preceded him through this terrain, endeavors to make sense of human conduct, to discover the uniformities of character among individuals, and to devise general principles to explain particular motives. My purpose in this book is to present for the undergraduate and graduate student of psychology a selection of competing and sometimes complementary theories of human nature that attempt to capture scientifically what some philosophers feel we intuitively already know about ourselves.

It rapidly becomes apparent, however, to even the most casual observer of personality psychology, that each theorist approaches the problem of human nature with rather different assumptions, scientific strategies, and different psychological objectives to be reached through his theory. Hence, what we *think* we know about humans and what *scientific* personality theorists have been willing or able to *capture* within their theories are widely separate accomplishments. The constraints imposed by scientific method upon the theorist of human conduct are given fuller exposition in the first chapter. For the present it is sufficient to point out that personality theories are, like nearly every other kind of theory in psychology, attempts to understand the understander.

No special prior knowledge about personality theory is required to use this book, but a background in general or introductory psychology will be helpful. Each chapter was written to stand alone as a self-contained unit requiring no lead in from the others. Thus, with the exception of the two chapters on Freud (2 and 3), the instructor is permitted maximum flexibility in assigning the sequence of theorists for his or her course. No single personality book ever contains exactly the selection of theories desired by every professor, but the relative independence of chapters in this book should go a long way toward allowing the teacher to shape his course to his own interests and expertise.

Sixteen theorists are given comprehensive treatment in the chapters that follow, a number far too large to be treated comfortably in a one-semester course. Yet this broad array is necessary to permit the instructor to bring to the course his own special emphases. Some teachers may stress the empirical and experimentally derived theories of personality like those of Lewin (Chapter 11), Miller and Dollard and Bandura and Walters (Chapter 14), or Eysenck (Chapter 15). Or the course may reflect the instructor's interest in Freudian and neo-Freudian views by emphasizing the theories of Freud (Chapters 2 and 3), Jung (Chapter 4), Adler (Chapter 5), Horney (Chapter 6), and Erikson and Fromm (Chapter 10). Other emphases will suggest themselves to individual teachers who will find a place of distinction for theorists like Kelly (Chapter 9), Allport (Chapter 12), Maslow and Rogers (Chapter 13), R. D. Laing (Chapter 8), and Harry Stack Sullivan (Chapter 7).

Within a chapter, each theorist's viewpoint has been presented with an emphasis on the intellectual origins or antecedents of the theory. Rather than simply presenting the theorist's conception as it existed in his final or most recent writing, each theory, so far as it is possible, was presented as it was developed: that is, as a slowly evolving set of ideas, hunches, principles whose form and content were influenced by other theorists, by discoverable errors, or by careful experimentation. In some cases, where the published information warranted this kind of inference, emphasis was given to the ways in which the theorist's personal life-circumstances affected his conception of human nature. My intention was to avoid the all too frequent textbook distortion whereby students are permitted a view of the theorist's destination without accompanying him on the journey. Understandably, students tend to view theories presented in this way as frozen and eminently forgettable sets of facts. Hence, each chapter in this book presents not merely the finished theoretical product but also the steps that led to its manufacture.

It is my privilege to acknowledge several debts of gratitude. Anna Freud was especially kind in permitting me to visit with her at her home in London, in July, 1974, to discuss the chapters on the work of her father. Carl Rogers, though he believes textbooks like this one merely rehash what he has already said better, was generous in sending along a bibliography and an unpublished paper for my use. Neal Miller's courtesy in providing reprints of his work and in reading and commenting upon the material in Chapter 14 concerning his collaboration with John Dollard is greatly appreciated. Marian Margaret Sullivan and the staff of Elizabeth Seton College library deserve my undying gratitude for arranging extended loan privileges during the years I worked on the book and for their customary excellence in fulfilling impossible demands. Dr. Eduardo Paderon, colleague and friend, provided many hours of stimulating discussion that shaped some of my ideas in presenting the theorists, and he was kind enough to read and comment upon several chapters. Finally, I owe much to my wife, Regina, both for her skillful editorial assistance and for communicating to me her special sense of curiosity and intellectual delight in new ideas.

C.F.M.

CONTENTS

10 ERIK ERIKSON AND ERICH FROMM
Psychoanalytic Social Psychology   344

11 KURT LEWIN
Field Theory   400

12 GORDON W. ALLPORT
Trait and Self Theory   444

13 ABRAHAM MASLOW AND CARL ROGERS
Self-Actualization Theory   480

BENEATH THE MASK

1 VARIETIES OF THEORY AND BASIC ISSUES

True, whoever looks into the mirror of the water will see first of all his own face. Whoever goes to himself risks a confrontation with himself. The mirror does not flatter, it faithfully shows whatever looks into it; namely, the face we never show to the world because we cover it with the persona, *the mask of the actor. But the mirror lies behind the mask and shows the true face.*

C. G. JUNG, *Archetypes of the Collective Unconscious*

Problem of the Mask: An Illustrative Case

Five-year-old Jean-Mary is either a *uniquely* deceitful, shrewd, vengeance-seeking, and aggressive rascal, or she is an intelligent but *typical* child driven by the press of circumstance to inventive desperation. The difference in interpretation is largely dependent on the interpreter. When Jean-Mary's own mother describes her, Jean-Mary is a lovable imp. But when Jean-Mary's best friend's mother describes her, she is a spiteful and vicious troublemaker. Imagine the following scene:

> Jean-Mary is playing tea party outside her house with her friend Roselle, also age five years. During the course of play, between innumerable servings of invisible tea, a dispute erupts that is marked by name calling and some one-sided hair pulling, and it culminates in Roselle's smacking Jean-Mary on the head with a toy broom handle. As Jean-Mary, tearfully surprised, hurt, and somewhat befuddled, bawls uncontrollably, Roselle takes her leave with the ultimate parting shot: "I'm not going to be your friend anymore!" Pique added to injury.
>
> Jean goes inside her house where Mommy repairs a wounded pigtail, cleans the tearful little puckered face, and soothes a bruised ego. Somewhat assuaged by Mommy's gift of a few coins for ice cream, Jean-Mary proceeds to the ice-cream truck parked on her street and purchases a luscious chocolate eclair pop with a delectably crunchy crushed-almond coating. Continuing down the block, delectable almond-covered bait in hand, Jean-Mary approaches Roselle's house and confronts the startled and wary former best-friend-life-

long-bosom-for-always-buddy. "I'm not mad, Roselle. Come back to my house to play. See, I bought you an ice cream."

Upon return to Jean-Mary's back yard, Roselle sits contentedly munching her almond-covered goody, and between mouthfuls of ice cream, talks to the other "guests" at the tea party. A rather generous bite of ice cream is interrupted by a toy broom handle brought smartly across the back of Roselle's no-longer-wary little head. Jean-Mary, rejoicing in her revengeful triumph, a happy state marred only by the smallest twinge of guilt, watches Roselle fling down the half-eaten almond-coated chocolate eclair ice-cream pop. Roselle has learned an important lesson about the world: Beware of playmates who turn the other cheek and proffer ice cream. Jean-Mary has learned two important lessons: (1) Don't use muscle when shrewdness will do. (2) It is pitiful to waste a perfectly good ice cream on revenge, but it feels good.

The parents of both young ladies come together in mutual hostility and distrust. It is incomprehensible to Jean-Mary's mother that Roselle's mother is unable to see that *her* daughter is an "instigator." Roselle's mother is convinced that Jean's unladylike behavior is surpassed only by the ignorance and blindness of her mother. Their mutual communication takes the form of screamed accusations.

Both Jean-Mary and Roselle, the chief characters of this drama, evidence behaviors, reactions, feelings that can be characterized as *personality.* But what exactly is "personality" in this adventure? Would precise knowledge of the meaning of *personality* aid in understanding Jean-Mary's and Roselle's actions? To be completely fair, it is important to point out before proceeding that, for psychologists, at least, these questions are unanswerable. More precisely, those psychologists who have answered them rarely find agreement among their colleagues.

Part of the problem lies in the difficulty of deciding on those characteristics of a person that evidence personality. Gordon Allport (1968, p. 377) framed the psychologist's difficulty with some precision: "How shall a psychological life history be written? What processes and what structures must a full-bodied account of personality include? How can one detect unifying threads in a life, if they exist?" If this small fragment ripped from the stream of episodes that compose the lives of Jean-Mary and Roselle has any meaning whatsoever, how shall it be construed by the investigator of personality? Are Jean's and Roselle's actions situationally determined? personally determined? biologically determined? parentally determined? Is this the *real* Jean-Mary we observe, the genuine *person* who has slipped out from behind the mask of childhood? Or is the incident so unusual as to have no connection to the "unifying threads" of Jean-Mary's ongoing life history? *Actor or mask? Person or situation? Enduring characteristic or transient response?* More fundamentally, it is possible to ask whether questions like these are of any use to psychologists.

Some Ways Personality Is Construed: Personality Theories

In this book, sixteen discrete, sometimes overlapping, theories of personality are presented. Almost always, a particular theorist's viewpoint is recounted with careful attention to the detail and emphasis that characterized the theorist's own development of those concepts. Each of the sixteen theories, in so far as it is possible, is given full and sympathetic treatment. The goal is to expose each theory in a light that reflects its contribution to the field of personality in its entirety and in a way that does not violate the theorist's own struggle to understand human nature.

The consequence of this sympathetic approach is that some residue of disappointment is inevitably deposited. "But which theory is right?" students protest. "That is an inappropriate question because it is unanswerable," instructors reply. To some extent, the student's question is a good one, an inquiry deserving of reply on its own terms. It represents the timeless desire to know with some precision whether human existence is meaningful; whether, in fact, anyone has discovered a strategy for making sense of human nature.

Yet, the teacher's traditional reply is a fair one, for it suggests that absolute truths, unbending certainties, are not to be found in psychology's study of personality. The Socratic dictum "Know thyself" is always interpreted, never merely obeyed. The dilemma boils down to a single issue: How is one to decide among the *interpretations* of human personality? Psychologists are reluctant to answer this question because a unified strategy of determining the validity of competing theories is not yet within reach. And if such validity tests were to be agreed upon, some theories are constructed in ways that defy tests of their accuracy.

Unfortunately, it is precisely such questions about the accuracy of personality theories that engender student frustration. A *scientific* theory of personality is likely to be a far different thing in structure and content from any common-sense notion of what a useful theory of human nature should be. Restrictions imposed by scientific method make it a near certainty that satisfying generalizations about human conduct will yield to unsatisfying, sometimes trivial, experimental abstractions. Carlson (1971, p. 207) has listed the limitations of current research methods in personality:

> We cannot study the organization of personality because we know at most only one or two "facts" about any subject. We cannot study the stability of personality, nor its development over epochs of life, because we see our subjects for an hour. We cannot study the problems or capacities of the mature individual, because we study late adolescents [i.e., college students]. We cannot study psychosexuality, because we avoid looking at distinctive qualities of masculinity and femininity as a focal problem. We cannot study how persons strive for their important goals, because we elect to induce motiva-

tional sets. We cannot study constitutional, temperamental variables because ... we do not consider biological bases of personality. We cannot study the development and power of friendship—nor the course of true love—because we choose to manipulate interpersonal attraction.

The picture does not have to remain so bleak, Carlson suggests, because it is possible to restore to personality research a concern for the "whole person":

> Obviously, no single scientist, no single study, no single research tradition can possibly deal "scientifically" with anything so complex as a whole person. But the attempt can be made collectively and cumulatively. [Carlson, 1971, p. 207]

None of the theories represented in the chapters that follow can convey the essence of Jean-Mary's personality as richly as a series of anecdotes can. Critical incidents in Jean-Mary's life are more satisfying, aesthetically more pleasing, than any scientific theory of personality could ever be. But no collection of anecdotes, no grouping of revealing crises, can effectively explain or predict *general* human behavior. If the question "Which theory is right?" remains unanswerable, it nevertheless requires some patience, some forebearance, to understand why.

A related issue concerns the reasons that some personality psychologists have preferred to be called *personologists.* This term is meant to indicate a distinctly different research tradition and conceptual strategy from that of psychologists who have traditionally been known as personality theorists. Henry A. Murray, an early pioneer of personology, defined the concept this way:

> The branch of psychology which principally concerns itself with the study of *human lives* and the factors that influence their course, which investigates *individual differences* and types of personality, may be termed 'personology' instead of 'the psychology of personality,' a clumsy and tautological expression. Personology, then, is the science of men, taken as gross units ... [1938, p. 4; italics added].

The personologist is concerned with the *life history,* the coherent stream of feelings, events, traits, and situations that characterize individual personalities. Thus, the question "How shall a psychological life history be written?" is a *personological* query. The question "Do subjects high in their need to achieve success cheat on exams more often than low need achievement subjects?" is not. The essential difference lies not so much in the content of the two inquiries as in the lack of breadth evidenced by the second one. Personologists are interested in whole persons, in their unique adjustment to the circumstances of their lives. The personologist would find the second question of interest only to the extent that research results obtained under its banner fit into an entire pattern of information about high need achievement subjects.

Although the use of the term *personology* lacks precision, its adoption by some psychologists who explore personality indicates the extent to which opinion differs in finding a way to understand human differences. Personality theories have been classified in an endless variety of ways. For present purposes, a fourfold scheme of classification will suffice to point up the similarities and differences among the theories that constitute this book.

Interpersonal Theory
(With a Detour through Phenomenology)

One way that psychologists define personality focuses on an aspect that has come to have increasing significance for a wide range of different theorists. The social context of a human life was given its strongest emphasis in the work of Harry Stack Sullivan: "... personality is the relatively enduring pattern of recurrent interpersonal situations which characterize a human life" (1953b, p. 111).

If we agree to conceptualize personality as a pattern of person-to-person relationships, Roselle's personality might be described as initially aggressive (she hits Jean-Mary first), independent (she storms off, "not wanting to be friends" any longer), and suspicious. Jean-Mary's personality, in terms of her relations with Roselle, might be described as initially meek, then cunning or deceitful, and capped with a dash of aggression. Of course, we would have to observe both girls in their relations to many "significant others," as Sullivan terms influential persons in one's life.

Sullivan would begin such a study with an investigation of the quality, intensity, and consistency of the relationship between the infant Jean-Mary and her "mothering one." Through nonverbal patterns of communication between mother and child, the person first develops an orientation to the world and its people. The manner in which the mother handles, feeds, and soothes the infant is decisive, in Sullivan's view, for shaping the child's later emotional expectancies in his dealings with his social world.

With the focus centered on interpersonal relationships, the kinds of questions deemed appropriate are relatively obvious. For example, Sullivan might ask, "How does Jean-Mary typically react when meeting people for the first time?" Or he might inquire, "Are there any common characteristics among the people Jean-Mary befriends?" Or, "What particular people have played the role of significant other in Jean-Mary's life?" Clearly, the interest of the interpersonal theorist lies in the pattern of communication between people. The interpersonal approach does not exclude such aspects of personality as fantasy, unconscious strivings, or physical and biological variables. It merely subsumes these person characteristics under the central concept of human relations.

The interpersonal approach may be extended to include attempts to understand the individual's unique perception of his social world. Though the emphasis remains on the quality of person-to-person contact, the *phenomenological* theorist wonders how those contacts look through the eyes of the involved individuals. "Phenomenology" is derived from a Greek root, *phainesthai,* meaning "to appear," "as it appears" (Shlien, 1963, p. 298). The preoccupation of phenomenologically oriented personality psychologists is the immediate sensory experience of the individual and the meaning he derives from it. How does he understand *his* reality? Shlien described the concerns of phenomenology well:

> If the mind could not think silently; if there were outwardly audible and visible signs directly indicating specific mental activities, we would all be rank behaviorists, and the history of psychology, to say the least, would have hinged on a very different set of data. But this is not the case. As things stand, we have both internal and external events *experienced* by the total organism; experienced, recorded at some level of awareness, and in some cases, given meaning. The phenomenologist is convinced that much goes on "inside," and that the behavioristic concept of the "empty organism" is narrow, and largely spurious. [1963, pp. 291–292]

Thus, for example, George Kelly (1955), whose theory is given consideration in Chapter 9, was convinced that every person holds an implicit personality theory that allows him to make sense of the people in his world. The object of personality investigation for Kelly was to develop means to assess the personal constructs (subjective meanings) used by a person in predicting the behavior of the significant figures in his life.

R. D. Laing, considered more fully in Chapter 8, combined the interpersonal strategy of Sullivan with the existentialism of Jean-Paul Sartre to create a social phenomenological theory (e.g., 1969b; Laing and Cooper, 1971; Laing, Phillipson, and Lee, 1966). To take only one example of Laing's phenomenology, consider the complexities involved in a husband-wife relationship that is based on mutual distrust. The wife feels her husband often deceives her. The husband feels that he is totally honest with her. Each of these people is certain that the other does not understand how he or she feels. The following phenomenal evaluations are thus possible:

wife feels:	"He deceives me."
husband feels:	"She deceives herself."
wife feels:	"He thinks I think He thinks I am foolish."
husband feels:	"She thinks I think She thinks I am dishonest."

The spiraling whorl of mismatched expectations and interpretations escalates until each partner is no longer responding to the other as he exists, but rather as he *thinks* the *other thinks.* Consequently, to understand this couple's *relationship* it is first necessary to make explicit all of the implicit partner expectations. To enter the phenomenal world of another is an exciting but supremely difficult task.

Trait Theory
(With a Detour through Dimensional Type Theory)

Another way of defining personality, and a way that is not necessarily antithetical to the interpersonal approach, is to seek enduring and stable "traits" within an individual that provoke him to action in some *consistent* way. Trait theorists observe and attempt to measure these enduring tendencies to action in an effort to allow comparisons to be made among individuals differing in the degree to which they possess the trait. Gordon Allport, whose theory is presented in Chapter 12, defined personality as "the dynamic organization within the individual of those psychophysical systems that determine his characteristic behavior and thought" (1961, p. 28).

Allport's definition stresses three aspects of the trait approach. Traits, in the first place, do not exist singly or in isolation. They form, instead, *patterns* or clusters with the individual's total personality. Secondly, the origin of traits is to be sought in some combination of *psychological* and *biological* processes, like the functioning of the endocrine and central nervous systems. Finally, the *pattern* that traits form within any individual is different from that formed in any other person: *individuals are unique.* The traits that persons possess are general, common to all men. The pattern or configuration, however, is the source of uniqueness.

Trait theories, indeed the concept of trait itself, have come under heavy criticism in contemporary psychology (e.g., Kelly, 1955; and Mischel, 1968). One of the chief criticisms has been that any trait attributed to a person by an observer, say, high aggressiveness, is more easily explained as a product of the *observer's* personal reactions or measuring instruments. In theory, a trait should be consistently translated into characteristic behaviors that transcend the immediate situation. But investigators have failed to find the degree of trait consistency that the concept implies.

Nevertheless, the notion of "trait" may yet prove useful to psychologists who, like Kelly, are interested in a person's own implicit theory of personality. The average layman, if such a creature exists, tends to judge others in terms of traits. Whether the traits actually exist in the person to whom they are attributed is irrelevant. They exist in the mind of the attributor (Asch, 1946; Heider, 1958; Bruner, *et al.,* 1958).

To say that Jean-Mary is *highly intelligent, cunning,* or *deceitful* is to impute three specific traits to her. Each of the traits may interact with another: High intelligence is conducive to extreme cunning, deceitfulness directs intelligence into antisocial behaviors, and so on. But precisely *how high* is Jean-Mary's intelligence compared to other individuals? Is she *more or less* cunning than the average five-year-old child? Questions of degree clearly indicate that some hypothetical scale, ranging from low to high, may be employed to locate Jean-Mary's constellation of traits in a universe of varying degrees. Thus, trait theory may be supplemented by *dimensional* concepts.

Dimensional theories usually postulate two or more opposite *types* of personality lying at extreme anchor points of the dimension. Thus, for example, Carl Jung (Chapter 4) proposed that individuals may be introverted or extroverted. Shy, retiring, withdrawn, intellectual, and anxious, the *introvert* represents one type of personality. The introvert's opposite type, characterized by a sociable, outgoing, optimistic, and impulsive nature, lies at the opposite end of this personality dimension and is described by the label *extrovert.* Thus, each type of personality is defined as a cluster of interrelated traits. The important point is that one's *degree* of introversion may vary from low to high. The less an individual's degree of introversion, the more his personality presumably leans toward extroversion.

Some place between the extremes, perhaps at dead center, lie the *ambiverts.* The ambivert personality is thus presumed to partake of traits in equal degree from both ends of the scale. Eysenck (Chapter 15) has proposed an experimentally based biological explanation for the dimensional types of Introvert and Extrovert (e.g., 1967). In Eysenck's scheme, however, one's type of personality is a product of a multiplicity of social and biological factors that are inferred from observable (i.e., measurable) traits.

Trait and type theorists, consequently, tend to ask questions about personality that involve some reliance on measuring devices. "What is Jean-Mary's *score* on the Standford-Binet test of intelligence?" "At what *rate* is Jean-Mary able to acquire a conditioned eye-blink reflex to the sound of a tone?" "How does Jean-Mary compare to other five-year-old children in the *rate* at which she can detect errors in a page of printed numbers?"

Psychoanalytic Theory
(With a Detour through Ego Psychology)

Inferences about the nature of internal states from observable behaviors are also characteristic of a third way in which psychologists define personality. Psychoanalytic theories assume the existence of *unconscious internal states* that motivate an individual's overt actions. Sigmund Freud (Chapters 2 and 3) proposed in his final model of the mind that sexual and aggressive motives could shape behavior without the direct awareness of the individual (e.g., 1933).

Remembered dreams, daytime fantasies, verbal associations, creative stories about ambiguous drawings, and, sometimes, directly observed behavior make up the data of the psychoanalytic approach. Each of these observable indices, when properly interpreted, allows the psychoanalytic observer to assess the unobservable state of the person's colliding and discordant motives.

Freud's conception of personality assumed the existence of three mental agencies engaged in complex mutual exchanges of energy. Instincts or biological drives, collectively known as the *id,* with their unceasing pressure for satisfaction, instigate the development of a reality-oriented *ego* whose function it is to obtain needed gratifications. Sometimes the ego transgresses learned ethical or moral standards in attempting to secure satisfactions. Anxiety and conflict are the result. So for Freud, and for many other psychoanalytic theorists, personality might be defined as: ". . . a certain constancy [which] prevails in the ways the ego chooses for solving its tasks" (Fenichel, 1945, p. 523; see also Freud, 1933, Lecture 31).

Psychoanalytic theory is sometimes characterized as *psychodynamic state theory* (Mischel, 1968, 1973; Bandura, 1969). The slightly altered label is designed to emphasize an important characteristic of Freud's and his co-workers' theories: Drives, instincts, or motives direct behavioral sequences by channeling energy from an unconscious reservoir into conscious *symbolic* equivalents. Behavior, whether neurotic symptom or recurring dream, is always a sign of the dynamic interaction that lies below the surface. Thus, we might assume that Jean-Mary's frustration tolerance is low and that her aggression level is high. Her elaborate deception in employing the ice-cream bait, her willingness to waste a precious treat, and her seeming indifference to possible parental censure might all suggest a weak conscience (superego in Freud's terms). Depending upon the consequences of her act, the psychodynamic (psychoanalytic) theorist might make predictions about the future development of Jean-Mary's susceptibility to anxiety-provoking impulses in similar situations. For both trait and state theories, situations change; individual's motives (states) do not (Mischel, 1973).

The psychoanalytic theorist is thus prompted to make rather different inquiries from those previously considered. "Did Jean-Mary's dreams reveal a healthy resolution of her early attachment to her father and resentment of her mother?" "Is Jean-Mary comfortable in her sex role or would she prefer to be more masculine?" "To what extent does Jean-Mary experience conflict between her impulses to express anger and her learned ethical sense of wrongdoing?"

Freud's psychoanalytic theory has been modified and extended by his followers. His daughter, Anna Freud, initiated a major change in theoretical direction with the publication of her monograph on ego defense mechanisms (1936). Restricting her own work to therapy with children, Anna Freud suggested that psychoanalytic theory and psychotherapy could profit from more direct investigation of the conscious ego and its relations to the world, to the unconscious, and to the superego. Thus, with Anna Freud, psychoanalysis was no longer to be regarded as exclusively a "depth" psychology. The interaction of conscious and unconscious determinants of personality was now to be explored with the methods made available by Sigmund Freud.

Among the foremost proponents of the "new" ego psychology was Heinz Hartmann (1964) who suggested that the nature of personality might be illuminated by investigations of the "conflict-free" sphere of the ego, that is, of ego qualities that arise independently of the id. Hartmann was not suggesting that psychoanalytic theory become a psychology of consciousness, but that reality functioning—i.e., adaptation to life—could best be understood as a cooperative effort of the unconscious and its equal partner, the ego (1964, Chap. 1).

Erik Erikson (Chapter 10) has also made significant contributions to psychoanalytic ego psychology. Erikson has developed a social and biological conception of the individual personality as a product of a series of interrelated *psychosocial crises* (e.g., 1950, 1959). For Erikson, the development of a personal sense of self, of what he calls *ego identity*, is a complex process involving the interaction of biological drives and the society in which the individual matures. The emphasis, of course, is on the individual's awareness of the identity society accords him and the sense of self he himself has struggled to shape.

Thus, with the ego psychologists, psychoanalytic theory shifted somewhat in the direction of social and interpersonal theory. Although unconscious instinctual conflict remained a significant part of the total picture, man's needs for autonomy and self-direction were now also considered suitable for psychoanalytic exploration.

Social Learning Theory
(With a Detour through Behaviorism)

Most views of personality, regardless of their theoretical viewpoint, assume that human behavior is malleable and shaped by its consequences (Skinner, 1953, 1974). Relatively enduring changes in behavior that result from the impact of environmental stimuli are the objects of a special field of study within psychology. Learning theorists, like Pavlov and Skinner, have used laboratory methods to study the ways in which organisms acquire a host of reliably repeatable responses. The advantage of such investigations was that the theorist confined himself to an analysis of *observable* responses. Inferences about unobservable internal states of the organism were avoided. John B. Watson (1913), the founder of a school of psychological thought known as *behaviorism,* went so far as to assume that all significant emotional, cognitive, or motivational aspects of an individual were learned responses subject to modification by proper manipulation of the stimuli that controlled them.

Radical behaviorism, as Watson's and some of his later coworkers' concepts were called, further assumed that conditioned responses were acquired more or less automatically, more or less independently of the subject's volition or expectations (Bandura, 1974). As sophistication in learning theory increased, it became apparent that a subject's expectations, knowledge, and willingness to perform have significant effects on the outcome of any learning situation. Furthermore, attention became focused on animal and human capacity for *imitation learning*, the ability to follow the behaviors of a model. The subject matter of learning theory was no longer restricted to enforced stimulus-response pairings like those investigated in Pavlov's laboratory. Nor was attention restricted to the effects of reinforcements on voluntary responses like those investigated in B. F. Skinner's laboratory. Social interactions as mediators of reinforcements became the objects of study. And with this broadening in focus came a concern for the long dismissed internal states of the organism (Bandura, 1974, p. 865).

Social learning theory, initiated by Miller and Dollard (1941), at first followed the ground plan developed by the early behaviorists. Higher mental processes were conceptualized as internal elaborations of simple conditioned responses. Slowly, this conception was modified to include the possibility of creative interaction between an individual and his environment. Not only can a person's behavior be shaped by appropriate schedules of reinforcement, but, more important, the person can reinforce himself for behaviors that he values. "The development of self-reactive functions gives humans a capacity for self-direction. They do things that give rise to self-satisfaction and self-worth, and they refrain from behaving in ways that evoke self-punishment" (Bandura, 1974, p. 861). Principled people who conduct their lives in accord with strongly held convictions of what is ethical or moral often receive few overt rewards for their conduct. Yet, behaviors that meet their internal criteria of "goodness" evoke self-reinforcing evaluations.

Bandura (e.g., 1969) has also introduced into social learning theory the idea that a person may acquire a response without direct reinforcement. Instead, observing a model perform a response that is reinforced may be sufficient (Bandura, 1965a). Bandura has suggested that a great many complex responses, some of which would be regarded by any theorist as evidencing "personality," are acquired in this indirect way. In watching a cowboy movie in which the hero (in the white hat) subdues the villain (in the black hat) and marches off into the sunset (with or without the heroine), children covertly imagine themselves in the place of the hero. They identify with his victories and suffer humiliation at his defeats.

Applying similar notions to Jean-Mary's personality, it is possible to analyze her interaction with Roselle in terms of her past reinforcement history and the nature of the models to which she had been exposed. It is likely that Jean-Mary had previously been reinforced for aggressive behaviors, or that she had observed an older brother or sister in a successful aggressive encounter. Perhaps Jean-Mary had been "instructed" by her mother and father "not to take guff from anyone—dish out what you get, and don't come crying to me!"

The kinds of questions provoked by a social-learning analysis of personality have a quality of simple precision lacking in some of the questions asked by other theoretical viewpoints: "Do the important models available to Jean-Mary demonstrate the rewarding consequences of aggression?" "Has Jean-Mary endured similar frustrations in the past?" "Was the outcome of her encounter with Roselle rewarding or punishing?"

The four varieties of personality theory we have surveyed are summarized in Table 1–1.

The Fundamental Questions: Jean-Mary Revisited

Despite the differences in emphasis and focus of attention, all these approaches (and there are other varieties) share several common concerns. All personality theories, to differing degrees, ask three fundamental questions about people:

1. *Developmental-Historical Question:* How did the person come to behave as he now does?
2. *Prediction-Consistency Question:* Will this person behave similarly in similar situations at a later time?
3. *Uniqueness-Generality Question:* To what extent are the effects of significant people and events on *this* individual similar to their effects on other individuals?

Even though there are real differences among theoretical strategies, a common core of assumptions may be discerned. Making these similarities and differences explicit would be a monumental undertaking. Some indication, however, of the general contrasts and agreements can be provided with the help of another critical episode from Jean-Mary's life.

Jean-Mary entered adolescence as an attractive young lady. One evening, when Jean-Mary was eighteen years old, a young man she was dating dropped by for an unexpected visit. He was told by her mother that Jean-Mary was in her room doing some ironing and would join him shortly in the living room.

Upon entering the living room to greet her date, Jean-Mary was sprayed in the face with whipped cream from an aerosol can deftly aimed by her hilariously laughing, jubilant boyfriend. She stood shocked and speechless, caught motionless between the impulse to tears and the urge to strike back. The upshot of the whole affair was that Jean-Mary ran tearfully from the spot to cry uncontrollably in the privacy of her room. She was to date that young man only once more in order to tell him that she was breaking off their relationship.

TABLE 1–1: OVERVIEW OF FOUR TYPES OF PERSONALITY THEORY

THEORY	DATA	PERSONALITY DEFINED
Interpersonal (and Phenomenological)	Observed interactions with significant others and/or verbal expressions of person's private interpretations of self and others.	Habitual ways of responding to others; person's interpretations of such interactions.
Trait (and Type)	Measured degree of response similarity across situations.	Enduring nervous and/or glandular system characteristics and structures; chronic biological drive levels.
Psychoanalytic (and Ego Psychology)	Dreams, slips of tongue, creative stories or art, free-associations, neurotic symptoms.	Characteristic ways of resolving unconscious conflicts of sexual and aggressive drives with learned ethical values, or conflicts of impulses toward self-fulfillment with impulses toward self-fragmentation.
Social Learning	Any behavior, some verbal reports of private experience, schedules of direct and vicarious reinforcements.	Acquired observable response repertoire that may have "private" (cognitive) components.

When asked later why a crude practical joke like this one produced such a reaction in her, Jean-Mary answered simply: "I don't know. I felt so—so degraded!"

It may profitably be asked what is revealed of Jean-Mary's personality in this incident when viewed through the perspective of interpersonal theory, trait theory, psychoanalytic theory, or social learning theory?

Interpersonal Theory

The first matter of significance is the extent to which this second critical episode reveals characteristics that are consistent with the insights gleaned from the first, ice-cream episode. If we assume that careful deliberation and a willingness to delay immediate aggressive impulse satisfaction are enduring characteristics of Jean-Mary's personal relationships, then there is clearly continuity between the episodes. Once again, Jean-Mary has terminated an interpersonal relationship after a pause to consolidate her thinking.

From the phenomenological point of view, Jean's image of self was probably that of an "elegant" young lady, to judge by her comments on the damaging effects of being whipped-creamed. Instead of complementing her role of "elegantly attractive woman," her admiring suitor revealed that he construed her as a suitable target for a practical joke. This violation of Jean-Mary's expectancy was both frightening and infuriating. Her past interpersonal relationships with significant others (e.g., Roselle) may have contributed to this need to be sure of the constancy and security of a relationship. Thus, for interpersonal theory both the prediction-consistency question and the developmental-historical question are answered by seeking continuities in the quality of person-to-person contacts. And in both cases, the answer that is acceptable involves pointing to observable behaviors and verbal reports from which phenomenological inferences can be made.

The uniqueness-generality question cannot be answered without a comparative baseline. Yet theorists like Karen Horney (Chapter 6) and Sullivan (Chapter 7) proposed that basic, unresolved anxiety evoked in infancy by an indifferent or detached mother would reliably produce an overblown adult need for security and personal control. The difficulty with interpretations such as these lies in the assumption of internal, unobservable psychological conflicts.

Trait Theory

Jean's inappropriate reaction to her boyfriend's primitive sense of humor betrays the existence of a high degree of anxiety. The trait of high anxiety that characterizes Jean-Mary's present behavior probably also characterized her earlier activities with Roselle. Additionally, the trait of aggression might be brought into the discussion to account for her more sophisticated revenge in this later episode. Instead of physical revenge, this time the more sophisticated and mature Jean-Mary responds with social revenge: the termination of their relationship.

The difficulty with the trait explanation is the problem of finding the traits. The developmental-historical question can be answered only if aggressiveness and anxiety, and their interaction, can be shown to have originated either in an inherited pattern of nervous system functioning or in previous learned responses. In either case, once a nervous system dimension is postulated (e.g., Eysenck), or once a past pattern of reinforcements is evoked, the concept of trait becomes superflous.

The question most easily handled by the trait approach is the prediction-consistency question. If measurements are made of Jean-Mary's anxiety level and of her degree of aggressiveness, then we should be able to predict with some reliability her future anxieties and aggressions in situations that resemble the measurement situation. The uniqueness-generality question may similarly be handled by trait theory's resort to comparative measurements.

Psychoanalytic Theory

Through the eyes of a psychoanalytic investigator, the whipped-cream episode reveals the ambivalent and conflicting nature of Jean-Mary's love relationships. The boorish behavior of the boyfriend brings to the surface the latent hostility that until now was submerged in favor of a stronger love. At the moment of the disaster, Jean-Mary is caught between the warring impulses, and she withdraws to find a suitable, reality-oriented outlet for her aggression.

The psychoanalytic approach has no difficulty with the developmental-historical question. Indeed, this dimension is of supreme importance to all psychodynamic approaches. Jean's earlier difficulty with Roselle and her present abrasive contact with her boyfriend would both be interpreted as evidence of continual love-hate ambivalence. The problem with such interpretations is to demonstrate the existence of the unobservable conflict. The prediction-consistency question also presents little difficulty for the psychoanalytic formulation. Continuity of instinctual motives is always assumed. Precise predictions, however, can rarely be made.

The uniqueness-generality question is handled in a peculiar way by psychoanalytic theory. Assuming that basic drives or instincts are essentially similar from person to person, psychoanalytic theory postulates the existence of *universal combinations* of instincts. One of these, the Oedipal conflict, is seen as the basis for the person's development of a sexual identity, of techniques to deal with stress, and of his typical patterns of dealing with others. The fact that people differ in their "choice" of responses to these universals is given explicit treatment by psychoanalytic theory only when the individual succumbs to neurotic disorganization. This point is treated more fully in Chapters 2 and 3.

Social Learning Theory

The basic assumption underlying social learning theory, namely, that all significant human personality characteristics are acquired through interaction with the environment, is not unique to this formulation. However, the focus of analysis in social learning theory is on the schedules of reinforcement, the social mediators, and the intensity of the organism's needs. The first two of these characteristics are strictly observable phenomena.

Jean-Mary's early experiences with Roselle and, from her point of view, the successful outcome of the carefully plotted revenge served to reinforce this pattern of dealing with hurtful others. The developmental-historical question is thus answered by pointing to the similarity of the *situations and consequences of behavior in the past.* The prediction-consistency question is consequently interpreted as a special case of the historical-developmental question. For the social learning theorist there is no need to distinguish between the two inquiries.

The uniqueness-generality question, however, poses some problems. Although a particular individual's past reinforcement history could, in principle, be known, it rarely is. Inferences based on contemporary patterns of responding are made about the precise pattern of previous reinforcements that shaped the person's style of social interaction. Presumably, the number of possible patterns of past reinforcements, significant models, and acquired expectations is infinitely large. Uniqueness is thus a product of a multiplicity of environmental, including social, contingencies of reinforcement. The advantage is that analysis is largely restricted, thought not exclusively, to observable behavioral referents.

Jean-Mary had learned to expect to be treated with courtesy and respect by her intimates. Whatever the pattern of social reinforcements responsible for this expectation, her boyfriend rudely violated the sequence with intensely aversive consequences. The fact that Jean-Mary's ice-cream revenge was successful probably is responsible for the continuity of her behavior in the present situation.

The Actor and His Mask: Constraints of Scientific Methodology

In all of the approaches to personality discussed thus far, there is a sense of something missing, something not quite intellectually or aesthetically satisfying. It is as if the surface of an individual were described without ever really touching the underlying person. Henry Murray posed the difficulty in precise terms in his description of the *peripheralist* view of personality:

> Now since we are reasonably certain that all phenomena within the domain of personology are determined by excitations in the brain, the things which are objectively discernible—the outer environment, bodily changes, muscular movements, and so forth—are peripheral to the personality proper and hence those who traffic only with the former may be called *peripheralists.* ... To repeat, the man we are distinguishing is a *peripheralist* because he defines personality in terms of action *qua* action rather than in terms of some central process which the action manifests, and he is an *elementarist* because he regards personality as the sum total or product of interacting elements rather than a unity which may, for convenience, be analysed into parts. [1938, p. 7]

Contrasted with the peripheralist is what Murray called the *totalist*. The totalist craves "to know the inner nature of other persons as [he] knows [his] own . . ." (1938, p. 8). But in his strategy of abandoning the observable characteristics of the person, the totalist simultaneously abandons hope of reliable analysis of his data.

The dilemma is crucial for those psychologists who seek to provide a comprehensive, yet scientifically defensible account of human personality. All of the various theories of personality must rely, at some point, on observed behavior. Each approach, however, begins with observable behavior to a different degree. Unconscious states, for example, are not directly observable in themselves. Yet even an orthodox Freudian analyst must focus his attention on what people *do*, how they *behave* because of these underlying states. In the end, whether the theorist postulates an unconscious conflict, frustration of a biological drive, arousal of a brain mechanism, or the reinforcing effects of social approval, he must rely on observable behavior to construct and test his theory.

In this sense, a scientific theory is very restricted in what may be included within its bounds (Popper, 1959, 1963). It is generally agreed that a scientific theory must be rooted in observational data if it is ever to be tested. Karl Popper proposed that such theories must, in principle, be refutable by observations that they themselves specify as incompatible. Thus, the logic of a scientific theory must proceed as follows:

1. Human beings behave in ways A, B, C because of variables 1, 2, 3.
2. If this assertion (A, B, C and 1, 2, 3) is true, then observations D, E, F should be possible. Furthermore, if this assertion is true, then observations G, H, I should *not* be possible.
3. Observations D, E, F are made and confirm the theory. Observations G, H, I are attempted, but cannot be accomplished. The theory is further confirmed. (Popper, 1963; Cf. Campbell, 1969; Monte, 1975)

Thus, according to Popper, a theory must state not only what people are expected to do, but what, according to its own logic, they should be expected *not* to do. In effect, the scientific theory must state what observations it would take to disprove it. If such disconfirmatory observations can be made, the theory is refuted. This *criterion of refutability* guarantees that scientific theories will be stated in empirical, testable terms—in principle. The problem is that the majority of personality theories are couched in terms that make it difficult to determine what phenomena *could* prove them wrong.

For example, the cliché con game of "heads I win, tails you lose" is a nonrefutable statement. If the coin comes up heads, my prediction is confirmed. If the coin comes up tails, my prediction that I win is again confirmed. Barring the unlikely event that the coin stands on its edge, there are no possible observable outcomes that can disprove the prediction. Some personality theories are stated in terms like these. No conceivable observable behavioral outcome could count as evidence against the theory.

Thus the theory is so general and inclusive that the validity of its explanations must always be suspect. To be compatible with any and all behavioral outcomes is to be an accurate explanation of none.

This restriction to observable, refutable phenomena removes the flavor, the fullness of explanation that would be intuitively and aesthetically satisfying. No theory, in the present state of the art, can both comprehensively and empirically account for the wholeness, for the uniqueness, for the universality of human propensities, foibles, drives, abilities, desires. The person represented in a scientifically testable way is not the real person demanded by common sense. When we ask questions such as "What is Jean-Mary really like?" we fully expect some readily understandable statements about the true, private, *inner person* that Jean-Mary *really* is. This expectation is irrelevant to the scientific psychologist at the present stage of his inquiries. He is more concerned with establishing general and valid propositions that can be confirmed and serve, therefore, as the reliable nucleus of further generalizations. He can achieve validity and reliability only by restricting his inquiry to the observables. The "real inner person" —if such an entity exists—will have to be ignored for the present.

A Useful Metaphor: The Mask

Gordon Allport traced the etymological roots of the word *personality*. In classical Latin, the word *persona* was employed with a variety of meanings:

1. as one appears to others (but not as one really is)
2. the part someone (e.g., a philosopher) plays in life
3. an assemblage of personal qualities that fit a man for his work
4. distinction and dignity (as in a style of writing). [Allport, 1937, p. 26]

Allport further traced the meaning of the term *persona* to an antecedent phrase in Latin: *per sonare,* meaning "to sound through." The noun *persona* had originated as the designation for the masks worn by Greek actors and later adopted by their Roman counterparts. Thus, the phrase *per sonare* referred to the mouthpiece of the theatrical mask through which the actor beneath the facade projected his voice. The four meanings cited previously demonstrate that the term *persona* slowly evolved to a more abstract designation indicating the dichotomy between appearance (the mask) and the actor. The Greek equivalent, *prosôpon,* also designated the theatrical mask and the distinction between superficial and fundamental characteristics (Allport, 1937, p. 25).

The implication of Allport's survey of the linguistic roots of "personality" is that below the surface of *public* behavior there is a private, and perhaps different, person concealed from view. Nevertheless, it is possible to question the further implicit assumption that the inner person is more real or genuine than the surface phenomenon. Most contemporary psychologists, with the exception of the humanists (e.g., Rogers, Maslow) take a dim view of this distinction. To them it seems a great deal like magical thinking because they see no reason to look for inner persons when overt behavior is adequate for scientific study (cf. Skinner, 1953, 1956, 1963, 1971, 1974; Lundin, 1963; Berlyne, 1968; Wilkinson, 1973; Eysenck, 1963b; Kelly, 1955).

By contrast, other psychologists, like Angyal (1941, 1965), Laing, Sullivan, and Allport feel that theories of personality that attend only to observable behavior with no inferences or assumptions about an inner core of experience lose contact with the very stuff they seek to understand. The legitimacy of the separation between the actor (inner person) and his observables (the mask) is assumed by these theorists to be a personality given—with the stipulation that eventually, as theoretical sophistication grows, personality psychology will be able to reconstruct the whole person, weld together the necessarily fragmented elements of actor and mask into a unified scheme.

Reducing Jean-Mary's and Roselle's personalities to a description of their past reinforcement histories or to a discussion of their degrees of introversion/extroversion seems far removed from the "real" Roselle or from the "real" Jean-Mary. For our purposes, therefore, it will be an acknowledged and convenient metaphor to conceptualize personality as the study of the actor and his mask, as the person and his *persona.* It is a metaphor, however, and not a precise description or evaluation of theoretical strategies. Convenient in its role of conceptualizing the degree to which a particular theory contacts the whole person, the actor-mask analogy increases the risk of creating pseudoproblems in personality psychology. It is a risk, however, worth taking. The majority of theorists in this book seem to agree by their use of the metaphor in their writings.

Throughout the following chapters, the many theorists who actually explicitly employ the actor-mask metaphor in their works will be indicated (e.g., Freud, Chapters 2, 3; Jung, Chapter 4; Adler, Chapter 5; Laing, Chapter 8; Kelly, Chapter 9; Erikson and Fromm, Chapter 10; Allport, Chapter 12; and Maslow and Rogers, Chapter 13). Theorists who prefer equivalent formulations to distinguish between central and peripheral personality phenomena (e.g., Horney, Chapter 6; Sullivan, Chapter 7; Lewin, Chapter 11; and Miller and Dollard, Chapter 14) demonstrate the universality of this problem. Other theorists "solve" the problem by simple omission or by direct contradiction that such a problem exists (e.g., Eysenck, Chapter 15; Bandura and Walters, Chapter 14). Yet, by their omission of inner and outer, central and peripheral distinctions, these theorists indicate the complexity of the task of conceptualizing real people.

The metaphor of the actor and his mask was used by Carl Jung (see the epigraph at the opening of this chapter) to indicate the public self of the individual, the image he presents to others, as contrasted with his feelings, cognitions, and interpretations of reality anchored in his private self. Without adopting Jung's entire theoretical formulation, this usage of the term *persona* or mask will serve as the definition followed in this book. Jung defined the *persona* in this way:

> Fundamentally the persona is nothing real: it is a compromise be-
> tween individual and society as to what a man should appear to be.
> He takes a name, earns a title, exercises a function, he is this or that.
> In a certain sense all this is real, yet in relation to the essential
> individuality of the person concerned it is only a secondary reality,
> a compromise formation, in making which others often have a greater
> share than he. [1935, p. 158]

Jung seems to be identifying the *persona* with the concept of social role. The same use of the metaphor has been made in recent times by Erving Goff-man (1959; cf. 1961). Goffman has suggested, as had Jung, that the mask may become more real than the actor.

> [An] . . . illustration may be found in the raw recruit who initially
> follows army etiquette in order to avoid physical punishment and
> eventually comes to follow the rules so that his organization will not
> be shamed and his officers and fellow soldiers will respect him. [1959,
> p. 20]

Goffman employs a number of other distinctions drawn from theatrical vocabulary to illustrate the difference between the performance of a role and the actor's genuine belief that he *is* the role.

Sidney Jourard (1971a, 1971b) has investigated the conditions under which an individual will reveal various kinds of personal information to another person.

> The most powerful determiners of self-disclosure thus far discovered
> are the identity of the person to whom one might disclose himself
> and the nature and purpose of the relationship between the two
> people. More specifically, it has been found that disclosure of one's
> experience is most likely when the other person is perceived as a
> trustworthy person of good will and/or one who is willing to disclose
> his experience to the same depth and breadth. [1971a, p. 65]

If Jourard is correct, it is small wonder that Carlson (1971) was provoked to lament psychologists' inability to penetrate to the person whose person-ality is being investigated. The mask may slip, but in the presence of a psychologist, the person is likely to take extreme and practiced measures to ensure its secure fit. The rare therapist, perhaps Freud, is privileged to locate the actor beneath his mask. The extent to which one feels satisfied with the human accuracy of a particular theory in the following chapters is the extent to which that theory has peered beneath the mask.

Psychology's Two Disciplines:
Correlational and Experimental Methods

The personality psychologist is fundamentally concerned with differences among people. No matter how he defines personality, regardless of the theorist's position on the actor-mask issue, personality research and theory always center on *individual differences:* Why is John different from Bill? How is John different from Bill? Are John and Bill alike in any way? Questions like these reflect the scientific nature of contemporary personality psychology because each question, in principle, is quantitatively answerable, provided suitable measuring instruments can be devised. But these questions also reflect an enduring dilemma for scientific psychologists. Difficulties in the study of personality arise when the psychologist who is interested in *individuals* tries simultaneously to discover generalizations and universal laws of behavior applicable to humanity at large. Conflicting theoretical aims, philosophical goals, and research strategies result from this individual versus people-in-general dilemma.

In his 1957 presidential address to the American Psychological Association, Lee J. Cronbach called attention to a division of research traditions in psychology. Cronbach referred to what he then saw as independent disciplines in the research strategies of the *experimentalist* and the *correlationist.*

Control is the essence of the experimental method. In the simplest design, for example, two groups of subjects are exposed to differing experimental treatments. The "experimental group" is exposed to some independent variable under the control of the investigator. A comparison group is denied access to the critical experimental treatment and given a placebo or mock treatment. Performance of both groups of subjects on some task is then measured, and if the independent variable is exerting some behavioral effect, differences between the experimental and control group should be measurable. Note that the experimentalist is interested in *group* differences. He is not particularly interested in how each individual in each group performed. Only the *average* performance of each group *taken as a unit* enters the experimentalist's critical measurement. In theory, the effect of the independent variable is responsible for differences in average performance level between the groups.

In contrast to the experimentalist's strategy, the *correlationist* seeks to exploit the variability that exists among the *individuals* he observes. The correlational strategy focuses on the individual differences displayed by subjects in their reactions to stimuli. Relationships between these individual differences and other measurable variables are then assessed. In short, where the experimental psychologist emphasizes differences *between groups,* the correlational psychologist attends to *individual differences within a group.*

In highlighting these two research traditions, Cronbach has pinpointed their essential strategies:

> The correlational psychologist is in love with just those [individual-difference] variables the experimenter left home to forget. He regards individual and group variations as important effects of biological and social causes. [1957, p. 674]

Experimental method, of necessity, has been anchored in the abstractions of the laboratory. Concerned with generalizing his results to all men, the experimentalist must ignore the peculiarities of some men. Correlational psychology, because of the circumstances of history, has been more closely tied to the real world, to practical applications of psychological research, and to the unique properties of the individuals it studies.

An illustration of the practicality and concern for individual differences that characterize the correlational strategy can be drawn from the circumstances surrounding the development of the first standardized intelligence test. Alfred Binet, the test's designer, in collaboration with a colleague, had set out in 1905 to solve some very practical problems with some very real people in mind. Paris school officials were concerned to find out how children of various intellectual capacities could be identified and appropriately placed for maximum *individual* educational benefit. These educators recognized that each child is different from the mythical "average" pupil for whom school situations were originally designed.

> The officials [of the school system] could not trust teachers to pick out the feeble-minded. They did not want to segregate the child of good potentiality who was making no effort and the troublemaking child the teacher wished to be rid of. Moreover, they wanted to identify all the dull from good families whom teachers might hesitate to rate low, and the dull with pleasant personalities who would be favored by the teacher. [Cronbach, 1960, p. 160]

Teacher biases, the intellectual and motivational characteristics of the pupils, and the properties of the school situation had all to be taken into account. What was required of Binet was no less an achievement than the creation of an objective assessment technique by which to fit individual personalities to generalized classroom environments.

Binet was thus confronted with an unusually practical problem. His task was not to discover the type of school situation that the "average" child requires, but to determine instead the most suitable school environment for the individual, unique child.

Cronbach urged in 1957 that experimentalists and correlationists find a way to merge their strategies. Laboratory precision and abstraction, characteristic of the experimentalist, must and can be profitably merged with the correlational psychologist's concern for individual differences. The experimentalist must consider that every controlled situation involves not only the characteristics of the experimental treatment but also an entire range of individual differences among the persons so treated:

> We can expect some attributes of persons to have strong interactions with treatment variables. These attributes have far greater practical importance than the attributes which have little or no interaction. In dividing pupils between college preparatory and noncollege studies, for example, a general intelligence test is probably the wrong thing to use. . . . We require [instead] a measure of aptitude which predicts who will learn better from one curriculum than from the other; but this aptitude remains to be discovered. Ultimately we should *design* treatments, not to fit the average person, but to fit groups of students with particular aptitude patterns. Conversely, we should seek out the aptitudes which correspond to (interact with) modifiable aspects of the treatment. [Cronbach, 1957, p. 681]

Personality investigations are, by definition, concerned with individual differences. But when experimental method is employed to study personality, the experimentalist must understand the range of possible person-situation interactions that threaten to cancel significant findings. An illustrative case will make this interaction clear.

An Illustrative Case: Introversion and the Reminiscence Effect

Hans Eysenck (1957, 1967), among the theorists represented in this book, comes closest to a true blending of the correlational and experimental strategies. Without becoming enmeshed in the details of his theory (see Chapter 15), a useful illustration can be drawn from Eysenck's work on a personality dimension called *introversion-extroversion.* An individual's personality type can be established on the basis of a paper-and-pencil personality inventory such as the *Eysenck Personality Questionnaire* (Eysenck and Eysenck, 1975 a and b). His score on such an instrument is compared to the distribution of scores of a norm group to ascertain his relative degree of introversion (or extroversion). Once established, the individual's personality type can be *correlated* with his performance on a series of laboratory tasks such as Pavlovian conditioning, rote-memory of nonsense syllables, and perceptual discriminations.

Eysenck has found that individuals who score high on the trait of *introversion* on his personality test generally condition more rapidly, learn verbal materials more quickly, and perform with fewer errors in perceptual tasks that require extreme attentiveness than extroverted individuals. On the basis of such correlations between test-score and laboratory-task performance, Eysenck has conceptualized the introvert as having very sensitive, highly aroused central nervous system processes. Extroverts, on the other hand, are conceptualized as having less sensitive, less highly aroused, and more inhibitory brain processes. It should be noted that these ideas are derived from the *correlation* between an individual's test score and his subsequent performance in the laboratory. However, each of the characteristics of introverts and extroverts described above is only a *general* statement of an observed relationship between personality type and task performance.

The unwary experimentalist might design an investigation to study the differences in verbal learning ability between introverts and extroverts without regard to other mediating individual differences. Thus, using Eysenck's personality questionnaire, or a similar instrument, a sample of introverts and extroverts is selected and required to learn under controlled conditions paired nonsense syllables, such as SIP-WOL, VIL-MUF, SEL-PON, and the like. Based on the *general* finding that introverts condition more quickly than extroverts, our unwitting experimenter would predict that introverts will learn these paired nonsense syllables more rapidly and remember them longer than extroverts.

A problem emerges, however, when we stop to consider another phenomenon that interacts with the learning of verbal materials. Experimental psychologists have demonstrated that performing a learned response *immediately after* acquiring it results in poorer performance than if some period of time is allowed to intervene between acquisition and performance. This effect is called *reminiscence.* Eysenck hypothesized that the improved performance after undisturbed rest was a result of a brain *consolidation process* whereby learned responses are made more permanent in reverberating neural circuits of the cortex. During the time consolidation processes are occurring, performance is hindered because the brain cannot both direct performance and make memories permanent at the same time. Thus, after a rest—when consolidation is finished—performance seems to improve.

Eysenck further hypothesized that introverts, having higher cortical arousal to begin with, would have the strongest consolidation effects. Thus, in a test of the introvert's memory against the extrovert's, the critical variable is *when performance is measured.* Knowledge of personality type of itself is not adequate to the task of making valid predictions. Nor is knowledge of the reminiscence effect by itself sufficient to prevent the experimentalist from making hasty generalizations. The "simple" prediction that introverts learn better than extroverts is not so simple: an accurate prediction depends upon knowledge of the experimental conditions under which a subject is tested *and* the individual's personality type. *If subjects are made to perform immediately after acquisition, extroverts will perform better than introverts.* Conversely, performance tests administered some time after acquisition will favor the introverts.

Eysenck is clearly proposing an *interaction effect* between personality and experimental treatment. It is equally clear that uncritical adoption of the traditional experimental strategy of disregarding individual differences might result in erroneous conclusions. Furthermore, if one had set out to test the reminiscence effect in its own right, slight accidental bias in the selection of subjects who were extroverts would wipe out the phenomenon entirely. Tested some time after learning, a group composed predominantly of extroverted individuals would show forgetting, not reminiscence, as their weak consolidation processes gradually succumb to time (Eysenck, 1972, p. 45; 1967, p. 50; 1953a, p. 448).

If the results of Eysenck's experiment were plotted over increasing periods of time, we would expect the performance curves for extroverts and introverts to intersect at some point along the time dimension. Thus, while extroverts start out with better recall, they should show increasing deterioration of performance with time, whereas the introverts should evidence increasing superiority of performance with increasing time since acquisition. This basic scheme is shown in Figure 1–1.

Eysenck summarized his results in this way:

> After practically no rest, extroverts remember almost twice as much as do introverts. After five minutes, the two groups remember about the same amount. After twenty-four hours, introverts remember almost twice as much as extroverts. . . . Introverts show a beautiful instance of reminiscence; over a twenty-four-hour period, the score

FIGURE 1-1: INTERACTION OF PERSONALITY TYPE AND REMINISCENCE SCORE

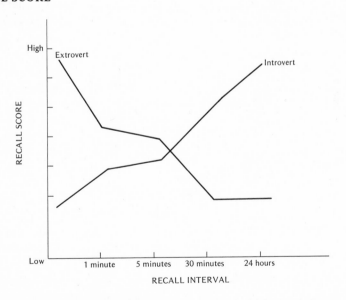

Note that extroverts start out with high recall scores and end with low ones. Introverts begin low and end high.

Based on Eysenck, 1972, p. 44; 1953, p. 448.

almost doubles! Extroverts instead show a beautiful instance of for-getting; over a twenty-four-hour period the score is almost halved. Take both groups together, and the score does not change at all. No wonder "reminiscence" became so difficult to pin down. Results de-pended entirely on the personality make-up of your group. Include a majority of introverts, and you see it; include a majority of extrov-erts, and you don't. [1972, pp. 44–45]

Cronbach has recently taken a return look at the field of psychology to assess the progress both disciplines have made in attempting a merger. In an article entitled "Beyond the Two Disciplines of Scientific Psychology" (1975), Cronbach has suggested that much significant change has occurred in the eighteen years that followed his original suggestions. Yet, Cronbach insists, psychologists are still seeking through experimental methods im-mutable universal "laws" of behavior. In the field of behavior, however, nothing remains unchanged from generation to generation (1975, p. 122). There are few, if any, universal laws.

Our troubles do not arise because human events are in principle unlawful; man and his creations *are* part of the natural world. The trouble, as I see it, is that we cannot store up generalizations and constructs for ultimate assembly into a network. It is as if we needed a gross of dry cells to power an engine and could only make one a month. The energy would leak out of the first cells before we had half the battery completed. So it is with the potency of our generaliza-tions. If the effect of a treatment changes over a few decades, that inconsistency is an effect, a Treatment X Decade interaction that must itself be regulated by whatever laws there be. Such interactions frustrate any would-be theorist who mixes data from several decades indiscriminately into the phenomenal picture he tries to explain. [Cronbach, 1975, p. 123]

Thus, Cronbach argues that psychological researchers have yet to resolve the most fundamental problem of research: namely, how to capitalize not only on individual differences, but how to profit from the fact of their change with time. The personality theorist, by his exclusive concern with individual differences, is at the very heart of the dilemma. Not only must he decide whether there is a mask to penetrate, but he must discover the long-range reliability of the concepts and tools he employs to decide such issues.

Summary

The concept of "personality" is a hypothetical construct designed to bring order and consistency to the explanation of an individual's behavior. The-oretical orientations vary in the way in which they construe the meaning of personality and in the kinds of questions they prompt the investigator to ask. Among the varieties are:

1. *Interpersonal Theory* (and phenomenology): Personality is the relatively enduring pattern of interpersonal situations that characterize a human life (Sullivan, 1953b, p. 111).
2. *Trait Theory:* Personality is the dynamic organization within the individual of those psychophysical systems that determine his characteristic behavior and thought (Allport, 1961, p. 28).
3. *Psychodynamic or Psychoanalytic Theory:* Personality is the certain constancy that prevails in the ways the ego chooses for solving its tasks of drive satisfaction and ethical mediation (Fenichel, 1945, p. 523).
4. *Social Learning Theory:* Personality is the cluster of interrelated responses interacting with stimuli.

The first three varieties of theory make assumptions about the nature of internal, unobservable states. Social learning theory, however, can avoid the issue by focusing on observables only. However, modern social learning theory has begun to take account of the subject's expectations and cognitions.

Sixteen theories of personality are considered in the chapters that follow. Sometimes questions arise about a theorist's position in history, or about his location in the chronology of men who preceded or followed him. A useful device for simplifying the conceptualization of the span of time involved in the construction of theories and of a particular theorist's position in the sequence may be obtained from Table 1–2. Only theorists represented in this book are listed, but from time to time, the reader may wish to return to the table to clarify for himself the position a particular theorist occupies with respect to influences from other theorists.

TABLE 1–2: **A CHRONOLOGY OF PERSONALITY THEORISTS**

SIGMUND FREUD	(1856–1939)
ALFRED ADLER	(1870–1937)
CARL G. JUNG	(1875–1961)
KAREN HORNEY	(1885–1952)
KURT LEWIN	(1890–1947)
HARRY STACK SULLIVAN	(1892–1949)
GORDON ALLPORT	(1897–1967)
ERICH FROMM	(1900–)
ERIK ERIKSON	(1902–)
CARL ROGERS	(1902–)
GEORGE A. KELLY	(1905–1969)
ABRAHAM MASLOW	(1908–1970)
NEAL MILLER	(1909–)
HANS EYSENCK	(1916–)
ALBERT BANDURA	(1925–)
R. D. LAING	(1927–)

A convenient metaphor for concretizing the dilemma that personality theorists face when they try to understand human nature is that of the actor and his mask. Personologists, exemplified by Henry Murray or Gordon Allport, are concerned to represent the individual person in the context of his life history. In more technical terms, a theorist may be concerned with peripheral variables that are easily observable (mask), or with central variables that touch upon the very core of some more "real" inner person (actor). Some contemporary psychologists (e.g., Skinner) feel that such a distinction between core and periphery is spurious. Behavior considered alone is adequate for an understanding of personality. Although the issue remains unresolved, personally satisfying, aesthetically pleasing accounts of human nature are restricted in their ability to penetrate the mask by considerations for the scientific refutability of the theory's concepts.

Karl Popper suggested that a theory must be rooted in empirical data that allow for a statement of what observations it would take to prove the theory wrong. "Heads I win, tails you lose" kinds of theory do not specify precisely what they predict as possible and not possible. The criterion of refutability is designed to assure the relative accuracy of the statements that can be incorporated into a theory.

Along these same lines, Cronbach has suggested that psychology is divided into two distinct disciplines: experimental versus correlational strategies. It is time, Cronbach argues, that the concern for universal "laws" of behavior be combined with an understanding of how experimental treatments interact with individual differences. Cronbach has recently suggested that psychologists' cherished "laws" may, even if discovered, change with time as the characteristics of the people on whom they are based change.

In all, it is probably not necessary to point out that the study of personality, the creation of personality theories, and the attempt to peer beneath the mask are all attempts to understand the understander.

FOR FURTHER READING

To obtain an initial orientation to the historical scope of personality psychology, the easiest route is to browse through the annual editions of the personality research review contained in *Annual Review of Psychology* (Palo Alto, Calif.: Annual Reviews Inc.). These volumes will be found in any large college or university library and contain useful, succinct surveys of psychology's various subfields. Along these same lines, though now somewhat dated, E. Borgatta and W. Lambert (Eds.) *Handbook of Personality Theory and Research* (Chicago: Rand McNally, 1968) contains informative reviews of several research traditions within personality psychology.

Rae Carlson's "Where is the Person in Personality Research?" (*Psychological Bulletin,* 1971, *75,* 203–219) deserves special study for its careful analysis of contemporary personality psychology's failings. Problems of applying scientific method to the study of social and personality phenomena are cogently discussed by Howard Gadlin and Grant Ingle in their article "Through the One-Way Mirror; The Limits of Experimental Self-Reflection" (*American Psychologist,* October, 1975, *30,* 1003–1009). In the same issue of the *American Psychologist* will be found a complementary analysis of methodological problems in social psychology that have some bearing on personality research in Alan C. Elms' "The Crisis of Confidence in Social Psychology."

The significance of testability and empirical refutability of scientific theories is nowhere better discussed than in Karl Popper's *The Logic of Scientific Discovery* (New York: Basic Books, 1959) and in his *Conjectures and Refutations* (New York: Basic Books, 1963). A more elementary discussion of these ideas will be found in Chapter 3 of Christopher F. Monte's *Psychology's Scientific Endeavor* (New York: Praeger, 1975).

Specific readings are recommended for each of the theorists discussed in this book at the end of the appropriate chapters. However, some secondary sources on the various theoretical orientations may be helpful at the beginning of one's study. The collection of chapters in Raymond Corsini's (Ed.) *Current Psychotherapies* (Itasca, Ill.: Peacock, 1973) surveys the therapeutic applications of many of the theories covered in this book. Each of these chapters was written by a specialist in the particular theoretical orientation. Richard I. Evans has for years filmed and taped interviews with the "greats" of psychology and published transcripts of these dialogues as separate paperbacks. Included in the series are conversations with Ernest Jones, Carl Rogers, Neal Miller, Albert Bandura, R. D. Laing, Erik Erikson, Jean Piaget, B. F. Skinner, Gordon Allport, Erich Fromm, and C. G. Jung, to name only those who have immediate relevance to personality. Condensed versions of all these interviews have recently been published in a single paperback, *The Making of Psychology,* edited by R. I. Evans (New York: Knopf, 1976), and each is well worth scrutiny.

Robert White's *The Enterprise of Living* (New York: Holt, Rinehart and Winston, 1972) is a particularly lucid and coherent account of the development of the healthy personality. Lois Barclay Murphy's *The Widening World of Childhood* (New York: Basic Books, 1962; available in paperback) demonstrates what systematic and sensitive observation can yield to the study of personality development. Case studies of moderately healthy personalities may be found in R. W. White's *Lives in Progress* (New York: Holt, Rinehart and Winston, 1966). The two volumes of *Carmichael's Manual of Child Psychology,* edited by Paul H. Mussen (New York: Wiley, 1970), despite their title, contain a wealth of information in detailed reviews of the subfields of personality development.

2

SIGMUND FREUD
Psychoanalysis: The Clinical Evidence

They cannot scare me with their empty spaces
Between stars—on stars where no human race is.
I have it in me so much nearer home
To scare myself with my own desert places.

ROBERT FROST, "Desert Places"

Writhing in her bed with the pangs of labor, evidencing most of the usual signs of advanced pregnancy, twenty-three-year-old Anna O. bore no child in her womb. The year, 1882, was to mark for Viennese physician Josef Breuer the termination of an intimate and lengthy doctor-patient relationship with this neurotic young girl. A two-year-long series of bizarre physical and mental symptoms was climaxing now with the most frightening and, for Breuer (who could intuitively read the symbolic meaning of the new symptom), the most painfully disconcerting outcome: pseudocyesis, or false pregnancy.

From Josef Breuer's work with Anna O. was to emerge a theory of hysterical nervous disorder, a method of psychological treatment nicknamed "chimney sweeping" by the patient herself, and the germ of a comprehensive theory of personality and psychotherapy yet to be formulated by Breuer's young colleague and friend Sigmund Freud.

The Hysterical Neurosis of Anna O.

Bertha Pappenheim, Anna O.'s real name (Jones, 1953, p. 223n.), was a charming, attractive, intelligent, and witty young lady who developed a series of disorders ranging from paralysis of limbs and disturbed vision to, at one point, a dual personality. The symptoms seemed to make their emergence subsequent to a protracted and fatal illness of her father. Though a variety of physicians was consulted, no physical basis could be found for her bewildering maladies. Breuer diagnosed Anna O.'s collection of symptoms as *hysterical neurosis*, a disorder that, though recognized from antiquity, had thus far defied satisfactory explanation.

The affliction received its name from the ancient Greeks' word *hystera*, meaning uterus. It was the ancient Greeks' opinion that hysteria was limited to women because the disease was the result of a wandering womb. By its travels to various parts of the body, the errant womb caused the symptoms of temporary paralysis of limbs or the dysfunction of sense organs whenever it came to rest in other than its customary place. Needless to say, Josef Breuer held no such mystical convictions about the nature of the disorder, although it can be said with equal certainty that he did not yet understand the full import of his observations on Anna O.

Breuer was originally consulted in the case because Anna had developed a severe and persistent cough while caring for her father during his terminal illness. She was twenty-one years old at this time. Some months later, in 1881, Anna's father died and her own health showed signs of profound impairment. She refused food, became weak and anemic, and she then began to develop the even more bizarre symptoms of paralysis, muscle contractures, visual hallucinations, and loss of feeling in her hands and feet —the so-called functional anesthesias. Breuer described Anna's alternating states as follows:

> Two entirely distinct states of consciousness were present [in Anna O.] which alternated very frequently and without warning and which became more and more differentiated in the course of the illness. In one of these states she recognized her surroundings; she was melancholy and anxious, but relatively normal. In the other state she hallucinated and was "naughty"—that is to say, she was abusive, used to throw the cushions at people, so far as the contractures [in her limbs] at various times allowed, tore buttons off her bedclothes and linen with those of her fingers which she could move, and so on. . . . There were extremely rapid changes of mood leading to excessive but quite temporary high spirits, and at other times severe anxiety, stubborn opposition to every therapeutic effort and frightening hallucinations of black snakes, which was how she saw her hair ribbons and similar things. . . . [Breuer, in Breuer & Freud, 1893–1895, p. 24[1]]

In addition to the emergence of an incipient dual personality, young Anna O. began to exhibit other forms of disturbance in her relations with people. She occasionally omitted necessary words from her spoken language, and she gradually increased these omissions until her speech was rendered virtually nonsensical and totally devoid of logical and grammatical construction. The inevitable consequence of such behavior then occurred: complete mutism for a period of two weeks. Although she struggled mightily to speak, all of Anna O.'s efforts resulted in soundless frustration.

[1]Reference citations throughout this chapter and the next that indicate the writings of Sigmund Freud (or, in this case, of Josef Breuer) refer to the volumes of the *Standard Edition of the Complete Psychological Works of Sigmund Freud,* translated under the general editorship of James Strachey, with the collaboration of Anna Freud, and published by the Hogarth Press, London. Citations to the *Standard Edition* will employ only the original publication date of the work in question, so that the reader may follow the chronology of Freud's thought.

When Breuer guessed that something had recently annoyed and offended her, causing her to resolve not to speak about it, his insistence that they discuss the problem robbed Anna's mutism of its efficacy (1893–1895, p. 25).

Anna, whose native tongue was German, now created a new symptom: She spoke only English. No amount of argument could convince Anna, who was seemingly unaware of her changed speech, that the people to whom she spoke English were as unable to understand her now as they had been during her weeks of silence.

"Clouds": Self-Induced Hypnosis

Anna O.'s father died in April, nine months after these speech disturbances developed. "This was the most severe psychical trauma that she could possibly have experienced. A violent outburst of excitement was succeeded by profound stupor which lasted about two days and from which she emerged in a greatly changed state" (Breuer, in Breuer & Freud, 1893–1895, p. 26).

Anna O.'s loss of feeling in her hands and feet and her paralysis returned, along with what would now be called "tunnel vision": that is, her field of vision was greatly narrowed as when one looks through a narrow cardboard cylinder. For example: ". . . in a bunch of flowers which gave her much pleasure she could only see one flower at a time."

> She complained of not being able to recognize people. Normally, she said, she had been able to recognize faces without having to make any deliberate effort; now she was obliged to do laborious "recognizing work" [she used this phrase in English] and had to say to herself "this person's nose is such-and-such, his hair is such-and-such, so he must be so-and-so." [Breuer, in Breuer & Freud, 1893–1895, p. 26]

During the day, Anna was always upset, and she presented a picture of a harassed and tormented victim of her disease. She hallucinated, talked incoherently, and experienced grave anxiety. Toward afternoon, Anna became sleepy and quiet, sinking into a deep autohypnosis by sunset. For these self-induced evening hypnotic states she created the English term "clouds." When Breuer visited her in the evening, she was able to recount to him her day's hallucinations, and it was in this state of "clouds" that Breuer and Anna O. made a joint discovery.

Her family had noticed from Anna's mumblings that the content of these daytime hallucinations seemed to resemble a fantasy story. Anna's fantasies were surprisingly sad, yet they were also pretty and poetic because they had probably been modeled on a book of Hans Andersen's fairy tales. After her father's death, these daytime hallucinations became even more tragic, and they usually involved, as at least one element of a complex structure, the character of an anxious young girl sitting near the bedside of a patient. Accidentally at first, a family member would repeat a few key words of Anna's mutterings, and this response would draw her out to narrate an entire story or hallucinatory fantasy. During her evening hypnotic clouds, Breuer took up the procedure of priming the conversation with several words or phrases from Anna's own fantasies. The significant point was that after Anna recounted the full content of her daytime hallucinations and stories to Breuer, she became quieter, more lucid and cheerful, and almost symptomfree for the rest of the night.

The Talking Cure: "Chimney Sweeping"

Little by little, through a combination of accident and intent, Anna and Breuer shaped a method to relieve Anna of her anxiety and symptoms, at least temporarily. By unburdening herself to Breuer in the evening, Anna was able to achieve some respite from her torment. She and Breuer had thus made an important discovery, a "talking cure" that involved a kind of verbal *catharsis* (literally, a cleansing or purifying).

Aristotle had used the term "catharsis" to describe the emotional release and purification engendered in the audience during their viewing of a tragic drama. Anna O., more to the point, perhaps, than Aristotle, called the emotional release produced by her semi-hypnotic conversations with Breuer "chimney sweeping."

The evening talking sessions were obviously beneficial for Anna O. and of medical interest to Breuer. Unfortunately for Breuer's scientific curiosity, however, no specific symptoms had yet been removed or explained by the cathartic talking-cure method.

That such symptoms as paralysis, blindness, and mutism might be not just manifestations of the irrationality of the hysteric personality, meaningless expressions of "craziness" to be expected of the neurotic, had already occurred to Breuer. He became firmly convinced that neurotic symptoms had an explainable and rationally understandable cause to be found in the patient's life history, and that the *form* of the symptom was rooted in a deeply *personal meaning* attached by the patient to the past event.

Catharsis: Expressing Strangulated Feeling

As the talking cure progressed, Breuer found that some of the symptoms of Anna O.'s illness permanently disappeared. He was particularly surprised when a long-standing symptom disappeared during an unplanned conversation with Anna. Breuer provided an account of the removal of this specific symptom:

> It was in the summer during a period of extreme heat, and the patient was suffering very badly from thirst; for, *without being able to account*

for it in any way, she suddenly found it impossible to drink. She would take up the glass of water she longed for, but as soon as it touched her lips she would push it away like someone suffering from hydrophobia. As she did this, she was obviously in an *absence* [self-induced hypnotic state] for a couple of seconds. . . . This [condition] had lasted for some six weeks, when one day during hypnosis she grumbled about her English lady-companion whom she did not care for, and went on to describe, *with every sign of disgust,* how she had once gone into that lady's room and how her [the lady-companion's] little dog—horrid creature!—had drunk out of a glass there. The patient [i.e., Anna O.] had said nothing, as she had wanted to be polite. After giving further *energetic expression to the anger she had held back,* she asked for something to drink, drank a large quantity of water without any difficulty and woke from her hypnosis with the glass at her lips; and thereupon the disturbance vanished, never to return. [1893–1895, pp. 34–35, italics added]

Here was the secret of the *origin* and the *form* of hysterical symptoms. An emotion had been experienced intensely, but it had been blocked from normal expression during the initiating event. The patient had been compelled to "strangle" the feeling, so to speak. However, even though the emotion had *then*—in the patient's past—been prohibited from expression, there was little cause, Breuer reasoned, to assume that the emotion had thereby ceased to exist. Indeed, the strangulated "affect," as Breuer and Freud would later call these unruly emotions, remained to haunt Anna O. She was able to solve partially the problem of the dammed-up disgust and anger by expressing these emotions behaviorally, symptomatically, as a feeling of disgust for, and as a refusal to drink, water. When the incident that had precipitated the *original* feelings had been recalled in hypnosis, those pent-up emotions were finally spent.

Following up his patient's success with that one symptom, Breuer systematically explored with Anna O. the possibility that other precipitating but no longer remembered incidents lay at the root of her remaining bizarre behaviors. Breuer adopted the procedure of asking Anna during hypnosis to tell him her thoughts on a particular symptom. The exploration was often difficult, and it required great concentration from both Breuer and his patient. On some occasions, the whole process ground to a halt because a particular symptom's initiating cause would not come to the surface of Anna's memory.

With time, however, concentrated effort relieved Anna of many of her difficulties. For instance, some of Anna O.'s visual disturbances, language problems, hallucinations, and the paralysis of her right arm were removed after she was able, under hypnosis, to recount the story of a particularly long and frightening night vigil she had spent at her sick father's bedside.

She fell into a waking dream and saw a black snake coming towards the sick man from the wall to bite him. . . . Her right arm, over the back of the chair, had gone to sleep and had become anaesthetic and paretic; and when she looked at it the fingers turned into little snakes with death's heads (the nails). (It seems probable that she had tried to use her paralysed right arm to drive off the snake and that its anaesthesia and paralysis had consequently become associated with the hallucination of the snake.) When the snake vanished, in her terror she tried to pray. But language failed her: *she could find no tongue in which to speak, till at last she thought of some children's verses in English, and then found herself able to think and pray in that language.* [Italics added]

... on [another] occasion, when she was sitting by her father's bedside with tears in her eyes, he suddenly asked her what time it was. She could not see clearly; she made a great effort, and brought her watch near to her eyes. The face of the watch now seemed very big—thus accounting for her macropsia [tunnel vision] and convergent squint. Or again, she tried hard to suppress her tears so that the sick man should not see them. [Breuer, in Breuer & Freud, 1893–1895, pp. 38, 39, 40]

Breuer's account of the case history ends shortly after this incident is recounted, but that is not the end of the story. Anna O., Bertha Pappenheim, developed a new symptom that was to frighten Breuer so intensely and to engender such guilt in him that he could look to psychology in the future only with great trepidation.

Anna O.'s Treatment Ends

Symptom by symptom, feeling-event by feeling-event, the thread of Anna's hysteria was unraveled with the assistance of Breuer and the cathartic method. During the course of the treatment, a period lasting almost two years, an intimate and intense relationship developed between Breuer and Anna O. Breuer's wife became jealous of her husband's fascinating patient, and she provoked in Breuer a strong reaction of guilt. He decided to end his treatment of Anna, a decision strengthened by her improvement, and he announced this intention to her. Ernest Jones, Freud's official biographer, provides an account, based on a conversation with Freud years later, of what followed Breuer's announcement to his patient:

... that evening ... [Breuer] was fetched back to find ... [Anna O.] in a greatly excited state, apparently as ill as ever. The patient, who according to him had appeared to be an asexual being and had never made any allusion to such a forbidden topic throughout the treatment, was now in the throes of an hysterical childbirth (pseudocyesis), the logical termination of a phantom pregnancy that had been invisibly developing in response to Breuer's ministrations. Though profoundly shocked, he managed to calm her down by hypnotizing her, and then fled the house in a cold sweat. The next day he and his wife left for Venice to spend a second honeymoon. . . . [Jones, 1953, p. 224. Freud himself hinted at this story in his *Autobiographical Study,* 1925a, p. 26.]

There can be little doubt that Breuer had read the unconscious meaning of Anna O.'s symptom clearly and that he felt directly responsible. Despite the scientific importance of this further discovery, Breuer lost almost all professional interest in hysterical neurosis.

Breuer's Contributions to Psychology

We should not overlook the immense contributions provided by Breuer's scientific astuteness prior to his embarrassing episode with Anna O. It was upon these contributions of Breuer that the young Sigmund Freud was to build the structure of psychoanalysis.

First, Breuer recognized that hysterical symptoms were *meaningful* and that they possessed a certain *emotional logic* beneath their bizarre appearance.

Second, Breuer regarded the *origin* of the hysterical symptom as some intense, *emotionally abrasive experience* in the life history of the patient. Though no longer remembered, the past experience *actively operated unconsciously,* pressing for release and goading the patient to find symbolic means of expressing the discomfort. It is not easy to determine how much Sigmund Freud contributed to this interpretation of hysterical symptoms. Freud was always generous in giving most of the credit to Breuer for the early theory of hysteria that they proposed in their joint publications, the "Preliminary Communication" of 1893 and their full monograph, *Studies on Hysteria* of 1895.

Third, the discovery that symptoms could be removed by promoting the expression of the strangulated emotion dating from the past traumatic experience gave further force to the theory that symptoms were the result of dammed-up emotional (affective) energy. The cathartic method, a joint discovery of Breuer and Anna O., was a uniquely *psychological* method for dealing with hysterical disorder. In the terminology of the *Studies on Hysteria,* the goal of the cathartic method was to enable the patient to "abreact" the painful feelings, literally to "react away" the trapped energy. As Breuer and Freud expressed the idea in their "Preliminary Communication," *"The hysteric suffers mostly from reminiscences"* (1893, p. 7).

It was also Breuer's conviction that the essential precondition for the occurrence of hysterical symptoms was the presence of a tendency to self-induced hypnotic states of consciousness. Thus, for Breuer, *any* intensely experienced emotion which occurred during one of these states of "absence" and which was prevented from immediate expression, could serve as the origin of a hysterical symptom. It was with this idea that Freud was later to disagree and that he would modify by the time *Studies on Hysteria* had been published.

The Cathartic Method in Freud's Hands: Hypnotism

The young Sigmund Freud, doctor in training at the University of Vienna, had been befriended by the older, more experienced Josef Breuer. In 1882, shortly after Breuer had terminated his treatment of Anna O., Freud heard the details of the strange case. He was greatly interested and requested Breuer to tell him the story again and again (Jones, 1953, p. 226). It was not until some years later, however, that Freud and Breuer began to treat cases together, employing for the most part the cathartic method. Apparently, Freud did not simply accept Breuer's technique on a wholesale basis. He was already experimenting with slight modifications in the application of the cathartic method to individual patients as the limitations of his hypnotic skill demanded.

Charcot

Freud's early reliance on the technique of hypnotism—a necessary adjunct to catharsis—had other roots besides Breuer's successful treatment of Anna O. In 1885, Freud had been awarded a traveling grant to attend the lecture-demonstrations of the famous neuropathologist Jean-Martin Charcot (1825–1893) in Paris, at the equally renowned Salpêtrière Hospital (Freud, 1925a, pp. 12–16).

Charcot was investigating the symptoms and causes of hysteria, and he had demonstrated that the bizarre behaviors associated with the disease could be removed and then restored under hypnosis at the suggestion of the physician. This famous French clinician had also demonstrated that hysterical symptoms parallel the hysteric's naïve conception of physical disorder. Thus, for example, the patient who has recently been involved in a frightening horse-drawn-carriage accident, but who emerges unscathed, may nevertheless exhibit all the symptoms of the paralysis he *expects* to have. Hence, in Charcot's view, *ideas,* rather than physical pathology, lie at the base of hysteria.

That a man of Charcot's professional standing could be scientifically interested in the clinical oddities of hysterical attacks was enough to impress Freud with the significance of the disease as a natural phenomenon worth investigation. Breuer's unusual experiences with Anna O. began to assume greater importance in Freud's estimation. He would, however, have a difficult time trying to convince the Viennese medical establishment to investigate what was then regarded as a malingerer's syndrome.

As if to underscore the incredulity with which the medical profession viewed hysterics' suffering, the Viennese society of physicians greeted the young Freud's report of Charcot's work with open hostility. Freud recounted in his *Autobiographical Study* the cool and unpleasant reception his presentation of Charcot's findings engendered (1925a, pp. 15ff.).

Nevertheless, Freud had learned his lessons well with Charcot: Hysteria *was* a legitimate psychological disorder; there *were* cases of male hysteria; there *were* symptoms that could be removed, modified, or reinstated by hypnotism; there *were* ideas underlying the patient's symptoms. Freud was later able to demonstrate these truisms to the members of the *Gesellschaft der Aerzte* (Society of Physicians), but they expressed only grudging approval and little interest.

Liebeault and Bernheim

Meanwhile, in another part of France, two physicians, Ambroise-Auguste Liebeault (1823–1904) and Hippolyte Bernheim (1837–1919), founded a clinic at Nancy that rivaled the Charcot school of Paris in its employment of hypnotism in the treatment of hysteria (cf. Watson, 1963, pp. 303–304; and Zilboorg, 1941, pp. 361–378). The physicians associated with the Nancy School, as it came to be known, differed from Charcot's group by their emphasis on the purely pragmatic efficacy of hypnotism as a cure for their hysteric patients. Liebeault and Bernheim were more interested in *treating* the disease than in developing theories to explain its origin, or the action of hypnotism. By contrast to Liebeault and Bernheim's practical viewpoint, Charcot was *theoretically* interested in both hypnotism and in hysteria as manifestations of altered mental processes. He conceived of hypnosis as an essentially pathological or disease state in itself, a state to which hysterics were peculiarly susceptible. Hypnotic trance, Charcot believed, was the precursor and necessary biological foundation on which the disease of hysteria built. (It was, incidentally, from Charcot that Breuer adopted the idea that hysteria required a "hypnoid state" or condition of "absence" in order for the damming up of feelings to take place.)

Liebeault and Bernheim held the rather different view that hysteria and hypnotism were not necessarily related. The members of the Nancy School believed, furthermore, that Charcot's findings about the malleability of hysterical symptoms were an artifact of hypnotism imposed by the physician, and, therefore, hypnotic states in themselves could not be the biological *cause* of hysterical disorder (Murphy & Kovach, 1972, p. 156). History seems to have supported the views of Liebeault and Bernheim.

In 1889, Freud traveled back to France, this time to visit the Liebeault-Bernheim clinic at Nancy in an attempt to refine his hypnotic technique (1925a, p. 17). He came away from Nancy with "... the profoundest impression of the possibility that there could be powerful mental processes which nevertheless remained hidden from the consciousness of men."

Hypnotism Fails:
Search for a New Technique

Throughout the late 1880's, Freud continued to employ the cathartic method, but the difficulties and the dissatisfactions he experienced in its use continued to mount. For one thing, not all his patients could be hypnotized. Some individuals could not achieve the trancelike state of somnambulism so necessary to reliving and releasing the strangulated emotion of the forgotten traumatic event. Furthermore, Freud had begun to understand that even in cases where hypnotism was successful, the success depended deeply on the personal relationship between the physician and the patient.

The efficacy of the hypnotic act was thus a function of the emotional quality of the person-to-person contact between himself and his patient. If for some reason or other this personal relationship was disturbed, "even the most brilliant results [of hypnotism] were likely to be suddenly wiped away . . ." (Freud, 1925a, p. 27). Breuer's unwitting intimate involvement with Anna O. was proof enough of the partially erotic nature of the process.

Clearly, it was necessary for Freud to abandon hypnosis altogether if he was to pursue unimpeded his psychological investigations. Consequently, Freud was compelled gradually to reduce his reliance on hypnosis. His search for a new technique received its first important, if altogether unintentional, guidance from a new patient, Frau Emmy.

Frau Emmy von N.

"Keep still!—Don't say anything!—Don't touch me!" These were the words with which Freud was greeted on an afternoon in May, 1889, when he visited his new patient, Frau Emmy von N., for the first time.

Frau Emmy was lying on a couch when Freud entered, and in the course of greeting her new physician, interposed between perfectly coherent and logical, softly spoken amenities, came the bizarre utterance: "Keep still!—Don't say anything!—Don't touch me!" She also evidenced several ticlike facial twitches, punctuated by grimaces of disgust and fear that contorted her pleasant face with each repetition of her magical formula: "Keep still!—Don't say anything!—Don't touch me!" Additionally, as if his new patient's behavior were not already strange enough, Frau Emmy had a tendency to stutter, and her speech was often accompanied by a smacking sound that Freud, quite straight-facedly, tried to convey to the reader by describing it as comparable to the call of a forest bird (Freud, in Breuer & Freud, 1893–1895, p. 49n). Freud's first suspicion was that these behaviors involved some form of protective ritual practiced by Frau Emmy to ward off a repetitive hallucination.

Frau Emmy had been ill almost since the death of her husband, fourteen years earlier, and she had traveled to Vienna with her daughters to seek medical help. Freud suggested that she place the girls with their governess and that Frau Emmy enter a sanitarium, where he would visit her daily.

Fortunately, in this, one of the first cases that Freud treated by hypnosis and the cathartic method, Frau Emmy, unlike his later patients, proved to

be an admirable subject. She was able to assume the sleeplike somnambulistic state readily, and she was cooperative in discussing her symptoms
and their origins—to a point.

Tracing Symptoms to Their Origins

As the therapeutic relationship progressed, Freud attempted to trace each
of Frau Emmy's symptoms to its root by asking her under hypnosis to
explain its meaning. For example, Freud asked her to explain the meaning
of her magical phrase, "Keep still!—Don't say anything—Don't touch
me!"

> She explained that when she had frightening thoughts she was afraid
> of their being interrupted in their course, because then everything
> would get confused and things would be even worse. The "Keep
> still!" related to the fact that the animal shapes [hallucinations] which
> appeared to her when she was in a bad state started moving and
> began to attack her if anyone made a movement in her presence. The
> final injunction "Don't touch me!" was derived from the following
> experiences. She told me how, when her brother had been so ill from
> taking a lot of morphine—she was nineteen at the time—he used
> often to seize hold of her; and how, another time, an acquaintance
> had suddenly gone mad in the house and had caught her by the arm;
> . . . and lastly, how, when she was twenty-eight and her daughter
> was very ill, the child had caught hold of her so forcibly in its
> delirium that she was almost choked. Though these four instances
> were so widely separated in time, she told me them in a single
> sentence and in such rapid succession that they might have been a
> single episode in four acts. [Freud, in Breuer & Freud, 1893–1895, pp.
> 56–57]

Thus far, as Freud's account clearly indicates, he held to the conception
of hysteria that Breuer had developed in working with Anna O. The
patient's unconscious memory had to be searched through hypnotism for
hidden emotional experiences that had not been fully expressed when they
occurred. By allowing Frau Emmy to reexperience the strangulated affect
of those events, catharsis was achieved. But it sometimes seemed as if Frau
Emmy's list of traumatic experiences was endless.

For one thing, although Freud used hypnotic suggestion to remove these
fears and the power of these memories to instill terror, Frau Emmy experienced relapses, and she sometimes succumbed to new fears and hallucinations. Freud realized that his hypnotic suggestions and emotional catharsis
were only partially successful. Tracing the symptom to its origin and
freeing the choked emotional energy could not of themselves explain why
a particular event had been traumatic.

First Clue in the Discovery of Free Association: Freud Learns to Listen

It is perhaps surprising that Frau Emmy von N., the first patient with whom Freud employed the cathartic method, would also be the person who provided the first clue to the discovery of a new technique of conducting therapy. That clue assumed great significance in later years as Freud experienced difficulty with the hypnotic method.

Frau Emmy, despite Freud's hypnotic suggestions to the contrary, continued to recall frightening experiences with animals and terrifying hallucinations based on animal content. Freud, quite willing to accept the fact that each new instance of anxiety had to be removed separately, took to quizzing Frau Emmy closely on each occasion. She had reported intense stomachaches, and Freud noticed that reports of stomach pains coincided with each new animal terror. He questioned her under hypnosis on the possible origin of the stomachaches, but she seemed reluctant to continue examining each symptom with such exactness:

> Her answer, which she gave rather grudgingly, was that she did not know. I requested her to remember by tomorrow. She then said in a definitely grumbling tone that I was not to keep on asking her where this and that came from, but to let her tell me what she had to say. [Freud, in Breuer & Freud, 1893–1895, p. 63]

Frau Emmy's offhand and somewhat petulant remark was a momentous occasion in Freud's intellectual history. Jones, Freud's biographer, remarks, with understatement worthy of Freud himself, that "he took the hint" and thus approached one step closer to a substitute for hypnosis.[2] (1953, p. 244).

In more concrete and immediate terms, Freud's acceptance of Frau Emmy's "suggestion" meant that he would allow more free rein in the handling of his patient. He would permit her own feelings and strivings to direct the flow and the content of their therapeutic conversation.

False Connections: Deceptions of Memory

Freud had already begun to suspect that certain of the contents of mental processes revealed during hypnosis might be forms of self-deception designed to screen deeper and more threatening material. Thus, he believed that one form of this self-protective deception involved an attempt by the unconscious mind to *falsely connect* one memory with another to obscure

---

[2]It is interesting to note that Ernest Jones, in an uncharacteristic lapse, attributes Frau Emmy von N.'s irritable remark to Fräulein Elisabeth von R., a patient Freud treated some six years after Frau Emmy. The Fräulein Elisabeth case was also a landmark step in Freud's development of psychoanalysis and will be considered at a later point.

the real connections between thoughts. Such real connections, left undisturbed, might lead to the eventual recall of a threatening memory.

On one occasion, for example, Frau Emmy had a restless morning because she was worried that the hotel where her children and their governess were staying had a faulty elevator. She herself had recommended that the children use the elevator, and she was now anxious over the thought that the elevator might fail. But a strange thing happened when Freud questioned Frau Emmy under hypnosis about the reason for her anxiety. Fully expecting to hear again the story of her concern for her children's safety, Freud was puzzled when Frau Emmy related instead a worry that her massage treatments would have to stop because her menstrual period might begin. The explanation for this hypnotic *non sequitur,* Freud reasoned, might be found in the self-protective tendency of the mind to distort and to obscure connections between anxiety-arousing ideas. Ideas can be rearranged into sequences that block conscious recognition of the correct sequence of ideas, the sequence that is connected to some anxiety-provoking thought.

Freud was able to decipher the meaning of Frau Emmy's jumbled thought train. Her real concern was for her oldest daughter, who was having some difficulty walking because of a severe attack of ovarian neuralgia. Frau Emmy had just that morning solicitously inquired of the children's governess if the girl, in her pain, had used the elevator to descend from the upper floor of the hotel instead of walking down. Then, blotting out the true source of her anxiety, her daughter's illness, Frau Emmy recalled only its oblique connection with the elevator. By displacing the anxiety to the least-threatening component of the sequence, the elevator, the thought sequence became transformed: NOT AFRAID OF CONSEQUENCES OF DAUGHTER'S ILLNESS, BUT AFRAID THAT ELEVATOR MIGHT FAIL.

The perceptive Freud noticed that the anxious impulse was not only displaced to another thought, but that the displacement had taken place along *meaningful* associative lines:

DAUGHTER'S MENSTRUAL PROBLEM $\longrightarrow$ HER OWN MENSTRUAL PROBLEM $\longrightarrow$ ELEVATOR FEAR

Consequently, during hypnosis only the topmost displacement, *fear of the elevator,* had given way to the next item in the sequence, *her own menstrual problem.* Even though hypnotic exploration with her physician had enabled penetration one layer down through the sequence, the fundamental layer —*anxiety over the daughter's menstrual problem*—was left untouched.

Relapse: Intensification of Symptoms

Within seven weeks of the beginning of treatment, Frau Emmy's condition was sufficiently improved to warrant her dismissal from the sanitarium. It appeared that the cathartic method had once again worked its miracle. But this happy outcome was not long-lasting.

Seven months later, Breuer received word from Frau Emmy that her oldest daughter had suffered a recurrence of her ovarian difficulties, and this time the daughter had succumbed to a "severe nervous illness" as well. The girl had visited a gynecologist for her difficulty, and during the treatment she had manifested all the signs of a severe emotional disturbance. Frau Emmy had concluded that Freud was responsible for the daughter's condition because he had treated the subject so lightly during his therapy with her. Thus, Frau Emmy relapsed into the state in which Freud had first encountered her. After much coaxing, Breuer persuaded Frau Emmy that Freud was not at fault, and one year elapsed before she again visited her old physician.

Overdetermination of Symptoms

Frau Emmy now began a period of self-inflicted semistarvation (anorexia). She refused to eat complete meals, and she drank very little. Freud ordered her to increase her intake of food and liquid, and there followed a somewhat uncharacteristic argument between patient and physician.

Two days passed and Frau Emmy mellowed a little. Freud put her into hypnosis and asked why she could not eat and drink normally.

> "I'm thinking how, when I was a child [Frau Emmy began], it often happened that out of naughtiness I refused to eat my meat at dinner. My mother was very severe about this and under the threat of condign punishment I was obliged two hours later to eat the meat, which had been left standing on the same plate. The meat was quite cold by then and the fat was set so hard" (she showed her disgust) ". . . I can still see the fork in front of me . . . one of its prongs was a little bent. Whenever I sit down to a meal I see the plates before me with the cold meat and fat on them. And how, many years later, I lived with my brother who was an officer and who had that horrible disease [venereal disease]. I knew that it was contagious and was terribly afraid of making a mistake and picking up his knife and fork" (she shuddered) ". . . and in spite of that I ate my meals with him so that no one should know that he was ill. And how, soon after that, I nursed my other brother when he had consumption so badly. We ate by the side of his bed and the spittoon always stood on the table, open" (she shuddered again) ". . . and he had a habit of spitting across the plates into the spittoon. This always made me feel so sick, but I couldn't show it, for fear of hurting his feelings." [Freud, in Breuer & Freud, 1893–1895, p. 82]

We can discern in Frau Emmy's reminiscences a phenomenon that Freud called *overdetermination.* Each symptom, Freud discovered, had not one cause, not one root, but *multiple* determinants which had become associatively bonded together in the patient's thoughts. Consequently, one overt symptom represented many emotional threads woven to a single pattern. Conversely, a branching network of *emotionally related* ideas, impulses, and meanings supported each symptom. In Frau Emmy's case, the unitary symptom of refusing to eat capped a latent amalgam of previous experiences that centered on the arousal of disgust for the act of eating: *cold meat and fat; fear of contracting a "foul" disease through shared eating implements;* and *revulsion at the act of spitting into a spittoon over dinner.*

Freud again helped his patient to abreact these strangulated emotions. From this time on, Frau Emmy was able to eat relatively normally, and she began to recover her composure in most other respects as well.

The Theoretical Yield from Frau Emmy's Therapy

The case of Frau Emmy von N. is important for a firm understanding of psychoanalytic theory because it provides a vivid illustration of the clinical data on which Freud exercised his powers of observation, imagination, and reason. There are at least five important features of the case that deserve consideration.

First, it would naturally be expected that a doctor employing a new method of treatment for the first time would rigidly adhere to the inventor's technique in order to gain facility with its use. In so doing, he should be concerned with maintaining correct form and be temporarily blind to the method's shortcomings and limitations during the period of attempted mastery. None of these expectations is confirmed in Freud's use of Breuer and Anna O.'s cathartic method. Freud was sensitive not only to the limitations of hypnosis, but to the shortcomings of catharsis as well in achieving an understanding of the network of strangled emotions.

Second, we must not forget that it was Frau Emmy who provided for Freud a service similar to the one provided for Breuer by Anna O., namely, a timely hint about how to proceed. Frau Emmy's irritation with Freud's incessant probing, questioning, ordering, and badgering led to her modifying her physician's technique. She wished to be allowed to speak her mind without interruption. Instead of question-and-answer sessions, the flow of therapeutic communication should be at least partially under the patient's control. This hint was to stand Freud in good stead several years later as he searched about for a way to modify his procedure with patients not susceptible to hypnotic suggestion.

Third, Freud had been led to hypothesize that the workings of the mind could be directed toward *defending* the person's conscious self or ego from the recognition of unpleasant, frightening, or unacceptable thoughts. Frau Emmy's concern over her daughter's illness had been obscured by a conscious, but associatively related, concern for the safety of her daughters in the hotel elevator. The link in the chain between the *conscious* fear that the elevator might not be safe and the *unconscious* anxiety over her daughter's *ovarian* difficulties was revealed during hypnosis as the non sequitur of Frau Emmy's worry that she might have to forgo massage treatment if her own *menstrual* cycle interfered. This worry was the last of a chain of displacements. The conscious shield memories (elevator fear, menstrual-interference-with-massage) served to distract thought from the more threatening idea of her daughter's illness. Defense, not confusion, was responsible for the displacements.

Fourth, we can see evidence from this early case that Freud's attention was directed to the importance of childhood incidents, childhood emotions, and childhood conflicts in establishing the basis of an intricate associative chain of ideas that influences adult behavior. Frau Emmy's early dinnertime experiences with cold meat and fat and her terrifying experiences with death and disease had certainly not passed from memory with time.

Fifth, Freud understood the importance of following each symptom back to its cause. Partial abreaction led only to partial relief. He accepted as proof that a symptom had been fully explained only the permanent removal of that symptom. He did not accept the patient's verbal expression of relief as sufficient evidence that a symptom had been traced to its fundamental cause. Only his patient's subsequent behavior could satisfy that requirement. In consequence, Freud puzzled over the recurrence of Frau Emmy's symptoms after he had employed hypnotic suggestion to remove the memory traces of the strangled emotions. Such symptoms, he discovered, were overdetermined. Multiple causes, complex chains of experiences, contributed to the formation of a single symptom. Hence, to account for the persistence of some symptoms in the face of massive hypnotic suggestion to abandon them, Freud found it necessary to hypothesize that the fundamental cause of the symptom had not been reached (cf. Freud, 1896c). Deeper probing had to be undertaken; recall of a single traumatic experience was not sufficient.

Breuer's cathartic method became, in Freud's hands, not only a therapeutic tool of increased flexibility, but a method of investigation to be employed in understanding the psychology of the human animal.

The Evolution of Method: Fräulein Elisabeth von R.

In 1892, Freud faced an intensification of his difficulties with the cathartic method: Fräulein Elisabeth von R., his latest patient, could not be hypnotized.

Hypnotism had been an invaluable adjunct in applying the cathartic method, widening the scope of the patient's consciousness and "putting within . . . [the patient's] reach knowledge which he did not possess in his waking life" (Freud, 1925a, p. 27). With some of his other patients Freud had experienced the same difficulty, and, in fact, some patients refused even to make any attempt to submit to hypnosis. Freud began to suspect that *unwillingness* to be hypnotized, whether verbally expressed or mutely evident in uncooperative behavior, formed the basis for all such failures (Freud, in Breuer & Freud, 1893–1895, p. 268).

Fräulein Elisabeth von R., therefore, posed a formidable problem because she was either unable or unwilling to achieve the customary somnambulistic state. Freud suspected that her hysterical symptoms of intense pain in her legs and her inability to stand or to walk for long periods were connected with some experience that she *could* recall if only she felt free enough. The greatest difficulty confronting Freud in the treatment of Fräulein Elisabeth was to devise a way to enable her to discuss her symptoms freely and without reservation in the absence of hypnosis.

Freud learned from Elisabeth that she had nursed her father after his heart attack for a period of one and a half years. She was quite dutiful, sleeping in her father's room, attending to his needs morning and night, forcing herself to remain cheerful and encouraging. She had experienced an attack of severe pain in her legs during this period, an attack so intense that she had had to take to her bed and become a patient herself. Two years after her father's death, the pains returned, unbearably, and she discovered that she could not walk at all. Furthermore, because of the death of her father, the happiness of the family reached a new low ebb. In consequence, when Fräulein Elisabeth's sister married a talented and ambitious man, who unfortunately did not respect their mother, Elisabeth found herself expressing resentment both toward her new brother-in-law and toward her sister for deserting the family.

Elisabeth's younger sister also married in this period, but, fortunately, the couple remained close to the family. This sister then became pregnant and died in childbirth. The widowed brother-in-law was overcome with grief, and he withdrew from Elisabeth's family to seek solace with his own. Thus, in the space of a few years, Elisabeth had lost by death or by alienation those most important to her. She now began a period of almost total social isolation.

For Freud, the case history as thus far related by Fräulein Elisabeth was a great disappointment. True, it was a heartbreaking tale, but it contained no overt indication of the cause of her hysterical symptoms. Freud felt stymied. In the past, such obstacles had been overcome by the judicious use of hypnotism. His frustration was not helped much by Elisabeth's often biting remarks about the lack of effect his treatment exerted on her symptoms. With his usual candor, Freud conceded: "I was obliged to admit that she was in the right" (Freud, in Breuer & Freud, 1893–1895, p. 145).

Second Clue to the Free-Association Method: The Concentration Technique

Freud's experiences with Bernheim at the Nancy Clinic came to his aid. He remembered an unusual demonstration during which Bernheim had suggested to one of his patients under hypnosis the negative hallucination that he, Bernheim, was no longer present in the room. Bernheim further encouraged her in the belief that no amount of effort would enable her to see him, despite any action he might take. Bernheim followed this hypnotic suggestion with a variety of threatening gestures directly in front of the subject's face, but she behaved in every way as if Bernheim truly no longer existed. Bernheim then added to his previous instructions the command to remember nothing of what had transpired, a typical posthypnotic amnesia command. Then, bringing the patient back to wakefulness, he proceeded to demonstrate just the opposite, that is, that the patient *could* recall what had transpired, despite the hypnotic amnesia, if only the hypnotist insisted strongly, urgently, and convincingly enough that the subject do so. To aid the process of recall, Bernheim would place his hand on the forehead of the awake subject and press firmly, while insisting that the memory of the previous events return. Much to Freud's surprise, the subject was able to recall the events of the hypnotic session. Thus, Bernheim had shown Freud that the patient does remember, but he does not know that he remembers until he is pressured to do so. Here was Freud's way out of his dilemma with the hypnotism-resistant Fräulein Elisabeth.

Willful concentration thus became the basis of Freud's new approach to therapy and the investigation of unconscious processes. Of course, the new concentration technique was no less dependent than hypnotism had been on the quality of the relationship between doctor and patient. The new method, in fact, was really another form of manipulating the patient's suggestibility. Freud described his new strategy as follows:

> I decided to start from the assumption that my patients knew everything that was of any pathogenic [disease-causing] significance and that it was only a question of obliging them to communicate it. Thus when I reached a point at which, after asking a patient some question such as "How long have you had this symptom?" or: "What was its origin?," I was met with the answer: "I really don't know," I proceeded as follows. I placed my hand on the patient's forehead or took her head between my hands and said: "You will think of it under the pressure of my hand. At the moment at which I relax my pressure you will see something in front of you or something will come into your head. Catch hold of it. It will be what we are looking for.—Well, what have you seen or what has occurred to you?" [Freud, in Breuer & Freud, 1893–1895, p. 110]

Employing the new concentration technique with Fräulein Elisabeth brought immediate results. After a long silence, she admitted that the pressure of Freud's hand had brought forth the recollection of an evening in which a young man had romantically escorted her home from the social affair they had attended, the pleasure of their intimate conversation during the walk, and her feelings of distress on returning home to nurse her father. Bernheim had been right! Apparently, even the reluctant Fräulein Elisabeth could recall events that seemed meaningful in context without hypnotism. Freud's faith in a deterministic explanation of mental events would not allow that seemingly spontaneous thoughts were random thoughts. Thus, whatever ideas were evoked by the pressure of the concentration technique *had* to be related to the problem at hand. The difficulty remained, however, to discover the relationship between these newly recalled incidents and the ongoing process of her neurotic symptoms.

Conflict, Symbol, Conversion, and Defense

Freud observed that Fräulein Elisabeth's memories bore a very special emotional quality. *They conflicted.* She had known the young man for a short time, and because he could not yet support a wife, and because Elisabeth was dutifully bound to her ailing father, she had resolved to wait until she and her young man were both independent before marrying. But at the same time, she felt that her feelings for the young man were somehow incompatible with her equally worthy resolve to care for her father. She recalled that the night of the social affair, after which she had walked home with the man, marked the height of the conflict between her affection for the young man and her responsibility to her father.

When Elisabeth returned home late that night, she found her father's condition worsened, and she reproached herself for having sacrificed her father's care to her own pleasure. Elisabeth never again left her father for a whole evening. As a result, she saw her young man only rarely thereafter.

At the death of Elisabeth's father, the young man seemed to withdraw, but he probably did so only out of respect for her mourning. Eventually, his business affairs caused him to travel to distant regions, and contact with Elisabeth was completely severed.

Not only was the loss of her first love a painful experience for Elisabeth, but the relationship's premature end deprived her of ever resolving the conflict between her feelings for the young man and her self-imposed duty to her father. In effect, the solution to the conflict was made inaccessible, while the abrasively emotional quality of the incompatible feelings remained untouched.

On the basis of these revelations developed through the concentration technique, Freud reasoned that Elisabeth's symptoms were a technique of defense by which she had unconsciously converted the painful conflicting emotions into a bodily manifestation. Fräulein Elisabeth confirmed Freud's interpretation by informing him that she now knew why her leg pains always began at the same point on her thigh: *This was the exact place upon which her father rested his leg every morning while she changed the bandages on his swollen leg.* Clearly, the pain in her own legs had arisen through association and symbolization with her father's painful leg. Furthermore, as Freud and Elisabeth discussed this interpretation, the pain in her legs intensified, or, as Freud put it: "her painful legs began to 'join in the conversation ...'" (Freud, in Breuer & Freud, 1893–1895, p. 148).

Freud followed up her several symptoms using the new concentration technique. When asked, for instance, why other areas of her legs were painful, Fräulein Elisabeth produced under the pressure of Freud's hands a whole series of recollections of other emotionally painful events. Moreover, each of these events was connected by association or by symbolization with her legs or with the act of walking. For the pain she felt while *standing,* she produced a memory of *standing* at the door when her father was brought home after his heart attack. In her fright on that occasion, she had been frozen in place. When Freud asked her what else the notion of "standing" meant to her, she reproduced a memory of *standing* "as though spellbound" by her sister's deathbed.

Yet, despite the insights that had been attained, there seemed to be some hesitation, some difficulty in recalling certain feelings, desires, or events. It was almost as if Elisabeth, though desirous of cooperating with Freud in the removal of her symptoms, was nonetheless *resisting* the recollection of some important ideas. Freud wondered whether the new concentration technique was already proving a failure, or was there another psychological process at work here?

Resistance: Defensive Barrier to Psychological Pain

On those occasions when Freud applied the concentration technique and Elisabeth reported that nothing had occurred to her, Freud detected behind her tense and preoccupied facial expression a hint that ideas *had* come to her. For some reason, Freud suspected, Elisabeth did not want to communicate her thoughts to him:

> I could think of two motives for this concealment. Either she was applying criticism to the idea, which she had no right to do, on the ground of its not being important enough or of its being an irrelevant reply to the question she had been asked; or she hesitated to produce it because—she found it too disagreeable to tell. [Freud, in Breuer & Freud, p. 153]

Freud therefore decided to proceed as if he had the greatest confidence in his technique. He informed his patient that he knew full well that she had thought of something under the pressure of his hand, and that if she continued to conceal it, she would never be rid of her pains.

Freud had correctly surmised that the cause of her recalcitrance was emotional resistance. Elisabeth ultimately, but reluctantly, complied:

ELISABETH:	"I could have said it to you the first time."
FREUD:	"And why didn't you?"
ELISABETH:	"I thought I could avoid it, but it came back each time," OR "I thought it wasn't what you wanted."

[Freud, in Breuer & Freud, 1893–1895, p. 154]

It was at this point, with the concept of resistance in hand, that Freud was able to gather the several threads of evidence he had been collecting from his patients into one elegant skein. Resistance to recalling significant emotional events is another form of defensive maneuver that the conscious mind employs to protect the individual from threatening thoughts. But such thoughts, though consciously resisted, may nevertheless continue to exert unconscious pressure in their striving for expression, if not in their original form, then in disguised form. Thus, Elisabeth's *symptoms* were not only the *result* of strangulated emotion, they were, indeed, the *unconsciously symbolic expression* of an unresolved conflict. The symptoms are substitute expressions of the conflicted emotions.

Such conflict has been pushed from conscious awareness because it has never been adequately resolved. It continues to be a source of painful and unacceptable self-perceptions. Fräulein Elisabeth's conflict over her duty to her father and her incompatible desire for the companionship of her young man certainly fit this mold. Yet, Freud discovered, there had to be more to it because the abreaction of these emotions had not completely removed Elisabeth's symptoms. There had to be a conflict still unresolved and continuing to operate behind some formidable resistance to its recall.

Symptoms as Self-Punishment

Covering old territory again from his new perspective, Freud began to requestion Elisabeth about the origins of her pains. Her thoughts turned back to the summer resort where she had stayed just before her sister died in childbirth, her worries over her mother's illness, and her feelings of despair and loneliness at having been unable to accomplish anything in life. Particularly strong at this period had been her desire for love, a desire that, contrary to her previous resolve to do without men after her unhappy love affair, had begun to soften her "frozen nature."

With these feelings uppermost in mind, the marriage of her sister to a man who cared lovingly and tenderly for her made a profound impression on Elisabeth. She knew that her sister regretted becoming pregnant again so soon after her first child's birth. But Elisabeth also knew, and marveled at, the way her sister bore the discomfort of the illness resulting from her pregnancy with absolute calm for the sake of her husband. At the summer resort, Elisabeth went on a walk with this brother-in-law. He had wanted to remain with his sick wife, but even she urged him to accompany Elisabeth, and he relented. Elisabeth tremendously enjoyed the afternoon she spent with her sister's husband because they talked freely and intimately, and, for the first time, she had the feeling that someone really understood her. In consequence, she became overwhelmed with the desire to possess a man like her brother-in-law. In fact, so strong was this desire that, a few days after their walk, Elisabeth returned to the place in the woods where they had been together and, in a reverie, dreamed of a man like him who might make her as happy as her sister. She arose from the reverie with her legs in pain.

The nature of her hidden conflict had become crystal clear to Freud: Elisabeth desired her brother-in-law, but she felt guilty over such feelings, particularly so because his wife—her own sister—was now ill and helpless. As clear as the conflict was to Freud, it was in the same measure obscure to Elisabeth. Because she had, apparently, never admitted the existence of these feelings, her guilty wish had remained utterly alien to her conscious personality. Ironically, several months after that fateful walk in the woods, Elisabeth's wish almost came true. She was called to her sister's sickbed but when she arrived, her sister was dead.

> At that moment of dreadful certainty that her beloved sister was dead without bidding them farewell and without having eased her last days with her care—at that very moment another thought had shot through Elisabeth's mind, and now forced itself irresistibly upon her once more, like a flash of lightning in the dark: "Now he is free again and I can be his wife." [Freud, in Breuer & Freud, 1893–1895, p. 156]

Here was the confirmation of Freud's burgeoning speculations about conflict and emotional resistance. Elisabeth had converted a series of painful ideas into bodily symptoms to exact a kind of self-punishment for the illicit wish for her brother-in-law and to atone for the reprehensible feeling of gladness at the thought that her sister's death had freed him to marry her. By the time she had come to treatment with Freud, the memory of her love and guilt had already been defensively isolated from her awareness.

Fräulein Elisabeth was devastated at the realization of her own feelings. Freud was kind to point out, however, that, strictly speaking, she was not responsible for her feelings and, more important, her symptoms and suffering were proof enough of her sound moral sense.

The Theoretical Yield from Fräulein Elisabeth's Therapy

Freud had progressed sufficiently in his use of the cathartic method with Fräulein Elisabeth to consolidate his observations into important theoretical concepts.

Concentration Technique

Fräulein Elisabeth's lack of susceptibility to hypnotism had initially prodded Freud into the search for a new therapeutic technique. Thus, Fräulein
Elisabeth von R. provided the occasion for Freud's incorporation of a
second clue in the process of formulating his final psychoanalytic method
of free association. Bernheim's demonstration at the Nancy Clinic that a
posthypnotic patient could willfully remember his previous hypnotic experiences if he was authoritatively pressured to do so became the prototype for Freud's hand-pressure concentration technique with the
recalcitrant Elisabeth. (Freud's first clue, it will be recalled, was Frau Emmy's acid remark that he should allow her to speak her mind without
interruption.)

Defense and Resistance

The discovery, through use of the concentration technique, that Elisabeth's
thought processes were directed by *active resistance* to unacceptable ideas
was a hard-won insight. Ironically, only through the loss of hypnotism as
a therapeutic tool could the significance, cause, and direction of the process
of resistance be uncovered. Because the patient in the hypnotic state is
freed from active avoidance of unacceptable impulses and ideas, the *defensive* nature of this "forgetting" in the conscious state could not be discerned.

Freud's discovery clearly had brought about a drastic change not only
in the way therapy was conducted, but in the theoretical conception by
which its effects were to be understood. Breuer's cathartic method focused
on the problem of breaching the patient's conscious amnesia through
hypnosis to reach dammed-up emotions. Once reached, these feelings
could finally be spent in a therapeutic reenactment of the traumatic moment. Then, hypnotic suggestion was employed to help the patient to
forget the unpleasantness of his experiences and to conduct his life without the troublesome symptom. Freud, in contrast, had reshaped the rules
of the game by zeroing in, not on the symptom and its backlog of unexpressed emotion, but on the patient's *unwillingness* to recall his painful or
unacceptable thoughts.

The goal of psychotherapy for Freud became the examination and interpretation of the patient's resistances in an attempt to enable the patient to
deal with conflicts that had festered, defensively protected from real resolution. Thus, by working with, rather than by circumventing, emotional
resistance, Freud discovered that hysterical symptoms were a form of
psychological defense against threatening ideas and wishes. The symptoms of the neurosis were symbolic and associative replacements for the
pain of unresolved, "forgotten" conflicts.

Repression and Conflict

If Fräulein Elisabeth could not willingly recall her desire for her sister's husband or her guilt feelings, and if she vigorously resisted the thought when pressured, then some psychological force that actively keeps the memory out of consciousness must have been operating. Furthermore, this same counterforce must have been responsible for originally removing the memory from awareness. Freud christened this hypothetical force *repression.*

Repression is a kind of motivated amnesia for certain impulses, ideas, or events. Resistance to recall is one evidence of motivated forgetting or repression. But the minute the word "motivated" is used, it becomes necessary to ask what that motive might be. The answer, it seemed clear to Freud, lies in the nature of the cognitive-emotional state known as conflict.

Not just any unpleasant thought, not just any painful memory succumbs to repression. Only memories, thoughts, ideas that are somehow connected to impulses or wishes *that are unacceptable to the individual's conscious ethical standards* are capable of the intense anxiety needed to trigger repression (Freud, 1910b, p. 24).

Removal from consciousness is one way of avoiding the emotional pain of the conflict when a solution to the discord is unavailable. Thus, the thought that she was glad that her sister was dead because her sister's death freed the husband to marry again was a totally unacceptable idea to Elisabeth's ethical self. If the problem had been only a momentary desire for her sister's husband, Elisabeth would probably have only *suppressed* (not *repressed*) the thought. Suppression involves the conscious or deliberate avoidance of certain ideas with the individual's full awareness that he refuses to entertain them. Repression, on the other hand, is characterized by the *unconscious, automatic* nature of the "forgetting" that it accomplishes. When repression operates, the individual is *not* aware that he is avoiding certain thoughts or impulses. In fact, we could say along with R. D. Laing, that when an individual represses an idea, he "forgets" it and then "forgets" that he forgot it (see Chapter 8 for Laing's treatment of this concept).

Sometimes suppression of a thought, though it begins as a deliberate act of mental avoidance, may grade imperceptibly into habitual "not-thinking" about the idea. When suppression has been practiced long enough, rigidly enough, and widely enough, it may become such an unthinking act that it is seemingly indistinguishable from an act of genuine repression. But the motive for such habitual "not-thinking" responses is vastly different from the motives that trigger repression, for repression is not brought about gradually but abruptly and automatically because its underlying conflict is unbearable.

In Elisabeth's case, this intensity of conflict was clearly present from the beginning. The fact that her illicit wish had become associatively connected with the even more reprehensible feeling of gladness that her sister was dead was too powerful a combination for Elisabeth to face consciously. The nascent conflict would become a two-pronged kernel of pain: the unacceptable wish for her brother-in-law and the wicked feeling of pleasure at her sister's death. Freud's most profound discovery about the nature of defensive repression was that it is not any *one* unacceptable thought that causes its removal from awareness; it is the *combination* of thoughts or feelings and their interrelationships that intensify psychological pain to the point where it cannot be consciously borne. Moreover, *each* element of the conflict clashes powerfully with the individual's ethical self-image.

A Dynamic Unconscious

Unfortunately, though removed from consciousness by repression, conflicts continue to operate unconsciously, producing symptoms that symbolically or through association with other ideas replace the conflict's psychological pain. Therefore, repression of wishes or impulses is not an adequate resolution of conflict at all. The symptom, Freud discovered, carries on the conflict in distorted form. In Fräulein Elisabeth's case, the symptoms of pain in the legs and the inability to walk or stand were shaped by a series of symbolic ("standing alone") and associative links (*standing* in shock by dead sister's bed; *walking* with her brother-in-law; *walking* with her first love while she should have been caring for her father; father placing *leg* on her *thigh* to be bandaged).

Breuer had been right: The energy of the strangulated emotion had to be expressed somehow. But the cause of the neurotic's symptoms was not simply the damming up of emotional energy. First, Freud realized, there had to be a wish or an impulse that was *incompatible* with that individual's conscious self-perception. Such a wish would be at odds with his everyday ethical principles. Only this incompatibility could carry the conflict to an ego-threatening intensity. *Then* the conflict's associated emotions could be dammed up by repression. Conflict of a wish with a conscious ethical principle—this is the essence of defense by repression. It is an active, dynamic process giving painful, if mute, evidence of the power of unconscious forces.

It is interesting to note that some early attempts at experimental testing of the Freudian hypothesis of repression sorely missed the point. Some of these experimenters naïvely assumed, in their enthusiasm to design experiments, that *any* anxiety-provoking idea could trigger repression.[3] Often,

[3]See Mackinnon & Dukes, 1962, for a review of the experimental literature on repression. Eriksen & Pierce, 1968, provide a broad overview of the methodological problems encountered in studying all defense mechanisms. See also Murray, 1938, Chap. 6, for some of the early studies on repression, and Rapaport, 1971, Chaps. 5, 7, 8, for a conceptual analysis of the early repression work. Interesting for the broad perspective it offers on experimental tests of Freudian hypotheses is the volume by Hans Eysenck and Glenn Wilson, 1973, which presents some of the original research reports and follows them with cogent, if pessimistic, criticism. A more optimistic view of the experimental tests of Freudian theory is given by Kline, 1972.

this unsophisticated version of the theory led to the creation of mild forms of anxiety or unpleasantness as experimental analogs of Freud's ideas. In a great number of cases these attempts did not come close to the kind and the quality of anguish that Freud conceptualized as the basis of repression. The mechanism of repression remains a difficult phenomenon to study in the laboratory (see Monte, 1975, Chap. 3).

Freud's Final Clue to the Method of Free Association

For his final modification of his developing therapeutic procedures, Freud followed yet another clue, a recollection from his own youth. One of his favorite authors, Ludwig Borne, had offered the following advice to those who wish to write creatively:

> Take a few sheets of paper and for three days on end write down, without fabrication or hypocrisy, everything that comes into your head. Write down what you think of yourself, of your wife, of the Turkish War, of Goethe, of Fonk's trial, of the Last Judgement, of your superiors—and when three days have passed you will be quite out of your senses with astonishment at the new and unheard-of thoughts you have had.[Quoted in Freud, 1920b, p. 265. See also Jones, 1953, p. 246]

The passage just quoted was part of a complete essay entitled "The Art of Becoming an Original Writer in Three Days." At the age of fourteen years, Freud was given a present of the collected works of Ludwig Borne. Ernest Jones reports that Borne had been such a favorite with the young Freud that only Borne's books survived Freud's adolescence to become part of his adult library (1953, p. 246). Freud himself acknowledged his debt to Borne for the latent kernel of an important idea that was to revise his therapeutic method completely.

Borne's startling proposal apparently left a lasting impression on Freud, for he now began to follow Borne's advice, not for writing, but for allowing his patients free play for their thoughts during therapy. Freud developed a technique of therapeutic communication designed to permit patients to roam freely through their fleeting thoughts, verbalizing each idea as it occurred. He permitted his patients to omit *nothing.* Freud instructed each of his patients in the new technique of *free association* in the following way:

> You will notice that as you relate things various thoughts will occur to you which you would like to put aside on the ground of certain criticisms and objections. You will be tempted to say to yourself that this or that is irrelevant here, or is quite unimportant, or nonsensical, so that there is no need to say it. *You must never give in to these*

*criticisms, but must say it in spite of them—indeed, you must say it precisely
because you have an aversion to doing so.* ... Finally, never forget that
you have promised to be absolutely honest, and never leave anything
out because, for some reason or other, it is unpleasant to tell it. [1913,
pp. 134–135; italics added]

Thus, the "fundamental rule" of psychoanalysis, as Freud called it, was
to say everything that comes to mind with no attempt to edit the stream
of thought logically or emotionally. Sometimes patients had great difficulty following the fundamental rule. Freud had observed a similar difficulty earlier when using the concentration technique on those occasions
when a patient would object: "As a matter of fact, I knew that the first
time, but it was just what I didn't want to say" (Freud, in Breuer & Freud,
1893–1895, p. 111). In fact, patients would employ the most devious techniques of escaping the new fundamental rule. They would engage Freud
in conversation about the decorations in his office, or in a discussion about
the state of the weather, or they would pursue some abstract and irrelevant
topic on which they considered themselves expert—anything rather than
abandon logical and emotional censorship over their thoughts.

With careful prodding and urging, and with constant reminders and
corrections, Freud eventually helped his patients to see the importance of
abandoning the mind to its own directions. Actually, the notion that the
associations dredged up in this way are "free" should not be taken to mean
that they are random or accidental. Quite to the contrary, Freud discovered, the unconscious is bound by its own emotional logic that strictly
determines the sequence, content, and speed of the flow of ideas.

Compromise Formation: The Meaning of Symptoms

Consider the following description of disordered behavior:

An eleven-year-old boy would not sleep each night until he had
performed the following compulsive ceremony. He recounted to his
mother every minute detail of the day; all scraps of paper, lint, or
rubbish on the carpet in his bedroom had to be picked up; the bed
had to be pushed up against the wall; three chairs, no more, no fewer,
must stand by the bed; the pillows must be placed in a particular
pattern on the bed. Finally, just before sleeping, the boy had to kick
out with his legs a certain specified number of times and then lie on
his side. Only then would sleep come. [Based on Freud, 1896b, p. 172]

The young boy's sleep ritual is evidence of a severe emotional disturbance known as *obsessional neurosis.* Obsessional neurotics practice a variety of ritualistic behaviors that bear the mark of anxiety. When the

obsessive is prevented from carrying out the behavior in question, he succumbs to an intense anxiety attack. The obsessive patient suffers from ostensibly unwanted but continually intruding ideas that threaten to flood his consciousness, despite his attempts to control them. Performance of a rituallike series of behaviors temporarily alleviates the discomfort produced by the constant succession of the obsessive ideas. The problem is to understand the connection between the obsessive ideas and the compulsive anxiety-reducing ritualistic behaviors. Utilizing his new conception of "defense," Freud sought to unlock the mystery of the obsessive's behavior by attempting to understand the *personal meaning* of symptoms.

> The nature of obsessional neurosis can be expressed in a simple formula. *Obsessional ideas* are invariably transformed *self-reproaches* which have re-emerged from *repression* and which always relate to some *sexual* act that was performed with pleasure in childhood. [1896b, p. 169]

Unable to sleep until his ceremonial acts involving chairs, pillows, bed, and rug had been accomplished, along with a detailed explanation to his mother of the day's events, the eleven-year-old boy was able to reveal in analysis the defensive nature of these compulsive behaviors. Some years earlier, a servant girl had abused him sexually at bedtime. She had lain on top of him in the bed and this memory was forgotten until a recent similar experience revived it. The defensive meaning of the ceremony became clear:

> The chairs were placed in front of the bed and the bed pushed against the wall in order that nobody else should be able to get at the bed; the pillows were arranged in a particular way so that they should be differently arranged from how they were on that evening; the movements with his legs were to kick away the person who was lying on him; sleeping on his side was because in the scene [with the servant girl] he had been lying on his back; his circumstantial confession to his mother was because, in obedience to a prohibition by his seductress, he had been silent to his mother about this and other sexual experiences; and, finally, the reason for his keeping his bedroom floor clean was that neglect to do so had been the chief reproach that he had so far had to hear from his mother. [Freud, 1896b, pp. 172n.–173n.]

Each of these compulsive behaviors served a double purpose. First, they served as a means of self-initiated, self-inflicted punishment for having engaged in behavior that was pleasurable but "bad." Second, performance of the ritual allowed the boy no time to think about the guilt-provoking memory or about possible future seductions. Thus, preventive distraction, as well as self-imposed penance, formed the basis of his symptoms.

Paradoxically, the obsessive ideas and the compulsive acts were also the means to gratify the pleasurable (yet anxiety-triggering) impulse involved in the taboo sexual activity. Each night, through the symptomatic ritual, the original seduction was recalled or relived. The symptoms, were, therefore, *compromise formations:* They balanced the anxiety and the guilt of the conscious personality against the pleasurable gratifications sought by the unconscious.

Only by assuming the defensively altered form of the somewhat magical ritual acts could the repressed memory of the seduction take a place in consciousness. In effect, the symptoms symbolically substituted for the sexual gratification that the boy would not allow himself in reality (Freud, 1916, vol. XVI, p. 368). The patient reproached himself for "bad wishes" and guilt-provoking experiences, expiating the guilt by ritual, while his symptoms achieved partial gratification of the very same wish that he sought to repudiate. In performing his defensive ritual against seduction, the young boy reenacted, not any the less completely, the very experience he struggled to escape.

Sexual Motives as the Basis of Conflict: Origins of the Hypothesis

The common denominator that Freud had discovered among his patients was the presence of erotic impulses from childhood that were frustrated or guilt-laden. Thus, to take but two examples, Fräulein Elisabeth suffered the pain of unacceptable desire for her brother-in-law as this desire clashed with her sense of moral responsibility; the eleven-year-old boy's sleep ritual involved the stress produced by a pleasurable, yet anxiety-laden, seduction. Many of Freud's other patients revealed sexual themes in their free associations and, in each such case, Freud was able to trace the themes back to incidents and experiences of childhood. Additionally, Freud recalled some years later in writing the *History of the Psycho-Analytic Movement* (1914b) that offhand comments of Breuer, Charcot, and a gynecologist named Chrobak about the sexual nature of neurotic disorders in women had shown that the idea had fleetingly passed through the minds of other workers in the field. Chrobak and Breuer later denied any knowledge of such comments, and Freud concluded that Charcot, too, would have joined them in denial had he had the opportunity (Jones, 1953, p. 248). Could a nineteenth-century Viennese physician foist on the Victorian world the hypothesis that *erotic* conflict was the basis of neurotic disorder? Freud did not hesitate.

Sexual Motives and the Seduction Hypothesis

Intrigued by the direction his clinical investigations were taking, Freud asked the logical question: Why should *sexual* experiences and *sexual* motives be the common denominator in the cases he had observed? The answer, he suspected, could be found only by examining the neurotic's fundamental defensive response: namely, repression.

Only emotional content intense enough to overwhelm the ego was ever subject to repression in the patients he had treated. One would, therefore, logically expect—if sexual motives were the common denominator—that any emotion connected with the sexual experiences of his patients would have been correspondingly intense. But there is a problem with this supposition. Most of Freud's patients were able through analysis to trace the critical sexual experiences to their childhood years when, presumably, their physical capacity for sexual stimulation had been undeveloped or nonexistent. Hence, the seduction by an adult in childhood could not have led to full understanding or to full sexual arousal with its normal accompaniment of emotional excitation. *How, then, could these relatively mild childhood feelings ever have been intense enough to trigger repression?*

The time sequence was wrong. Logically, the sequence should have been, first, some sexual experience like a forceful seduction by an adult; then, repression of the experience because of the intensity of the conflict between feelings of pleasurable arousal and feelings of guilt or anxiety; and, finally, the outbreak of neurotic symptoms on behalf of the repressed impulses. But if the traumatic seduction had taken place in childhood, as many of his patients reported, this sequence was impossible. There could not have been sufficient sexual arousal or pleasure in a child to establish an intense enough conflict to trigger repression *at that time.*

In order for repression to have occurred, a new, inverted sequence had to be postulated, placing repression at the end of the process: Sexual experience (seduction) occurs first; then amnesia for it until some stimulus or situation triggers by its similarity recall of the incident *at maturity;then,* finally, repression and symptom formation *after maturity has been reached.* In other words, neurosis was not a *product* of childhood, but a *process* begun in those early years and brought to fruition in maturity (Freud, 1896b, 1896c, and 1898, vol. III, pp. 279–285).

Logic of the Seduction Hypothesis

Freud examined the new hypothesis carefully. Ordinarily, he knew, when thoughts are entertained that have sexual content, the *adult* thinker responds with simultaneous arousal of the sexual organs. This primary bodily arousal is always more intense than any later, secondary *memory* of the experience. But if his reasoning up to this point was correct, a sexual seduction experienced *before* physical maturity (that is, before eight to ten years) would be experienced only as a somewhat faded recollection years later in maturity. It becomes necessary, therefore, to assume that the memory is intensified from some other source of energy (cf. Freud, 1954, Letter No. 52, p. 174).

Suppose that source of energy was the bodily arousal associated with sexual excitation. Further suppose that physical sexual arousal could be rechanneled into psychological emotional arousal. In effect, the result would be a conversion of *physical,* biological energy into *mental,* psychological energy. If such a process was possible, then the *memory* of the earlier experience (that is, the seduction) would initiate the *deferred* bodily arousal some years after the experience, when the individual had developed the biological capacity for appropriate somatic response. In this delayed version it is the *memory* of the experience that leads to the kind of intense physical arousal that is stronger than the original passive-seduction experience itself.

Proportionate *adult* anxiety and guilt would accompany and augment the memory image—intensifying it—to bring about the conflicting psychological state of affairs that was not possible during the actual experience in childhood (cf. Freud, 1896b, pp. 172–175 and pp. 166n.–167n.; see also 1916, Lecture XXIII, vol. XVI, pp. 361–371). Thus, Freud reasoned, a memory could be more potent than the actual experience that it represented *if* there was a biological process that lagged behind the psychological development of children. At maturity there would be sufficient incremental emotional arousal, freshly fueled by the slower-developing biological events, for repression to operate.

Freud had managed to answer the key question as to why *sexual* content, above all else, was the basis of the neurotic disorders he had seen. Only the *sexual* experiences of individuals are subject to the delay in physical development that human biology imposes. So, of all the experiences and motives of childhood, only the *sexual* among them would succumb to repression because only the *sexual* experiences become intensified by the developments of puberty. *Neurotics, indeed, suffer from reminiscences.*

Abandonment of the Seduction Theory

The seduction hypothesis was an elegant one, for it accounted in one stroke for two observations: the reports of childhood seductions by his patients, and the fact that his patients had been mentally healthy throughout childhood, succumbing to neurotic disorder only in adulthood. However, two new questions posed themselves: *What accounts for the period of childhood amnesia during which the seduction experience remains dormant?* and *What stimulates the recollection of these early seductions in adulthood?* In supplying answers to these questions Freud discovered that he had made a near-fatal error.

Reviewing the evidence on which the seduction hypothesis had been based, Freud discovered that he had been a victim of his own naïveté. In a letter written to his friend Wilhelm Fliess on September 21, 1897, Freud revealed how some critical rethinking had caused the collapse of his seduction theory (1954, pp. 215–217). He frankly enumerated the reasons: (1) the high improbability of universal sexual abuse of children by their fathers, though for a time it had seemed credible; (2) the failure of his patients' revelations of such seductions to accomplish any lasting therapeutic effect; (3) his hard-won insight that the unconscious cannot distinguish between reality and fantasy, an insight that had forced the conclusion that the reports of childhood seduction were not of real events but of *imagined* happenings; and (4) the discovery that, even in the severe psychoses, when the unconscious contents flood consciousness, no infantile sexual seductions are revealed.

Freud could only comment, years later:

> ... If the reader feels inclined to shake his head at my credulity, I cannot altogether blame him. ... When, however, I was at last obliged to recognize that these scenes were only phantasies which my patients had made up or which I myself forced on them, I was for a time completely at a loss. [1925a, p. 34]

Toward a Revised Theory: Childhood Sexuality

Freud did not long remain in this bewildered state. He began to revise his thinking in the light of the new evidence that seduction tales were fantasies, products of the imagination.

> If hysterical subjects trace back their symptoms to traumas that are fictitious, then the new fact which emerges is precisely *that they create such scenes in phantasy,* and this psychical reality requires to be taken into account alongside practical reality. This reflection was soon followed by the discovery that these phantasies were intended to cover up the autoerotic activity of the first years of childhood, to embellish it and raise it to a higher plane. And now, from behind the phantasies, the whole range of a child's sexual life came to light. [1914b, pp. 17–18; italics added]

Freud was gradually coming to the view that children are not *passive* participants in erotic activities imposed on them, as the seduction hypothesis had it, but they are, instead, *active initiators* of behaviors designed to bring sensual pleasure. Moreover, Freud had begun to understand the importance of fantasy in the mental economy of his patients. Imaginary events, he realized, occupied the same status as real events *in the unconscious.* It was only a short jump from this realization to the discovery that neurotics are not unique in this characteristic.

Personal Sources of the Hypothesis: Freud's Self-Analysis

In the months before he announced to Fliess his not-quite-fatal error of the seduction hypothesis, Freud had begun to subject his own dreams and thoughts to careful scrutiny through the method of free association (Kris,

1954, p. 30; Jones, 1953, pp. 319–323). Beginning in the summer of 1897, Freud embarked on a process of self-exploration that was to occupy him for the rest of his life. Although we cannot trace the entire progress of his self-analysis here, several crucial discoveries deserve our consideration both for what they reveal about Freud and for the light they throw on the origins of some of his ideas. For, much to his own amazement, Freud uncovered a quasi-erotic love for his mother and an equally disturbing hostility toward his father, discoveries that were later to be incorporated into psychoanalytic theory as central tenets (Freud, 1900, pp. 318, 583).

The triggering incident for Freud's application of psychoanalytic method to himself seems to have been the emotional aftermath of his father's death in October, 1896. Though Freud did not at this time begin his "official" self-analysis, the emotional upheaval of the loss and some resultant family discord over proper funeral rites occasioned a dream about his father that provoked in him some residue of unexpected guilt. The dream led Freud to suspect that he was not as sorry for the loss of his father as he should have been. Yet, as he wrote to Fliess, he experienced a feeling of "being torn up by the roots," and he continued to be troubled in this way for some months (1954, letter No. 50, p. 170). Some years later, in *The Interpretation of Dreams* (1900, vol. IV, p. xxvi), Freud acknowledged that his father's death was "the most poignant loss of a man's life" and had played a significant part in both his self-analysis and in the writing of that book.

Another motive for Freud's undertaking the task of self-analysis was his discovery in himself of several mild neurotic symptoms (Schur, 1972, esp. chap. 4). In addition to a very uncharacteristic overconcern with the prospect of an early death prompted by some cardiac symptoms, Freud also evidenced a phobia regarding travel. His concern for his health and the fear that he was developing severe heart disease may have had some element of neurotic anxiety at its core, though the physical symptoms were certainly genuine (Jones, 1953; Schur, 1972). Indeed, the only time in his life when he would abstain from his cherished cigars occurred during this period of somewhat superstitious worry over the possibility of an early, nicotine-aggravated death. To understand how out of character for Freud such concerns were, consider that, years later, stricken with cancer of the mouth and facing the certainty of an unpleasant death, he clung to his cigars all the more fervently.

A somewhat different neurotic symptom concerned Freud's behavior when setting out on the journeys he professed to love so much. Throughout his life, he would frequently turn up at a railway station hours before his train was scheduled to depart, apparently in the compulsive attempt not to miss his train. But he would just as often enter the wrong rail station or board the wrong train. Freud recognized that these were symptomatic acts suggestive of anxiety and an unconscious unwillingness to embark on a journey.

Ever willing to face and accept the truth, Freud's passion to be master of his fate must have played no small role in his decision to turn on himself the same method of exploration he was so carefully shaping with his patients.

Self-Discovery of Sexual Feelings: The Oedipus Complex

The most pertinent aspect of Freud's self-analysis for our consideration of his developing theory involved his discovery within himself of what he would later call the Oedipus Complex. As his self-analysis progressed, he was able to reconstruct and, with his mother's help, corroborate several memories from childhood. These reconstructions allowed him to piece together a fairly accurate account of his own childhood emotional life. One such memory fragment concerned a recollection of an elderly woman who had been the infant Freud's nurse along with the memory of a seemingly unconnected but especially important train ride with his mother:

> ... the "prime originator" [of my troubles] was a woman, ugly, elderly, but clever, who told me a great deal about God Almighty and Hell and who gave me a high opinion of my own capacities; and that later (between the ages of two and two-and-a-half) my libido [sexual interest] was stirred up towards *matrem,* namely on the occasion of a journey with her from Leipzig to Vienna, during which we must have spent the night together and I must have had an opportunity of seeing her *nudam.* . . . [1897, vol. I, Letter No. 70, p. 262]

This passage from Freud's correspondence with Fliess is remarkable for a number of reasons. First, it is a clear indication of the importance of an idea that Freud had been toying with for some time: namely, that the child experiences sexual impulses toward his mother. By "sexual" Freud meant to include all pleasurable and affectionate interactions, commonly called *love,* between mother and child (see, for example, Freud, 1925a, p. 38). (We will again pick up this idea at a later point in the chapter.) Further on in this same letter, Freud hinted that his anxiety over travelling could be dated to the train ride with his mother and the residue of guilt that remained from his feelings toward her.

The second important aspect of this memory fragment is Freud's admission of such feelings in himself. Notice, however, that both the word for "mother" *(matrem)* and the word for "naked" *(nudam)* are in Latin, as though writing them in his native German would have made them all the more unpalatable. Clearly, Freud experienced first hand the kind of emotional resistance that his patients often exhibited.

Third, Freud evidenced another characteristic typical of a patient undergoing psychoanalysis, an erring sense of time. Freud could not have been only two or two-and-a-half years old, as he states. Ernest Jones, after careful research, places the date of the train ride somewhat later, at around the age of four years (1953, p. 13). Max Schur, Freud's more recent biographer, concurs with Jones' estimate (1972, p. 120). Indeed, Schur suggests that it is probable that the infant Freud had many times observed some intimate scenes between his mother and father in the crowded conditions of their home.

Fourth, the "prime originator" mentioned in the letter was the nursemaid who had cared for Freud as an infant and for several years of his childhood. This enigmatic old woman had popped in and out of Freud's memories for years, haunting him like a ghost with a message to tell but no voice with which to announce it. During his self-analysis the memory finally yielded its secret. To substantiate his analysis, Freud asked his mother, now in her old age, to confirm the facts of his recollection.

She told him that he had indeed had a nurse who was elderly but clever, and that she had been arrested for stealing his gold coins and toys. At the time of the incident, Freud's mother was in bed in the last stages of pregnancy with Freud's younger sister, Anna. In consequence, it was Freud's older half-brother, Philipp, who had gone to fetch a policeman to arrest the treacherous maid. Furthermore, Freud's mother revealed, the maid had been *imprisoned* for ten months. With these facts in hand, Freud could ask of himself even more probing questions:

> I said to myself that if the old woman disappeared so suddenly [on account of her imprisonment], it must be possible to point to the impression this made on me. Where is that impression, then? A scene then occurred to me which for the last 29 years has occasionally emerged in my conscious memory without my understanding it. My mother was nowhere to be found: I was screaming my head off. My brother Philipp, twenty years older than me, was holding open a cupboard for me, and, when I found that my mother was not inside it either, I began crying still more, till, *looking slim and beautiful,* she came in by the door. What can this mean? Why was my brother opening the cupboard, though he knew that my mother was not in it, so that this could not pacify me? And then suddenly I understood. *I had asked him to do it. When I missed my mother, I had been afraid she had vanished from me just as the old woman had a short time before* [i.e., the maid's imprisonment]. Now I must have heard that the old woman had been locked up and consequently *I must have thought that my mother had been too—* or rather had been "boxed up"; for my brother Philipp, who is 63 now, is fond to this very day of talking in this punning fashion. *The fact that it was to him in particular that I turned proves that I knew quite well of his share in the nurse's disappearance.* [1897, vol. I, Letter No. 71, pp. 264–265; italics added]

Freud's memory had condensed the account of the maid's disappearance with the memory of his mother's pregnancy. Analysis of the reconstructed memory revealed a peculiar pattern of motivation. There was the implied accusation against Philipp to the effect that he has made Freud's mother vanish. Philipp was represented as a rival who controlled the whereabouts of Freud's mother, a rival, that is, who possessed adult authority. From other details of Freud's life it was clear that Philipp also represented specifically a father-substitute. Note, too, that Freud's mother appeared in the memory as "slim and beautiful," emphasizing that her pregnancy was terminated.

Three elements, then, required interpretation: concern over his mother's pregnancy; the demand that his half-brother open the *cupboard;* and an implied connection between Philipp's causing the maid's disappearance and the disappearance of his own mother. Freud's self-analysis allowed him to clarify the relations among these three elements, as he reported some years later in *Psychopathology of Everyday Life:*

> Anyone who is interested in the mental life of these years of childhood will find it easy to guess the deeper determinant of the demand made on the big brother [i.e., the request to open the cupboard]. The child of not yet three [i.e., Freud himself] had understood that the little sister [Anna] who had recently arrived had grown inside his mother. He was very far from approving of this addition to the family, and was full of mistrust and anxiety that his mother's inside might conceal still more children. *The wardrobe or cupboard was a symbol for him of his mother's inside.* So he insisted on looking into this cupboard and turned for this to his *big brother, who* (as is clear from other material) *had taken his father's place as the child's rival.* Besides the well founded suspicion that this brother had had the lost nurse "boxed up," there was a further suspicion against him—namely that *he had in some way introduced the recently born baby into his mother's inside.* [1901, p. 51n.; italics added]

The young Freud's disappointment when the cupboard was opened and his mother was not to be found inside was assuaged only by his relief when she reappeared *slim and beautiful,* that is, without any other unwanted children. Key emotions contained in these disturbing memories involved the desperate fear of losing his mother to an adult rival, the vague understanding that men somehow put babies inside women, and the defensive telescoping of the maid's having been "boxed up" at the hands of the same adult rival with the memory of his mother's disappearance. Freud had thus discovered within himself the essential elements of the emotional constellation to be known later as the Oedipus complex.

It should perhaps again be mentioned that Freud never ceased his self-analysis, reserving the last half-hour of his day throughout his life for such self-exploration (Jones, 1953, p. 327). Yet it was from the earliest self-analytic attempts that Freud derived his most fertile ideas, those which he sought to further corroborate with his patients. The implication of these early disturbing self-insights was clear: *Children are capable of diffuse sexual feelings and the first objects of their erotic endeavors and resulting jealous aggression are their parents, the people with whom they have had the most intimate contact.*

It becomes necessary at this point to break off our essentially chronological treatment of psychoanalytic theory to gather together the several threads of Freud's continually evolving views of sexual development.

Psychosexual Development

Human infants are born essentially helpless and vulnerable to all manner of painful and potentially lethal stimulation. It is only through the efforts of their caretakers that infants survive the first several years of life.

Autoerotic Activity and Erotogenic Bodily Zones

Consider the situation of the well-cared-for infant. When he experiences hunger, his cries bring his mother with nourishment in the form of breast or bottle. The sucking response with which he meets the nipple, though reflex at first, not only provides the needed nourishment to terminate the hunger pains, but soon itself becomes a pleasurable source of stimulation. Gentle stimulation of the lips and mouth, the infant quickly learns, is quite satisfying and sensually pleasing. Thus, even a thumb may become an object of sensual pleasure. In a sense, then, he is finding satisfaction through the stimulation of his own body; he is, in Freud's terms, behaving *auto*erotically (1905, pp. 181–182). The pleasurable activity of the mouth may be thought of as the prototype for various other potentially pleasurable zones of the body that yield satisfaction to rhythmic stimulation. Primary of such *erotogenic zones,* as they are called, are those areas of the body characterized by the presence of a mucous membrane, for example, the anus. But the infant's body pleasures are not restricted to mucous membrane areas. With time, these mucous membrane prototypes yield their dominance so that almost any part of the body may become an erotogenic zone. Thus, the skin when tickled or stroked produces great delight; the anus during elimination provides a sense of satisfaction at the pleasure of discharging tension, and so on.

The important point is that the child searches his own body, seeking the sensations of pleasure that it will offer to the knowing touch. Consequently, Freud concluded, the infant's chief aim is the attainment of bodily or "organ pleasure" based on his experiences with the world, his body, and its caretakers. Food and the breast provided the first such experience and the mother was the medium through which that learning took place. Because the mother is directly connected with almost every other important—pleasurable and unpleasurable—activity of the infant's life, it follows that it will be the mother who becomes the object of the child's constantly developing modes of seeking new pleasures.

Libido and the Widened Meaning of "Sexual"

The biological force underlying the child's pleasure-seeking activity is the sexual drive or *libido* (cf. Freud, 1905, p. 135; and 1916, vol. XVI, Lecture XX, p. 313). (*Libido* is a concept that will be given much more detailed consideration in the context of Freud's theory of instincts in Chapter 3 of this book.) The term "sexual" cannot be confined to the adult sense in which it is customarily used to indicate *genital,* procreative activity. Genital primacy, one component of the generalized sexual instinct or libido, is a relatively late, postpubertal development. Genital sexuality has origins far more diffuse and deeply rooted in infantile pleasure-seeking activity than is ordinarily realized. Thus, libido must be thought of as a drive for generalized bodily or sensual pleasure. Adult, genital sexuality is only the final step in a long apprenticeship to pleasure.

The Oedipus Complex

The Oedipus complex occurs as a kind of emotionally climactic midpoint in the developmental sequence of the child's ever-increasing interest in pleasurable sexual activity. In the first stages of psychosexual development, the child's dominant erotogenic zones are the oral and the anal areas. Eventually, however, through exploration of his own body, he discovers the pleasure to be derived from manipulation of a new zone, the genital area. It is at this point, when the mother first discovers the child's errant hand seeking out that "taboo" part of his body, that she is likely to take measures to prevent such "perversity." Her admonitions may take the form of direct or veiled threats to remove the tempting organ, or, more typically, she may delegate the responsibility to father (Freud, 1940, p. 189). Parental practices like these may have been widespread in the Victorian age, but it is doubtful that a contemporary mother or father would resort to such extreme threats. Freud nevertheless thought that children may invent such threats for themselves from even the most remote references to punishment.

If the threat is at first unbelievable, it easily becomes more real when it is reinforced by the sight, however accidental, of the female genitals. The young boy becomes convinced that castration is not only possible, but, in fact, has already been accomplished in some individuals. The distinction between the sexes is still obscure to the frightened and chastened boy.

> In some diffuse and vaguely understood way, the pleasurable sensation produced by self-manipulation of the sexual organs is perceived by the child as connected with his relationship to his mother, displacing his earlier oral and anal interests.
>
> At this point in the developmental sequence, the child senses that his mother's attention and her warmly soothing ministrations are not exclusively his. Besides troublesome siblings, mother must be shared

with father, and the child soon comes to resent and to be jealous of this interloper. Freud assumed that with increasing sophistication the child develops a belief that his father knows, or at least suspects, how much he would like to be rid of him. Anxiety-stricken and guilty, the young boy feels certain that his intense anger and avid pleasure-seeking are impossible to conceal. His submissive and overtly loving behavior, he feels, is but a transparent façade to an all-knowing, all-powerful father. What more appropriate retribution could father plan to exact than the removal of that organ that provides the most pleasure at this stage? Castration by the father becomes the over-whelming fear for the child's burgeoning ego, and this imag-ined outrage must be dealt with by the mechanisms of defense. Most notable of these is the mechanism of repression. [Monte, 1975, p. 100]

The period during which this emotional constellation of love, jealousy, and castration fear occurs is called the *phallic stage* of psychosexual devel-opment. Emotional ambivalence is the hallmark of the phallic stage, for the young boy not only must learn to give up his chosen love-object, he must also reconcile his contradictory feelings of love for and anger at his father.

The Electra Complex

"Anatomy is destiny" was Freud's paraphrase of Napoleon and his own indication of the nature of the female version of the Oedipus complex (1924b, vol. XIX, p. 178).

In the boy, it seemed clear that the Oedipus complex was dissolved by the real or fantasied threat of castration. However, since the girl, by virtue of her anatomical development, does not fear the *loss* of a penis, she must assume that its absence indicates that she has *already* been deprived. Con-sequently, for her the realization that she has been castrated *initiates* the Oedipus complex. Freud alternately rejected and then seemingly accepted the term "Electra complex" for the distinctly different feminine version of this emotional constellation (cf. Freud, 1931, p. 229 for his arguments against the use of the term; and 1940, p. 194, for his apparent acceptance). Regardless of the term employed, the Oedipus complex in the female involves several highly distinctive processes that differentiate her from the male.

ATTACHMENT TO MOTHER: "PENIS ENVY." Just as the little boy takes his mother as the first love-object, the little girl likewise attaches herself intimately to her mother. Thus, like the little boy, she will also eventually have to relinquish her first love-object. More significantly, however, she will also have to relinquish her first erotogenic zone of pleasurable genital stimulation, the clitoris. When she first discovers that her clitoris is not a penis: ". . . she envies boys its possession; her whole development may be said to take place under the colours of envy for the penis [Freud, 1940, p. 193]."

With the discovery that she lacks what, in her view, is an essential anatomical item, the girl at first tries to convince herself that her perception is wrong. She has seized on the clitoris as the nearest approximation to the external male genitalia, but the choice has not been successful. Maturation forces her to abandon even more fully any notion of a comparable external genital to that of boys. Ultimately, the girl is forced to the realization that she is lacking not only the penis, but all the virtues of maleness that possession of such an organ implies.

A variety of outcomes is possible: The girl may develop a *masculinity complex,* in which she devoutly protests the injustice she perceives and comes to assume all the essential male personality characteristics in defiance of her alleged inferiority; or she may abandon sexual activity altogether in her attempts to avoid any reminder of her inferiority (Freud, 1931, p. 230).

DEVALUATION OF MOTHER. In the light of her discovery that lack of a penis is a universal attribute of girls, devaluation of the mother and abandonment of her as a love-object occurs (Freud, 1931, p. 233). Hostility accompanies this breaking off of the attachment for a variety of reasons. Some of these may include the real or fantasied idea that her mother deprived her of pleasures rightfully hers, or that her mother shortchanged her in affection, or, most important, that it was mother who deprived her of the envied organ. The hostility can reach a climax when a sibling is born:

> . . . what the child grudges the unwanted intruder and rival is not only the suckling but all the other signs of maternal care. It feels that it has been dethroned, despoiled, prejudiced in its rights; it casts a jealous hatred upon the new baby and develops a grievance against the faithless mother. . . . [Freud, 1933, p. 123]

Consequently, it is to the father that the young girl now turns in her effort to obtain that which she "knows" her mother cannot provide.

SEARCH FOR A PENIS SUBSTITUTE. Freud's earlier work with neurotic female patients had revealed the almost universal presence of a seduction-by-anadult fantasy. In most of his published writings of the period he alluded to seduction, but Freud barely hinted that the seduction was accomplished by the patient's own father. He had, however, made the role of the father in the seduction tales of his patients known to his friend, Wilhelm Fliess, during the course of their correspondence (1897, p. 259; also in 1954, Letter No. 69, p. 215). In later published writings, Freud indicated that indeed it was the father who had been reported to have early seduced his own child

(1925a, p. 34). It was not until 1931, however, almost thirty-five years after his ideas on the role of childhood sexuality had replaced the original seduction hypothesis, that Freud revealed, in a paper on female sexuality, that *mothers,* too, had been indicted in the seduction fantasies (1931, p. 238; see also 1933, pp. 120–121).

Of course, both types of seduction fantasy now made sense: they were products not of a perverse whimsy of hysterical patients, but of the female Oedipal stage of development. In the pre-Oedipal phase, the object of the seduction fantasy is the mother for both boys and girls. During the Oedipal period proper, the father becomes the focus of the girl's fantasy. She wishes for a penis from her father, since she cannot obtain one from her mother, who likewise lacks this vital equipment, or she desires a symbolic penis-substitute, a baby. With the wish for a "penis-baby," the girl fully enters the Oedipal phase (Freud, 1925b, p. 256).

Resolution of the Oedipus Complex

Although a fully detailed description of the resolution of the Oedipus complex for the boy requires some knowledge of Freud's final model of the mind—and for that reason detailed discussion will be deferred until Chapter 3—some general indications can be provided now. In a general way, Freud summarized the dissolution of the boy's Oedipus complex:

> In boys . . . the complex is not simply repressed, it is literally *smashed to pieces by the shock of threatened castration.* Its libidinal cathexes are abandoned [i.e., the attachment to mother], desexualized and in part sublimated. . . . [1925b, p. 257; italics added]

In his final model of the mind, Freud extended this line of reasoning to show that the dissolution of the Oedipus complex results in the identification of the boy with his father and in the establishment of a "superego" or special agency of morality incorporated from the parents.

For the girl, however, the Oedipus complex (or Electra complex) has no such clear-cut, final issue. Because the threat of castration, the motive for its dissolution in the boy, has effected the *beginning* of the Electra complex, the same fear cannot be the basis for its resolution. Instead, the female complex may undergo slow fading with time, or, in some cases, may meet its end through massive repression (Freud, 1925b, p. 257). The male and female Oedipus complexes are summarized in Table 2–1.

From the differences between boys' and girls' resolutions of the Oedipus complex, Freud drew several conclusions that today would be considered antifeminist. Among these was the notion that women do not develop as strong a conscience (superego) as men: Only the *full* resolution in the face of castration threat allows the Oedipal strivings to become the basis of strong conscience, a topic to be treated in Chapter 3.

TABLE 2–1: THE SUCCESSIVE STAGES OF THE OEDIPUS AND ELECTRA COMPLEXES CONTRASTED

OEDIPUS COMPLEX (BOY)			ELECTRA COMPLEX (GIRL)		
MOTIVE	CONSEQUENCE	OUTCOME	MOTIVE	CONSEQUENCE	OUTCOME
1. Attachment to mother (feeding, bodily care)	Jealousy of rivals, particularly of father	Feelings of hostility toward father	1. Attachment to mother (feeding, bodily care)	Jealousy of rivals	General feelings of inferiority; discovery of genital difference from males
2. Castration fear (sight of female genitals; possible threats)	Fear of punishment by father for his desires to possess mother	Intensification of rivalry with father; development of need to camouflage hostility	2. Penis envy (sight of male genitals)	Jealousy of male organ and of male privileges	Devaluation of mother and of female role; adoption of male behaviors
3. Need to appease father and prevent imagined attack	Creation of facade of meekness and love for father	Repression of hostility and fear; relinquishment of mother; identification with father	3. Attachment to father as more powerful than mother	Seeking from father penis substitute—a baby	Identification with female behaviors to appeal to father; slow fading of penis envy and mother devaluation

Stages of Libidinal Organization: Psychosexual Development

Along with the discovery that sexuality is wider in scope than adult, genital activities imply, Freud was able to discern a sequence in the development of the expression of libido. Characteristic patterns of sexual instinct organization prevail at each stage; each pattern centers on an erotogenic zone that dominates the given age.

Actually, a midpoint in psychosexual development, the Oedipus complex serves as a climactic demarcation between two earlier, *pregenital organizations* of libido and two subsequent *genital organizations* of the sexual instinct.

Pregenital Organizations: Oral and Anal Periods

Libido is organized, in the first year of life, around the pleasurable activities of the mouth. Thus, the attachment to the breast is a prototype of pleasurable behavior for the infant, a behavior that is, incidentally, clearly pregenital in character (Freud, 1916, vol. XVI, p. 328). In fact, as has already been mentioned, children are capable of finding pleasurable satisfaction in a variety of ways, from a variety of sources. If the same means of obtaining pleasure prevailed in adulthood, they would be labeled "perverse." For this reason, Freud characterized the infant as "polymorphously perverse" (literally: "many-formed perversity") (1905, p. 191).

Although the phrase is often misunderstood out of the context of the entire scheme of pregenital development, Freud meant to indicate by this description only the essentially malleable and plastic nature of the sexual instinct as it emerges in infancy. Adult sexuality must be thought of, consequently, as the long-range result of the unification of several component instincts that come to focus on genital sexuality only after an extended period of "polymorphously perverse" infantile expression.

The oral phase is marked, first, by the pleasure obtained from feeding, then by the development of purely sensual sucking in which the infant obtains oral pleasure by sucking nonnutritive objects like his thumb. In this way, his own body provides sensual pleasure and this part of the oral period can be justly characterized as autoerotic (Freud, 1905, pp. 179–181). Further development tends toward the decreasing importance of autoerotic activity and a seeking for an *external* love-object. Clearly, the dominant erotogenic zone during the oral phase is nongenital, but its flow of pleasure is analogous to adult-intensity sexual satisfaction:

> No one who has seen a baby sinking back satiated from the breast and falling asleep with flushed cheeks and a blissful smile can escape the reflection that this picture persists as a prototype of the expression of sexual satisfaction in later life. [Freud, 1905, p. 182]

With the development of his first teeth and with the possibility of chewing rather than simply swallowing food, the child enters a phase of development characterized by a shift from a *passive* to an *active* orientation to his environment. From now on, the central concern for the infant is the attainment of self-mastery. From around the age of eighteen months through the second year of life, the child is subject to increased manipulation and discipline by the mother as she attempts to toilet train him. He discovers that retention and expulsion of feces sets a rhythmic pattern of tension and relief that is associated not only with pleasure but with social approval and motherly love. When he retains his feces, or expels them in inappropriate places, he incurs his mother's wrath. When, on the other hand, he accomplishes fecal elimination in a suitable place, at the appropriate time—a series of demands that must seem absurd to the child—he receives approval and other loving communications. Because he is becoming biologically capable of controlling his sphincter muscle, he is also learning an important lesson about mastering the functions of his own body, with the anus as the prototype of such experiences. Again, the pleasures derived from elimination and self-mastery are clearly pregenital (1905, pp. 186–187).

Transient Genital Organization: The Phallic Period

Some time at the end of the third year or in the beginning of the fourth year of the infant's life and extending into his fifth year, a phase of libidinal organization is entered in which the genital organs play a brief and not yet adult role. Through his bodily self-explorations and through the attentions of his mother to his physical care and cleanliness, the child discovers that manipulation of the genital region produces pleasurable sensations. There ensues a period of infantile masturbation, and because the child does not yet know shame, he expresses an unabashed curiosity about the genitals of others, along with a guiltless exhibitionism of his own (Freud, 1905, p. 194). It is during this period of "sexual researches" that the Oedipus complex arises (Freud, 1908a). Freud called this period the *phallic stage* of psychosexual development because for both the boy and the girl, in their own ways, it is the male organ that dominates their thinking and inquiry.

Latency Period

The sexual forces dating from infancy become subject to mounting counterforces of suppression that require the sexual impulses to be rechanneled into nonsexual outlets. In the sixth year of life, the child's sexual activities, along with the Oedipus complex, are temporarily dethroned from their status as major elements of the child's developmental history, but the sexual drive does not cease to exist. Instead, libidinal impulses become latent, obscured by the overlay of learned shame, disgust, and morality. Freud, however, was of the opinion that the sexual impulses would become dormant at this stage even without cultural pressures because the phenomenon of latency is biologically determined (1905, pp. 177–178). In any event, the period of latency extends from the sixth to about the eighth year of life, or roughly from the resolution of the Oedipus complex to the onset of puberty. At puberty, truly adult, primarily genital, sexuality emerges.

The Genital Period

Biologically capable of procreating because his hormonal and anatomical development permit the production of viable sex cells, the pubescent child's sexuality is no longer dominated by its earlier infantile aim of the attainment of pleasure to the exclusion of all else. The adult sexual aim is the discharge of sexual products. It is probably an understatement to point out that this adult sexual aim also provides individual pleasure, despite its essentially altruistic, species-preserving goal (Freud, 1905, vol. VII, p. 207).

The important point is that the lengthy periods of development leading up to the adult's sexual status had as their ultimate goal the establishment of genital primacy. Stimulation of the genitals and the resulting production of sexual tension is the first step toward the species-preserving goal of procreation. Three sources of sexual stimulation are now possible for the adult: memories and impulses from the pregenital periods; direct manipulation and stimulation of the genitalia and other erotogenic zones; stimulation from the chemical, hormonal discharges from within the interior of the body (Freud, 1905, p. 208). Thus, the genital period is the culmination of all those trends in development of the libido, begun in infancy, and played out through the biological development of the mature organism.

Fixation and Regression

Of course not all outcomes of the sequence of psychosexual development are satisfactory. *Fixation of libido* may occur at any of the stages, thereby stunting and distorting the sequence of development that follows.

Essentially, fixation involves a "lagging behind" in development of one of the components of the maturing sexual drive before genital activity becomes dominant. Thus, one of the child's pregenital modes of attaining pleasure may cease its progression toward adult expression. It then becomes a dominant, rigid means of attaining satisfaction. For example, the pleasure derived from periodic tension and tension-release through retention and expulsion of feces during the anal phase may be so intense that the adultlike renunciation required by the mother's toilet-training program is impossible for the child to accept. Though he eventually submits to the stress of the cleanliness routine, his final socialization may be fixated on the attainment of anal pleasures that were forcibly and prematurely relinquished. As an adult, compulsively defensive traits like stinginess ("not letting go") and compulsive concern about filth make their appearance.

An Illustrative Character Type: "The Anal-Erotic Personality"

One kind of fixated personality is the anal-erotic character. In adulthood, this person is characterized by the presence of a triad of related traits: *orderliness, thriftiness,* and *obstinacy.* Freud pointed out that for those adults who exhibit all three traits in unusual potency, a common pattern of experiences occurred during the anal stage of their psychosexual development.

As children, they had more than the usual difficulty with toilet training, and they exasperated their parents by refusing to empty their bowels when, as Freud put it, "they were placed on the pot." Thus, these children expressed their defiance and self-mastery in an anal way, forcing their parents to more and more extreme measures to accomplish this necessary act of socialization.

Knowing no shame or disgust at this early age, anal-erotic children find pleasure in examining or playing with feces and pleasure in retaining them until release of tension produces the greatest satisfaction. Eventually they succumb to parental pressures for rigid orderliness and cleanliness and to a learned disgust for unclean products of the body. By adulthood, therefore, anal-erotic children have had to develop defensive measures to guard against reemergence of the taboo pleasures. The result is a personality overladen with defensive reactions against its own impulses to obtain pleasure in anal, i.e., "dirty," ways. The anal-erotic adult, consequently, becomes a model of cleanliness and orderliness, but a model who bears the hallmark of exaggeration in the pursuit of these desirable goals. Excessive, even compulsive, desire for order, neatness, and antiseptic spotlessness develops in order to ensure that the earlier and opposite traits remain submerged.

The trait of obstinacy is clearly related to the child's attempts at self-mastery as indicated by his refusal to "go on demand." Instead, he prefers to "let go" only when *he* decides to experience the pleasure of tension reduction, and the anal-erotic child prolongs this release until an optimal amount of satisfaction can be obtained. Even today, as Freud pointed out in very modest language, we point to the buttocks and make suggestions to caress them as a gesture of defiance to someone who makes demands on us. Who has not thwarted a rival's aggressive utterances with a defiant shout of "Kiss my arse"?

Thriftiness is also related to early developments in the anal period, as can be seen from the similar tendency of the stingy adult who "never lets go" of anything. Tightness with money may unconsciously represent earlier attempts to control fecal elimination against the demands by others to "let go." In adulthood, money may come to be associated linguistically with filth—"filthy lucre" or "dirty greenbacks"—just as that other once desirable possession, feces, was labeled filth by adults in authority. A stingy person may even express his unwillingness to part with his money by saying, "Who would want the filthy stuff," or, "Money only brings ruin."

Tongue-in-cheek, Freud remarked in a letter to Fliess that, because he was immersed in working out the details of the anal period of libidinal development and because he had begun to see its wide significance for adult behavior, he considered himself to be the "new Midas," for everything he now touched turned to shit (1954, letter No. 79, p. 240). (See also Freud, 1908b for a more detailed account of anal character types.)

Regression

Another difficulty in psychosexual development may occur when there is cause for a return to an earlier stage's mode of response. Such a return is called *regression of libido,* and it usually implies a primitivization of behavior in the service of the personality's defense against stress. For example, the six-year-old who, for one reason or another, finds his school experiences anxiety provoking and intolerable may return to his infantile mode of attaining peace and tranquillity in the face of stress by narrowing his attention to pleasurable oral stimulation. He consequently regresses to thumb sucking, much to the dismay of parents and teacher.

Fixation and *regression* bear an important relationship to each other. The more intense the fixation of libido at early stages of development, the more susceptible that individual will be to regression (Freud, 1916, pp. 339–341).

Summary

Anna O.'s long array of hysterical symptoms were interpreted by her physician, Josef Breuer, not in their usual way as bizarre and meaningless ravings of a diseased mind, but as a coherent array of meaningful behaviors possessing a hidden emotional logic. Breuer soon discovered with Anna O.'s help that the coherence and logic had origins in strangulated emotions. Unable to be expressed during some traumatic incident, strangulated emotions survive unconsciously and are converted into bodily symptoms.

Sigmund Freud, Breuer's young colleague, was greatly interested in the case of Anna O., especially after his visit with Charcot in Paris, during which he observed the master remove and produce hysterical symptoms through hypnosis. Practicing Breuer and Anna O.'s method of catharsis, the "talking cure," Freud soon found that hypnosis could be achieved only with a rare few of his patients. His search for a new method led, eventually, to the technique of free association, for which the fundamental rule of speaking aloud all thoughts, no matter how arbitrary or perverse they may seem, had several sources. Frau Emmy's reprimand to let her do the talking, a demonstration by Bernheim that posthypnotic subjects could recall their behaviors enacted under hypnosis if pressured to do so, and a remembrance of the words of advice of a favorite author, Ludwig Borne, came to Freud's aid in developing free-association technique.

With the method of free association in hand, Freud soon discovered what had been hidden by hypnosis—emotional resistances. Examining and removing these resistances revealed to Freud one of the fundamental notions of his psychology, the mechanism of repression. Unacceptable wishes, ideas, or impulses, which by virtue of their incompatibility with the conscious, ethical standards of the individual's personality had caused psychical pain, had to be removed from consciousness. Repressed ideas and impulses require a continual outlay of energy to prevent their return to consciousness, and the symptoms of neurotic disorder may be viewed as the return of the repudiated thought in compromise form. Symptoms allow the simultaneous satisfaction and rejection of the unacceptable impulse or idea in symbolic form.

Much to his own amazement, Freud found that sexual impulses were the common denominator for classifying unacceptable thoughts. In every case, the underlying cause of the symptoms could be traced to an erotic urge or to a sexual wish that had been repressed because of its potential threat to the ethical side of the conscious personality. For a time, Freud was convinced that the strongest evidence for the correctness of the sexual hypothesis was the almost universal occurrence among his neurotic patients of childhood seductions by their fathers. Soon, however, Freud saw how untenable the idea of universal childhood seduction was, and simultaneously he faced a momentous truth: Children are not merely passive recipients of sexual attentions by adults, but, rather, they are active sexual creatures who seek pleasure in a variety of diffuse ways before the onset of purely genital sexuality at puberty. His patients' seduction tales were fantasies, not realities, and were to be construed as the products of an important emotional conflict in relation to the sexual instinct during childhood.

For the infant, pleasure seeking is connected to developing erotogenic zones in a sequence of psychosexual maturation that shows the sexual instinct to be very much broader than adult notions of genital sexuality ordinarily admit. An emotional climax in sexual development is the Oedipal phase, in which the male child focuses his pleasure-seeking activities on the mother, and he views siblings and father as hostile rivals. The girl, on the other hand, who also initially takes her mother as the first love-object, relinquishes mother for father when she realizes that girls, including mother, do not possess a penis. Penis envy, then, is the origin of the girl's Electra complex. It is from penis envy that the girl turns to her father to obtain that which is not available from her mother. The boy's Oedipus complex is resolved by the real or imagined threat of castration; the girl's Electra complex is initiated by her discovery that she has already been castrated. Freud was unclear about the matter of the girl's resolution of the Electra complex, but he seems to have decided that it simply fades slowly with time.

The Electra and Oedipus complexes are only one part of Freud's scheme of psychosexual development, a scheme that involves five phases: (1) the oral stage in which pleasurable activities center on the activities of the mouth; (2) the anal stage in which the critical developments involve retention and expulsion of feces, as well as learning generalized self-mastery; (3) the phallic stage, the time period of the Oedipus and Electra complexes; (4) the latency stage, during which time the child's sexual interests and impulses lie dormant until puberty; and the (5) genital stage of adult sexuality and interest in the opposite sex.

Sometimes development does not proceed smoothly through the five stages because anxiety, threat, or frustration block further maturation. Such blocking is termed *fixation* in the Freudian scheme, and it is intimately related to another phenomenon of development called *regression*. Regression is a partial return to an earlier form of impulse gratification when current stresses frustrate the normal progression of the sex drive's development. Fixation and regression work hand in hand, so to speak, for the blocking of psychosexual developments in current living is the cause of a child's regression to previous developments.

In the next chapter we will take up the matters of Freud's dream theory, his changing views of the instincts, and his final model of the mind.

FOR FURTHER READING

Freud's writings in psychology span over forty-three years of theorizing and fill twenty-three volumes in the definitive translation of *The Standard Edition of the Complete Psychological Works of Sigmund Freud,* translated by James Strachey in collaboration with Anna Freud (London: Hogarth Press, 1953–1974). Perhaps the single best overview of Freud's early ideas is contained in his *Five Lectures on Psychoanalysis,* which has been published in paperback as *The Origin and Development of Psychoanalysis* (Chicago: Henry Regnery, 1965), and may also be found in Vol. 6 of *The Standard Edition.*

Freud's early neurological model of the mind deserves some scrutiny by the serious student of psychoanalysis and may be found under the title "A Project for a Scientific Psychology" in Vol. 1 of *The Standard Edition* and in a different translation as part of *The Origins of Psychoanalysis: Letters to Wilhelm Fliess,* edited by Marie Bonaparte, Anna Freud, and Ernst Kris (New York: Basic Books, 1954). Understanding this model is a difficult task that can be made somewhat easier with the help of Peter Amacher's scholarly commentary, *Freud's Neurological Education and Its Influence on Psychoanalytic Theory* (Psychological Issues, vol. IV, *16,* New York: International Universities Press, 1965). Along these same lines, Karl Pribram's "The Neuropsychology of Sigmund Freud" is an attempt to assess the contemporary significance of Freud's neurological model, and it may be found in *Experimental Foundations of Clinical Psychology*, edited by A. J. Bachrach (New York: Basic Books, 1962). A particularly lucid account of the neurological model is provided by Raymond Fancher in *Psychoanalytic Psychology: The Development of Freud's Thought* (New York: W. W. Norton, 1973), ch. 3.

The clinical evidence on which Freud based his early concepts is to be found in Joseph Breuer's and Sigmund Freud's *Studies on Hysteria* (1893–1895, vol. 2 of *The Standard Edition;* also available in paperback from Beacon Press, Boston.) Other case histories that have a bearing on Freud's developing theory of sexuality may be found in vol. 10 of *The Standard Edition* under the titles "Analysis of a Phobia in a Five-Year Old Boy" and "Notes Upon a Case of Obsessional Neurosis" (1909; also available in paperback editions edited by Philip Rieff: *The Sexual Enlightenment of Children.* New York: Collier, 1963; and *Dora: An Analysis of a Case of Hysteria.* New York: Collier, 1963).

An unusual opportunity is afforded the reader who would like to hear both sides of the story of a psychoanalytic patient's treatment by the publication of *The Wolf-Man by the Wolf-Man* (New York: Basic Books, 1971). This volume contains Freud's original case history of this young Russian nobleman whom he had treated for obsessional-compulsive neurosis and an account by the young man himself of his treatment with Freud.

Basic background reading into the details of Freud's personal life is best begun with Ernest Jones' three-volume masterwork *The Life and Work of Sigmund Freud* (New York: Basic Books, 1953, 1955, 1957). Max Schur, Freud's personal physician during the last years of his life, provides a glimpse into the personal incidents of Freud's life that shaped his attitude toward death in *Freud: Living and Dying* (New York: International Universities Press, 1972). Finally, Freud's correspondence with Carl Jung (whose theory is treated in Chapter 4) has been recently published as *The Freud/Jung Letters* (Princeton, N.J.: Princeton University Press, 1974). These letters provide a rare glimpse into the personal lives of Freud and Jung, their attitudes toward their contemporaries (not always flattering), and the emotional abrasiveness of their theoretical and personal falling-out.

Additional recommended readings for Freud's theory are provided at the end of Chapter 3 and concern more directly his later theoretical efforts.

3 SIGMUND FREUD
Psychoanalysis:
The Dynamic Model
of the Mind

But these two discoveries—that the life of our sexual instincts cannot be wholly tamed, and that mental processes are in themselves unconscious and only reach the ego and come under its control through incomplete and untrustworthy perceptions—these two discoveries amount to a statement that the ego is not master in its own house.

SIGMUND FREUD, 1917a, p. 143

Dreams as Wish Fulfillments

Consider the following dream of Freud's daughter Anna:

> My youngest daughter, then nineteen months old, had had an attack of vomiting one morning and had consequently been kept without food all day. During the night after this day of starvation she was heard calling out excitedly in her sleep: "Anna Fweud, stwawbew-wies, wild stwawbewwies, omblet, pudden!" At that time she was in the habit of using her own name to express the idea of taking possession of something. The menu included pretty well everything that must have seemed to her to make up a desirable meal. [Freud, 1900, vol. V, p. 130]

Clearly, as can be discerned in Anna's menu, children's dreams are relatively transparent embodiments of wishes come true. There is no disguise here to obscure Anna's blatant craving for goodies that had necessarily been denied her during her illness. Anna's dream was an undisguised wish receiving undisguised fulfillment.

Freud had already come to the conclusion that dreams were mental states designed to bring about the fulfillment of wishes or desires. The dream, he reasoned in the "Project for a Scientific Psychology" (1895, vol. I), is a hallucinatory state that serves to structure dream events, not as they are in the external world, but as we would like them to be. Sometimes, however, unconscious desire clashes with conscious restraint, so the dream processes pursue devious paths to wish fulfillment. Freud stated the fundamental implication of this insight in the dictum *"The interpretation of dreams is the royal road to a knowledge of the unconscious mind"* (1900, vol. V, p. 608).

By examining a dreamer's nighttime productions, the skilled observer can detect those motives and wishes that are hidden from view during waking life, motives and wishes that the dreamer himself can entertain only in the disguised, compromise form that dream imagery represents. Compared with the dreams of children, adult productions rarely evidence the simplicity of Anna's stwawbewwies-and-pudden fancy.

Disguised Wish Fulfillment: The Karl and Otto Dream

Compare the following adult dream with Anna's innocently lucid construction:

> The patient, who was a young girl, began thus: "As you will remember, my sister has only one boy left now—Karl; she lost his elder brother, Otto, while I was still living with her. Otto was my favourite; I more or less brought him up. I'm fond of the little one too, but of course, not nearly so fond as I was of the one who died. Last night, then, I dreamt that *I saw Karl lying before me dead. He was lying in his little coffin with his hands folded and with candles all round—in fact just like little Otto, whose death was such a blow to me.* [Freud, 1900, vol. IV, p. 152]

If it is true that dreams are the fulfillment of wishes, then surely this dream by one of Freud's patients must embody the wish that little Karl had died instead of little Otto.

Assured from *his knowledge of his patient* that she was not cruel, Freud considered the dream carefully. He asked her to tell him everything that came to mind when she thought of the separate elements of the dream. It is important to note that the interpretation of the dream is possible only when the past history of the dreamer, as well as the context provided by the dreamer's personality, is known to the analyst. Dreams are the dreamer's unique productions.

Thus, Freud knew that after his patient had been orphaned, she had been raised in the house of an elder sister. A particular male visitor to the sister's home, nicknamed the Professor by virtue of his occupation as professional lecturer, had made quite a romantic impression on Freud's patient. After marriage plans had been disrupted between the girl and the Professor, he ceased to visit the sister's home. Freud's patient nonetheless secretly longed to see and to be with him. On the other hand, through hurt pride, she tried to convince herself to relinquish any romantic attachment to him. Her resolve was not an easy one to keep. Whenever she learned that he was to give a public lecture, she quietly became a part of the audience. Yet, she would observe him only at a discreet distance, and she never allowed herself to confront him directly. In fact, she seized upon every opportunity, however trivial, to see her professor friend. *She had even experienced a moment of happiness at the funeral of little Otto when her professor had made an appearance to express his condolences.* It was this continual vacillation between approach and withdrawal that chiefly characterized Freud's patient.

Here, of course, was the key to her dream. If little Karl were to die, his funeral would provide another opportunity to see her professor without any direct attempt on her part to bring about the meeting. *Her wish, therefore, was not directly for Karl's death, but only for a meeting with her professor.* The dream had created from her past history of associations a perfectly logical pretext for furthering the satisfaction of her ambivalent desire. Thus, the lucidity and directness of Anna's stwawbewwy dream is not to be found here.

There is clearly great similarity between adult dream processes and hysterical symptoms if we make the assumption, as Freud did, that both dreams and symptoms conceal ideas that are not acceptable to the conscious personality. Freud found evidence in several of his own dreams that particularly objectionable desires were frequently the kernels from which nighttime fantasies grew.

Analysis of Two of Freud's Dreams

We saw in Chapter 2 that Freud had begun a self-analysis in the summer of 1897, and that the precipitating incident for that task was his emotional disturbance over the death of his father. Throughout *The Interpretation of Dreams,* and in one or two of his other works, Freud employed his own dreams, elucidated by self-analysis, as examples of his concepts. Like his patient's Karl and Otto dream, Freud's own dreams revealed how important it was for the analyst to understand the personal symbols and meanings of the dreamer.

Immediately following his father's funeral, Freud had a dream about a sign hanging *in a barber shop that he visited everyday.* In a letter to his friend Wilhelm Fliess, Freud reported that the dream occurred the night *after* his father's funeral; whereas in *The Interpretation of Dreams* he states that it occurred the night *before* the funeral (see 1954, Letter No. 50, p. 170). The analysis given in *The Interpretation of Dreams* provides the more detailed account:

> During the night before my father's funeral I had a dream of a printed notice, placard or poster [in a barber shop]—rather like the notices forbidding one to smoke in a railway waiting-room—on which appeared either
>
> "You are requested to close the eyes"

OR

"You are requested to close an eye."...

Each of these two versions had a meaning of its own, and led in a different direction when the dream was interpreted. I had chosen the simplest possible ritual for the funeral, for I knew my father's own views on such ceremonies. But some other members of the family were not sympathetic to such puritanical simplicity and thought we should be disgraced in the eyes of those who attended the funeral. Hence one of the versions: "You are requested to close an eye," i.e., to "wink" or "overlook" [the simplicity of the services]. Here it is particularly easy to see the meaning of the vagueness expressed on the "either-or." [Freud, 1900, p. 318]

The dream was, upon analysis, clearly a form of self-reproach or self-chastisement for not providing the "proper" full-fledged funeral that members of the family expected and desired. Simultaneously, the dream represented the ultimate act of filial duty: namely, the closing of his father's eyes at death. It was as though the dream condensed the idea of "failing to do your duty" with the idea of "filial duty" in a clever word picture.

Freud suspected that the dream was in some way connected with even deeper feelings of guilt. Might it be that he had not loved his father as much as he consciously protested? The family thought so, because on the day of the funeral Freud was actually late in arriving because he had been detained in *a barber shop.* The seemingly inexcusable lateness, coupled with his desire for relatively austere last rites for his father, must have seemed to members of Freud's family indications of supreme lack of respect. The important point is that to Freud, too, such behavior was an admission of an ambivalent attitude toward his father.

Another of Freud's dreams indicates the complexity of the verbal linkages that may be employed to defensively obscure threatening wishes. In his seventh or eighth year, Freud's self-analysis revealed, he had dreamt of his mother with a "peculiarly peaceful, sleeping expression on her features." In the dream, he saw her being carried into a room by two or three people with birds' beaks and laid upon a bed (Freud, 1900, p. 583). The bizarre creatures with birds' beaks brought to Freud's mind the association of the illustrations of bird-masked people in a particular edition of the Bible called the *Phillippson's* Bible.

Further analysis revealed an association to the name "Phillippson" in the form of a memory of an "ill-mannered boy" named Philipp, who was the first person to reveal to the young Freud the vulgar word for sexual intercourse. In German, the word *vogeln* is slang for copulation, and it is derived from the proper form of the word *Vogel,* which means "bird." Hence, the associative chain from people with *birds'* beaks to the *Phillippson* Bible to the boy named *Philipp* had revealed a sexual connotation to the dream images.

The expression of his mother's face in the dream reminded Freud of his dying grandfather, whom he had observed in a coma a few days before the grandfather's death. Therefore, the dream seemed to signify that Freud's mother was dying or dead. However, when the young Freud awoke from the dream, he had rushed into his parents' room to wake his mother and was quite relieved to discover that she was indeed alive.

Why, then, had the dream depicted her in a state similar to death—a state, that is, similar to his grandfather's coma? Surely the dream could not have been the representation of a wish that his mother die? On the contrary, Freud's anxiety at the thought of her death had forced him upon awakening to rush into her room to confirm that she was still alive. Perhaps the anxiety over her death was a form of disguise to prevent recognition of the sexual longing the dream had really depicted, a sexual longing for his mother.

Further analysis might be made along the path of the association of the grandfather's death. Could "grandfather" be a disguise for "father" so that the dream actually conveyed not only a sexual wish for mother but a death-wish toward father? Unfortunately, Freud did not carry the analysis that far in his published writings.

Freud's dreams, however, point up the difficult nature of the task that Freud undertook. He sought no less an accomplishment than the explanation of how dreams are structured to conceal significant but unacceptable motives from consciousness, and how dreams can satisfy in fantasy desires conceived in reality.

Manifest and Latent Dream Content: The Mask

In light of the disguised nature of wish fulfillment in adult dreams, even the most elementary description of dream processes must include a distinction between the readily accessible disguise and the less accessible ideas that lie behind the distortion. Freud referred to the dream's facade or mask consisting of all those recalled sights, images, ideas, sounds, and smells that compose the story of the dream. Behind the facade, beneath the mask of recallable elements, lie the "perverse," unacceptable impulses that, like "masked criminals," are far commoner in mental life than straightforward, undisguised urges (Freud, 1925c, p. 132).

Freud's use of the mask metaphor is an apt analogy for his more technical distinction between the *manifest* and *latent* content of the dream. The manifest content corresponds to the mask, whereas the impulses thus disguised like "masked criminals" are properly termed latent content. Manifest content is generally easily recalled by the dreamer. By contrast, the latent content can be arrived at only by careful interpretation of the manifest content.

The mental processes that convert strivings, wishes, and needs into the disguised images of the manifest content are called collectively *dream work.* In a sense, the analyst's interpretation of a dream is an attempt to undo the dream work, to unmask the manifest content and reveal the more fundamental latent content from which the dream was constructed.

Sources of Dream Distortion: The Dream Work

Once distortion or disguise is recognized as a general phenomenon of dream imagery, it becomes necessary to search for a cause of the distortion. Freud postulated that the wishes or needs that initiate the dream are unacceptable to a special agency of the conscious mind called the "censorship system." The censorship system is actually on the frontier of consciousness, a border guard, so to speak, between the unconscious and conscious systems of the mind.

The censorship system is very selective about the wishes and needs it will allow the dreamer to entertain or remember consciously. Wishes that are morally unacceptable to the awake dreamer will also be unacceptable to the sleeping dreamer's censorship system. In consequence, wishes or urges that arise from the unconscious during sleep are heavily censored by this ethical arm of the mental apparatus. Thus the distortion in those wishes as they appear in the manifest dream is a direct result of the efforts of the ever-watchful preconscious dream censor.

The two systems of the mind, the unconscious system from which the wishes emerge and the preconscious censorship system that prevents those wishes from freely entering consciousness, constitute the mechanism of dream formation (Freud, 1900, pp. 144–145). Unacceptable wishes can be prevented from gaining access to consciousness in only one way. The censorship system must selectively distort the wish, transforming it into an alternate form that does not clash with the conscious ethical standards of the personality. Conversely, the only way the unconscious can achieve satisfaction for its pressing urges is to evade the censor by masquerading the unacceptability of its wishes behind a facade of related but more neutral ideas. Hence, the distortion in dreams is a joint product of two architects: the unconscious system and the censor. Freud was able to isolate four separate processes in the dream work of these two architects that account for the form of the manifest dream.

The Work of Condensation

One of the mundane facts about the interpretation of a dream, but a fact that contains a significant clue about dream distortion, is that a remembered dream (i.e., the manifest content) can be recounted in relatively few words. In contrast, the *interpretation* of the manifest dream, penetrating to the latent content, may produce as much as twelve times the amount of information (Freud, 1900, p. 279). Freud concluded, therefore, that the manifest content is an unsurpassed model of compression, or *condensation* as it was called in Freud's technical vocabulary.

It might be possible to conclude hastily that the work of condensation is merely a one-way editing process whereby only a select few elements of the mass of unconscious material are chosen for representation in the manifest content. In this simplistic view, condensation is accomplished by a process of omission. But free association to the few manifest elements of a dream usually reveals that each manifest element has multiple, two-way relationships with every other element, and each component is, there-fore, at least partially redundant. Borrowing a concept from the study of hysterical symptoms, it can be said that the manifest dream content is *overdetermined*. Several unconscious ideas band together to contribute *as a group* some energy to direct the choice of *one* common manifest element. Simultaneously, each manifest element has connections to several other manifest elements, which, of course, have their own connections to other groups of unconscious, latent ideas that have similarly banded together. The picture that Freud paints of condensation is more like an associative web than it is like a chain.

Condensation, consequently, is not a process of simple omission. It is a technique of creative compression by telescoping elements together. Each segment of the manifest content is a nodal point upon which a great number of latent ideas converge (Freud, 1900, p. 283). The latent dream thoughts are thus condensed into the manifest dream content much as a composite photograph of a single person is constructed from the character-istics of several individuals: It may "look like *A* perhaps, but may be dressed like *B*, may do something that we remember *C* doing, and at the same time we may know that he is *D*" (Freud, 1916, p. 171).

The Work of Displacement

Displacement is a technique the censorship agency of the mind employs to replace a latent dream element in consciousness by a more remote idea, or to accomplish a shifting of the dream's recalled emphasis away from an important idea and toward an unimportant one. Thus displacement may proceed by two paths: replacement of one idea with a remote associate, or the shifting of emotional accent from one thought to another. The dreamer is left with the impression of having dreamed a very strangely connected sequence of thoughts, or of having very absurdly made "much ado about nothing."

Freud employed an amusing anecdote in his *Introductory Lectures* to illus-trate the concept of displacement:

> There was a blacksmith in the village, who had committed a capital offence. The Court decided that the crime must be punished; but as the blacksmith was the only one in the village and was indispensable,

and as on the other hand there were three tailors living there, one of *them* was hanged instead.[1916, pp. 174–175]

Where condensation was responsible for compressing the latent thoughts into the abbreviated form of the manifest content, displacement is responsible for the "choice" of elements from which the manifest dream is constructed.

Beginning with the latent, unacceptable wish at the center, the dream work of displacement spins outward from this nucleus a web of increasingly remote associations. Each strand of this associative web is connected both to the central latent wish and to every other associated idea in the network. Hence, manifest elements are redundant in the sense that the unacceptable wish is dispersed simultaneously into many interconnected and mutually excitatory strands of the web. Because each of these strands shares a common origin, the nuclear wish, recollection of the ideas along any one strand excites recollection of nearby, connected strands of ideas.

One way to view the manifest dream, therefore, is to conceive of it as an associative "beating-around-the-bush," whereby the unacceptable nucleus wish of the latent content is dispersed into any available channel of the web *except* one that leads directly back to the origin. The pattern of associatively connected, overlapping, and redundant ideas evoked by the dreamer during free association to a manifest element is evidence of this delicately tangled skein. Displacement robs the latent content of its normal sequence of ideas, substituting the sequence of the associative web, and it likewise rechannels the latent content's original focus of emotional intensity into the diffuse lattice of the web.

The Work of Visual Representation

Abstract ideas, wishes, and urges that form the latent thoughts of the dream are by themselves colorless and ephemeral. Within the scope of the dream, these abstract thoughts must be converted into concrete visual images with the kind of primitive pictorial quality that readily lends itself to the manipulations of condensation and displacement (Freud, 1900, p. 339). While not all the elements of the latent content are converted into visual images, on the whole the translation of abstract thoughts into concrete pictures constitutes the essence of a dream (Freud, 1916, p. 175).

The translation of abstract thoughts into visual imagery typically follows the path of converting the symbolic labels representing the idea into a physical and concrete act. For example, the abstract idea of "possession" can be converted into the visually concrete act of "sitting on the object." Children often employ this strategy to protect a treasured possession from the grasp of an overwhelming playmate (Freud, 1916, p. 176n.).

To take another illustration, Freud reported the recollections of Herbert Silberer, who, in a sleepy, twilight state, often converted some abstract intellectual task into visual imagery. On one occasion, Silberer thought of having to revise an uneven or rough passage in an essay he was writing. He then pictured himself planing a piece of wood (Freud, 1900. vol. V, p. 344). In another episode, Silberer had the experience of losing his train of thought so that he had to return to the beginning to pick up the thread of logic. Silberer subsequently had the visual image of a printer's type-setting form for a page of print with the last lines of type fallen away (Freud, 1900, p. 345).

It is easy to see that the translation of abstract thoughts into visual imagery represents a process of *personal, idiosyncratic symbolization*. The dreamer creates concrete pictures to represent his abstract thoughts. The images he will employ are likely to be a function of his own creativity, unique experiences, and sophistication. But it is important to keep in mind that this kind of symbol formation proceeds from the abstract to the concrete, as opposed to the more usual literary case of transforming concrete acts into abstract symbols.

The Work of Secondary Revision

All the mechanisms of the dream work discussed thus far have as their common goal the appeasement of dream censorship. The dream work can condense, displace, and represent in visual form the latent dream thoughts in its attempt to disguise them. For the most part, these three mechanisms attend to distorting and to breaking apart the latent elements' form and organization. Thus, these mechanisms usually produce an absurd product. When the dreamer tries to recall and to make sense of his dream, however, the gaps, distortions, and substitutions strike a note of disharmony to his conscious mind. The dreamer's waking need is for logical coherence and consistency in his mental activities. Consequently, to bring order to what otherwise would be experienced as chaos, that part of the mind that is between unconsciousness and consciousness exerts an organizing, sense-making influence on the confused and bizarre story. In those twilight moments just before waking from a dream, it is the preconscious system of the mind that struggles to mold the dreamer's creations into a form comprehensible to his waking intelligence.

The preconscious thus attempts to patch together, into an understandable, coherent whole, the scattered and apparently nonsensical elements of the latent dream. In so doing, the preconscious is, in effect, subjecting the dream to an interpretation before the dreamer is fully awake. Whatever that interpretation is, the elements of the dream will be fitted to its outlines until what was scattered and diffuse becomes organized and reasonable.

It is this preinterpretation that introduces further distortion into the recalled manifest content. Freud called this process of constructing a coherent whole from the scattered dream elements *secondary revision*. In a sense, the preconscious treats the dream elements to a kind of further elaboration designed to mold what is patently unconnected and absurd into a logically consistent structure.

Sometimes the secondary revision occurs during the dream itself. For instance, a particular dream may be so laden with unpleasant emotional intensity that the various patterns of distortion introduced by the mechanisms of condensation and displacement are not sufficient to satisfy all the demands of the dream censorship. If the ever-watchful dream censor were to be aroused to action, the dreamer's sleep would surely be disturbed or disrupted in an effort to halt the dream. To lessen the impact of such a dream without recourse to interrupting the dreamer's sleep, there occurs instead a kind of judgmental interpretation on the part of the dreamer that, after all, *"it's only a dream"* (Freud, 1900, p. 489).

Study of the Dream: The Theoretical Yield

Psychoanalytic dream interpretation is a careful labor of elucidating the apparent absurdities of the recalled dream by accepting such productions as evidence of the dreamer's nonconscious mental achievements. Accurate interpretation of the dream, therefore, lifts the disguise, makes intelligible the distortions, and replaces absurdity with understanding. The long hidden logic of the unconscious is made accessible.

Freud considered the study of the dream one of his most fundamental and lasting achievements. A brief survey of the theoretical yield is in order.

The Regressive and Archaic Nature of Dreams

The medium of dreams is visual imagery. It was Freud's opinion that visual imagery represents an earlier and more primitive mode of mental operation than verbal thought. Thus, the dream is an *archaic production*—a return to a mode of thought characteristic of the early years of childhood before language achieves its prominence in our relations to the world. Each individual initially begins mental life, Freud asserted, with sensory impressions and memory images of such impressions. Words are attached to these images only later in development, so that, at the outset, the child does not code his mental activities into language labels (Freud, 1916, pp. 180–181; see also Freud, 1900, pp. 189 ff.).

Dreams are a return to this archaic mode of mental functioning, and often, when correctly translated, a dream's latent content may contain a wish that dates from childhood: *". . . to our surprise, we find the child and child's impulses still living on in the dream"* (Freud, 1900, p. 191). Dream processes, then, are a *regression* to the earlier years of the dreamer's mental life.

Sexual and Aggressive Motives of Childhood

On the whole, adults retain very few memories of the first five or six years of life. With rare exception, most uf us can recall but one or two incidents that we now presume, precisely because they are remembered, to have been overwhelmingly important at the time. But key memories and feelings are conspicuously absent from adult consciousness. Recollection of our Oedipal sexual and aggressive strivings remains inaccessible to consciousness because an *infantile amnesia* obscures the great wealth of experiences of the childhood epoch.

However, it was Freud's discovery that these memories are not simply "forgotten." Instead, they are only inaccessible or latent, and, having become part of the unconscious, these childhood memories, strivings, and wishes may emerge during dreams when triggered by some current, thematically similar, incident.

The "Hellish" Unconscious

Consider the necessity of censorship in dreams. The dreamer entertains wishes and desires that would seem so perverse and unethical to him if he were awake that the dream work must disguise these thoughts beyond conscious recognition. What is the source of these monumentally "evil" inclinations? Obviously, since dreams are a product of the unconscious, the unconscious must be the source of the impulses that the conscious personality, the ego, finds objectionable. But during sleep, the censorship agency is less stringent, more easily pacified by partial disguise, and it allows the ego to be flooded with material that is customarily held in check.

> The ego, freed from all ethical bonds, also finds itself at one with all the demands of sexual desire, even those which have long been condemned by our aesthetic upbringing and those which contradict all the requirements of moral restraint. The desire for pleasure—the "libido," as we call it—chooses its objects without inhibition, and by preference, indeed, the forbidden ones: not only other men's wives, but above all incestuous objects, objects sanctified by the common agreement of mankind, a man's mother and sister, a woman's father and brother. . . . Lusts which we think of as remote from human nature show themselves strong enough to provoke dreams. Hatred, too, rages without restraint. Wishes for revenge and death directed against those who are nearest and dearest in waking life, against the dreamer's parents, brothers, and sisters, husband or wife, and his own children are nothing unusual. *These censored wishes appear to rise up out of a positive Hell; after they have been interpreted when we are awake, no censorship of them seems to us too severe.* [Freud, 1916, pp. 142–43; italics added]

Are we to conclude, on the basis of the seemingly reprehensible content of adult dreams, that dreams simply expose the inherently evil character of humanity? On the contrary, Freud protested. It is not that dreams expose evil, hellish strivings of adults, but that the adult *interprets* such feelings in himself as evil when he becomes aware of them. Actually, the egoistic, unrestrained sexual and aggressive urges found in dreams date from childhood, when ethical and realistic standards of conduct, which we attribute to adult understanding, were yet undeveloped.

Against the standards of adult ethics, such wishes as sexual desire for a parent and murderous intent directed toward rivals are absolutely wrong, shocking, and condemnable. But for the infant such reactions are the typical responses of an organism that is at once helpless, yet dominated by his urgent need for immediate gratification of his wishes. That gratification can come only from those persons who are in charge of his care, and who, therefore, are in intimate contact with him. For the *infant* it is not morally outrageous to desire the exclusive possession of his mother; it is not shocking that *he* expects this accustomed fulfiller of his every pleasure also to be the object of his sexual explorations and curiosity; it is not a condemnable quality of the *infant* that he harbors wishes for the annihilation of brothers, sisters, and father, along with anyone else who rivals his insistent and pressing commitment to mother, the satisfier. To the *infant*, unschooled in shame, disgust, or morality, such desires are the mere commonalities of day-to-day existence. To the *adult*, recollecting these feelings in dreams, guilt and horror seem the only appropriate responses.

It is with these memories, wishes, and strivings, then, that the ethical and realistic demands of later socialization will clash. The forces of repression will thrust them into the unconscious: *". . . what is unconscious in mental life is also what is infantile"* (Freud, 1916, p. 210). Adult dreams regress to the archaic and amoral level of infancy, and they deceptively appear to shed light on the vileness of the adult unconscious.

The obvious question arises: "What triggers the reemergence of these latent, infantile strivings in adult dreams?" Freud suggested that something in the dreamer's current waking life, an incident, a frustrated desire, the emotionally abrasive happenings of the day, somehow connect by association to the stored memories of the unconscious and, together with them, initiate a dream. Archaic wishes in the unconscious link up with these "day's residues," as Freud called them, to produce the dream thoughts. Dream thoughts are thus dominated by events that have given us pause for reflection during the day and which bear some associative similarity to the archaic wishes in the unconscious. The explanation, of course, may apply the other way round: events that give us pause during the day do so because they are connected with repressed wishes in the unconscious (Freud, 1900, pp. 169, 174).

Indeed, in either case, dreams *are* the royal road to an understanding of the unconscious mind.

Counterwishes: Anxiety Dreams

If dreams are indeed wish fulfillments, then why do we sometimes dream dreams that apparently run counter to our most cherished desires? Indeed, why do our dreams sometimes contain elements of our most dreaded fears? To answer these questions, and to account for the apparent contradiction, we must ask a further question: "*Whose* wish is fulfilled by a dream?"

> No doubt a wish-fulfillment must bring pleasure; but the question then arises "To whom?" To the person who has the wish of course. But as we know, a dreamer's relation to his wishes is a quite peculiar one. He repudiates them and censors them—he has no liking for them, in short. So that their fulfillment will give him no pleasure, but just the opposite; and experience shows that this opposite appears in the form of anxiety. ... *Thus a dreamer in his relation to his dream-wishes can only be compared to an amalgamation of two separate people who are linked by some important common element.* [Freud, 1900, pp. 580–581; this passage was added as a footnote in 1919; the same paragraph is included in Freud, 1916, pp. 215–216; italics added]

The amalgamated personage referred to in this passage describes, of course, the conflicting relationship between the dreamer's *unconscious,* the source of the wish, and his *preconscious* censorship agency, the source of the repudiation. Thus, while the wish fulfillment embodied in the dream brings pleasure to the unconscious, the anxiety element introduced by the distortion of the dream work is meant to satisfy the ever watchful censor. Freud employed a clever analogy to describe how a wish could bring both pleasure and unpleasure simultaneously:

> A good fairy promised a poor married couple to grant them the fulfillment of their first three wishes. They were delighted, and made up their minds to choose their three wishes carefully. But a smell of sausages being fried in the cottage next door tempted the woman to wish for a couple of them. They were there in a flash; and this was the first wish-fulfillment. But the man was furious, and in his rage wished that the sausages were hanging on his wife's nose. This happened too; and the sausages were not to be dislodged from their new position. This was the second wish-fulfillment; *but the wish was the man's, and its fulfillment was most disagreeable for his wife.* You know the rest of the story. Since after all they were in fact one—man and wife —the third wish was bound to be that the sausages should come away from the woman's nose. ... *if two people are not at one with each other the fulfillment of a wish of one of them may bring nothing but unpleasure to the other.* [Freud, 1900, p. 581; italics added]

If we conceive of the mind as divided between the two agencies—the unconscious pleasure-seeking system, and the preconscious censorship system—the compromise nature of anxiety dreams becomes apparent. On the one hand, the unconscious is allowed *some* expression and *some* satisfaction of its repressed urges in the dream. On the other hand, the ethical arm of personality is allowed *some* control over the unacceptability of the wishes (Freud, 1900, vol. V, p. 581). *Dreams, just like neurotic symptoms, are compromise formations that allow both an outlet for the discharge of the wish's tension and a censorship mechanism to repudiate the now gratified, but still unacceptable, wish.*

Repression and the Unpleasure Principle

Consider once again the state of the human infant. Striving to obtain satisfaction for his needs and to avoid the unpleasure of mounting somatic tension, the infant soon learns the distinction between a fantasied and a real satisfier. Frustration and unpleasure are his tutors in a curriculum that includes the lessons that fantasied food cannot be eaten, hallucinatory milk cannot be drunk, and an ephemeral mother cannot be cuddled. In order to survive, the infant must learn that the wish fulfillments embodied in dream states and fantasies have to be pursued in reality. When *real* satisfactions for its desires are not forthcoming, the infant experiences psychological and sometimes bodily pain that Freud termed *unpleasure.* Conversely, when the unconscious obtains gratification of its desires, the result is the physical and mental state of *pleasure.*

There is, however, a further set of lessons that must be mastered in order to ensure a comfortable and safe existence. This "unpleasure principle" is a two-edged sword, not only motivating the naïve infant to avoid the discomfort of hallucinatory need satisfaction, but also pressing on his awareness the importance of *actively avoiding painful or noxious stimulation* as well. Hence, the newly developed *preconscious* reality-scanning system may operate to promote escape or flight from certain forms of excitation when, on the basis of past experience, it recognizes some stimuli as potentially threatening. This class of unpleasure-producing stimuli might include, for example, as the child matures, lighted matches, hot radiators, and angry-in-the-mood-for-a-spanking-mother.

Furthermore, even the internal, *mental representations* of such stimuli would trigger avoidance responses in the mental apparatus. But in the case of internal stimulation, the mental apparatus cannot engage in the physical act of flight. Instead, mental withdrawal occurs which takes the form of a removal of *cathexis*[1] (charges of mental energy, or the diversion of atten-

---

[1]The term *cathexis* is a translation of a German term Freud had first used in his "Project for a Scientific Psychology" (1895, vol. 1). The "Project" was a detailed neurological model of the mind in which Freud postulated coordinated systems of neurons within the brain as the basis of various psychological processes, including repression and dreams. Certain of the neurons in this model become permeable to the flow of energy (electro-chemical discharges) within the nervous system and they "fill-up" with quantities of it. Freud used the German word *Besetzung,* which roughly means "to fill up," or "to occupy," in describing the flow of energy in and out of the neurons. His translators converted the German word to the more technical sounding *Cathexis* from a Greek root meaning "to hold onto." Freud abandoned the neurological model, but not the analogous idea of psychic energy systems that could fill up and discharge their quantities of energy, that is, their *cathexis* of excitation.

tion) from the *memory image* of the noxious stimulus. In brief, this "ostrich policy" is the prototype of the mechanism of repression.

The Reality Principle

The infant's newest mental attainment under the tutelage of the unpleasure principle is the ability to delay the motor activity that he normally employs in obtaining gratification. He will now wait until there is a clear indication of reality from the preconscious perceptual system. It is this reality-testing orientation to the world that provides the infant with a reliable income of pleasure. We might, therefore, redefine a wish in these terms: *a wish is a quantity of unpleasurable excitation resulting from a need that can be completely satisfied only by a real object or by specific and instrumental activity in the external world.*

Thus, the infant's intercourse with the world is governed not only by the pleasure-unpleasure principle, but by the *reality principle* as well. With the adoption of this more sophisticated mental strategy, external reality increases in importance in the economy of the infant's mental life, along with the rising significance he now attaches to his sense organs. The infant will gradually increase the use of his senses to scan the environment for appropriate objects of satisfaction demanded by the reality principle (Freud, 1911, p. 220).

Primary and Secondary Process Thought

Our description of the unpleasure and reality principles is incomplete because their joint functioning is more complicated than this rigidly dualistic picture might suggest. The unconscious system, for example, apparently knows no bounds to its wishfulness, and it is well satisfied with only hallucinatory wish satisfaction. Behaving as if reality did not exist, the unconscious does not by itself discriminate between real and fantasied objects. Its only interest is in the distinction between pleasure and unpleasure. Moreover, as revealed in manifest dreams and in neurotic symptoms, the unconscious system's sum total of mental energy is highly mobile and capable of all sorts of shifts, condensations, and displacements. All of these mental acrobatics are, of course, directed to the attainment of satisfaction *at all costs.* Freud characterized this state of affairs in the unconscious as *primary process thinking.* The chief characteristics of primary process thinking are the urgency with which tension reduction is sought, the plasticity or mobility of its energy, and its disregard for reality.

In contrast to the primary process functioning of the unconscious system, the preconscious system operates in accord with the reality principle by delaying gratification until appropriate moments. This kind of mental functioning, characterized by an *interest in the demands of reality* and an ability to *delay gratification,* Freud termed *secondary process* thinking. Because secondary process mental functioning develops later than primary process thinking, and because such reality-oriented mental activity is characteristic of truly adult thought, Freud considered secondary process thought to be a clear developmental advance over primary process functioning. Of course, during dreams, even the most mature adult regresses to primary process thought as the unconscious system gains control of the mental apparatus.

The Meaning of "Unconscious" in Psychoanalysis: "Metapsychology"

The way in which Freud had used the term "unconscious" in his early writings led to some confusion about the reasons for which an idea might be removed from consciousness. Freud, therefore, distinguished three ways in which the term "unconscious" was used in psychoanalysis.

The first meaning, indicating the existence of ideas that are not *now*— at this precise moment—in consciousness, is a purely *descriptive* one. Thus, for example, while few of us keep our own phone number in the forefront of our minds at every minute of the day, we can nevertheless recall that item when necessary. Our phone number is only temporarily out of immediate awareness. There is no a priori reason why it cannot be brought into consciousness at will. Such items that can easily be made conscious are conceptualized as residing in the preconscious system (Freud, 1912, p. 262). Hence, this first meaning of "unconscious" is *descriptive* of those occasions when the limitations of consciousness and the human attention span necessitate the simple omission of some content.

In contrast with this purely descriptive sense, there are memories of early childhood incidents, impulses, and desires that are unacceptable to the conscious ego and cannot be recalled no matter how great the effort. Such memories are *repressed* from consciousness. Hysterical symptoms owe their existence to such unconscious ideas that, despite their intensity and their activity, remain apart from conscious awareness. *Repressed memories are never admitted to consciousness so long as repression operates successfully.* Because this meaning of "unconscious" indicates the forceful and energetic activity of ideas not in consciousness and implies the continual expenditure of energy required to keep them out of awareness, it is called the *dynamic* meaning (Freud, 1912, pp. 263–264). (Freud employed another explanatory term in connection with the concept of a dynamic unconscious. He would often refer to the fact that a dynamic conception of the energy that is required to keep a thought repressed raised questions of an *economic* nature, i.e., of attempts to *quantify* various degrees of energy expenditure [1923a, p. 14].)

Last, Freud's investigations of dream processes had revealed that there are at least two types of mental functioning, the primary and secondary processes. The unconscious is characterized by the high mobility of its cathexes of energy as evidenced in its ability to condense, displace, and distort ideas. Furthermore, the unconscious responds to the demands of the pleasure principle by its continual press for immediate gratification of wishes, in contrast with the delayed, inhibitory, reality-testing orientation of the preconscious. In consequence, the unconscious must be conceptualized as a unique *system* operating in accordance with its own local rules of conduct side by side with the other systems of the mind that, likewise, operate in conformity with their intrinsic standards of conduct. This usage of the word "unconscious" conveys the *systematic* meaning of the term, indicating the independent status of the unconscious as a system among systems.

In summary, Freud distinguished among three meanings of the term "unconscious": the descriptive, the dynamic, and the systematic. Each of these usages might be thought of as corresponding to a question: *What* is unconscious? *(descriptive)*; *Why* is it unconscious? *(dynamic)*; and *Where* is the unconscious idea? *(systematic)*.

When we are able to understand a given psychological process in all three of its meanings, we have entered the realm of what Freud called "metapsychological presentation" (1915c, p. 180). Thus, Freud had resolved the ambiguities in the usage of the term "unconscious" by the expedient of delineating each of the possible meanings. He realized, however, that psychoanalysis was far from providing a comprehensive explanation of all psychological states in their descriptive, dynamic, and systematic properties. Freud acknowledged, therefore, that psychoanalysis had only begun to develop a metapsychology (1915c, p. 181). The concept of repression, one of his earliest discoveries, was quickly redefined in terms of the new metapsychological perspective.

Metapsychology of Repression: Balance of Pleasure and Unpleasure

Repression, it will be recalled, is the way in which the mental apparatus deals with wishful impulses from which physical flight is impossible. Instead, these unescapable and unacceptable impulses are denied direct access to awareness. Consider the paradox involved in proposing a mechanism like repression. Wishful impulses demand satisfaction because when it is forthcoming, the experience of pleasure is the usual result. But in the case of a repressed impulse, something has happened to a wishful idea that makes satisfaction so *unpleasurable* that denial of its existence is the only means of dealing with it. Yet, paradoxically, the impulse continues to press for release.

It thus seems that one of the preconditions for an impulse to be subject to repression is that satisfaction of the impulse be simultaneously pleasurable and unpleasurable. The only way to account for this disparity of aims is to assume that the reason a repressed impulse has been denied release into consciousness is because its satisfaction would create pleasure for one mental system at the expense of the even more grave unpleasure evoked in a competing system. Here, of course, we have the conflict between the unconscious wishful demands and conscious restraint.

Freud clearly conceived of repression as the expression of a *balance* between these two motives: *the seeking after pleasure* and *the avoidance of unpleasure.* In the case of a repressed impulse, however, the motive force of unpleasure is more intense than the pleasure to be obtained from satisfaction of the impulse. Repression occurs, consequently, when the balance between pleasure and unpleasure is tipped in the direction of unpleasure.

The process of repression requires that the preconscious system prevent the emergence of the unconscious impulse into awareness by withdrawing a sum of mental energy (cathexis) from the offending impulse. However, having lost the cathexis of the preconscious, the unacceptable impulse may still retain the cathexis of energy from the unconscious, where it originated. Consequently, the repressed impulse can continue to make assaults on the preconscious system indefinitely, drawing on its reserve of energy in the unconscious. The simple expedient of withdrawing preconscious energy from the impulse is not sufficient to prevent the impulse from unendingly repeating its attempts at entry into consciousness (Freud, 1915c, p. 180).

What is needed to accomplish the permanent subjugation of the impulse is another, opposing quantity of energy, strong enough to resist the unconsciously endowed impulse's cathexis of energy. Such an opposing supply of energy would, in effect, serve as a barrier against the reemergence of the rejected impulse. Freud called this barrier that is set up by the preconscious an *anticathexis.* Anticathexis is the primary mode of dealing with unacceptable unconscious content. Clearly, to enable repression to remain effective, an anticathexis requires a *continual* expenditure of energy by the preconscious.

Primal Repression and Repression Proper

With the development of the theoretical concept of anticathexis, Freud could account for the creation and presence of repressed derivatives in consciousness, like symptoms and seduction fantasies. He now conceived of repression as a two-stage process to effect this theoretical advance.

In the first stage, the ideational representative of the unacceptable impulse is denied access to consciousness by the preconscious setting up an anticathexis as a barrier. This first stage is called *primal repression. The immediate result of primal repression is that the repressed idea or impulse is fixated or frozen in development.* No further modification or maturation of the repressed content can occur (Freud, 1915b, p. 148). Significant acts of primal repression occur during the first six or eight years of life, and in their role of immobilized, unconscious memories they become important sensitizing or predisposing factors for later acts of adult repression.

The second stage of repression is called *repression proper,* and it is directed against any derivatives or associates of the originally repressed impulses that may enter consciousness. Repression proper is rather like an "after pressure," to use Freud's descriptive phrase, whereby ideas, trains of thought, or perceptions that are associatively linked to the primally repressed impulse are also denied access to consciousness. *Repression proper consists of the preconscious system's withdrawing its cathexis* [energy] *from the derivative.* Repression proper thus cooperates with primal repression to ensure that unacceptable impulses and associated ideas remain out of conscious awareness.

Thus, repression is not a unitary act. Or, more precisely, repressions of primal derivatives that occur after infancy depend on the mass of primally repressed impulses *already* present in the unconscious. An idea or an impulse cannot be removed from awareness by repression proper *unless there has already been an act of predisposing primal repression to exert a "pulling effect" on subsequent derivatives.* At the same time, the preconscious system actively strives from its vantage point on the threshold of awareness to eject these offending ideas by pushing them away from consciousness (cf. Freud, 1900, p. 547n.).

Instincts of the Unconscious

Terms like "excitation," "impulse," "wish," and "tension," dating almost from the very beginning of Freud's psychological writing, were replaced in his later work by the term *instinct.*

In his 1915 metapsychological paper, "Instincts and Their Vicissitudes," Freud carefully delineated the meaning of the term in psychoanalysis. In the first place, Freud distinguished between a stimulus and an instinct by pointing out that physical stimuli impinge on the organism from the external environment, whereas instinctual urges develop from within the organism. Although the organism, through the use of reflexes, may escape or even terminate *external stimulation,* internal *instinctual* demand cannot be escaped by flight. An organism cannot flee the demands of its own body.

As a second distinguishing feature of instinct, Freud pointed out that stimulation originating in the environment is only *temporary* in its impact on the organism. Instinctual, internal excitation is *constant,* terminating only when the tissue need giving rise to the instinct is satisfied. Thus, instincts may be thought of as needs seeking appropriate satisfactions (Freud, 1915a, p. 119).

Freud returned in his discussion of instinct to an earlier idea of his and Breuer's of the nervous system as an apparatus that functions to reduce stimulation and excitation to the lowest possible level. In Freud's view, the nervous system is assigned the task of "mastering stimuli" by discharging excitation almost as soon as it builds up (1915a, p. 120). Called the "principle of constancy" by Breuer and Freud, this idea of repeated returns to some optimal state of minimum arousal is similar to the modern biologist's concept of homeostasis. It follows, in consequence, that this essential task is complicated in the case of an instinct because the nervous system cannot master instinctual demands by the expedient of flight. Furthermore, because the nervous system is governed by the pleasure principle—the seeking after pleasure by the discharge of unpleasurable mounting tension—instincts must not be dealt with in a way that merely avoids their demand; the nervous system must find a way to reduce the biological deficit (or to satisfy the urge) that the demand represents.

For Freud, then, the concept of instinct was both a psychological and a biological one, a "frontier concept" on the border between bodily and mental phenomena. *An instinct is a mental representation of a physical or bodily need* (1915, p. 122).

Characteristics of Instincts

Freud distinguished four characteristics of an instinct.

Pressure

The amount of force or the strength of the demand made by the instinct on the mind is described as *pressure.* Thus, for example, deprivation of food for twenty-four hours produces greater instinctual pressure (hunger) than deprivation for only four hours. A twenty-four-hour-deprived individual is more strongly impelled to seek food, think about food, and to devour it, when food is available, than he would be after only four hours without a meal.

Aim

Instinctual impulses all strive toward one goal: satisfaction or tension reduction. While satisfaction is clearly the universal *aim* of an instinct, a given instinct may operate to achieve its aim in differing ways, as circumstances dictate. Freud distinguishes, therefore, between *ultimate aim,* the immediate gratification of demand, and *intermediate aim,* the devious, roundabout, or substitute forms of satisfaction for which an instinct may strive when blocked from a directly suitable goal. The sexual instinct is particularly prone to this widening of its aims. For example, the aim of the sexual instincts is "organ pleasure," a pleasing sensation attached to a particular part of the body when stimulated. With maturation, the sexual instincts become focused on the aim of reproduction (Freud, 1915a, p. 126). The path from the goal of diffuse pleasurable sensation in infancy to the stage of genital primacy at puberty is a long and tedious journey.

Object

In order to obtain its ultimate aim of satisfaction, the instinct must seek some concrete, usually external, *object* that has the power to reduce its tension. For example, an infant's hunger drive is directed toward the object of food; for the sexually aroused individual, an appealing member of the opposite sex is the appropriate and satisfying object.

However, the object of an instinct is its most variable characteristic. Appropriate objects may be changed many times during the course of the instinct's vicissitudes. Thus, displacement from one satisfying object to another, a process so characteristic of the wish fulfillments in dreams, is possible. Prisoners, for example, confined with members of their own sex often resort to masturbation or to homosexual gratification as substitutes for heterosexual satisfaction, only to return to exclusive heterosexual gratification upon release.

Conversely, it is equally possible for a single object to satisfy several instincts simultaneously. Thus, thumb sucking may partially alleviate the infant's hunger, soothe his teething discomfort, and also provide pleasurable stimulation as a prelude to shutting out the world before sleep.

Source

The origin of all instincts, as we have seen, is to be sought in the physical-chemical processes of the body. These processes give rise to the tissue-needs of the organism that make their demands felt in the mental operations that guide much of our behavior. The sexual instincts, for example, have their *source* in the genital zone of the body (and in some central nervous system activities), while the hunger instinct originates in the viscera (and also in some parts of the central nervous system). It was Freud's opinion, however, that physical and chemical processes were beyond the scope of psychology.

Dualistic Division of the Instincts: Hunger versus Love

It is clear that Freud viewed the instincts, though biologically based, as essentially malleable and plastic in the course of an organism's life history. During their collision with life's circumstances, the instincts may undergo modifications or reversals of expression. These vicissitudes, to use Freud's translators' term, share the common motive of avoiding the psychological or biological discomfort that would result from free, undisguised expression of an instinctual urge. Repression, as we have seen, is one of the vicissitudes that an instinct may undergo.

Although instincts may be expressed and satisfied in diverse ways, Freud was hesitant to catalog a seemingly infinite list of biological demands and their mental representatives. Instead, he proposed a concise, bipolar division of all instincts into two great classes: instincts in the service of the preservation of the individual's life, and instincts directed toward the attainment of pleasure. *Life maintenance* and *pleasure*—these are the poles around which the operations of the mental apparatus are organized.

According to this dualistic scheme, Freud asserted that the ego was the seat of the organism's instincts for self-preservation, whereas striving for pleasure was a function of the child's developing sexual equipment. Though Freud did not provide a name for the energy of the ego instincts, he employed the term "libido" to denote the energy of the sexual or pleasure instincts (e.g., 1916, p. 313). Libido, to reiterate an important concept, was to be broadly conceived as general pleasurable stimulation rather than be restricted to genital, sexual pleasure. Thus, Freud's original dualistic classification of the instincts pitted the ego instincts against the sexual (pleasure) instincts: survival versus libido.

The ego instincts have as their main goal the preservation and continuance of the safety and bodily integrity of the *individual.* Sexual (pleasure) instincts, on the other hand, are directed mainly toward the attainment of pleasure during the years of infancy and childhood and, only after puberty, when the genital organs assume dominance, are the sexual instincts directed to the preservation of the *species.* Consequently, in Freud's original dualism, the ego instincts are individual-centered and the sexual instincts are, ultimately, species-centered. This dichotomy, Freud pointed out, is roughly similar to the division between hunger (individual self-preservation) and love (other-centered pleasure).

Freud introduced this division of the instincts in a paper in 1910b (p. 214; see Editor's footnote), and he maintained the dualism of which he was so fond for a number of years. The bulk of his writing in subsequent years, however, was focused on the sexual instincts with the effect of obscuring by neglect the role of the ego instincts. But the ego instincts were to come into their own in psychoanalysis as Freud's clinical practice revealed some disconcerting anomalies and violations of the dualistic hunger-love scheme.

Exceptions to the Hunger-Love Dichotomy: Narcissism

In the dualistic conception of the instincts, libido, the energy of the sexual or pleasure instincts, should be a separate quantity from that of the ego instincts. Freud noted a disconcerting exception to this separation hypothesis in the case of some psychotic patients.

One of the main characteristics of some forms of schizophrenia is the withdrawal of the patient's interest from the external world. He behaves as if reality no longer existed and in every way as though only his own ideas, feelings, or urges mattered. Freud's instinct theory would characterize such withdrawal as the retraction of libido from external objects and persons. Simultaneously with this retraction of libido, however, there occurs what seems to be an *expansion* of ego instinctual energy, an increase in the ego's self-interest. In short, the psychotic overvalues his own ideas, his own body, his own person. Why should this reciprocal increase in ego instinct occur at the same time outwardly directed libido is diminished—unless the two forms of energy are *not* separate? Freud had to conclude that libido could be turned back on the ego and that libido could donate to the ego's disposal some of the energy normally expended outwardly.

> The libido that has been withdrawn from the external world has been directed to the ego and thus gives rise to an attitude which may be called narcissism. [1914a, p. 75]

Clearly the energies of the ego and sexual instincts are not separate. They commingle, one drawing on the reserves of the other at various times. Freud had thus introduced a new distinction into his theory of instincts. He postulated that in the earliest stages of life there is a supply of libidinal energy in the ego that produces a primary state of narcissism or self-love. It is from this pool of primary ego libido that the later, external object libido emerges. But the original pool of ego libido remains in the ego, and it is this supply that is expanded or contracted in the narcissism of psychosis. In consequence, ego instinctual energy and sexual instinctual energy are not completely independent, but initially emerge from a common pool. Thus, in the beginning all instinctual energy was one, libido. Later developments cause the differentiation into ego libido and object libido.

Freud had thus revised his dualistic notion of the instincts, altering the nature of the conflict from that of a clash between ego instincts and sexual instincts to that of a clash between two forms of libido: *ego libido* conflicts with *object libido*. This seemingly unitary or monistic scheme of instinctual energy is more apparent than it is real. Freud was fond of dualistic, bi polar explanations of events and certainly ego and object libido fit the favored pattern. Yet even this partial dualism did not satisfy Freud, and he ultimately would again revise his conception of the instincts.

Return to a Dualistic Instinct Theory: Life against Death

By considering the narcissistic pool of ego libido the primal source of all significant interactions with the world, Freud had virtually erected libido as the unitary scheme of explanation. He was not, as some of his critics accused, attempting to sexualize all human behavior. His distinction between the self-preservative nature of ego libido and the pleasure-seeking orientation of object libido had maintained and paralleled his original division between ego and sexual instincts. But the problem for Freud was that his clinical experience had uncovered the essentially conflict-ridden nature of human behavior and neurosis. A unitary scheme of instinctual dynamics based solely on libido deprived psychoanalytic theory of the ability to specify the elements of the conflict precisely. What was needed was a new dualistic scheme in which libido (both object and ego libido) could be contrasted against some other, independent pool of instinctual energy.

In 1920, Freud solved the problem. He published a startlingly speculative account of a profoundly revised instinct theory whereby libido was contrasted with a newly discerned instinctual energy, the *death instinct*. Thus, Freud returned to a dualistic conception of mental energy. At the same time, he traveled beyond his earlier model of the mind by transcending even the seemingly secure dominance of the pleasure principle. For in revising his instinct theory, Freud replaced the pleasure principle as the fundamental mental rule with an even more basic "law," the *compulsion to repeat*. It is no wonder that Freud entitled the book in which he made these radical, and for some psychoanalysts disturbing, revelations *Beyond the Pleasure Principle*. Freud's changing views of how the instincts were organized are summarized in Figure 3-1.

FIGURE 3-1: FREUD'S CHANGING VIEWS OF THE INSTINCTS

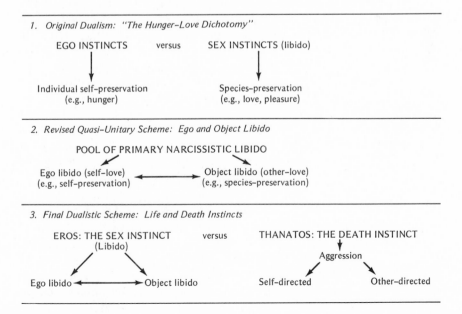

1. Original Dualism: "The Hunger–Love Dichotomy"

EGO INSTINCTS   versus   SEX INSTINCTS (libido)

Individual self-preservation   Species-preservation
(e.g., hunger)   (e.g., love, pleasure)

2. Revised Quasi–Unitary Scheme: Ego and Object Libido

POOL OF PRIMARY NARCISSISTIC LIBIDO

Ego libido (self–love) ⟷ Object libido (other–love)
(e.g., self-preservation)   (e.g., species–preservation)

3. Final Dualistic Scheme: Life and Death Instincts

EROS: THE SEX INSTINCT   versus   THANATOS: THE DEATH INSTINCT
(Libido)   Aggression

Ego libido ⟷ Object libido   Self-directed   Other-directed

Behaviors beyond the Pleasure Principle: The Clinical Evidence

Ernst's "Gone" Game

At one and a half years, Freud's eldest grandson, Ernst, played a strangely symbolic game. He would momentarily take hold of any available small object, throw it into a corner of the room or under the bed, and croon loudly the German word for "gone" *(Fort)* with a peculiarly long, drawn-out "o-o-o-o" pronunciation. Immediately upon throwing his toys away from himself, Ernst would retrieve them only long enough, it seemed to Freud, to begin the dispersal again. Freud soon realized that the sole use Ernst made of his toys was to play this strangely compelling game of "gone."

Ernst was singularly attached to his mother and especially sensitive to periods of her absence. Not that Ernst ever cried or showed any other obvious form of protest to separation from his mother. In all respects, Ernst was a "good" child. In September 1915, while Freud was spending several weeks with his daughter Sophie at her home in Hamburg, he had the opportunity to observe Ernst's extraordinary game (Jones, 1957, p. 267). Freud found himself peculiarly moved by Ernst's pastime.

As if to confirm his growing feeling that the "game" was somehow strangely symbolic of Ernst's sense of loss at his mother's absence, Freud was able to make the following further observation: Ernst had as one of his toys a wooden reel (probably similar to a thread spool) with a piece of string firmly attached.

> It never occurred to [Ernst] to pull it along the floor behind him, for instance, and play at its being a carriage. What he did was to hold the reel by the string and very skillfully throw it over the edge of his curtained cot, so that it disappeared into it, at the same time uttering his expressive "o-o-o-o." He then pulled the reel out of the cot again by the string and hailed its reappearance with a joyful *"da"* ["there"]. *This, then, was the complete game—disappearance and return.* [1920a, p. 15; italics added]

On another occasion, when Ernst's mother had been away for several hours, her return was greeted by her son's exclamation, "Baby o-o-o-o!" In the light of Freud's earlier observations, such an utterance could only be meant to communicate: "Ernst (baby) was gone!"—an interpretation that was confirmed when it was discovered that Ernst had tried a variation of his "gone" game with a full-length mirror. Not quite reaching the floor, the mirror had provided the inventive Ernst with the opportunity to make himself "gone" each time he crouched below its bottom edge (Freud, 1920a, p. 15n.).

"Gone" was more than a game. It was a form of self-discipline by which Ernst had sought to master the unpleasurable prospect of his mother's periodic absences. He could not, however, symbolically act out the pleasurable *return* of a missing love object until he had first staged its unpleasurable *disappearance.* In his "game," Ernst was particularly successful because the disappearance and return of his toys were directly under *his* control, as contrasted with the absences of his mother, which he could experience only as a circumstance imposed from without.

Ernst had developed a technique of symbolically *repeating* an unpleasurable experience. In its original form, the experience had to be endured *passively.* By his re-creations, Ernst could *actively* control the event, and he could express a kind of defiance: "All right, go away—I don't need you!"

Sadly, when Ernst was almost six years old, his mother died of pneumonia; in his terms, she was permanently "gone."

On the theoretical level, Freud offered Ernst's game as one example of a violation of the pleasure principle. It showed clearly that unpleasurable events could be reworked, repeated, and relived, despite their painful quality, until they were mastered. Yet, Ernst's game was not a definitive example. Freud pointed out that such cases could be interpreted as consistent with, rather than beyond, the pleasure principle because the *eventual* outcome was pleasurable. He searched about for another example of a behavior beyond the pleasure principle.

Recurring Posttraumatic Dreams

In the dreams of patients suffering from hysterialike paralysis and apparent physical illness following upon some life-threatening accident like a railway collision or exposure to stress on the battlefield, Freud found another illustration of an urge to repeat unpleasant experiences. Traumatic neurosis resembles hysterical symptomatology in that the afflicted individual shows no organic basis or demonstrable physical cause for his symptoms. But, more important, in many such cases the individual experiences recurring dreams that each night re-create the traumatic situation of the accident or battlefield. By contrast, such patients in their waking state are usually more concerned with forgetting the trauma than with reliving it. The dream, however, instead of pleasurably fulfilling some wish, *returns* the patient to the situation and to the fright he once helplessly endured.

Reliving Painful Memories during Psychotherapy

As a last example of an apparent violation of the dominance of the pleasure principle, Freud cited an observation from the realm of psychotherapy. Often, during a psychoanalysis, the patient treats the analyst as if he were a particular authority figure from his own past. He thrusts onto his therapist attitudes and desires that would be appropriate only to the real figures of his past life. In effect, the patient *relives* significant experiences and attitudes of his life history with the therapist as his present target. ". . . [The patient] is obliged to *repeat* the repressed material as a contemporary experience instead of, as the physician would prefer to see, *remembering* it as something belonging to the past" (Freud, 1920a, p. 18).

Transference is the name that Freud gave to this tendency of the patient to react to his therapist with emotions reproduced from childhood. Because the material that is thus repeated originates in the unconscious, and because the conscious ego is occupied with the repression of that material, Freud concluded that the compulsion to repeat must also originate in the unconscious. Therefore, in the conflict between the ego and the unconscious, reexperience of the repressed material must figure as a potent source of unpleasure for the beleaguered ego.

For every instance cited—Ernst's game, traumatic dreams, transference in therapy—the common denominator seems to be that these individuals are acting under the *compulsion endlessly to repeat unpleasurable experiences*.

Reduction of the Pleasure Principle to a Pleasure "Tendency"

Freud had in mind cases like Ernst's game, transference, and traumatic dreams when he modified his conception of the pleasure principle from a dominating influence to that of a trend in mental life:

> If such a dominance [of pleasure] existed, the immense majority of our mental processes would have to be accompanied by pleasure or to lead to pleasure, whereas universal experience completely contradicts any such conclusion. The most that can be said, therefore, is that there exists in the mind a strong *tendency* towards the pleasure principle, but the tendency is opposed by certain other forces or circumstances, so that the final outcome cannot always be in harmony with the tendency towards pleasure. [1920a, pp. 9–10]

The opposing forces were, of course, those underlying the *compulsion to repeat* unpleasurable experiences until, like Ernst's, they are mastered. Freud was now prepared to embark on a speculative reexamination of his previous accounts of the mental apparatus. His intention was to bring his discrepant findings about violations of the pleasure principle into harmony with the rest of psychoanalytic theory.

The Nirvana Principle: Tension Reduction

The overwhelming necessity governing the operation of the mental apparatus is the reduction of excitation, tension, or drive, and the need to maintain a relatively stable state of stimulation-free existence. Freud, following Breuer, had originally adopted the term "constancy principle" to describe the tension reduction efforts of the nervous system. Breuer had borrowed the term from the psychophysicist Gustav Fechner.

In *Beyond the Pleasure Principle,* Freud incorporated some new terminology from Barbara Low to replace the constancy principle. Freud now employed "Nirvana principle" to indicate the homeostatic trend of nervous system functioning whereby it attempts to divest itself of disturbing tensions and excess stimulation. In fact, Freud had thought that the Nirvana principle and the pleasure principle were essentially intimately related so that the nervous system's adherence to the Nirvana principle was guaranteed by the operation of the pleasure principle. That is to say, reduction of tension and the maintenance of an almost stimulation-free state implied by the Nirvana principle are pleasurable. However, in a paper written in 1924, Freud changed his mind and distinguished between the two principles.

The distinction was necessary, Freud thought, because certain states of pleasure require *increases* in excitation rather than the reduction of excitation. One state, for example, that would violate the Nirvana principle, but accord with the pleasure principle, is sexual excitation, in which rising amounts of bodily tension in the genitals produce pleasurable sensation (Freud, 1924a, p. 160). Therefore, the Nirvana principle and the pleasure principle were distinguished as separate, but complementary, trends in mental life.

The Conservative Nature of the Instincts

As Ernst played his evocative game of "gone," and as traumatic neurotic patients relive their frightful experiences in nightly dreams, so too the instincts, when viewed from the perspective of the nervous system's ultimate goal of tension reduction, seem to function to *repeat the past. Instincts operate to return to an earlier state—to the excitation-free state prior to stimulation.*

> *It seems, then, that an instinct is an urge inherent in organic life to restore an earlier state of things* which the living entity has been obliged to abandon under the pressure of external disturbing forces ... or, to put it another way, instincts are the expression of the inertia inherent in organic life. [Freud, 1920a, p. 36]

Freud was postulating that mental life is essentially *conservative* in quality. The mental apparatus is periodically disturbed by outside stimulation and internal needs but, on the whole, strives to maintain itself in the state of quietude that characterizes its functioning prior to such disturbances. A "Nirvana-like" state of peaceful freedom from need is the principal goal of the mental apparatus, for it is this satiety that conforms faultlessly to the pleasure principle.

As primitive organisms evolved, however, their trend toward maintaining a constant state and inertial resistance to change would have been overcome by the continuous flux of external conditions, the constant change of environmental pressures, which make their demands on living things. Thus, the instincts developed in unison with the increasing biological complexity of the evolving primitive organisms in order to maintain the capacity of the organism perpetually to restore an internal state of harmony in the face of a changing environment. The hunger instinct is a good example. When hunger tension mounts, one seeks food and achieves satisfaction, but within a few hours, food again must be sought to return to the state of satisfaction, and so on.

Such striving is always aimed at *returning to* or *repeating* the earlier state of quietude before the world or internal needs made their demands. In its most fundamental form, the compulsion to repeat is the ultimate conservative trend: an urge to gain *complete* quietude, *total* freedom from stimulation and need, and *absolute* independence of the world. In short, the aim is death.

> It would be in contradiction to the conservative nature of the instincts if the goal of life were a state of things which had never been attained. On the contrary, it must be an *old* state of things, an initial state from which the living entity has at one time or other departed and to which it is striving to return by the circuitous paths along which its development leads. If we are to take it as a truth that knows no exception that everything living dies for internal reasons— becomes inorganic once again—then we shall be compelled to say that *"the aim of all life is death"* and, looking backwards, that *"inanimate things existed before living ones."* [Freud, 1920a, p. 38]

Accidental death arising from *external causes* would cheat the organism of the completion of its *cycle* by merely terminating organic life. The organism would be deprived of achieving a *return* to the earlier state of inorganic existence that is an intrinsic part of its cellular structure. In consequence, accidental death, illness, injury merely short-circuit the process and circumvent the aim of life. The organism must gain death in its own way—the gradual burning out of the life energies. Any other means of death is evolutionary heresy.

Revision of Instinct Theory: Eros and Death

Freud's bold proposal of a death instinct brings the new theory into direct conflict with his original dualistic model of the instincts whereby one half of the dichotomy was asserted to be constituted of self-preservative ego instincts. Of what use to the organism are self-preservative instincts if the ultimate aim of life is death? Freud ingeniously answered this question by placing the ego instincts in the service of the death instincts as their agent of successful discharge:

[Self-preservative instincts] . . . are component instincts whose function it is to assure that the organism *shall follow its own path to death,
and to ward off any possible ways of returning to inorganic existence other
than those which are immanent in the organism itself* . . . What we are left
with is the fact that the organism *wishes to die only in its own fashion.*
Thus these guardians of life [i.e., self-preservative instincts] too, were
originally the myrmidons of death. [Freud, 1920a, p. 39; italics added]

Although Freud himself never, except in conversation with colleagues,
used the term *Thanatos* to refer to the death instinct, his followers have
almost universally adopted the term as the official name (Jones, 1957, p.
273). (*Thanatos,* incidentally, is the name of the Greek god of death and
was first used to refer to the death instinct by Freud's pupil Paul Federn.)
   The other half of the original dualistic classification of the instincts, the
sexual instincts, presented yet another problem to the hypothesis of a
death instinct. How could instincts that serve the continuity of life, the
longevity of a species, be brought into line with the penultimate conserva-
tism of the death instinct in its striving toward the dissolution of life? The
answer is that these two forces *conflict.*

Eros and Immortality

The instincts that guard the development of the germ cells, sperm and egg,
that provide them with safety during their time of generativity, and that
motivate the union of male and female are the sexual instincts, collectively
termed *libido.* Clearly the sexual instincts are the true *life* instincts since
they operate against the forces of death and dissolution by attempting to
immortalize the organism through its progeny. Paradoxically, the other
class of instincts, ego instincts, subserve death by striving to promote the
self-preservation of the organism *until it dies in its own way,* of its own
immanent causes. Thus, in *Beyond the Pleasure Principle,* the ego instincts
presented Freud with a problem of classification. In which group, life or
death, should the ego instincts be included? Freud eventually combined
the ego instincts with the sexual instincts and considered them to be part
of the libido's press for the continuity of life while they nevertheless serve
the inexorable aims of death.
   Freud had retained much of his desired dualistic classification by opposing the death instincts to the combined life instincts (ego and object libido)
(1920a, p. 41). In honor of the changed scheme, Freud assigned to the
unified sexual and ego instincts the term Eros, the name of the god of love
and passion. Consequently, the dichotomy in Freud's theory was changed
from the conflict between love and hunger to the opposition between life
and death. All organisms die. If they bear the spark of immortality it is
evidenced only in their ability to confer equally transient life.

Eros and Bisexuality: Return to Unity

Freud had one further problem that had to be solved before his life-death dualism could be brought into the main body of psychoanalytic theory. How is Eros governed by the compulsion to repeat, a compulsion that is basic to all instincts? The death instinct operates to *return* the organism to the prior evolutionary state of inorganic existence. But what is Eros attempting to repeat; *to what does it seek return?*

The answer, Freud speculated, lies in the origin of the two sexes. He suggested, hesitantly at first, that Plato's myth of the origin of the human race may be a poetic representation of a fundamental truth. In the *Symposium,* Plato, speaking through the character of Aristophanes, recounts a myth in which the original human sexes existed in three varieties: male, female, and the union of the two. Those bisexual humans had double sets of hands, feet, and sexual organs, but, because they offended the gods, Zeus decided to cut them into two. After the division, each half-human, desiring its missing component, sought out its mate. They threw their arms about each other, eager to merge again into unity. Freud commented:

> Shall we follow the hint given us by the poet-philosopher, and venture on the hypothesis that living substance at the time of its coming to life was torn apart into small particles, which have ever since endeavoured to reunite through the sexual instincts? that these instincts, in which the chemical affinity of inanimate matter persisted, gradually succeeded, as they developed through the kingdom of protista, in overcoming the difficulties put in the way of that endeavour by an environment charged with dangerous stimuli—stimuli which compelled them to form a protective cortical layer? that these splintered fragments of living substance in this way attained a multicellular condition and finally transferred the instinct for reuniting, in the most highly-concentrated form, to the germ cells? [1920a, p. 58]

Freud had returned to the concept of the inherently bisexual nature of the human constitution as the basis of the compulsion to repeat in Eros. Humans are striving in their sexual activity to attain the wholeness of sexuality that once was the hallmark of the earliest organisms. The compulsion to repeat is evidenced by Eros in the active striving of males and females to consummate sexual union—that is, in their striving to repeat evolutionary history.[2]

[2]It is interesting that Freud later rejected this formula of the compulsion to repeat in Eros. In one of his last considerations of the subject, *An Outline of Psycho-Analysis* (1940), Freud came to the conclusion that the hypothesis that living substance was once a unity that, having been separated, now struggles toward reunion could not be supported by biological fact (1940, p. 149n.). He did not, however, offer any alternative basis for Eros' repetition compulsion, and by his omission, he left himself open to the criticism that Eros no longer fits his own definition of an instinct (cf. Fromm, 1973, Appendix).

Death Instinct Derivatives: Aggression and Hate

Operating silently and invisibly, the death instinct is rarely observable in pure form. The existence of the death instinct can only be inferred from the operation of its more observable derivatives: namely, a tendency in humans to behave aggressively and their capacity to harbor destructive intent. These more observable derivatives of the death instinct emerge when the life instinct, Eros, succeeds in preventing the full self-destructive expression of Thanatos. Thus, when Thanatos is deprived of expression within the individual, it emerges as other-directed, displaced aggression. Eros succeeds in preventing the death instinct from achieving the destruction of the *individual* by diverting the death instinct's energy to other individuals. The price of Eros' success is high.

Yet, it was Freud's opinion that the death instinct and Eros are generally mingled throughout life. He believed that Eros generally succeeds in preventing Thanatos from attaining the organism's dissolution at the cost of creating outwardly directed human hate and aggression. Where Eros succeeds in constructive unification of humans, the death instinct wins a victory for human misery (Freud, 1930, p. 119).[3]

The Final, Structural Model of the Mind

In 1923, in a book entitled *The Ego and the Id,* Freud again embarked on a major theoretical adventure. During the course of his career, he had

[3]While it is not the purpose of this book to survey the body of criticism that exists for each personality theory, it should perhaps be pointed out that the concept of a death instinct aroused enormous controversy and criticism from sources within and outside psychoanalysis.

Ernest Jones, Freud's biographer and himself a psychoanalyst, found very little support in biology or in medicine for the death instinct, and he suggested that Freud's proposal of the concept could be understood only in terms of Freud's personal reaction to the prospect of his own death. That eventuality was periodically impressed on Freud's mind by the loss of members of his own family, some early recurring cardiac problems to which Freud reacted somewhat superstitiously, and by his ultimately fatal protracted illness of jaw cancer (Jones, 1957, p. 278).

Max Schur, Freud's personal physician during the latter part of his life, criticizes the death instinct along much the same lines as Jones in his insistence that the theoretical concept served an important role in Freud's personal mental economy (1972, Chap. 12). Schur, however, goes a step farther and concludes that the death instinct is based on an act of circular reasoning, an error very uncharacteristic of Freud. Thus, according to Schur, the conservative nature of the instincts is proposed as the basis of the Nirvana principle, while the Nirvana principle is seen as the cause of the conservative trend of instincts to repeat compulsively (1972, p. 323).

Erich Fromm, a leading psychoanalytic thinker, accuses Freud of playing the game of theory construction by different rules at different times. In his most recent book, Fromm points out that Freud confused the tendency to *repeat* with the motive to *destroy*. In so doing, Freud failed to bring the death instinct into line with his own semibiological definition of an instinct that emphasized the achievement of bodily satisfaction through tension reduction. The death instinct strives not for tension reduction within the organism, but for the actual dissolution of the organism's life integrity (Fromm, 1973, p. 366).

constructed two major models of the mind. The first was a neurological model (1895,) which he soon abandoned.[4] The second, proposed in Chapter 7 of the *Interpretation of Dreams* (1900, vol. V), was a distinctly psychological theory based on a spatial or topographical analogy. It was from this topographical model that terms like *unconscious* and *preconscious* originated. Both of these previous models, however, had serious flaws and ambiguities, chief of which was their inability to depict unambiguously the interplay of combining and competing forces within the personality.

In *The Ego and the Id* (1923a), Freud created a final, *structural* model of the mind that no longer represented mental functioning as divided among sharply separated and rigidly frontiered subsystems. Freud's new structural strategy depicted the mind as a complex of melding, combining forces whereby parts of the conscious personality could also harbor unconscious content. Three newly named agencies, the *id,* the *ego,* and the *superego,* subsumed all of the mental functions previously assigned to the unconscious and the preconscious.

Id, Ego, Superego Terminology

Because the unconscious could no longer be restricted to a distinct region of the mind, and because it could not be employed solely as a description of momentarily latent thoughts, the term "id" would from now on indicate that part of the human person's selfhood that is alien to or isolated from his conscious self, or ego. Freud adopted the term "id" (or the simple German equivalent for "it") from Georg Groddeck (1922), a physician who had become interested in psychoanalysis. Freud's translators converted the terminology to Latin equivalents to preserve in English translation the technical flavor of the terms.

The Id

Developmentally, the id is the oldest portion of personality. The existence of the id dates from birth. "Originally, to be sure, everything was id . . ."

[4]In conversation with Anna Freud in July, 1974, at her home in London, she suggested to me that her father had "dismissed" the neurological model he created in 1895 because he could advance no further with it. She was quite adamant that contemporary presentations of psychoanalysis, like this one, should exclude the neurological model from consideration because psychoanalysis is a *psychological* theory, not a modified neurology. She conceded that her father's early training in neurology had been influential in shaping his thinking and that his habit of framing his thoughts in biological terms was not easily overcome. When I suggested that, were her father alive today, he might adopt for his use some of the recent advances in biology and neurology, she again insisted that her father had created a psychology and not merely a neurology translated into psychological language. Apart from its historical significance, Freud's 1895 neurological model of the mind has little relevance to psychoanalytic theory or therapy as it is practiced today. She reemphasized that her father would not have returned to his neurological ideas under any circumstances.

(Freud, 1940, p. 163). Because the id is the most archaic portion of personality, already operative before the infant has had much in the way of transactions with the world, it must contain all of the unlearned, innate strivings that we have come to know "psychoanalytically" as the instincts. Thus, Freud characterized the id as a "cauldron full of seething excitations," fueled by the energies of the organic processes of the instincts and striving toward one goal: *immediate satisfaction of its wishes.*

The id is to be regarded as the pool of mental representatives of the biological processes underlying bodily needs, a pool populated, therefore, by Eros and the death instinct: ". . . but it has no organization, produces no collective will, but only a striving to bring about the satisfaction of the instinctual needs subject to the observance of the pleasure principle" (Freud, 1933, p. 73).

Like its precursor, the unconscious, the id is an untrammeled, primeval chaos free of the laws governing logical thought. Contrary impulses exist side by side without canceling each other; the passage of time exerts no influence on the id; and wishful impulses, after the passage of decades, behave as if they had just occurred (Freud, 1933, p. 74). Freud summarized the characteristics of the id in much the same way as he had previously spoken of the unconscious:

> The id of course knows no judgments of value: no good and evil, no morality. The economic or, if you prefer, the quantitative factor, which is intimately linked to the pleasure principle, dominates all its processes. *Instinctual cathexes seeking discharge—that, in our view, is all there is in the id.* It even seems that the energy of these instinctual impulses is in a state different from that in the other regions of the mind, far more mobile and capable of discharge. . . . [1933, p. 74; italics added]

Because it is ruled by primary process thinking, condensations and displacements of its energy are not only possible for the id, they are an inevitable result of the id's striving for satisfaction without due regard for the goodness, evilness, realness, or appropriateness of its objects. In many ways, the id operates on the principle that whatever brings satisfaction to a want, desire, or wishful impulse is good; whatever hinders or frustrates such satisfaction is bad. "The id obeys the inexorable pleasure principle" (Freud, 1940, p. 198).

The Ego

Left to itself, the id's unbridled striving would bring about the destruction of the organism. The id's lack of organization, its diffuseness and disregard for reality must be tamed in the service of survival. It is to the ego that the task of self-preservation falls.

The ego develops out of the id. In fact, the ego is a differentiated part of the id that has become specialized and organized in response to its constant exposure to external stimulation. Thus, the ego is conceived as having an intimate relationship with the outermost layer of the organism, the perceptual and conscious systems that are localized in the cortical layer of the brain.

Clearly, Freud pictured the ego as developing from the id in response to the organism's need for a mediator between its internal needs and the demands of reality. The ego is thus the reality-oriented arm of the mental apparatus, though it is simultaneously responsive to internal conditions as well.

With reference to the *external environment,* the ego's functions are familiar ones: to become aware of stimuli and their location; to avoid excessively strong stimulation; and to learn to bring about changes in the external world that would be to its own advantage in pursuing survival. For this last activity, the ego must govern the muscular apparatus of the organism (Freud, 1933, p. 75).

Correspondingly, with reference to the *internal environment,* including the id, the ego functions to gain control over the expression of the instincts. The ego must decide whether the instincts are to be *immediately* satisfied as the id demands, or if their satisfaction is to be *postponed* to later times more favorable to wish fulfillment, or, finally, whether the instinctual demand should be totally denied expression, i.e., whether the instinct should be *repressed.*

With the development of the ego as a specialized and efficiently organized portion of the id, the organism correspondingly increases in the degree of sophistication with which it approaches the tasks of life. For one thing, the pleasure principle is "dethroned" by the reality principle as the ego seeks to provide safe and realistically appropriate pleasures for the id. "To adopt a popular mode of speaking, we might say that the ego stands for reason and good sense while the id stands for the untamed passions" (Freud, 1933, p. 76).

Metaphorically, the ego is fighting a battle on two fronts: It must not only protect the organism from excessively strong demands from within, it must also seek to satisfy these demands in an external world fraught with danger. Such external dangers can be dealt with by flight, that is, by the removal of the organism from the dangerous situations. Internal threats to the integrity of the organism, that is, impulses whose satisfaction would bring the organism into contact with external dangers, are dealt with by the ego in an analogous way, namely, by *mental flight* or repression.

Thus, there is a portion of the id-ego amalgam that becomes separated from the conscious functioning of the ego. That separated part, the repressed, then behaves in every way as if it were part of the unconscious. This zone of alien content is nevertheless part of the ego, though *functionally, dynamically* separated from it.

It is important in this context of defense by repression to note that it is the id that is the great reservoir of libido or sexual energy. In his previous writings, Freud had characterized the ego, in his then broad usage of the term, as the reservoir of libido. But actually there is no contradiction, for the ego is a specialized aspect of the id, and while it is only the very tip of a deep iceberg, the ego is nonetheless an integral part of that mass (Freud, 1923a, pp. 30, 38).

In the original state of being at birth, the total energy of Eros, libido, is available to the undifferentiated id-ego amalgam. Eros' presence serves to neutralize the death instinct (Freud, 1940, p. 149). The ego is, therefore, primarily narcissistic at this stage, and it cathects *itself* with libido. Only when the ego becomes differentiated from the id will it direct its cathexes of libido to external objects. Once a quantity of its libido is externalized as object libido, the ego's remaining store of libido comes into opposition with the death instinct. Ego libido, as contrasted with the externalized object libido, thus works in the service of the organism's own preservation, and ego libido operates to keep the organism from premature harm that might cheat the death instinct of its opportunity to bring the organism to its immanent destiny. Thus, it is the particular developmental stage that determines whether it is the undifferentiated id-ego unity or the id alone that occupies the focus of attention as the reservoir of libido.

While the ego is fighting a two-front battle with the internal and external worlds, there is yet a third front that the ego is compelled to consider during its intercourse with life and death. This third front is the *superego*.

The Superego

When the id is forced by circumstances beyond its control to give up its love-objects, as for example, in the child's renunciation of his mother at the resolution of the Oedipal complex, it is compensated for the loss by the ego (Freud, 1916, p. 249; 1923a, p. 23 ff.). The ego undergoes an alteration by which it takes on the characteristics of the lost love-object. This same process can be seen more clearly in adulthood when one marriage partner is widowed. After the immediate shock of the death, the powerful sense of loss is almost too painful for the remaining partner to bear. The surviving spouse may then unconsciously adopt the habits or the speech patterns of the deceased, or an item of the deceased's apparel, as if to compensate for the loss by reinstating at least a part of that person's identity in his own behavior.

> When the ego assumes the features of the [lost] object, it is forcing itself, so to speak, upon the id as a love-object and is trying to make good the id's loss by saying: "Look, you can love me too—I am so like the object." [Freud, 1923a, p. 30]

This process of modeling itself on the lost love-object, as the ego attempts to pacify the id, is called *identification*. Identification is an important part of the processes by which the superego is formed.

Recall that the child's first erotic love-object is his mother. Since his first, and in some ways his most important, contact with the mother is through feeding, it is this most satisfying activity that serves as the prototype for the child's desire to possess this eminently pleasurable creature. When, however, during the phallic stage of libidinal development, the child continues to seek his mother as desirable love-object in the new sexual sense, he comes to perceive that his father is his competitor. Without recapitulating the entire progress of the Oedipal situation (Chap. 2), it will be recalled that the child relinquishes his mother as his love-object, identifies with his father in order to be like him because father possesses desirable objects, and the child represses his libidinal cathexes toward mother.

There is an obvious inconsistency in this formulation of identification, as Roger Brown has pointed out (1965, p. 379). According to Freud's account, since the boy must relinquish his *mother* as a love-object, he should identify with *her*, not with his father. Likewise, the girl, having relinquished her father, should identify with him. Obviously this sequence won't do since, except in the most pathological cases, boys correctly assume their masculine sexual identity and girls similarly correctly identify with their mothers. Freud noted the discrepancy between his proposed mechanism of identification and the actual outcome (1923a, p. 32). As a result he returned to one of his long-standing ideas and concluded that the *inherent bisexuality* of human nature determines the outcome of the identification. Because boys are *more* male than female, they identify only partially with mother, but *mostly* with father. The converse is true for girls. As Brown put the matter, the assumption of inherent bisexuality makes the theory work, but "if that assumption is acceptable to Freud he does not need all the rest of his theoretical apparatus . . ." (1965, p. 379).

Undaunted by his own discovery of the inconsistency and relying on the concept of bisexuality, Freud proposed that the full Oedipus complex is comprised of both positive and negative aspects. It is *positive* in the sense that the boy *actively* strives to be like his father, to identify with him. But the Oedipus complex may also have negative properties because of the child's inherent feminine components. The boy may behave *passively* or "girlishly" toward the father because he has partially identified with mother when he was forced to renounce her as love-object. In this way, the boy may also attempt to appease his father by an overtly submissive attitude. For girls, of course, the opposite set of behaviors dominates, for the girl has partially identified with father and so behaves in subtle *masculine* ways (Freud, 1923a, p. 33). The final outcome, however, is as expected: Boys identify with their fathers, and girls model themselves on their mothers.

Sometime around the age of five years, the child internalizes (identifies

with) the standards of rightness, morality, and goodness that were originally enforced by his parents. Where the parents had watched over him,
guided him, and reprimanded him for "bad" behaviors, a new internal
agency continues *from within* to exercise these judgmental functions autonomously. In terms of psychoanalytic theory, a *superego* has been formed.
Through the process of identification with the mother and father, the
superego becomes the "heir of the Oedipal complex." This formulation
will require some explanation.

In becoming like the father, the child has internalized the standards of
adult authority, but, more important, he has also internalized a number of
prohibitions that will form the basis of his superego. The child's ego not
only must strive to be like the all-powerful-father-who-possesses-the-all-
desirable-mother, it must also establish the boundaries that limit the degree to which he acts the role of father (Freud, 1923a, p. 34). Out of fear
of his competitor, the child must not carry the identification as far as actual
possession of the mother. Before they arouse the hostility of father, he
himself must repress the id's Oedipal desires. Hence, the child *internalizes*
the prohibitions that he imagines his father might enforce. Timely compliance thus averts what his hesitation would otherwise provoke. As a direct
result, the superego is formed. The superego is a combination of the active
striving to be like the father and the anxiety-motivated attempts to anticipate the father's proscriptions.

The next step in the sequence is for the child to repress his Oedipal
strivings. Repression of desire for mother and hostility toward father is not
an easy undertaking for the boy's ego. The force that such repression
requires is a measure of the strength of the internalized superego. For it is
the superego that embodies the anxiety and resultant identification with
authority that remain after the Oedipal strivings are repressed. To say it
another way, *the superego replaces the strength of the Oedipal wishes in the
mental economy with the equal or stronger energy of the father identification.* Or,
as Freud repeatedly stated it: "The super-ego is the heir of the Oedipal
complex." Like the father, the superego can stand apart from the ego and
master it (Freud, 1923a, p. 48).

Superego as Conscience

An important quantitative relationship may be inferred from the fact that
the superego becomes the repository of the quantity of energy that was
required to master and to repress the Oedipal desires (Freud, 1923a, pp.
34–35; and 1930, p. 123). *The greater the instinctual gratification that is renounced, the more severe the superego grows in its judgments of the ego* (Freud,
1923a, p. 54; 1930, p. 129).

In effect, the intensity of the impulse or desire that is mastered is
assimilated by the superego, increasing its supply of energy for future
moral judgments. In less technical language, the greater the temptation to
which one *fails to yield,* the greater will be the pangs of his conscience in

future temptations. In short, the superego is fed by the energy of the renounced id-impulse, and it grows more scrupulous with each moral triumph.

Since the superego is the internalized character of the father (through identification), the more fearsome and wrathful the child perceived that character to be, the stronger was the ego's fear of the id's unacceptable wishes. Consequently, a child in the Oedipal phase who harbors intensely aggressive feelings toward his father will be required for the sake of his ego to internalize an even more intense fear of the father's potential wrath in order to master his hatred. Thus, it is the child who has renounced the strongest aggressive urges who will have the strongest sense of guilt about them and about similar desires in the future. The aggression not expressed toward the father becomes available to the superego for use against the child's own ego.

The paradox is clear: *The more aggression you virtuously renounce, the more your conscience reproaches you.* Common sense, contrary to psychoanalytic theory, suggests that the stronger a man's conscience, the more virtuous he will be. Freud reversed the temporal sequence in this apparent truism, and he suggested that

> ... the more virtuous a man is, the more severe and distrustful is ... [the behavior of his conscience], so that ultimately it is precisely those people who have carried saintliness furthest who reproach themselves with the worst sinfulness. [1930, pp. 125–126]

Clearly, Freud meant to emphasize that once the superego was established within the personality to be fed by the energy of renounced id impulses, it could be as harsh and unyielding in its demands as the id continually is in its relationship to the ego. "From the point of view of instinctual control, or morality, it may be said of the id that it is totally non-moral, of the ego that it strives to be moral, and of the super-ego that it can be super-moral and then become as cruel as only the id can be" (Freud, 1923a, p. 54).

Id, Ego, and Superego Interactions

Because the superego was formed at a stage in developmental history when the child idealized his parents and saw in them every perfection, it follows that the standards of the superego will likewise have the character of their *idealized* image (Freud, 1933, p. 64). Conscience is thus a standard of perfection, an ideal, rather than a realistic appraisal of behavior. Consequently, in their rearing of children, parents exemplify not so much a standard of experience tempered by a realistic appraisal of life, but rather the idealistic standard of their own superegos (Freud, 1933, p. 67).

Freud employed a diagrammatic summary of his new structural model that, reproduced here as Figure 3–2, will be helpful in recapitulating the essential points.

Figure 3–2 shows the location of the three mental structures: id, ego, and superego. It also indicates the important relationships that bind them.

The ego is situated near, and oriented toward, the perceptual-conscious end of the organism, and it is thus in direct contact with the external world. But the diagram also clearly demonstrates that the ego extends into the lower regions of the system, where it merges into the unconscious id. A segment of the ego, then, is in closer contact with the unconscious than it is with consciousness or perceptual activity. Furthermore, there is a segment of the ego that is equally rooted in the unconscious, but that is sharply separated from the rest of the ego's conscious activities. Even though this segment forms a structural part of the ego, it functions *dynamically* like the unconscious system.

In Figure 3–2 this ego-alien segment is illustrated in its separation from conscious ego activity by two diagonal lines that define the boundary of repressed content. The ego is thus both conscious in its orientation toward the perceptual end of the apparatus and dynamically unconscious by virtue of its repressions.

Although Freud did not include the superego in the diagram that he employed in *The Ego and the Id* (1923a, p. 24), by the time he had written

FIGURE 3-2:   THE DYNAMIC MODEL OF THE MIND

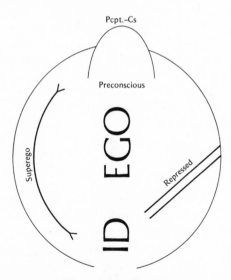

Note that the diagram depicts the three agencies of the mind with no sharp boundaries between them. In Freud's last model, the mind was represented as an amalgam of blending, combining, and competing forces. See text for explanation.

After Freud, 1933, p. 78.

his *New Introductory Lectures,* almost ten years later, he found a way to include the superego in such diagrammatic summaries. Lying along the left-hand margin of the drawing in Figure 3–2, the superego clearly merges into the unconscious id, for, as "the heir of the Oedipus complex it has intimate relations with the id; it is more remote than the ego from the perceptual system" (Freud, 1933, p. 79).

The superego, therefore, is structured of both conscious and unconscious components, and, as a moral or ethical agency, it functions both consciously and unconsciously. That is to say, the superego has relations with both the ego and the id.

In several respects, Freud pointed out, the diagrammatic summary of Figure 3–2 is misleading. For one thing, the space occupied by the unconscious id should be greater than that of the ego or preconscious. For another thing,

> In thinking of this division of the personality into an ego, a superego, and an id, you will not, of course, have pictured sharp frontiers like the artificial ones drawn in political geography. We cannot do justice to the characteristics of the mind by linear outlines like those in a drawing or in a primitive painting, but rather by areas of colour melting into one another as they are presented by modern artists. After making the separation we must allow what we have separated to merge together once more. [Freud, 1933, p. 79]

The ego's task is to balance the passions of the id against the censure of the superego while it simultaneously appraises reality and its exigencies. In Freud's words, for the ego "Life is not easy!" When the ego is overwhelmed and compelled to recognize its own weaknesses in carrying out successfully its Herculean tasks, anxiety results. Such anxiety may be the result of fear of the external world, fear of the id's passions, or fear of the superego's censure. Life for the ego is certainly not easy.

Freud's Changing Conceptions of Anxiety

In the earliest days of Freud's theorizing, he came to view anxiety as the result of unexpressed or dammed-up libido. The neurotic's badly distorted relations with the world and its people are often expressed in sexual difficulty. Normal, satisfying sexual relations are frequently forgone as a welter of neurotic symptoms and other defensive measures sap the individual's capacity for joyous living. Unexpressed libido, the dammed-up energy of the sexual impulses that have thus succumbed to repression, is then explosively released in a transformed state, the state of anxiety. In short, in Freud's early thinking, repression of sexual impulses is the cause of anxiety (Cf. Freud, 1894; 1896a; 1896b; 1896c; and 1898).

According to this early view, anxiety was instinctual, arising from the repressed unconscious sexual urges. But if it were true that such feelings were restricted to unconscious origin, the conscious ego as depicted in the new structural model with its separation from the repressed would never experience the unpleasant affect of anxiety. Furthermore, if the ego did not experience the anxiety, it would never trigger repressive counterforces to cast the unacceptable, anxiety-producing impulses from consciousness in the first place (Freud, 1926, pp. 140; 161). Freud's new structural model demanded that the ego be the seat of anxiety, and so Freud was required to rethink the problem.

Birth Trauma as the Prototype of Adult Anxiety

Through a slow return to and development of his neurological ideas, Freud renounced the view of anxiety as transformed libido. In his early neurological model of the "Project for a Scientific Psychology," Freud had experimented with the idea that anxiety originates in the feeling of overwhelming helplessness (1895, vol. I). The ego experiences the perception of being overpowered or flooded with too much stimulation. In infancy, the first of such experiences is the act of birth. The neonate is thrust from its warm, dark, safe, parasitic existence in the mother's body into the confusing, demanding, changing, and irritating external environment (Freud, 1926). In successive stages of life, other situations will evoke the same emotional response of helplessness, stimulus flooding, and the feeling of being overpowered. Separation from the mother (recall Ernst's "gone" game) provokes distress in most infants, and such separation is a good example of a later life situation that harbors the threat of helplessness.

The common denominator in all such cases of anxiety is the sense of abandonment, the feeling that life's demands will overwhelm the isolated ego because of its helplessness. When anxiety mounts to a level that the individual feels will threaten his survival, neurotic symptoms may be formed as attempts to stifle the tide of mental confusion and emotional pain. In a very real sense, the adult neurotic develops symptoms to control his anxiety over threats that he perceives as truly life threatening, just as life threatening as early abandonment by mother. Overt symptoms thus unconsciously replace what he can no longer consciously bear (Freud, 1933, p. 85). The question of significance thus changed for Freud from how libido could be transformed into anxiety, to how anxiety was produced from the ego's perceptions.

As early as 1909, in a footnote to the *Interpretation of Dreams*, Freud pointed out that ". . . the act of birth is the first experience of anxiety, and thus the source and prototype of the affect of anxiety" (1900, vol. V, pp. 400–401). In effect, Freud was postulating that the birth situation is every individual's first experience with the unpleasurable state of anxiety, and that it is this first experience that serves as the model against which the ego compares future situations in making its responses to reality and to the demands of the id and superego.

A colleague of Freud's, Otto Rank, broadened the concept of birth trauma beyond its status as the prototype for anxiety. Rank established the birth trauma as the central emotional constellation in psychological development (Rank, 1929; 1932). In emphasizing the significance of the birth trauma for neurotic symptomatology, Rank almost inadvertently dethroned the main psychoanalytic concepts of the Oedipus complex and sexual strivings from their etiological importance. For Rank, the trauma of birth was the nucleus from which all human development, neurotic and normal, proceeds. Freud thus felt compelled to repudiate Rank's ideas.

The essential point about anxiety-producing impulses or situations is that they represent states of intense excitation, so intense that, like the moment of birth, they possess the potential to overwhelm the ego (Freud, 1933, p. 93). Thus, for example, separation from mother at birth is equivalent to separation from her in childhood, for in both situations the mounting tension of bodily needs threatens to overwhelm the ego (Freud, 1926, p. 137; 1933, p. 93). When the ego responds to situations like these with the affect of anxiety, it triggers the pleasure-unpleasure machinery so that such impulses will be effectively defended against by the ego.

An Illustrative Case of Anxiety: Jean-Mary Revisited

To illustrate Freud's concept of anxiety as a reaction to a danger situation that involves an overwhelming of the ego through fear of separation from one's source of need satisfaction and security, we can return to Jean-Mary, the young lady introduced in Chapter 1. It will be recalled that Jean-Mary was a rather intelligent child who skillfully planned the ice-cream revenge against her friend Roselle, and who later suffered indignity at the hands of her boyfriend and a can of whipped cream.

Some facts about Jean-Mary's life in the period between these two events are pertinent. Throughout her childhood, Jean-Mary suffered from a congenital heart defect that required constant medical care and protracted hospital stays. Besides the limitations imposed on Jean-Mary's physical activity, a hardship any child would find frustrating, her frequent separations from home, family, and especially from mother, did little to establish the normal, reliable, repetitive routine of childhood so essential to a sense of security and trust. It would often be heartbreaking to observe Jean-Mary beg and plead with her parents, saying that she would "be good" if only they would not take her to the hospital. For her parents, fully aware of the medical necessity of hospital care, each incident was almost too painful to bear. It was from this background that Jean-Mary's rather strange behavior emerged:

Traveling alone with her mother on an ocean voyage to England when she was twelve years old, Jean-Mary developed a series of bizarre, compulsive behaviors that kept her awake through the better part of each night on their journey. As she slept beside her mother in the dark cabin, Jean-Mary would listen intently to the rhythm of her mother's breathing. She was fully aware that an ocean voyage alone with her mother was no small undertaking. She knew, too, that her total well-being and safety in these strange surroundings were centered in this one familiar person. Thus, Jean-Mary mentally ticked off each of her mother's breaths with anxious precision and an overwhelming dread that the sounds might stop.

The thought that her mother might die in her sleep, the possibility of being left alone in strange surroundings—again—were so frightening that Jean-Mary felt compelled to reach to the switch overhead and periodically flood the cabin with light. Each of these occasions was an attempt to observe her mother's breathing and movement when a change in her position obscured the sound. Needless to say, when these momentary illuminations gradually increased in number to twelve or thirteen a night, they became a source of great consternation to Jean-Mary's mother. Actually, Jean-Mary's mother was more irritated at the strangeness of her daughter's behavior than at the loss of sleep.

Armed with excuses about being unable to sleep and wanting to read or to visit the bathroom, the twelve-year-old sentinel persisted in her maternal sleep-deprivation campaign clear to England. Jean-Mary has never revealed to her mother the cause of her seemingly whimsical nighttime rituals. To this day, however, she clearly remembers the awful feeling that she might be left alone aboard the huge liner in the company of strangers.

As if to underscore the reality of her terror, Jean-Mary's worst fears were partially realized when, on the return voyage across England by rail, her mother left the train car to purchase some tea from a platform attendant. The train pulled out without her. Panic-stricken, Jean-Mary could only remember her mother's often repeated admonitions, originally applicable to New York subway rides, to get off the train and wait for her at the next stop. Unfortunately, the next stop was over one hundred miles away.

Some three hours later, mother and daughter were reunited, but not before this new abomination had taken its toll by producing an almost inconsolable Jean-Mary. For years afterward, Jean-Mary could not bring herself to go to summer camp or even to spend the night at a friend's house. She remained firm in her resolve never to be away from home.

Clearly, Jean-Mary's separation anxiety was more intense and more exaggerated than most children's, but her early experiences with hospitals and frightening stays away from home make her sensitivity explicable. Overwhelmed by so many past occasions of threat, her ego was ever vigilant to the prospect of new separations. Her entire personality development underwent a defensive inhibition or constriction. The possibility of leaving home, for any reason whatsoever, brought with it the familiar ego signal of anxiety. Thus, in this one area of her life, for a long time throughout childhood, Jean-Mary was defensively isolated from change.

Summary

Anna Freud's "stwawbewwies" dream reveals with stark simplicity the essential nature of dream processes: the fantasied fulfillment of wishes. As Freud investigated dream processes, however, he soon learned that adult dreamers' productions were far from the lucid creations of children. The adult dreamer's unconscious presses for the release of unacceptable and anxiety-provoking impulses, for amoral childhood wishes, and for sexual and aggressive desires that can be entertained by the conscious self only in disguised form. Distortion and disguise are introduced into the story of the dream by the mechanisms of dream work, including displacement, condensation, visual representation, and secondary revision. Thus, Freud found, dreams have both a latent and a manifest content, as distinguishable from each other as the actor and his mask.

Freud embarked on a revision and a tightening of his psychological theory in a series of important "metapsychological" papers. He tackled such topics as repression and the nature of the unconscious from a new vantage point, the perspective of dynamic explanations. Thus, Freud now saw repression as a two-stage process: In the first stage, a *primal repression* against early unacceptable impulses is erected by the preconscious system opposing the unacceptable unconscious impulse with an expenditure of energy called an anticathexis. Later derivatives and associates of primally repressed content are subject to the "after pressure" of a *repression proper,* whereby the preconscious withdraws cathexes of energy from the idea in consciousness as it is pulled back into the unconscious by the mass of primal repressions.

Because of the basic conflict underlying the neurotic behavior of the patients he observed, Freud sought to conceptualize the instincts in a dualism that contrasted the self-preservative instincts (e.g., hunger) with the instincts of pleasure (sex, libido). The dualistic classification of hunger versus love had eventually to be revised when Freud's speculations revealed the presence of an even more fundamental dichotomy in instinctual life: life versus death.

In *Beyond the Pleasure Principle* (1920a), Freud created a new picture of the workings of the mind. This altered view included Freud's argument that the nervous system had evolved in such a way as to minimize the excitatory level of the organism by directing the organism's efforts to satisfy needs immediately. The ultimate aim of an instinct is to return the organism to the unstimulable state of inorganic matter, namely, to the state of death. Since the death instinct cannot be directly observed, its derivatives of hate, anger, and aggression are the only overt evidence of its existence. When the life instincts, or Eros as Freud now called the combined ego and sexual instincts, oppose the death instinct, the energy of destruction is turned outward from the individual and displaced onto other individuals.

Freud proceeded from his revision of instinct theory to a total revision of his conception of the mind. He created a structural model that depicted the mind as a blending, merging amalgam of forces. The structural model had three divisions: id, ego, and superego. The id, formerly the unconscious, is the seat of the instincts, and is a cauldron of fury, striving to gain immediate satisfaction of its urges. To accommodate the id's desires and needs, a specialized portion, the ego, emerges from the id to steer a safe course through reality and to maintain satisfactory relations with the world. By the age of five or six, another agency, the superego, is internalized within the child. The superego is the "heir of the Oedipal complex," for it is based on identification with the parents, and assimilates the energy of the renounced Oedipal desires. The superego is the moral or ethical arm of personality, and it has final say in matters of ego-id relations.

Freud's conception of anxiety changed over the years from the view that anxiety is the result of dammed-up sexual impulses, to the concept that the ego responds to a variety of perceived threats with signals of unpleasure. Freud experimented with the idea that the prototype of anxiety is the trauma of birth, but more generally, anxiety is an ego reaction to perceptions of being overwhelmed or flooded helplessly by intense stimulation.

Though the scope of this and the preceding chapter on Freud is extensive, it should not surprise the reader that the material presented merely scratches the surface of the mass of ideas and hypotheses that are to be found in Freud's collected works. For that reason, the reader is encouraged to pursue topics of interest in Freud's own writings.

FOR FURTHER READING

The best overviews in Freud's own writings of his later theory are to be found in two complementary sets of lectures. The first of these dates from his prestructural model of the mind and is entitled *Introductory Lectures on Psychoanalysis,* vol. 15 and 16 of *The Standard Edition,* or in paperback under the title *A General Introduction to Psychoanalysis* (New York: Washington Square Press, 1960, or W. W. Norton). The second set of lectures dates from his development of the id-ego-superego model and can be found in vol. 22 of *The Standard Edition* under the title *New Introductory Lectures on Psychoanalysis* (also available in paperback [New York: W. W. Norton, 1964]).

Freud's own historical accounts of the development of his system bear scrutiny. *An Autobiographical Study (The Standard Edition,* vol. 20; paperback ed.: W. W. Norton) was Freud's attempt to survey personal and intellectual factors that shaped his theorizing. A further historical effort by Freud, dating from somewhat earlier in his career (1914), can be found in *On the History of the Psychoanalytic Movement* (*The Standard Edition,* vol. 14; also in *The Basic Writings of Sigmund Freud,* translated and edited by A. A. Brill, New York: Random House, 1938).

Freud considered *The Interpretation of Dreams* to be his masterpiece (vols. 4 and 5 of *The Standard Edition;* also in *The Basic Writings of Sigmund Freud,* edited by A. A. Brill, New York: Random House, 1938), and Chapter 7 of this work contains the direct translation of his early neurological model into a topographical model of the mind. The serious student of psychoanalysis will also want to consult a series of papers collectively termed Freud's "Metapsychology," and published as "Instincts and Their Vicissitudes" (1915); "Repression" (1915); "The Unconscious" (1915); "Metapsychological Supplement to the Theory of Dreams" (1917); and "Mourning and Melancholia" (1917) (all contained in vol. 14 of *The Standard Edition*). These papers form the heart of Freud's midcareer theorizing and his attempts to reconcile ambiguities and inconsistencies in his early formulations.

Freud's final model of the mind is to be found in his *The Ego and the Id* (1923) in vol. 19 of *The Standard Edition* (also in paperback [New York: W. W. Norton, 1960]), and in more concise form in one of his last publications, *An Outline of Psycho-Analysis* in vol. 23 of *The Standard Edition* (and in paperback [New York: W. W. Norton, 1949]).

Freud's changing conception of defense and anxiety can be discerned by a comparative reading of one of his early papers, "The Neuro-Psychoses of Defence" (1894) and his later *Inhibitions, Symptoms and Anxiety* (1926) (vol. 20 of *The Standard Edition,* or in paperback under the title *The Problem of Anxiety* [New York: W. W. Norton, 1936]). Anna Freud elaborated her father's conception of neurotic defense mechanisms in a book that has now become a psychoanalytic classic and essential reading for all students of psychoanalysis, *The Ego and the Mechanisms of Defense,* rev. ed. (New York: International Universities Press, 1966).

Critical commentaries and summaries of Freud's thinking abound. A survey and analysis of the experimental study of Freudian concepts is provided by Paul Kline in *Fact and Fantasy in Freudian Theory* (New York: Harper & Row, 1972; originally published in Great Britain by Methuen). Where Kline is relatively optimistic about the empirical testability and validity of Freud's ideas, Hans Eysenck and Glen Wilson in their *Experimental Study of Freudian Theories* (New York: Harper & Row, 1973; originally published in Great Britain by Methuen) reproduce and sharply criticize several "classic" experiments purporting to demonstrate the validity of Freudian hypotheses. Richard Wolheim has edited a collection of philosophical essays and methodological criticisms of Freud's ideas that will repay the careful reader of his *Freud: A Collection of Critical Essays* (New York: Doubleday, 1974). A similarly critical viewpoint from a more psychological perspective is maintained throughout the essays contained in *Critical Essays on Psychoanalysis,* edited by Stanley Rachman (New York: Macmillan, 1963). Erich Fromm's *The Anatomy of Human Destructiveness* (New York: Holt, Rinehart and Winston, 1973) contains an incisive criticism of Freud's death instinct.

The areas of personality research in which Freud's theory have been applied are so numerous as to defy classification, but two clinically oriented studies deserve attention. Peter Blos has modified and extended Freud's ideas for application to the stormy period of adolescence in two books: *On Adolescence* (New York: Free Press, 1962) and *The Young Adolescent: Clinical Studies* (New York: Free Press, 1970). The latter volume presents two detailed case histories of Susan and Ben, young people for whom psychoanalytic therapy proved invaluable. Kenneth Keniston's *The Uncommitted: Alienated Youth in American Society* (New York: Dell, 1960) brilliantly applies Freudian theory, especially the Oedipus complex, to the task of explaining why young, affluent, and well-educated males become disaffected with society and with their own lives.

4 CARL G. JUNG
Analytical Psychology

It would be so much simpler if I knew nothing; but I know too much, through my ancestors and my own education.

C. G. JUNG, *Analytical Psychology: Its Theory and Practice*

The truly "mysterious" object is beyond our apprehension and comprehension, not only because our knowledge has certain irremovable limits, but because in it we come upon something inherently "wholly other," whose kind and character are incommensurable with our own, and before which we therefore recoil in a wonder that strikes us chill and numb.

RUDOLF OTTO, *The Idea of the Holy*

Experimental Study of Associations

In April, 1907, after only a few exchanges of letters and one brief visit to Freud's home, Carl Gustav Jung became Freud's handpicked successor. On April 7, Freud wrote to Jung "that you have inspired me with confidence for the future, that I now realize that I am as replaceable as everyone else and that I could hope for no one better than yourself, as I have come to know you, to continue and complete my work" (Freud/Jung, 1974, p. 27). Part of Freud's enthusiasm for his younger colleague rested on Jung's published acknowledgement that Freud's ideas had been useful in his own clinical work; and part rested on some clinical experiments that Jung had conducted with his cousin, Franz Riklin, that purported to demonstrate unconscious mental processes.

Subjects in Jung and Riklin's experimental studies of word associations typically found themselves confronted by the following circumstances. Professor Jung or Professor Riklin would sit or stand opposite the subject, 1/5-second stopwatch in hand, and instruct him to "answer as quickly as possible with the first word that occurs to you" at each of one hundred stimulus words. A small sampling from Jung's list of stimulus words provides some of the flavor of the experimental subject's experience:

1. head	72. to beat
5. death	75. family
15. to dance	79. happiness
22. angry	84. to fear
28. to sin	87. anxiety
40. to pray	88. to kiss
42. stupid	89. bride
53. hunger	95. ridicule
60. to marry	100. to abuse

[From Jung, 1909a, p. 440]

A variety of grammatical forms was included among the various stimulus words. The full list was arranged in a specific sequence that Jung's experience had shown was suitable for eliciting maximum emotional reaction. In later experiments, Jung and his colleagues employed additional procedures besides the simple stopwatch timing of the subject's reactions. Sometimes, the subject's respiration rate was measured, along with a recording of his galvanic skin response (GSR). The GSR measures the skin's decrease in resistance to electrical current during sensory and emotional changes, a variable akin to one of the measures used in the modern "lie detector" or polygraph.

The word-association experiment was not unique to Jung's laboratory (cf. Woodworth & Schlosberg, 1954, Chap. 3 for a brief history of the method; and Jung, 1909a). Jung's contribution lay in his use of the method to study the subject's nonconscious emotional reactions. He found, for example, that "normal" men and women do not respond similarly to the stimulus words. Individual differences in reaction time, respiration rate, GSR, and ideational content were the rule. More important, in word-association experiments with neurotic and psychotic patients, Jung found that the method could aid in uncovering latent emotional difficulties by exposing content areas that produced hesitation, perseveration, or total inhibition of response.

Emotional Complex Indicators

Usually, the stimulus word that triggered the subject's hesitation or inability to respond was connected *symbolically* with a deeply personal and emotionally abrasive set of ideas or experiences. Because such latent difficulties were often collections of various thoughts held together by common emotional themes, Jung and Riklin termed them *complexes*. A complex is thus a personally disturbing constellation of ideas connected together by common feeling-tone (Jung, 1913, p. 599). For example, the individual caught up in a conflict over relations with his father would be said to have a "father complex"; or the individual experiencing anxiety and frustration in sexual matters would be characterized as having a "sex complex."

Complexes are revealed in word-association experiments through a number of diagnostic signs:

1. Longer than average reaction time
2. Repetition of the stimulus word by the subject as if he had not heard it
3. Mishearing of the stimulus word as some other word
4. Expressive bodily movements like laughing, twitching
5. Reaction composed of more than one word
6. Very superficial reaction to stimulus word, as in rhyming to the sound: e.g., to sin—subject responds with "to win"
7. Meaningless reaction: made-up words
8. Failure to respond at all
9. Perseveration of response: continuing to respond to previous word even after new stimulus word is presented
10. Defective reproduction: subject drastically altering his responses when list is administered for second time
11. Slips of the tongue: stammering

In addition to these eleven unique patterns of response, there were, Jung discovered, also characteristic and stable differences between men and women, and between educated and uneducated subjects' responses. Consider Table 4–1:

TABLE 4–1: EDUCATIONAL LEVEL AND REACTION TIME (in seconds)

	EDUCATED SUBJECTS	UNEDUCATED SUBJECTS
Men	1.3	1.6
Women	1.7	2.2
Average	1.5	1.9

From Jung, 1905, vol. 2, p. 227.

In Jung's laboratory, women characteristically took longer to respond to the stimulus words than their male counterparts at both educational levels. Generally, Jung found that educated people responded faster than uneducated.

An Illustrative Case of Word-Association Diagnosis

One of Jung's clinic patients, a thirty-year-old woman, had been diagnosed as a depressed schizophrenic, and most of the hospital staff agreed that the prognosis for her recovery was poor. Jung felt otherwise. He therefore administered a modified form of the association test. Some of the woman's responses were very suggestive. Consider the graph of her responses in Figure 4–1.

FIGURE 4-1: RELATIVE REACTION TIMES FOR CRITICAL STIMULUS WORDS

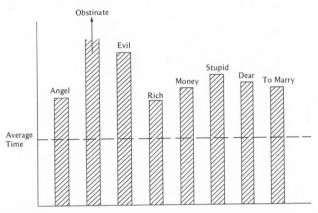

Based on Jung, 1968, p. 59.

Each of the words graphed in Figure 4–1 has a reaction time that exceeds the average reaction time for an educated woman. The height of the bars indicates the relative differences in length of reaction time above the mean for educated women. Most outstanding of the woman's responses was her inability to offer any reply to the word "obstinate." Jung confronted the woman with the results of her word-association test. He asked her to comment on the various stimulus words that had produced such lengthy reaction times.

To "angel," the woman replied: "Of course, that is my child whom I have lost." There followed a great upheaval. To "obstinate," she responded: "It means nothing to me." To "evil," she again refused to comment. But to the word "blue" (not illustrated in the graph) she replied: "Those are the eyes of the child I have lost." Jung asked her why the child's eyes had so impressed her: "They were so wonderfully blue when the child was born." Jung noticed that this last reply was accompanied by much emotion. He again asked her why she was upset: "Well, she did not have the eyes of my husband." With further questioning, the entire story was told.

The child's eyes had so upset her mother because they resembled the eyes of a former lover. In the town where she was born, the woman had fallen in love with a wealthy young man of the aristocracy. Being herself of a well-to-do but nonaristocratic family, the girl and her parents had concluded that a romance with the young man was not feasible. At the insistence of her family, she married another young man and remained happy until the fifth year of the marriage. A friend from her home town came to visit in that fifth year and informed her that her present marriage had hurt and displeased the wealthy aristocrat she had once loved. For the first time she was made to realize that he had loved her in return. She immediately repressed her feelings.

Two weeks later, as she was bathing her two children, a small boy and the wonderfully blue-eyed girl, she noticed the girl sucking on the bath sponge. The woman knew she should stop the child because there was good reason to believe that the town's water supply was infested with typhus, and the bath water had not been boiled. She hesitated and finally purposefully did not interfere. Shortly thereafter, the girl got typhoid fever and died, but the little boy survived.

The act was symbolic, a denial of her marriage through murder of the first child. Jung felt obligated to confront her with the fact of her crime, the significance of which she seemingly failed to understand. Within three weeks she was sufficiently recovered from her depression to be released from the hospital:

> I traced her for fifteen years, and there was no relapse. That depression fitted her case psychologically; she was a murderess and under other circumstances would have deserved capital punishment. Instead of going to jail she was sent to the lunatic asylum. I practically saved her from the punishment of insanity by putting an enormous burden on her conscience. For if one can accept one's sin one can live with it. [Jung, 1968, p. 61]

Practical Uses of the Word-Association Test

Jung became quite adept in the use of the word-association test for diagnosis of unconscious complexes. He even adapted the method for use in cases involving criminal proceedings. The guilt or innocence of the accused could be established by careful interrogation with the help of modified word lists containing critical words relating to key aspects of the crime (Jung, 1905, pp. 318 ff.).

Jung and his associates also employed the word-association tests for comparisons of unconscious complexes among members of a family. Thus, for example, Jung and Furst (1909b, pp. 466 ff.) investigated the associations of the members of twenty-four families, collecting in the process some 22,000 responses. The resulting data were analyzed in a variety of ways, but the outstanding overall result was the similarity of content among members of a single family. For example, the associations of a mother and daughter in different sessions to the same stimulus words were quite revealing:

STIMULUS WORD	MOTHER	DAUGHTER
law	God's commandment	Moses
potato	tuber	tuber
strange	traveler	travelers
brother	dear to me	dear
to kiss	mother	mother
merry	happy child	little children

[from Jung, 1909b, p. 469]

Not only do the content of the mother's and daughter's associations match, but the choice of response word is virtually identical in several cases. Clearly, the fleeting thoughts of members of a family are not random and richly varied, as one might expect. Rather, there is a striking mutuality of expression and feeling (cf. Laing's study of the family in Chapter 8 of this book).

Jung's Conception of Libido

At the beginning of his career, Jung saw the possibility that his word-association studies could offer objective support for Freud's psychoanalytic concepts. It is easy to understand why. Subjects' inhibitions and long reaction times to the stimulus words, along with their heightened physiological responsivity, could serve as *quantitative* evidence that these individuals had latent feeling-toned ideas that they would or could not directly express but that produced demonstrable verbal and physiological reactions.

He had, Jung realized, developed a method of exploring the unconscious comparable to Freud's investigations of that domain with free association. In the early days, Jung and Freud agreed on what they found there: namely, repressed, unacceptable infantile sexual and aggressive strivings.

As Jung continued his explorations of the unconscious, he found it more and more difficult to accept Freud's insistence that sexual motives were the basis of neurosis (Jung, 1961, Chap. 5). The central Freudian concept of libido as a generalized and universal pleasure drive rooted firmly in an individual's developing sexuality caused Jung no small amount of difficulty. Early in their relationship Jung wrote to Freud and inquired:

> Is it not conceivable, in view of the limited conception of sexuality that prevails nowadays, that the sexual terminology should be reserved only for the most extreme forms of your "libido," and that a less offensive collective term should be established for *all* the libidinal manifestations? [Freud/Jung, 1974, p. 25]

Freud's reply to Jung's suggestion bears reporting:

> I appreciate your motives in trying to sweeten the sour apple, but I
> do not think you will be successful. Even if we call the unconscious
> "psychoid," it will still be the unconscious, and even if we do not call
> the driving force in the broadened conception of sexuality "libido,"
> it will still be libido. . . . We cannot avoid resistances, why not face
> up to them from the start? [Freud/Jung, 1974, p. 28]

Jung's objections to Freud's sexual hypothesis abated for a while. But
increasingly, as his own powers of perception and professional judgment
grew, Jung discovered forces and content within the unconscious quite
unlike anything in the Freudian scheme.

For Jung, then, the fundamental psychic energy was still to be termed
libido, but his conception of this primal force drastically differed from the
classical psychoanalytic view. In fact, in his English publications, Jung
began to employ the word *horme* for libido because he felt that the substitution avoided confusion with the established Freudian usage. *Horme* is a
Greek word that means "force," "attack," "press," "urgency" (Jung, 1914,
p. 190n.). Thus *horme* more adequately conveyed Jung's conception of
libido as a general psychic energy.

Jung and Freud Contrasted

Where Freud saw in human behavior a similarity of dynamic pleasurable
energy among bodily needs like hunger, thirst, and sex, Jung glimpsed
". . . only a continuous life-urge, a will to live which seeks to ensure the
continuance of the whole species through the preservation of the individual" (1912, p. 136).

Where Freud had viewed libido as the basis of the human pleasure
appetites, Jung observed "an energy value which is able to communicate
itself to any field of activity whatsoever, be it power, hunger, hatred,
sexuality, or religion without ever being itself a specific instinct" (1912, p.
137).

Where Freud discovered at the root of neurotic behavior *personal* conflict over unacceptable sexual and aggressive motives, Jung found *transpersonal, universal* symbols of the human race's life experiences that transcend
the individual's immediate conflicts (1912, p. 139).

Where Freud found damaged reality functioning in his neurotic and
psychotic patients, Jung mined their fantasies and dreams, and he perceived the channeling of libido or life energy into a general myth-making
or analogy-producing process (1912, p. 141).

Where Freud anchored his concepts in the workings of the body and
brain, Jung found within those confines the roots of spirit (1948, p. 55).

The Principles of Equivalence and Entropy

It is clear that for Jung libido was a more neutral form of general psychic energy, corresponding to an *intentionality* in living things (1912, p. 137). Libido, as a form of energy, may be shaped, channeled, suppressed, repressed, blocked, or expressed. In all cases, however, it is to be understood as a *creative* life force, the same creative force that underlies myths, religious dogma, and neurosis.

If libido is dammed up, repressed, an equivalent or substitute expression must take its place in consciousness. Hence, for Jung, as for Freud, repressed libido obeys what Jung called the *principle of equivalence*: When conscious psychic energy is repressed, an unconscious substitute, or symbolic alternative idea, assimilates the energy of the banished idea and takes a place in consciousness (Jung, 1948, p. 19; 1912, pp. 143–144). Following the laws of thermodynamics, Jung agreed with Freud that psychic energy never ceases to exist, despite transformations in form. Repressed ideas embodying psychic energy simply find expression in *equivalent* symbolic forms. Unlike Freud, Jung did not regard these transformations as necessarily neurotic. Rather, Jung defined such modifications as potentially healthy "canalizations of libido," that is, as creative, almost poetic, transfers of psychic energy to mythic or allegorical symbols.

Transformations or canalizations of libido are more than mere examples of psychic energy equivalence. Canalizations of libido from one form of expression to another are guided in man by an inherent tendency toward symbol making. A symbol is, therefore, a "libido analog." Throughout human history, man has created symbols and woven them into themes called myths. He has practiced rituals, both religious and magical, that center around unconsciously created symbols. In work with neurotic and psychotic patients, Jung found evidence that this process of converting libido into symbolic expressions has a certain continuity with the symbol making of our primordial ancestors. Though Freud had pointed to the symbolization of dreams as personally necessary disguises of unacceptable motives, Jung now focused attention on the transmission of symbol-making processes from human forebear to human descendant.

The principle of equivalence has a necessary and complementary co-principle in Jung's theory. Based on the second law of thermodynamics, as the principle of equivalence had been based on the first law, Jung formulated a psychological counterpart to physical *entropy*. According to Jung's *principle of entropy*, transformations of psychic energy are possible only because there is a gradient of intensity among ideas. Some mental representatives are more intense, hold more energy, than others. The principle of entropy says, in effect, that psychic energy will flow from the most intensely energized ideas to the least intensely energized ideas. Ultimately, the mental system strives to an equalization of differences (Jung, 1948, p. 26). Thus, for example, when an individual is torn between two opposite attitudes or feelings, he will eventually resolve the conflict by assuming a less intense third course of action or thinking comprising the energy of the two intense extremes (1948, p. 26).

Transcending the Personal Unconscious: Sources of the Hypothesis

The Sun's Phallus "Hallucination"

Staring out the window of the hospital corridor, a young schizophrenic patient beckoned Jung to his side. If you half shut your eyes, he told Jung, and stared at the sun, you could see the sun's phallus. If you then moved your head side to side, the sun's phallus would also move. The young man concluded his strange remarks to Jung with the matter-of-fact assertion that *the movement of the sun's phallus was the origin of the wind* (Jung, 1931, pp. 151–152; 1912, pp. 100 and 157; and 1936, pp. 50–51).

Jung had this enigmatic encounter with a psychotic thirty-year-old clerk in 1906. Under normal circumstances, Jung would have dismissed the episode as one more strange hallucination or fantasy characteristic of schizophrenia. Four years later, however, in 1910, while researching in the field of mythology, Jung came across a book that reproduced the rituals of the ancient Mithraic Greek religious cult. Professor Albrecht Dieterich, the author of the book, quoted one of the cult's visions:

> *And likewise the so-called tube, the origin of the ministering wind.* For you will see hanging down from the disc of the sun something that looks like a tube. And towards the regions westward it is as though there were an infinite east wind. But if the other wind should prevail towards the regions of the east, you will in like manner see the vision veering in that direction. [Quoted in Jung, 1931, pp. 150–151; italics added]

Jung was startled by the correspondence between this ancient pre-Christian myth and the young schizophrenic clerk's hallucinatory vision. There was no doubt that the clerk could not have read Dieterich's book, having been institutionalized before its publication. Nor could Jung explain the correspondence as a product of the young man's educational and cultural training because he had only the equivalent of a secondary-school education and his occupation and habits precluded any possibility of travel. Further mythological study convinced Jung that the notion of a sun phallus, or its equivalent, a divine phallus, was a common theme in many cultures of the past. The problem remained to account for the presence of the myth in the unconscious and conscious mind of a contemporary schizophrenic.

The Snake Dream

Another of Jung's patients, a young military officer, succumbed to a hysterical neurosis characterized by three symptoms. First, he suffered severe attacks of pain in the chest. Second, he experienced several episodes of choking "as if there were a lump in his throat." Finally, he was unable to walk normally because of stabbing pains in his left heel (Jung, 1931, p. 146).

In psychotherapy with Jung, the source of the first two symptoms was uncovered and followed the usual patterns of hysterical neurosis. The young man had been hurt and humiliated by a love affair that terminated when the girl became engaged to another man. He had denied his hurt and shattered self-esteem, but unconsciously he felt that "his heart was broken," and the idea that she had terminated the affair was "hard to swallow." Thus, as Freud had suggested, a painful psychological experience had been converted into a painful and symbolic cluster of bodily symptoms. Though the pain in the throat and the choking attacks, along with the chest pains, were eliminated when these feelings were made conscious, the young soldier's third symptom, a stabbing pain in his left heel, remained intractable.

Jung turned to an analysis of the man's dreams. The officer reported a dream in which *he was bitten in the heel by a snake and instantly paralyzed.* Analysis of the dream revealed the expected associations of the girl as a "snake" who had betrayed him; of a mother who had overprotected and thus "crippled" him; of a certain tendency to "girlishness" in himself for which he overcompensated by joining the military. But Jung felt that he detected something more fundamental, more primitive and universal in the man's dream. It was as though the Genesis saying: "And I will put enmity between thee and the woman, and between thy seed and her seed; it shall bruise thy head, and thou shalt bruise his heel . . ." had been transformed by the man's unconscious mind into a personal mythic symbol of his recent romantic upset.

For some reason, this singularly unreligious soldier had felt the *need for mythic expression* of his psychic pain. Jung concluded that the man's knowledge of the Bible, scanty though it was, had lain dormant until his unconscious seized upon it (1931, p. 147). For the Bible story had provided just the right medium for conversion of a personal conflict into an opportunity to express a deeper sentiment in allegorical fashion (Jung, 1968, p. 116). Certainly, the soldier's unconscious could have chosen a more secular form of symbolism to express his pain. But, in fact, he chose a universal myth.

Consequently, Jung was convinced that there is a part of the unconscious mind that transcends the personal experiences of the individual, as exemplified by the sun's phallus fantasy. This unconscious subsystem embodies some of the past experiences of the human race. Moreover, that same transpersonal unconscious domain may employ personal experience as a vehicle for mythological, allegorical expression of age-old themes, as exemplified by the soldier's snake dream, "for the dream of the snake reveals a fragment of psychic activity that has nothing whatever to do with the dreamer as a modern individual . . ." (Jung, 1931, p. 148). Such a dream could not be a product solely of the soldier's personal experiences. Fantasies like the sun's phallus and the snake dream could have originated only in the individual's recognition of the cumulative experiences of the human race. To the part of the mind responsible for universal myth transmission Jung gave the name *collective unconscious.*

Personal Sources of the Hypothesis

Jung's writings are studded with a seemingly endless array of mythological examples and their similarities to the dreams, paintings, and fantasies of normal and abnormal personalities. But there was an even more fundamental source of Jung's conviction that a suprapersonal unconscious exists. In his autobiography, *Memories, Dreams, Reflections,* written just before his death in 1961 with the collaboration of his personal secretary and confidante, Aniela Jaffé, Jung provided his readers with a series of rare and penetrating glimpses into his inner life, indeed, into the intimate workings of his own unconscious. The entire book is laden with gods, spirits, and fantasy figures that populated Jung's inner mental life. One event in particular is relevant in the present context of our discussion of the collective unconscious because out of it grew Jung's conviction that "... there are things in the psyche which I do not produce, but which produce themselves and have their own life" (1961, p. 183).

Jung reported that between 1913 and 1917 he was seized by a series of visions, fantasies, or mystical experiences. Several personages made contact with Jung during these experiences, that is, they emerged from his collective unconscious. Several of these figures subsequently had long conversations together with Jung about topics of which Jung could have consciously known very little. One particular figure, whom Jung named Philemon, arose from the metamorphosis of an earlier fantasy figure, Elijah:

> Philemon was a pagan and brought with him an Egypto-Hellenistic atmosphere with a Gnostic coloration. His figure appeared to me in the following dream. There was a blue sky, like the sea, covered not by clouds but by flat brown clods of earth. It looked as if the clods were breaking apart and the blue water of the sea [was] becoming visible between them. But the water was the blue sky. Suddenly there appeared from the right a winged being sailing across the sky. I saw that it was an old man with the horns of a bull. He held a bunch of four keys, one of which he clutched as if he were about to open a lock. He had the wings of a kingfisher with its characteristic colors. [1961, pp. 182–183]

At first Jung did not understand the dream. He tried to impress it upon his memory by painting it. During the time he was painting that picture, he discovered in his garden a dead kingfisher bird. "I was thunderstruck, for kingfishers are quite rare in the vicinity of Zürich and I have never since found a dead one" (1961, p. 183).

For Jung, the significance of the Philemon figure lay in the insight that such apparitions represented a force beyond himself, and beyond his personal experiences and personal unconscious mind. Philemon said things during the fantasies that Jung felt he himself had not consciously thought. "He confronted me in an objective manner, and I understood that there is something in me which can say things that I do not know and do not intend, things which may even be directed against me" (1961, p. 183).

The Philemon "fantasy" occurred sometime between the middle of December and early January, 1913, approximately one year after Jung's acrimonious break with Freud. Jung had been extending his theoretical talents in directions that Freud found quite unacceptable both because Jung's ideas clashed with his own and because he felt sure Jung was heading in a mystical direction. For Jung's part, he saw himself poised on the edge of a precipice. Visions and fantasies had been bombarding his consciousness and threatening to take complete control. Jung knew, as, of course, a trained psychiatrist would, that he might be on the verge of engulfment by a fullblown psychosis. In his view, therefore, he was faced with a momentous decision: Should he attempt to fight off these assaults of the unconscious to remain, as it were, in the land of the living, or should he willfully make the descent and attempt to make rational sense of his experiences?

> My enduring these storms was a question of brute strength. Others have been shattered by them—Nietzsche, and Hölderlin, and many others. But there was a demonic strength in me, and from the beginning there was no doubt in my mind that I must find the meaning of what I was experiencing in these fantasies. When I endured these assaults of the unconscious I had an unswerving conviction that I was obeying a higher will, and that feeling continued to uphold me until I had mastered the task. [Jung, 1961, p. 177]

Thus, between 1913 and 1917 Jung conceived of himself as engaged on a voluntary exploration of his own personal and collective unconscious. There is considerable division of opinion over whether Jung's descent into his fantasies and dreams was as voluntary as he suggested in his memoirs. On at least one occasion, for example, after Jung had allowed himself to be engulfed by a vision in which he and a "brown-skinned savage" murdered a mythological Germanic hero, he was so overcome with disgust that he came close to suicide. He heard a voice that demanded he immediately interpret the vision or shoot himself with the loaded revolver he kept in his night table drawer (1961, p. 180). Experiences like this one, so characteristic of psychotic disorganization, have caused scholarly commentators on Jung to be divided into two camps.

The first of these schools of opinion is represented by writers like Aniela Jaffé (1971) and Laurens van der Post (1975) who have accepted Jung's own view that his 1913 to 1917 "stormy period" was a careful and deliberate voyage of exploration. According to this view, Jung was a visionary, who, with courage and determination, skillfully charted unknown psychological realms. Jung phrased it this way:

> It is of course ironical that I, a psychiatrist, should at almost every step of my experiment have run into the same psychic material which is the stuff of psychosis and is found in the insane. This is the fund of unconscious images which fatally confuse the mental patient. But it is also the matrix of a mythopoeic imagination which has vanished from our rational age. . . . Unpopular, ambiguous, and dangerous, [such an imagination] is a voyage of discovery to the other pole of the world. [1961, pp. 188–189]

In the contrasting school of opinion, represented by writers like Paul J. Stern (1976), there exists the equally certain conviction that Jung's voyage was not visionary but psychotic; not voluntary but uncontrollable. It must immediately be pointed out, however, that the question cannot be definitively answered on the basis of the published evidence. Each reader will form his or her own opinion, but it is important that such opinion be informed. For even if one decides that Jung had indeed undergone a psychotic episode, one cannot deny that he emerged from his descent with ideas and concepts that stand as creative, if yet untested, contributions to psychology.

The 1913–1917 period of engulfment was not an isolated episode of visionary experience for Jung. From childhood, Jung engaged in confrontations with his own, seemingly independent, inner life. Many of the concepts of his later theoretical writings can be traced to Jung's gift for universalizing and externalizing his inner turmoil.

Major Themes of Jung's Boyhood

To judge from the evidence of his memoirs and from information provided by his biographers, Jung appears to have been beset with a series of (perhaps) serious emotional difficulties in childhood. Two personal themes in particular seem to have arisen by the age of twelve from Jung's attempts to deal with his difficulties. The first theme was embodied in his conviction that he was actually two persons: the child he objectively seemed to be and an authoritative wise old man who had lived in the eighteenth century, some hundred years before Jung had been born. So powerful was his belief that at least part of him belonged to the previous century, that, occasionally in doing school work, he would write "1786" instead of the correct date, 1886. The second theme, closely allied to the first, was contained in

Jung's secretly held belief that certain thoughts, dreams, visions, and fantasies he periodically experienced were truly important, externally derived revelations, "secret" wisdom that only rare few people were privileged to acquire.

Both of these themes, as we shall later see, became cornerstones of Jung's theoretical style. But it is important at the outset of our brief survey of the personal sources of his concepts to acknowledge with Paul Stern (1976, p. 10) that an examination of the origins of Jung's ideas in no way prejudges their validity.

THE STONE. Between the ages of seven and nine years, Jung had several experiences from which his belief that he was two personalities emerged. The first experience involved a game that Jung played with a large chunk of stone that jutted from a garden wall. Frequently, when alone, Jung would mount the stone and pass the time in revery:

> "I am sitting on top of this stone and it is underneath." But the stone also could say "I" and think: "I am lying here on this slope and he is sitting on top of me." The question then arose: "Am I the one who is sitting on the stone, or am I the stone on which *he* is sitting?" This question always perplexed me, and I would stand up, wondering who was what now. The answer remained totally unclear, and my uncertainty was accompanied by a feeling of curious and fascinating darkness. [Jung, 1961, p. 20]

Jung's ability to shift mental perspective to that of the stone was interpreted by him as his first discovery of the "mysterious" in life. When the very religious adults around him (his father was a minister and his mother a minister's daughter) tried to "pump" religious teachings into him, Jung would think to himself: "Yes, but there is something else, something very secret that people don't know about" (1961, p. 22).

THE MANNEQUIN. When Jung was ten years old, he carved from a wooden ruler a small male figure, a "mannequin" approximately two inches long. With ink and small bits of wool, Jung created for the mannequin a frock coat, shiny black boots, and a top hat; and from a wooden pencil case, he devised a little bed for the figure. Inside the pencil case, Jung deposited, along with the mannequin and makeshift bed, an oblong blackish stone that he had painted with water colors: "This was *his* [the mannequin's] stone. All this was a great secret. Secretly I took the case to . . . the attic at the top of the house . . . and hid it with great satisfaction on one of the beams under the roof—for no one must ever see it! . . . I felt safe, and the tormenting sense of being at odds with myself was gone" (Jung, 1961, p. 21).

Thereafter, whenever Jung felt under stress, he would conjure up in his mind the image of his hidden mannequin and feel secure. Sometimes he would create for the mannequin small scrolls of paper on which, in a secret language of his own invention, he would write a particularly pleasing saying. Each addition of a scroll was treated as a solemn ceremonial act to be guarded as an inviolable secret, "for the safety of my life depended on it" (1961, p. 22).

It is possible to interpret both the philosophical stone dialogue and the creation of the wooden mannequin as attempts by Jung to concretize and therefore control his frightening belief that he was two persons. The stone and the mannequin may be thought of as externalizations of the second personality that Jung felt he harbored. Jung's own interpretation was that he had early come into contact with one of the great secrets of human nature: the existence of the collective unconscious from which these urges and actions had emerged. However, in the light of Jung's family circumstances, it seems possible that there were more mundane causes for his actions.

Jung's father, the Reverend Dr. Paul Jung, had many of his own boyhood dreams crushed. Failing to become a university professor of Oriental languages, he settled for the vocation of country parson, a wife who was stronger willed and an opposite personality, and a life-long history of worry over his health. Jung reports that his father's depressed spirits and morose personality were due to a religious crisis in which his father was consumed by doubts (1961, p. 73). Toward the end of his life, his father became extremely hypochondriacal and believed that he suffered from a variety of diseases.

Jung's mother, Emilie, was, on the surface, an exact opposite personality to his father. Relations between Jung's parents were strained, and at least part of his own childhood sorrow stemmed from the parental disputes he observed. To make matters worse, Jung was convinced that his mother was possessed of two personalities: one, the observable character of the pleasant, plump housewife; the other, a witch, prophetess, and seeress who communicated with spirits. Jung described his mother in this way:

> By day she was a loving mother, but at night she seemed uncanny. Then she was like one of those seers who is at the same time a strange animal, like a priestess in a bear's cave. Archaic and ruthless; ruthless as truth and nature. [1961, p. 50]

The "uncanny" personality in his mother seems to have emerged only at special moments. "She would then speak as if talking to herself, but what she said was aimed at me and usually struck to the core of my being, so that I was stunned into silence" (1961, p. 49). Jung early decided to keep his own inner life hidden from her because he was unsure just how much control the uncanny personality exerted over the housewife personality.

Jung's propensity for endowing people with two personalities may have had its origins in his need to cope with feelings of inferiority. Thus, his mother's uncanny personality emerged frequently when she was scolding young Carl or trying to instill in him good manners so that he would not embarrass the family with friends. It may have been easier for him to believe that a second personality within his mother administered these lessons. Likewise, his conviction that he himself was two persons seems to have emerged completely during a scolding he received from a friend's father for some misbehavior related to the man's boat.

> ... I was seized with rage that this fat, ignorant boor [i.e., the friend's father] should dare to insult ME. This ME was not only grown up, but important, an authority, a person with office and dignity, an old man, an object of respect and awe. Yet the contrast with reality was so grotesque that in the midst of my fury I suddenly stopped myself, for the question rose to my lips: "Who in the world are you, anyway? ... Then, to my intense confusion, it occurred to me that I was actually two different persons. One of them was the schoolboy who could not grasp algebra and was far from sure of himself; the other was important, a high authority, a man not to be trifled with, as powerful and influential as this [friend's angry father]. This "other" was an old man who lived in the eighteenth century, wore buckled shoes and a white wig, and went driving in a fly with high, concave rear wheels. ... [Jung, 1961, p. 34]

The exact imagery of Jung's other personality had been adopted from a piece of terra cotta sculpture that depicted a well-known medical doctor of the day and his patient. The motive for adoption of this second personality is transparently clear in Jung's own account. It is similar to the motives that lay behind his earlier confusion regarding who was the stone and who was the stone-sitter:

> ... it was strangely reassuring and calming to sit on my stone. Somehow it would free me of all my doubts. Whenever I thought that I was the stone, the conflict ceased. "The stone has no uncertainties, no urge to communicate, and is eternally the same for thousands of years," I would think, "while I am only a passing phenomenon which bursts into all kinds of emotions, like a flame that flares up quickly and then goes out." I was but the sum of my emotions, and the Other in me was the timeless, imperishable stone. [Jung, 1961, p. 42]

Jung's uncertainties and doubts drove him near the edge of madness, for two dreams revealed to him secrets so blasphemous that he was terrified even to think them.

THE PHALLUS GOD. The first of Jung's terrifying secret dreams occurred between the ages of three and four years. Descending a stone stairway, he came upon a rounded archway closed off by a green curtain. In the dream, he pushed aside the curtain to expose a large rectangular chamber constructed of stone. In the center of the chamber stood a magnificent golden king's throne:

> Something was standing on [the throne] which I thought at first was a tree trunk twelve to fifteen feet high and about one and a half to two feet thick. It was a huge thing, reaching almost to the ceiling. But it was of a curious composition: it was made of skin and naked flesh, and on top there was something like a rounded head with no face and no hair. On the very top of the head was a single eye, gazing motionlessly upward. [Jung, 1961, p. 12]

Jung was paralyzed with terror at the sight of this huge column of flesh and was consumed with the fear that at any moment it would crawl off the throne. "At that moment I heard from outside and above me my mother's voice. She called out, "Yes, just look at him. That is the man-eater!" (1961, p. 12) The dream haunted Jung for years, causing him night-mares when he could sleep, and enormous fear on those nights when sleep would not come.

Jung later interpreted the dream as a condensation of his childhood fears of "Jesuits," about whom he had heard some frightening things. The column of flesh was, of course, a phallus, a phallus-god, in fact. For Jung, the Lord Jesus was the "above-ground" counterpart of this subterranean monster. "Lord Jesus never became quite real for me, never quite accept-able, never quite lovable, for again and again I would think of his under-ground counterpart, a frightful revelation that had been accorded me without my seeking it" (1961, p. 13).

It is possible that the Christian doctrine Jung had been taught by his mother and father, and which had engendered such skepticism, Jung later thought to have been somehow connected with this dream. In any event, on its surface, the dream suggests a small child's confusion about the Christian doctrine of eating the body and blood of Christ condensed with the notion of "man-eater" in the form of a wormlike column of flesh. It is also possible that in his later recollection of the dream, Jung added to it some of the anger he felt when being "pumped" full of religious teach-ings.

THE THRONE. Jung experienced one other dreamlike vision that has rele-vance to our discussion. One afternoon upon leaving school, his thoughts were occupied with the beauty of the day, the beauty of the nearby cathedral roof glinting in the sunlight, and the magnificence that God displayed in such creations. The image of God sitting on his golden throne in the beautiful clear blue sky came into Jung's mind. Suddenly he froze. No other thoughts would come, but deep within he knew that something momentous, something monstrous and blasphemous, was about to occur to him. For days he went about in a fog, attempting to ward off the dreaded thought and fearing that were he to entertain the idea, he would be plunged immediately into hell.

Three nights later, awaking from a restless sleep, Jung was struck with the thought: "Now it is coming, now it's serious! *I must think.* It must be thought out beforehand. . . . Who wants to force me to think something I don't know and don't want to know?" (1961, p. 37). Jung finally convinced himself that it was God who intended that he think the unthinkable as a critical test of faith. Gathering his courage, Jung allowed the image he had been choking back for three days and nights to flood into awareness:

> I saw before me the cathedral, the blue sky. God sits on His golden throne, high above the world—and from under the throne an enormous turd falls upon the sparkling new roof, shatters it, and breaks the walls of the cathedral asunder. [1961, p. 39]

Jung immediately experienced relief from his turmoil. He explained to himself that his image of God befouling his own cathedral was God's way of revealing to him that "God could be something terrible." This dream became Jung's boyhood sorrowful secret, a secret that motivated him to explore his father's theological books in search of further clarification and reassurance. But the only result was his conviction that all these wise authors could shed very little light on genuine religious experiences.

The net effect of Jung's dreams and visions was the creation of a lonely and withdrawn boy:

> My one great achievement during those years was that I resisted the temptation to talk about it with anyone. Thus the pattern of my relationship to the world was already prefigured: today as then I am a solitary, because I know things and must hint at things which other people do not know, and usually do not even want to know. [1961, pp. 41–42]

We have thus come full circle, returning to the two major themes of Jung's life with which we started. The first theme, it will be recalled, was the conviction that he was actually two persons. It is now easy to see the motives that shaped this belief. Jung's family dissatisfaction, his sense of inferiority, his religious skepticism in a home where religion was paramount, and his desire for inner peace necessitated the creation of the second personality as a haven, an immutable and stress-immune sanctuary. The second theme, namely, that his inner experiences originated from some external source of revelation, later became the basis for Jung's ideas on the *collective unconscious,* the *archetypes* or inherited images that reside there, and *synchronicity* between internal psychic events and external equivalents. Each of these concepts will be taken up in subsequent sections of this chapter.

Jung seems to have experienced an intense need to endow an external source, or at least an entity apart from himself, as the genesis of the feelings, dreams, and visions he experienced. In some acutely anguished way, Jung found it necessary to find a more believable substitute for the God that he suspected his own father doubted. He thus regarded his two personalities as real, that is, as genuine psychological achievements and as manifestations of higher, perhaps religious, wisdom. He viewed his visions and dreams as gifts of the same kind of wisdom, bestowed from the same unimpeachably holy source. He was thus adamant that his personalities were not evidence of a personality "split" or schizophrenic dissociation (1961, p. 45), and equally sure that his descent into the unconscious was a foray after psychological truth, not a folly of psychotic delusion. Whatever the reader's opinion on these matters, the indisputable fact remains that Jung's theorizing was shaped by his personalities.

Structure of the Psyche: Ego, Personal and Collective Unconscious

In light of his clinical observations with schizophrenic patients like the young visionary clerk, along with his own self-analysis from 1913 to 1917, Jung's approach to personality theory was necessarily different from Freud's. In Jung's view, the chief problem was to explain the individual's construction of fantasies and dreams that embody symbols and themes unlikely to be part of the individual's strictly personal experiences. He hypothesized, therefore, that the mind or total personality was divided into three major zones: the *conscious ego,* the *personal unconscious,* and the *collective unconscious.*

The Conscious Ego

The conscious ego, for Jung, corresponds roughly to what Freud meant by the same term. Functioning as the conscious part of personality, the ego includes all sense impressions and self-awareness. Consciousness, therefore, consists of all those internal and external events that are within our awareness at a given moment. By the same token, the ego can experience all that is conscious by simply directing attention to one or another sensory experience or to memories of such experiences.

The Personal Unconscious

Jung conceived of the second division of the mind, the personal unconscious, in a somewhat different way than did Freud. Mental content that through disuse or inattention does not at the moment occupy our awareness, but which can become conscious at will, is classed as unconscious. (Freud would have called such momentarily latent content *preconscious.*)

Even out of awareness, however, all the activities that normally take place consciously can also occur unconsciously (Jung, 1931, p. 144). Therefore, the personal unconscious consists of all those contents that became unconscious simply because they lost their intensity and were forgotten or not attended to. Jung agreed with Freud, however, that the personal unconscious also contains ideas and impulses that have been actively withdrawn from consciousness by repression. Such content is unconscious because in the personal experience of the individual it involved motives unacceptable to his ego (1931, p. 151).

Despite the apparent agreement with Freud, Jung viewed the personal unconscious as more complex than simply the repository of *past* experience. For Jung, the unconscious is both *retrospective* and *prospective*. It is oriented not only by the individual's past, but by anticipations of his future. Jung's patients often had dreams that could aptly be described as "forward looking" in the sense that, though the individual was not yet aware of his decision or feelings, the dream revealed that the unconscious had already solved some problem or had already made some decision (1916, p. 255).

The unconscious also has a *compensatory* function. When an individual's conscious attitude leans too one-sidedly in a single direction, the unconscious may compensate for the imbalance by producing dreams or fantasies that emphasize the opposite tendency (Jung, 1916, pp. 252–253). Compensation may also be seen in dreams that make available to consciousness all that was subliminal or not attended to during the day.

Prospection and *compensation* may combine to aid in the individual's adaption to life, as for example when the individual is confronted with a difficult problem. Upon waking in the morning, he may find the solution popping suddenly into mind as if he had been continuously working on the problem while sleeping.

The Collective Unconscious

At a deeper level than the personal unconscious lies the *impersonal* or *transpersonal* unconscious. This transpersonal domain is "detached from anything personal and is common to all men, since its contents can be found everywhere" (Jung, 1917, p. 66). Consequently, as previously pointed out, Jung termed the transpersonal layer of the unconscious the collective unconscious.

Stored within the recesses of the collective unconscious are the primordial images and ideas that have been common to all members of the race from the beginning of life. These images are not preformed; they have no concrete content. They are simply *possibilities* of action; *predispositions* to respond to external events in specific ways; *potentialities* of shaping experience in certain directions. They are, in short, flexible templates or models for current experience to follow (Jung, 1936, p. 66ff.).

These primordial images of the collective unconscious were termed by Jung the *archetypes,* in the sense of *prototypes* or molds of emotional reaction. As a kind of template or model, the archetypes serve to organize and shape the course of an individual's interactions with his external world and with his inner world of the personal unconscious. In this sense, Jung seems to have conceived of the *personal* unconscious as only the most superficial veneer of the entire unconscious domain.

Origin of the Archetypes

The collective unconscious is not a development of any *individual's* experience. It is inherited. Jung's arguments in this regard bear careful scrutiny because his various writings on the subject are often vague, contradictory, and abstract to a degree that makes unequivocal interpretation impossible.

Within the course of the history of the human race, certain fundamental day-to-day events *had* to be experienced by all members of the human family. For example, the rising and setting of the sun surely did not escape the notice of even the most primitive humans.

> One of the commonest and at the same time most impressive experiences is the apparent movement of the sun every day. We certainly cannot discover anything of the kind in the unconscious, so far as the known physical process is concerned. What we do find, on the other hand, is the myth of the sun-hero in all its countless variations. It is this myth, and not the actual physical process, that forms the sun archetype. The same can be said of the phases of the moon. *The archetype is a kind of readiness to produce over and over again the same or similar mythical ideas. Hence it seems as though what is impressed upon the unconscious were exclusively the subjective fantasy-ideas aroused by the physical process.* We may therefore assume that the archetypes are recurrent impressions made by subjective reactions. [Jung, 1917, p. 69; italics added]

Archetypes, therefore, are the cumulative effect of perpetually repeated experiences on the human nervous system's development. To say it another way, perhaps more precisely, it is *not* the memory of the actual *physical experience* itself that is inherited. The repetitive *subjective emotional reaction* to the event is impressed on human unconscious mental processes, and it is this *internal state,* this predisposition to react in a similar way to repetitions of the physical event, that is transmitted to future generations. Thus, the collective unconscious's archetypes are a residue of ancestral emotional life (Jung, 1917, p. 77).

Archetypal Myths: Symbol-Making Processes

Jung himself asked the most significant question of his theory: "... why does the psyche not register the actual process, instead of mere fantasies about the physical process?" Jung's answer centered around some well-known hypotheses about the mind of primitive man, namely, James George Frazer's notion of *sympathetic magic* and Lévy-Bruhl's treatment of the *"participation mystique."*

Frazer postulated that early man interpreted his world magically by assuming that events though separated in time or space could nevertheless affect one another. Frazer called this assumption "sympathetic magic." Such mental functioning is based on the conviction that through some *mysterious* or *unknowable* means, events and objects may exert a mutual reaction, a kind of sympathetic effect without physical causality. For example, some early men believed that the fingernail clippings and hanks of hair they stole from an enemy could be used to gain control over that individual. What was done to the nail fragments and hair, would, mysteriously, be done to their owner (Frazer, 1963).

Lévy-Bruhl went a step further and suggested that for the primitive mind the distinction between self and object, between what is "me, mine" and what is external to me, was vague and confused. For the primitive, what happens outside *is* happening inside him (Jung, 1931, p. 154).

For early man, then, what was of supreme importance was not the external physical event, or an objective conception of cause and effect. In fact, he probably did not make these distinctions. For him, the ultimate reality was himself, his emotions and his desires. Crucial for early man was the net effect of reality *on him,* for "his emotions are more important to him than physics; therefore what he registers is his emotional fantasies. . . . It is not thunder and lightning, not rain and cloud that remain as images in the psyche, but the fantasies caused by the affects they arouse" (1931, pp. 154–155).

Hence, the descendants of early man do not store within their brains the exact photographic copies of their ancestors' experiences. Each successive culture, each individual, creates afresh the myth of the sun god, or the hero, or the god of thunder when external events demand reaction. The *mythological tendency,* the predisposition to respond to these external events in specific ways, and the disposition to be emotionally affected by such events are the real legacy of past generations. "The primitive mentality does not *invent* myths, it *experiences* them" (Jung, 1940, p. 154).

Jung subsequently devoted a significant part of his life to discovering and elucidating specific archetypal images as they appeared in mythological stories, dreams, fantasies, and in paintings. Presumably, there is no a priori limit to the number of archetypes that are possible. Among the most frequently appearing, however, were the following.

The Child-God Archetype

The Christ child and personifications of children as elves or dwarfs are depicted throughout legend and religious lore as having divine or mystical powers. Among his patients Jung discovered cases of women who believed that they had an imaginary child. Symbolically, in a purely psychological sense, a *child* represents what Jung called "futurity." That is to say, the child is *potentially* an adult, he is in the process of becoming. A child may symbolize anticipation of future events and is likely to make its appearance as an archetype when an individual is in the process of important life decisions (Jung, 1940, p. 164).

The Mother Archetype

This archetype may be elicited from an individual's collective unconscious in response to a real mother, mother-in-law, grandmother, or stepmother. Even figurative mothers may provoke the emergence of the Mother archetype as symbolized by a wife, Divine Mother (Virgin Mary), an institution: Alma Mater, the Church, or any event, place, person associated with fertility and fruitfulness.

The Mother archetype can be either positive or negative, light or dark, good or evil. For example, the goddess of fate (Moira) can be kind and generous, or remorseless and heartless. Evil-Mother archetype symbols abound: the witch, the dragon (or any devouring and entwining animal) (Jung, 1938, p. 82). Thus, the Mother archetype includes both the loving and the terrible mother.

The Trickster or Magician Archetype

Jung explored the figure of the Trickster or Magician through a variety of myths, most notably in American Indian mythology. Characteristic of this mythical figure is his fondness for sly jokes, malicious pranks, and his dual nature: half animal, half human. The demonic figures of the Old Testament, even the characterization of Yahweh himself as Trickster undergoing transformation into a divine savior, embody this age-old myth (Jung, 1954, p. 256).

The Hero Archetype

According to Jung, the finest expression of the symbol-making capacity of the collective unconscious is the figure of the Hero, or its opposite, the demon (e.g., Anti-Christ, Satan). Hero myths are common to many cultures and tend to share the same characteristics. The Hero defeats evil, slays the dragon or monster, usually near water, suffers punishment for another, or rescues the vanquished and down-trodden (Jung, 1917, p. 99).

The Shadow as Archetype

Within our personal unconscious there are repressed, unacceptable motives, tendencies, and desires. There is thus within us an inferior, undesirable aspect to our personality. Jung calls this side of our inner life the

Shadow, the "dark half" of personality. It is the side of ourselves that we would prefer not to recognize.

Mythologically, Shadow symbols include demons, devils, and evil ones. This archetype may be evoked in our relations with another when we feel terribly uncomfortable with a person but are unable to specify exactly what provokes the distress. We sense an immediate dislike for some people without being able to verbalize the cause. In such cases we may be projecting our shadow side onto him because we recognize in this person something that we do not like in ourselves (Jung, 1917, p. 95).

There is danger in the Shadow archetype. If we fail to recognize the "inferior" dark side of ourselves, there is the possibility of dissociation of the Shadow from the ego. In this case, the personality would be incomplete, truncated. One or the other aspect could gain dominance. Thus, the Shadow is common to all men. It is both a personal and a collective unconscious phenomenon (Jung, 1968, pp. 21–22). It may be used as a synonym for the personal unconscious, or as the name of an archetype.

Animus and Anima Archetypes

No man is entirely masculine, exclusively male. Feminine elements, attitudes, intuitions are sealed into every man's character. Traditionally, men strive to repress their "weak, soft, feminine" traits. Such repression causes a buildup of libido tension within the unconscious. In striving to win a woman as a mate, a man unconsciously projects these feminine traits and the feminine image of himself that he has so actively repressed (Jung, 1917, p. 189). This internalized feminine image is based on his real experiences with women (his mother, sister, etc.) and on the collective experiences of men throughout history (Jung, 1917, p. 190). The projected image of femininity from a man's collective unconscious is his *anima*. The anima determines a man's relationship to women throughout his life and shapes his understanding of those relationships. In a sense, a man's anima helps to compensate for the otherwise one-sided masculine nature of his interactions with and perceptions of others.

Likewise, the woman has her inherited masculine image, her *animus*. "If I were to attempt to put in a nutshell the difference between man and woman in this respect, i.e., what it is that characterizes the animus as opposed to the anima, I could say only this: as the anima produces moods [in the male], so the animus produces [in the female] *opinions* . . ." (Jung, 1917, p. 207). Jung suggested that the opinions of a woman's animus have the character of solid convictions with unassailable validity. The moods of the man's anima are often expressed in sudden changes in temperament, or character, so that a man may say, "I was not myself today."

The woman's animus, unlike the man's anima, usually does not consist of a single personification, but rather of a plurality of masculine figures. "The animus is rather like an assembly of fathers or dignitaries of some kind who lay down incontestable 'rational' *ex cathedra* judgments" (Jung,

1917, p. 207). The animus is thus the embodiment of all of a woman's ancestral experiences of man.

The danger of the anima and the animus lies in the possibility that the entire psyche may come under the exclusive sway of these images so that a man loses his masculinity and a woman her femininity (Jung, 1917, p. 209). Yet, without recognition of their inherent opposites, man and woman run the risk of incompleteness.

The Persona Archetype

Persona is the Latin word for the mask that actors in Roman and Greek drama wore to depict their roles (see Chapter 1). Thus, the persona in Jung's scheme is the front we present to others because social living makes demands for certain kinds of behavior. Society establishes certain expectations and certain roles around which we must shape our public selves, and behind which we hide our "private" selves (Jung, 1917, p. 192).

There is danger in the persona, for "people really do exist who believe they are what they pretend to be" (Jung, 1917, p. 193). When the mask and the ego become identical, the personal unconscious must find an alternate means of expression and representation for its demands in consciousness. Thus, "Whoever builds up too good a persona for himself naturally has to pay for it with irritability" (Jung, 1917, p. 193).

As described thus far, the persona is an individual creation, rather than an archetypal form. But there is also an *impersonal* or *transpersonal* aspect to the persona. It comes into existence to smoothe the individual's *collective* existence as an individual among individuals. "It is, as its name implies, only a mask of the collective psyche, a mask that *feigns individuality*, making others and oneself believe that one is individual, whereas one is simply acting a role through which the collective psyche speaks" (Jung, 1917, p. 157).

Fundamentally, therefore, the content and form of the individual's persona is a projection of the collective unconscious. There are individual differences in the choice of collective unconscious themes that the individual will role-play, but the themes themselves are born of universal and impersonal archetypal images. The persona is an ideal image, a desirable actor's part, a compromise between the individual and humanity as a whole, past and present, as to what a man should appear to be (Jung, 1917, p. 158).

Archetypes and Synchronicity

Archetypes invariably involve great emotion. Jung pointed out that sometimes an archetype may even take control of the personality so that individual behavior from that point onward is modified and directed by the collective unconscious. In fact, Jung felt that groups of people, whole civilizations, may project a given archetype at a single moment in history. The course of that civilization may thus be directed by the universal theme that emerges. For example, a satanic or demonic archetype may have made its appearance during the years of the rise to power of the Nazis under Adolf Hitler. The reverse may, of course, also occur. A return to religious commitment or faith may be preceded by the emergence of the God archetype or the Wise Old Man.

On an individual basis, archetypes may make their appearance in times of tension, whether or not the individual consciously experiences the stress. Jung even suggested that the archetypes could transcend causality as we know it. He proposed a principle called *synchronicity* to account for events that are related through meaning rather than by the usual cause-and-effect sequence. For example, one might dream of a relative with whom little contact has been had in recent years. A day after the dream, a telegram announces that relative's death. The two events, dream and relative's death, are not related *causally*. The dream did not cause the relative's death any more than his future demise could have caused an anticipatory dream. Nonetheless, the two events are related through *meaningful simultaneity,* which Jung termed *synchronicity* (1952).

Jung's explanation of synchronicitous events involved the emergence of an archetype from the collective unconscious. During moments of great stress, the individual's collective unconscious knows more than the individual himself. In the case cited, the dream and death, the archetypical figure of death had begun to penetrate into the dreamer's consciousness. For the collective unconscious, time is relative; future, present, and past are one. For the dreamer, the dream and subsequent death are uncannily coincidental, but to the collective unconscious the death of the relative was a certainty. In a sense, the collective unconscious experienced the dream imagery and the actual future death as one and the same, as happening simultaneously.

Jung's concept of the collective unconscious and its archetypes was severely criticized, unfairly he thought, as akin to the discredited Lamarckian notion of evolution. In Lamarck's view parental *experiences* could be transmitted to offspring. Modern biologists no longer accept the view that characteristics acquired in the organism's lifetime can be transmitted to offspring. Only those traits coded into the organism's genes are capable of transmission. Jung's critics interpreted his concept of the collective unconscious as a special case of inheriting acquired characteristics. Jung's repeated explanations did not help much in dispelling the suspicion, for Jung often treated the subject abstractly and with vague, imprecise language that could be interpreted as supporting a Lamarckian view. Yet, on the other hand, biologists readily confess that we have only begun to understand patterns of inheritance and their mechanisms. The optimist and Jung supporter will interpret such statements as indications that potential hard evidence for the collective-unconscious concept is just around the corner.

Jung's View of Freud and Adler: Interpreting a Case of Neurosis

Here is a brief description by Jung of a case of neurotic misery:

A young woman begins to have attacks of anxiety. At night she wakes up from a nightmare with a blood-curdling cry, is scarcely able to calm herself, clings to her husband and implores him not to leave her, demanding assurance that he really loves her, etc. Gradually a nervous asthma develops, the attacks also coming during the day. [Jung, 1917, p. 35]

A strictly Freudian approach to this woman's difficulty, according to Jung, would begin by eliciting from the patient her associations to the nightmare, exploring her past anxiety dreams, and by investigating the circumstances of her childhood and familial relations. With such a thorough evaluation of the patient the following facts would be discovered: (1) Her prior dreams involved ferocious bulls, lions, tigers, and evil men attacking her. (2) She had lost her father when she was fourteen; but before his death, when she was on an outing in Paris with him at the *Folies Bergères,* a dancer had looked at her father in a brazen way, and he had returned her gaze with an "animal look." From then on, the girl's relationship with her father changed. The patient reported that the dancer's gaze and her father's return stare had reminded her of the look in the wild animals' eyes in her dreams, and of the look of a former lover of her own who had treated her badly. (3) The first appearance of her neurosis came when she had her second child and discovered that her husband advanced a "tender interest" in another woman. (4) One additional fact is pertinent: After her father's sudden death, she succumbed to fits of uncontrolled weeping followed by equally uncontrollable episodes of hysterical laughter.

Jung pointed out that the Freudian interpretation of this data would center on the woman's inability to break with her father as a young girl, her Electra complex, and on the sexual imagery of the animals in her dreams in relation to her father's animal stare at the dancer. Furthermore, the connection between her own husband's "tender feelings" for another woman after she herself had become a *mother* for the second time bore a powerful unconscious similarity to the relationship of her own mother and father. Her hysterical laughing and weeping fits betrayed the ambivalence she felt toward her husband, and more fundamentally, toward her father.

What would happen, Jung wanted to know, if the same case history were subjected to a different theoretical analysis? Alfred Adler, one of Freud's early colleagues, developed a different way of approaching such cases. For Adler, the key human motivation was a struggle to compensate for any perceived sense of inferiority. Compensation for inferiority feelings takes the form of a struggle for its opposite, superiority, and emerges as a fight for power in human relationships (Adler, 1959; Adler's theory is given a full exposition in Chapter 5 of this book). Thus, according to Jung's application of Adlerian theory, Adler would see in this same case a struggle to dominate the father's attention, jealousy provoked by the dancer episode, and a repetition of these same motives in the woman's relationship with her husband. Her "sickness," asthma, her terrible plea for her husband not to leave her, and her demands for assurances of love are all techniques of interpersonal domination and striving for power (Jung, 1917, p. 39).

Whether Adler and Freud would have agreed with Jung's application of their viewpoints is an unanswerable question. What is important, however, is that Jung was troubled by the drastic difference in interpretation that resulted from different psychological theorists viewing the same case. Each would approach the personality of his patients from the perspective of his own theory—and from the constraints imposed by his own personality.

Jungian Attitude Types: Freud the Extrovert and Adler the Introvert

For Jung, the Freudian and Adlerian explanations both had merit, and neither could be totally dismissed (1917, p. 41). Jung felt that the key problem was to account for the difference in approach between two skilled men treating the same case. The essence of the difference, Jung hypothesized, lay in the two men's personalities. Not only were Freud and Adler different in intellectual skills and theoretical viewpoint, but, more important, each was a distinctly different *type* of personality.

The Freudian interpretation of the case just discussed centers on the woman's problem with unresolved sexual and affectional dependence on the father. That pattern of dependence on a significant *external love object* is repeated, in the Freudian view, throughout the woman's life (e.g., with her husband). For Freud, according to Jung, the key element is the individual's conscious and unconscious relationship to people and things in the external world (1917, p. 41).

For Adler, on the other hand, the focus is more *subjective* with the accent on the individual's striving for *inner* security and compensation for perceived *personal* inferiority, as interpreted by Jung.

Out of his ruminations on the differences in approach of Adler and Freud, Jung formulated a problem:

> The spectacle of this dilemma made me ponder the question: are there at least two different human types, one of them more interested in the [external] object, the other more interested in himself? [1917, p. 43]

Adler, it seemed to Jung, was an *introvert* whereas Freud appeared to be more of an *extrovert*.

> The first attitude [introversion] is normally characterized by a hesitant, reflective, retiring nature that keeps itself to itself, shrinks from objects, is always slightly on the defensive and prefers to hide behind mistrustful scrutiny. The second [extroversion] is normally characterized by an outgoing, candid, and accommodating nature that adapts easily to a given situation, quickly forms attachments, and, setting aside any possible misgivings, will often venture forth with careless confidence into unknown situations. [Jung, 1917, p. 44]

Thus, personality type constrains an individual's perception of events. Freud and Adler each was bound by his personality type to see only one viable interpretation of the psychology of others.

Jung proposed that the differences between the introvert and the extrovert in relation to subjective and objective experience were not absolute. In some cases, the introvert will be more interested in the objective, external world, *when that world affects his inner life.* Conversely, the extrovert is more interested in the subjective world *when the objective world has caused him disappointment.* Then, the extrovert will withdraw into moodiness and subjective, egocentric behavior.

At all events, it is clear that Jung was not satisfied with the simple division of personality into two gross, rigid types (1921, p. 6). He postulated, in addition to the attitude types of introversion/extroversion, four *functional types:* (1) sensation; (2) intuition; (3) thinking; (4) feeling. Thus, the introvert and extrovert personalities admit of gradations and variety. In all, disregarding the infinite variety that *degree* of expression may provide, there are eight combined attitude-function types of introvert and extrovert. A brief consideration of the four functions is in order before a survey of these eight types is undertaken.

The Functions of the Psyche

Jung postulated that the mind has a number of specific functions directed on the one hand to mediating intercourse with the external world, and on the other, focused on relations with one's own inner world, the world of the personal and collective unconscious. To those functions of consciousness directed outwardly to the world, Jung gave the name *ectopsychic.* To the functions of the unconscious in its relations with the ego, Jung gave the name *endopsychic* (1968, p. 11). The endopsychic functions were not emphasized in Jung's theory and they will be omitted in the present discussion.

Ectopsychic Functions

The ectopsychic functions were those that Jung emphasized in constructing his introversion/extroversion typology. The first ectopsychic function
is *sensation,* "which is the sum total of external facts given to me through
the functions of my senses" (Jung, 1968, p. 11). Thus sensation is concerned with orientation to reality: "Sensation tells me that something *is;*
it does not tell me *what* it is" (Jung, 1968, p. 11; 1921, p. 461, definition
47).

The second ectopsychic function is *thinking* and is complementary to
sensation, for thinking "in its simplest form tells you *what* a thing is. It
gives a name to the thing" (Jung, 1968, p. 11; 1921, p. 481, definition 53).
For Jung, the term *thinking* was to be restricted to "the linking up of ideas
by means of a concept, in other words, to an act of judgment, no matter
whether this act is intentional or not" (1921, p. 481).

The third ectopsychic function is *feeling.* For Jung, the concept of feeling
had a somewhat restricted meaning. "Feeling informs you through its
feeling-tones of the values of things. Feeling tells you for instance whether
a thing is acceptable or agreeable or not. It tells you what a thing is *worth*
to you" (1968, p. 12).

Feeling may give rise in isolated circumstances to *mood,* an emotional
state of acceptance or rejection. Thus feeling is a subjective process that
is independent of external stimuli (Jung, 1921, p. 434, definition 21).

The fourth and last ectopsychic function is *intuition.* Sensation tells us
that a thing is; thinking tells us what that thing is; and feeling tells us what
that thing is worth to us. The only conscious function left is an awareness
of time, the past and the future of a thing, where it has come from and
where it is going. Intuition is comprised of hunchlike feelings about the
origins and the prospects of a thing (Jung, 1968, p. 13). Jung found it very
difficult to define intuition, but he pointed to the conditions, familiar to
mostly everyone, under which we employ intuition: "Whenever you have
to deal with strange conditions where you have no established values or
established concepts, you will depend upon that faculty of intuition"
(1968, p. 14). Thus, intuition is the psychological function that mediates
perceptions in an unconscious way so that our experience of intuitive
problem solutions is that they spring on us suddenly, without conscious
intent (Jung, 1921, p. 453, definition 35).

Rational versus Irrational Ectopsychic Functions

The four ectopsychic functions can be further classified as *rational* or
irrational, depending upon the degree of judgment or reasoning involved.
Hence, *sensation* and *intuition* are classed as *irrational* because conscious
reasoning is, by Jung's definitions, virtually absent. By contrast, *feeling* and

thinking are classed as *rational* functions because both involve the judg-mental process and the "supremacy of reason" (Jung, 1921, pp. 359 ff.; and 1968, p. 12).

During the course of his famous Tavistock Lectures, Jung employed the diagram shown in Figure 4–2 to summarize the four ectopsychic functions and their relationships in the psyche. In the central circle of Figure 4–2 is the ego, the center of conscious self-awareness and possessor of the psy-chic energy. At the top of the compasslike diagram is thinking (T) and its direct opposite on the lowest spoke, feeling (F). Thus, the diagram repre-sents the type of person whose *superior function* (topmost in the diagram) is reason or thought, and whose *inferior function* (lowermost spoke) is feeling, "for when you think, you must exclude feeling, just as when you feel you must exclude thinking" (Jung, 1968, p. 16).

To represent the opposite type of personality, the individual for whom feeling is the superior function and thinking the inferior, the T and F spokes would be reversed. The two other possible types of personality may be represented, depending upon the dominance of either sensation or intuition, by rotating the spokes of the compass accordingly.

Each of these four functional types may dominate the basic introvert or extrovert attitude orientation. The eight resulting personality types are summarized in Figure 4–3.

Jung's typology of introversion/extroversion bears careful scrutiny be-cause it has been a source of fruitful empirical research for a variety of investigators in recent years. Foremost among these has been Hans Ey-senck. His experimental and factor analytic work in exploring the biologi-cal bases of introversion/extroversion and neuroticism/normality dimensions has progressed for nearly thirty years (Eysenck, 1967; see Chapter 15 of this book for an account of Eysenck's theory).

FIGURE 4-2: THE FUNCTIONS OF THE PSYCHE

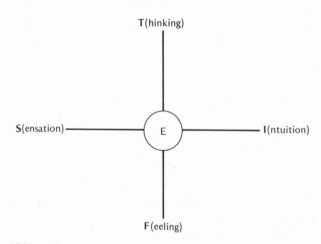

After Jung, 1968, p. 59.

FIGURE 4-3: **THE JUNGIAN COMBINED ATTITUDE AND FUNCTION TYPOLOGY**

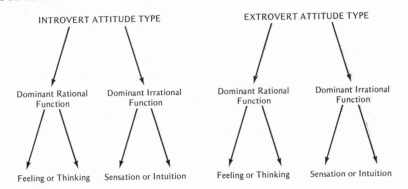

The Extrovert Types

From our discussion thus far, it is clear that Jung's typology is not a gross classification of individuals into mutually exclusive categories. Rather, Jung pictured his typology as having the breadth and flexibility to allow for an infinite number of possible permutations of function, attitude, and degree. However, because they exemplify in clear-cut fashion the characteristics of pure types, extreme cases were the dominant illustrations Jung employed in delineating his scheme.

The extrovert, it will be recalled, is dominated by the external object to the detriment of subjective experience. Powerfully influenced by his social surroundings, the extrovert is consequently shaped by the moral and ethical climate of his culture, and therefore by the opinions and values of those close to him. Greatest of the dangers for the extreme extrovert is that he gets "sucked into objects and completely loses himself in them" (Jung, 1921, p. 336). Thus, in Jung's view, the most typical neurosis of the extrovert is hysteria, for hysterical reactions are essentially primitive, dependent attitudes toward people and things in the environment. Eysenck (e.g., 1967, 1953a and b) has marshalled a good bit of empirical evidence that supports this view.

Extrovert Thinking Type (Rational): Objective, Rigid, Cold

The *thinking extrovert* is "captured" by external ideas and objects; he is unable to escape their influence in solving problems. He may give the impression of a certain shortsightedness or lack of freedom in the drawing of logical conclusions because he refuses to go beyond the objective facts at hand.

Emotionally, the thinking extrovert subjugates everything to the intellect, refusing to see any other principle for himself or others to follow than the power of his own decision making. His moral code is correspondingly rigid and intolerant of exception. His struggle is for objective and valid universal truths (Jung, 1921, p. 347). "Oughts" and "musts" dominate the thinking extrovert's approach to values, and his thinking tends to be dogmatic.

Since thinking is his superior function, the feeling side of his life is suppressed. He may, therefore, give the impression of being cold or indifferent. Key concise trait descriptions are *objective, rigid,* and *cold.*

Extrovert Feeling Type (Rational): Intense, Effervescent, Sociable

Dominance by the feeling function is most characteristic of women, according to Jung (1921, p. 356). Like the thinking extrovert, the *feeling extrovert* seeks harmony with the external world. His/her thinking function is kept suppressed behind a facade of loud gushing talk and intense displays of extravagant emotional responsivity. There is, of course, a tendency to make friends easily and to be influenced by the feeling-tone of social situations. Key trait descriptions are *intense, effervescent,* and *sociable.*

Extrovert Sensation Type (Irrational): Realistic, Sensual, Jolly

The *sensation extrovert's* life-style is a search for new sensory experiences and the accumulation of actual experiences of concrete objects (1921, p. 363). He may refine his sensory powers to a high pitch so that he is not merely a gross sensual type, but rather a connoisseur of fine wines, a discriminating judge of art. The sensation extrovert is usually good company, for he suppresses any tendency to introspection and self-concern, favoring instead minute attention to objective, external detail.

He tends to be well adjusted to reality and concerned for the welfare of others. Key trait descriptions are *realistic, sensual, jolly.*

Extrovert Intuitive Type (Irrational): Visionary, Changeable, Creative

The *intuitive extrovert* has difficulty maintaining an interest in any one thing for very long. Usually, this type flits from one novel idea to another, and he stays with each only until the novelty wears off. Because in the intuitive type thinking and feeling, the rational functions, are at a minimum, this individual tends to make decisions without conscious, reflective thought. Yet his decisions are likely to be good ones, though based on hunches, because the intuitive extrovert is closely in touch with the wisdom of his own unconscious. Consideration for the welfare of others is

weakly developed in the intuitive extrovert. However, the intuitive extroverts are valuable to society because they have the capacity to inspire
confidence and enthusiasm for new causes and adventuresome undertakings. Thus, key trait words describing the intuitive extrovert are *visionary*,
changeable, and *creative*.

The Introvert Types

The introvert attitude, it will be recalled, implies that the individual is
aware of external conditions, but that he emphasizes his subjective reactions to them as decisive. The introvert's orientation to life may be characterized as a struggle to keep his ego independent of external influences and
tugs. Typically, if the extreme introvert succumbs to neurosis, it will be to
psychasthenia. This neurosis is, as might be expected, characterized by
intense anxiety reactions, chronic fatigue, and exhaustion. Eysenck has
marshaled evidence that this neurotic disposition was more than a haphaz-
ard guess on Jung's part.

Introvert Thinking Type (Rational): Theoretical, Intellectual, Impractical

When the introvert's consciousness is dominated by the thinking function,
he presents a picture of the stereotypical intellectual, the "egg head."
Concerned with abstractions and with the creation of theories for their
own sake, the *thinking introvert* has a tendency to ignore the practicalities
of everyday living. "His judgment appears cold, inflexible, arbitrary, and
ruthless, because it relates far less to the [external] object than to the
subject [himself]" (Jung, 1921, p. 384).

The *thinking introvert* develops an intense desire for privacy and is
horrified when anyone threatens to invade his solitary domain. Hence, the
key trait descriptions of the thinking introvert are *theoretical, intellectual,
impractical*.

Introvert Feeling Type (Rational): Silent, Childish, Indifferent

More common among women, dominance of consciousness by feeling in
the introvert produces a picture of cold indifference to others. Sometimes
this impression is fostered by a suggestion that "still waters run deep." The
feeling introvert seemingly has no concern for the feelings or opinions of
others. There is even a faint air of superiority and critical neutrality in the
feeling introvert's relations with others. Emotional expression is kept to a

minimum, for inwardly the feeling introvert's emotions are intense and troublesome. Sometimes, his emotions are so intense that they are expressed in the writing of poetry that is scrupulously kept from the prying eyes of others. Key trait descriptions are *silent, childish,* and *indifferent.*

Introvert Sensation Type (Irrational): Passive, Calm, Artistic

The *sensation introvert* is dominated by the changing flux of external events. Their subjective influence is of paramount importance, for the only thing that matters to the sensation type of introvert is his personal reaction to objective sensory events. His thinking and feeling functions are primitively expressed, and he is oriented mythologically or poetically to interpret his world. That is to say, he evaluates his sense impressions in terms of clear-cut categories of good and evil—strictly, of course, with reference to what is good and evil *for him.* He sometimes misinterprets reality and becomes separated from the external world, but he remains calmly undisturbed when others point this out to him. Key trait descriptions are *passive, calm,* and *artistic.*

Introvert Intuitive Type (Irrational): Mystical, Dreamer, Unique

When intuition gains the ascendancy in the introvert, he tends to be aloof and unconcerned about concrete reality or external events. He presents the stereotypical picture of the "peculiar artist" or the slightly "mad genius" whose productive efforts result in strange but beautiful creations. Perception is the *intuitive introvert's* main problem, for he is enmeshed in shaping meaning from his perceptions that will satisfy his inner self. Thus, he may become estranged from those around him and be viewed as a "wise man gone wrong" or as a crank and "oddball." Key descriptive traits are *mystic, dreamer,* and *unique.*

Summary

Jung emphasized that the extremes depicted in the previous list of eight combined attitude-function types rarely exist in pure form. Furthermore, he suggested that an individual of a given type may undergo change as conditions of his personal and collective unconscious change (1921, p. 405). Precisely which of the functions will be superior or differentiated fully within an individual's total personality will depend on his need for auxiliary or compensatory functions to achieve adaption to his life circumstances.

The Process of Individuation: "Enantiodromia"

With Jung's emphasis on the collective unconscious, inherited archetypal images, and on the classification of personality types, it might seem that he was uninterested in *individual* personality development. Nothing could be further from the facts. Jung spent a good deal of the latter part of his life exploring the processes by which a person becomes a complete individual. That is to say, Jung investigated the psychological processes of *differentiation* by which an individual develops his unique pattern of traits and his idiosyncratic relationship to his personal and collective unconscious. Jung called this development of a clearly personal pattern of traits *individuation*. Individuation, in short, is the process by which a person harmonizes his unconscious with his ego (1939, p. 287).

Jung believed that every human has an innate tendency to pursue this inner harmony, and he called it the *transcendent function*. The transcendent function is the motive force behind the individual's desire to come to terms with all aspects of himself and guides his need to accept the content of his unconscious as "mine" (Jung, 1916, p. 73). Individuation and the transcendent function are thus opposite sides of the same coin. Individuation refers to the attainment of full development of all sides of oneself into a unique configuration. The transcendent function is the guiding force in the achievement of this idiosyncratic "wholeness."

Jung's method of helping his patients to attain individuation involved the process of *active imagination*. Jung instructed his patients in the art of consciously focusing on dream images or on fantasy figures in an effort to elaborate them willfully and to embellish such unconscious creations purposefully. Active imagination might best be compared to a form of meditation that enables the individual to capitalize knowingly on self-knowledge that would otherwise remain untapped. By active imagination, Jung's patients could truly examine every aspect of their personalities.

Within every personality Jung discerned a multiplicity of conflicting themes, discordant opposites, and antagonistic forces. Thus, for the anima, there is the animus; for introversion, there is extroversion; for thinking, sensation; for sensation, feeling; for the personal unconscious, there is the collective unconscious; the ego is opposed by the shadow; the God archetype has its counterpart in the Demon; causal explanations should be complemented with acausal, synchronistic ones; and dreams can be analyzed not only in terms of the dreamer's past, but in terms of his future.

Jung employed a term from Heraclitus, the fifth century B.C. Greek philosopher, to label the conflicting, sometimes complementary, but usually opposed themes of the human condition. Jung referred to these opposites as examples of *enantiodromia*, literally as a "running counter to" (1921, p. 425, definition 18). Initially, Jung restricted the term to the emergence of an unconscious function or idea that was opposite to an individual's conscious dominant function. Eventually, however, Jung began to see the development of personality as a goal-directed enterprise, marked by a striving toward the *equal* development of *all* parts of the psyche. Thus, opposites must coalesce in the individuated person. Each of us must develop not only his rationality, but must accept his irrationality with equal fervor; not only must we strive to adapt our egos to life, but we must recognize the shadow's influence; not only must we venerate what is God-like in ourselves, we must respect what is most base. Failure to recognize the opposite tendency within ourselves can lead only to the feeling of being torn apart (Jung, 1917, p. 73; 1957, pp. 302 ff.). Success at individuation means the acceptance of inherent enantiodromia.

Individuation, however, is a product of the mature years. Throughout life, the individual's development is oriented toward the attainment of one goal: the reconciliation of opposites. Within the fully differentiated, individuated personality, then, there develops a final psychological organization that embodies all the discordant elements, slighting none, emphasizing all equally. To this reconciler of opposites, Jung gave the name *self* (1950, p. 267). "In the end we have to acknowledge that the self is a *complexio oppositorum* precisely because there can be no reality without polarity" (Jung, 1950, p. 267). The self is the ultimate individuation.

Development of the Self: A Teleological View of Life

Jung had treated a variety of middle-aged patients who, while not mentally ill by any definition, were nonetheless discontent. They were ill at ease with themselves and alienated from any possible satisfaction in life. These patients had, in Jung's view, developed altogether too one-sidedly. One particular psychic function had become differentiated at the cost of others. These alienated middle-aged patients could be helped by psychotherapy only if Jung could aid them in developing the stunted functions of their psyches. In short, the process of individuation, the creation of the self as reconciler of opposites, had not occurred for them.

These individuals had arrived at middle age with their sense of purpose completely undeveloped. For Jung, life does not proceed randomly. It is purposive or *teleological,* and shaped by beckoning goals. The purpose of an individual's life is attained when he is fully integrated, completely in harmony with himself. Some individuals find their purpose in religion, some discover their life's goal in helping their fellow man, and yet others find purpose in simply living each day with care. But in every case, the purposive individual has accepted the basic enantiodromia of life.

The Self as Archetype

The most perfect mythological symbol of the self is Christ. "He [Christ] is our culture hero, who regardless of his historical existence, embodies the myth of the divine Primordial Man, the mystic Adam. . . . *Christ exemplifies the archetype of the self.* He represents a totality of a divine or heavenly kind, a glorified man, a son of God *sine macula peccati,* unspotted by sin" (Jung, 1950, pp. 36–37).

Even the divine archetypal figure of the self is a composite of opposites: Christ and Anti-Christ, God and Satan, the Prince of Light and the Prince of Darkness (1950, p. 44).

Thus the self, that totality of opposites, that unique combination of perfection and baseness, was prefigured in man's mythology and religion by symbols of the God-man. The early Christian concept of Christ implied an "all embracing totality that even includes the animal side of man" (1950, p. 41). It is clear, therefore, that Jung regards man's need for religion, for God, as an inherent drive directed toward self-fulfillment. Without God to aspire to, man is forever condemned to the incompleteness of his own existence. For Jung's theory the question of God's existence is nearly irrelevant because it can never be answered with certainty. What is important is man's *belief* in God's existence, for without that belief, his inherent need for wholeness is denied.

Jung found in his explorations of mythology and alchemy that the self was often archetypically symbolized by a *mandala.* Mandala is a Sanskrit word meaning "circle." In various mythologies, religious rituals, and in the dreams and fantasies of his patients, a variety of mandalalike figures could be observed. Sometimes the mandala is divided into four segments around which is drawn the characteristic circular enclosure. Figure 4–4 illustrates a mandala drawing by one of Jung's patients. The coiled snake within the circle is seemingly trying to wend its way out of the enclosure. Jung himself was seized on occasion with the compulsion to create mandala figures in paint.

> Only gradually did I discover what the mandala is: "Formation, Transformation, Eternal Mind's eternal recreation [*Faust*]." And that is the self, the wholeness of personality, which if all goes well is harmonious, but which cannot tolerate self-deceptions. [Jung, 1961, pp. 195–196]

In the delicately balanced harmonies of the mandala, Jung discerned a mythic expression of the self as the reconciler of opposites. The precise juxtaposition of colors and shadings and the fourfold spatial division of the circle symbolize the harmony of the self. This fourfold division of many mandalas is the instinctive expression of man's desire to create organization from chaos, to plot on a schema of four coordinates the confusing flux of his inner and outer life. Each individual's approach to the attainment of self-harmony is unique and occurs only once in time, as the Christ figure symbolizes. But even the Christ figure has to be expressed in antagonistic terms, a complementarity of opposites.

Figure 4–5 expresses an analogy of the self through the historical and mythical figure of Christ. "As an historical personage Christ is unitemporal [once in time] and unique; as God, universal and eternal. Likewise the self:

FIGURE 4-4: A MANDALA DRAWING BY ONE OF JUNG'S PATIENTS

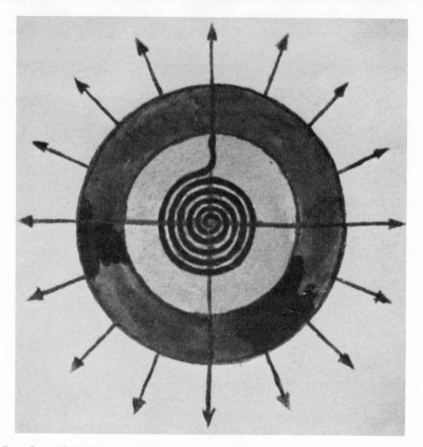

From Jung, 1950, "Concerning Mandala Symbolism."

as the essence of individuality it is unitemporal and unique; as an archetypal symbol it is a God-image and therefore universal and eternal" (Jung,
1950, p. 63).

Christ also embodied another fourfold division of opposites: *Good*
(Christ) versus *Evil* (Anti-Christ) and *spiritual* (Divine) versus *material*
(man). Thus, Jung illustrated this composite of opposites with another set
of coordinates, shown here in Figure 4-6.

Because the self is a totality, it must embody both light and dark, good
and evil. The fully individuated person can freely accept both aspects of
his psyche, and he can willingly strive to unite the two into wholeness.

In consequence, for Jung, the goal of psychotherapy, indeed, the goal
of the well-lived life, is the attainment of wholeness, the individual's
recognition of the opposites within himself, and the achievement of harmony through the articulation of the separate parts.

Jung was able to face ambiguity and uncertainty. In fact, it would be

FIGURE 4-5: CHRIST AS AN ARCHTYPE OF THE SELF—THE FIRST SET OF OPPOSITES

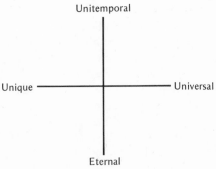

After Jung, 1950, p. 63.

FIGURE 4-6. CHRIST AS AN ARCHTYPE OF THE SELF—THE SECOND SET OF OPPOSITES

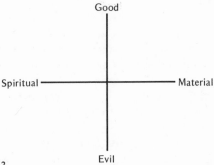

After Jung, 1950, p. 63.

fair to say that Jung was fascinated by antimonies and by paradoxes. Toward the end of his life, Jung was able to accept the rational and the irrational as copartners in the events of the psyche. He was, furthermore, capable of welcoming the mysterious with a relish no less than his acceptance of the merely logical. Perhaps the period of his own turmoil in childhood, and his self-analysis of the 1913–1917 "stormy period" prepared the way for his resignation to the conflicting pulls of a complex existence.

Summary

Beginning his career in the tradition of classical clinical psychiatry, Carl Gustav Jung soon developed a tool of investigation that brought his thinking close to that of Sigmund Freud. The word-association test, in Jung's innovative hands, revealed that normal and neurotic subjects harbored latent and inexpressible ideas and feelings. These emotional complexes, as Jung called them, could be objectively demonstrated in the pauses, hesitations, and inhibitions of the subject as he or she reacted to a list of stimulus words. Jung realized that the recorded reaction times and various other physiological measures could serve as hard evidence that Freud was right about the nature of unconscious conflict.

Eventually, however, Jung pursued a path different from Freud's when he found himself unable to accept the exclusively sexual nature of Freud's "libido." In working with his own patients, Jung discovered residues of racial history in their fantasies. His own childhood experiences with visions and alternative personalities had prepared him to accept the possibility that some psychic content might arise from sources external to the individual. His self-analysis (from 1913 to 1917) of the dreams, visions, and nightmares that flooded his consciousness convinced him more strongly that a "higher" power was responsible for at least some of the content of mental life. He therefore postulated a personal unconscious similar to Freud's concept, and a collective unconscious that transcends the personal experiences of the individual.

Within the collective unconscious there are stored inherited predispositions to respond with great emotion to specific events. These predispositions, which Jung called *archetypes,* include the animus and anima, the Hero, God, the shadow, and the persona. Jung felt that the archetypes were solid evidence of the innate symbol-making tendency man had inherited from his ancestors.

In trying to resolve the differences between himself and Freud, and between Freud and Adler, Jung postulated two personality types: the introvert and the extrovert. The introvert is characterized by his withdrawal from social stimulation, his intensely subjective interest in things intellectual, and his reliance on the power of his own feelings. The extrovert, much the opposite, is dominated by objective, external reality and is socially oriented. In addition to these attitude types, Jung proposed four functions: thinking and feeling (rational), and intuition and sensation (irrational). Introverts and extroverts can each be dominated by one or more of these functions leading to an eightfold combined typology.

In his later years, Jung came to emphasize the spiritual side of man's existence. He discovered individuals for whom life had lost its purpose. Jung postulated that to achieve full individuality, or *individuation* as he called it, the person must form a psychological organization that can reconcile all of the opposing and contradictory trends within the psyche. To this reconciler of opposites, Jung gave the name self. Within the history of mankind, the self has been mythologically prefigured by the Hero archetype, and most eminent of the hero myths is the Christ figure as the God-man.

Jung's tolerance for ambiguity and the mysterious finds great disfavor among contemporary, hard-nosed empirical psychologists. Fortunately, Jung's popularity as a theorist who expresses the spiritual side of man is currently on the rise among a generation of young students and professional psychologists.

FOR FURTHER READING

Jung wrote for various purposes three relatively concise introductions to his work that will serve as useful first contacts with his writing. In order of value to the serious student these introductions are: *Analytical Psychology: Its Theory and Practice* (New York: Pantheon, 1968), which is the published version of Jung's Tavistock Lectures, and the most readable of his writings; *Two Essays on Analytical Psychology* (vol. 7 of *The Collected Works of C. G. Jung* [Princeton, N.J.: Princeton University Press, 1953]), a work that is somewhat more difficult but also more characteristic of Jung's style; and *Man and His Symbols* (New York: Doubleday, 1964; available in paperback), which is a lavishly, though at times superficially, illustrated compendium of Jungian thought by both Jung himself and several of his collaborators as an attempt to more widely disseminate Jung's thinking to contemporary readers.

To gain some of the flavor of Jung's religious and spiritual researches, his *The Archetypes of the Collective Unconscious* (vol. 9 of *The Collected Works* [Princeton, N.J.: Princeton University Press, 1968], though difficult in style, will introduce the reader to his characteristic form of presenting hypotheses drawn from clinical, mythological, and historical sources.

Two recent biographies of Jung present drastically different pictures of the same man and should be read together to achieve balance. Laurens van der Post's *Jung and the Story of Our Time* (New York: Pantheon, 1975) is a spiritual rather than intellectual account of Jung's life and influence based on van der Post's personal relationship with Jung. Very sympathetic and mystical, approaching almost hero worship, van der Post emphasizes Jung's image as a "wise old man." A somewhat more realistic view that sometimes borders on hostility is provided by Paul J. Stern in *C. G. Jung: The Haunted Prophet* (New York: Braziller, 1976). Stern attempts to make the case for Jung's personal psychotic episodes as the basis of his later theoretical ideas and succeeds in providing a more objective view of Jung's personality than van der Post. Neither of these biographies should be consulted without Jung's own account of his life and work given in his *Memories, Dreams and Reflections*, edited by Aniela Jaffé (New York: Pantheon, 1961). Further personal insights may be gleaned from *The Freud/Jung Letters*, edited by William McGuire (Princeton, N.J.: Princeton University Press, 1974), in which the development, course, and final break-up of Freud and Jung's relationship may be witnessed.

Richard I. Evans' interview with Jung is contained in *Conversations with Carl Jung and Reactions from Ernest Jones* (Princeton, N.J.: Van Nostrand, 1964), or in condensed form in Evans' *The Making of Psychology* (New York: Knopf, 1976). Gerhard Adler's *Studies in Analytical Psychology* (New York: Putnam, 1969) shows Jungian therapy at its best through studies of dreams and detailed case histories. A view of how the contemporary Jungian analyst operates may be obtained from E. C. Whitmont and Y. Kaufmann's "Analytical Psychotherapy," in Raymond Corsini (Ed.), *Current Psychotherapies* (Itasca, Ill.: Peacock, 1973), ch. 3.

Aniela Jaffé, Jung's long-time student and colleague during the later part of his life, attempts to explicate some controversial aspects of Jung's thinking and career in her *From the Life and Work of C. G. Jung* (New York: Harper & Row, 1971; available in paperback). Jaffé's essays are particularly worthwhile in the areas of explaining Jung's alleged antisemitism and his equally dubious sympathy for the Nazi philosophy. In contrast, Gustav Jahoda provides some criticism of Jung's ideas, especially his concept of synchronicity, in *The Psychology of Superstition* (Baltimore: Penguin, 1969), ch. 7.

Three paperback books attempt to provide a comprehensive treatment of Jung's ideas. The classic one and the easiest to read is Frieda Fordham's *An Introduction to Jung's Psychology* (Baltimore: Penguin, 1953). Anthony Storr's *Jung* (New York: Viking, 1973) is more detailed than Fordham's book and somewhat less authoritative. Calvin Hall and Vernon Nordby's *A Primer of Jungian Psychology* (New York: New American Library, 1973) is the most sympathetic and uncritical account of the three.

For comparative purposes, the reader may want to explore Chapter 15 of the present book for a detailed account of Hans Eysenck's formulation of an experimentally testable introvert-extrovert typology. Eysenck began, but did not long remain, with Jung's conceptions.

5 ALFRED ADLER
Individual Psychology

The most important question of the healthy and the diseased mental life is not whence? but, whither?

ALFRED ADLER, *The Individual Psychology of Alfred Adler*

The neurotic striving for power . . . is born out of anxiety, hatred and feelings of inferiority. To put it categorically, the normal striving for power is born of strength, the neurotic of weakness.

KAREN HORNEY, *The Neurotic Personality of Our Time*

The Cemetery That Wasn't There

The men and women who create personality theories have sovereign personalities of their own. Consequently, some part of each theorist's comprehension of human character is always a reflection of his self-comprehension. For the young Alfred Adler the reigning themes of childhood existence were fear and anger: fear in the face of death, and anger at the frailty thus imposed. Adler was able to recall a particularly revealing episode of his boyhood attempts to master what his five-year-old mentality perceived as cowardice:

> I remember that the path to the school led over a cemetery. I was frightened every time and was exceedingly put out at *beholding the other children pass the cemetery without paying the least attention to it, while every step I took was accompanied by a feeling of fear and horror.* Apart from the extreme discomfort occasioned by this fear I was also annoyed at the idea *of being less courageous than the others.* One day I made up my mind to put an end to this fear of death. Again, I decided upon a treatment of hardening. I stayed at some distance behind the others, placed my schoolbag on the ground near the wall of the cemetery and ran across it a dozen times, until I felt that I had mastered the fear. [Adler, 1959, pp. 179–180; italics added]

Of significance to Adler-the-theorist was the fact that this recollection showed Adler-the-child attempting bravely to confront his fear and to master the sense of helplessness and inferiority it evoked.

At the age of thirty-five, in conversation with a childhood school chum, Adler learned that there had never been a cemetery on the way to their school (Adler, 1959, p. 180; Orgler, 1963, p. 37). This poignant "memory" had been a "poetic" expression of Adler's striving to overcome the fear of death. Death had been Adler's ready companion throughout childhood, and the struggle to overcome it, Adler later recognized from his theoretical perspective, was the central goal of his life.

The Fear of Death and the Anger at Being Helpless

Adler's unconscious had woven what Freud called a "screen-memory" around an illusory cemetery and feelings of fear and anger. This screen-memory was the culmination of a childhood series of brushes with death. As a young boy, Adler had twice been run over in the streets, and he could recall regaining consciousness on the living-room sofa (Orgler, 1963, p. 2). When he was only three years old, Adler's younger brother died in a bed beside his. At the age of five, the period to which the cemetery recollection dates, Adler became so profoundly ill with pneumonia that the family physician gave him up for lost. Fortunately, another physician prescribed some treatment and within a few days the "lost" boy was well on his way to recovery. Adler recounted the lasting emotional significance of this brush with death:

> In the joy over my recovery, there was talk for a long time about the mortal danger in which I was supposed to have been. From that time on I recall always thinking of myself in the future as a physician. *This means that I had set a goal from which I could expect an end to my childlike distress, my fear of death.* Clearly, I expected more from the occupation of my choice than it could accomplish: The overcoming of death and the fear of death is something I should not have expected from human, but only from divine accomplishments. Reality, however, demands action, and so I was forced to modify my goal by changing the conscious form of the guiding fiction [life-goal] until it appeared to satisfy reality. So I came to choose the occupation of physician in order to overcome death and the fear of death. [Adler, in Ansbacher and Ansbacher, 1956, p. 199; italics added]

But even as a physician Adler could not tolerate death. Hertha Orgler (1963), Adler's biographer and friend, reports that Adler gave up his general medical practice after the death of several of his diabetic patients. Powerless to forestall these patients' deaths in the days before the discovery of insulin, Adler was overwhelmed by his old enemy.

In addition to his intimate contacts with death throughout his youth, Adler was a chronically sick and weak child. He suffered from rickets, a deficiency disease that results in softening of the bones. He was thus unable to compete well with his older brother or with peers in the physically active pastimes of childhood (Orgler, 1963; Bottome, 1957). Another of Adler's childhood recollections drawn from the age of two years again indicates his special sensitivity to feelings of inferiority:

> I remember sitting on a bench bandaged up on account of rickets, with *my healthy elder brother* sitting opposite me. *He could run, jump, and move about quite effortlessly,* while for me, movement of any sort was a strain and an effort. *Everyone went to great pains to help me* and my mother and father did all that was in their power to do. [Quoted in Bottome, 1957, pp. 30–31; italics added]

The importance of this memory lies in Adler's comparison of himself with his older brother, who apparently made Adler feel all the more acutely his physical limitations. Moreover, as Mosak and Kopp (1973, p. 158) point out in their analysis of Adler's early recollections, the young Adler had discovered that there was much to be gained from one's organ defects in the way of sympathy and concern from the powerful people in one's life.

In addition to his acute sense of inferiority, Adler succumbed to a deep resentment over the birth of his younger brother, for this child "dethroned" him from his place of distinction in his mother's heart. It was, however, the mother, not his younger brother, who became the target of Adler's resentment. Therefore, Adler came to prefer his father, who encouraged his son to master life's difficulties on his own terms.

By the age of three years, Adler had come to the extraordinary insight that another of his physical problems, contractures and spasms of his vocal cords, was caused by his own feelings of anger and resentment toward his mother and older brother. As with his fear of the cemetery, or more precisely the fear of death, he resolved to confront these unruly feelings and to bring his anger and resentment under control (Orgler, 1963, p. 215). He became a model young man, sociable, affable, outgoing, and altruistic. The hallmark of his style of life was concern for the welfare of others, a theme of existence for which Adler coined a new German word, *Gemein-schaftsgefühl* (most meaningfully translated as *social interest*), in his later theory of personality.

Three essential elements, then, marked Adler's early personality development and, consequently, the structure of his theory of personality. First among these personal elements were his repeated brushes with death, his own and that of loved ones. Second, his physical disability and clumsiness in comparison with his older brother and peers forced Adler into a position of inferiority he struggled consciously to overcome. Finally, he harbored resentment toward his mother for transferring her affections to his younger brother; what degree of guilt emerged from this childish anger when the younger brother died Adler's biographers do not tell us. The key element in Adler's early life history remains his boyhood exposure to and attempts to master the fear of death. Perhaps with his own life history in mind, Adler was later to theorize:

> In all probability none but human beings are conscious of the fact that death is in the destiny of life, and this consciousness alone is enough to give mankind a sense of being terribly overpowered by Nature. If a child experiences a brusque contact with death at an early age, the whole style of life may be largely moulded by that single impression. In such a case the importance of death to life is invariably over-valued, and we can often perceive how the child's actions and reactions are so directed as to find relief from this oppressive idea, or compensate for it. [Adler, 1929b, p. 145]

Adler further suggested that the confrontation with death could have far-reaching consequences for the direction the remainder of the child's life might take. To circumvent his personal death, an individual may seek to *prolong his life through his children* and thereby to gain a small measure of immortality through his contribution to the continuity of the species. Other individuals may seek to defy death through *the attainment of personal greatness in art or science,* thus assuring their survival in the works and ideas they leave for posterity. Finally, the fear of death may be allayed by commitment to *the belief in the immortality of one's soul,* a religious faith that, after all, death is not the final victor of life's struggle. Clearly Adler chose for himself the second of these directions, for in the act of selecting the vocation of physician, he chose to struggle actively against death.

Adler's, Freud's, and Jung's Early Recollections Compared

Interestingly, there is some evidence to suggest that among personality theorists, Adler was not alone in according death a special place among the influences of his life. Mosak and Kopp (1973) compared Adler's early recollections with several of Freud's and Jung's early memories, drawn from their own and their biographers' writings. Freud's early memories seem to indicate that he was a doubter and a skeptic, but once convinced of death's inevitability, his doubt was supplanted by awe:

> When I was six years old and was given my first lessons by my mother, I was expected to believe that we were all made of earth and must therefore return to earth. This did not suit me and I expressed doubts of the doctrine. My mother thereupon rubbed the palms of her hands together—just as she did in making dumplings, except that there was no dough between them—and showed me the blackish scales of *epidermis* produced by the friction as a proof that we were made of earth. My astonishment at this ocular demonstration knew

no bounds and I acquiesced in the belief which I was later to hear expressed in the words: *"Du bist der Natur einen Tod schuldig"* ["Thou owest Nature a death"]. [Freud, 1900, vol. IV, p. 205]

In light of Freud's later theory of the death instinct as an inexorable force inherent in living matter, it is not difficult to agree with Mosak and Kopp that Freud was awed by death. (See Chapter 3 of this book for a discussion of Freud's death instinct.)

Jung, on the other hand, was fascinated by death, attracted by the mystery and uncertainty of it. Two incidents he recorded from approximately his fourth year of life are suggestive of his attitude:

> And once there was a great flood. The river Wiese, which flowed through the village, had broken its dam, and in its upper reaches a bridge had collapsed. Fourteen people were drowned and were carried down by the yellow flood water to the Rhine. When the water retreated, some of the corpses got stuck in the sand. When I was told about it, there was no holding me. I actually found the body of a middle-aged man, in a black frock coat; apparently he had just come from church. He lay half covered by sand, his arm over his eyes. Similarly, I was fascinated to watch a pig being slaughtered. To the horror of my mother, I watched the whole procedure. She thought it terrible, but the slaughtering and the dead man were simply matters of interest to me. [Jung, 1961, p. 15]

It is possible to interpret each theorist's early recollection of an experience with death as one indicator of that person's style of life. Mosak and Kopp contrasted the significance of each theorist's early recollections for understanding the life goals of Adler's, Jung's, and Freud's adult personalities:

> Although all three show an interest in death, they differ in their approach to it. Jung is intrigued by death, Freud is awed by death's inevitability, while Adler resolves to work to overcome death. . . . Finally, the dominant life goals of each man emerge from their recollections. Adler's goal is to overcome inadequacy through effort and resolve. Freud strives to comprehend through analysis and interpretation, while Jung moves toward communion with nature through sensual awareness. [1973, pp. 164–165]

For Freud, death was a biological process he struggled to comprehend *intellectually, theoretically,* perhaps in an effort to master his own uneasiness. For Jung, death was but another aspect of an already paradoxical existence, inviting one to explore its spiritual and psychological reality. For Adler, death was the ultimate enemy, the supreme obstacle to self-fulfillment, the paramount state of helplessness against which one must struggle at all costs.

Freud and Adler: Dissent over the Fundamental Human Motive

It is small wonder, given Adler's early life history, that he disagreed drastically with Freud over the issue of the central motive force in human personality. Adler felt that human motivation could not be subsumed under the exclusive category of pleasure or sexuality, however broad these concepts had become. A new model of personality was needed, a model that accorded weight to other fundamental human strivings. As Robert White (1960) succinctly put the matter, with the neo-Freudians like Horney, Fromm, and Adler, the libido instinct model was replaced by the interpersonal model. Man's search for success, for superiority, for freedom from his own helplessness, for escape from his own fears, and for perfection and personal completeness became Adler's fundamental coordinates upon which to plot human lives in process. While Freud labored to demonstrate the sexual and pleasure-seeking strivings that underlie a broad range of human behaviors, Adler was already inwardly attuned to a human desire he considered more fundamental: *the striving to compensate for one's own perceived inferiorities, for one's enforced states of helplessness.* As Adler had learned, nothing can make one feel more inferior, more powerless than death.

Although there is some confusion over the exact sequence of events, Adler's and Freud's biographers seem to agree that in 1902 Freud sent Adler and several others an invitation to meet with him for informal seminars (cf. Jones, 1955; Furtmuller, 1973; Ansbacher, 1973, p. 336n.). Sometime shortly before this invitation, Adler had written a defense of Freud's *Interpretation of Dreams* in one of Vienna's foremost newspapers; thus Freud was apparently motivated to contact what he believed to be a kindred spirit. However, Adler's published defense of Freud has never been located. In any event, it seems clear that even though Adler joined the select group of intellectuals surrounding Freud, he was never as completely committed to the Freudian viewpoint as most of the others.

By 1911, as the culmination of continually widening personal and theoretical differences, Adler resigned from the Freud group to pursue his own psychological formulations. Some of Freud's recently published correspondence with Jung reveals the depth of personal and intellectual animosity that arose between himself and Adler. In March 1911, shortly before Adler's resignation, Freud wrote to Jung, expressing his disappointment at the direction Adler's theorizing was taking:

> I see now that Adler's seeming decisiveness concealed a good deal of confusion. I would never have expected a psychoanalyst to be so taken in by the ego. In reality the ego is like the clown in the circus, who is always putting in his oar to make the audience think that whatever happens is his doing. [Freud, in Freud/Jung, 1974, p. 400]

Freud's own opinion about the significance of the ego would change drastically by the 1920s; but at this juncture in history Freud was convinced that Adler's psychology was too superficial, too concerned with conscious functioning, and too neglectful of the unconscious determinants of behavior. Freud was particularly alarmed that Adler seemed to ignore the most fundamental tenet of psychoanalytic motivation theory:

> The crux of the matter—and that is what really alarms me—is that [Adler] minimizes the sexual drive and our opponents will soon be able to speak of an experienced psychoanalyst whose conclusions are radically different from ours. Naturally in my attitude toward him I am torn between my conviction that all this is lopsided and harmful and my fear of being regarded as an intolerant old man who holds the young men down, and this makes me feel most uncomfortable. [Freud, in Freud/Jung, 1974, p. 376]

The members of the informal seminar group, who now called themselves the Vienna Psychoanalytic Society, decided to clear the air by having a formal debate on the differences between Freud and Adler. Adler was therefore invited to give a systematic presentation of his ideas, beginning on January 4, 1911, and extending over the course of the next several sessions. On February 22, after the members of the group had discussed Adler's ideas and Freud had commented on the significance of the difference between Adler and himself, Adler resigned from the presidency of the Vienna Psychoanalytic Society. By May 24, Adler terminated all contact with the group, and at Freud's suggestion withdrew as co-editor of the *Zentralblatt,* an important psychoanalytic journal. Freud wrote to Jung in early June:

> I have finally got rid of Adler. After I had pressed Bergmann [the journal's publisher] to dismiss him from the *Zentralblatt,* he twisted and turned and finally came up with a strangely worded statement which can only be taken as his resignation. At least, this interpretation is supported by his announcement that he is leaving the Psychoanalytic Society. And then he came out with what he had been holding back: "Despite its unprecedented resolution at one time to that effect, the Society has not had sufficient moral influence on you to make you desist from your old personal fight (!!) against me. Since I have no desire to carry on such a personal fight with my former teacher, I hereby announce my resignation." The damage is not very great. Paranoid intelligences are not rare and are more dangerous than useful. As a paranoic of course he is right about many things, though wrong about everything. [Freud, in Freud/Jung, 1974, p. 428]

For Adler's part, the society's meetings devoted to the differences between himself and Freud had allowed him to crystallize the essential tenets of his own developing viewpoint. It will be especially useful before undertaking a study of Adler's theory to briefly explore Adler's own presentation of his divergence from orthodox psychoanalysis.

Adler's View of His Theoretical Differences with Freud

Years after his original dispute with Freud, Adler published an essay summarizing his differences from orthodox psychoanalysis (Adler, 1931, in 1973). The views he expressed in this essay are a useful means of understanding the directions his theorizing took upon his official break with the Freudian circle.

THE EGO. Adler viewed the ego not as the servant of the id's desires but as a creative intelligence independently operating to effect a healthy adaptation to life's circumstances. For him, the ego was the seat of the individual's sense of wholeness, of the person's identity as a complete and willful organism (1931, p. 206). Freud, of course, initially viewed the ego as only one part of a complex series of interactions between the individual's drives and reality. The emphasis, for Freud, was on the ego's *relationship to the unconscious,* not upon the ego's interactions with reality. Adler focused his attention on the ego as a mediator of social and physical reality, upon, that is, the individual's conscious striving to be someone.

THE OEDIPUS COMPLEX. In Adler's view, the Oedipus complex was not to be interpreted as a purely sexual phenomenon in which the child vainly attempts to possess the mother. Rather, he felt that equal if not greater weight should be attached to the child's striving to compete with the father, to secure for himself equal strength and power, not merely equal pleasure. The personality theorist must recognize not only the sexual attraction between child and mother but also the fact "that the boy wants to grow beyond himself, wants to attain a superiority over his father" (Adler, 1931, in 1973, p. 207).

NARCISSISM. When Freud developed the concept of narcissistic ego libido, he had in mind a protective channeling of energy into the self, a healthy self-interest or self-love. Adler, however, felt that the Freudian notion of narcissism indicated a personality turned in on itself, a style of life that by definition excluded healthy *social* interest. The narcissistic attitude, contrary to Freudian theory, is not innate or instinctual, but learned or acquired by those personalities that doubt their own strength. The narcissistic individual fears that he is essentially too weak, too powerless to survive, and he thus can control his fear only by excluding any obligation to others (1931, in 1973, p. 208).

FRAGMENTATION OF PERSONALITY. Adler felt that Freudian theory had fragmented the person into a set of competing parts that defied any attempt to understand the person as a *whole entity,* as a complete functioning unity. For Adler, as we shall later see, personality can be understood to have one fundamental, innate, evolutionary tendency: to grow, to become whole, to seek happiness by becoming fully what one is, rather than by satisfying one's discrete drives. For Adler, human motivation cannot be understood in terms of attempts to reduce the discomfort of mounting biological tensions like sex, hunger, and fatigue; humans struggle *toward* goals they set for themselves, not away from states of deprivation. Adler put the matter this way:

> The main problem of psychology is not to comprehend the causal factors as in physiology, but the direction-giving, pulling forces and goals which guide all other psychological movements. [1931, in 1973, p. 216]

THE MEANING OF DREAMS. Adler disagreed strongly with Freud's conception of the function of dreams. According to Freud, a dream is a disguised fulfillment of a wish that would be quite unacceptable or unattainable in the waking state (cf. Chapter 3). Thus, the dream story that can be recalled by the dreamer is bizarre, confused, and incomprehensible to the dreamer to protect him from recognition of his own unacceptable id impulses. The distortion and disguise of the manifest content is merely a protective mask defensively obscuring illicit latent urges.

For Adler, dreams were not to be interpreted as the fulfillment of unacceptable wishes; rather, they represent the dreamer's attempt to resolve problems he is unwilling or unable to master with his conscious powers of reason (Adler, 1973, p. 214). Like Freud, Adler felt that the dream was disguised, but in marked contrast to Freud, Adler was convinced that the *purpose* of the dream was to be *not understandable:*

> It is the intention of the dreamer not to understand his dreams. He *wants* to withdraw the dream from understanding. This must mean that something happens in the dream which he cannot justify with reason. *The intention of the dream is to deceive the dreamer.* The person attempts in a certain situation to deceive himself. I have also understood why one does not understand the dream. Its purpose is only to create a *mood.* This emotion must not be clarified; it must exist and act as an emotion, created from the individuality of the dreamer. This apparently corresponds to the desire to solve a problem by an emotional episode and in accordance with his life style, since he is not confident of solving his problem in accordance with the common sense. [Adler, 1973, p. 214]

Thus, for Adler the dream is an attempt by the dreamer's unconscious to create a mood or emotional state upon waking that will force him to take action that he was reluctant to attempt. In effect, the dream provides him with the excuse and the strength to actualize his true feelings.

In Freud's view, the dream itself is satisfying, while in Adler's view, the dream is merely the means to an end, an act of emotional fortification enabling one to live what one thinks. When the dreamer cannot provide a conscious and logical justification for his actions, he creates a dream that will leave behind a residue of emotion to stimulate action, to provoke the behavior he had been hesitant to accept.

There are many other differences between Freud's and Adler's approaches to personality, and some of these will become apparent in subsequent sections. The five areas we have surveyed—the ego as mediator of social reality, the Oedipus complex as a striving for superiority, narcissism as unhealthy self-centeredness, fragmentation of personality into parts versus the goal striving of the unified person, and dreams as problem-solving self-deceptions—signify substantial differences of opinion between Freud and Adler in their basic view of man's nature.

Freud and Adler never reconciled their differences, and, as Freud's system continued to evolve, Adler's disenchantment with his former teacher grew. Freud's increasing pessimism and fatalism about the nature of man was in direct contrast to Adler's view of man as an essentially good creature capable of altruistic social concern. In 1930, Freud gave vent to his pessimism in a remarkable passage in *Civilization and Its Discontents,* where he commented on the age-old precept: "Thou shalt love thy neighbor as thyself":

> What is the point of a precept enunciated with so much solemnity if its fulfillment cannot be recommended as reasonable? ... Not merely is this stranger in general unworthy of my love; I must honestly confess that he has more claim to my hostility and even my hatred. He seems not to have the least trace of love for me and shows me not the slightest consideration. If it will do him any good he has no hesitation in injuring me, nor does he ask himself whether the amount of advantage he gains bears any proportion to the extent of the harm he does to me. Indeed, he need not even obtain an advantage; if he can satisfy any sort of desire by it, he thinks nothing of jeering at me, insulting me, slandering me and showing his superior power; and the more secure he feels and the more helpless I am, the more certainly I can expect him to behave like this to me ... Indeed, if this grandiose commandment had run "Love thy neighbour as thy neighbour loves thee," I should not take exception to it. ...
>
> The element of truth behind all this, which people are so ready to disavow, is that men are not gentle creatures who want to be loved, and who at the most can defend themselves if they are attacked; they are, on the contrary, creatures among whose instinctual endowments

is to be reckoned a powerful share of aggressiveness. As a result, their neighbour is for them not only a potential helper or sexual object, but also someone who tempts them to satisfy their aggressiveness on him, to exploit his capacity for work without compensation, to use him sexually without his consent, to seize his possessions, to humiliate him, to cause him pain, to torture and to kill him. *Homo homini lupus* [Man is a wolf to man]. [Freud, 1930, pp. 110–111]

Adler was genuinely shocked by Freud's statement (Orgler, 1963). It seemed to him contrary to all reasonable views of man's nature to assume that man was inherently evil:

And, indeed, if we look closely we shall find that the Freudian theory is the consistent psychology of the pampered child, who feels that his instincts must never be denied, who looks on it as unfair that other people should exist, who asks always, "Why should I love my neighbour? Does my neighbour love me?" [Adler, 1931, p. 97]

Inferiority-Superiority: From Minus to Plus Self-Estimates

In light of Adler's childhood infirmities and his experiences with death, it is not surprising that he gave to psychology the concept of the *inferiority complex* (1927, 1929a, 1931, 1964). An individual's sense of helplessness, of powerlessness in the face of death, is not the only way that the person may arrive at the conclusion that he is inferior. The child may, as had Adler himself, experience the physical inferiorities of damaged or diseased organs that prevent successful competition with peers. Or he may perceive that his elders are powerful controllers of his fate, of his satisfactions, of the very direction his life is to take. In comparison with these potent manipulators, the child feels weak, impotent, and inferior, and like Adler himself, he embarks on a life-long struggle to compensate for his perceived inferiority, to erect a façade of compensatory superiority to conceal his sense of worthlessness.

For Adler, the striving to master inferiority feelings, whatever their origin, is an inherent characteristic of living things, a product of organic evolution: "Set in motion at one time or other the material of life has been constantly bent on reaching a plus from a minus situation. . . . This movement is in no wise to be regarded as leading to death; on the contrary, it is directed towards achieving the mastery of the external world and does not by any means seek a compromise with it or a state of rest" (Adler, 1964, p. 97). For Adler, in contrast to Freud, the basic striving of life is not to achieve pleasure, nor final rest; the fundamental urge of life is to achieve "superiority," to achieve, that is, a sense of competence and fulfillment.

It may be helpful at the outset to indicate the sequence of changes through which Adler's thinking progressed on the subject of the organism's striving from minus to plus self-estimates. The concepts of superiority and inferiority underwent several transformations as Adler sought to refine his theory. At first, Adler began with a very concrete, physiological conception of inferiority as rooted in physical *organ defects.* Slowly, this medical conception was modified in the direction of a psychological theory to account for the person's own perception of physical inferiorities. Adler's interest subsequently shifted from this emphasis on the *perceived sense of inferiority* to the individual's strivings to compensate for his inadequacy. Cultural and social factors were thus brought into the theory. *Aggressive* impulses, the *masculine protest, superiority* strivings, and *perfection* strivings rapidly took their respective places as successive transitions in Adler's developing theory of personality. A schematic overview of these transitions is provided in Figure 5–1 as a prelude to more detailed discussion in the sections that follow.

Organ Inferiority: Compensatory Strivings

Adler had fought his own childhood battles with organ inferiority in struggling to compete with his older brother and peers in physical activities despite the weakness induced by rickets. When he later chose the vocation of physician in his continuing efforts to combat his own sense of helplessness, he characteristically located his first medical office in a lower-class Viennese neighborhood, where his patients would be drawn from society's least economically favored working men and women.

Situated near the famous Prater amusement park, Adler's practice brought him into contact not only with the "common man" of Viennese society but with the entertainers, acrobats, and artists of the Prater. Adler's interest in organ inferiority may have therefore received some impetus from the unusual nature of the patients who sought his help. Furtmüller (1973) has suggested in his biographical essay on Adler that the entertainers of the Prater directed Adler's attention to the importance of physical strength and weakness in making a successful adaptation to life:

> All these people [i.e., Prater entertainers], who earned their living by exhibiting their extraordinary bodily strength and skills, showed to Adler their physical weaknesses and ailments. It was partly the observation of such patients as these that led to his conception of overcompensation [for perceived inferiority]. [1973, p. 334]

In 1907, Adler published a novel theory of disease that would now be classed as a contribution to psychosomatic medicine. Entitled "Study of Organ Inferiority and Its Physical Compensation," the essay sustained the

FIGURE 5–1: AN OVERVIEW OF ADLER'S CHANGING VIEWS OF HUMAN MOTIVATION

ORGAN INFERIORITY ——→	AGGRESSION DRIVE ——→	MASCULINE PROTEST ——→	SUPERIORITY STRIVING ——→	PERFECTION STRIVING ——→
Least or most poorly developed organ succumbs fastest to environmental demands. Disease strikes only such predisposed organs.	Hostile attitude toward perceived helplessness in obtaining satisfactions. May be reversed into an opposite drive of humility or submission.	Every child desires to be competent, to be superior or and in control of his own life. Overcompensation to be "manly" and admired results.	Inherent biological urge toward self-expansion, growth, and competence.	Seeking after a chosen goal, or dream, fulfillment. Based on subjective or fictional estimates of life's values.

assertion that every man succumbs to disease in that organ which has been less well developed, less successfully functioning, and generally "inferior" from birth. Thus, for example, some people are born with weak eyes, weak stomachs, badly functioning hearts, or damaged limbs. Whatever the inherent bodily weakness, environmental demands and stresses have their greatest impact on the inferior organ, and the way the individual adapts to life is likely to be shaped by his reaction, both physical and psychological, to his organ inferiority.

The notion of organ inferiority did not mean, in Adler's development of the concept, that the individual suffers disease only in terms of inherited organ defects. Rather, organs that are biologically inferior to the demands made upon them by the environment are the ones most likely to become sites of origin for physical disease. Adler later emphasized the individual's subjective reaction to his physical infirmities as of crucial importance for the direction his life would take. The entertainers of the Prater—jugglers, acrobats, and strongmen—would be a case in point. Organ inferiority, one's attempts to compensate for it, and one's sense of self-worth are inextricably interwoven with the individual's biological-medical status and his unique reaction to his social environment:

> We wish to replace the obscure concept of "pathological disposition" by the following proposition: Disease is the resultant of organ inferiority and external demands. The latter are limited in duration and to a particular cultural environment. Changes in the external demands represent cultural progress, changes of the mode of living, or social improvements. [Adler, 1907, p. 25]

Adler postulated that because the entire organism is governed by a principle of equilibrium or balance, the inferior organ under the guidance of the central nervous system would *compensate* for the defect of underdevelopment or damage. Physiologist Walter B. Cannon would some years later propose a similar principle called *homeostasis.* Undergoing increased growth and functioning power, the initially inferior organ, or allied organs, may "overcompensate" for the previous deficit as the individual consciously centers his attention on that area of functioning. For example, the individual with an early speech defect may become so involved in mastering his stuttering that he turns his inferiority into a career. Becoming a speech therapist, or an orator, or an actor, the individual overcompensates for what had been a perceived inferiority (1907, p. 29).

In this early stage of his theorizing, Adler did not yet include his characteristic later emphasis on the individual's subjective perception of inferiority. Compensation and overcompensation were still conceived of as biological-environmental processes in the service of equilibrium or homeostasis.

The Aggression Drive

Adler's next step, taken in 1908, was the assertion of an inherent drive of aggression in man. Ironically Freud himself was not ready to admit the possibility of aggressive strivings in man on an equal footing with the drive of sexuality. Yet, from his attempts to work within the frame of psychoanalytic thought, Adler developed this very concept. He was still within the circle of Freud's followers, and sought to account for behavior in terms of Freud's basic pleasure principle.

Thus Adler proposed that two basic drives govern the course of the individual's life: the drives of sexuality and of aggression. Along with these two primary biological urges, a number of diverse secondary drives associated with sensory processes like seeing, smelling, and hearing had to be included in any account of motivated behavior. But Adler's key contribution to this scheme was that no drive stands alone. Drives always enter into a *confluence,* an amalgam of interaction whereby each separate component drive is subordinated to the whole (Adler, 1908, p. 30). Furthermore, drives could be transformed and displaced from their original form and goals into new channels of expression.

A. *Transformation of drive into its opposite:* the unconscious drive to eat, for example, becomes the conscious refusal to eat;

B. *Displacement of drive to another goal:* unconscious love for father becomes a conscious love for a teacher or other authority figure;

C. *Direction of drive to one's own person:* the unconscious repressed drive to see, becomes the conscious drive to be looked at, in other words, exhibitionism;

D. *Displacement of the accent on a second strong drive:* the repression of one drive may enhance the expression of another. Thus, blocking of the sex drive's direct expression may increase the drive to "look" at sexual objects. [Adler, 1908, pp. 32–33]

In his paper "Instincts and Their Vicissitudes" (1915a), Freud elaborated the first two of these transformations, for which he gave Adler some credit. Adler, however, developed the concept of "confluence of drives" in a different direction from Freud. The drive of aggression became the dominant and governing force shaping the confluence of drives:

From early childhood, we can say from the first day (first cry) we find a stand of the child toward the environment which cannot be called anything but hostile. If one looks for the cause of this position, one finds it determined by the difficulty of affording satisfaction for the organ [i.e., the sites of drive; e.g., hunger]. This circumstance as well as the further relationships of the hostile, belligerent position of the individual toward the environment indicate a drive toward fighting for satisfaction which I shall call "aggression drive." [Adler, 1908, p. 34]

Pure expressions of this superordinate striving toward aggression take form as fighting, beating, biting, and outright cruelty. But aggression, following the principle of transformation or plasticity of drives, may also be expressed in less direct form. Athletic competition, religious conflict, social, national, and race struggles, politics, and even art embody this fundamental human motive. When the aggression drive is turned inward, the individual displays the resultant opposite traits of humility, submission, or in the extreme case, masochism (Adler, 1908, p. 35).

This ability of aggression to be reversed into its opposite at the demands of cultural and parental censure lends the complexity of a "hidden-figure puzzle" to human motivation:

> Charity, sympathy, altruism, and sensitive interest in misery represent new satisfactions on which the drive, which originally tended toward cruelty, feeds. If this seems strange, it is nevertheless easy to recognize that a real understanding for suffering and pain can only come from an original interest in the world of torment. The greater the aggression drive, the stronger will become this cultural transformation. Thus the pessimist becomes the preventor of dangers, Cassandra becomes a warner and prophet. [Adler, 1908, p. 36]

In contrast to his emphasis on the aggression drive as the basic striving governing the confluence of lesser drives, Adler also pointed out the importance of love and affection in the development of the child's personality. Parts of the drives to look, to touch, and to listen join in a unique confluence called the *need for affection:*

> Children want to be fondled [i.e., to be touched] loved, and praised [i.e., to be looked at]. They have a tendency to cuddle up, always to remain close to loved persons, and to want to be taken into the bed with them. [Adler, 1908, p. 40]

Where Freud had seen sexual strivings, Adler found striving for affection. Manipulation of the child's drive for affection is the parents' tool of education, for by partially satisfying the child's love needs, his behavior can be shaped in the direction of social interest, concern for his fellow beings. By partially denying them, he can be taught healthy independence.

Masculine Protest: A General Striving for Superiority

Adler's theorizing to this point emphasized the biological nature of the organism and its defects: organ inferiority and the confluence of drives. In

1910, however, Adler shifted his focus to purely psychological phenomena. These psychological formulations were, of course, derived from his early physiological concepts of inferiority and aggression, but now the center of interest was the individual's *interpretation,* his phenomenal experience, of his organ inferiorities.

Adler first coordinated the biological fact of organ inferiority with its psychological counterpart, the *feeling* of inferiority. Thus, children with marked defects like stuttering, clumsiness, deafness, visual deficits, or extreme ugliness or disfigurement develop a subjective feeling of inferiority in relation to the stronger, more competent persons in their sphere. "Such children are thus often placed in a role which appears to them as unmanly. All neurotics have a childhood behind them in which they were moved by doubt regarding the achievement of full masculinity" (Adler, 1910, p. 47).

In an unfortunately chosen metaphor, Adler had identified "superiority" feelings with masculinity and "inferiority" feelings with femininity. Masculinity and femininity were to be understood in their *cultural meanings* as well as biological genders:

> ... any form of uninhibited aggression, activity, potency, power, and the traits of being brave, free, rich, aggressive or sadistic can be considered masculine. All inhibitions and deficiencies, as well as cowardliness, obedience, poverty, and similar traits, can be considered as feminine. [Adler, 1910, p. 47]

In Adler's view, then, the child begins life with one conviction pressed on his awareness in relation to the powerful adults around him: *he is powerless, weak, and dependent* (Adler, 1927, p. 66). When the adults in his world insensitively treat their children as passive "toys" to be guarded as valuable property, or dismiss them as worthless "freight," the child learns that there are only two things in *his* power: "the pleasure or displeasure of his elders" (Adler, 1927, p. 66).

In consequence, the "feminine tendency" toward passivity provokes in the child a need to combat his enforced inferiority. A *"masculine protest"* or overcompensatory striving to demolish his dependency, to assert his autonomy, and to achieve *superiority* similar to that which he witnesses in those around him emerges. It should perhaps be pointed out that girls too engage in the "masculine protest." The identification of inferiority with femininity and masculinity with superiority may have been a poorly chosen set of terms, but until recently they were culturally accurate metaphors. Neither boys nor girls, according to Adler, wish to be locked into the "minus" role assigned to the traditional concept of the female. All persons, therefore, engage in *protest to be superior;* Adler happened to succumb to the historical moment in choosing to call this phenomenon "masculine."

Relation Between Inferiority and Superiority

The core of the feeling of inferiority is organized around a network of character traits that have as their common denominator the feeling of "smallness" and "powerlessness." On this emotional pattern of fundamental inferiority, the masculine protest overlays a defensive network of *compensatory traits:* for timidity there is courage; for submissiveness there is rebelliousness; for feelings of smallness, feelings of grandeur substitute, and so on as illustrated in Table 5–1 (p. 183).

Striving for superiority, or in contemporary terminology, the need for an income of self-esteem, is a two-phase process. In the first phase, the child's sense of inferiority in relation to the adults around him and perhaps founded on a biological handicap fosters a timid, passive, and insecure feeling of smallness.

In the second phase, a superordinate striving for superiority, for autonomy, and for assertive expression of "masculinity" compensates for the inferiority feelings. In the special sense that the terms have been used in this book (cf. Chapter 1), the compensatory traits of the masculine protest can be seen as the mask covering the actor's fundamental character flaws.

At a later point in his theorizing, Adler understood that these compensatory "superior" traits were more than attempts at mere cover-up of one's inferiority. They were, instead, indicators of the individual's interpretation of his inferiority, for the traits he chooses to outwardly adopt are shaped by his perception of those he inwardly despises. Therefore, such compensatory traits are *signs of what the individual has planned to do about his inferiority.*

The Mask Must Fit the Drama

The remainder of an individual's life takes shape and direction in accordance with his unconscious plan to overcome his sensed inferior traits. He creates, to use Adler's later terminology, a *fictional goal,* that is, a subjective guiding ideal that represents *to him* mastery of his character flaws. This fictional ideal of mastery, furthermore, becomes the achievement toward which, throughout life, his every fantasy, thought, and action are directed. The mask of compensatory "superior" traits must be consonant with this abiding life goal and must, in an unconscious fashion, foreshadow this most desirable of all possible life outcomes. Adler himself employed the metaphor of the actor and his mask to describe this fundamental continuity of personality:

> The fictional, abstract ideal is the point of origin for the formation and differentiation of the given psychological resources [of the individual] into preparatory attitudes, readinesses, and character traits. The individual then wears the character traits demanded by his fictional goal, just as the character mask *(persona)* of the ancient actor

INFERIORITY CHARACTER TRAITS	MASCULINE PROTEST COMPENSATORY TRAITS
timidity	impudence
indecision	stubbornness
insecurity	rebelliousness
shyness	impertinence
cowardliness	courage
increased need for support	defiance
submissive obedience	fantasy of hero, warrior,
fantasies of smallness	grandeur
masochism	

Based on Adler, 1910, p. 53

> had to fit the finale of the tragedy. . . . The self-ideal [i.e., fictional goal] . . . carries within itself all abilities and gifts of which the so-disposed child considers himself deprived. [Adler, in 1956, pp. 94–95]

We will return to Adler's notion of the fictional final goal or self ideal at a later point. First, we must turn to an illustrative case history to translate into more concrete human terms the abstraction of striving for superiority.

An Illustrative Case: Lying for Superiority

Philip, age nine years, tells lies that portray him as a fearless hero, able to master all obstacles, willing to enter on new and bold adventures. "For example, he says: 'I was in England. From where I was standing *I looked around the corner of a wall,* and I saw a tiger' " (Adler, 1930a, p. 97; italics added). Adler commented:

> In itself, this is a big lie. But what interests me particularly is that he does not just look, he looks "around the corner of a wall." This is virtuosity. Not everyone can do it. And it tells us even more: The boy's interest is particularly marked, and he is eager to conquer difficulties—difficulties which would be insurmountable for anyone else. [1930a, p. 97]

Philip has a visual problem; he is cross-eyed (strabismus). For this acutely felt organ inferiority, Philip has learned to compensate with adventuresome tales that involve acrobatic feats in the visual mode: "I looked around the corner of a wall." He has turned a handicap into a marvelous feat.

Philip is described by his mother as a "problem child" because he is terribly restless and unable to learn. In school, Philip feels unsure and "unequal to the demands of the situation." But in everyday life, in his play on the street, he misses nothing. He is paradoxically incompetent at tasks favored by his parents and teachers, and quite competent at those of his own choosing. His mother describes him further as cowardly: "He is afraid of everything and runs away from any kind of danger."

Philip's mother understands that he would like to be brave and smart in school, and to be a person that everyone admires. She tries to help him, but Adler reveals that her "help" is more like pampering. She makes his decisions for him; she decides what dangers force her to protect him; she cares for his every need. Her husband confirms Adler's conclusion, for he too feels that she "spoils" Philip. Adler was very specific in his definition of the pampered child:

> A pampered child is one who has been relieved of his independent functioning. Someone else speaks for him, recognizes the dangerous situations, and protects him from them. In short, the child is taken in tow by someone else. *He has another person at his disposal, and he builds his life in symbiosis with her. Such a child has a parasitic trait: he tries to get everything he wants through the aid of his mother.* [Adler, 1930a, p. 97; italics added]

Despite his mother's attention, Philip is unlikely to give up his lies, for lying is the only source of independent superiority. In fact, the sole route open to Philip is to construct ever more subtle lies in an effort to avoid losing what remains of his own sense of selfhood: " . . . he cannot give up his lying and run the risk of appearing to be a 'zero' . . ." (Adler, 1931, p. 99).

Philip's lies continued to grow. For a school theme he wrote about a trip he and his father had made to a cemetery. The entire account was fictional, but Philip went so far as to indicate that he had even surpassed his father in courage: His father had cried, but "I didn't cry. A man doesn't cry."

Unable to win any sense of personal worth without lying for superiority, Philip's response was flight, the flight into a *fantasy* of superiority.

Fictionalism: The Philosophy of "As If"

To a considerable extent, the young Philip lived by a fiction. Philip's fiction was not identical with the lies he told but rather with the *motive* underlying his specific tales: namely, his desire to be brave, assertive, aggressive, and independent. The resulting lies and exaggerations were merely the tissue covering a skeleton of *subjectively real* interpretations by which Philip managed to navigate the obstacles of his life.

Philip's "lies" were transparent fictions, easily detectable by virtue of their exaggeration. With somewhat less transparency, most people live by similar objectively false ideals. Despite their contradiction of reality, such idealistic "fictions" as "all men are created equal" serve us well as rules-of-thumb or as working hypotheses in daily living (Ansbacher & Ansbacher, 1956, p. 77). Hans Vaihinger (1911) published a book devoted to explaining the ways in which people create and live by such "as if" thinking. Entitled *The Philosophy of "As If,"* Vaihinger's book so impressed Adler that he modified and adopted several of its concepts for his theory.

For Vaihinger, fictions are *subjectively useful interpretations of reality* that, despite their falsity, are valuable to the user in making sense of his life. Thus, although Vaihinger was personally skeptical, he acknowledged that behaving "as if" there were a God lent meaning to man's life. Similarly, the legal profession must operate "as if" corporations were persons. Physicists sometimes proceed "as if" electricity were a fluid or "as if" light were discrete packets of energy. Some behavioristic psychologists conduct human experimentation "as if" mind does not exist.

Vaihinger specified five types of fiction whose precise definitions need not occupy us here. The important point is that all such fictions are cognitive devices for representing reality in understandable, livable terms. The fiction may not coincide with the "truth" or objective fact it seeks to represent, but it does capture the essence in a form that is useful to the thinker. For Vaihinger, "truth is merely the most expedient degree of error, and error the least expedient degree of ideation;" but all ideation (thinking) is nevertheless fictional. What counts to the pragmatic Vaihinger is the degree of usefulness of any idea, the degree to which the idea is productive in negotiating the demands of life.

What seemingly attracted Adler's interest in Vaihinger's philosophical position was Vaihinger's emphasis on the *subjective perceptions* of the thinker. As Adler saw it, what matters to a given personality is not what is, but what he thinks is. Moreover, Adler was impressed by Vaihinger's stress upon the *individual, idiosyncratic* nature of the process of creating fictions. Each individual creates fictions that are unique to him, that are singular creations of his personal inventiveness. Vaihinger even made clear that at least part of the time the creation of fictions was "carried on in the darkness of the unconscious," a proposition for which Adler's psychoanalytic experiences had prepared his ready acceptance (cf. Ansbacher & Ansbacher, 1956, p. 88).

Like the "liar" Philip, each personality can be understood fully only when we expose to scrutiny the fictions by which goals and dreams, passions and promises are created.

Personality as Unified Goal Striving: Fictional Finalism

Vaihinger's concept of fictions became for Adler the means to understanding the goal directedness of personality. He adopted the notion of a "fictional" *final goal* in the sense of an *ultimate* ambition that stands at the center of a person's existence. Although Adler eventually dropped the term *fictional* from his designation of this ultimate goal, the three meanings of the concept derived from Vaihinger remained in his usage: *the goal is subjective and personally meaningful; the goal is created by the individual to navigate the obstacles of existence; and the goal is unconscious* (Ansbacher & Ansbacher, 1956, p. 90).

The immediate motive underlying the creation of the fictional goal is the need to gain superiority, attain a state of "plus existence" from a position of minus:

> ... the movement of the psyche is analogous to the movement of organic life. In each mind there is the conception of a goal or ideal to get beyond the present state, and to overcome the present deficiencies and difficulties by postulating a concrete aim for the future. *By means of this concrete aim or goal the individual can think and feel himself superior to the difficulties of the present because he has in mind his success of the future.* [Adler, 1929a, p. 2; italics added]

Adler pictured the creation of this superordinate goal, or process of *fictional finalism,* as beginning in early childhood. Like the "liar" Philip, the child formulates a "prototype" of his later mature personality in interaction with his environment from the base of his feelings of inferiority:

> A child, being weak, feels inferior and finds itself in a situation which it cannot bear. Hence it strives to develop, and *it strives to develop along a line of direction fixed by the goal which it chooses for itself.* ... Children look for the strongest person in their environment and make him their model or their goal. It may be the father, or perhaps the mother, for we find that even a boy may be influenced to imitate his mother if she seems the strongest person. ... Later on, the ideal may become the doctor or the teacher. For the teacher can punish the child and thus he arouses his respect as a strong person. [Adler, 1929a, pp. 3–4]

Thus, Adler strongly emphasized the *teleological* or goal-directed character of the human personality, the "mysterious creative power of life." In Adler's own words, the creativity of the personality is "that power which expresses itself in the desire to develop, to strive and to achieve—and even to compensate for defeats in one direction by striving for success in another" (1929a, p. 1).

In 1912, Adler introduced new terminology for this final fictional goal. He referred to a "guiding self-ideal" as the unifying principle of personality, as in the ideal of the role-models referred to in the previously quoted passage. Consequently, Adler's view of personality began to emphasize more strongly the "wholeness" or unity of personality as it is entwined with goal-seeking, ultimate "becoming."

Striving for Perfection: Focus on the Normal Personality

In his earliest treatments of the subject, the striving for superiority that emerges from feelings of inferiority is conceptualized by Adler as concerned with power, aggression, and a need to be "masculine." However, Adler began to modify his views of superiority as he moved his focus from the neurotic personality's defensiveness to the normal's goal centeredness.

Adler had described the core of the neurotic personality as a balance between inferiority and the striving for compensatory superiority as expressed in gaining power over others: "We can consequently always recognize, as the unconscious premises of the neurotic goal-striving, the following two facts:

1. *Human relations in all circumstances represent a struggle.*
2. *The feminine sex is inferior and by its reactions serves as the measure of masculine strength."* [1913a, p. 35]

Note that Adler was not asserting that the feminine sex *is* inferior, but that the neurotic personality, man or woman, believes in that inferiority as part of the struggle, masculine protest, to achieve superiority. The neurotic personality struggles with an overexerted sense of his importance, his "godlikeness," in his efforts to win security:

All neurotic symptoms have as their object the task of safeguarding the patient's self-esteem and thereby also the life-line [later, life-style] into which he has grown. *To prove his ability to cope with life the patient needs arrangements and neurotic symptoms as an expedient.* He needs them as an oversized safeguarding component against the dangers which, in his feeling of inferiority, he expects and incessantly seeks to avoid in working out his plans for the future. [Adler, 1913b, p. 263; italics added]

Thus in Adler's view, the essential characteristic of the neurotic is his self-centeredness, his inflated perception of self and his overcompensation for his feelings of inferiority. For the neurotic the dominant goal is *self* security through personal *superiority*. A healthy interest in the being of others, in their welfare, in their commonality with him, is excluded from the neurotic's personality development and life plan.

All men have feelings of inferiority, in Adler's view, but only the neurotic has blown them up into the central fact of existence. While the normal is always ready to abandon his fictional goals, his self ideals, as he matures beyond them, the neurotic is fixated, defensively rigid, unable to budge:

More firmly than the normal individual does the neurotic fixate his God, his idol, his personality ideal, and cling to his guiding line, and with deeper purpose he loses sight of reality. *The normal person, on the other hand, is always ready to dispense with this aid, this crutch.* In this instance, the neurotic resembles a person who looks up to God, commends himself to the Lord, and then waits credulously for His guidance; the neurotic is nailed to the cross of his fiction. The normal individual, too, can and will create his deity, will feel drawn upward. But he will never lose sight of reality, and always takes it into account as soon as action and work are demanded. *The neurotic is under the spell of a fictional life plan.* [Adler, 1912, pp. 246–247; italics added]

Adler had clearly evolved a new scheme for interpreting the striving for superiority. He now saw this motive as a ceaseless *yearning for perfection,* a yearning that is inherent to organic life:

The origin of humanity and the ever-repeated beginning of infant life impresses with every psychological act: "Achieve! Arise! Conquer!" This feeling, this longing for the abrogations of every imperfection, is never absent. ... The unreluctant search for truth, the ever-unsatisfied seeking for solution of the problems of life, belongs to this longing for perfection of some sort. [Adler, 1956, pp. 103–104]

The striving for perfection in one's life is inherent to the processes of life itself, "something without which one could not even conceive of life" (Adler, 1973, p. 31). Adler construed the striving for perfection as one more evolutionary trend evidenced in the Darwinian principle of adaptation to the environment. The striving for perfection is a never-ending struggle to better adapt to the world; it is, however, a *"victorious* adaption to the external world."

The Completed Transition: From Organ Inferiority to Perfection-Striving

With the concept of perfection striving as a basic evolutionary process of adaption to life's circumstances, Adler had maintained continuity with his earliest notions of organ-inferiority and the striving to compensate and win a sense of superiority. By the assumption of an inherent biological trend toward better adaption (i.e., toward perfection), Adler also maintained the goal-seeking or teleological aspect of his personality theory. The steps involved in Adler's achievement of this final conception of perfection-striving as the superordinate goal of life are summarized in Table 5–2.

It may be of some help to compare the contents of Table 5–2 with the items outlined previously in Figure 5–1.

TABLE 5-2: TRANSITIONS IN ADLER'S CONCEPTION OF HUMAN MOTIVATION

ANTECEDENT OR CAUSE	MOTIVE OR PERSONALITY GOAL
1. Physiological-environmental interaction	Organ Inferiority
2. Frustrated biological needs and perceived helplessness	Aggression Drive
3. Cultural attitudes toward "maleness," and feelings of passivity or inferiority	Masculine Protest
4. Evolutionary trend toward successful adaption; personal feelings of inferiority	Superiority Striving
5. Subjective interpretation of life's meaning, life's values, the fictional final goal	Perfection Striving

Social Interest: The Tasks of Life

Though the striving for perfection is common to normal and neurotic personality alike, the neurotic's motives are isolated from any interest in the rest of humanity. Indeed, they are isolated from any interest even in those closest to him. Adler indicated the essentially normal sympathy of feeling for one's fellow man by a German coinage: *"Gemeinschaftsgefühl,"* a term that defies precise translation. Eventually, the English equivalent of "social interest," which Adler himself favored, was decided upon as the uniform translation of Adler's unique German neologism (Ansbacher & Ansbacher, 1956, p. 134).

Social interest is the key difference between the neurotic's striving for superiority and the normal's:

> It is always the want of social feeling, whatever be the name one gives it—living in fellowship, co-operation, humanity, or even the ideal-ego—which causes an unsufficient preparation for all the problems of life. [Adler, 1964, p. 110]

The problems of life, which can be successfully solved only by a person with strong social interest, are grouped under three major headings. Each of these tasks was conceptualized by Adler as a universal life problem that every human must master because he is embedded in a social fabric:

(a.) *Occupational Tasks.*   In the selection and pursuit of a vocation as a productive mode of existence, a man "arrives at a feeling of his worth to society, the only possible means of mitigating the universally human feeling of inferiority. The person who performs useful work lives in the midst of the developing human society and helps to advance it" (Adler, 1933, p. 132).

(b.) *Societal Tasks.*   Because each human lives within the context of mankind, he must adapt to others and interest himself in them. Friendship, social interest, is man's normal means of adapting to societal life: "it was only because man learned to cooperate that the great discovery of the division of labor was made, a discovery which is the chief security for the welfare of mankind" (Adler, 1933, p. 132).

(c.) *Love Tasks.*   The relationship between the sexes is the last significant task of life to be mastered. "On his approach to the other sex and on the fulfillment of his sexual role depends his part in the continuance of mankind" (Adler, 1956, p. 132).

Adler emphasized the relatedness of the three tasks:

> The three problems are never found apart, for they all throw cross lights on one another. A solution of one helps towards the solution of the others, and indeed we can say that they are all aspects of the same situation and the same problem—*the necessity for a human being to preserve life and to further life in the environment in which he finds himself.* [Adler, 1956, pp. 132–133; italics added]

The individual who embodies a healthy social interest is expressing an evaluative attitude toward life: *"To see with the eyes of another, to hear with the ears of another, to feel with the heart of another"* (Adler, 1956, p. 135).

Style of Life: Individual Psychology

Adler chose the phrase *individual psychology* to identify his system for what by now must be obvious reasons. He emphasized the essential subjective nature of the individual's goal striving, the innate creativity of human psychological adaption, and the wholeness of the individual's unified personality. Each of us, in an analogy to evolution, fits into his own niche in his own way. And then, the individual subordinates all drives, needs, strivings to the context of his entire style of life, the very pattern of his existence as a social being *as he creates it.*

> The goal of superiority, with each individual, is personal and unique. It depends upon the meaning he gives to life; and this meaning is not

a matter of words. It is built up in his style of life and runs through it like a strange melody of his own creation. . . . Understanding a style of life is similar to understanding the work of a poet. A poet must use words; but his meaning is more than the mere words he uses. The greatest part of his meaning must be guessed at; we must read between the lines. . . . The psychologist must learn to read between the lines; he must learn the art of appreciating life-meanings. [Adler, 1931, pp. 57–58]

To the degree that the individual has developed a healthy social interest, his striving for superiority will be shaped into a style of life that is warmly respective of others and focused on friendship and interpersonal ties. He will be characteristically expectant that other people are similarly warmly respective of him and are therefore sources of satisfaction and pleasure.

Style of life, then, is based on the individual's unique interpretation of his inferiority. Adler illustrated his meaning for "style of life" with the following analogy:

Perhaps I can illustrate this by an anecdote of three children who were taken to the zoo for the first time. As they stood before the lion's cage, one of them shrank behind his mother's skirts and said, "I want to go home." The second child stood where he was, very pale and trembling, and said, "I'm not a bit frightened." The third glared at the lion fiercely and asked his mother, "Shall I spit at it?" The three children really felt inferior, but each expressed his feelings in his own way, consonant with his style of life. [1931, p. 50]

The individual's style of life is the product of a *creative* personality trend to overcome his unique sense of inferiority. The goal that beckons an individual becomes the guiding force of his life because it is *his* goal. He decides to shape his life in the direction of that goal because *his* feelings of inferiority form a unique constellation with *his* striving for superiority.

Every individual represents both a unity of personality and the individual fashioning of that unity. The individual is thus both the picture and the artist. He is the artist of his own personality, but as an artist he is neither an infallible worker nor a person with a complete understanding of mind and body; he is rather a weak, extremely fallible, and imperfect human being. [Adler, 1956, p. 177; see also 1930c, p. 24]

In Adler's view, therefore, the individual is a *creative artist* of personality, an *active constructor* of his life events (cf. Kelly, Chapter 10, for a similar proposition).

An Illustrative Case: Jean-Mary's Life Style

That the life style of a child may be shaped by personal reaction to a perceived inferiority or to a physical limitation is illustrated by the direction Jean-Mary's life followed. Recall that Jean-Mary suffered from a congenital heart defect that required constant medical supervision and hospitalization during her childhood.

> When Jean-Mary was six years old, the congenital heart defect from which she suffered imposed a low ceiling on the physical activities that she could pursue. Unable to run, skate, or skip rope as well as the other children, Jean-Mary never assumed for a moment that there was anything wrong with *her.* It was simply a matter of ability. Her strengths lay elsewhere.
> For example, when the girls on the block skipped rope, Jean-Mary was always a "steady-ender," the girl who turned the rope as the others jumped. But when it came to school activities, Jean-Mary was at the top of her classes.
> Slowly her whole style of life was shaped in the direction of intellectual pursuit, helped on the one hand by her lack of physical prowess, and on the other by her positive intellectual superiority. Most of her spare time was spent devouring books. So great was her appetite for reading that daily trips to the library for new books were not unusual. In fact, a book was usually begun on the walk home, a journey that consequently took a meandering snail's pace. Once, while deeply absorbed in a particularly juicy romance, Jean-Mary walked headlong into a sidewalk tree, excused herself without looking up, and continued homeward oblivious to the fact that her politeness had been inappropriately bestowed. Her later choice of career was therefore not surprising. As a manuscript editor for a university publisher, Jean-Mary was more concerned with Elizabethan prose than with the demands of daily life, as her friends would often tell her.

Jean-Mary's style of life was shaped by two important factors: Her physical restrictions fostered the development of interest in things intellectual, and her native superior intelligence made her interest fruitful. Thus, Jean-Mary's style of life was a product of inferiority and superiority merging into a unique and unified personality.

Personality Types: Degrees of Social Interest

Adler developed a scheme of personality types based on the degree of social interest and activity level embodied in different personalities. His personality typology was not strongly emphasized in his whole personality system, but is of some interest in relation to other theorists' typologies.

Adler had early written about the four classic types of temperament described in the writings of Hippocrates and Galen in ancient Greece. According to temperament theory, individual personality types can be classified into four categories on the basis of individual dominance of one of four body fluids or humors: blood, black bile, yellow bile, and phlegm. The *sanguine personality,* for whom blood is the decisive determinant of temperament, is accepting of life, greets it on its own terms with a certain joyousness. The sanguine individual does not take things too seriously, and he optimistically attempts to see the good side of things. In terms of Individual Psychology, "The Sanguine individual seems to be that one who has been least exposed to the feeling of inferiority in his childhood, who has shown fewest important bodily infirmities, and has been subjected to no strong irritations, with the result that he has developed quietly with a certain love for life . . ." (Adler, 1927, p. 148). Thus, Adler conceptualized the sanguine type as the healthiest of the four.

The *choleric type,* for whom yellow bile is the dominant humor, is irascible and easily irritated. Explosions of anger and perpetual pessimism are characteristic of the choleric type. In Adler's terms, "the choleric individual is one whose striving for power is so tense that he makes more emphatic and violent movements, feeling that he is forced at all times to produce evidence of his power. He is interested only in overcoming all obstacles in a straight-line aggressive approach" (Adler, 1927, p. 147).

The *melancholic type,* in whom the influence of black bile is strongest, is introspective and brooding, sad and "melancholy." "Individual Psychology sees in him the outspokenly hesitating neurotic who has no confidence in ever overcoming his difficulties or of getting ahead, who prefers not to risk a new adventure, who would rather remain standing still than proceed to a goal . . ." (Adler, 1927, p. 148).

Finally, the *phlegmatic type,* for whom, of course, phlegm is the dominant humor, is the slow, lethargic, uninterested-in-life individual. He makes few friends and "of all types he perhaps stands at the greatest distance from the business of living" (Adler, 1927, p. 148). In individual psychology, the phlegmatic temperament is interpreted as "a defense mechanism, a meaningful response to the challenge of existence . . ." (Adler, 1927, p. 150).

In 1935, Adler expanded his views on personality types and created new terminology to describe them. Though the four new personality types correspond to the four classical Hippocratic types, Adler stressed two new variables in their classification. The *degree of activity,* or what would probably now be called arousal level (cf. Eysenck in Chapter 15), and the *degree of social interest* were used to define and categorize the newly named *ruling, getting, avoiding,* and *socially useful* types.

Some individuals can be described in terms of activity level from childhood as wild or unbridled, while others are characteristically shy, withdrawn, and calm. The individual's style of life will be molded in some degree by the basic attitude he has acquired in interaction with his environment through his activity level. We would expect the wild, unbridled type of personality to have a more active, aggressive attitude toward life than the quieter, more withdrawn type. The four specific types are as follows:

(a.) *The Ruling-Dominant Type.*   This personality is assertive, aggressive, and active. He manipulates and masters the life situation and the people in it. His activity level is high, but it is combined with minimal social interest. The danger is that the activity will be directed into antisocial behavior.

(b.) *The Getting-Leaning Type.*   This type of individual expects others to satisfy his needs and to provide for his interests; he is a "leaner." The getting-leaning type is a combination of low social interest and low activity level.

(c.) *The Avoiding Type.*   This type of individual is inclined to achieve success by circumventing a problem, by withdrawing from it. In effect, he achieves mastery by avoiding defeat. His social interest is about as low as that of the getting-leaning type, but his activity level is even lower.

(d.) *The Socially Useful Type.*   This personality type is the healthiest of them all in Adler's view. The socially useful person attacks problems head on with a realistic appraisal of their difficulty. This type is socially oriented and prepared to cooperate with others to master the tasks of life. Thus, the socially useful person has a combination of high activity level and high social interest (Based on Adler, 1935, pp. 167–168).

In all cases, the important consideration for Adler was the degree of social interest embodied in a particular type, for the feeling of human empathy is the determinant of a goal-directed life that avoids the excesses of self-centered neurotic striving. The four social interest types correspond to the classical humoral types and Adler's early description of them. These correspondences have been summarized in Table 5–3.

TABLE 5–3: HIPPOCRATIC AND ADLERIAN TYPES

CLASSICAL GREEK TYPES		ADLER'S SOCIAL INTEREST TYPES	
HUMORS	TYPES	TYPES	SOCIAL INTEREST
Yellow bile	Choleric	Ruling-dominant	Low
Phlegm	Phlegmatic	Getting-leaning	Low
Black bile	Melancholic	Avoiding	Lowest
Blood	Sanguine	Socially useful	High

Note that the sanguine and socially useful types were considered by Adler to be the healthiest personalities because of their degree of social interest and willingness to tackle the problems of life, namely, vocational, social, and love tasks.

Early Recollections as Indicators of Style of Life

Adler employed a number of diagnostic indicators in dealing with his patients. Among these he employed dream analysis, interpretation of early recollections, and the birth-order sequence within a family. Adler felt that one of the most significant roads to investigating an individual personality could be traveled by an analysis of his earliest recollections. We have already seen an application of this technique to aspects of Adler's own life. The incidents, feelings, and people that the individual recalls from early in life are significant exactly because these and no others are available to the individual's conscious recollection. With them he expresses the meaning he has placed on his life:

> There are no "chance memories": out of the incalculable number of impressions which meet an individual, he chooses to remember only those which he feels, however darkly, to have a bearing on his situation. Thus his memories represent his "Story of My Life"; a story he repeats to himself to warn him or comfort him, to keep him concentrated on his goal, and to prepare him by means of past experiences, so that he will meet the future with an already tested style of action. [Adler, 1931, p. 73]

Thus, if he lives his life "as if" others are always trying to humiliate him, the memories he is likely to recall are those of humiliation or those that he can interpret as humiliating experiences (Adler, 1956, p. 351).

The most significant of the individual's early recollections is the one that he chooses to verbalize first. This incident will reveal his basic life attitude, "his first satisfactory crystallization of his attitude." Adler in no way accepted the individual's recollections as statements of fact. He seems, rather, to have treated them more as a form of projective test whereby the *individual's construction* of meaning, not the objective truth of the memory, is the key indicator. "What is altered or imagined is also expressive of a patient's goal . . ." (Adler, 1956, p. 352). Adler thus adhered to the same conviction that Freud had established as a major principle of psychology: Psychical events are determined. Or, as Adler stated it: "There are no chance memories." However, where Freud viewed the determinism of mental life as located in the patient's past, Adler interpreted early recollections as shaped by the patient's goal, that is, by his view of the future.

An Illustrative Case: Early Recollections of a Pampered Child

Adler treated a thirty-two-year-old man, suffering for two years with hysterical aphasia. He could not speak above a whisper. He had been involved in an accident on the street in which he fell suddenly against the window of a taxi. For two days, he vomited and suffered intense headaches; he probably sustained a concussion. At this time he lost his voice, although his throat showed no organic changes and no signs of injury from the accident. Eventually, the man decided to sue the taxi company for damages resulting from his injuries. As Adler diplomatically stated it: "We can understand that he is in a much better situation with his lawsuit if he can show some disability. We need not say that he is dishonest; but he has no great stimulus to speak loudly" (1931, p. 86). Adler asked the man for his earliest memory:

> "I was hanging in the cradle, lying on my back. I remember seeing the hook pull out. The cradle fell and I was badly hurt." [1931, p. 87]

Adler suggested that the man's recollection revealed an important aspect of his style of life: Because his mother had been horrified when she discovered his mishap, and because she showered him with atypical attentiveness, he learned a technique to gain her attention. It was his opinion that he deserved the increased concern and attention because before the accident "she did not take good enough care of me." Indeed, the accident occurred largely because, in the man's opinion, his mother had failed to prevent it. Of course the taxi incident followed the same pattern, for the company and the cab driver "did not take good enough care of him" (Adler, 1931, p. 87).

The character of these recollections suggested to Adler that the man had been a "pampered child," a favorite descriptive phrase for Adler. By that description Adler meant to indicate a child whose daily life involved the delegation of responsibility for living to others. Allowed to make none of his own choices, protected from every danger, the child soon fails to develop genuine autonomy, and he resents people who do not shower him with favor. The previous case history of Philip "the liar" is a similar example of a pampered child.

The man's next recollection followed in this path: "At the age of five I fell twenty feet with a heavy board on top of me. For five or more minutes I was unable to speak" (1931, p. 87). Again, his mother was horrified and excited, and, of course, very attentive. Adler's interpretation needs no elaboration:

> He was a child who wanted to be pampered, to be the center of attention. We can understand how he wants to be paid for his misfortunes [i.e., the taxi accident]. Other pampered children might do the same if the same accidents happened. Probably, however, they would not hit on the device of having a speech defect. This is the trademark of our patient; it is part of the style of life he has built up out of his experiences. [1931, pp. 87–88]

Early recollections, as employed by Adler, are an adjunct to psychotherapy that aims to reorient the patient's life, to enable him to reinterpret his past misinterpretations of his experiences (cf. Dreikurs, 1963, p. 254). The technique can be used, of course, to interpret patients' early recollections from a variety of theoretical viewpoints (Mosak, 1958).

Ordinal Position within the Family as Indicator of Style of Life

Another diagnostic indicator Adler pioneered by systematizing his clinical insights was interpretation of the birth-order relationships of children within a family. Adler pointed to the myriad of differences that exist between the first born and the last born, to the differences between an only child and a child with many siblings, and so on. *First born, second born, youngest child,* and *only child* are considered significant roles by Adler.

First Born (Oldest)

Because he is first born, the oldest child lives a favored existence for a time as an "only child." He is given central place until another child is born to remove his favored status. Adler comments:

> Now he must share the attention of his mother and father with a rival. The change always makes a great impression and we can often find in problem children, neurotics, criminals, drunkards and perverts that their difficulties began in such circumstances. They were oldest children who felt deeply the arrival of another child; and their sense of deprivation had moulded their whole style of life. [1931, p. 144]

Though he is skillful at gaining attention, the oldest child eventually learns that mother is too busy, too harassed, or too unconcerned to tolerate his demands. He turns to father. By directing his attention-getting behaviors to father, the deprived oldest child seeks to "reproach his mother" (1931, p. 146). The outcome of this family struggle is that the oldest child "trains himself for isolation." He masters the technique of surviving alone and independently of the need for anyone's affection or attention. Because the happiest time of his life was *before* the birth of the new child, oldest children often show an unusual interest in the past. "They are admirers of the past and pessimistic over the future" (1931, p. 147).

A healthy outcome is also possible. An oldest child may imitate father and mother in their attentions to the other children. As such imitation progresses, the oldest becomes a helper to the younger children or a father figure to playmates.

Second Born

From birth, a second-born child is raised in a world in which mother divides her attention and ministrations between her two children. This second child's existence is the most favored of the two since he has, so to speak, a "pacemaker" in the form of an older brother or sister. He is thus stimulated, or perhaps provoked, to match the older child's exploits.

> He behaves as if he were in a race, as if someone were a step or two in front and he had to hurry to get ahead of him. He is under full steam all the time. [Adler, 1931, p. 148]

When, however, the oldest child, the pacemaker, beats the younger sibling, the younger child is likely to feel incompetent. The most difficult combination occurs when the oldest is a boy and the second child is a girl. If the girl beats the older boy at his own game, he fares worse than if the younger child had been another boy. On the other hand, if the older child sets a pace to which the girl cannot match her stride, her personal and culturally reinforced feelings of inferiority will be intensified. Generally, however, the second child is the conqueror, using direct and devious means to surpass the pacemaker (Adler, 1929b, p. 106).

The Youngest Child

Although in a large family each succeeding child "dethrones" the previously born one, the last or youngest can never be removed from his pampered position. This child has many pacemakers, but because he retains the position of "most pampered," the baby of the family group, he often outstrips his brothers and sisters in achievements.

Adler felt, however, that the second largest proportion of problem children come from the group of youngest:

> The reason for this generally lies in the way in which all the family spoils them. A spoiled child can never be independent. He loses courage to succeed by his own effort. Youngest children are always ambitious; but the most ambitious children of all are the lazy children. Laziness is a sign of ambition joined with discouragement; ambition so high that the individual sees no hope of realizing it. [1931, p. 151]

Because of the multiplicity of his pacemaker models, the youngest child is driven to desire success in everything. Because universal accomplishment is unlikely, he may be driven to discouragement.

The Only Child

The only child's rival is his father. Pampered by his mother because she is afraid of losing him, he becomes "tied to his mother's apron strings." In later life, when no longer the center of attention, his enforced timidity and passivity will operate to his detriment.

> Only children are often very sweet and affectionate, and later in life they may develop charming manners in order to appeal to others, as they train themselves in this way, both in early life and later. . . . We do not regard the only child's situation as dangerous, but we find that, in the absence of the best educational methods, very bad results occur which would have been avoided if there had been brothers and sisters. [Adler, 1929b, pp. 111–112]

Adler's homely positional psychology is another outstanding example of his differences from Freud. While Freud focused on the instinctual interactions between children and parents, Adler preferred the common-sense approach of direct observation of children's behavior. His formulations contain many insights recognized from antiquity as "truisms," but like all homespun theory, the exceptions to the rule outnumber the agreements.

Conclusion

Adler's chief contribution was to provide the framework for a unified, holistic account of personality. His emphasis on man's creativity is matched by later theorists (e.g., George Kelly, R. D. Laing, Carl Rogers, Abraham Maslow), and his assumption of the goal-directed characteristics of human motives was given fuller scientific expression in the work of Kurt Lewin (see Chapter 11).

But Adler's influence on contemporary psychology has been slight, with improving prospects in recent years largely through the systematic efforts of the Ansbachers (1956, 1973). As contemporary theorists seek to formulate theories more adequate to the task of dealing with man's humanity, Adler's stature will rise. But only when Adler's clinical and insightful hypotheses are translated into empirically testable constructs, if that is possible, will his system achieve a place in the broader field of a unified behavioral science.

Summary

As a child, Alfred Adler had been singularly sensitized to cues indicating his own frailty and powerlessness. Poor health prevented him from competing successfully with his older brother and peers in the athletic pursuits of boyhood. Repeated brushes with death impressed Adler with the fragility of human nature and with the necessity for struggling against imposed helplessness. A powerful resentment toward his mother and older brother was also influential in shaping Adler's conception of human nature, for he became convinced that such undesirable impulses had to be controlled and replaced by a healthy concern for others. In his later theory of personality, Adler referred to this essential quality of the healthy personality as *Gemeinschaftsgefühl* ("social interest").

Having joined Freud's intellectual circle in Vienna in 1902, Adler, never completely committed to psychoanalysis, slowly drew farther and farther apart from orthodox Freudian theory. By 1911, the split between Freud and Adler reached a climax, and Adler set off to develop his own school of Individual Psychology. His differences from Freud were many, but key theoretical discrepancies can be discerned in the following six areas: (1) The ego was not merely the handmaiden of the id, but an independent, creative entity mediating intercourse with social reality. (2) The Oedipus complex was not exclusively a sexual phenomenon but an indication of the boy's attempts to gain superiority and power as possessed by the father. (3) Narcissism was not a retraction of energy into the ego as a protective self-interest, but an unhealthy, antisocial and egocentric withdrawal of interest in others. (4) Personality could not be studied piecemeal or in fragments of discrete id, ego, superego functioning; the *human person is a whole entity,* striving towards self-determined goals. (5) Dreams are attempts to create a mood that will induce the awake dreamer to take action he was previously reluctant to pursue; dreams are not satisfactions, as Freud held, but attempts to solve problems from waking life. (6) Freud's pessimism concerning the inherent evil of human nature offended Adler's philosophical convictions to the contrary.

For Adler the central core of personality is a state of perceived inferiority for which the individual feels compelled to compensate by striving for superiority. The notion of inferiority compensation underwent several changes in Adler's thinking:

Organ ———▶ Aggression   Masculine   Superiority   Perfection
Inferiority   Drive ———▶ Protest ———▶ Striving ———▶ Striving

Adopting Vaihinger's concept of "fiction," Adler postulated that every person has a *fictional final goal* in the sense of a *subjective* (fictional), unconscious, and creative striving to master the obstacles of his life. Each individual's life-meaning can be understood only by comprehending the goal toward which he strives. The neurotic's choice of goal, unlike the healthy personality's, is directed by egoistic, self-centered strivings for personal superiority and security. The normal personality's goal is largely centered in his social interest, that is, in his fellow feeling. It is this empathy with others that allows the normal personality to solve the tasks of life. Vocational, societal, and love tasks can be solved only by the individual who is willing to face life head-on and in cooperation with others.

Adler developed a typology of personality organized on the principles of activity level and degree of social interest. Four personality types were described: ruling-dominant (choleric); getting-leaning (phlegmatic); avoiding (melancholic); and the socially useful (sanguine) type. Adler felt that only the socially useful type, embodying a high degree of social interest and a high degree of activity, was healthy enough to master successfully the three life tasks.

Adler's diagnostic indicators employed in psychotherapy included the analysis of early recollections and the interpretation of the child's ordinal position within his family. Early recollections are important indicators because they reveal the central concerns and unconscious goals (fictions) of the personality through its conscious choice of key memories. Positional or ordinal psychology is concerned with the child's relationship to his parents and siblings. The first born is independent and initially favored; the second born is also favored because he has the "pacemaker" older sibling to model himself after, though there is the danger that he may feel incompetent by comparison, as had Adler with his older brother; the youngest child has many pacemakers to follow, and he is customarily the "most pampered;" and, finally, the only child who, like the first born, learns to be independent, is initially pampered, but may ultimately become timid and passive because he lacks pacemakers and siblings with whom to compete.

FOR FURTHER READING

Adler's definitive work is *The Practice and Theory of Individual Psychology* (Totowa, N.J.: Littlefield, Adams, 1959). Two biographical accounts are worth pursuing for what they reveal of the sources of Adler's ideas on inferiority and superiority. The most comprehensive biography is Phyllis Bottome's *Alfred Adler: A Portrait from Life* (New York: Vanguard, 1957). More concerned with explicating Adler's concepts than his life is Hertha Orgler's *Alfred Adler: The Man and His Work* (New York: Putnam, 1963).

Harold Mosak, an eminent Adlerian therapist, has edited a collection of papers that place Adler's work in historical perspective and evaluate his contemporary influence: *Alfred Adler: His Influence on Psychology Today* (Park Ridge, N.J.: Noyes Press, 1973). Some of the papers in this collection seek to extend Adlerian theory to family and child therapy. In a similar vein, Rudolf Dreikurs and Loren Grey develop an approach to child rearing and teaching from the Adlerian perspective in *A New Approach to Discipline: Logical Consequences* (New York: Hawthorne Books, 1968).

Heinz and Rowena Ansbacher have collected some of Adler's writings and edited them into a coherent account of his theory in *The Individual Psychology of Alfred Adler* (New York: Harper & Row, 1956); this volume will serve as an excellent source book for students of Adlerian psychology. The Ansbachers have performed the same service with a collection of Adler's later writings in *Superiority and Social Interest: A Collection of Later Writings* (New York: Viking, 1973), and this volume contains Furtmüller's previously unpublished biography of Adler. An interesting collection of case histories with Adler's comments is provided in *The*

Problem Child (New York: Putnam, 1963) and in *Problems of Neurosis,* edited by Philip Mairet (New York: Harper, 1929).

For contrasting points of view on why Adler and Freud ended their relationship, the reader should consult vol. 2 of Ernest Jones' *The Life and Work of Sigmund Freud* (New York: Basic Books, 1955) for the Freudian camp's opinion. The Adlerian consensus on the break-up may be gleaned from H. Mosak and R. Dreikurs' "Adlerian Psychotherapy," in R. Corsini (Ed.), *Current Psychotherapies* (Itasca, Ill.: Peacock, 1973), ch. 2.

6 KAREN HORNEY
Psychoanalytic Interpersonal
Theory

People can renounce food, money, attention, affection so long as they are only renouncing satisfaction, but they cannot renounce these things if without them they would be or feel in danger. . . .

KAREN HORNEY, *New Ways in Psychoanalysis*

. . . the deepest hatred grows out of broken love. . . . To have to recognize that a deep love was an error, a failure of intuition, so compromises us before ourselves, so splits the security and unity of our self-conception, that we unavoidably make the object of this intolerable feeling pay for it.

GEORG SIMMEL, *Conflict*

The Way the World Looks: Coping

Individuals differ in the way they view the world and in their perception of the best way to conduct their lives in relation to the people in it. Some individuals are human doormats, inviting an endless succession of significant (that is, emotionally important) others to tread all over them. These compliant personalities behave as if the most crucial aspect of existence were to please and pacify other people.

At the opposite extreme, there are persons who operate with a typically hostile strategy for dealing with others. These aggressive personalities seem to be behaving in a world that they view as dangerous. Only by constant vigilance, they seem to believe, can the continually hostile efforts of others be thwarted.

Yet a third form of interpersonal strategy is exemplified by the individual who remains coldly aloof and withdrawn from any genuine interaction with significant others. This detached personality seems to construe the world and its people as essentially troublesome and unjustly demanding. The only reasonable solution, he feels, is avoidance.

Karen Horney brilliantly described these three views of the world and the corresponding coping strategies. While nearly everyone adopts from time to time each of these stances toward others, the neurotic is unable to shift posture. Because he has become entangled in the web of his own efforts to ward off anxiety, the neurotic personality adopts *one* mode of

interaction as a rigidly unshakable coping technique. The first task, therefore, in exploring Horney's account of personality is to understand the
neurotic's strivings for safety and control over his world.

The Neurotic Trends: Strivings for Control

On the basis of theoretical assumptions derived partly from psychoanalytic theory and partly from her own clinical observations, Karen
Horney postulated that the neurotic personality is governed by one or
more of ten needs or trends. Each of these trends is directed toward *interpersonal control and coping;* that is, toward making life and its necessarily
people-oriented contacts bearable. Horney separated herself from the rest
of the psychoanalytic school in an important way:

> Freud believed that the [neurotic] disturbances generate from a con-
> flict between environmental factors and repressed instinctual im-
> pulses. Adler, more rationalistic and superficial than Freud, believes
> that they are created by the ways and means that people use to assert
> their superiority over others. Jung, more mystical than Freud, be-
> lieves in collective unconscious fantasies which, though replete with
> creative possibilities, may work havoc because the unconscious striv-
> ings fed by them are the exact opposite of those in the conscious
> mind. *My own answer is that in the center of psychic disturbances are
> unconscious strivings developed in order to cope with life despite fears, help-
> lessness, and isolation.* I have called them "neurotic trends." [1942, p.
> 40; italics added]

Each of the neurotic trends is characterized chiefly by its *compulsive rigidity.*
While a neurotic trend for affection, to take one example, may resemble
the normal need for love, the neurotic is unaware of the *indiscriminate*
nature of his need. His need for affection is out of all proportion to reality:
"If it is affection that a person must have, he must receive it from friend
and enemy, from employer and bootblack" (Horney, 1942, p. 41). Thus,
the ten neurotic trends superficially resemble healthy values, but are
different in four important respects: They are *disproportionate in intensity;
indiscriminate in application* to all other persons; evidence an extreme *disregard for reality;* and show a tendency to provoke *intense anxiety* when they
remain unsatisfied. These ten neurotic "needs" are (Horney, 1942, pp.
54–60):

1. *The neurotic need for affection and approval:*   an indiscriminate desire to
please others and to be liked and approved of by others. The person's
"center of gravity" is in others, not in self.
2. *The neurotic need for a "partner" who will take over one's life:*   a partner
who will fulfill all expectations the neurotic has in life; who will take
responsibility for good and evil, success and failure. The neurotic so in-

clined has a tendency to overvalue "love" because love can solve everything.

3. *The neurotic need to restrict one's life within narrow borders:* a necessity to be undemanding and contented with little; a need to remain inconspicuous, belittling one's potential.

4. *The neurotic need for power, for control over others, and for a facade of omnipotence:* domination over others craved for its own sake; essential disrespect for others; indiscriminate adoration of strength and contempt for weakness; belief in the power of reason and intelligence; extreme value placed on foresight and prediction; tendency to relinquish wishes and to withdraw because of dread of failure.

5. *The neurotic need to exploit others and get the better of them:* others evaluated primarily according to whether they can be exploited or made use of; dread of being exploited or made to look "stupid."

6. *The neurotic need for social recognition or prestige:* self-evaluation dependent entirely on public acceptance; all things and people evaluated only in terms of prestige value.

7. *The neurotic need for personal admiration:* inflated image of self; need to be admired not for what one possesses or presents in the public eye, but for the imagined self.

8. *The neurotic ambition for personal achievement:* self-evaluation dependent on being the very best—lover, sportsman, writer, worker—particularly in one's own mind, recognition by others being vital too, however, and its absence resented.

9. *The neurotic need for self-sufficiency and independence:* necessity never to need anybody, or to yield to any influence, or to be tied down to anything; necessity to avoid any closeness that involves the danger of enslavement.

10. *The neurotic need for perfection and unassailability:* ruminations or recriminations regarding possible flaws; relentless driving for perfection; feelings of superiority over others because of being perfect.

There are obviously many overlaps and similarities among the ten needs or trends. Horney in fact devoted a great deal of her later theoretical efforts to grouping and categorizing these ten discrete trends into clusters descriptive of particular personalities. The important fact to be kept in mind is that none of these trends is by itself abnormal; only when the trend is disproportionate, indiscriminate, relentless, and anxiety-provoking when frustrated can it be classed as neurotic.

Basic Anxiety and Basic Hostility

Very much like Adler, Horney assumed that one of the child's most potent early perceptions of himself was the discovery of his helplessness. In the face of powerful and authoritative, manipulative and decisive "giants" like

parents, he perceives himself to be weak and small. The child thus soon
learns that his needs, his safety, and his comfort are wholly dependent on
these powerful people. His very survival depends on his evoking in them
a favorable and responsive attitude toward himself.

Parental Indifference: The "Basic Evil"

Horney felt that the "basic evil" that lies at the source of later neurosis is
a coldly indifferent, perhaps hostile, rejecting attitude of the parents toward the child:

> The basic evil is invariably a lack of genuine warmth and affection.
> A child can stand a great deal of what is often regarded as traumatic
> —such as sudden weaning, occasional beating, sex experiences—as
> long as inwardly he feels wanted and loved. . . . *The main reason why
> a child does not receive enough warmth and affection lies in the parents'
> incapacity to give it on account of their own neuroses.* . . . we find various
> actions or attitudes on the part of the parents which cannot but
> arouse hostility, such as preference for other children, unjust re-
> proaches, unpredictable changes between overindulgence and scorn-
> ful rejection, unfulfilled promises, and not least important, *an attitude
> toward the child's needs which goes through all gradations from temporary
> inconsideration to a consistent interfering with the most legitimate wishes of
> the child,* such as disturbing friendships, ridiculing independent
> thinking, spoiling its interest in its own pursuits . . .—*altogether an
> attitude of the parents which if not in intention nevertheless in effect means
> breaking the child's will.* [1937, pp. 80–81; italics added]

The main result of such parental indifference, inconsistency, and interference is the creation within the child of an attitude of *basic hostility.*

Basic Hostility: Repression for Survival
and Security

Like a mature person, the child senses the injustice of his treatment at the
hands of his emotionally manipulative elders, and he rightfully resents
both the manipulation and the manipulators. Unfortunately, unlike the
mature adult, the child is in no position to alter the circumstances by a
direct expression of his hostility and anger; he must repress his angry
feelings—drive them right out of awareness—in the service of his continued survival. Repression of the hostility is triggered by a combination of
feelings on the child's part: feelings of helplessness, fear, love, or guilt
(Horney, 1937, p. 85). But whatever the motive for repression, the result
is the creation of feelings of increased unworthiness and anxiety. Because
he is caught between dependence on his parents and the growing feeling

of hostility toward them, he may actually intensify the conflict by turning those feelings against the only available "safe" target, himself. His feelings of helplessness are thus magnified and the need to maintain the repression of hostility is reinforced. In mottolike form, the child's behavior says: "*I have to repress my hostility because I need you*" (Horney, 1937, p. 86).

In some cases, parents actively strive to dominate their children by teaching them fear of the world and its people. They impress the child with the "great dangers of life": germs, cars, strangers, other children, and on and on. In consequence, the child becomes apprehensive lest he be unable to survive in such a dangerous world without his parents' help. Furthermore, he learns to fear the parents themselves because they have the awesome power to evoke images of the dangers. For this child, repression of hostility is a product of his fear: he does not *dare* to express it. "*I have to repress my hostility,*" his motto goes, "*because I am afraid of you*" (Horney, 1937, p. 86).

In other families, where genuine affection and warmth are lacking, there occurs a kind of verbal substitute expression of love in the form of continual protestations by the parents of how much they are sacrificing for the child. In this case, the child may cling desperately to this mock emotion and feel: "*I have to repress my hostility for fear of losing love*" (Horney, 1937, p. 86).

All three cases are essentially similar in that the child's fundamental motive is to sustain satisfying contact with the powerful people of his world. Survival need, fear, and love are in most ways closely related by the thread of helplessness that runs through the child's entire pattern of existence.

Basic Anxiety: Lonely and Helpless in a Hostile World

The danger of the child's repression of basic hostility toward his parents is that he will generalize that "grudging and anxious" attitude to people in general. The more he covers his hostility and his "grudge against his own family," the more likely he is to project his anxiety to the outside world and its people. He will soon convince himself that the whole world is, as his parents' behavior may have suggested, a dangerous place:

> The condition that is fostered or brought about by the factors I have mentioned . . . is an insidiously increasing, *all-pervading feeling of being lonely and helpless in a hostile world.* . . . This attitude as such does not constitute a neurosis but it is the nutritive soil out of which a definite neurosis may develop at any time. Because of the fundamental role this attitude plays in neuroses I have given it a special designation: *the basic anxiety;* it is inseparably interwoven with a *basic hostility.*
> [Horney, 1937, p. 89; italics added]

Horney's concept of *basic anxiety* sounds similar to Adler's notion of the inferiority feelings of childhood. Her explicit definition of basic anxiety strengthens the similarity:

> It [basic anxiety] may be roughly described as a feeling of being small, insignificant, helpless, deserted, endangered, in a world that is out to abuse, cheat, attack, humiliate, betray, envy. [Horney, 1937, p. 92]

The most immediate consequence of the combination of basic hostility and the resultant basic anxiety is the creation of a characteristic mode of reacting to the world and to significant others. Originally, Horney proposed four such character types (1937, p. 96); later, however, in keeping with her tendency to formulate concepts in threes, she reduced the number (1945).

If a child comes to feel that he can survive only by *complying with others* and by placating them:—"*If you love me, you will not hurt me*"—he may solve his survival problem by offering the world a passive, nonassertive, appeasing personality. (Horney, 1937, p. 97).

Another child may develop the attitude that life is a struggle that must be fought by maintaining an aggressive stance toward others: "*If I have power, I shall not be hurt*" (Horney, 1937, p. 97). This child's characteristic interaction with others solves his survival problems by keeping others at arm's length or by exerting dominance over them.

Lastly, a child may solve the conflict between unexpressed basic hostility and anxiety by withdrawal from others: "*If I withdraw, nothing can hurt me*" (Horney, 1937, p. 99). His habitual mode of dealing with others is to create a protective shell of isolation, thereby removing himself from *any* significant emotional interactions.

Each of these character attitudes will be given fuller treatment. For now, however, it is important to retrace the sequence of Horney's ideas about the nature of personality development to emphasize the importance of basic hostility and basic anxiety.

Out of the fundamental feelings of hostility and anxiety develops a set of values for living. As we have seen, Horney initially proposed ten such values or neurotic trends, and later she regrouped them in terms of the three character attitudes of *compliance, aggression,* and *withdrawal.*

The child has been made aware that his feelings of hostility and anger cannot be openly displayed; he represses them and the repression is reinforced by parental indifference, inconsistency, or withdrawal of love. His feeling of helplessness is thus also intensified. The world and its people become a source of anticipated pain and anxiety. Out of these anticipations the child develops a series of needs that are rigid, compulsive, and indiscriminate strivings to predict, control, and survive the manipulations and the indifference of a hostile world. These concepts are best illustrated in the context of a real personality. For this reason, we turn next to the case history of Clare.

An Illustrative Case: Clare, an Unwanted Child

Despite several of her mother's abortion attempts, Clare was born into the unhappy marriage. Her parents' first child, a boy, had been born at a time when the marriage was a happy one, and in some ways he remained the only object of genuine parental approval and affection. Not that Clare was in any material way mistreated or abused. She always received the same quantity and quality of gifts, trips, lessons, and educational opportunities as her brother.

> But in less tangible matters she received less than the brother, less tenderness, less interest in school marks and in the thousand little daily experiences of a child, less concern when she was ill, less solicitude to have her around, less willingness to treat her as a confidante, less admiration for looks and accomplishments. [Horney, 1942, p. 49]

Always away from home, Clare's father, a doctor, became the object of the mother's ridicule and loathing. As the "dominating spirit" of the family, mother's evaluation of father soon was converted into a family law of contempt. So great was the bitterness against the father that open death wishes were often expressed by Clare's mother and these "contributed much to Clare's feeling that it was much safer to be on the powerful side" (Horney, 1942, p. 49).

The most immediate result of the family atmosphere on Clare's development was her lost opportunity to develop a sense of confidence and self-trust. As Clare matured, her feelings of unworthiness and her sense of total unlikableness grew:

> This shift from essentially true and warranted accusations of *others* to essentially untrue and unwarranted *self-accusations had far-reaching consequences. . . . And the shift meant more than an acceptance of the majority estimate of herself. It meant also that she repressed all grievances against the mother. If everything was her own fault, the grounds for bearing a grudge against mother were pulled away from under her.* [Horney, 1942, p. 50; italics added]

Clare thus relinquished any possibility of genuine rebellion against the injustice of her own treatment at the hands of her family. Instead, she became a "joiner," a compliant member in the circle of admirers surrounding the powerful mother. "By admiring what in reality she resented, she became alienated from her own feelings. She no longer knew what she herself liked or wished or feared or resented" (Horney, 1942, p. 51). In short, she began to act on the unconscious premise "that it is safer to admire others than to be critical." In a word, Clare had become *compliant.*

The essentially self-effacing quality characteristic of compliance was expressed in a variety of ways in Clare's behavior. One way was her compulsive modesty, a tendency to "put herself into second place," and to judge herself more critically than anyone else ever could. In effect, Clare had lost the capacity to take control over her own life; she lived life only to appease and placate others. Beneath the facade of compliance, passivity, and modesty, however, there developed an unconscious need to excel others, to beat them at their own game, a striving aimed at restoring some much needed self-esteem. But of course that need had to remain submerged.

At the age of thirty, Clare felt the need of analytic treatment. As an editor for a magazine, she had submerged her ambition to do creative fiction writing. Her life and interests had become so constricted in the service of compliance that she was able to perform only routine work on the writing of others, but was totally incapacitated when it came to original or creative writing of her own.

Fortunately an incident occurred that allowed Clare to see the anxiety that underlay her compulsive humility and modesty. She had developed a plan for improving the magazine, a plan she knew to be sound but which would occasion much protest and argument from other members of the staff. During the staff meeting at which she was to present her plan, she experienced several moments of panic. She even had to leave the room at one point because of a sudden attack of diarrhea. However, when the discussion began to favor her proposal, she was able to control herself and the panic diminished. After her plan proved successful in operation, she received much recognition and acclaim. Instead of viewing her success as a critical victory, she was able to view it only as a lucky escape from great danger.

Eventually, with continued analytic treatment, Clare was able to recognize that her self-effacement was a striving for security. She came to enjoy her successes and to take pride in her considerable abilities. A final indication of her slowly burgeoning self-confidence and realistic pride was embodied in a dream she had during the final phase of her psychoanalysis:

> . . . she drove with her friend in a strange country and it occurred to her that she, too, might apply for a driver's license. Actually she had a license and could drive as well as the friend. The dream symbolized a dawning insight that she had rights of her own and need not feel like a helpless stranger. [Horney, 1942, p. 84]

Real Self, Actual Self, and Ideal Self: "Tyranny of the Shoulds"

Confronted by the intense conflict between his feelings of helplessness and his unexpressible hostility toward his parents, the child has slowly developed a characteristic *defensive* way of perceiving himself. His *"real self,"* he has been made to realize, is despicable, unlovable, and unworthy; his parents' inconsistent and indifferent reactions to him have made that clear. The hostility that he has had to repress has been turned against the self to further buttress the notion that he is unlovable and unworthy. This so-called "real" self is not real at all. Since the picture he holds of this personage is based on *false* evaluations by others, it is "real" only to the extent that *he* believes it (Horney, 1945, p. 98). When his image of this "real" self is this negative, it would more appropriately be designated as the "despised self."

The child necessarily begins to develop a defensive restructuring of his image of the despised real self into an *idealized image of the self he should be* in order to survive the hostile world and gain needed love and approval.

> In contrast to authentic ideals, the idealized image has a static quality. It is not a goal toward whose attainment he strives but a fixed idea which he worships. . . . The idealized image is a decided hindrance to growth because it either denies shortcomings or merely condemns them. *Genuine ideals make for humility, the idealized image for arrogance.* [Horney, 1945, p. 99; italics added]

The idealized self-image substitutes for genuine self-confidence and pride. It is based on a wishful-thinking style that is betrayed in all of its unrealistic compulsivity later in adulthood when the neurotic continually refers to his "shoulds":

> "Forget about the disgraceful creature you actually *are* [i.e., the despised real self]; this is how you *should* be. . . ." He should be the utmost of honesty, generosity, considerateness, justice, dignity, courage, unselfishness. He should be the perfect lover, husband, teacher. He should be able to endure anything, should like everybody, should love his parents, his wife, his country; or, he should not be attached to anything or anybody, nothing should matter to him, he should never feel hurt, and he should always be serene and unruffled. He should always enjoy life; or, he should be above pleasure and enjoyment. He should be spontaneous; he should always control his feelings. He should know, understand, and foresee everything. He should be able to solve every problem of his own, or of others, in no time. He should be able to overcome every difficulty of his as soon as he sees it. He should never be tired or fall ill. He should always

be able to find a job. He should be able to do things in one hour which can only be done in two to three hours. [Horney, 1950, p. 65]

This seemingly endless list of things the neurotic feels he ought to be or do was termed by Horney the "tyranny of the should" (1950, pp. 65 ff.). The contradictory and uncompromising nature of the items in the list suggests the compulsive, inexorable process of personality distortion that has resulted from the creation of the idealized self-image. With time, the idealized self-image becomes converted into an ideal self, no longer to be recognized as a fiction. It is now seen as a state of being that is nearly impossible to attain (Horney, 1950, p. 158). Nevertheless, the neurotic is compelled to strive toward this unreachable ideal in what Horney called the "search for glory" (1950, p. 23). Indeed, the ideal self slowly becomes more real to the neurotic than his "real" despised self ever was. The idealized self becomes the *comprehensive neurotic solution,* for it actualizes the fantasied image by which all problems can be solved, all difficulties surmounted. With the creation of the ideal self, the neurotic "solves" the conflict between his feelings of basic anxiety and hostility; *he learns to deal with the world and its people through the shoulds of the ideal self.*

In her later work, Horney created a further distinction among the images the neurotic has of himself. Originally the term *real self* was used to indicate the damaged self-image produced in the child by his parents' reinforcement of his feelings of helplessness. Horney later changed the usage somewhat by employing "real self" to designate the true core of a person's being, his very center of existence. The real self harbors all of his potential for growth and health: "clarity and depth of his own feelings, thoughts, wishes, interests; the ability to tap his own resources, the strength of his will power, the special capacities or gifts he may have; the faculty to express himself, and to relate to others with his spontaneous feelings" (Horney, 1950, p. 17). It is this core that is damaged by parental indifference. The goal of the real self is the striving for self-realization, that is, the accomplishment of the person's *own* values and aims in life. In this sense, Horney began to use the term "real self" to indicate a "possible self," that is, a self that the individual *can* realistically learn to express.

To a large extent, the real self is a product of the person's own perceptions, his own interpretations of what he is. To distinguish from this phenomenally real self the objective sum of what the person is at any moment in time as observed by others Horney used the term *actual self.* The actual self is thus the totality of everything, physical and mental, that the person "really" is, independent of the person's own perceptions. In summary, the real self is the core of the person's existence as he perceives it and perhaps despises it; the ideal self is a glorified image of what he should be, an image that is impossible to attain; the actual self is the sum of objectively observable characteristics of the person at one moment in time.

It should be pointed out that for Horney the goal of psychotherapy was to provide the individual with the means to free his real self, to accept its character, and to allow it full and spontaneous expression without the curtailment of learned defensiveness (Horney, 1946, pp. 202 ff.).

The Core Neurotic Conflict: Alienation from Real Self

The central neurotic conflict can now be rephrased. Recall that Horney originally described it as the contradictory trend between unexpressed hostility and anxiety over feelings of helplessness. These feelings are generalized to people at large from their original focus against the family, causing the individual to adopt one of three possible orientations to the world. On the basis of those needs he values most, he may adopt a strategy of compliance, aggression, or withdrawal. Now, however, the central conflict was rephrased in terms of Horney's developing ideas of the real and idealized selves.

The basic anxiety experienced in childhood and coupled with basic hostility that could not be expressed causes an alienation of the individual from his real self. The central neurotic conflict is furthered by the adoption of an idealized self at the expense of one's spontaneity, self-trust, and independence. In essence, the neurotic attempts to mold himself into something he is not to gain that which he has lost: security. Since other people are the key agents in what has become a dangerous world, he adopts defensive strategies for dealing with them: "He feels what he *should* feel, wishes what he *should* wish, likes what he *should* like" (Horney, 1950, p. 159; italics added).

> In other words, the tyranny of the should drives him frantically to be something different from what he is or could be. And in his imagination he *is* different—so different, indeed, that the real self fades and pales still more. Neurotic claims, in terms of self, mean the abandoning of the reservoir of spontaneous energies. Instead of making his own efforts, for instance, with regard to human relations, the neurotic insists that others should adjust to him. [Horney, 1950, p. 159]

Three consequences of the individual's alienation from his real self can be discerned in the neurotic's feelings of being removed from himself (Horney, 1950, pp. 159–161):

1. *Abandonment of self-responsibility for his behavior:* The neurotic comes to feel that "I am driven instead of being the driver" (1950, p. 159).
2. *Active moves away from the real self:* His own inner creative forces lie fallow as he succumbs to the idealized self and the search for glory embodied in his "shoulds"; at all costs the ideal image must be striven for, perpetually and inexorably, since only by investing all energy in these strivings can the despised real self be left behind.

3. *Active moves against the real self:*   The individual experiences bouts of self-hate, with the idea of "being oneself" becoming terrifying and appalling. The neurotic has an unconscious interest in not being himself, in not having a clear self-perception. In short, the neurotic treats himself *impersonally,* as an object.

Interpersonal Coping Strategies: Moves Toward, Away from, and Against Others

Unlike Freud, who saw conflict between repressed instincts and the forces of the ethical side of personality as the core of neurosis, Horney observed a different kind of conflict, interpersonal and intrapersonal conflict:

> They [i.e., the conflicts] operated between contradictory sets of neurotic trends, and though they originally concerned contradictory attitudes toward others, in time they encompassed contradictory attitudes toward the self, contradictory qualities and contradictory sets of values. . . . [1945, p. 15]

Horney viewed the neurotic's symptoms and interpersonal strategies as attempts to "solve" his basic conflicts. Compulsive and indiscriminate strivings, contradictory and conflicted needs for perfection, power, affection, and independence, are all anxiety-allaying techniques designed to maintain the alienation between his despised real self and his ideal self, and between the real self and significant others. The ten neurotic trends or needs began to be more comprehensible to Horney as *clusters of strivings* directed toward dealing with people and their demands. Horney organized the ten needs into three patterns of traits, illustrated by the three hypothetical personalities with which we began. It is necessary to examine those three character types from the perspective of Horney's concept of self-alienation.

Moving Toward People: The Self-Effacing Solution

Recall that the first solution to neurotic conflict that Horney described was originally termed "moving towards others" (Horney, 1945, pp. 48 ff.). This type of individual manifests the neurotic traits that are conducive to compliance, much as Clare had learned to do. These traits include intense needs for affection and approval, a need for a partner in the form of friend, husband, wife, or lover, and a necessity to be undemanding, restricting one's life within narrow borders:

> In sum, this type needs to be liked, wanted, desired, loved; to feel accepted, welcomed, approved of, appreciated; to be needed, to be of

importance to others, especially to one particular person; to be helped, protected, taken care of, guided. [Horney, 1945, p. 51]

The goal of the compliant type's "moving towards others" is on the surface a need to be in harmony with them, to avoid friction. But contradictory trends may also be served by this strategy. Compliance on the surface may mask a strong inner need to compete, to excel, to dominate (Horney, 1945, p. 56). Below the surface, within the real self, there boils an unrecognized rage, anger, and residual hostile sentiment. The compliant neurotic's need to be liked by others thus serves to conceal his need to be aggressive. Occasionally, the repressed impulses of anger will explode into fits of irritability or into temper tantrums. Or, he may make demands on others only "because he is so miserable—'poor me.' " Of course, he never recognizes that such demands are manipulative of others, or that they are attempts to satisfy his aggressive strivings: "He cannot help feeling at times that he is so unfairly treated that he simply can't stand it any longer" (Horney, 1945, p. 58).

In her later statement of neurotic conflict (1950, pp. 214 ff.), Horney referred to the "moving towards others" strategy as the *self-effacing solution* to neurotic conflict. In effect, the self-effacing person has identified his ideal self with his restricted and subdued despised self:

> He is *his subdued self;* he is the stowaway without any rights. In accordance with this attitude he also tends to suppress in himself anything that connotes ambition, vindictiveness, triumph, seeking his own advantage. In short he has solved his inner conflict by suppressing all expansive attitudes and drives and making self-abnegating trends predominant. [Horney, 1950, p. 216]

The self-effacing type has idealized the qualities of suffering, helplessness, and martyrdom, *for only by viewing himself as "saintly" can he supply himself with a good reason to endure the basic hostility he has never allowed himself to express.* If one is a saint, then it is reasonable that one must suffer. And suffering becomes even more enjoyable if you can spread the misery to others. He thus is unable to identify with his idealized and glorified self-image. He can identify only with his victimized distortion of it. Horney felt that the self-effacing "solution" was the most damaging because intrinsic to this strategy is intense subjective unhappiness.

Moving Against People: The Expansive Solution

The aggressive, expansive solution to neurotic conflict is based on a different view of life: on a belief that the world is a hostile place and that life "is a struggle of all against all . . ." (Horney, 1945, p. 63). This individual characteristically behaves toward others in aggressive ways; he is best described as "moving against others." He has a kind of Machiavellian facade of suave politeness and good fellowship that is designed to facilitate satisfaction of his need for control and power. The aggressive individual needs to excel by exploiting others, to attain recognition by exerting dominance and power over those he perceives to be underlings. Success and prestige are the yardsticks to his sense of self-worth:

> Any situation or relationship is looked at from the standpoint of "What can I get out of it?"—whether it has to do with money, prestige, contacts, or ideas. *The person himself is consciously or semiconsciously convinced that everyone acts this way,* and so what counts is to do it more efficiently than the rest. [Horney, 1945, p. 65; italics added]

Where the compliant type who moves toward others has a need for a mate or partner stemming from his feelings of helplessness, the aggressive type desires a partner who can enhance his prestige, power, or wealth.

Horney later rechristened this type who "moves against" people as the expansive solution to neurotic conflict: the appeal of mastery (1950, pp. 187 ff.). In almost every respect, the expansive solution is the direct opposite to the self-effacing solution. *The expansive type glorifies and cultivates in himself everything that leads to mastery of others* (1950, p. 214).

> The appeal of life lies in its mastery. . . . He should be able to master the adversities of fate, the difficulties of a situation, the intricacies of intellectual problems, the resistances of other people, conflicts in himself. The reverse side of the necessity for mastery is his dread of anything connoting helplessness; this is the most poignant dread he has. [Horney, 1950, p. 192]

Horney distinguished among three subvarieties of the expansive type, each characterized by a different reason to move against others:

1. *Narcissistic Type:* Moving against others is based on a firmly inflated estimate of his own worth. "He has (conspicuously) no doubts; he *is* the anointed, the man of destiny, the prophet, the great giver, the benefactor of mankind" (1950, p. 194).

2. *The Perfectionistic Type:* Moving against others is based on the belief that his personal standards involving moral and intellectual capacity are superior to others. "His arrogant contempt for others, though, is hidden —from himself as well—behind polished friendliness, because his very standards prohibit such 'irregular' feelings" (1950, p. 196).

3. *The Arrogant Vindictive Type:* Moving against others is based on a need for triumph, victory, and glory. "He is convinced that everybody at bottom is malevolent and crooked, that friendly gestures are hypocritical, that it is only wisdom to regard everyone with distrust unless he has been proved honest" (1950, p. 199).

Horney summarized the three types of expansive solution:

> The *narcissistic type* can be friendly and generous under certain condi-
> tions, out of a feeling of abundance, even though this arises on a
> partly spurious basis. The *perfectionistic type* can show friendliness
> because he *should* be friendly. The *arrogant-vindictive type* tends to
> crush friendly feelings and to scorn them. There is much hostility in
> all of them, but in the *narcissistic* it can be overruled by generosity;
> in the *perfectionistic* it is subdued because he *should* not be hostile; in
> the *arrogant-vindictive* person it is more out in the open and . . . poten-
> tially more destructive. [1950, pp. 212–213; italics added]

The common denominator that binds together all of the expansive, aggressive solutions to neurotic conflict is the identification of the neurotic's real
self with his glorified idealized self. Unlike the compliant, self-effacing
type who identifies with his despised real self, the aggressive person has
come to believe that he *is* his ideal self, that he *is* the glorified image
toward which he strives. All of the aggressive type's behavior can be
understood as an attempt to actualize the ideal self (Horney, 1950, p. 192).

Moving Away from People: The Solution of Resignation

The third "solution" to neurotic conflict is practiced by those individuals
who develop a protective "I don't care about anything" attitude. They
become detached from human affairs and resigned to an emotionally flat
life. For if he does not allow himself to care about anything or anyone, he
can deceive himself that he will never be hurt. Horney characterized this
individual's dominant strategy as "moving away from people" (1945, pp.
73 ff.). The resigned individual evidences intense needs of self-sufficiency,
perfection, and unassailability. He tends to restrict his life within narrow
confines much as the compliant type does, but for the resigned individual
the motive is the need *never to be dependent on anyone.*

Neurotic detachment is considerably different from the normal feelings
each of us experiences on those occasions when we would like to be alone
with our own thoughts. The neurotic has *persistent* feelings of indifference
and withdrawal based on an "intolerable strain in associating with people"
(Horney, 1950, p. 73).

> What is crucial is their inner need to put emotional distance between
> themselves and others. More accurately, it is their conscious and
> unconscious determination not to get emotionally involved with oth-
> ers in any way, whether in love, fight, co-operation, or competition.
> They draw around themselves a kind of magic circle which no one
> may penetrate. [Horney, 1945, p. 75]

By his resigned attitude and detachment, the neurotic who moves away from others has removed himself from the "inner battlefield" of his own conflicts. His "don't care" demeanor provides him with a sense of superior distance, haughty removal from his own and others' "petty" problems. He becomes an onlooker at himself and his life to the degree that even in therapy he remains detached and views the process of his own inner explorations as a "fascinating entertainment" (Horney, 1950, p. 261).

A consequence of his "moving away from others" is the total lack of any striving for achievement or success in the ordinary meaning of these terms. He belittles his own assets. Unconsciously, he denies any desire to achieve success or to exert effort on his own behalf. He lacks goal-centeredness. As a result, he is hypersensitive to coercion or advice, which he perceives as essentially similar, and he rejects both in his attempts to remain independent.

Horney identified three modes of stilted and joyless living that characterize various subvarieties of the resigned neurotic:

1. *Persistent Resignation:* This individual is characterized by a continual emotional inertia. He fulfills as few of the tasks of life as are necessary to guarantee his freedom. He may pass for essentially normal, though without any observable joy in living. His persistent resignation may be only a mask covering a feeling of rebelliousness. Instead of active resistance to life, he practices passive resistance: a total uncooperation with the demands of living.

2. *Rebelliousness:* The appeal of freedom and independence from others is so strong for this individual that he *actively* resists the "trivia" of life. He may turn the rebellion against the self and struggle against his own inner tyrannies and shoulds. In this sense, his rebellion may actually be liberating and therapeutic.

3. *Shallow Living:* This type of individual "moves to the periphery of life"; he is without hope or any positive commitment. In worse condition than the persistently resigned type, the "shallow liver" finds life worthless. Eventually he will settle for superficial enjoyments, "high living," without meaning or direction, or he will pursue opportunistic success in business. But beneath the mask of sociability he is merely a "well adapted automaton" (Horney, 1950, pp. 286–287). He goes through the motions of life, but he is without genuine concern or involvement. He lives with others, takes over their conventions, codes of conduct, and morals. But inwardly he never accepts any of these codes as truly relevant to him. In short, he becomes other directed and completely without responsibility for his own life.

The common denominator that binds the three types of detached or resigned neurotic is the presence of vacillation between identification with the despised real self and identification with the glorified ideal self. The detached neurotic strives halfheartedly toward actualization of his ideal self, but fundamentally he has surrendered any hope of making the glorified image come true. In effect, he is unsatisfied with his despised real self, but simultaneously afraid to strive toward the goals of the ideal self. He desires to be free *from* all demands, rather than to be free *for* the pursuit of desirable activities.

Horney's description of the three patterns of neurotic conflict-solution points up an important premise of her theory. Each of the patterns is designed to minimize anxiety in *dealing with people.* Thus, Horney's conceptualizations emphasize her position that the neuroses are evidence of damaged *interpersonal processes.* Horney summarized the three attitude types in these terms:

> As we have seen, each of the basic attitudes toward others has its positive value. In moving toward people the person tries to create for himself a friendly relation to his world. In moving against people he equips himself for survival in a competitive society. In moving away from people he hopes to attain a certain integrity and serenity. As a matter of fact, all three attitudes are not only desirable but necessary to our development as human beings. *It is only when they appear and operate in a neurotic framework that they become compulsive, rigid, indiscriminate, and mutually exclusive.* [1945, p. 89; italics added]

The three attitude types are presented together with their dominant neurotic needs in Table 6–1.

Auxiliary Conflict Solutions

In addition to the basic attitudes for dealing with others, Horney suggested that several secondary or auxiliary techniques might be employed by the neurotic personality in his striving for security. Each of these techniques is to be conceptualized as a "secondary defence" in the service of buttressing the primary attitudinal "solution" to neurotic conflict.

Externalization

Though the neurotic personality seeks to bridge the distance between his idealized self and his real self, all of his efforts paradoxically broaden the gap. In the most extreme case, when the gap between the idealized self and the real self becomes so great that the person can no longer tolerate the discrepancy, he must turn elsewhere than to himself for the solution. "The only thing left then is to run away from himself entirely and see everything as if it lay outside" (Horney, 1945, p. 116).

Externalization is the auxiliary neurotic defense technique by which the individual shifts his "center of gravity" from the self to others. Although

TABLE 6–1: "SOLUTIONS" TO NEUROTIC CONFLICT

SELF-EFFACING SOLUTION: LOVE "Moving Toward" (Compliance)	EXPANSIVE SOLUTION: MASTERY "Moving Against" (Aggression)	RESIGNATION SOLUTION: FREEDOM "Moving Away" (Detachment)
Need for:	Need for:	Need for:
1. Affection and approval	4. Power and omnipotence and perfection	3. Restriction of life to narrow borders
2. Partner to take control	5. Exploitation of others	9. Self-sufficiency
3. Restriction of life to narrow borders	6. Social recognition and prestige	10. Perfection and unassailability
	7. Personal admiration	
	8. Personal achievement	
"If you love me, you will not hurt me."	*"If I have power, no one can hurt me."*	*"If I withdraw, nothing can hurt me."*
Identification with the despised real self	Identification with the ideal self	Vacillation between despised real self and ideal self

Based on Horney, 1945, chaps. 3, 4, 5; 1942, chap. 2; and 1950, chap. 3.

somewhat similar to the defensive technique described by Freud as projection, externalization is much more comprehensive, for it involves the shift outward to others not only of unacceptable feelings, but of *all* feelings, all emotion. Other people become the center of all the neurotic's emotional life: these external individuals become the nucleus of all important strivings that would normally be directed to and experienced by the self. Thus, the person may be angry with himself, but instead he attributes the anger to another: *He* is angry with me. A profound consequence for his dealings with others emerges from his tendency to externalize:

> When a person feels that his life for good or ill is determined by others, it is only logical that he should be preoccupied with changing *them,* reforming *them,* punishing *them,* protecting himself from *their* interference, or impressing *them.* . . . Another inevitable product of externalization is a gnawing sense of emptiness and shallowness. . . . Instead of feeling the emotional emptiness as such, the person experiences it as emptiness in his stomach and tries to do away with it by compulsive eating. Or he may fear that his lack of bodily weight could cause him to be tossed about like a feather—any storm, he feels, might carry him away. He may even say that he would be nothing but an empty shell if everything were analyzed. [Horney, 1945, p. 117; italics added]

Horney's description of the emptiness of the self resembles Laing's description of what he called the experience of implosion or the vacuum of the empty self (see Chapter 8). By externalizing his very being, the individual can forgo any feelings of humiliation, self-hate, or self-contempt; he merely assigns these damaging functions to others. He still feels unworthy but now he has provided himself with a rational reason for the self-hatred: others have no use for him since he is *nothing.*

Creation of Blind Spots

The magnitude of the difference between a neurotic's ongoing behaviors and his idealized picture of himself can sometimes be so great that outsiders marvel that he never himself detects the discrepancy. The fact that the neurotic never consciously admits the difference is evidence for the existence of a *blind spot,* that is, the creation of a defensive "refusal to see" his own defenses.

> A patient, for example, who had all the characteristics of the compliant type and *thought of himself as Christlike,* told me quite casually that at staff meetings he would often shoot one colleague after another with a little flick of his thumb. True enough, the destructive craving that prompted these figurative killings was at that time unconscious; but the point here is that the shooting, *which he dubbed "play,"* did

not in the least disturb his Christlike image. [Horney, 1945, p. 132; italics added]

Compartmentalization

Similar to blind spots, *compartmentalization* involves pigeonholing one's life into rigid and exclusive categories: thus, there is a compartment for friends, for enemies, for family, for outsiders, a compartment for professional activities separate from personal life, and so on (Horney, 1945, p. 133). The important point is that anything that occurs in one compartment cannot contradict, influence, or support what transpires in another. "Compart-mentalizing is thus as much a result of being divided by one's conflicts as a defense against recognizing them" (Horney, 1945, p. 134). A widely cited example is that of the man who ruthlessly runs his business affairs during the week, taking no real interest in the hurt or humiliation he causes his competitors, and on Sunday serves as the deacon of his church. Religion and business are in separate compartments, and so too, unfortunately, is his humanity.

Rationalization

Horney treated the defense of *rationalization* pretty much as had other theorists, including Freud. "Rationalization may be defined as self-decep-tion by reasoning" (Horney, 1945, p. 135). Thus, when the person rational-izes he creates a good reason for some action where the reason would be unacceptable to his self-esteem. For example, the compliant type offers as his reason for "giving in" to others his desire to make *them* happy, when, in fact, he seeks to bring them under his control. Where he consciously offers an altruistic reason, a desire for dominance lurks.

Excessive Self-Control

In her clinical practice, Horney found that the tendency for excessive self-control was so pervasive that she originally classed it among the ten neurotic trends or needs: *the need to restrict one's life within narrow borders.* Individuals who are exerting excessive self-control are attempting to pre-vent being caught up in emotion: they "will not allow themselves to be carried away, whether by enthusiasm, sexual excitement, self-pity, or rage. . . . In short, they seek to check all spontaneity" (Horney, 1945, p. 136).

Arbitrary Rightness

Because the inner conflicts that have shaped the individual's life always produce doubt and hesitation, the individual is sometimes paralyzed, un-able to take *any* course of action. All of his energy is spent in keeping the conflicts under control. Therefore, almost any outside influence will tip the scales, even temporarily, in one direction or another. To an outsider, it appears that the neurotic decides important events arbitrarily and then defends his decisions with rationalizations.

Horney felt that the most "fertile soil" for such rigid rightness was the development of aggressive tendencies coupled with feelings of detachment from others (1945, p. 138). For example, a neurotic may end a family dispute by preemptively declaring that he will do what he has already decided to do since he is right. He then storms off, effectively ending the argument by absenting himself to pursue a course of action chosen more in spite than by reason.

Elusiveness

Sometimes the only way the neurotic can avoid the inherent contradictions of his life is to avoid making any decisions whatsoever. Completely opposite to the arbitrarily right neurotic, the *elusive* neurotic seeks never to be pinned down to anything, never to state any issue or opinion clearly. "They have a bewildering capacity to becloud issues. It is often impossible for them to give a concrete report of any incident; should they try to do so the listener is uncertain in the end just what really did happen" (Horney, 1945, p. 138).

Cynicism

To defend against the recognition of inner conflict, the neurotic may adopt a *cynical* stance toward life and its traditional moral and ethical values. By treating such issues derisively, the neurotic can forestall any conflict over deciding what his own position is. In effect, he adopts the Machiavellian attitude "Do what you please, so long as you don't get caught" (Horney, 1945, p. 140).

The Price of Protection

For Horney, the development of personality is an interpersonal process involving the achievement of self-confidence and the capacity for spontaneity. The character attitudes of compliance, aggression, and withdrawal, coupled with the auxiliary defenses, constitute an entire *protective structure*. The protective structure is designed to provide the neurotic with a sense of security, however falsely based, and with the means continually to fend off any potential new threats to his idealized self-image.

It must not be forgotten, however, that for these attainments of security, the neurotic pays a heavy price: He must abandon the realization of his true potentialities, the fruition of his genuine skills for living, and the expression of his authentically felt needs.

Modification of Freudian Psychoanalysis

Horney's jumping-off point was, of course, traditional psychoanalytic technique and theory. She accepted, for example, Freud's orientation toward psychological determinism. For Horney, as for Freud, every mental event was caused (1939, p. 18). Furthermore, that the cause of each mental event may be found in unconscious processes and motives, another fundamental Freudian tenet, was a postulate Horney easily accepted. The basic concept of unconsciously motivated defenses against self-disturbing perceptions also was taken over from psychoanalysis by Horney, as can be seen in her list of defensive strategies for coping with others.

Where Horney radically differed from Freud was in the area of motivational *content*. She reinterpreted the Oedipus complex, for example, as a culturally determined, occasional process of jealousy and aggression within some families (1939, p. 84). For Horney, the roots of the Oedipal situation were not so much sexual as *interpersonal attitudes:*

> The typical conflict leading to anxiety in a child is that between dependency on the parents . . . and hostile impulses against the parents. Hostility may be aroused in a child in many ways: by the parents' lack of respect for him; by unreasonable demands and prohibitions; by injustice; by unreliability; by suppression of criticism; by the parents dominating him and ascribing these tendencies to love. . . . If a child, in addition to being dependent on his parents, is grossly or subtly intimidated by them and hence feels that any expression of hostile impulses against them endangers his security, then the existence of such hostile impulses is bound to create anxiety. . . . The resulting picture may look exactly like what Freud describes as the Oedipus complex: passionate clinging to one parent and jealousy toward the other or toward anyone interfering with the claim of exclusive possession. . . . *But the dynamic structure of these attachments is entirely different from what Freud conceives as the Oedipus complex. They are an early manifestation of neurotic conflicts rather than a primarily sexual phenomenon.* [1939, pp. 83–84; italics added]

Thus Horney desexualized the Oedipal conflict and transferred the dynamics of its emotional constellation into the realm of disturbed interpersonal relations.

Along these same lines, Horney found Freud's libido theory to be a grossly inaccurate representation of feminine psychology. The concept of "penis envy" by which Freud sought to explain women's feelings of inferiority and subsequent development into the role of motherhood Horney found to be based on inadequate and biased interpretations of "evidence" from neurotic women (1939, pp. 104 ff.; see also Horney, 1967, for a selection of her early papers on feminine psychology in which she adhered more closely to the orthodox views of the psychoanalytic school).

Horney differed with Freud on other issues in personality theory, but the central distinction that divided the two theorists was Horney's resculpting of human motivation theory in cultural terms. Consequently, for Horney, personality development cannot be understood exclusively in terms of *instinctual* or biological dynamics. Personality is meaningful only when the individual's cultural setting, his familial interactions, and his wider interpersonal relationships are taken into account. Basic anxiety and basic hostility can be conceptualized only as interpersonal outcomes; masculinity and femininity can be understood psychologically only as cultural products.

Summary

Karen Horney developed a psychoanalytically oriented interpersonal theory of personality and neurotic conflict. Fundamental to her conception of personality development and its distortion by neurotic strivings are two basic emotions: basic anxiety and basic hostility. When the parental attitude toward the child is cold, inconsistent, or abusive, the foundation is laid for the child to develop a sense of basic hostility toward them, and perhaps toward people in general. Since he cannot openly express his anger for fear of abandonment by these powerful "giants," he represses these feelings. Unable to recognize the hostility that boils below the surface, the child develops a facade of pleasing lovableness. But because unconsciously he still fears abandonment and the potential chaos of his own helplessness, basic anxiety shapes his dealings with significant people in his life.

With his personality development blocked from its natural directions of growth, the neurotically disposed child begins to develop compulsive, indiscriminate, and unrealistic needs to control himself and others. Resembling in a superficial way the normal values or needs, the neurotic's strivings are insatiable and anxiety provoking when frustrated. Horney eventually grouped the ten needs (affection and approval; partner; restriction of life; power and omnipotence; exploitation of others; social recognition; personal admiration; personal achievement; self-sufficiency; and perfection and unassailability) into three character patterns: moving toward, away from, or against others.

With the development of neurotic needs and strategies for dealing with others, the individual becomes alienated from his real self. For Horney, the real self is the source of all spontaneous personal growth toward happiness, health, and spontaneity. The individual develops an idealized self-image, which typically is composed of a long list of things he *should* be. Horney wrote brilliantly of the "tyranny of the shoulds" by which the neurotic's life becomes shaped in a never-ending struggle to attain that which is impossible.

In distinction from the real self and the ideal self, Horney also described the person's actual self, which is the objective sum total of traits, needs, and physical and mental characteristics of the individual as they actually exist independently of his interpretation of them. Thus the core of neurotic conflict can be phrased as the alienation of the individual from his real self and his struggle to identify with his idealized image, the image of the shoulds. With that struggle, he loses his spontaneity, his genuine concern for others, and relinquishes any contact with his true feelings.

In addition to the major coping techniques of compliance, aggression, and withdrawal, Horney suggested that several secondary defenses are employed by the neurotic in his struggle for security. These secondary techniques include externalization, blind spots, compartmentalization, rationalization, excessive self-control, arbitrary rightness, elusiveness, and cynicism.

Horney's theory emphasizes the cultural and interpersonal factors in neurotic conflict. Her disagreements with Freud were many, but the central difference between their positions concerned Horney's reconceptualization of human motivation in cultural and social terms. She desexualized the Oedipal conflict, rejected the universality of penis envy in feminine development, and restored to personality theory an emphasis on understanding man as a person struggling for survival, identity, and security.

FOR FURTHER READING

Horney did not publish as extensively as some of the other personality theorists. Her first book, *The Neurotic Personality of Our Time* (New York: W. W. Norton, 1937), contains lucid descriptions of neurotic coping mechanisms. She elaborated her differences from Freud and criticized fundamental psychoanalytic tenets in *New Ways in Psychoanalysis* (New York: W. W. Norton, 1939). By far the most comprehensive presentation of her thinking is to be found in her *Neurosis and Human Growth* (New York: W. W. Norton, 1950).

A collection of Horney's papers that show both her agreement and disagreement with the Freudian view of women is to be had in *Feminine Psychology* (New York: W. W. Norton, 1967). Some of Alfred Adler's ideas served as the jumping-off point for Horney's conception of basic hostility and inferiority. Adler's *The Practice and Theory of Individual Psychology* (Totowa, N.J.: Littlefield, Adams, 1959) will provide some basis for comparison with Horney.

Two volumes edited by H. Kelman, *New Perspectives in Psychoanalysis: Contributions to Karen Horney's Holistic Approach* (New York: W. W. Norton, 1965) and *Advances in Psychoanalysis: Contributions to Karen Horney's Holistic Approach* (New York: W. W. Norton, 1964), will provide some indication of Horney's influence in psychiatry. A critical examination of her modification of psychoanalysis is provided by Benjamin Wolman in "Psychoanalysis without Libido: An Analysis of Karen Horney's Contribution to Psychoanalytic Theory," *American Journal of Psychotherapy* (1954), *8,* 21–31. Some of Horney's ideas on social influences were shaped by Georg Simmel; his *Conflict and the Web of Group Affiliations* (New York: Free Press, 1955) will give some indication of his thought.

7 HARRY STACK SULLIVAN
Interpersonal Theory

A multiple personality is in a certain sense normal. . . . What we have here is a situation in which there can be different selves, and it is dependent upon the set of social relations that is involved as to which self we are going to be.

GEORGE HERBERT MEAD, *Mind, Self and Society*

Properly speaking, a man has as many social selves as there are individuals who recognize him *and carry an image of him in their mind. To wound any of these images is to wound him.*

WILLIAM JAMES, *Principles of Psychology*

An Infant's View of the Universe

During approximately the first four months of life, an infant's world is identical with the infant himself. When he closes his eyes, or when an object is moved out of sight, the world and the object cease to exist. Consider, for example, an observation made by Jean Piaget of his infant son, Laurent, reacting to the disappearance of his bottle:

> If the bottle disappears from his perceptual field this is enough to make it cease to exist from the child's point of view. At 0;6 (19) [six months, 19 days], for instance, Laurent immediately begins to cry from hunger and impatience on seeing his bottle (he was already whimpering, as he does quite regularly at mealtime). *But at the very moment when I make the bottle disappear behind my hand or under the table* —he follows me with his eyes— *he stops crying.* As soon as the object reappears, a new outburst of desire; then flat calm after it disappears. I repeat the experiment four more times; the result is constant until poor Laurent, beginning to think the joke bad, becomes violently angry. [1954, p. 32; italics added]

From observations such as this one, Piaget attempted to construct a picture of the infant's universe. Laurent's behavior at the disappearance of his bottle may be taken as evidence that objects in the infant's world do not have independent and permanent existence once they are outside his perceptual field.

For another example, consider what happens if a child of five to seven months is shown a dangling pocket watch. He will reach up to grab for it, more or less smoothly coordinating his perception with his motor responses. But if the pocket watch is suddenly removed from his line of sight, dropped behind the edge of his crib, for instance, its sudden disappearance elicits no systematic search behavior by the child. At this stage of his life, the infant does not seek out the watch, for once out of sight it ceases to exist. It is *not,* however, a case of the old maxim "out of sight, out of mind," because that saying implies simple forgetting as the cause of the child's lack of continued interest. Rather, in the infant state, out of sight means *out of existence,* for there is no mental image of the sensory object to be forgotten.

Piaget concluded that in the early months of infancy, the child's universe has no real stability or permanency. Objects exist only to the extent that they are immediately present as sensory experiences. Stop the flow of sensation, and the continuity of experience is erased. In Piaget's terms, the infant lacks a sense of *object permanence.*

To return for a moment to Laurent's behavior at the disappearance of his bottle, Piaget drew from this observation a further inference about the nature of Laurent's universe. Just because he ceases to cry when the bottle disappears, Piaget reasoned, does not mean that:

> . . . the vanished bottle has been fundamentally forgotten; the child's ultimate rage reveals clearly enough that he believes he can count on the object. But this is precisely because *he considers it as being at the disposal of his desires* . . . and not as having a substantial existence under my hand or under the table. Otherwise he would behave quite differently at the moment of its disappearance; he would manifest, at that exact moment, a still more intense desire than during normal perception [i.e., while the bottle is in view]. [1954, p. 32; italics added]

In short, not only does the infant lack object permanence, but his conception of the object when present is an *egocentric,* magical view that *his* desires, *his* wishes are responsible for its timely appearance. Piaget referred to this world view as *magico-phenomenalistic* causality (Piaget & Inhelder, 1969, p. 18). "Magical" refers to the fact that the infant has no conception of physical causality governing the sequence of events he experiences; "phenomenalistic" is meant to indicate the subjective immediacy of the infant's interpretations of reality: *his* wishes, *his* desires are what count, for *his* power controls *his* universe.

Jean Piaget, the Swiss psychologist-biologist, has for more than half a century studied the development of children's awareness and interpretations of reality. What is remarkable is that Piaget's descriptions of the child's progressively abstract constructions of reality are similar to the developmental sequence proposed by Harry Stack Sullivan to account for the same cognitive-emotional phenomena. In fact, Sullivan himself, in the first book he wrote, though delayed from publication for over forty years, called attention to Piaget's observational techniques and findings (1972, pp. 40n.–41n.).

Those phenomena that Piaget's scheme terms "magico-phenomenalistic" were termed by Sullivan the "parataxic" mode of experience. For both Sullivan and Piaget, parataxic and magico-phenomenalistic organization of reality are middle stages in a sequence of development that begins with even more primitive interpretations of events and ends with logical, predictive thought.

Modes of Experience: Prototaxic, Parataxic, Syntaxic

Piaget's description of the child's development of the concept of causality and of his eventual recognition of a permanently existing universe of which he is only one part is organized into a progressive sequence of six stages. For present purposes, the stages can be grouped into pairs, each pair roughly corresponding to one of Sullivan's three stages of experience: prototaxic, parataxic, and syntaxic. By considering Piaget and Sullivan together, we can lend some descriptive precision to Sullivan's terms. Piaget's observations also provide approximate age ranges and coordinated behavioral referents lacking in Sullivan's account. Indeed, it is probable that Sullivan had Piaget's early observations in mind when he conceived of the three modes of existence (cf. Sullivan, 1972, p. 41n.).

Prototaxic Experience: A Serial Flow of Sensation

The simplest, crudest, and most exclusive mode of experiencing reality at the beginning of life is what Sullivan called the *prototaxic mode* (1953b, p. 29). For the first few months of life the infant's world is composed of a stream of sensory experience upon which he is unable to impose order or consistency. The infant's contact with and representation of the universe is limited to the continually changing flow of information provided by his sense organs. Generally, each sensory experience in the prototaxic mode is isolated from and uncoordinated with all other sensory experiences. As a result, the world is perceived, or "prehended" as Sullivan would say, as a flux of *unconnected* and *discrete* moments of sensation (1953b, p. 108). Even though some sensory events may be repetitive, the infant is unable to generalize from one event to another. Experiences occur in succession, but he does not apprehend that one event "goes with," "goes before," or "comes after" another.

In Piaget's terms, prototaxic experience corresponds to the first two stages of the development of causality: stage one is called *global causality*, and stage two is termed *feelings of efficacy* (1954, pp. 250 ff.). In the first stage, extending roughly from the first few weeks of life to approximately four months, the infant makes no distinction between self and not-self. All his experience is fused into one global mass in which all that is "self" and all that is "not-self" are the same, a proposition with which Sullivan agreed. Some of Piaget's observations of his son's behavior in the early days of life had shown, for example, that the infant is unable even to keep track of the parts of his own body:

> Laurent at 0;0 (21) [21 days] is lying on his right side, his arms tight against his body, his hands clasped, and he sucks his right thumb at length while remaining completely immobile. . . . I take his right hand away and he at once begins to search for it, turning his head from left to right. As his hands remained immobile due to his position, Laurent found his thumb after three attempts: prolonged sucking begins each time. But once he has been placed on his back, he does not know how to coordinate the movement of the arms with that of the mouth and his hands draw back even when his lips are seeking them. [1952, p. 27]

Objects do not exist permanently or independently of the child's experience of them. A simple change of bodily position is sufficient to cause Laurent to "lose" his thumb.

Around the fifth month of life, extending to approximately seven months, the child's experience of the world becomes slightly more organized. He begins to recognize that some events do go together; that, for example, a given smell accompanies food, or a particular face is present when the bottle is available. But, as Sullivan suggested, the child is unable to anticipate one stimulus (food) from the presence of the other (face). They occur together, and they are responded to similarly, but the presence of only one does not evoke an "image" of the other. Piaget calls this period of development the *stage of feelings of efficacy* in the sense that the infant believes that his *desires* are responsible for the presence of both stimuli. When he is hungry, mother-with-bottle appears. Sullivan would call this personification of mother the "mouth mother." The infant does not, of course, understand that his crying is a *causal* signal to his mother that feeding time is at hand. If left unfed, the infant's crying would reach rageful proportions, and he would be confused as to why this time his feelings of hunger went unsatisfied. But he would not necessarily comprehend that it was mother's failure to bring the bottle that was responsible for his frustration.

Consequently, from the child's point of view, he understands that something is happening, but he does not know *why*. He senses his own existence, but only in egocentric fashion. *His* existence is everything that exists, for without *his* immediate perception of objects, there simply are none. By the end of the stage of feelings of efficacy, the child's reflexes like sucking and crying have become organized into sequences of reliable habits. At this point, when events have *temporal connection,* Sullivan speaks of the parataxic mode of experience. Thus Piaget's second stage overlaps and grades into Sullivan's second mode.

The Parataxic Mode: A Sequential Flow of Sensation

The cycle of mounting hunger tension and its reduction when food is available leads eventually to the child's *foresight* or *anticipation* of satisfaction when he experiences hunger (Sullivan, 1953b, p. 38). Before this achievement, the infant's experience of tension, or "disturbed euphoria," as Sullivan conceptualized it, and his eventual satisfaction after eating are simply two successive and unrelated events. With the establishment of the ability to predict or anticipate one event from another's presence, the dimension of time is imposed on the infant's universe. Temporal contiguity, the occurrence of one event immediately after or immediately before another event, comes to the center of the infant's attention. This dominance of temporal sequence as the only conception of causality is what Sullivan calls the *parataxic mode* of experience.

Sullivan made no precise statements on the duration of the period of parataxic experience in the infant's developmental history. If we take Piaget's observational sequence as a guide, the period extending from about the eighth month through the eleventh month probably encompasses the same phenomena Sullivan termed parataxic. The period is divided into two stages in Piaget's scheme: eight to nine months is the stage of *magico-phenomenalistic causality,* with which we are already familiar; from the end of the ninth through the eleventh month the child is in the stage of *elementary externalization of causality.*

Parataxic thinking is magical thinking, for in the parataxic mode events that occur close together in time are construed as causally related. For example, consider the following observation made by Piaget of his daughter Jacqueline:

> At 0;8 (9) [eight months, nine days] Jacqueline is lying down looking at a saucer which I swing 50 centimeters in front of her eyes. She reveals a lively interest and expresses her pleasure by the well-known behavior of arching herself upward, with her weight on her feet and shoulder blades, and then letting herself fall in a heap. I pass the saucer before her again. She watches it smiling, then stares at it seriously and attentively and arches upward a second time. When

Jacqueline has fallen back again I pass the object before her once more; the same play three more times. After this I hold the object motionless before her; she arches herself again two or three times, then proceeds to something else. I resume twice; as soon as the saucer is motionless Jacqueline arches upward again. I then definitely pause in my game; Jacqueline nevertheless draws herself up five or six times more, while looking at the object, then tires of it. Every time the child's gesture has been followed by the saucer's movement, Jacqueline has manifested great satisfaction; otherwise, an expression of disappointment and expectation. [1954, p. 269]

Jacqueline believes that her arching response is the *cause* of the saucer's movement. Because in her past experience, the two events—arching and movement of saucer—have occurred in close *temporal* sequence, she assumes that her arching is the cause of the movement. Parataxic thinking is like Jacqueline's magico-phenomenalistic response. The infant understands that he may *intend* to bring about some effect. But what he fails to comprehend is the physical and spatial contact necessary to success. If she wants the saucer to move, either she or someone else must move it. Simple desire and unrelated body movements (arching) have no power to cause the observed effect. Most superstitions are based on parataxic reasoning. If a gambler on a losing streak at the roulette table suddenly strikes it lucky, he is likely to assume that the young lady who just sat down next to him is the cause of his good fortune.

When the infant enters the parataxic mode of experience, he has progressed to the point at which he can generalize his experiences and identify similarities and differences among events. He is thus now able to respond differentially to different stimuli on the basis of his past experience (Sullivan, 1953b, pp. 82–83). For example, the infant is able to see that it is the same person who ministers to his different needs: The mother who produces a nipple when he cries with hunger is the same mother who produces a blanket when he cries with cold. Prior to this achievement, in the prototaxic mode, each of these personages was identified only by the bodily zone through which satisfaction was obtained: thus there was a "mouth mother," a "skin mother," an "anus mother," and so on.

Piaget's fourth stage, *elementary externalization and objectification of causality,* extending from nine to eleven months, also overlaps with Sullivan's concept of parataxic thinking. In this stage, according to Piaget, the child is able to distinguish crudely between that which is "self" and that which is not. Sullivan, in a concept that will be more fully examined later, proposed that parataxic thinking is accompanied by the ability to differentiate the body from the rest of the world (1953b, p. 163). Out of this differentiation emerges a personification of self called the "not-me."

Though the child's egocentrism is diminished during the stage of elementary externalization, he still tends to judge events only in terms of their effects on him. For example, though he realizes there are other people in his world, and that he, like them, is a member of an even larger universe, the only importance others have is in terms of what they do for and to him.

The Syntaxic Mode of Experience: Causally Connected Sensations

The syntaxic mode of experience corresponds to adult, logical, analytic thought. Syntaxic experience of reality thus presupposes the ability to understand physical and spatial causality, and the ability to predict causes from knowledge of their effects. As an example, consider another of Piaget's observations:

> At 1;4 (4) [one year, four months, four days] Laurent is seated in his carriage and I am on a chair beside him. While reading and without seeming to pay any attention to him, I put my foot under the carriage and move it slowly. Without hesitation, Laurent leans over the edge and looks for the cause in the direction of the wheels. As soon as he perceives the position of my foot he is satisfied and smiles. [1954, p. 335]

Laurent was able to infer from the movement of his carriage that something was the cause of it; that something, he surmised, had to do with the wheels on which the carriage must roll. From experience of the effect (movement), he was able to hypothesize a cause and test his hypothesis (looked at the wheels).

This kind of logical synthesis of present, past, and future experience is what Sullivan calls the syntaxic mode. It is characteristic of adult functioning. Piaget locates the origins of this kind of logical thought in two separate stages: *real objectification and spatialization of causes* (12–15 months) and *representative causality* (18 months–2 years). From the twelfth to the fifteenth month, the child is able to perceive that causes of the events he experiences are located *outside himself.* No longer magically-phenomenalistic, nor totally egocentric, the child can perceive himself as an object in a world of independently existing and relatively permanent objects. He realizes that he is only one cause among many causal agents.

In the last Piagetian stage, *representative causality,* the child of approximately eighteen months to two years has learned to use a new tool to structure reality: language. As Sullivan had pointed out, in a vein similar to that of Piaget:

> . . . the first instances of experience in the syntaxic mode appear between, let us say, the twelfth and the eighteenth month of extrauterine life, when verbal signs—words, symbols—are organized which are actually communicative. [Sullivan, 1953b, p. 184]

and

... I should stress that syntaxic symbols are best illustrated by words that have been *consensually validated.* A consensus has been reached when the infant or child has learned the precisely right word for a situation, a word which means not only what it is thought to mean by the mothering one, but also means that to the infant. [Sullivan, 1953b, pp. 183–184; italics added]

Sullivan, like Piaget, also emphasized the predictive function of syntaxic thought (1953b, p. 233). Language allows the child to store information from past experiences for use in understanding future novel events. Not only can he generalize from past experience, the syntaxic thinker can choose to focus on only certain events that make sense in terms of his past accomplishments:

At 1;8 (11) [one year, eight months, eleven days] Jacqueline, observing from her window the mists on the side of the mountains, says, "Mist smoke papa." The next day, confronted by the same sight, she says, "Mist papa." The following day, on seeing me smoke my pipe she says, "Smoke papa." It would seem to me difficult not to interpret the first of these circumstances by a causal relation which can be formulated as follows: "It is papa who has made those mists with his pipe," or more cautiously, "There is in those mists something connected with the smoke papa makes with his pipe." [Piaget, 1954, p. 335]

Jacqueline's explanation of mist as pipe smoke may be wrong, but she has sought to apply her knowledge of similar events in a causal way. It is not the particular error that is important. From the child's point of view she has made an estimate of the high probability that because pipe smoke and mountain mist are similar, they have a common cause: Papa Piaget.

The three modes of experiencing, and their correspondences to Piaget's stages of causal thinking, are summarized in Table 7–1.

Schizophrenia as Parataxic Experiencing: Dissociation

Sullivan began his psychiatric career with an intense interest in schizophrenia. Influenced strongly by the then innovative ideas of Carl Jung and Sigmund Freud, Sullivan tried to account for the bizarre, seemingly unconnected cognitive and verbal processes of his psychotic patients. He adopted from Jung the concept that the disorganized thoughts of schizophrenics were the products of ideas and feelings that had been split off from waking consciousness and thereby freed from control by the ego (Sullivan, 1962, p. 19).

TABLE 7–1: A COMPARISON OF SULLIVAN'S MODES OF EXPERIENCE AND PIAGET'S STAGES OF CAUSAL THOUGHT

SULLIVAN'S MODES	PIAGET'S STAGES	CHARACTERISTICS OF EXPERIENCE
Prototaxic (Literally, "placing one before the other in series")	1. Global causality (birth to 4 months) 2. Feelings of efficacy (5 to 7 months)	Lack of object permanence; egocentric interpretation of world as indistinguishable from self; constant flux of sensory events, unconnected and discrete; causality is vague conception of power when events accidentally coincide with desires.
Parataxic (Literally, "placing side by side without causal connection")	3. Magico-Phenomenalistic (8 to 9 months) 4. Elementary externalization and objectification of causality (9 to 11 months)	Discovery that one may intend an action; egocentrism persists; temporal connection between events perceived as causal; magical or superstitious thinking based on view that intentions are causes; causes are partially externalized in others, but only to extent they affect self; self/not-self distinction; crude memory.
Syntaxic (Literally, "placing together in logical, connected order")	5. Real objectification and spatialization of causes (12 to 15 months) 6. Representative causality (18 months to 2 years)	Egocentrism absent; perception of difference between physical and temporal connections; language used to predict causes from their effects; consensual validation; mutually agreed-upon meanings; past, present, and future can be synthesized; interpersonal contacts grow in importance.

Set adrift from the rest of the personality, these "disassociated complexes," as Jung called them, ceased to obey the usual laws of logic and reason. They appeared, instead, to be isolated fragments of experience absurdly and madly strung together by the patient and spewn forth in jumbled speech patterns called "word salad."

Jung had also proposed another idea adopted by Sullivan. Employing his word-association tests with psychotic patients, Jung had detected a similarity between the "meaningless" verbal productions of the schizophrenic and the fantastic distortions of thought that occur during normal dreaming. Freud had elucidated the mechanisms of dream work—displacement and condensation, among others—that produce the disguised manifest content of the dream story. Furthermore, he had shown that the construction of dreams in normal personalities obeyed the same laws of impulse disguise that govern neurotic symptom formation (see Chapter 2). Jung sought to apply these principles to an explanation of schizophrenic thought processes. Sullivan picked up the threads of this psychoanalytic tradition, and from them and others he eventually created the fundamental tenets of his theory of personality.

An Illustrative Case of Schizophrenic Dissociation

It will be recalled that Jung had employed the method of word association in diagnosing and treating his patients (see Chapter 4). A particularly informative illustration of the factors that shaped Sullivan's early conception of what, with a slight change in terminology, he called *dissociation* can be discerned in one of Jung's cases.

Jung's patient, an unmarried dressmaker, was admitted to the Burghölzli Asylum in Switzerland with the diagnosis of dementia praecox. This diagnostic category was later to be renamed schizophrenia by Jung's immediate superior at the Burghölzli, Eugen Bleuler. Her symptoms were not uncommon for schizophrenic patients: She heard accusing voices, responded in kind to them, and had once contemplated suicide by drowning. Her explanation for the voices was that she was in the presence of "invisible telephones":

> They called out to her that she was a woman of doubtful character, that her child had been found in a toilet, that she had stolen a pair of scissors in order to poke out the child's eyes. [Jung, 1907, p. 99]

To the stimulus words of Jung's word-association test she responded with strange, often inexplicable statements. Jung tried, as was usual in his procedure, to get the patient to explain her responses. She would not or could not do so. He tried a variation of the technique of free association adopted from Freud. He would repeat back to his patient key words or phrases from her mumblings and pronouncements, and then keep track of her string of responses. One of her often repeated words was "Socrates," employed in such phrases as "I am Socrates." Jung therefore began with "Socrates" as the stimulus word:

> *Socrates:* "Pupil—books—wisdom—modesty—no words to express this wisdom—is the highest ground-pedestal—his teachings—had to die because of wicked men—falsely accused—sublimest sublimity—self-satisfied—that is all Socrates—the fine learned world—never cut a thread—I was the best dressmaker, never left a bit of cloth on the floor—fine world of art—fine professorship—is doubloon—25 francs —that is the highest—prison—slandered by wicked men—unreason —cruelty—depravity—brutality." [Jung, 1907, p. 112]

In the Socrates associations and others, Jung detected a clear thread of meaning. It seemed that the woman identified herself with Socrates in a kind of metaphorical expression of her own life situation. Jung provided the missing logical connections:

> The explanation of her stereotypy "I am Socrates" . . . is that she is the "best dressmaker" who "never cut a thread" and "never left a bit of cloth on the floor." She is an "artist," a "professor" in her line. She is martyred, she is not recognized as the owner of the world, she is considered ill, which is a "slander." She is "wise and modest," she has achieved "the highest." *All these things are analogies of the life and death of Socrates. She therefore wishes to say: 'I am like Socrates, and I suffer like him.'* With a certain poetic licence, such as appears also in moments of strong affect, she says outright: "I am Socrates." [Jung, 1907, p. 112; italics added]

Jung concluded that the really pathological element in the woman's use of the Socrates metaphor was her total identification with it. She regarded it as so real that she expected everyone to understand it. The woman lived as though in a perpetual dream-state, a state, as for normal persons, characterized by allegories, symbols, and metaphors with the intensity of reality. With awakening, the normal person readjusts to reality, and he either interprets, represses, or dismisses the dream. But the schizophrenic patient operates with dreamlike imagery in her waking state. Her thought processes proceed as if the elements of the metaphor, linked together by strong emotion, had become a *complex* disassociated from conscious control, freed from the restraints normally imposed by the reality-oriented ego.

> The basic thoughts—I am an excellent dressmaker, have lived a respectable life and am therefore worthy of respect and financial reward—are understandable enough. . . . Before her illness the patient

was always poor and came from a low-grade family (her sister is a prostitute). *Her thoughts and wishes express her striving to get out of this milieu and attain a better social position* ... *All strong wishes furnish themes for dreams and the dreams represent them as fulfilled,* expressing them not in concepts taken from reality but in vague dreamlike metaphors. *The wishfulfilling dreams appear side by side with associations from the waking state,* the complexes come to light and, the inhibiting power of the ego-complex [i.e., conscious rational functioning] having been destroyed by the disease, they now go on weaving their dreams on the surface, just as they used to do under normal conditions in the depths of the unconscious. [Jung, 1907, p. 124; italics added]

Jung therefore became convinced that the schizophrenic patient could be understood, that the meaningless and absurd utterances were not meaningless or absurd at all. When once their function as wish fulfillments was understood, and the tendency for some mental content to be split off from consciousness recognized, then the physician had the key to unlock the meaning of the patient's symptoms.

"Her baroque mumble of words can now be seen in a different light: they are arrangements of an enigmatic inscription, bits and pieces of fairy-tale fantasies which have broken away from hard reality to build a far-off world of their own. ... The patient can spare only a few mysterious symbols for the dim, dismal realm of reality; *They need not be understood, for our understanding has long ceased to be necessary for her*" (Jung, 1908, p. 177; italics added).

Implications of Jung's Conceptions for Sullivan's Theory

Jung's innovative approach to schizophrenia, particularly his early adoption of unpopular Freudian concepts, does not seem particularly startling or unique from the perspective of the present (cf. R. D. Laing in Chapter 8). No contemporary psychological investigator regards schizophrenic thought processes and verbal productions as meaningless or totally chaotic. Yet, at Jung's period in history, and even later in Sullivan's day, such insights were novel and controversial. Particularly controversial were the psychoanalytic tenets that Jung introduced into the clinical treatment of psychotics. Some of the implications of Jung's work bear summarizing, for these concepts, among others, were the building blocks from which Sullivan constructed many of his important conceptions of personality dynamics.

First, Jung's approach emphasized the possibility that certain feelings and thoughts could be split off from the bulk of conscious functioning, yet remain in consciousness in an isolated, encapsulated form. In a sense, the disassociation of these ideas and feelings was a case of repression in reverse. Instead of submergence to the unconscious, these unacceptable feelings were separated from the ego but kept within awareness as isolated fragments deprived of apparent meaningful connection with each other and with the self or ego. Sullivan construed schizophrenic functioning in much the same way. But Sullivan extended the idea of disassociation (or dissociation) to include normal personality developments. Each of us, Sullivan postulated, develops an aspect of self that is dissociated from the bulk of our self-conceptions. Called the Not-Me, this personification of self embodies all the unacceptable behaviors that are accompanied by "uncanny" feelings of anxiety. These emotions prevent our recognizing some behaviors as "ours." Not-Me will be considered in more detail shortly.

Second, Jung saw no reason to assume that the processes of schizophrenic thought were different in kind from normal thought. As Freud saw neurotic and normal mental processes lying on the same continuum, Jung felt that "when we penetrate into the human secrets of our patients, the madness discloses the system upon which it is based, and *we recognize insanity to be simply an unusual reaction to emotional problems which are in no wise foreign to ourselves*" (1908, p. 165; italics added). Compare to Jung's formulation Sullivan's later statement of his position:

> In approaching the subject of mental disorder, I must emphasize that, in my view, persons showing mental disorder do not manifest anything specifically different in kind from what is manifested by practically all human beings. . . . From my viewpoint, we shall have to accept as a necessary premise that what one encounters in various stages of schizophrenia—the odd, awe-inspiring, terror-provoking feelings of vastness and littleness and the strange strewing-about of relevance—are part of the ordinary experience of these very early stages of personality development in all of us [namely, parataxic thinking and the Not-Me]. Most of us, however, experience these processes in later life only as strange fragments carried over from sleep or in our fleeting glimpses of what I call anxiety. [1956, p. 3]

Sullivan was quite explicit that schizophrenia was to be regarded as lying within the range of processes found in normality:

> Schizophrenic thinking shows in its symbols and processes nothing exterior to the gamut of ordinary thinking, including therein that of revery and of dreams. . . . It is, as a whole, a peculiarly inadequate adaption of the cognitive processes to the necessities of adult life. . . . [1962, p. 92]

Sullivan's reference to the normal personality's experience of the mental state of the schizophrenic only in dreams is reminiscent of Jung's conceptualization. Sullivan, of course, took matters a step farther by establishing a developmental chronology of events leading to schizophrenia. Furthermore, Sullivan's emphasis on the continuity of mental processes from normality through psychosis led him to a rather important philosophical statement of human similarities. "Everyone and anyone is much more simply human than otherwise, more like everyone else than different" (1962, Frontispiece). This concise statement was originally called the species identity theorem by Sullivan in his early unpublished notebooks, and later expanded to the *one-genus postulate:*

> ... the differences between any two instances of human personality —from the lowest-grade imbecile to the highest-grade genius—are much less striking than the differences between the least-gifted human being and a member of the nearest other biological genus. *Man* —however undistinguished biologically—*as long as he is entitled to the term, human personality, will be very much more like every other instance of human personality than he is like anything else in the world.* [1953b, pp. 32–33; italics added]

Because "everyone and anyone is much more simply human than otherwise," Sullivan felt it necessary to rescue psychiatry from the "ivory tower myth" of objective, uninvolved commitment to "scientific" truth finding (1964, p. 15). For Sullivan, the psychiatrist is certainly a scientific observer of behavior; but he is also a *participant observer* who is no less human, no less involved, no less of a participant, and no less changed than the patients he treats. As Sullivan pithily summarized his concept, "The crying need is for observers who are growing observant of their observing" (1964, p. 27).

The third implication of Jung's work for Sullivan's theory was Jung's emphasis that the wish-fulfilling tendencies observed in the schizophrenic's bizarre speech and thoughts *are derived from important concerns of his life before his illness began.* Jung had summarized his view in this way:

> ... we can assert that the pathological ideas dominate the interests of the patient so completely *because they are derived from the most important questions that occupied him when he was normal.* In other words, what in insanity is now an incomprehensible jumble of symptoms was once a vital field of interest to the normal personality. [1908, p. 173; italics added]

Sullivan's later conceptualization of schizophrenic personality development is nearly identical to Jung's:

> The disorder [i.e., schizophrenia] is one in which the total experience of the individual is reorganized. ... It is a disorder which is determined by the previous experience of the individual—regardless of whether it is excited by emotional experience (psychic traumata), by the toxaemia of acute disease, by cranial trauma, or by alcoholic intoxication. [Sullivan, 1962, p. 12]

and

> Schizophrenia is considered tentatively as an evolution of the life
> process in which some certain few motivations assume extraordinary
> importance to the grave detriment of adjustive effort on the part of
> the individual concerned. This disturbance of adjustive effort is
> shown as an interference in the realm of social experience. [Sullivan,
> 1962, p. 160]

The comparison between Jung's approach to schizophrenia stemming from
his adaptation of psychoanalytic theory and Sullivan's early conceptualizations of the disease could be extended into several other areas. That
Sullivan read widely in the psychiatric literature, and adopted for his own
purposes the conceptions that most suited his interpersonal theory, is an
example of one of the common processes of science. To name just a few
of Sullivan's intellectual antecedents and influences, we can list Piaget,
Freud, Jung, Adler, William Alanson White, George Herbert Mead, and
Kurt Lewin. But Sullivan's development and interweaving of their concepts resulted in a unique product.

Anxiety: The States of Euphoria and Tension

From his work with schizophrenics, Sullivan had observed the effects of
dissociated systems of experience in extreme form. The cause, it seemed
clear, was the patient's struggle to master unacceptable and anxiety-
provoking interpersonal situations. Because he intended to provide a developmental scheme of personality description, Sullivan's chief questions
became: *"How does the experience of anxiety originate? and How does the experience of anxiety cause dissociation of certain feelings and ideas?"*

> It is demonstrable that the human young in the first months of life
> . . . exhibits disturbed performance when the mothering one has an
> "emotional disturbance." . . . Whatever the infant was doing at the
> time will be interrupted or handicapped—that is, it will either stop,
> or it will not progress as efficiently as before anxiety appeared. . . .
> I have reason to suppose, then, *that a fearlike state can be induced in an
> infant under two circumstances:* one is by the rather *violent disturbance
> of his zones of contact with circumambient reality;* and the other is *by
> certain types of emotional disturbance within the mothering one.* [Sullivan,
> 1953b, pp. 8–9; italics added]

Sullivan had embarked on a theoretical assumption that anxiety was
communicable from mother to child, and from child to mother. Sullivan
conceptualized anxiety, however, in a very specific way. He distinguished

between two hypothetical states of the organism: *absolute euphoria* and *absolute tension.* Absolute euphoria is roughly similar to total peace, complete freedom from desire and need, a state of utter well-being experienced, for example, by the infant in the state of deep sleep (Sullivan, 1953b, p. 35). Absolute tension is defined as the "maximum possible deviation from absolute euphoria," as, for example, the state of terror or panic. These bipolar opposites are hypothetical extremes that are only rarely experienced by any individual. Most of the organism's lifetime is spent in states of experience lying near the middle of the extremes.

Sullivan's next major assumption about personality development concerned the reciprocal relationship between mother's and child's tensions: *"The observed activity of the infant arising from the tension of needs* [e.g., hunger, thirst] *induces tension in the mothering one, which tension is experienced as tenderness and as an impulsion to activities toward the relief of the infant's needs"* (1953b, p. 39). In simpler language, Sullivan conjectured that bodily tensions of hunger cause the infant to cry, and this pattern of behavior induces a state of tension in the mother that can be satisfied only by attending to the infant's needs. Thus, from the earliest moments of life, anxiety and tension involve interpersonal relationships.

The Communication of Anxiety

Because tension arising in the infant can induce tension in the mother, then it follows that tensions arising in the mother are likewise communicable to the infant: *"The tension of anxiety, when present in the mothering one, induces anxiety in the infant"* (Sullivan, 1953b, p. 41). Since the infant experiences reality in the prototaxic mode, his experience of anxiety is fragmented, isolated from other experiences, and diffuse. From *his* perspective, anxiety is another increase in tension similar to tensions produced by needs like hunger and thirst. In fact, because the infant does not yet differentiate himself from his environment, but experiences himself and his world as one global, fused mass, the mothering one's anxiety *is* his anxiety. They are linked by *empathy,* the capacity of the child to feel the mother's feelings, and vice versa.

Since he cannot differentiate the experience of anxiety from other unpleasurable tensions, the infant possesses as yet no specific means of reducing the anxiety. In order for him to reexperience the comforting state of euphoria, he must rely on the mothering one to reduce his anxiety as he relies on her to satisfy his bodily needs. But because *she* is the origin of his anxiety, she cannot of herself reduce his tension until she eliminates hers:

> ... the infant's capacity for manipulating another person is confined, at the very start, to the sole capacity to call out tenderness by manifesting needs; and the person who would respond to manifest need

in the situation in which the infant is anxious is relatively incapable of that response because it is the parental anxiety which induces the infant's anxiety. . . . Therefore, there is, *from the very earliest evidence of the empathic linkage, this peculiar distinction that anxiety is not manageable.* [Sullivan, 1953b, p. 43; italics added]

Once experienced, the affect of anxiety cannot be removed, nor destroyed, nor escaped for the remainder of the organism's life (Sullivan, 1953b, p. 53). Having been inoculated with the first dose of this unmanageable emotion, the human organism is made a human person, sensitive, vulnerable, insecure. Thus, anxiety is the most potent, the earliest, and the most pervasive interpersonal force that can affect the human infant.

Nursing as the Prototype for Interpersonal Situations

Because the infant experiences reality in the prototaxic mode, the sum of his perceptions is no more than momentary and fleeting states of sensory awareness. One of the most important of his sensory experiences is nursing, or more specifically, the experience of "nipple-in-the lips." He "prehends" the nipple-in-the-lips event as a series of discrete bodily sensations including tactile, thermal, and olfactory stimuli.

From the repetitive nature of the experience, the infant slowly begins to develop a rudimentary conception of the nipple-person, the mothering one. His conception of her in no way corresponds to the completeness of reality. Instead, the infant's prototaxic, and later parataxic, experience of these discrete sensations constitutes a *personification* of the mother. She becomes identified with her primary transactions with him, namely, the nipple-in-the-lips image. In this sense, the nipple *is* the mothering one.

Depending upon the degree of satisfaction supplied by her feeding behavior, the infant develops several different personifications of the nipple-in-the-lips mothering one:

1. *Good-and-Satisfactory Nipple* personification is the nipple in the lips that supplies milk when the infant is hungry [Good Mother];

2. *The Good-but-Unsatisfactory-Nipple* personification is the nipple that supplies milk when the infant is not hungry [Good Mother];

3. *Wrong-Nipple-in-the-Lips* is an unsatisfactory nipple because it does not supply milk when he is hungry; infant rejects this nipple and searches for a better nipple [Bad Mother];

4. *Evil-Nipple* is the nipple of an anxious mother which communicates a profound degree of anxiety and tension; this tension is a signal for avoidance; "not that nipple in my lips" [Bad-Anxious Mother]. (Based on Sullivan, 1953b, p. 80)

Thus, the nursing situation is an important prototype for the development of the infant's relationships with future "significant others":

> ... the infant is bound to have two personifications of any mothering person [Good and Bad Mother], barring the most incredible good fortune, and ... the infant in the earliest stages of life need have only two personifications for any number of people who have something to do with looking after him. [Sullivan, 1953b, p. 122]

Differentiation of Self from the Universe

Toilet training and bodily care for urine and fecal elimination are clearly interpersonal situations that bear enormous potential for the learning of new personifications about oneself, and about one's own body. The way in which the mothering one responds to the infant's body—with disgust, with delight, or with simple acceptance—will be the key determinant in the infant's personification of himself. Coupled with these interpersonal effects are the infant's first clues that he is an independent object in the universe. As Piaget, too, has suggested, the infant learns he is a self through the activity of his hands, feet, and mouth.

For example, the infant lies in his crib and studies the movement of his own hands. He may grasp an object, bring it unsteadily to his mouth, and then insert it into his lips. He soon discovers that it is not a nipple; but he also discovers that *he—his* hand—has brought about the event. When, moreover, he brings an *empty* hand to his mouth, and sucks the thumb, he learns an even more important lesson:

> ... That the thumb is uniquely different from any nipple by reason of its being *in itself* a source of zonal sentience. *The thumb feels sucked.* [Sullivan, 1953b, p. 136]

Sucking the thumb is also different from the nursing situation in an important way: Unlike his attempts to bring mother-with-satisfactory-nipple *on demand,* his attempts to bring his thumb to his mouth are always successful, and invaryingly satisfying.

> The thumb-in-the-lips is dependable, and is independent of evoking the good mother; the infant can bring it into being, as it were, without cooperation—in isolation from any of his personifications, whether of the good mother or the bad mother. [Sullivan, 1953b, p. 139]

By his experiences with self-evoked satisfactions, the infant learns to foresee and to control some of his own behaviors. More important, he learns that *he is;* that he has a certain independence from the sequence of activities that engulf him. When, however, he naturally seeks further exploration of himself, in the genital or anal zones, he unwittingly brings the personification of the bad mother, the anxious mother, into play:

> The hand manipulating the anus, as any mother knows, will shortly be the hand that is in the mouth; thanks to the great development of the doctrine of germs and to the doubts about physical and sexual purity and cleanliness . . . many mothers feel that a finger conveying anything from the perineal region to the mouth would be disastrous. . . . *And even if these things are not so regarded by the mothering one, she will know that they are so regarded by a large number of other people.* [Sullivan, 1953b, pp. 143–144; italics added]

Thus the infant quickly discovers that although he is an independent being, he is not independent of the mothering one's "forbidding gestures" directing him not to experience certain parts of himself.

Personifications of Self: Good-Me, Bad-Me, Not-Me

For Sullivan, it is clear, the most important kinds of learning in infancy, indeed throughout life, occur in the discovery that some behaviors eliminate or reduce the intensity of interpersonal anxiety (1953b, p. 152). The great steersman of development is the *gradient of anxiety* attached to different behavioral situations. By trial and anxious-error, the infant gauges the desirability of particular behaviors in his repertoire:

> The infant plays, one might say, the old game of getting hotter or colder, in charting a selection of behavioral units which are not attended by an increase in anxiety. [Sullivan, 1953b, p. 159]

The gradient of anxiety ranges from relatively mild tension-evoking behaviors to behaviors that elicit such intense feelings of emotion that they are best described as "uncanny," "*awe*-full," or "*dread*-full." Out of his games of hot or cold, the infant shapes his conceptions of "me."

Good-Me Personification

All those infant behaviors to which the mothering one has responded with tenderness, praise, emotional warmth, or physical reward become amalgamated into a self-perception of *Good-Me.* The Good-Me personification is thus a product of satisfying or pleasing interpersonal relations with this significant other, the mothering one (1953b, p. 162). The Good-

Me personification is largely conscious and usually indicated in verbal behavior by everything to which a person can freely apply the pronoun "I," as in "I am ..." or "I would like to be ..." or "I have. ..."

Bad-Me Personification

Increasing degrees of anxiety and tension on the part of the mothering one are directed to certain behaviors of her infant: touching objectionable parts of his body, unruly crying, refusal to eat certain foods, struggling over bodily care like bathing. All those behaviors that occasion increasing tension in the mother also evoke anxiety in the infant. Over time, these undesirable, anxiety-provoking behaviors become amalgamated into the personification of the *Bad-Me.* The Bad-Me personification is also conscious to a large degree, but it may grade imperceptibly into behaviors that are unconscious because they evoke stronger degrees of anxiety.

Not-Me Personification

The *Not-Me* personification is almost outside the realm of description. It is the part of personality that is rarely experienced consciously by the normal person, except perhaps during dreaming. For the schizophrenic, on the other hand, experience of the Not-Me personification is continual. The Not-Me is the dissociated cluster of feelings and images that exists side by side with the more neutral content of consciousness, but which seemingly does not belong to consciousness. Thus the Not-Me lies outside the realm of description by language. It is a product of intense, "uncanny" emotion in the parataxic mode:

> This [Not-Me] is a very gradually evolving personification of an always relatively primitive character—that is, organized in unusually simple signs in the parataxic mode of experience, and made up of poorly grasped aspects of living which will presently be regarded as "dreadful," and which still later will be differentiated into incidents which are attended by awe, horror, loathing, or dread. [Sullivan, 1953b, p. 163]

The feelings of dread and terror, disgust and loathing that attend the Not-Me personification are difficult to place in words because they were attached to certain behaviors and perceptions through forbidding gesture and empathic expression of anxiety from the mothering one. To a greater or lesser extent, all personalities have a Not-Me personification, a part of oneself that seems alien and hideous. For a good example of Not-Me experience common to everyone, turn to the next chapter (Chapter 8) and consult page 281.

Another rather potent example from the case history of one of Sullivan's schizophrenic patients may serve to indicate the "uncanny," "*awe*-ful" nature of dissociated feelings of the Not-Me. This patient, among other dissociated systems operating in his psychosis, evidenced strong homosexual and incestuous impulses so loathesome and frightening that they had been split off from the rest of consciousness. In the development of the normal personality, if we are to take Freud at face value, incestuous and erotic impulses of childhood are repressed along with autoerotic wishes at the time of the resolution of the Oedipus complex. In addition, the child's normally uninhibited desire to play with and to smear his own feces is abandoned after "education" in the shame and disgust lessons of parental example and horror. In Sullivan's patient, most of these impulses lingered on in consciousness, but only in the dissociated form that intruded into his conscious fantasies and delusional thinking. Particularly problematic was his habitual masturbation accompanied by fantasies that could be described in the normal personality only as Not-Me:

> He masturbated frequently, to the accompaniment of homosexual anal phantasies. *On an occasion when about 17,* he, having inserted a candle into the rectum "to increase satisfaction," as the orgasm approached, withdrew the candle and thrust it into his mouth. The orgasm, he remembers vividly, was very powerful. This recollection was strongly resisted. He had never repeated the procedure. [Sullivan, 1962, p. 36]

The revulsion one experiences upon reading of this schizophrenic's behavior is some evidence of the uncanny Not-Me nature of the oral–anal impulses that we have learned to disconnect from one another early in infancy. Because of the reaction of the mothering one, all normally socialized adults have acquired a sense of loathing and disgust for anything connected with anal or fecal content.

Ordinarily, the close association between the mouth and the anus for the infant is not connected with disgust or revulsion until shame, learned through anxiety, is established. From that point, the early willingness to manipulate feces, to smear them, or to raise them to the mouth evokes intense horror. Any connection between oral and anal impulses and genital sexual activity is likewise deeply submerged. In effect, these impulses have become Not-Me:

> The not-me is literally the organization of experience with significant people that has been subjected to such intense anxiety, and anxiety so suddenly precipitated, that it was impossible for the then relatively rudimentary person to make any sense of, to develop any true grasp on, the particular circumstances which dictated the experience of this intense anxiety. [Sullivan, 1953b, p. 314]

The Self-System: Security Operations

From his experiences with reward and anxiety, with forbidding and tender gestures, the infant learns another important lesson: Anxiety can be reduced by certain specific behaviors that are approved by the mothering one; and anxiety is sometimes increased to an unbearable degree by behaving in ways that she disapproves. In effect, it is desirable to be the Good-Me; undesirable to be the Bad-Me; and unthinkable to be the Not-Me.

In order to maintain the division between "good" and "bad" forms of living, the infant learns to interact only in certain ways with the significant others of his world. The habitual pattern of behaviors that the infant develops to gain the greatest satisfaction and to keep anxiety at a minimum in dealing with significant others is the *self-system*, or *self-dynamism*. The self-system is thus a cluster of "security operations."

In Sullivan's attempt to establish a scientific conception of interpersonal relations, he chose the term *dynamism* to indicate habitual patterns of behavior like the self-system because it offered the possibility of objectivity. Like the physicist, the psychiatrist should be able to specify what *energy transactions* characterize the human life he is studying because:

> . . . the present view of the universe, as held by a great majority of mathematicians, physicists, and other scientists, makes the discoverable world a dynamism. This is implied in the fundamental postulate that the ultimate reality in the universe is energy, that all material objects are manifestations of energy, and that all activity represents the dynamic or kinetic aspect of energy. [Sullivan, 1953b, p. 102]

For Sullivan, the study of the personality is really the investigation of the organism's energy transactions with the world of things and people. Sullivan therefore defined dynamism in psychological and biological terms:

> . . . the ultimate entity, the smallest useful abstraction, which can be employed in the study of the functional activity of the living organism is the dynamism itself, *the relatively enduring pattern of energy transformations which recurrently characterize the organism in its duration as a living organism.* [1953b, p. 103]

The concept of dynamism may be thought of in psychological terms as a *habitual reaction pattern*. As always, Sullivan emphasized his fundamental belief that we are all "much more simply human than otherwise" by suggesting that minor variations in habitual reaction patterns were relatively unimportant. It was his opinion that such variations were merely "the envelope of insignificant particular differences." Thus, his earliest definition of personality was constructed along these same lines:

Personality is the relatively enduring configuration of life-processes characterizing all of the person's total activity pertaining to such other persons, real or fantastic, as become from time to time relevant factors in his total situations. [1972, p. 47]

In Sullivan's final, definitive lectures on his conceptualizations, he changed the definition of personality somewhat to emphasize the concept of person-to-person contact as the fundamental unit of study:

Personality is the relatively enduring pattern of recurrent interpersonal situations which characterize a human life. [1953b, pp. 110–111]

Personality is thus composed of a series of interpersonal dynamisms; of, therefore, *habitual patterns of relating to others.* Originally founded on the need to reduce anxiety and obtain satisfaction for needs, the self-system is the dynamism of "educative experience called into being by the necessity to avoid or to minimize incidents of anxiety" (1953b, p. 165). The self-system's sole function is to aid the infant in reducing anxiety, first with the mothering one, and later as an adult, with all significant others.

Unfortunately, the self-system also embodies some troublesome characteristics. Since it is the product of parental censure and praise, it embodies the prevailing cultural standards by which the parents themselves have been molded. The self-system, therefore, functions to screen the child's repertoire of possible behaviors and to focus them into a smaller number of socially acceptable ones. Thus the self-system narrows attention to those aspects of living that generate praise and blame, and it attempts to perpetuate only those experiences that are least likely to generate anxiety. In this sense, the self-system is a stumbling block to growth:

[The self-system] permits a minute focus on those performances of the child which are the cause of approbation and disapprobation, but, very much like a microscope, it interferes with noticing the rest of the world. *When you are staring through your microscope, you don't see much except what comes through that channel.* So with the self-dynamism. It has a tendency to focus attention on performances with the significant other person which get approbation or disfavor. [Sullivan, 1953a, p. 21; italics added]

The self-system refuses awareness to all experiences, all impulses, that are not relevant to parental approval and disapproval. Experiences that generated parental approval become part of the Good-Me; experiences that generated disapproval become part of the Bad-Me; but experiences that generated superdisapproval, intense disfavor, are dissociated from the personality and relegated to the Not-Me. In effect, the self-system is a selective filter, restricting attention, and consequently personality growth, to the reflected appraisals of others (Sullivan, 1953a, p. 29). This process of selective filtering was termed by Sullivan selective inattention.

Selective Inattention

Selective inattention may occur in emergency situations, for example, when it is necessary to focus awareness only on the problem at hand. In this case, selective inattention is a very adaptive and useful response. But when selective inattention to important aspects of living is habitual in the service of allaying anxiety, it is a mechanism of defensive perception, a "security operation."

To illustrate, Sullivan reported an experience with a patient who provided an elegant and extreme example of selective inattention. Sullivan had been seeing this patient every week for a number of years and soon became accustomed to the man's ritualistic way of beginning the therapeutic hour. Each week the patient would recount an experience he had while on the train enroute to Sullivan's office. Each week it was the same experience. And each week the man reported the experience with the same fresh amazement, as if none of the other reported experiences had happened. Sullivan commented:

> I had heard it perhaps two hundred times when one day, for some reason or other, all the factors added up in my mind and I interrupted before he finished. After he had recounted his fantasy of kissing some man and then biting a piece out of his ear I said, "And you were amazed!" He said, "Yes, what do you mean? . . . I *was* amazed. But why did you say so? What do you know about it?" [Sullivan responded:] "Why, only that you have told me the same story two or three hundred times. . . ." [1956, pp. 44–45]

To a large extent, selective inattention resembles Freud's mechanisms of denial and repression. But Sullivan saw selective inattention as an integral part of the self-system's functioning. On this basis, Sullivan proposed a *Theorem of Escape:*

> The self-system unlike any of the other dynamisms . . . is extraordinarily resistant to change by experience. This can be expressed in the theorem that *the self-system from its nature . . . tends to escape influence by experience which is incongruous with its current organization and functional activity.* [1953b, p. 190]

As maturity is attained, whole segments of activity related to anxiety are relegated to the self-system. Like the train-riding man, parts of the self are isolated from the rest of personality. Though we behave in particular ways, we may be reluctant to recognize our actions as our own, or to incorporate new experiences into the self.

Me-You Personifications

Even in maturity, the individual's self-system and its processes of selective inattention operate to shape in important ways his conception of himself and of significant others. For example, consider the possibilities inherent in the multiple relationships of Mr. A to Mrs. A in the course of their married life. Because both partners' self-systems are differentially attuned to reality, and to maintaining self-images founded on others' reflected appraisals, they respond to *personifications* of the other, not to the reality of the other's presence. As the conditions of the interpersonal situation change, Mr. A's image of his wife will shift. He may personify her one moment as the illusory image "loving and tender wife-mother," and in the next situation she will become for him the illusory image "feminine viper and tauntress." Likewise, Mrs. A responds not to the objective Mr. A, but to a series of multiple "you's" she has created in relationship to her personification of herself, her "me" image.

In a sense, there are at least eight personages involved (based on Sullivan, 1965, pp. 46 ff.):

Mr. A and Mrs. A as they really are

Mr. A¹ as his wife personifies him [loving husband]

Mr. A² as his wife personifies him in another situation
   [selfish and despicable husband]

Mrs. A¹ as her husband personifies her [loving wife]

Mrs. A² as her husband personifies her in another context
   [viper and tauntress]

Mr. A³ as he sees himself [peace maker; long suffering]

Mrs. A³ as she sees herself [victim; belittled wife]

Additionally, the list of personifications might be supplemented with the subsequent changes in self-perception as the other's "you" image changes the situation and is reflected in changed self-images: Mr. $A^{4,5,6,7}$ $\cdots$ and Mrs. $A^{4,5,6,7}$ $\cdots$ and so on.

If we could observe a quarrel between Mr. and Mrs. A we could record the shift in me-you patterns that takes place. In the quarrel, Mrs. A has assumed the role of victimized wife; she resents frequently being left alone on her husband's nights out. Mr. A, on the other hand, remarks to his wife that her choice of friends is so utterly boring and ridiculous that he can barely tolerate being present. That is why he seeks out his own friends. Mrs. A now unleashes some pent up fury to inform the man she now views as an *utterly selfish belittler of women* not to "judge my friends by the fools you spend your evenings with . . ." (Sullivan, 1964, p. 45). In response Mr. A assumes the role of *wounded husband, long-suffering peace maker* who has finally suffered enough at the hands of this malicious person. In his view,

Mrs. A has become "the epitome of malicious persecutions, a human viper whom the law protects while she taunts him with her ability to destroy his every chance of happiness" (Sullivan, 1964, p. 45).

The interaction between Mr. A and Mrs. A has shifted among mutual *illusory* "me-you" patterns. The fact that the partners can respond to each other, to each other's image of self, and to their own illusory personifications of the other led Sullivan to propose that:

> The incongruity in the coincident me-you patterns may grow to such a point that [Mr.] A comes to think "something is wrong" with Mrs. A, and consults a psychiatrist about her. He reports that "she seems to have undergone a complete change. She misunderstands everything I do, thinks I deceive her about everything. . . ." [1964, p. 47]

Thus, the label "mental illness" may be applied to one partner on the basis of discrepant mutual and illusory me-you personifications. For Sullivan, the goal of psychiatry is "the study of the phenomena that occur in interpersonal situations, in configurations made up of two or more people, all but one of whom [the psychiatrist-observer] may be more or less completely illusory" (1964, p. 33).

R. D. Laing has extended Sullivan's concepts of me-you personifications into an elaborate and sophisticated set of postulates. In addition, with his colleagues, Laing has constructed a paper-and-pencil instrument to assess the impact of incongruent mutual perceptions. Laing et al. (1966, p. 3) rather poetically summarized these ideas:

> The human race is a myriad of refractive surfaces staining the white radiance of eternity. Each surface refracts the refraction of refractions of refractions. Each self refracts the refractions of others' refractions of self's refractions of others' refractions. . . . Here is glory and wonder and mystery, yet too often we simply wish to ignore or destroy those points of view that refract the light differently from our own.

In the next chapter, we shall consider Laing's work in some detail.

Developmental Epochs: From Infancy to Late Adolescence

Sullivan divided the course of personality development into six epochs. Each of these is marked by a distinctly different quality of interpersonal relations and by functioning in one of the three modes of experience. The six epochs are infancy, childhood, juvenile epoch, preadolescence, early adolescence, and late adolescence.

Infancy

Extending roughly from birth to the development of language, the period of infancy is primarily prototaxic in nature. The infant experiences reality as a discrete flux of momentary states. He does not differentiate self from the world; his experience of reality is global, diffuse.

Most significant of the developments of infancy are the personifications of self and significant other. Good-Me, Bad-Me, and Not-Me have already been surveyed, as well as the personifications of the Good and Bad Mother (nipple). Out of his experiences with the significant others of his world, the infant develops a particular orientation to the world. These dynamisms can include *apathy* and *somnolent detachment* when the infant's experiences with the mothering one have been anxiety provoking and frustrating.

Apathy refers to the capacity of the infant to deal with emergency situations of unsatisfied needs by developing a withdrawing "I don't care" orientation to his own experiences of hunger, thirst, and pain (Sullivan, 1953b, p. 55). (See Horney's description of the detached personality in Chapter 6.)

Somnolent detachment literally means the separation from reality that occurs by being sleepy. In effect, the infant's withdrawal response of apathy may be extended to cope with anxiety situations that are persistent and prolonged. Somnolent detachment is not distinguishable observationally from apathy in the infant. However, from the infant's point of view, somnolent detachment involves not only a "don't care" attitude about objects of need satisfaction, but also a forthright *indifference to significant persons* responsible for the neglected satisfactions. Apathy is called out by aggravated and unsatisfied needs; somnolent detachment is evoked by prolonged anxiety in interpersonal contacts (Sullivan, 1953b, p. 57).

An example of what prolonged anxiety and unsatisfied emotional needs can do to a child is provided by the work of René Spitz, a psychoanalytically oriented developmental psychiatrist. Spitz conducted studies of severely emotionally deprived children in hospitals and nursing homes. These children were provided with every material necessity but were totally lacking in experiences of emotional warmth and security, tender mothering, or even simple intellectual stimulation. For one reason or another, usually illness, they were separated from their mothers for an unbroken period of two to three months. A characteristic pattern of behavior emerged in these children which Spitz named *anaclitic depression* on the basis of psychoanalytic theory. The term "anaclitic" literally means "leaning on," "dependent," or "attached" (cf. Freud, 1914a, vol. XIV, p. 87). It is an approximate translation of a German word that Freud used to describe one form of narcissistic object choice. Spitz observed a reliable sequence in the establishment of anaclitic depression through the first three months of separation:

> *first month:* The children become weepy, demanding and tend to cling to the observer when he succeeds in making contact with them.

second month: The weeping often changes into wails. Weight loss sets in. There is an arrest of the developmental quotient.

third month: The children refuse contact. They lie prone in their cots most of the time. . . . Insomnia sets in; loss of weight continues. There is a tendency to contract intercurrent diseases; motor retardation becomes generalized. Inception of facial rigidity. [Spitz, 1965, pp. 270–271]

If satisfactory reunion with the mother is not accomplished within five months, permanent and irreversible physical and psychological effects result. In Sullivan's terms, these children are extreme cases of somnolent detachment.

Childhood

The childhood epoch extends roughly from the acquisition of language to the appearance of a need for playmates or "compeers" (1953b, p. 33; 1953a, p. 37). The basic mode of experience in childhood is parataxic. Though language is present, it is used in some very magical, parataxic ways:

. . . in so far as a verbal statement by a child is taken by the acculturating adults to have a superior quality of reality to other of his behavioral acts, the child is being trained to be incapable of dealing with life. . . . in a good many homes, the following kind of statement is a conspicuous ingredient in the alleged education of the young: "Willie, I told you not to do that. Now say you are sorry." . . . If Willie dutifully says he is sorry, that is supposed to markedly mitigate the situation, although it is something that Willie is almost absolutely incapable of understanding. [Sullivan, 1953b, pp. 200–201]

To extend Sullivan's example, we can return to Jean-Mary. Her magical use of language illustrates the same phenomenon. She, too, had learned to say "sorry" or "pardon me" or "no offense" as a propitiatory gesture. She assumed that therefore it was all right to say or do anything to a playmate as long as one followed it with a "sorry" or a "no offense." Thus, she would say to a playmate that her dolly was ugly or funny-looking, following this crass insult with a "no offense!" Having offered the magical cancellation, Jean-Mary was always amazed when her playmate was hurt or argumentative.

Another important development of the childhood epoch is the possibility for the child to undergo what Sullivan called a *malevolent transformation* (1953b, p. 213):

For a variety of reasons, many children have the experience that when they need tenderness, when they do that which once brought tender cooperation, they are not only denied tenderness, but they are treated in a fashion to provoke anxiety or even, in some cases, pain. A child may discover that manifesting the need for tenderness toward the potent figures around him leads frequently to his being disadvantaged, being made anxious, being made fun of ... Under those circumstances, the developmental course changes to the point that the perceived need for tenderness brings a foresight of anxiety and pain. The child learns, you see, that it is highly disadvantageous to show any need for tender cooperation from the authoritative figures around him, in which case he shows something else; and that something else is the basic malevolent attitude, *the attitude that one really lives among enemies.* ... [Sullivan, 1953b, p. 114; italics added]

Later, in adolescence, the child who has learned that this is a hostile and unfriendly world may deliberately behave in ways that make it impossible for anyone to love him or to show him affection and kindness. In effect, he has learned to forgo any demonstration of a need for tenderness, and he treats others with a similar malevolence.

On the positive side, the epoch of childhood is marked by a number of *"as if" performances* or role playing the significant behaviors modeled by parents. "As if" performances may eventually be practiced as defensive maneuvers by the child who has been exposed to manipulative and anxiety-provoking rearing.

Instead of a healthy identification with parents, the child may play roles to conceal his real feelings in the *dramatization* of behaviors demonstrated by mother and father (1953b, p. 209). In a dramatization the "as if" performance shifts from "acting like" the parents to acting as if he *were* the parents. For the most part, however, dramatizations are an essential and normal part of the childhood epoch, and they facilitate adoption by the child of his appropriate male or female role.

The second kind of "as if" performance is the technique of seeming preoccupied with something in order to be left alone. The child learns to behave "as if" some activity were highly important to him, riveting his attention and demanding all his energy. In actuality, the seeming preoccupation is really a technique of avoiding disturbing and painful interactions with anxiety-provoking significant others, or it is a means of escaping their demands (1953b, p. 210).

Juvenile Epoch

The transition from childhood to the juvenile epoch is marked most clearly in Sullivan's thinking by the changing role of playmates in the child's estimation. In childhood, the need for a playmate was essentially egocentric, even selfish. Children play side by side, but they do not necessarily interact. Though the child is aware of his playmate, more important to him are his own pursuits, his own ideas, his own speeches. He may even invent an imaginary playmate in order to satisfy *his* wishes. But in the juvenile epoch, there emerges a true need for mutuality of experience, a need for genuine cooperative play (Sullivan, 1953b, p. 226).

The juvenile epoch thus extends from the grammar school years through that phase when the child experiences a need for an intimate relationship with a same-sexed "chum." Most of the juvenile's experiences are in the syntaxic mode, and language has become his chief tool of coping with the demands of authority.

Education and the authority figures of the school play a significant role in the juvenile's life. The chief contributions to personality development occur through two avenues of social activity. *Social subordination* occurs when the child learns to respect and to obey a succession of parental authority substitutes: the teacher, the crossing guard, the gym coach, and so on. *Social accommodation* involves "a simply astounding broadening of the grasp of how many slight differences in living there are; how many of these differences seem to be all right, even if pretty new; and how many of them don't seem to be right, but nonetheless how unwise one is to attempt to correct them" (Sullivan, 1953b, p. 229). In short, through exposure to a variety of new and significant others, the child learns to tolerate familial and social diversity.

Preadolescence

The key characteristic of preadolescence is the strong emergence of a trend that was already present in the juvenile epoch: namely, the need for intimacy with a "chum" or best friend of the same sex. The preadolescent epoch thus extends from the establishment of an intimate friendship with a same-sexed peer to the emergence of an interest and a need for a partner of the opposite sex.

The significance of the need for a chum is in the character of the relationship. For the first time, the chum is a person who has equal importance to self; his interests, his needs, his fantasies are on the same level of importance as the preadolescent's own. The preadolescent has developed a real sensitivity to the needs of the other person.

> And this is not in the sense of "what should I do to get what I want," but instead "what should I do to contribute to the happiness or to support the prestige and feeling of worth-whileness of my chum." [Sullivan, 1953b, p. 245]

The relationship which develops between chums is termed *collaboration* because each of the chums validates the personal worth of the other. They collaborate to mutually validate desires, conceptions of the world, and interpretations of the self:

> Because one draws so close to another, because one is newly capable of seeing oneself through the other's eyes, the preadolescent phase

of personality development is especially significant in correcting autistic, fantastic ideas about oneself or others. [Sullivan, 1953b, p. 248]

Early Adolescence

Extending from the emergence of genital sexuality, that is, from puberty,
to a focused interest in the opposite sex, early adolescence is characterized
by feelings of "lust" (1953b, p. 263). The adolescent has experienced
orgasm and the feelings of sexual arousal are a new and continual component of his self-image.

A variety of collisions between the feelings of lust and the needs for
security and intimacy occurs. It is typical of adolescence that the burgeoning sexual needs cause a reevaluation of the self-image in the light of
growing doubts about sexual competence and proficiency.

> Ridicule from parents and other elders is among the worst tools that
> are used on early adolescents. Sometimes a modification of ridicule
> is used by parents . . . and this modification takes the form of inter-
> fering with, objecting to, criticizing and otherwise getting in the way
> of any detectable movement of their child toward a member of the
> other sex. [Sullivan 1953b, p. 268]

There are also collisions between the need for intimacy and lustful feelings. Not uncommonly, the adolescent feels awkward and clumsy in his
first advances to a member of the other sex, particularly so when that
person has already been idealized and idolized. Male adolescents may
create among their groups distinctions between "good" girls and the more
permissive ones. Genital activities are thought to apply only to the latter
group, with the "good" girls reserved as more or less potential marriage
partners.

Late Adolescence

Late adolescence extends from the focused expression of genital sexual
activity through the establishment of a full repertoire of adult interpersonal relations (1953b, p. 297). The predominant mode of experience is, of
course, syntaxic. The most important behavioral characteristics of late
adolescence are the establishment of vocational identity or the decision to
pursue an educational course leading to some professional role.

For the first time, the adolescent may experience real "restrictions in
living." Inhibitions or hindrances based on past developmental failures or
other handicaps stemming from his past emotional interactions may curtail
his range of adult choices for a job, for education, or for a mate. Respect
for self must be based on learned respect for others; without this mutuality
of concern and performance, the adolescent is likely to develop a variety

of techniques for isolating and preventing further development to full maturity.

The developmental epochs are summarized in Table 7–2.

Summary

Sullivan viewed personality as the set of characteristic and habitual interpersonal relations that mark a human life, the most significant of which is with the mothering one in infancy. Because the mothering one can communicate anxiety to the infant, and because the infant's needs arouse in her a corresponding need to show her infant tenderness, Sullivan characterized the relationship as an "empathic linkage."

The ways in which the mothering one responds to the infant's behaviors will shape the three personifications of the self: Good-Me, Bad-Me, and the uncanny Not-Me. Out of his work with schizophrenic patients, and from his knowledge of the work of Jung and Freud, Sullivan formulated his view of dissociated feelings and ideas. These dissociated components of personality are to be found even in the normal personality as revealed in dreams and momentary states of stress.

With the focus on interpersonal relations, Sullivan also emphasized the unity of human endeavor in his species identity theorem: We are all much more simply human than otherwise. Thus even the psychiatrist's professional activities are to be conceptualized as *participant* observation, for he too brings to the therapeutic relationship strictly human experiences and qualities.

As the infant progresses through the various stages of growth and psychological development, he experiences reality in vastly more abstract ways than were possible in the first months of existence. As Piaget had also shown, the infant's first perceptions of himself and his universe are fused, vague, and in continuous flux. Called the prototaxic mode, this early form of experience is primarily sensory, not cognitive, and predominantly egocentric. As the infant progresses to the parataxic mode, temporal contiguity is interpreted as causality. Jacqueline's arching movements to control the moving saucer illustrate Piaget's concept of magico-phenomenalistic causality and Sullivan's conception of magical thinking. Finally, the child enters the syntaxic mode in which reality is interpreted on its own terms, and the most important tool that the child brings to bear is language. Now, for the first time, the child is capable of employing consensually validated symbols, words that have shared and accepted meanings in the larger social community.

Sullivan's conception of "me-you" patterns of personification was yet another indication of his growing sense of the importance of social interaction as the basic datum of psychiatry. In a close dyadic relationship, for example a marriage, the partners respond not to the reality of each other's

TABLE 7-2: SULLIVAN'S DEVELOPMENTAL EPOCHS

DEVELOPMENTAL EPOCH	CHRONOLOGY	OUTSTANDING ACHIEVEMENTS/FAILURES
1. Infancy	Birth to language (0 to 18 months)	Prototaxic experience of reality; differentiation of Good, Bad, and Not-Me; personifications of Good/Bad Mother; defensive reactions of apathy and somnolent detachment.
2. Childhood	Language use to need for playmates (18 months to approx. 5 years)	Parataxic experience of reality; egocentric relationship with peers; magical use of language; malevolent transformation possible; "as if" performances: dramatizations and preoccupations.
3. Juvenile Epoch	Grammar school to need for a chum (6 to 8 or 9 years)	Parataxic and syntaxic experiences of reality; mutuality and cooperation in play; social subordination and social accommodation in school experiences.
4. Preadolescence	Intimate friendship to puberty (9 to 12 years)	Mostly syntaxic experience of reality; need for a same-sexed chum; strong collaboration with chum; consensual validation of experiences; establishment of a capacity for selfless love.
5. Early Adolescence	Puberty to interest in other sex (13 through 17 or 18 years)	Syntaxic experience of reality; need for expression of lust; need for partner of opposite sex; collisions between lust and security-intimacy needs.
6. Late Adolescence	Heterosexual activity to adult interpersonal relationships (19 or 20 years to maturity)	Syntaxic experience of reality; vocational identity established; restrictions in living experienced on basis of past developments; establishment of adult friendships; need for a life-partner of other sex.

Based on Sullivan, 1953b.

person, but to illusory images of the other created in the situational context. R. D. Laing later extended some of Sullivan's ideas on interaction into a sophisticated interpersonal theory of perception-personality processes.

Sullivan divided personality development into six epochs: infancy, childhood, juvenile epoch, preadolescence, early adolescence, and late adolescence. The significant advances represented by the successive stages center, of course, on the child's acquisition of more sophisticated modes of experiencing reality and on his growing need for intimate relationships with significant others.

Sometimes classed as a neo-Freudian theorist, Sullivan's interpersonal theory is more similar to Horney's theory or to Adler's than to Freud's. Yet, Sullivan did freely borrow psychoanalytic conceptions from Freud and Jung. But what Sullivan molded from the psychoanalytic tradition can be described as a unique blend of social, cognitive, and clinical psychology.

The most important aspect of Sullivan's view of personality may be summarized by pointing out that this is a people-world, and feelings—painful and joyful—are wisely or unwisely tied up with our relations to significant others.

FOR FURTHER READING

During his lifetime, Sullivan published rarely. His major work, *The Interpersonal Theory of Psychiatry* (New York: W. W. Norton, 1953), is actually a series of lectures skillfully edited into a coherent work. To gain some historical perspective on the development of Sullivan's ideas, the reader will find the recently published *Personal Psychopathology* (New York: W. W. Norton, 1972) quite illuminating. Sullivan had postponed the publication of this volume several times during his career, until it was finally published posthumously.

Some of Sullivan's early papers on schizophrenia and psychotic disorganization have been organized into a single volume under the title *Schizophrenia as a Human Process* (New York: W. W. Norton, 1962); a careful reading of these papers will reveal Sullivan's debts to Jung and to Freud. Another collection of Sullivan's papers, *The Fusion of Psychiatry and Social Science* (New York: W. W. Norton, 1964), more clearly exposes his methodological assumptions, including his one genus (species identity) theorem. Sullivan's other published works are cited throughout the chapter, and a careful reading of any of them will repay the effort involved.

For comparative purposes, the reader may want to explore some of R. D. Laing's works, in which Laing expands and modifies some of Sullivan's conceptions on interpersonal perception. Particularly useful in this regard are Laing's *Divided Self* (Baltimore: Penguin, 1959), and his *Self and Other* (New York: Pantheon, 1969). (Laing's work is treated in Chapter 8 of this book.) A reading of George Herbert Mead's *Mind, Self and Society from the Standpoint of a Social Behaviorist* (Chicago: University of Chicago Press, 1934; available in paperback) will reveal another source of Sullivan's ideas on the nature of selfhood.

Indirectly influenced by Sullivan, Jurgen Ruesch has written two books that emphasize the power of language in shaping a person's world view. The two volumes are *Disturbed Communication* and *Therapeutic Communication* (New York: W. W. Norton, 1957 and 1961, respectively).

The papers published in Patrick Mullahy's *The Contributions of Harry Stack Sullivan: A Symposium on Interpersonal Theory in Psychiatry and Social Science* (New York: Hermitage Press, 1952) attempt to place Sullivan's work in historical perspective.

8 R. D. LAING
Existential Phenomenology

The lie is the specific evil which man has introduced into nature. . . . In a lie the spirit practises treason against itself.
                                                    MARTIN BUBER, *Good and Evil*

The self may be said to be made up of reflected appraisals. If these were chiefly derogatory, as in the case of an unwanted child who was never loved . . . then the self dynamism will itself be chiefly derogatory. It will facilitate hostile, disparaging appraisals of other people and it will entertain disparaging and hostile appraisals of itself.
                                    HARRY STACK SULLIVAN, *Conceptions of Modern Psychiatry*

Fly on the Wall of an Insane Place

You are to be accorded a rare privilege. Largely unnoticed and unhindered, you will spend some weeks in a mental hospital. As one of eight pseudopatients, you are a faker, a "normal" individual, perhaps even a professional mental health worker, who, by deception and guile, has gained voluntary entry to the hospital. As a disguised observer, you will be the proverbial fly on the wall, from whose view nothing is concealed, from whose hearing nothing is withheld.

There are, however, some duties that attend this privilege. For one thing, you will have to forgo your personal freedom, your real identity and name, and your normal daily activities. Most of your time will be spent taking notes, recording personal interactions between staff and patients, and making observations of your own reactions to the environment of the hospital. You will be, in effect, consumed by days and nights devoted to covert social psychological observation.

Despite your initial misgivings, it was relatively easy to commit yourself to the institution. Presenting yourself at the admitting office, you reported a straightforward complaint: "I hear voices that say 'empty,' 'hollow,' and 'thud.' " Though you displayed no bizarre behavior nor acted in any way other than normally, the diagnosis of "schizophrenia" was affixed to you and to six of your seven comrades enacting the same drama in hospitals of five other states.

The chances of being detected as "sane" were unbelievably slim once the diagnostic label had been applied. None of the pseudopatients was, in fact, released from the hospital in less than a week. The longest period of time in which a pseudopatient went undetected was fifty-two days, and nineteen days was the average length of time for the group as a whole. In all cases, when release finally came, it was not because you were discovered to be a sane faker. Your discharge diagnosis read: "Schizophrenia in remission."

Thus, the absence of symptoms was interpreted as "spontaneous" recovery. Even more surprising, no hospital administrator, nurse, attendant, or physician ever discovered the true state of any pseudopatient's mental health. Only the real patients ever caught on to the deception: "You're not crazy. You're a journalist or something. You're checking up on the hospital."

The Illness of Mental Myths

David Rosenhan (1973), the man responsible for the design and execution of the pseudopatient study of mental hospitals, attacked several myths implicit in psychology and psychiatry. One myth states that the *"normal are detectably sane."* Rosenhan, who served as the first pseudopatient, and the seven other men and women enacting that role, went undetected as sane by people who presumably should be able to do so—but not by the real patients.

Another myth debunked by the Rosenhan study is the age-old tradition in the mental health professions that a trained diagnostician can correctly identify the specific "mental illness" syndrome from which a patient suffers. A corollary of this myth states that having diagnosed the patient's illness, the differential diagnostic label affixed to him is a humane and reliable guide for therapeutic procedure. Both of these myths evaporated under Rosenhan's critical scrutiny.

To illustrate, in a substudy related to the one described, Rosenhan informed the staff and professional workers of a teaching mental hospital that during the next three months one or more pseudopatients would attempt to gain admission to their facility. The staff were particularly skeptical about Rosenhan's previous results so they were even more on guard than the implied challenge to their professional competence would indicate. During the three-month period, judgments about 193 patients admitted to the hospital were obtained from the staff who had primary contact with them. "Forty-one patients were alleged, with high confidence, to be pseudopatients by at least one member of the staff. Twenty-three were considered suspected by one psychiatrist *and* one other staff member. Actually, no genuine pseudopatient . . . presented himself during this period" (Rosenhan, 1973, p. 252).

Rosenhan's findings imply that diagnostic labels and professional acumen are weak in two ways. In the first place, it is clearly possible to affix a diagnostic label indicative of "mental illness" to someone who suffers no disease. On the other hand, it is possible to err on the side of overcaution and skepticism. *If one's suspicions are aroused,* it is possible to label as *sane* people who come for treatment out of a sincere belief in their own illness, as was the case with the alerted hospital staff. Evidently, therefore, in the normal order of things, when the physician does not expect patients to give false reports, all the people who present themselves for admission to a mental hospital are uncritically accepted as ill. They receive a diagnostic label that brands them members of a special class of people who suffer from *disease* that is "mental." The label is likely to follow them for the rest of their lives, influencing everyone with whom they come into contact, from relatives and friends to employers and government agencies.

Thomas Szasz (1960, 1961, and 1970) has been arguing for a long time that the concept of *mental illness* is a myth. It is his thesis that the so-called mentally ill are not *ill* in the medical sense. Disordered behavior does not fit the pattern of disease states. Neurotic and most psychotic reactions, according to Szasz, are more accurately conceived of as failures to adjust, mistakes in socialization, and as problems in assuming the tasks of living. In his view, so-called mental illness falls more sensibly within the scope of social, ethical, legal, and political specialists.

Most recently, Szasz has traced the history of the medical model of mental illness as a transition from the witchcraft explanation of disturbed behavior. Initially, the medical model was heralded as a more rational and more humane conception than its predecessor model of demonic possession. But, Szasz argues, adoption of the medical model's view of disturbed persons as sufferers of disease unfortunately did not include the abandonment of depersonalizing and dehumanizing techniques in dealing with them (1970, chap. 8). Just as accused witches were persecuted by the members of the medieval Inquisition clinging to their belief in demons and spirits, modern psychiatry clings to its myth that disturbed persons suffer disease. Torture wrung from many a "witch" her confession of complicity with the devil, and her inquisitors felt secure in having thus obtained salvation for her soul. Similarly, as compulsory salvation was practiced for witches, modern psychiatry treats its patients as people who have to be saved—even against their own will (Szasz, 1970, p. 112).

It is possible to interpret Rosenhan's pseudopatient study as supporting Szasz's contention that however personally disruptive and painful psychological disorder may be, it cannot be classed as a clear-cut, diagnosable, medically treatable illness. Yet, there is the equally strong possibility that *some* difference between "normal" and "mad" individuals exists, for *real* patients were able to detect the sane.

R. D. Laing, like Szasz, has argued that schizophrenia is not a "disease." The schizophrenic patient's behavior is explicable, not as a medical disorder, but as a desperate attempt to survive conflicting and irrational demands made upon him by a world that, more than the patient, deserves the label "mad." *From the viewpoint of the patient himself,* it is the situations into which he is thrust, not his mind, that are disordered. Laing's argument is an extreme position that, like the medical model it seeks to redress, is not by itself adequate to the task of describing and explaining disordered personalities. But, as we shall see, arguments like Szasz's and Laing's have served as much needed correctives to rigidly narrowed conceptions of disordered human lives (see also Goffman, 1959 and 1961).

The Pseudopatients' Experiences

Life within a mental hospital is unbelievably boring, consisting of tedium and regimentation, broken very rarely by normal social enjoyments. This fact rarely intrudes itself into the professional staff's awareness because they themselves have little experience with enforced monotony.

> One psychiatrist pointed to a group of patients who were sitting outside the cafeteria entrance half an hour before lunchtime. To a group of young residents he indicated that such behavior was characteristic of the oral-acquisitive nature of the [schizophrenia] syndrome. It seemed not to occur to him that there were very few things to anticipate in a psychiatric hospital besides eating. [Rosenhan, 1973, p. 253]

The psychiatrist's medical orientation, betrayed in his interpretation of the patients' cafeteria "waiting behavior," forces him to mold every observation, every patient-trait into a uniform picture consistent with "disease." Given that he believes institutionalized patients suffer from mental illness, then surely it must follow that their every action is a result of the disease. For a mental patient, boredom is not possible. To illustrate, when Rosenhan's pseudopatients first entered the hospital, they kept their note-taking secret. However, when no staff member paid attention to them, they began openly recording their observations. " 'Patient engages in writing behavior' was the daily nursing comment [in the patient's chart] on one of the pseudopatients who was never questioned about his writing" (Rosenhan, 1973, p. 253). Thus, even this activity was made consistent with his role as patient, for "writing *behavior*" is surely different from the normal person's "writing."

To obtain a clear conception of the atmosphere of the psychiatric hospital and the flavor of the patient-staff interactions, consider the encounters recorded by the pseudopatients, as shown in Table 8–1.

The percentages recorded are based on the observations of Rosenhan's pseudopatients with thirteen psychiatrists and forty-seven nurses. To flesh out the figures a bit, consider the quality of a typical encounter between a professional staff member and a pseudopatient. When the pseudopatient approached to ask: "Pardon me, Dr. X, could you tell me when I am eligible

TABLE 8-1: STAFF-PATIENT ENCOUNTERS (in percent)

TYPE OF CONTACT	PSYCHIATRISTS	NURSES—ATTENDANTS
Moves on, head averted	71	88
Pauses and chats	2	2
Stops and talks	4	0.5

Adapted from Rosenhan, 1973, p. 255.

for grounds privileges?" the psychiatrist's reply was: "Good morning, Dave. How are you today?" (Moves off without waiting for a response.) Rosenhan points out that the psychiatrist's reply can be classed only as bizarre, and his behavior as strangely aloof (1973, p. 255). As Table 8–1 indicates, the majority of patient-staff contacts are aloof (71–88 percent), and only rarely is the depersonalizing environment transcended by simple human amenity (2–4 percent).

Rosenhan concludes his report by emphasizing that the hospital environment, and all it implies by way of atmosphere, expectations, and efficiency, is essentially countertherapeutic. Rosenhan cautions, however, against attributing the pseudopatients' experiences to malice or stupidity of the hospital staff. Quite to the contrary, Rosenhan's impression of the hospital staff was that they were concerned, dedicated, and uncommonly intelligent. "Where they failed, as they sometimes did painfully, it would be more accurate to attribute those failures to the environment in which they, too, found themselves than to personal callousness" (1973, p. 257). To emphasize the role that environmental setting plays in shaping staff and patient roles, Rosenhan entitled his published study: "On Being Sane in Insane Places."

Implications of the Rosenhan Study

The one implication that emerges clearly from Rosenhan's study is the immensity of the task confronting the mental health worker. Should he conceptualize mental illness and disordered personality as a disease state? Or, perhaps, the professional specialist should follow Szasz's recommendations that such patients be treated as people with problems in living? The question is reducible to the form: "How shall disordered personality be construed?"

R. D. Laing provides an answer to this question that favors the social, problems-in-living approach. Laing, however, would ask: "How does the *patient* view his 'disordered' behavior?"

Going a step further than Szasz's position that mental illness is a myth, Laing has suggested that the schizophrenic experience has its own validity as a mode of being, as a strategy of coping with an insane world (1964 and 1967, p. 115). Laing feels that *some* individuals are labeled mentally ill or schizophrenic when their mode of adapting to an insane situation conflicts with commonly held convictions about appropriate or "healthy" forms of behavior (1959, p. 36). Rosenhan's pseudopatient study concretizes and lends some support to Laing's thesis. But Rosenhan's findings should not be taken as a definitive rebuttal of the medical model of mental disorder, nor as the ultimate verification of Laing's position. Rosenhan's results should be interpreted as one indication of the degree to which mental-health workers have continued need to refine and reshape their conceptions of the disordered personality.

Laing's View of "Mental Illness"

To describe patients waiting outside the cafeteria as people evidencing the "oral-acquisitive nature of the syndrome" is an act of utter obscenity to Laing. For him, such facile application of terminology confuses labeling with explanation. Labels drawn from classical clinical psychiatric models obscure the fundamental humanity of patients who strive to make sense of the existence *they perceive as theirs*. Laing gave an extraordinary example of the discrepancy in viewpoints between the physician and the patient in his re-analysis of a classic lecture "demonstration" of schizophrenia by Emil Kraeplin, a pioneer in psychiatry. The following passage is part of Kraeplin's account (1905) to a lecture room of his students of a patient diagnosed as catatonic (quoted by Laing, 1959, p. 29):

> The patient I will show you today has almost to be carried into the rooms, as he walks in a straddling fashion on the outside of his feet. On coming in, he throws off his slippers, sings a hymn loudly, and then cries twice (in English), 'My father, my real father!' He is eighteen years old. ... The patient sits with his eyes shut, and pays no attention to his surroundings. He does not look up even when he is spoken to, but he answers beginning in a low voice, and gradually screaming louder and louder. When asked where he is, he says, 'You want to know that too? I'll tell you who is being measured and is measured and shall be measured. I know all that, and could tell you, but I do not want to.' When asked his name, he screams, 'What is your name? What does he shut? He shuts his eyes. What does he hear? He does not understand; he understands not. ...'

Kraeplin, committed to the medical model, which he had had a hand in creating, interpreted the patient's lack of responsiveness and seeming excitable incoherence as symptoms of the *disease* called catatonia. He concluded that the patient had not provided a single piece of useful information to the series of questions because his disease fostered catatonic disorganization.

Laing suggested that there is another way to interpret the same behaviors. If the psychiatrist had been successful in entering the patient's phenomenal world *to see things as the patient saw them,* Kraeplin would have understood that the patient was mocking him:

> Surely [the patient] is carrying on a dialogue between his own parodied version of Kraeplin, and his own defiant rebelling self. 'You want to know that too? I tell you who is being measured and is measured and shall be measured. . . .' Presumably he deeply resents this form of interrogation which is being carried out before a lecture-room full of students. He probably does not see what it has to do with the things that must be deeply distressing him. But these things would not be 'useful information' to Kraeplin except as further 'signs' of a 'disease.' [Laing, 1959, p. 30]

The patient expressed not only his resentment at being "demonstrated" before an audience, he also adopted a survival strategy. He failed to cooperate with the "demonstrator," "his real father," and he resisted this authority figure's probing questions by parrying all inquiry with queries of his own. Of course, for Kraeplin, such resistive behavior was additional evidence of the effects of disease. For Laing, such behavior is rational and explicable once the psychiatrist is able to escape the case history approach to patients.

Existential Phenomenology

Laing's viewpoint might be characterized as existential phenomenology. In his early writings, Laing shares much with the European existential psychiatric tradition expressed in the work of Ludwig Binswanger and Medard Boss. Though we cannot survey the major tenets of existential psychology within the scope of this chapter, some comment on the existential tradition is necessary.

Owing much to the philosophy of Heidegger and Jaspers, Binswanger and Boss adopted an existential phenomenological approach to the treatment of their patients. They had found classical psychoanalysis to be wanting when it came to understanding their patients as pained human beings. In the United States, a foremost exponent of the existential approach has been Rollo May, and he, perhaps more than anyone, has lucidly defined the existential viewpoint:

> [The existential approach] is the endeavor to understand the nature of this man who *does* the experiencing and to *whom* the experiences happen. [1961, p. 12]

and

> Existentialism means centering upon the *existing* person; it is the emphasis on the human being as he is *emerging, becoming.* The word "existence" comes from the root *ex-sistere,* meaning literally "to stand out, emerge." [1961, p. 16]

Thus the existential psychologist is concerned with a *process* conception of human nature. Existentialism emphasizes the *living immediacy* of experience as the *individual lives it.* There is, consequently, an emphasis on the *here* and the *now,* in contrast to psychoanalysis' emphasis on the patient's past.

In some ways, though the existentialists find much of value in Freud's work, existential psychology can be understood as a reaction to classical psychoanalysis. Where Freud had adopted a deterministic conception of behavior as a product of *past* causes, the existentialists prefer to view the human person as a complex of conscious *processes,* ongoing, changing, and continually striving toward a *future* state of self-fulfillment. Man is unique among creatures of the living world, the existentialists point out, for he alone has the capacity to become aware of his own strivings, of his own *being.* Binswanger and other existentialists employ the German word *Dasein* for this aspect of human existence. *Dasein* may be translated literally as "being" *(sein)* and "there" *(da).*

> *Dasein* indicates that man is the being who is *there* and implies also that he *has* a "there" in the sense that he can know he is there and can take a stand with reference to that fact. The "there" is moreover not just any place, but the particular "there" that is mine, the particular point *in time* as well as space of my existence at this given moment. Man is the being who can be conscious of, and therefore responsible for, his existence. [May, 1958, p. 41]

As May indicates, the term *Dasein* is not exhausted by the English translation "being." It is extraordinarily difficult, most commentators agree, to speak and write about *being* with the full meaningfulness of the term as used by the existentialists. In English, the word *being* has a connotation of a thing, of a static state, or of a unit that contains being as in "a human being." For the existentialists, *Dasein* indicates a dynamic state, *becoming,* a continual *process*—the activity of *being something* not yet realized. In consequence, May (1958, p. 41) has suggested that the term "becoming" probably conveys the import of *Dasein* more meaningfully to English-speaking readers.

Freud named his approach to the study of human nature psychoanalysis because he conceived of his task as the elucidation of the connection between mental states and their underlying physical processes. The existentialists, on the other hand, reject any assumption of a split between mind and body. For them, what is of importance in man is *being*—in both mind and body—as an inseparable amalgam of physical and spiritual. Thus, the existentialists term their approach *Daseinanalyse.*

Where Freud conceived of anxiety as the threat of deprived instincts, the existentialist conceptualizes anxiety as the threat of nonbeing. Anxiety as the existentialist describes it is a sense of *dread,* of being *choked out of life,* a sense of exquisite *anguish* that the being he is and has must change with life's circumstances, causing him to forfeit present security in his striving to become future potentiality (May, 1958, pp. 51, 55; Binswanger, in May, 1958, p. 315).

Modes of Being: World as Meaningful to Man

Man's being is not isolated within him—*He is being-in-the-world.* For the existentialists, man is interrelated with his *world.* They frown on the word "environment" because it bespeaks a conceptualization of the human person that is fragmented. Existentially, *man implies his world,* and *his world implies him:* ". . . there is neither without the other, and each is understandable only in terms of the other" (May, 1958, p. 59).

> *World is the structure of meaningful relationships in which a person exists and in the design of which he participates.* Thus world includes the past events which condition my existence and all the vast variety of deterministic influences which operate upon me. But it is these *as I relate to them,* am aware of them, carry them with me, molding, inevitably forming, building them in every minute of relating. For to be aware of one's world means at the same time to be designing it. [May, 1958, pp. 59–60]

Hence, the existential conception of *world* is not restricted to what is ordinarily meant by environment. It is more forward looking and centered more on *possibility* than on biological givens. The existentialists have refined their concept of world by distinguishing three *modes of world* which each person embodies as being-in-the-world.

1. *Umwelt,* translated literally as "world around," includes the biological drives, needs, and instincts of the individual. *Umwelt,* considered alone, corresponds roughly to what we mean by environment, the impersonal world of natural law and biological cycle. Even if one were totally without self-awareness, the *Umwelt* would continue to exist (May, 1958, p. 61). In some respects, Freud's conception of human nature focused almost exclusively on the *Umwelt,* a narrowness of vision with which the existentialists profoundly disagree.

2. *Mitwelt* is literally the "with-world," the world of being-with-others, one's fellowmen. *Mitwelt* is not to be confused with the concept of group behavior, for *Mitwelt* includes the *meaning* I make out of my relationship with others, and the *meaning* that these others design into the relationships. The essence of *Mitwelt* interrelationship is that *"in the encounter both persons are changed"* (May, 1958, p. 63). Laing, although he does not employ

the term, has focused much of his theorizing on the *Mitwelt,* and he probably would not have much difficulty in accepting this terminology.

3. *Eigenwelt,* or "own world," is the mode of relationship to one's self. "It is a grasping of what something in the world—this bouquet of flowers ... means to *me*" (May, 1958, p. 63). Thus the concept of *Eigenwelt* is not restricted to the inner, subjective world, but includes one's subjective reactions to the world at large. Again, since Laing has emphasized what he calls the individual's *metaperspective,* as we shall see, he would have no difficulty in accepting the terminology of *Eigenwelt.*

The three modes of world, *Umwelt, Mitwelt,* and *Eigenwelt,* are lived in simultaneously. One's reality of being-in-the-world is lost or damaged if one of the modes is emphasized to the detriment of the other two. To understand an individual's being-in-the-world is a task of enormous complexity, requiring literally that the observer crawl inside the observed's three modes of world and that he live them as the observed lives them. In brief, this is the meaning of the phenomenological method that the existentialists have adopted.

Phenomenology as practiced by the existentialists is almost atheoretical. In order to see the world as another sees it, one must abandon most of one's theoretical preconceptions to let experience speak for itself (see Macleod, 1964). Thus, the assumption of phenomenology is that *the more categories of analysis the psychologist employs,* like drives, instincts, libido, *"the more you are talking about abstractions and not the existing, living human being"* (May, 1961, p. 18). The phenomenological strategy means that the psychologist accepts the individual's experiences on that individual's terms, unaltered by strategies of analyses, unshaped by theoretical predictions, and unhampered by technical verbalizations. The raw data of existence, the unprocessed, unvarnished *experiences,* are the existential phenomenologist's field of study.

R. D. Laing follows closely in this tradition, as evidenced in his criticism of Kraeplin. For what Laing proposes to do is nothing less than to accept the phenomenological world of the patient as real, as valid, and as essential to an understanding of what that patient is striving to do in those of his behaviors that outsiders construe as diseased. However, Laing does not follow the existentialists' preference for leaving the machinery of theory behind. He prefers a form of abstraction that closely follows the contours of experience, but a form of abstraction that is nonetheless theoretical.

Ontological Insecurity: The Loss of Self

For Laing, the central problem in the development of human personality is what the existentialists call *ontological insecurity,* or the feeling that one is threatened by nonbeing. In his first major work, *The Divided Self* (1959),

Laing remained very much within the mainstream of existential phenomenology, and he described three modes of ontological insecurity.

Engulfment: Loss of Identity

Some persons' sense of self is so tenuous that any relationship *(Mitwelt)*
with another threatens to overwhelm them (i.e., to cancel the *Eigenwelt*).
Any such interaction fosters the feeling that even minimal contact with
another is a struggle to preserve their own existence, to maintain their own
identity (Laing, 1959, p. 44).

The most typical strategy employed by persons fearing engulfment is
to isolate themselves totally, to provide themselves with a cloak of total
"aloneness." Laing has dramatically illustrated the phenomenological
sense of engulfment in one of the intricate poems of *Knots* (1970, pp.
14–16), a collection of patterns of "human bondage" written in the metalanguage of experience. What follows is an abbreviated excerpt of one of
these knots, the knot of engulfment:

> Once upon a time, when Jack was little,
> he wanted to be with his mummy all the time
> and was frightened she would go away
>
> later, when he was a little bigger
> he wanted to be away from his mummy
> and was frightened that
> she wanted him to be with her all the time
>
> when he grew up he fell in love with Jill
> and wanted to be with her all the time
> and was frightened she would go away
>
> when he was a little older,
> he did not want to be with Jill all the time
> he was frightened
> that she wanted to be with him all the time . . .
>
> Jack feels Jill is devouring him.
> He is devoured
>   by his devouring fear of
>   being devoured by
>   her devouring desire
>   for *him* to devour *her*, ...

It can easily be seen that Laing has managed to capture the flavor of
subjectively experienced emotional and cognitive states from the perspective of the perceiver's confusion. Laing is here suggesting that early experience of emotional knotting in relation to the other is a pattern of bondage
that will haunt one throughout life.

Implosion: The Vacuum of an Empty Self

When the individual senses that at any moment the external world will rush in and "obliterate all identity as a gas will rush in and obliterate a vacuum," he experiences what Laing (1959, p. 45) calls *implosion*. In effect, the ontologically insecure individual experiencing this dread assumes that like the vacuum, he is empty. He may long for the emptiness to be filled, but he dreads that eventuality, for his emptiness, he suspects, is all that he can be.

Phenomenologically, the experience of implosion has this flavor (Laing, 1970, p. 83):

> One is inside
> then outside what one has been inside
> One feels empty
> because there is nothing inside oneself
> that inside of the outside
> > that one was once inside
> > once one tries to get oneself inside what
> > one is outside:
> > to eat and to be eaten
> > to have the outside inside and to be
> > inside the outside. . . .

Petrification and Depersonalization:
The Doubt of Being Alive

Petrification is a form of terror that one will be turned into stone, made into a robot or machine without feelings, without subjectivity, without awareness. The feeling of petrification can be described by an outside observer as depersonalization. Petrification is accomplished in the act of treating another as not human, as an object, not as a being (1959, pp. 46–48). From the petrified person's viewpoint this fear that others may manipulate the self through indifference is described this way (Laing, 1970, p. 24):

> . . . You are frightened of being boring, you
> try to be interesting by not being interested,
> but are interested only in not being boring.
>
> You are not interested in me.
> You are only interested that I be interested in you.
>
> You pretend to be bored
> because I am not interested
> > that you are frightened
> > > that I am not frightened
> that you are not interested in me.

Depersonalization of the subject, however, may also be a product of his attempts to dehumanize another, for the act of greeting the other as an object reduces the actor to object (1959, p. 57).

On Driving One Mad: Embodied and Unembodied Selves

Use your imagination to construct images of the following acts (after Laing, 1969a, p. 92):

1. Swallow the saliva in your mouth.
2. Take a glass of water; sip and swallow it.
3. Spit in the glass; swallow the saliva-water mixture.
4. Sip some water; spit it back up into a glass; sip and swallow what you have spat back.

While the above demonstration is not Laing's creation, he used it effectively to illustrate the distinction most people phenomenologically make between "inside" and "outside." Most individuals are unable to perform all four acts, and are disgusted particularly by numbers 3 and 4. "One is aware that there is a difference between saliva inside one's mouth, and that same saliva, one inch in space outside one's mouth. . . . *We* feel ourselves to be inside a bag of skin: what is outside this bag is not-us. Me—inside. Not-Me outside" (Laing, 1969a, p. 92).

Gordon Allport, a personologist, used roughly the same example in describing the self as a compartmentalized entity: "What I perceive as belonging intimately to my body is warm and welcome; what I perceive as separate from my body becomes, in the twinkling of an eye, cold and foreign" (1955, p. 43).

If you remain unconvinced that what is intimately a part of you may nonetheless become revolting and alien, try Allport's suggestion to imagine having pricked your finger with a needle. Few of us would hesitate to raise that finger to our lips to gently suck the wounded tip. But now imagine a bandage over that finger soaked in your blood. Further imagine sucking the blood from the bandage, the same blood that came from your pin-pricked finger: *your own blood.* This "bandage-blood" is no longer mine; it is something hideously alien.

The shortest route to madness is traveled by those persons who lose their abiding conviction that they are one within their bodies. An uncanny feeling of disembodiment, of being external and alien to self, a material object apart from a subjective mind, floods the waking consciousness of many schizophrenics. For the "mad," the distinction between "inner" and "outer" is heightened to the point that the individual feels himself to be two selves: a *true,* authentic *self* that is the core of his very being, and a *false self* that is the empty shell of the detached material body (Laing, 1959, p. 69).

The divorce of true self from body-shell produces a peculiar split in consciousness by which the schizophrenic experiences himself both as perceiver and as perceived, both as observer and as observed, as *me* and as *other*. Sometimes, such states of dissociation occur in "normal" people under great stress. For example, prisoners in concentration camps tried to disembody their feelings and perceptions as a technique of survival. The goal was to produce the protective feeling expressed in such phrases as "this is a dream," "this is not happening to me," "this seems unreal" (Laing, 1959, p. 79).

The strategy of the individual who compartmentalizes many aspects of self is to escape or to transcend the real external world by relegating all interaction with it to one compartment—to the false self. In this way, safety is sought, but emptiness is achieved. The inner compartment, true self, becomes like a vacuum, empty and devoid of experience, activity, and need. "The detachment of self means that the self is never revealed directly in the individual's expressions and actions, nor does it experience anything spontaneously or immediately. The self's relationship to the other is always at one remove" (Laing, 1959, p. 80).

Characteristics of the False Self: The Mask

Because the individual relegates all intercourse between himself and others, or between himself and the world, to a system "within his being which is not 'him,' then the world is experienced as unreal, all that belongs to this system is felt to be false, futile and meaningless" (Laing, 1959, p. 80). Thus, much as Jung (cf. Chapter 4 of this book) had spoken of individuals who too closely identified with their persona, Laing interprets disordered behavior as a product of the individual's striving to produce a false front. The false self is a façade through which others cannot penetrate to his security.

The most important immediate result of the establishment of a false self is that the "individual's acts are no longer self-expressions" (1959, p. 94). Laing is another of many theorists who employ the imagery of the actor and his mask. He is at pains to point out that the false self, or mask, is fairly typical in situations other than madness. " 'A man without a mask' is very rare" (1959, p. 95; see also 1969b, p. 31). To some extent, all of us wear masks, but there is a key difference. In the normal individual, the mask or false front presented to others is not the medium of that individual's gratification of true-self desires. For the normal individual, the mask is a convenient social necessity. For the schizophrenic, the mask is the very vehicle of survival—a necessity without convenience.

Indeed, the false-self system is at once the most dangerous and the most treasured component of the schizophrenic's life. It is cherished and nurtured as a buffer between others and the real self; but the false-self mask is nevertheless fearsome in its power to assimilate the whole of being.

In a very real sense, the false self is a product of the individual's struggle to comply with *his* world, with the significant people who mold his life, with the members of his immediate family on whom his life security is dependent. When interaction with these significant others is not bearable, or the demands of intimate living become intolerable, the false self is formed to comply with and to pacify these others. All the while, the mask protects the true inner self from likewise having to comply with unpleasant reality.

Thus, the inner self stagnates. It pursues a course of development divorced from what transpires in the world. In its role of mediator with the external world, the false self may so effectively mimic normality that the distortions of experience transpiring in the protectively isolated genuine self go undetected for some time. Impersonating the characteristics of those others from whom withdrawal is attempted, the false self caricatures the personalities and traits of the very individuals most hated and feared by the true self.

The false self presents to the world what the world's troublesome people expect. To the extent that the false self adopts the behaviors modeled by significant others for the purpose of pacifying them and preventing these people from penetrating to the true self, it is playing a role. More precisely, *the false self is role-playing normality.* Laing called this kind of role playing *impersonation* (1959, p. 100). Impersonation is a minimizing technique. By superficial adoption of the other's behaviors, the false self prevents total loss of identity that would come with global commitment to the trappings of normality.

The Split Between Behavior and Experience

All of Laing's early theorizing can be brought into focus around two central propositions, much as the spokes of a wheel are arranged around its hub. The first proposition is that *for the individual who succumbs to ontological insecurity, there is a massive discrepancy between his behavior and his experience.* For such individuals, who incidentally are likely to get themselves diagnosed "schizophrenic," an unbridgeable gulf exists between what they phenomenologically experience, and what they publicly do. Yet their behavior is intelligible once *their* experience is understood. Because only his "mask" behaviors receive validation from others, the gap between the actor and mask eventuates in the actor's annihilation.

Second, the discrepancy between inner self and outer public behavior is a product of social interaction that is duplicitous and unintentionally designed by others to drive one "mad." The focus of Laing's investigations of such pathogenic social interaction began with the study of two-person combinations called "dyads." He then expanded his view to the study of families, for it is within the family that the first and most important forms of public and private, "inner" and "outer," communications are experienced.

On Being Unwanted: The Personal Sources of Laing's Ideas

Laing's model of personality and personality disturbance stresses interpersonal communications, expectations, and frustrations as the crucial factors shaping human existence. Personality theorists of widely different theoretical perspectives have argued that a child's view of self and of significant others is sculpted, wittingly or unwittingly, to the design modeled by his family. When the family pattern, by intention or accident, is disturbed, the child struggles to cope with the mismatch between what he has learned of life and its people within the irrational family cloister and what he glimpses of life's meaning beyond it.

Laing's sensitivity to the irrationality of some family interactions seems to have grown from his experiences with his own. Born on October 7, 1927, Laing spent his boyhood in Glasgow, Scotland, amid a particularly raucous set of relatives. In a semiautobiographical essay (1976a), he has described some of the events of his boyhood in the same matter-of-fact (yet poetic) style he has used in describing the phenomenal world of others. In deliberately ambiguous and disjointed prose, he has implied that the central theme of his childhood in Glasgow was his discovery that he was unwanted by his parents:

> My parents and I lived in a three-room flat.
> My mother and I slept in one room in separate beds, and my father slept in another room.
> According to both of them, all sexual activity had ceased between them irrevocably before I was conceived.
> My mother and father still swear they do not know how I was conceived.
> But there is a birthmark on his right knee and one on mine.
> A fact against immaculate conception. [1976a, p. 8]

Laing further reports that his father could not "admit" his son's birth for several days after the event. His mother immediately entered a "decline," and a nurse was engaged to care for the newborn Laing. Unfortunately, this woman "turned out to be a drunken slut." A second nurse likewise proved to be a drunken slut, so Laing's mother resumed caring for the infant.

Laing's father's reluctance to reveal to others the birth of his child seems to have originated in a long-term family "rule" or taboo concerning sexual intercourse. As Laing remembers, "My father was the only one in his family to marry and, with one possible exception, the only one ever to commit sexual intercourse" (1976a, p. 3). So fraught with negative emotion was the topic of sexual relations that Laing had only the vaguest idea of "the facts of life" well into his midteens.

At the age of ten months, Laing's maternal grandmother and a maternal aunt arrived to live with Laing's family for eight months. In a nearby house, the paternal side of the family set up their housekeeping arrangements. The maternal and paternal branches of the family thus brought into such close proximity did not get along well together. Laing became rapidly aware of the impossibility of coping with so many conflicting adult viewpoints:

> From as far back as I can remember, I tried to figure out what was going on between these people. If I believed one, I couldn't believe anyone else. Especially at the time when my mother, my mother's mother, and my mother's younger sister were all part of the same household—from ten months to eighteen months—I could not believe all of them, one of them, or none of them. [1976a, p. 4]

As we shall later see, in establishing the phenomenological portion of his theory, Laing was to make much of the effects on family members of their own conflicting viewpoints.

The pervading sense of adult irrationality to which Laing was exposed and to which he refused to completely submit is revealed in several of Laing's family anecdotes. For example, his father was convinced that his own father had "systematically murdered" Laing's grandmother over the years. On one occasion, when "old Pa," as Laing's paternal grandfather was called, visited the Laing household, a fight erupted between Old Pa and Laing's father. Old Pa had told Laing's mother to shut off the radio, whereupon Laing's father told her not to touch the radio. The verbal dispute escalated to a physical struggle in which Old Pa and Laing's Pa fought a battle throughout the house. The outcome of this bizarre struggle was a clear but bloody victory for Laing's father. Dragging Old Pa into the bath, Laing's father submerged him in cold water and then "heaved him out [of the bath] drenched with blood and water, dragged him to the door, kicked him out, and threw his cap after him. Then he stood at the window and waited to see how [Old Pa] would manage to stagger or crawl away. 'He held himself up very well,' Dad said. 'You've got to hand it to him'" (Laing, 1976a, pp. 4–5).

Physical battles around the Laing household were not confined to those between Laing's father and grandfather. Old Pa's younger brother, "Uncle Jack," reputed to have gone "daft" with heat stroke in China during World War I, allied himself with Old Pa. For some years after the critical battle between Old Pa and Laing's Pa, Uncle Jack would occasionally come to the Laing household seeking to avenge his brother's defeat. Each of these reenactments was carefully orchestrated, and each time the outcome would be the same. First, Laing's mother would push all the furniture aside, then diplomatically leave the room. Hiding behind the curtains, the young Laing would watch his father and uncle go at each other, until Jack was down and called it quits. Before leaving, Uncle Jack would pause for a cup of tea provided by Laing's mother (because she felt sorry for him), and he would press a coin or two into Laing's hand. The entire sequence was enacted with chilling deliberateness, or so it must have seemed to young Laing.

Laing's perception of the irrational and unspoken rules that governed his family life was sharpened in adolescence. At the age of sixteen, Laing's father deemed it time to instruct his son in that most taboo of all topics, the facts of life. Hitherto the mere mention of sex was cause for grave anxiety. To escape the parental lecture, Laing lied: "Dad, it's all right. I've learned about them at school. . . . (This was the first lie I had told for, as far as I can remember, over eight years. I was terrified he would try to tell me. I didn't know what they [the facts of life] were, but I did not want to hear them from him. And by now I was so sorry for him I wanted to spare him the ordeal" (1976a, p. 10).

Laing eventually established for himself what the facts of life were by covertly consulting, among other sources, the *Encyclopaedia Britannica* in the library and the local bookstore's selection of volumes on venereal disease. But more important, Laing had learned the potential power of others to shape one's experience and one's self-experience:

> For as early as I remember I never took my self to *be* what people called me. That at least has remained crystal clear to me. Whatever, whoever I may be is not to be confused with the names people give *to* me, or how they *describe* me, or what they *call* me. I am not my name.
>
> Who or what I am, as far as they are concerned, is not necessarily, or thereby, *me,* as far as I am concerned.
>
> I am presumably *what* they are describing, but not their description. I am the territory, what they say I am is their map of me. And what I call myself to myself is, presumably, my map of me. What, o where, is the territory? [Laing, 1976a, p. 24]

The Medical School Years

It is not difficult to detect a note of rebelliousness in Laing's self-description, an unwillingness to be contained by the perceptions and expectations of others. It is small wonder, then, that this characteristic unwillingness to be another's object extended to his years at medical school in Glasgow. Laing found medical practice to be lacking in human warmth, in human concern for those to be treated. During his internship, Laing attended a childbirth that had extended through sixteen hours:

> Finally it started to come—grey, slimy, cold—out it came—a large human frog—an encephalic monster, no neck, no head, with eyes, nose, froggy mouth, long arms. . . . Maybe it was slightly alive. We didn't want to know. We wrapped it in newspaper—and with this bundle under my arm to take back to the pathology lab, that seemed

to cry out for all the answerable answers that I ever asked, I walked along O'Connell Street two hours later.

I needed a drink. I went into a pub, put the bundle on the bar. Suddenly, the desire to unwrap it, hold it up for all to see, a ghastly Gorgon's head, to turn the world to stone. [Laing, 1967, pp. 178–179]

In the cool professionalism that pervaded his medical training Laing had found no precedent for what he felt at this childbirth. We can surmise that the physicians and nurses attending this birth had shown no shock, horror, or sadness. And we can further speculate that Laing somehow wanted to express his own shock and sadness by shocking others.

When Laing began to specialize in psychiatry, as we shall see in more detail later, he observed what he felt were something less than humane methods of dealing with the troubled. In his fourth year in medical training, he witnessed an interview between a psychiatric consultant and a seventeen-year-old boy whose chief observable difficulty was an extensive case of acne. At one point in the interview, the patient stated that he was afraid that people were looking at him in the street. To this item of information, the psychiatrist replied to the effect that he, the boy, was really afraid that other people knew he masturbated. From there, the psychiatrist proceeded to interrogate the boy as to the details of his masturbation. Laing recalled the effect of that demonstration on his developing view of psychiatry:

I had never heard the word "masturbate" used "in public" before. I cringed in terror at the prospect of the [psychiatric] consultant asking us the questions he asked this patient, but he did not. [1976a, p. 90]

Although Laing later trained in psychoanalytic technique and theory, he never forgot the lessons of his boyhood and years as a medical student. If one were to treat disordered persons, one must not forget in the welter of psychological theory and speculation that it is a *person* to whom the label "disordered" is attached. The ideas and tools of Freudian psychoanalytic theory were profoundly useful to Laing, but they were also constraining and insufficient to the task of accounting for the facts of life as the person himself lives them.

Intrauterine Life as a Reflection of Things to Come

Laing has recently carried the theme of the effects of being unwanted by one's parents a giant step backward, to the time when the fetus is carried in the mother's womb. Could it be, he asks, that prebirth existence in the womb and the processes of birth set up causes whose effects will be felt

only later, only in analogous ways, only in ways that are somehow "resonances" of life before birth?

> ... it seems plausible to me that the intrauterine experience, from
> conception to birth and afterbirth experiences are mapped into our
> system in some way or another, and stored to express themselves
> later, especially surfacing after physical growth ends, and postpuber-
> tal life begins. One discovers as one gets older that the present situa-
> tion, whatever it happens to be, doesn't entirely seem to account for
> one's present behavior. [Laing, 1976b, p. 5]

To take one, perhaps trivial, example of a "resonance," Laing reports that
at 5:15 P.M. each day for several years he was taken with the desire for a
drink (vodka, whiskey, or the like). The time of his birth was 5:15 P.M.
Often, he says, he knows when it is 5:15 P.M. by the feelings that well up
within him, a desire for the calming effects of alcohol being only one of
these subjective indicators.

Thus the act of birth itself may be an unnecessarily brutal experience
that sets up life-long resonances to be experienced and reexperienced in
diverse ways. Following this line of logic, Laing suggests that it might be
possible for the feeling of being unwanted to also be communicated to the
fetus—perhaps even from conception. Carried to its most extreme form,
Laing argues, it may be that some schizophrenic patients need literally and
metaphorically to be reconceived, to be reborn—this time to confront
volitionally the prospect of a hostile, rejecting world, prepared anew to
master the cues that signal unwantedness (1976a, p. 72). Laing has, in fact,
adopted the procedure of "birthing" some of his patients, modeling his
technique on that of the late Elizabeth Fehr, a New York therapist he
admired.

Extending this line of reasoning in another direction, Laing asks
whether it is possible that the physical environment surrounding the un-
born fetus might become the prototype or analog for later interpretations
of life. To take one example, the placenta is the most critical tissue connection between fetus and mother, for it permits the exchange of nourishment
and oxygen from mother to child, and the elimination of wastes from
child's to mother's bloodstream:

> Could the placenta
> be the original
> life giver
> life sucker
> our first friend or our first persecutor
> tormentor?
>
> [Laing, 1976a, p. 61]

Laing credits Francis J. Mott, a relatively neglected writer on this subject,
with having proposed this analogy. Laing extends the analogy in specific

psychological ways. Thus, physically, chemically, the placenta is the membrane that serves as the two-way (in and out) physiological door through which the fetus receives nourishment and expends its wastes:

$$(in)fetus \xrightleftharpoons[\text{food}]{\text{feces}} placenta\ (out)$$

Psychological analogs of these primary "in-out" functions may be indicated by the following metaphors (modified from Laing, 1976a, p. 63):

$$life \longrightarrow death$$
$$death \longleftarrow life$$
$$loss \longrightarrow$$
$$\longleftarrow renewal$$
$$giving \longrightarrow$$
$$\longleftarrow receiving$$
$$going \longrightarrow$$
$$\longleftarrow coming$$
$$exports \longrightarrow$$
$$\longleftarrow imports$$
$$money \longrightarrow$$
$$\longleftarrow energy$$

Laing is here hypothesizing that our earliest interactions on the purely physiological level are impressed psychologically upon "our organism" (awareness?) before we are born. Afterbirth life may thus be a complex set of resonances of these, our first patterns of transaction with another.

Whatever may be Laing's intention regarding the possibility of incorporating such resonances into his procedures for treating disturbed personalities, it is clear that Laing is only at the beginning of his efforts to explicate the interactions between persons, and between persons and the lasting effects of their environments.

A Science of Persons: Social Phenomenology

"I cannot experience your experience. You cannot experience my experience. We are both invisible men. All men are invisible to one another. Experience is man's invisibility to man" (Laing, 1967, p. 54).

With these words, Laing sought to erect a science of persons' experience that would bridge the gulf between the superficial study of the mask and the phenomenological penetration to the actor's perspective.

For the individual constructing a false self to appease the world of others, there is an irredeemable split between his inner experience and his outer behavior. Experience is a very private matter, invisible to all, even to the experiencing agent. But it is *experience* that Laing sees as the central datum for his science of persons:

> We can see other people's behavior, but not their experience. . . . The other person's behavior is an experience of mine. My behavior is an experience of the other. The task of social phenomenology is *to relate my experience of the other's behavior to the other's experience of my behavior.* Its study is the relation between experience and experience: its true field is *interexperience.* [1967, p. 17; first italics added]

It is now clear why Laing would find the psychiatrist's comment about the "oral-acquisitive" nature of schizophrenia obscene. The comment is not merely an error; it betrays a monumental presumption that the observed person's experience of the act, *his* interpretation of what *he* does, is irrelevant.

For Laing, as for the existentialists, the normal condition of modern man is estrangement from himself, from his experience of self and from others' experience of his self:

> As a whole, we are a generation of men so estranged from the inner world [of experience] that many are arguing that it does not exist; and that even if it does exist, it does not matter. [1967, p. 54]

To some degree, we are all self-divided: "Man cut off from his own mind, cut off equally from his own body—a half crazed creature in a mad world" (1967, p. 55). But, "The 'normally' alienated person, by reason of the fact that he acts more or less like everyone else, is taken to be sane" (1967, p. 27). Therefore:

> Long before a thermonuclear war can come about, we have had to lay waste our own sanity. We begin with the children. It is imperative to catch them in time. Without the most thorough and rapid brainwashing their dirty minds would see through our dirty tricks. . . . By the time the new human being is fifteen or so, we are left with a being like ourselves, a half-crazed creature more or less adjusted to a mad world. This is normality in our present age. [Laing, 1967, p. 58]

Laing's proposal for a science of persons, a discipline to study the interaction and interexperience of humans adjusting to a mad world, might be regarded as pessimistic, indeed as cynical, if Laing's assumptions are valid. Specifically, Laing finds it offensive that from birth we are taught *what* to experience, instructed to *act* on what we experience at the behest of others, indoctrinated in what *not* to experience in compliance with their demands. Eventually, we act, reflect upon our actions, act on our reflections, or even "act out" our reflections because we have been molded by the most violent force available to man: love by and for significant others (Laing, 1967, p. 59). For it is with love that parents socialize their children into the culture by which they themselves are shaped. It is in the name of love that schools socialize students into the intellectual and practical skills that normalize their lives in the culture. It is for spiritual love that religions coerce the faithful into forfeiting experience for transcendent ethics. And it is for love that one marries and produces novices to initiate into this tradition of split experience. Sadly, these recruits are programmed to perpetuate the cycle of violence.

In Laing's view, then, a science of persons is the study of *political* violence in the original meaning of the word "politic" as relating to a citizen of a particular culture:

1. wise, prudent, sagacious in devising and pursuing measures; shrewd, expedient; . . .
2. prudently or artfully contrived; . . .
3. crafty, unscrupulous, cunning . . .

(Webster's Unabridged Dictionary, 2d ed.)

Laing wrote two books in which the titles juxtaposed the word "politics" with more traditional psychological subject matter: *The Politics of Experience* (1967) and *The Politics of the Family* (1969a). The central theme of both books is that "madness" is a prudent, sagacious, and cunning measure artfully contrived to make an insane situation livable.

Study of Dyads: Two-Person Perspectives on Experience

The split between inner experience and outer behavior is a problem for the schizophrenic only because he has failed to master the division and is torn apart. This self-division is the core of Laing's view of disordered personality. The task at hand is to understand how the split originates.

When two individuals interact, communicate, interpersonally behave, they each bring to the situation a set of expectations, cognitions, and desires. Sometimes their two perspectives uniformly mesh; sometimes they clash. It is the clash that is most instructive.

To illustrate: Peter is upset about something. Paul hopes to help him by himself remaining calm. Peter, however, feels that Paul is not genuinely friendly because a true friend would share his upset. Paul is unaware of Peter's expectation, and he does not communicate the friendly solicitude that underlies his exterior calm. And he remains unaware of his failure to communicate his concern. Consider the following resulting *spiral of reciprocal perspectives,* ignoring for the moment the bracketed notations:

PETER	PAUL
1. I am upset. [Pt → Pl]	1. Peter is upset. [Pl → Pt]
2. Paul is acting very calm and dispassionate. [Pt → Pl]	2. I'll try to help him by remaining calm and just listening. [Pl → (Pl Pt)]
3. If Paul cared about me and wanted to help, he would get involved and show some emotion also. [Pt → Pl → (Pl Pt)]	3. He is getting even more upset. [Pl → Pt] I must be even more calm. [Pl → (Pl Pl)]
4. Paul knows that this upsets me. [Pt → (Pl Pt)]	4. He is accusing me of hurting him. [Pl → Pt → (Pl Pt)]
5. If Paul knows that his behavior upsets me, he must be intending to hurt me. [Pt → Pl → (Pl Pt)]	5. I'm really trying to help. [Pl → (Pl Pt)]
6. He must be cruel, sadistic. Maybe he gets pleasure out of it. [Pt → (Pl Pt)]	6. He must be projecting. [Pl → Pt → Pl → Pt]

Modified from Laing, Phillipson, & Lee, 1966, pp. 21–22.

A basic sense of mistrust is responsible for Peter's and Paul's mismatched experiences of their relationship. Laing, Phillipson, and Lee (1966, p. 23) call the result a spiral of reciprocal perspectives. Each of the involved individuals is capable of assuming at least three different levels of interpretation or *metaperspectives* of their mutual experiences.

First of these perspectives are the various *direct views* by each person of himself and of the other. *Direct perspectives* come in four varieties.

The Direct Perspectives

The following four direct perspectives and the notations employed by Laing and his coworkers are simply a list of the logical possibilities inherent in the dyadic situation:

1. Peter⟶Peter: "Peter's view of himself."
2. Peter⟶Paul: "Peter's view of Paul."
3. Paul ⟶Peter: "Paul's view of Peter."
4. Paul ⟶Paul: "Paul's view of Paul."

The notation system thus far is relatively uncomplicated; the arrows simply denote the subject's view of the other or of himself. Laing and his colleagues, however, emphasize that each participant in the dyad may have a direct perception not only of himself and the other, but of his own perception of the other's perception of himself, and of the other's perception of his perception of the other, and so on. In essence, the important perspectives of the dyad are the individual's views of these *relationships* between one's self with one's self, between one's self and the other, and between the other's self and himself, etc.

At first these multiple perspectives seem mind boggling and arouse the suspicion that Laing, Phillipson, and Lee are parodying schizophrenic discourse. The algebraic notation system created by Laing and his team, which further abstracts these person-perspectives into a more or less workable form, does not do much to dispel the suspicion of a possible "put-on." If there is some element of whimsy in Laing's system it is present with a purpose, for in using the notation system one is rapidly put into the position of struggling desperately to comprehend the meaning of communications from multiple viewpoints. This struggle perhaps is the point.

To express the direct perspective of each individual's relationship to himself and to the other, Laing, Phillipson, and Lee (1966, p. 53) adopt the following shorthand:

1. Peter's relationship with himself   (PtPt)
2. Peter's relationship with Paul   (PtPl)
3. Paul's relationship with himself   (PlPl)
4. Paul's relationship with Peter   (PlPt)

By "relationship," Laing and his team mean to symbolize the phenomenologically experienced feelings, as in "Peter *likes* or *dislikes* himself" (PtPt), or "Peter *likes* or *dislikes* Paul" (PtPl), and so on. The relationship may take any form; the notation simply records the existence of the relationship. There is a further complication, however, in the fact that each of these individuals' unique *perception of the relationship* must also be specified:

PETER⟶
1. Pt⟶(PtPt): "Peter's perspective of Peter's relationship with Self"
2. Pt⟶(PtPl): "Peter's perspective of Peter's relationship with Paul"
3. Pt⟶(PlPl): "Peter's perspective of Paul's relationship with himself"
4. Pt⟶(PlPt): "Peter's perspective of Paul's relationship with Peter"

Likewise, Paul may experience his own direct perspective of the four relationships. Paul's direct perspectives can simply be added to the notation for Peter's. They are read backwards, from right to left:

PETER⟶ ⟵PAUL
1. Pt⟶(PtPt)⟵Pl: (Paul's perspective of Peter's relationship with Peter)
2. Pt⟶(PtPl)⟵Pl: (Paul's perspective of Paul's relationship with Peter)
3. Pt⟶(PlPl)⟵Pl: (Paul's perspective of Paul's relationship with himself)
4. Pt⟶(PlPt)⟵Pl: (Paul's perspective of Peter's relationship with Paul)

Metaperspectives

To completely capture the process of spiraling perspectives in dyadic relationships, it is necessary to describe the possible *metaperspectives* that may accrue to the direct perspectives of Peter and Paul. In phenomenological language we have not only: "My view of myself," but also "my view of the other's view of me," and, "how I think you see *me*" (Laing et al., 1966, p. 5). This form of internalizing the other's view of self, a kind of second-level perspective, is called a metaperspective.

Whereas "How I see me" defines my ego identity, "How I think *you* see me" defines my *metaidentity*. Self-identity (my view of myself) and metaidentity (my view of your view of me) may interact so that my views of others' views of myself begin to define a new self-identity (Laing et al., 1966, p. 6). Laing's conception of identity and metaidentity is very similar to what Harry Stack Sullivan meant by the Self being a product of "reflected appraisals" (e.g., 1953a, p. 22; see also the opening quotation for this chapter).

It is consequently theoretically possible to have not only a first-order metaperspective of a person-to-person relationship, but second and third orders of metaperspective as well: *meta-meta,* and *meta-meta-metaperspectives.* In fact, the layering of perspectives upon perspectives can continue indefinitely—in theory. However, mere practicality limits the layers that can be piled to a number that is within the reasonable grasp of the observer. Perspectives numbering much beyond the meta-metaperspective level would be so removed from the phenomenological description of the event that they would be useless. Laing, Phillipson, and Lee do not exceed the meta-metaperspective in their presentation.

In the relationship that we have been considering, Peter's perception of Paul is the result of the objective-Paul who exists *and* of the *Paul-for-Peter* that Peter constructs from his expectations, fantasy, and imagination. To extend the Peter/Paul example, assume that the issue of immediate significance is Peter's upset over Paul's seeming indifference. The following layered metaperspectives are possible:

(1) Peter's view of Peter's upset [direct]
(2) Peter's view of Paul's view of Peter's upset [meta]
(3) Peter's view of Paul's view of Peter's view of his upset [meta-meta]

The complementary perspectives from Paul's point of view are, of course, possible. To gain facility with the notation system, the reader should try to compile Paul's three perspectives.

If we convert Peter's layered perspectives to Laing's notation system it looks, with some modifications for clarity, like this:

(1) Pt⟶(upset) [direct]
(2) Pt⟶ Pl⟶(upset) [meta]
(3) Pt⟶ Pl⟶ Pt⟶(upset) [meta-meta]

To grasp what these notations mean, number three can be translated into words: "Peter's view of Paul's view of Peter's view of his upset." It is important to recognize that the "upset" in parentheses is always *Peter's* in all three notations. Of course, as always, Paul's complementary views are equally possible. Both Peter's and Paul's differing metaperspectives may be combined and expressed in abbreviated form. If we let X stand for the issue of "Peter's upset," then:

PETER$\longrightarrow$ $\longleftarrow$PAUL
   (1) Pt$\longrightarrow$(X)$\longleftarrow$Pl [Direct]
   (2) Pt$\longrightarrow$Pl$\longrightarrow$(X)$\longleftarrow$Pt$\longleftarrow$Pl [Meta]
   (3) Pt$\longrightarrow$Pl$\longrightarrow$Pt$\longrightarrow$(X)$\longleftarrow$Pl$\longleftarrow$Pt$\longleftarrow$Pl [Meta-meta]

To grasp the meaning, consider how number three is translated into words from *left to right* for Peter: "Peter's view of Paul's view of Peter's view of Peter's upset." And, from *right to left,* the translation for Paul is: "Paul's view of Peter's view of Paul's view of Peter's upset."

At this point, armed with a knowledge of the workings of the notation system, return to the original Peter-Paul reciprocal spiral and translate for yourself the bracketed notations on page 292. A clear conception of the system in context should emerge.

Assessing Patterns of Person Perception: The IPM

Laing, Phillipson, and Lee have developed a self-report inventory called the *Interpersonal Perception Method* (IPM) (1966). The IPM may be employed by two individuals in a dyadic relationship to ascertain their direct, meta, and meta-metaperspectives on sixty important issues. These sixty issues may be grouped into six categories:

A) Interdependence and autonomy
B) Warm concern and support
C) Disparagement and disappointment
D) Contentions: fight/flight
E) Contradiction and confusion
F) Extreme denial and autonomy

[Laing et al., 1966]

Husbands and wives, for example, may answer the items of the IPM, a process that takes about seventy minutes, to compare their direct, meta, and meta-metaperspectives on such issues as "He/she loves me." Within each of the six classes of issue, complementary questions are provided in separate booklets for each partner. Each set of questions on a particular issue is given in three levels with four choices in each question. The respondent's own direct perspective on one of the sixty issues is called an *A-level* question; *B-level* questions on the same issue provide an assessment of the respondent's metaperspective on the issue: "How he/she thinks the *other* has answered the equivalent question"; and *C-level* questions measure the respondent's meta-metaperspective on that issue: "How he/she feels the other feels he/she has answered the question."

After careful sorting and classification of the responses, their mutual three-level perspectives may be evaluated in terms of their similarities and differences, or *conjunctions* and *disjunctions* of perspective, as Laing and his coworkers call them. To illustrate, here are three questions on one issue from the IPM at each of the three levels. Note the change in phrasing of the stem of the question from level A through level C. The questions are answered by indicating with appropriate plus and minus signs for each of the four choices whether it is *very true* (++); *slightly true* (+); *very untrue* (− −); or *slightly untrue* (−).

A-LEVEL: How true do *you* think the following are? [direct perspective]
1. She belittles me [H⟶(WH)]
2. I belittle her [H⟶(HW)]
3. She belittles herself [H⟶(WW)]
4. I belittle myself [H⟶(HH)]

In brackets beside each of the above A-level choices is the notation for the particular issue under scrutiny. In the real test booklet, of course, the notations are not included. Here is the B-level item on the same issue, measuring the husband's metaperspective, that is, how he thinks his wife has answered the questions in her booklet:

B-LEVEL: How would SHE answer the following? [metaperspective]
1. I belittle him. [H⟶W⟶(WH)]
2. He belittles me. [H⟶W⟶(HW)]
3. I belittle myself. [H⟶W⟶(WW)]
4. He belittles himself. [H⟶W⟶(HH)]

and

C-LEVEL: How would SHE think you have answered the following?
1. She belittles me. [H⟶W⟶H⟶(WH)]
2. I belittle her. [H⟶W⟶H⟶(HW)]
3. She belittles herself. [H⟶W⟶H⟶(WW)]
4. I belittle myself. [H⟶W⟶H⟶(HH)]

The C-level item has the phenomenological meaning: "How do you think she thinks you think." Thus, taken together, the total complex of items on the IPM provides an overall assessment of:

$$H \rightarrow W \rightarrow H \ (X_{60}) \leftarrow W \leftarrow H \leftarrow W$$

where X indicates one of the sixty issues. The important result of the IPM is not the mere matching of responses and detection of discrepancies or disjunctions. "What matters instead is whether or not the husband's *view* of how his wife treats him is concordant or discordant with how *she sees herself* to be in treating him, and how *she sees him* viewing her treatment of him" (Laing et al., 1966, p. 60; italics added).

IPM Profiles of Reciprocal Perspectives

Laing and his coworkers have also developed a technique to profile the relationship between the two points of view assessed by the IPM. In purely operational terms, several important patterns of reciprocity emerge. Laing's team emphasizes the following particular comparisons:

Agreement/Disagreement

A comparison between the two person's direct perspectives on the sixty issues provides a measure of their agreements or disagreements. In notation form, the comparison is:

$$H \rightarrow (X_{60}) \text{ compared to } (X_{60}) \leftarrow W$$

In more concrete terms, disagreement/agreement comparisons involve tabulations of the A-level responses for husband and wife. To take one item as an illustration, if the husband answered the A-level item: *She belittles me* with the response of "very true," and the wife answered her A-level item: *I belittle him* with the response of "very true" it is clear that they agree that she belittles him. The truth or falsity of the assertion is another matter. The point is that they agree.

Understanding/Misunderstanding

A comparison of the metaperspective of one dyad member with the direct perspective of the other provides an estimate of the pair's understanding of each other's viewpoint. In notation, the comparison is given by:

$$H \rightarrow W \rightarrow (X_{60}) \text{ compared to } (X_{60}) \leftarrow W$$

The complementary comparison of the wife's metaperspective with the husband's direct perspective is also made. If the comparison shows that the other person is *aware* of the first person's view by being able to predict that person's A-level answer, then understanding may be said to exist. For example, to the level B question: "How would SHE answer the following: *I belittle him*"—the husband replies "very true." But to the level-A, direct-perspective complementary question in the *wife's* booklet: *I belittle him,* she answers "very untrue." It is then clear that the *husband* misunderstands the wife's viewpoint because he cannot predict her answer to her question. It may be true that she does *not* belittle him, but the point is that the husband fails to understand her interpretation of the issue. Of course, once again, the reverse comparison of the wife's understanding of the husband's point of view is also made:

$$W \longrightarrow H \longrightarrow (X_{60}): (X_{60}) \longleftarrow H.$$

Realization of Being Understood/Misunderstood

Comparison of one person's metaperspective to the other's meta-metaperspective provides an estimate of whether the first person realizes that he is understood by the other. Simply being understood by the other is of no benefit unless the understood *knows* he is understood. In notational form, the comparison involves:

$$H \longrightarrow W \longrightarrow (X_{60}) \text{ compared to } (X_{60}) \longleftarrow W \longleftarrow H \longleftarrow W$$

To illustrate in more concrete terms, suppose that the husband's response to a level-B question: "How would SHE answer the following: *He belittles himself*" is "very true." The wife agrees in her answer to the complementary level-C item: "How would HE think you have answered the following: *He belittles himself?*" She responds "very true." In this case, the wife's reply indicates that she knows her husband understands her, for he can predict her reply, and *she realizes that he can.*

If the wife had responded "very untrue" to the level-C item, her reply would indicate that she fails to realize that her husband understands her point of view, for she is *unable* to assume *his point of view* of her viewpoint. In neither case do the replies indicate the truth or falsity of the response. Wives may belittle husbands and vice versa, but the significant issue is whether they realize that the other realizes how they feel. If this last fails to make sense to you, it is time to put the book down and take a rest. I know how you feel. And we both understand that I know that you realize I know you are confused.

Feeling of Being Understood/Misunderstood

Comparison between one person's meta-metaperspective and his own direct perspective provides an indication of whether he feels understood or misunderstood by the other. This category of comparison is on the order of an *emotional* estimate of the experience of understanding, rather than the cognitive state of *recognizing* the other's understanding. In phenomenological language, the feeling of being understood may be expressed: ". . . if what I feel about something is compared to what I think you think I feel, I see whether I feel that you understand me or not" (Laing et al., 1966, p. 61). In notational shorthand, the feeling of being understood/misunderstood involves:

$$H \longrightarrow (X_{60}) \text{ compared to } H \longrightarrow W \longrightarrow H \longrightarrow (X_{60})$$

To illustrate, assume that the husband responds to the level-C question: "How would SHE think you have answered the following: *I belittle her?*" with the response "very true." Further assume that the husband's own answer to the level-A question in the same sequence: "How true do you think the following are: *I belittle her?*"—with the response "very untrue." This comparison indicates that the husband does *not* feel that his wife understands how he feels, for *he* predicts her answer to be *different* from his own. Similarly, for the wife's feeling of being understood/misunderstood the reverse comparison is made: $W \longrightarrow (X_{60})$ compared to $W \longrightarrow H \longrightarrow W \longrightarrow (X_{60})$.

It is therefore possible for the individual to be correct or incorrect about his feelings of being understood. Thus, *I may feel:*

understood and I am understood (correct)
understood and I am not understood (incorrect)
misunderstood and I am misunderstood (correct)
misunderstood and I am not misunderstood (incorrect)

[After Laing et al., 1966, p. 62]

It thus follows that the IPM measures the dyad members' *views* of their relationship; the *IPM does not directly measure the relationship itself.* There are three basic measures of the dyad's views of their relationship:

1. Agreement (A) and Disagreement (D)
2. Understanding (U) and Misunderstanding (M)
3. Realization (R) and Failure of Realization (F)

The various combinations of A, D, U, M, R, and F make a considerable number of potential profiles.

Despite the complexity of their method, Laing and his colleagues have focused attention on the intricacy of human relationships. It is doubtful that, once having wended one's way through the maze of the notation system, one can ever again view a dyadic interaction as a straightforward relationship of one person to another. With Laing's abstractions in mind, any such relationship will seem crowded with at least four personages.

In some cases, the convoluted thinking required to score and interpret the results of the IPM questionnaire seems to be more burdensome than the relationship being observed. But certainly Laing and his coworkers' strategy has the desired effect of making explicit what Sullivan calls "reflected appraisals" of the self. Laing has forced psychologists to conceptualize the knotted, often discrepant, viewpoints, perceptions, and perceptions of perceptions that are involved in human encounters.

Disturbed Communication: The Double-Bind Hypothesis

Ponder the following communication to her son from a mother who is feeling hostile and simultaneously guilty over her hostility (Bateson et al., 1956, p. 214):

"Go to bed, you're very tired and I want you to get your sleep."

Overtly, this statement is an expression of parental concern and love; covertly, the statement is a knot of conflicting messages. It asserts, in the first place, that the outside observer, mother, can detect an internal feeling state in the observed, her son, before he himself is aware of it.

In the second place, *her* interpretation of that alleged state is the only one that is valid: "You're very tired." Her son's genuine state of feeling may directly contradict her assertive appraisal of his condition, but the *tone* of her statement, "Go to bed," precludes any possibility of protest or correction by the son. His feelings are automatically classified as irrelevant because his mother asserts her point of view: "*I* want. . . ." Only at the cost of the implied punishment of withdrawal of love can the boy correct her assertion.

In the third place, the statement is simultaneously a command and a denial that it is a command by the expedient of coupling to the order an implied loving concern: "I want you to get *your* sleep."

In the fourth and last place, the initial purpose of the communication is concealment. She must hide her hostility and guilt from the target of her message *and* from herself. But the mother's tone of voice, bodily gestures, and verbal timing will nonetheless convey all of these conflicting feelings to the son.

If the mother said, "Listen, I'm absolutely fed up with you. Go to bed and get out of my sight!"—the child could deal with the message without being torn in two directions at once. In this case, although the message is hardly pleasant, at least both parties to the communication agree on its content, the reason for its content, fair or unfair, and the emotional tone of the situation. The child can go to bed, recognizing that mother is angry, and that he in turn is angry, or he can thumb his nose at mother, give her half the peace sign, and suffer the consequences. But at least the reason for *his* feelings, *her* feelings, and *her* command are clear to both parties. The command may not be just or pleasant, but it is after all openly acknowledged to be a command. It is, therefore, understandable. In the case of the first communication, however, "the result is that the mother is withdrawing from him and defining this withdrawal as the way a *loving* relationship should be" (Bateson et al., 1956, p. 214).

Laing has acknowledged the influence of Bateson's group on his own conceptualization of the importance of disturbed communications within families of schizophrenics (Laing, 1969b, Chap. 9). Gregory Bateson and his colleagues named the general class of knotted communications like the one we have been considering *metacommunications,* using the Greek prefix in its meaning of "along with," or "after." Jurgen Ruesch (1961, p. 423) has provided a concise definition of metacommunication as all ". . . the events that go along with language—specifically, a device which the speaker uses to instruct the receiver and which the latter uses to interpret a statement." Following Ruesch, metalanguage may be conceptualized as "communications about communication," in the sense that gestures, verbal tone, phrasing, and timing may change the meaning of verbal content. Bateson's team has focused on one particular variety of metalanguage which they called the *double-bind* communication.

A double-bind communication is a message that conveys at least two meanings, and sometimes three, all of which conflict with the ostensible purpose of the message. The first meaning is a primary negative injunction: "Do not do so and so, or I will punish you." The punishment typically takes the form of withdrawal of love or a thinly disguised expression of hate and anger. The second meaning is another injunction, enforced by the same threats. This time, however, the receiver is enjoined to "not see this command as punishment; do not see me as punisher; do not question my love, or do not think of what you must not do" (Bateson et al., 1956, p. 207; cf. Bateson, 1972). The third meaning is yet another injunction, a tertiary injunction that implicitly prohibits the victim of the double bind from escaping the situation. This prohibition is enforced by the statement's implication that endurance of the conflict (primary and secondary injunctions) will evoke love or acceptance.

An overweight child at a birthday party is invited by the guest of honor to have some ice cream. The child's own mother stares coolly at her son, not wishing him to eat more goodies than necessary because his overweight reflects poorly on her, and she says: "*You don't want any more ice cream, do you?*" Again, this message is laden with auxiliary meanings and enforced interpretations. It sets up a full-fledged double-bind "can't win" situation. If the child says, "I *do* want more ice cream," he violates the primary and secondary injunctions and provokes the threatened withdrawal of love. If the child says, "O.K., I don't really want more ice cream," he thereby accepts his mother's definition of *his* feelings. *He* thus deprives himself in the presence of other conspicuously consumptive children whose obvious enjoyment serves as an additional cue that his self-imposed denial is without reasonable foundation. In short, he's damned if he does, and damned if he doesn't.

Bateson's group proposed that single instances of double-bind commu-

nications could not by themselves cause distorted personality development. Only a constant environment of double binds is sufficient to evoke
disorder. However, when the individual has been repeatedly exposed to
double-bind communications, his mode of perception becomes permanently altered to accept "can't win" situations as normal. The complete
ingredient package is no longer necessary; he has internalized this mode
of "madness" to the extent that double-bind communications are autonomously present in *his* response to others' messages even when such messages are simply ambiguous.

In the simplest case of disordered communication, taking the mother as
the only double-bind inflicter, Bateson has suggested that the crux of the
problem is her constant sending of messages that simultaneously convey
hostility and simulated love. When the child responds to the latent hostility by withdrawing, she ambiguously verbalizes *his* apparent lack of
love and provokes *his* guilt. Schizophrenia, in Bateson's view, is very much
a case of disturbed communication between the "victim" and significant
others.

In Laing's terms, the split between a person's behavior and his inner
experience is fostered by such disturbed communications. The resultant
spiral of reciprocal perspectives is the very heart of double-bind communication. To map the ice-cream situation into Laing's notation system of such
spirals is relatively easy. The mother wishes to replace the son's perspective of his liking or desire for ice cream with her own perspective of how
he should view ice cream:

$$\text{From: } \text{Son's} \longrightarrow (\text{S ice cream})$$
$$\text{To: } \text{M} \longrightarrow \text{S} \longrightarrow (\text{S ice cream})$$

She further hopes that the substitution of perspectives will not be discovered, or will be discovered only at great cost.

Family Rules and Metarules

For Laing, disturbed communication patterns are not only the cause of
disordered behavior, but also the result of prior communication disturbances. Thus, schizophrenia is evoked in the child by disturbed communication or metacommunication from the members of his family, and in turn,
he responds to their disturbances with tangled metacommunications of his
own design. His deranged utterances are more than mere response; they
are strategies of survival. He must master not only the metalanguage and
meta-metalanguages of the network of persons, he must also learn to obey
the covert rules on which the communications are based. For these hidden
rules dominate the family's existence.

Every family, disturbed or otherwise, develops a set of rules that govern
the behavior and the expectations of its members. The disturbed family,

however, also develops *metarules* which are injunctions "not to see the rules." There can likewise be meta-metarules that are comprised of injunctions not to see the prohibitions against seeing the rules, and so on.

To illustrate the flavor of family rules, consider the dichotomy "good" and "bad." Within the family, certain events and persons are overtly labeled "good" and some are labeled "bad." There are "good" relatives and there are "bad" relatives. In a family dominated by one parent, all the "bad" relatives are, of course, on the side of the other spouse. Each member of the family is "good" or "bad" to the degree "one has good thoughts about what one is supposed to think good about, and bad thoughts about what one is supposed to think bad about" (Laing, 1969a, p. 104). Or, one may be "bad" if one thinks bad about things one is supposed to think good. Double-bind communication establishes the boundaries for such evaluative thinking. Mother to six-year-old son: "What do you mean you don't want to go to Grandma's house? You know you like to visit Grandma!" Mapping this statement into Laing's notation system, we can see that the mother tries to replace the son's expressed viewpoint of his relationship with Grandma [S—→(SG)] with her own: [M—→S—→(SG)].

There may be further sets of family rules about what is to be put into words and "what words one may use to put something into" (Laing, 1969a, p. 111). One *must* say that a visit to the bathroom is to "wash my hands," when in fact one has to urinate. One may *not* say "I have to urinate in the bathroom." But one may say, "I have to take a leak" if one is imitating Uncle Harry's use of this phrase because Uncle Harry is a "good" relative who is always humorous.

As if rules and metarules were not complex enough, some rules may be contradictory, paradoxical, or incompatible. "A paradoxical order is one which, if correctly executed, is disobeyed: if disobeyed, it is obeyed. Don't do what I tell you. Don't believe me. Be spontaneous" (Laing 1969a, p. 110). For example, the Great Subway Token Hustle practiced by scores of parents is an order not to do something in order to comply with what I have ordered you to do. Specifically, a mother gives her two girls, eleven and twelve years old respectively, tokens for the subway, but she instructs them to try to pass under the turnstile for free while she engages the token seller in conversation. If he notices the hustle, she angrily demands of them: "Are you trying to pull that stunt again? You're not six years old anymore. Didn't I give you the tokens?" All the while, of course, the unspoken premise is "I'm only yelling at you to save me from embarrassment at the hands of this outsider." But sometimes the game goes too far. When caught in the act, the mother may genuinely scold her offspring, forgetting the game, because they have put her into a position of intolerable jeopardy. "Don't do what I tell you. Don't believe me *before*, believe me now."

The problem with rules and metarules of the family is that sometimes the members develop a conception of the family not as a collection of individual persons, but as a set of relations among rule makers and rule followers. This internalized conception of one's family Laing indicates by surrounding the word with quotation marks: "family." An individual may become more aware of his experience of the "family" than of the family (Laing, 1969a, p. 6).

It is easy to see why the "family" is important to survival. The "family" is the *internalized set of person relations* that makes living sensible, makes survival possible, and serves as a "bulwark against total collapse, disintegration, emptiness, despair, guilt, and other terrors" (Laing, 1969a, p. 14). Because it is a fully shared image, the world can be dichotomized into "Us" and "Them."

"Schizophrenics" in the "Family" Nexus

The complex influence of mutually exerted perspectives within the family became the focus of concern for Laing's research. It was clearly a logical outgrowth of his concern with dyadic perspectives, for the family can in some ways be conceptualized as multiple dyads and triads. As had many personality theorists before him, Laing turned to the clinical "laboratory" of disordered personality to find support in the data of raw experience for his ideas about interpersonal processes. With a colleague, Aaron Esterson, Laing (1964) published an important social-phenomenological study of families of eleven women diagnosed by at least two independent psychiatrists as schizophrenic.

The premise on which Laing and Esterson's original research attempt was based included a genuine reluctance to accept the existence of schizophrenia as a disease entity. For Laing and Esterson, and later for another of their colleagues, David Cooper (1967, 1970; cf. Speck & Attneave, 1973), "schizophrenia" is another word to be used only in quotation marks to indicate the tenuous nature of the concept's reality. The only significance of the concept of "schizophrenia" is the social one evidenced in the number of psychiatrists willing to label the behavior of some individuals "schizophrenic." The problem, as we have seen from the outset, is that, having diagnosed "schizophrenia" as the source of the person's "problem," the psychiatric profession deceives itself into believing it has thus explained the person. The person's family is equally but deceptively secure now that the "problem" has been named, recognized, and located in one blamable, avoidable, treatable member of the "family" (cf. 1969a, p. 44).

Laing and Esterson framed a deceptively simple question about the families of "schizophrenics" (1964, p. 12): *". . . are the experience and behaviour that psychiatrists take as symptoms and signs of schizophrenia more socially intelligible than has come to be supposed?"* [Italics added.]

The question clearly contains its own implicit affirmative answer. Laing and Esterson were able to demonstrate in their eleven case histories, and in later publications (Esterson, 1970), that the behavior and experience of the family member consensually designated the "schizophrenic" was explicable in terms of the relations among family members. The "schizophrenic" patient's "psychotic" behaviors made rational sense when viewed from the *patient's* perspective of her own family. The pattern of communication, the system of rules and metarules that the "schizophrenic" had internalized as the "family," could make her and her relatives' behavior intelligible.

Laing and Esterson borrowed some terminology from Jean-Paul Sartre to describe the variables that operate within the family. Their primary interest was the family *nexus,* "that multiplicity of persons drawn from the kinship group, and from others who, though not linked by kinship ties, are regarded as members of the family (Laing & Esterson, 1964, p. 21; cf. Laing & Cooper, 1971 for an indication of the importance that Laing attaches to Sartre's philosophy. However, this book is so dense as to be nearly unreadable). The important attribute of the family nexus for making intelligible the "schizophrenic's" behavior is the face-to-face influence that members of the network exert on each other's behavior and experience.

An entire pattern of relationships must thus be studied to make sense of family or individual events and to discern the *process* of *what* is going on within the network (cf. Speck & Attneave, 1973). The "what" in the last sentence refers, of course, to the flavor of communications within the network and their effect on the members of the network. But it is also important to know *who* within the nexus is doing the *what* with, for, or against the group. When an observer is able to specify the *who* of the process, he is concerned with *praxis. Praxis* and *process,* the who and the *what* distinctions, are terms borrowed from Sartre. The important point remains that the "schizophrenic" behavior attributed to the "ill one" could rationally be described as more or less successful coping strategy in her struggle to survive the world *she* has experienced within the nexus (Laing, 1967, p. 115). Her behavior "made sense" once the praxis and the process were made explicit.

Coping Strategies against Disturbed and Disturbing Communications

Family experience is not only tolerated but actively sought and maintained as a form of personal protection. Protection against what? Against real or invented dangers. When real danger cannot be found, the family nexus must invent it to insure the maintenance of a reason for its existence as a "family" (Laing, 1967, p. 87). The result is a family fantasy of the external world as extraordinarily dangerous to the "family":

> The family's function is to repress Eros; to induce a false consciousness of security; to deny death by avoiding life; to cut off transcendence; to believe in God, not to experience the Void; to create, in

short, one-dimensional man; to promote respect, conformity, obedi-
ence; to con children out of play; to induce a fear of failure; to
promote a respect for work; to promote a respect for "respectability."
[Laing, 1967, p. 65]

Families, it should not be surprising, foster in Laing's view the adoption
among the members of coping strategies against *disturbing* communication
with the threats of the world, against *disturbed* communications of other
family members who have succumbed to such threats, and against the
possibility of *being disturbed* further by recognition of *disturbance* within
the family. Laing calls such coping strategies "operations," and some of
them may be conceptualized as similar to the classic psychoanalytic defense mechanisms like repression, projection, reversal. These coping techniques, Laing points out, are properly characterized by the psychoanalysts
as "mechanisms" because the person adopting them feels them imposed
on his being like impersonal machinery (Laing, 1967, p. 35; 1969a, p. 13).
They are *intrapersonal* techniques of acting on oneself and treating the self
as object.

But defenses are not only intrapersonal, they can also be *transpersonal*
in the sense that they operate on another's experience. The development
of direct, meta, and meta-metaperspectives in dealing with others can be
forms of transpersonal defense in the same way that a double-bind inflicter
tries to control self and other. However, there are also several specific
transpersonal defenses whereby *"self attempts to regulate the inner life of the
other in order to preserve his own"* (Laing, 1969a, p. 13). Within the triads and
dyads of the family, transpersonal coping mechanisms are shared, traded,
clashed, and supported to maintain the integrity of the nexus. Some of the
main forms of these transpersonal strategies are: *complementary identity,
confirmation* and *disconfirmation,* and *collusion.*

Complementary Identity

Sometimes one's identity can be realized only in terms of the other. In
fact, for some persons, identity does not exist in the absence of a complementary personality. A mother, for example, cannot be a mother without
a child (Laing, 1969b, p. 66). But sometimes complementarity may be
carried to extreme forms. The mother who comes to *need* her child to
maintain her self-integrity is a good example of complementarity carried
to the realm of transpersonal defense. For the mother must maintain her
identity by manipulating the identity of her child in ways that are not
consistent with the child's need for autonomy. Without the child, she is
a different person to herself.

To illustrate, Laing cites the case of John, son of an emotionally rigid
naval officer and a prostitute. Entrusted to his father's care at the age of
six, John experienced a changed world living with this new and exacting
"stranger." As John grew up, he disappointed his father in many ways: he

failed to become a naval officer; he failed the university entrance exam; he even disgraced himself by failure as a common seaman. John's father was thus prompted to remark repeatedly that he was *unsure such a boy could be his son.* Eventually, John's father, severing all ties and kicking the boy out of his house, made good the symbolic threat and completely disowned his "fatherhood." "What his father taught him was: 'You are my son if I say you are, and you are not my son if I say you are not' " (Laing, 1969b, p. 79).

John eventually succumbed to an acute manic psychosis by which he adopted a basic premise for living: *he could be anyone he wanted, merely by snapping his fingers.* His father had destroyed his identity by withdrawing his own identity as father. His son was able to recover only when he realized that he was not who his father said he was (i.e., "nobody"), any more than he was what his father said he was not (i.e., his father's son). John's "psychosis" had been another form of identity deception by which he deluded himself into negating his father's negation.

Confirmation and Disconfirmation

A sign of recognition from another confirms one's presence in the world. All forms of interaction between persons require some minimum of confirmation from the other to maintain the interaction. Total disconfirmation, absolute indifference to the other's existence, is a fine strategy for driving one mad. Irrelevant recognition, that is, paying attention only to the marginal details of another's existence, is as powerfully damaging as the total disconfirmation of absolute indifference.

To illustrate, Laing cites the case of a five-year-old who runs into his mother holding up a big fat worm. He says: "Mummy, look what a big fat worm I have got." She says: "You are filthy—away and clean yourself immediately" (Laing, 1969b, p. 85).

The mother's response to the boy is irrelevant, or what Ruesch has called a tangential response. The mother expresses no horror, delight, disgust, approval, or disapproval of the *worm*. She instead responds by calling attention to an aspect of the boy that he himself has not considered. "She may be saying either, 'I am not interested in looking at your worm unless you are clean,' or 'Whether or not you have a worm is of no importance to me—all that matters to me is whether you are clean or dirty, and I only like you when you are clean' " (Laing, 1969b, p. 86). The mother has failed to confirm the boy's being.

Collusion

Collusion is a "game" played by two or more people whereby they agree to deceive themselves. Their agreement to deceive and be deceived may not be conscious, but then part of the "game" is the rule not to see the game

(Laing, 1969b, p. 90). The dynamics of collusion involve one or more persons' projecting a false self that is somehow more desirable than his real self. Then, the projector must find others who will confirm the existence of his false self image by behaving in ways that are consonant with the projection:

> Collusion is always clinched when self finds in other that other who will 'confirm' self in the false self that self is trying to make real, and vice versa. [Laing, 1969b, p. 93]

To illustrate, some families must maintain the myth of being a "happy family." If one member is unhappy, he must conceal his unhappiness from his family and from himself in order to maintain the myth of "happy family," for if he did not deny his unhappiness to himself, his membership in the family would demolish its happiness. He thus projects an image of happiness. Conversely, the other members of the family must deny they detect unhappiness in any of their members and collude with the individual's projection. But colluding to keep unhappiness a secret causes unhappiness over having to keep it a secret. However, if the secret is well guarded by mutual denial and collusion, then unhappiness cannot arise in such a happy family (Laing, 1969a, pp. 99–100).

Summary

Like Thomas Szasz, R. D. Laing has taken the position that the label "schizophrenia" does not necessarily indicate a disease entity. The "schizophrenic's" behaviors are more intelligible if viewed as a strategy for coping with his intolerable life. In this respect, David Rosenhan's pseudopatient study of psychiatric hospital environments lends some credence to Laing and Szasz's position by demonstrating that diagnostic labels are more a function of the situation and the psychiatric staff's expectations than of the behavior of the person so labeled.

Laing's theorizing may be classed as a modified form of existential phenomenology. The existentialists, notably Binswanger, Boss, and May, interpret man as being-in-the world. Man's unique gift is for self-awareness, a consciousness that he *is*. Man's being, his *Dasein*, is conceived of by the existentialists as a process of continual development, of growth toward fulfillment. Unlike the psychoanalytic conception of man as product of his past, the existentialists view man as potentiality, guided more by his choices for the future than by his clashes with his own history. Each person occupies three modes of world, *Umwelt, Mitwelt*, and *Eigenwelt*. The *Umwelt* is the natural world of biological cycle and drive; the *Mitwelt* is the world of others, of relationships with one's fellow man; and the *Eigenwelt* is one's subjective experience of inner and outer reality. Laing's emphasis has been on the last two modes, and he has developed a unique phenomenological style of representing *Mitwelt* and *Eigenwelt.*

In his semiautobiographical essay, the most recent of Laing's publications, he has recounted the early irrationalities of family living to which he was exposed. In addition to a strictly enforced taboo on matters concerning sexuality, Laing's relatives fought some quite literal battles in the family living room. His medical school experiences left with Laing the impression that medicine as a profession, in particular the specialty of psychiatry, is sometimes coldly inhuman—as inhuman as it seemingly construes the "diseases" it attempts to treat.

Laing has extended the theme of unwantedness from his own childhood into the beginnings of a theory to account for parental rejection of children from conception to birth, the period of intrauterine life. Laing suggested that certain physical and chemical patterns rhythmically established for the fetus during its mother's pregnancy may produce afterbirth "resonances," that is, psychological analogs of the physiological patterns of life before birth. In some extreme cases, schizophrenic and other psychotic patients may need to be metaphorically "reborn" to reestablish a satisfactory relationship with the circumstances and people of their lives.

Laing and his colleagues have developed a notational system to represent the individual's perspectives of himself, of the other, and of his own perceptions of the other's perception. More important, Laing has also developed means to concretize the very complex ways that the members of a dyad perceive the relationships between each other, and between the subject and himself.

Out of his concern with understanding experience as the individual experiences it, Laing and his team developed the Interpersonal Perception Method (IPM) to assess the direct, meta, and meta-meta perspectives of intimately related twosomes. Both parties' direct, meta, and meta-metaperspectives may be compared to assess their understanding, their agreement, and their realization of understanding.

Bateson's work with double-bind communications has served as an important influence on Laing's conceptualization of disturbed communication in families. A double-bind communication involves tangled statements of commands and denials of the statement's commanding aspects, coupled with implied punishments for noncompliance with the denied command. Laing suggests that the families of "schizophrenics" practice such disturbed communication to the extent that some family members can cope with the "can't win" situation thus constructed only by erecting a false self to pacify them.

Laing has pointed out that a variety of transpersonal coping mechanisms are possible, in addition to the traditional defense mechanisms elucidated by Freud and his followers. Thus, whereas classic psychoanalytic defense mechanisms like repression, denial, and projection are intrapersonal because they operate on the self, Laing has described coping techniques designed to operate on the experiences of others: Complementary identity involves defining one's own identity in terms of another's being; discon- firmation is the failure to respond to another as a human person, dismissing him as object; and collusion is the active striving of two or more persons to deceive and be deceived in accepting false projected self-images.

FOR FURTHER READING

The development of Laing's thought from Freudian psychoanalytic premises through his existential-phenomenological modifications can be surveyed by successive reading of three books: *The Divided Self* (Baltimore: Penguin, 1959), the first statement of his position; *The Politics of the Family* (New York: Vintage, 1969), which contains some of his propositions on the importance of interpersonal rela- tionships in guiding the individual's interpretation of reality; and *Self and Others* (New York: Pantheon, 1969), which sets forth his concept of how individuals feel themselves forced to distort reality by the demands of significant others.

An interview with Laing, along with one of his previously unpublished papers on the genetic basis of schizophrenia (and the futility of this concept), are con- tained in R. I. Evans' *R. D. Laing: The Man and His Ideas* (New York: Dutton, 1976; the interview may also be found in condensed form in Evans' *The Making of Psychology* [New York: Alfred Knopf, 1976]). A semiautobiographical account of some of the sources of his ideas is provided by Laing in his most recent work, *The Facts of Life* (New York: Pantheon, 1976). This same book contains his speculations on the importance of uterine life in shaping one's later feelings of acceptance or rejection within the family.

David Cooper, a colleague of Laing's, has carried forward some of Laing's propositions on the pathological potential of family life in *The Death of the Family* (New York: Vintage, 1970). Cooper has also set forth his own unique criticisms of classical psychiatry with a major debt to Laing in *Psychiatry and Anti-Psychiatry* (London: Paladin, 1967). Along these same lines, the collection of papers in Robert Boyers and Robert Orrill's *R. D. Laing and Anti-Psychiatry* (Harper & Row, 1971) provides a useful overview of Laing's growing impact on the mental health profes- sions. Ross Speck and Carolyn Attneave describe an approach to family therapy heavily influenced by Laing's concepts in *Family Networks* (New York: Vintage, 1973).

Thomas Szasz's criticisms of the medical model of mental illness, which share much with Laing's philosophical assumptions, can most easily be had in *The Myth of Mental Illness: Foundations of a Theory of Personal Conduct* (New York: Harper & Row, 1961; available in paperback) and in *The Manufacture of Madness* (New York: Dell, 1970). Bruno Bettelheim's recent review of Laing's *The Facts of Life* contains some interesting comparisons of Szasz's work with Laing's, and may be read in *The New York Times Book Review,* May 30, 1976, p. 5.

9 GEORGE A. KELLY
Personal Construct Theory

Each time one man reveals himself in privacy to another, a secret society springs into being.

SIDNEY M. JOURARD, *The Transparent Self*

On Wednesday, when the sky is blue,
And I have nothing else to do,
I sometimes wonder if it's true
That who is what and what is who.

A. A. MILNE, *Winnie-the-Pooh*

When What Is Who

When George A. Kelly turned his hand to theorizing about human nature, he abandoned time-honored concepts like motivation, drive, the unconscious, emotion, and reinforcement. Instead, Kelly saw each individual to be like himself, a unique theorist of human nature. The person is a personality scientist who devises and tests predictions about the behavior of significant people in his life. In Kelly's view, each of us constructs anticipations of others' behavior on a what-for-who basis: What makes some whos similar, and what makes them different? Consequently, an individual who came to Kelly for counseling would be asked to make explicit his private personality theory. He would complete one or more versions of Kelly's *Role Construct Repertory Test* (REP) to provide some indication of how he construed important people in his life. The reader is herewith invited to participate.

REP TEST PART A: ROLE TITLE LIST

Instructions

Write the name of the persons indicated in the blanks provided below. Do not repeat names. If a role title appears to call for a duplicate name, substitute the name of another person whom the second role title suggests to you.

1. Your mother or the person who has played the part of mother in your life.

   1._____

2. Your father or the person who has played the part of a father in your life.

   2._____

3. Your brother nearest your age. If you have no brother, the person who is most like one.

   3._____

4. Your sister nearest your age. If you have no sister, the person who is most like one.

   4._____

5. A teacher you liked or the teacher of a subject you liked.

   5._____

6. A teacher you disliked or the teacher of a subject you disliked.

   6._____

7. Your closest girl (boy) friend immediately before you started going with your wife (husband) or present closest girl (boy) friend [Ex-Flame].

   7._____

8. Your wife (husband) or closest present girl (boy) friend.

   8._____

9. An employer, supervisor, or officer under whom you served during a period of great stress [Boss].

   9._____

10. A person with whom you have been closely associated who, for some unexplainable reason, appears to dislike you [Rejecting Person].

    10._____

11. The person whom you have met within the past six months whom you would most like to know better [Sought Person].

    11._____

12. The person whom you would most like to be of help to, or the one whom you feel most sorry for [Pitied Person].

    12._____

13. The most intelligent person whom
    you know personally.   13._____

14. The most successful person whom
    you know personally.   14._____

15. The most interesting person whom
    you know personally.   15._____

REP TEST PART B: CONSTRUCT SORTS

Instructions

The sets of three numbers in the following sorts refer to the numbers 1 to 15, inclusive, in Part A.

In each of the following sorts three numbers are listed. Look at your Part A sheet and consider the three people whom you have listed for these three numbers.

In what important way are two of these three people alike and at the same time, essentially different from the third?

After you have decided what that *important* way is, write it in the blank opposite the sort marked CONSTRUCT.

Next encircle the numbers corresponding to the two people who are alike.

Write down what you believe to be the opposite of the construct in the blank marked CONTRAST.

NUMBERS Sort	Part A	CONSTRUCT (EMERGENT)	CONTRAST (IMPLICIT)
1.	9,11,14	_____	_____
2.	10,12,13	_____	_____
3.	2,5,12	_____	_____
4.	1,4,8	_____	_____
5.	7,8,12	_____	_____
6.	3,13,6	_____	_____
7.	1,2,9	_____	_____
8.	3,4,10	_____	_____

9.	6,7,10	_____	_____
10.	5,11,14	_____	_____
11.	1,7,8	_____	_____
12.	2,7,8	_____	_____
13.	3,6,9	_____	_____
14.	4,5,10	_____	_____
15.	11,13,14	_____	_____

Based on Kelly, 1955.

When all of the construct and contrast blanks are filled, the Role Construct Repertory Test is completed. The form of the test that appears here is a slightly modified and shortened version of an early form of the Group REP Test. Number combinations making up the fifteen sorts are, for practical purposes, virtually unlimited. In fact, the subject could be asked to repeat his construct and contrast evaluations with a new set of sorts, depending on the judgment of the administering psychologist.

The ways in which the psychologist can choose to analyze the subject's sorts are also virtually unlimited. Generally, however, he either embarks on an informal *impressionistic* analysis, guided by the give and take of the clinical situation in which the counselee has provided comments and answered questions about his constructs and contrasts; or he analyzes the themes revealed in the construct and contrast columns more *objectively* by tabulating the frequency with which key phrases are repeated, and the relations among the descriptions assigned to various crucial figure-combinations like Mother–Father, Teacher–Boss, Husband–Ex-Flame.

A sample REP protocol of a subject identified by Kelly as "Mildred Beal" appears in Table 9–1. Only five of her sorts need be reproduced for the sake of illustration (after Kelly, 1955, pp. 242 ff.).

A number of interesting personal meanings stand out from Mildred Beal's partial protocol. For example, in sorts numbers 3 and 11, the description "easygoing" is applied by Mildred to Father, Liked Teacher, and Boyfriend. In sorts numbers 4 and 11, Mother is described as "hypercritical of other people," and as "socially maladjusted." It is clear that Mildred construes her sister as different from her father and boyfriend in the same way that her mother is. Impressionistic analyses like these yield important insights about the way Mildred construes the people in her world, and the relationships of the various figures in Mildred's estimation.

SORT NUMBER	SIMILAR FIGURES	SIMILARITY CONSTRUCT	DISSIMILAR FIGURES	CONTRASTING CONSTRUCT
2.	Rejecting Person (10) Pitied Person (12)	Very unhappy persons	Intelligent Person (13)	Contented
3.	Father (2) Liked Teacher (5)	Very quiet and easy going	Pitied Person (12)	Nervous, hypertensive
4.	Mother (1) Sister (4)	Look alike Both hypercritical of people in general	Boyfriend	Friendliness
11.	Mother (1) Ex-Flame (7)	Socially maladjusted	Boyfriend (8)	Easygoing, self-confident
13.	Disliked Teacher (6) Boss (9)	Emotionally unpredictable	Brother (3)	Even temperament

Grid Form of the REP: The Person's Own Personality Theory

Mildred's responses to the role constructs of the REP test may also be analyzed with the tools of mathematics. Factor analysis and its more lowly cousin, the correlation coefficient, can be applied to a grid form of the test. In this version, the subject is asked to make the sorts several times, applying each of his constructs developed in response to particular pairs of figures successively to all fifteen roles. (Actually, the full form of the REP test may include twenty-two figures, of which the *Self* is one; it has been shortened in this presentation for the sake of simplicity.)

The first time around, the subject is presented with the standard sort-combinations in the form of a 15 × 15 grid, as illustrated in Figure 9–1. He is instructed to indicate which two of the figures in the first sort (9, 11, 14) are similar by placing an "X" in the appropriate circles of the grid. The circles are placed in each line only in the boxes corresponding to the three figures the subject is asked to compare. Thus, for example, in Figure 9–1, Mildred has placed an "X" in the circles of numbers 9 and 14, Employer and Successful Person, indicating that she construes these two as similar (Emergent Pole). She has left number 11 unfilled, indicating that Sought Person is, in her view, different from the other two. On the first line of the emergent pole column, she then writes in her own words the way in which 9 and 14 are similar. Likewise, in the implicit pole column, she writes her

FIGURE 9–1:   A GRID ANALYSIS OF MILDREN BEAL'S ROLE CONSTRUCT REPERTORY TEST

Role figures (columns):

1 Mother
2 Father
3 Brother
4 Sister
5 Liked Teacher
6 Disliked Teacher
7 Ex-Flame
8 Boyfriend (Wife/Husband)
9 Employer
10 Rejecting Person
11 Sought Person
12 Pitied Person
13 Intelligent Person
14 Successful Person
15 Interesting Person

SORT NUMBER	ROLE FIGURES	EMERGENT POLE (Two as Similar)	IMPLICIT POLE (One as Different)
1	9, 11, 14	Are related to me	Unrelated
2	10, 12, 13	Very unhappy persons	Contented
3	2, 5, 12	Quiet and easygoing	Nervous, hypersensitive
4	1, 4, 8	Look alike, hypercritical	Friendliness
5	7, 8, 12	Feel inferior	Self-confident
6	3, 13, 6	Socially better than adequate	Unpleasant
7	1, 2, 9	Hypersensitive	Easygoing
8	3, 4, 10	Hypercritical	Understanding
9	6, 7, 10	Feelings of inferiority	Assured of innate worth
10	5, 11, 14	Pleasing personalities	High-powered, nervous
11	1, 7, 8	Socially maladjusted	Easygoing, self-confident
12	2, 7, 8	Relaxing	Uncomfortable to be with
13	3, 6, 9	Emotionally unpredictable	Even temperament
14	4, 5, 10	Look somewhat alike	Look unlike
15	11, 13, 14	Dynamic personalities	Weak personality

After Kelly, 1955, pp. 242 ff.

idea of what makes figure 11, Sought Person, different. Reading from Figure 9–1, Mildred regards Employer and Successful Person as similar because they are "related to me." Sought Person is different by being "unrelated."

The second time, after Mildred has completed all fifteen sorts and listed her constructs, she is asked to make systematic comparisons of her fifteen similar and different constructs to all of the remaining figures on each line. Mildred is thus instructed to start again with the constructs she listed for sort number one, namely, "related to me" versus "unrelated," and systematically consider this dichotomous construct in relation to the twelve remaining figures on line one. For each figure to which the construct of Sort 1 applies, Mildred is asked to place a *check mark* in that figure's box on the Sort 1 line.

Mildred proceeds down the remaining fourteen constructs, repeating her search for applicable figures for each of the constructs on that line. For the sake of simplicity, Sort 11 has been abstracted from the total grid and enlarged in Figure 9–2. The first time that Mildred sorted the figures of line 11, she chose Mother and Ex-Flame as similar by placing an "X" in the circles for those roles. Now Mildred is asked to take the remaining twelve roles and to indicate whether her construct "Socially maladjusted" versus "Easygoing, self-confident" applies to any of them. For the sake of illustration, figures 4,6,9,10, and 11 have been checked to indicate that Mildred feels the similarity construct "Socially maladjusted" applies to them. Those she has left blank indicate that the similarity (emergent pole) construct cannot be used to describe them.

The resulting grid pattern of checks and "X's" may be converted to a series of numbered coordinates without reference to Mildred's verbal labels. All that matters is the *pattern* of expressed similarity and difference indicated by the check marks, not the verbal labels that led Mildred to assign these marks. The procedures employed in mathematically analyzing the data are very complex and need not concern us here.

The grid or matrix of Mildred's REP test represents her own unique personality theory, the system of personal constructs or interpretations by which she conducts her life. Reading *across* Mildred's grid we can answer questions about the *figures* she construes as similar on a particular dimension of her theory. Reading *down* the columns, we can ask questions about *how* Mildred construes each person on a whole series of *dimensions*. To illustrate, consider what is learned about the way Mildred construes the world when columns 1 (Mother) and 12 (Pitied Person) are read *downward* together, as shown in the table on page 319.

In a way, Kelly's approach is similar to Laing's (cf. Chapter 8 of this book), in that both of these theorists are interested in the ways that the subject interprets his world and the significant people in it. Where Laing employs the terms "direct, meta-, and meta-metaperspectives," Kelly prefers the term *construct*. There are some important differences between Kelly and Laing, but one clear similarity emerges: Both Kelly and Laing are

FIGURE 9–2: A SINGLE CONSTRUCT FROM MILDRED BEAL'S GRID REP ANALYSIS

	1	2	3	4	5	6	7	8	9	10	11	12	13	14	15	SORT NUMBER	ROLE FIGURES	EMERGENT POLE (Two as Similar)	IMPLICIT POLE (One as Different)
	Mother	Father	Brother	Sister	Liked Teacher	Disliked Teacher	Ex-Flame	Boyfriend (Wife/Husband)	Employer	Rejecting Person	Sought Person	Pitied Person	Intelligent Person	Successful Person	Interesting Person				
	⊗			✓		✓	⊗	○	✓	✓		✓				11	1, 7, 8	Socially maladjusted	Easygoing, self-confident

318

(1) MOTHER	(12) PITIED PERSON
(1) Are related to me	(1)
(2) Very unhappy person	(2) Very unhappy person
(5) Feels inferior	(5) Feels inferior
(7) Hypersensitive	(7) Hypersensitive
(8) Hypercritical	(8)
(9) Feelings of inferiority	(9) Feelings of inferiority
(11) Socially maladjusted	(11) Socially maladjusted
(13) Emotionally unpredictable	(13)
(14) Looks like sister and rejecting person	(14) Looks like sister and rejecting person

primarily interested in the way an individual *experiences* his world through the meaning that *he* attaches to others' behavior. In fact, both Laing and Kelly focus their attention on the way the individual *anticipates* the feelings and behavior of significant others. Where Laing assesses the individual's metaperspective (how he thinks the other thinks), Kelly evaluates the individual's anticipations of important people's roles.

"Man the Scientist": The Fundamental Postulate

Tongue-in-cheek, Kelly caricatured the traditional attitude of most psychologists: " 'I, being a *psychologist,* and therefore a *scientist,* am performing this experiment in order to improve the prediction and control of certain human phenomena; but my subject, being merely a human organism, is obviously propelled by inexorable drives welling up within him, or else he is in gluttonous pursuit of sustenance and shelter' " (1955, p. 5).

The psychologist's *professional* pursuit of the sometimes elusive goals of prediction and control tends to dominate his habitual mode of being with others. But of course, in his view, those others never themselves create or test hypotheses about him or about the behavior of other people with whom they have contact. In consequence, the psychologist easily succumbs to the fallacy of believing that *his* theoretical constructs are real *things* with objective existence in the people he observes. These mere mortals are likely to surprise him when their behavior suggests that they too seek understanding—about themselves, about him, about people in general (Kelly, 1955, p. 5; 1958a, p. 87).

Out of preconceptions like these, countless theoretical constructs have been created to predict and to control human behavior, only to be discarded when Man the Scientist got a real look at Man the Human. Kelly suggested that psychologists would do better to take the long-range view of man by adopting a perspective of centuries to chart the influences that shape the direction of the species' progress. Such a broadened perspective, Kelly predicted, would reveal that questions of appetite, tissue needs, and sex impulses were largely secondary to a more fundamental human characteristic: *Man's need to know and to control his universe.*

> Might not the individual man, each in his own personal way, assume more of the stature of a scientist, ever seeking to predict and control the course of events with which he is involved? Would he not have his theories, test his hypotheses, and weigh his experimental evidence? [Kelly, 1955, p. 5]

A return look at Mildred Beal's REP protocol easily demonstrates the truth of Kelly's hypothesis that each of us behaves *as if* he were a scientist. Mildred has created explanatory hypotheses about her mother and father and the rest of the significant figures in her life. She presumably can predict their behavior on the basis of her past experiences with them; she can even discern similarities and differences among subgroups of these important people. In short, she has made sense of her world by attempting to *anticipate* the behavior of the people in it.

Kelly divorced himself from the view of man as a *reactive being,* perpetually provoked by his environment to mere survival behaviors. For Kelly, man is a *creative* creature with the capacity to abstract meaning from his environment and to impose his own representations on it (1958b). Because he can create his own interpretations of what he experiences, man is not restricted to inexorable reactions—unless he *chooses* to interpret his life that way. Furthermore, his Being is not restricted to one-time interpretations; he is endlessly free to change his mind, to place *alternative constructions* on his experience when it is different from expectation. Thus, every person shares with the scientist an enduring need to practice his skill as predictor and hypothesis tester.

Kelly described his position on man's freedom to create alternative explanations of his world as *constructive alternativism* (1955, p. 15):

> We take the stand that there are always some alternative constructions available to choose among in dealing with the world. No one needs to paint himself into a corner; no one needs to be completely hemmed in by circumstances; no one needs to be the victim of his biography.

The central notions, then, in Kelly's approach to understanding human nature involve a belief in man's *active striving to understand,* his *creativity* in construing events of importance, and his *freedom* limitlessly to revise his "theories" about his world: *"A person lives his life by reaching out for what comes next and the only channels he has for reaching are the personal constructions he is able to place upon what may actually be happening"* (1955, p. 228).

It is not surprising, therefore, that the fundamental postulate by which

Kelly described his theoretical position on man's nature is couched in the language of the scientist's attempts to predict and control:

FUNDAMENTAL POSTULATE: *A person's processes are psychologically channelized by the ways in which he anticipates events* (1955, p. 46).

Kelly did not seem to be completely comfortable with the label "phenomenological" for his theory (1955, p. 517). Nevertheless, his emphasis clearly demonstrates a concern with immediate experience and the individual's interpretation of it. The key word in the fundamental postulate is "anticipates," because it is man's need for reliable knowledge that Kelly sees as the distinguishing feature of human existence. Were it not for this urge to "anticipate," Kelly's theory would be virtually devoid of motivational concepts (cf. Sechrest, 1963, p. 212).

Sources of Kelly's Conception of Human Nature

Toward the end of his life, Kelly traced, as well as the deceits of memory permitted, the possible origin of his ideas about Man the Scientist. Kelly recounted his first exposure to psychology as a graduate student in a lecture class and the mounting disappointment that he experienced with classical psychology. One day the professor wrote on the blackboard an "S" with an arrow pointing to an "R." Anticipating that after several weeks of dull course work, the crux of psychology's explanation of man was about to be discussed, Kelly listened attentively: " . . . [T]he most I could make of it was that the 'S' was what you had to have in order to account for the 'R' and the 'R' was put there so the 'S' would have something to account for. I never did find out what the arrow stood for—not to this day—and I have pretty well given up trying to figure it out" (Kelly, 1963, pp. 46–47).

So much for stimulus-response psychology. Kelly graduated from the University of Iowa in 1931 with a doctor of philosophy degree, and he ran headlong into the Great Depression. He spent twelve years at a small college in western Kansas, the "dust bowl" region, and soon discovered that his professional training in academic physiological psychology and speech pathology was useless in helping the young people who did not know what to do with their lives during the Depression. At first, he returned to Freudian theory, having once dismissed it as preposterous in his student days, and now found that Freud had skillfully described the same pain and despair that he was discovering in his informal attempts to counsel students. "Through my Freudian interpretations, judiciously offered at those moments when clients seemed ready for them, a good many unfortunate persons seemed to be profoundly helped" (Kelly, 1963, p. 51).

Although Kelly experienced no out-and-out failures with his new Freudian orientation, something gnawed at him, the kind of unscratchable itch that sometimes precedes discovery of the obvious. Consequently, despite his apparent success with Freud's "language of distress," he continued to grow uneasy: "It was that I was beginning to take them [Freudian concepts] for granted. And ideas, like women, when too long taken for granted are likely to turn fickle" (1963, p. 52). In short, Kelly found his Freudian "insights" too certain, too pat, too prescriptive, and too boring.

In the depression climate of the 1930's, Kelly's informal Freudian psychological counseling was regarded by the local Kansasans as "pretty far out." His Freudianisms may have seemed strange, but they worked most of the time because Kelly's clients' unsophisticated acceptance of them, their anticipation that to be effective such interpretations had to be bizarre, guaranteed success. Thus, there was precious little in his patients' ready acceptance of his seemingly authoritative interpretations to pose challenge, scant few problems to provoke questions. In consequence, Kelly tried an informal experiment:

> . . . I began fabricating "insights." I deliberately offered "preposterous interpretations" to my clients. Some of them were about as un-Freudian as I could make them—first proposed somewhat cautiously, of course, and then, as I began to see what was happening, more boldly. My only criteria were that the explanation *account for the crucial facts as the client saw them,* and that it *carry implications for approaching the future in a different way.* [1963, p. 52; italics added]

Kelly might tell a client, for example, that his nervous stomach was "rebelling against nourishment of all kinds—parental, educational, and nutritional." Surprisingly, his clients felt that his interpretations were worth a try, and they often successfully changed the direction of their lives by adopting the new outlook implied in Kelly's "preposterous" suggestions. In Kelly's terms, they had developed alternative constructions about themselves.

Additional evidence began to mount for Kelly's slowly developing view that clients could change their own lives if somehow they would make the deliberate attempt to see things differently. When, for instance, more clients than he could handle applied to him for treatment, he started the practice of spending just a little time with these people to give them a few hints about what to do in the period while waiting their turn. Months later, when their turn came, Kelly often found that without formal therapy they had solved or were well on the way to resolving the difficulty for which they had initially come to see him. His few "hints" about how to proceed while waiting were sufficient to muster the client's own creative resources in restructuring his perspective of the problem. These patients had not been "cured" in the interval, but they viewed the problem as now more manageable.

Kelly therefore began to formulate a new clinical perspective of his own. " . . . I began to pursue the notion that one's current acts and undertakings might have as much to do with the development of his personality as did the imprint of events with which he came in contact or the insights he was able to conjure up with the help of his therapist" (1963, p. 56).

With the help of some graduate students, he established a statewide traveling clinic to visit schools and other agencies in an effort to reach those many people experiencing difficulty in living through the circumstances of a nation in crisis. Often, during a visit to one or another school, teachers would make a complaint about a student's behavior. To Kelly it seemed clear that such teacher complaints represented the child's disruptive influence on the *teacher's* life, and were not a description of that child in his life situation. A teacher's complaint of "laziness," for example, was hardly useful to the psychologist as a motivational construct, because the label described the teacher's construction of events, not the child's character. The child was lazy when it came to doing things the teacher thought he should do.

To obtain a picture of how the person himself construes his life, Kelly and his students began using an early personality test called the Maller Inventory. This test consisted of cards containing self-descriptive statements the subject was asked to sort in various ways; for example, those most like self, next most like, and so on. It was an early version of the Q-sort technique used by Stephenson and Rogers and a forerunner of Kelly's own REP test. From the person's responses, Kelly and his students would write a characterization of the person that differed in significant ways from the way he viewed himself. An attempt was made to make the description embody a new outlook on life and to offer specific examples of how this outlook would influence behavior. The "person" described was sometimes given a new name to emphasize the difference between the client's previous constructions and this new viewpoint. The client was then invited to pretend he was this "new person" and to enact the role for two weeks or so.

This role-playing procedure later became the basis of what Kelly called *fixed-role therapy* (1955, Chap. 8). Role playing helped the client to construe afresh the events of his life. Fixed-role therapy is thus an invitation to the client to experiment with alternative modes of living. In principle, Kelly conceived of his procedure as a means of freeing the curious and inventive scientist that lies hidden in each of us. Although not a panacea, fixed-role therapy helped a great many clients to see things differently, to anticipate life with more relish, and to construe themselves and the significant people in their lives in wholly new and productively fresh ways. In the words of the Fundamental Postulate: *"A person's processes are psychologically channelized by the ways in which he anticipates events."*

Kelly created eleven corollaries to the Fundamental Postulate that provide the overall skeleton of Personal Construct Theory. It may be of some help to preview this basic outline and the grouping of the eleven postulates that is followed here. For the better part of the remainder of this chapter we will be concerned with examining these eleven corollaries:

FUNDAMENTAL POSTULATE

1. Construction Corollary   3. Organization Corollary
2. Individuality Corollary   4. Dichotomy Corollary

     5. Choice Corollary
     6. Range Corollary
     7. Experience Corollary

8. Modulation Corollary   10. Commonality Corollary
9. Fragmentation Corollary   11. Sociality Corollary

Construction and Individuality Corollaries: The Person as Process

As Laing had been concerned with the power of labels to shape an observer's perception of the person so labeled, Kelly too had expressed concern lest psychologists be trapped by the traditions of Western civilization's language habits. Consider, for example, what happens when a person labels himself:

> . . . on occasion I may say of myself . . . "I am an introvert." "I," the subject, "am an introvert," the predicate. The language form of the statement clearly places the onus of being an introvert on the subject —me. What I actually am, the words say, is an introvert.
>
> . . . the proper interpretation of my statement is that *I construe* myself to be an introvert, or, if I am merely being coy or devious, I am inveigling *my listener into construing me* in terms of introversion. The point that gets lost in the shuffle of words is the psychological fact that I have identified myself in terms of a personal construct— "introversion." [Kelly, 1958a, p. 70]

The form of the statement easily deceives the listener into believing that it is *objectively* true, that when a predicate is applied to a subject, the subject must undoubtedly *be* what the predicate asserts.

> . . . when I say that Professor Lindzey's left shoe is an "introvert," everyone looks at his shoe as if this were something his shoe was responsible for. Or if I say that Professor Cattell's head is "discursive," everyone looks over at him, as if the proposition popped out of his head instead of out of mine. Don't look at his head! Don't look at that shoe! Look at me; I'm the one who is responsible for the statement. After you figure out what I mean you can look over there to see if you make any sense out of shoes and heads by construing them the way I do. [Kelly, 1958a, p. 72]

Thus, the focus of Kelly's theory is on the person and on his interpretations of events, not on the events themselves. Kelly believed that the person erects a structure of meaning to be imposed on the events he experiences, and this structure embodies both similarity and contrast. The person notes the similarities among various events, and he groups them together under one construct; but that same construct derives some of its meaning from those events that were excluded by contrast. Hence, the construct "introvert" not only indicates all traits the person associates with introversion but also defines what for him introversion is not.

Time exerts an important influence on the manner in which a person construes his world. With the passage of time, the individual is able to detect recurrent themes, repetitive events, and their onset and termination. "Once events have been given their beginnings and endings, and their similarities and contrasts construed, it becomes feasible to try to predict them, just as one predicts that tomorrow will follow today" (Kelly, 1955, p. 53).

Kelly therefore formulated a first corollary to the fundamental postulate:

> CONSTRUCTION COROLLARY: *A person anticipates events by construing their replications* (1955, p. 50).

This Construction Corollary says that man is able to deal with his life because he is able to detect and interpret through time similarities, regularities, and recurrences of events. He is, in short, able to make sense out of the chaos of the future only by predicting its occurrence on the basis of past experience. But most important, it is *his* past experience and *his* construction of that experience that dominates his life, not the events as they actually exist.

It follows from Kelly's emphasis on *personal* interpretation that individual differences in construction of events may exist. Kelly called this common-sense proposition the

> INDIVIDUALITY COROLLARY: *Persons differ from each other in their constructions of events* (1955, p. 55).

Hierarchy of Experience: Organization and Dichotomy Corollaries

A person's system of constructs is not static. The interpretations he imposes on the universe constantly change and are perpetually modified by new experience. Often, contradictions and conflicts between constructs emerge. The individual must then develop a way to resolve or to transcend the inconsistency—*if he perceives it.*

One way to resolve the conflicts that are perceived is to organize one's constructions of events into a hierarchy in which particular constructs may subsume many other constructs in the system. When one construct subsumes another it is called *superordinal;* conversely, the construct so subsumed is termed *subordinal.* It is possible sometimes for super- and subordinal constructs to change places in the hierarchy depending upon the demands of immediate events. For example, the construct *good* vs. *bad* may include the two poles of the *intelligent* vs. *stupid* dimension of experience. *Good* subsumes *intelligent,* and *bad* subsumes *stupid. Good* and *bad* may, of course, assimilate other constructs as well. Furthermore, *good* and *bad* may change ordinal position with *intelligent* and *stupid:*

GOOD———BAD (Superordinal)   INTELLIGENT———STUPID
Intelligent   Stupid (Subordinal)   Good   Bad

Another way in which constructs may be ordinally ranked is for one to create categories that subsume complete dimensions under *one* pole of a superordinal construct. For example, the *good-bad* construct might itself be subsumed under one pole of a broader superordinal construct: *evaluative* vs. *descriptive.* Thus, the pair *good-bad* would be globally subsumed under *evaluative,* whereas other constructs like *light* vs. *dark* would be subsumed under *descriptive:*

EVALUATIVE——————DESCRIPTIVE
Good   Bad   Light   Dark

In order to make sense out of his world, man systematizes his constructs into hierarchies for convenience in anticipating occurrences of events.

Kelly formulated an Organization Corollary to embrace his hypotheses about the systematization of constructs:

ORGANIZATION COROLLARY: *Each person characteristically evolves, for his convenience in anticipating events, a construction system embracing ordinal relationships between constructs* (1955, p. 56).

Kelly postulated that ordinal groupings were not the only way in which personal constructs are "filed." Each construct has meaning for the individual only because it is applicable to some events and is clearly inapplicable to others. A personal construct has a *range of convenience,* a collection of events that the individual construes as similar. For these events, the construct is "convenient." But the construct's range of convenience would make little sense if it were not precise enough to *exclude* some events as opposite or different. Kelly therefore proposed that every personal construct is dichotomous, bipolar in structure. In order to derive meaning from a construct, it must indicate at least two elements as similar, and a third as contrasting. Recall the structure of the REP test in which the subject is asked to find similarity between two figures and to determine how they differ from a third.

To illustrate further, suppose that there are two men, A and B. There is also a woman, C. An individual may abstract these people on the basis of a construct concerned with sex. A and B are construed as similar because they are men; C is outside the range of convenience of this construct that denotes "Masculine Sex." But note that the concept of masculinity would be meaningless were it not for the implied contrasting construct of "Femininity."

Suppose further that the individual had the following elements in mind: A and B (men), C (woman), and D (a dog). If the individual's personal construct is "masculinity," would he now group C and D, woman and dog, together as equally different from A and B? Of course not, because the woman and dog are different from the concept "masculinity" in different ways. The woman is much "more relevantly unmasculine" than the dog (Kelly, 1955, p. 60). It is *her* femininity that is opposite to masculinity. The dog is only relevant to the construct's range of convenience if the person chooses to abstract the dog as "feminine dog" or as "masculine dog." Even then, however, the construct "dog" would still fail to be as relevant to the construct "masculinity" as the woman is in establishing *human* masculinity.

Kelly's assertion that persons think in terms of dichotomies does not accord with classical logic. He felt, however, that it would accurately represent the way people actually think. In classical logic, a thing is either "A" or "not-A": masculine or not-masculine; feminine or not-feminine. But in Kelly's system, *three* elements are required to establish the identity of a thing: two similar and one contrasting. In the formal language of a theoretical postulate, the fifth thus far, Kelly formulated these implications into a corollary:

DICHOTOMY COROLLARY: *A person's construction system is composed of a finite number of dichotomous constructs* (1955, p. 59).

The word "finite" suggests that Kelly viewed the breadth of a person's construction system as limited. Indeed, several variables serve to set limits to the individual's anticipations.

Choice, Range, and Experience Corollaries: Limitations of Anticipation

Individuals are perpetually confronted with choices between the dichotomous poles of their anticipations of events. The person must adopt as his guiding construct one or the other pole of a contrasting pair. It is at this point that the person experiences uncertainty, the conflict of decision. Two choices confront him: He may decide to widen his perspective, including more, and therefore possibly uncertain, elements into his decision making; or he may decide to restrict his perspective, to "stand pat" with what he already knows as a means of assuring his continued predictive power with familiar people and events. In either case, whatever his conduct, he will be changed by it, for "he places relative values upon the ends of his dichotomies" (Kelly, 1955, p. 65). As the individual chooses one of each of his dichotomous constructs to live by, he simultaneously chooses among and thereby ranks his values.

The person is guided in his choice of personal constructs by a basic urge to enhance and maintain his ability to anticipate events reliably. Thus, his eventual choices will be those that in his view provide greater or more reliable predictive power. His choices are designed to achieve what in other psychologists' language would be called self-security, defense of the self, or anxiety reduction. Kelly formulated his sixth corollary around these ideas about the individual's choices:

CHOICE COROLLARY: *A person chooses for himself that alternative in a dichotomized construct through which he anticipates the greater possibility for extension and definition of his system* (1955, p. 64).

A seventh corollary stated the limits of the individual's choices:

RANGE COROLLARY: *A construct is convenient for the anticipation of a finite range of events only* (1955, p. 68).

Thus, the individual's personal construction system is limited in its range of application by his interpretation of what is relevant to him and to the reliability of his predictions. For example, if we wish to ascertain what an individual means by the construct "respect vs. contempt," we need to know not only those acts or behaviors that he regards as evidencing "respect," but also those he considers on the basis of his experience as evidencing "contempt." So far we are on familiar ground. For to understand an individual's construction of "respect," we must know both what he *excludes* from one pole of the construct and what is considered by him as relevant to the other. This concept was previously implied by the Dichotomy Corollary. But there is a further implication contained in the Range Corollary.

The Range Corollary implies, according to Kelly's elaboration of its stark language, that any construct is *limited* to a finite range of events that fall within the *experience of the individual* and that he considers *relevant*. *Relevancy* is the limiting factor. What is outside the range of a given construct is not considered as contrasting or opposite; it is viewed as *irrelevant*.

People do change their interpretations of relevancy, include more or fewer events in their world-view, as experience demands. Kelly was prompted to take the fact of change into account by proposing an eighth proposition:

> EXPERIENCE COROLLARY: *A person's construction system varies as he successively construes the replications of events* (1955, p. 72).

When an individual's anticipation of an event is violated and fails to conform to his expectation, he is compelled to modify his construct system. He changes his predictions. If he did not change with changing events, the person would grow more and more distant from reality. But the individual is never a merely passive reflection of life's stream of events:

> A person can be a witness to a tremendous parade of episodes and yet, if he fails to keep making something out of them, or if he waits until they have all occurred before he attempts to reconstrue them, he gains little in the way of experience from having been around when they happened. *It is not what happens around him that makes a man experienced; it is the successive construing and reconstruing of what happens, as it happens, that enriches the experience of his life.* [Kelly, 1955, p. 73; italics added]

Clearly, Kelly meant to emphasize that it is only the individual who actively participates in his world who is changed by it. For in striving to make sense of the continuous flux of life's events, the individual simultaneously changes himself with each imposition of a new sense-making construction. The need to know what to expect is therefore the great driving force of human nature.

Taken together, the Choice, Range, and Experience corollaries were designed to make obsolete such classical psychological terminology as drive, motivation, anxiety, and learning. It is not that Kelly abandoned these concepts. Rather, he viewed them as inherent in the more fundamental process of the individual's attempts to predict, control, and modify his predictions in the light of experience. For Kelly, man is the intellectual animal.

Motivation in Kelly's system may therefore be subsumed under the concept of man's need to predict; anxiety is construed as the product of the violation of his anticipations; and learning is inherent in the process of continual modification and definition of his construction system as the individual attempts to preserve the order and regularity he has imposed on life.

Modulation and Fragmentation Corollaries: Variation versus Stability

When a person makes a change in his construction system, that alteration is in itself an event capable of being construed. The person construes himself as changing. In fact, the very changes he is likely to make emerge only from the framework of his entire system of constructs. Any change in construction must therefore be placed in context, must be interpreted in the light of its effect on the entire system. Just as the scientist may use his theory as a guide to making new observations, the individual employs his construction system to make new constructions. And just as the scientist's theory may become a set of intellectual blinders, the individual's construction system permits him to see as possible only certain changes.

Certain of the individual's constructs are uniquely susceptible to change. Such constructs are said to be *permeable*. "A construct is permeable if it will admit to its range of convenience new elements which are not yet construed within its framework" (Kelly, 1955, p. 79). Conversely, constructs that will admit of no new elements are said to be *impermeable*. The implications of permeable and impermeable constructs were formulated by Kelly into a ninth proposition:

MODULATION COROLLARY: *The variation in a person's construction system is limited by the permeability of the constructs within whose range of convenience the variants lie* (1955, p. 77).

For example, early in life an individual may divide the people in his world into the two classes of the construct "fear vs. domination." There are, consequently, in his view those whom he fears, and those whom he may dominate. With the passing of years, this dichotomy may be interpreted as somewhat childish. The notion of "childishness," being itself a construct, has, of course, its opposite pole: "maturity." If this new construct, "childishness vs. maturity," is *permeable,* the individual may be able to subsume his previous construct, "fear vs. domination," under "childishness" as a rejected value. Under the pole of "maturity" he incorporates a totally new construct: "respect vs. contempt." He is now, consequently, in a position to redivide his acquaintances in what he perceives to be a more mature fashion: those whom he respects versus those whom he holds in contempt (1955, p. 82).

The permeability of the superordinal construct, "childishness vs. maturity," allows for this *modulation* or "fine-tuning" of the construct system whereby the respect-contempt variant is assimilated under the permeable "maturity" construct.

Sometimes, however, an individual may employ subsystems of permeable superordinal constructs in such a way that one subsystem is not logically derivable from another. Yet, on the whole, from the point of view of the entire construct system, the new construct is compatible with the individual's broad view of life. Kelly termed this theoretical assumption, his tenth, the

FRAGMENTATION COROLLARY: *A person may successively employ a variety of construction subsystems which are inferentially incompatible with each other* (1955, p. 83).

Kelly emphasized the significance of the Fragmentation Corollary:

> It should make even clearer the assumed necessity for seeking out the regnant construct system [that is, the larger whole system and its dominant themes] in order to explain the behavior of men, rather than seeking merely to explain each bit of behavior as a derivative of its immediately antecedent behavior. [1955, p. 83]

It is thus possible for a person to act in a way that is contradictory to his previous views, but which he *feels* is consistent with a momentarily dominant interpretation of events. Despite the piecemeal inconsistencies, the entire pattern of his life, his global anticipations of his world are always consistent with his *immediate* behavior. It is in this larger sense that a person's behavior is "logically" derivable from his "master life plan."

> . . . while a person's bets on the turn of minor events may not appear to add up, his wagers on the outcome of life do tend to add up. He may not win each time, but his wagers, in the larger contexts, do not altogether cancel themselves out. [Kelly, 1955, p. 88]

Kelly's Modulation and Fragmentation corollaries strike an intuitively satisfying balance between the inconsistency that we observe in people's daily activities, and the general trend for individuals to behave in ways that are recognizably typical of them.

Commonality and Sociality Corollaries: Shared Experience

Two people may be exposed to the same objective events but construe them differently. If their constructions, that is, the meanings that they impose on events, are different, then their experience of the events is different. This argument is the essential burden of the Individuality Corollary, previously discussed. But, if individuals can construe things differently, it follows that at least sometimes individuals may construe events similarly. Hence, in addition to an Individuality Corollary, there is a need for a Commonality Corollary.

> COMMONALITY COROLLARY: *To the extent that one person employs a construction of experience which is similar to that employed by another, his psychological processes are similar to those of the other person* (Kelly, 1955, p. 90).

Kelly added some important distinctions to clarify the Commonality Corollary:

> It is important to make clear that we have not said that if one person has experienced the same events as another he will duplicate the other's psychological processes. . . . One of the advantages of this position is that it does not require us to assume that it would take identical events in the lives of two people to make them act alike. Two people can act alike even if they have each been exposed to quite different phenomenal stimuli. It is in the similarity in the construction of events that we find the basis for similar action, not in the identity of the events themselves. [1955, pp. 90–91]

It is probably worth pointing out that nowhere does R. D. Laing come as close to Kelly's position as in his similarity to Kelly's discussion of shared anticipations. In fact, Laing, as we have seen, employed stunningly similar terminology. Where Laing labeled the process of mutual expectations a *spiral of reciprocal perspectives,* Kelly had used the term *spiralform model* to describe the way personal construct theory could be applied to interpersonal experiences:

> James anticipates what John will do. James also anticipates what John thinks he, James, will do. James further anticipates what John thinks he [James] expects John will do. In addition, James anticipates what John thinks James expects John to predict that James will do. And so on! [Kelly, 1955, p. 94]

The similarity of concept and language between Kelly and Laing is striking, but not surprising, for both theorists are deeply concerned with phenomenal processes.

If two interacting people share similar constructions of the events in which they are involved, it follows that they may socially influence each other. Kelly's statement of this potential mutual influence is again so similar to Laing's later elaboration of the concept as to give the reader familiar with Laing's position a feeling of *déjà vu:*

> In order to play a constructive role in relation to another person one must not only, in some measure, see eye to eye with him but must,

in some measure, have an acceptance of him and his way of seeing things. We say it in another way: the person who is to play a constructive role in a social process with another person *need not so much construe things as the other person does as he must effectively construe the other person's outlook.* [1955, p. 95; italics added]

As Laing systematized his similar formulation of direct and metaperspectives, Kelly formulated his thinking into his eleventh and last proposition:

SOCIALITY COROLLARY: *To the extent that one person construes the construction processes of another, he may play a role in a social process involving the other person* (1955, p. 95).

Kelly clearly meant to emphasize that the basis of social interaction was interpersonal *understanding,* not simply shared experience. If one person can anticipate (predict) the other's behavior, he can modify his own behavior in response.

An important part of the Sociality Corollary is its use of the concept of social role. Kelly defined roles as "psychological processes based upon the role player's construction of aspects of the construction systems of those with whom he attempts to join in a social enterprise" (1955, p. 97). To put it another way, the behavior of a person evoked by his interpretation of the other's interpretation of the task on which they are engaged is his role. In Laing's terms, a role is how you act because you think the other thinks such and such about this task. Kelly's definition of role is consistent with the cognitive orientation of his theory. The definition emphasizes the subjective interpretation of the role player and his audience.

With Kelly's personal-construct theory, the imagery of the actor and his mask is again offered as an appropriate analogy of the personality that runs the risk of yielding to confusion of the role player with his role:

It may be helpful at this point to ask ourselves a question about children at Halloween. Is the little youngster who comes to your door on the night of October 31st, all dressed up in his costume and behind a mask, piping "trick or treat, trick or treat"—is that youngster *disguising* himself or is he *revealing* himself? Is he failing to be spontaneous? Is he *not* being himself? Which is the *real* child—the child behind the mask or the barefaced child who must stand up in front of adults and say "please" and "thank you"? I suspect costumes and masks worn at Halloween time, as well as uniforms worn by officers on duty, doctoral degrees, and the other devices we employ to avoid being seen as we are, are all ways we have of extricating ourselves from predicaments. . . . *But masks have a way of sticking to our faces when worn too long.* [Kelly, 1964, p. 158; last italics added]

Kelly used the mask analogy to illustrate how individuals may be trapped by "objective" language labels into believing they are the label that they portray. A social role may be played without the awareness of one or both parties to the performance, or played even when both parties do not share the same understanding of the task on which they are engaged.

Kelly's Construction of "Personality"

As Sechrest (1963, p. 229) has pointed out, Kelly's two-volume *Psychology of Personal Constructs* does not contain an explicit definition of personality. No doubt Kelly would point to the Fundamental Postulate and the eleven corollaries and say that they are his definition. In a later paper, Kelly came close to saying exactly that with a summary statement: "[Personality is] our abstraction of the activity of a person and our subsequent generalization of this abstraction to all matters of his relationship to other persons, known and unknown, as well as to anything else that may seem particularly valuable" (quoted by Sechrest, 1963, p. 229).

Kelly's basic system emphasizes the intellective nature of man. He does not dismiss unconscious determinants or dynamics, but rather construes them with the same "as if" decision-making formulation that characterizes his approach to fundamental human character. Man may not actually be a scientist, but for Kelly it is theoretically useful to construe him as if he were. Man is an anticipatory animal, not a reactive one.

The CPC Cycle: An Illustrative Case

Consider the predicament in which Jean-Mary found herself when some key personal constructs were threatened with obsolescence and note the phases through which her thinking progressed as she wrestled with various solutions:

> In the fall of her thirteenth year, when Jean-Mary was in the eighth grade, a teacher precipitated a crisis in the relationship between Jean-Mary and her younger sister, Robin. Called from her own to the sixth-grade classroom by a note from Robin's teacher, Jean-Mary was startled to find her sister tear-stained, hotly flushed, and trembling beside the blackboard in front of the class. Unable to complete an arithmetic problem in long division to the satisfaction of the teacher, Robin had to endure a tirade from the teacher, the gist of which was an unfavorable comparison to her former student, Jean-Mary.
>
> Jean-Mary appraised the situation, caught in the conflict between obedience to a respected authority figure and compassion for and

loyalty to her own sister. Unable to decide between defiance and submission, Jean-Mary froze. She was finally made to solve the long-division problem for Robin in view of the whole class. But in her own perceptive way she understood the damage that had been done to her sister and to their relationship.

In that moment of humiliating comparison a wall had been built separating the two sisters in a way that neither of them could verbalize, though the emotional import was intense.

For her part, Jean-Mary was faced with an awful realization. Up to this time, teachers had always been objects of respect and admiration. They were people to be obeyed without question. But clearly, as her experience had so painfully shown, teachers could be cruel and stupid. The problem was a triple conflict: She felt guilt for having participated against her own sister in a situation that required the wit to change one's views quickly and decisively; she experienced anger at her own gullibility in having uncritically accepted teachers as paragons of virtue; she struggled against an emerging distaste for all teachers and for schoolwork in general.

Surmounting her personal difficulties, Jean-Mary was able to reason that *some* teachers are less than perfect, and that *sometimes* being a teacher was no safeguard against cruelty and stupidity. Jean-Mary was even able to redefine her own self-image to admit that she had acted with less courage than her personal values had demanded. She resolved never again to be an unwitting pawn of her own preconceptions.

Jean-Mary's predicament illustrates a cyclic sequence of thought involving the reconstruction of important anticipations. Up to the time of her experience with the long-division episode, her construction of "teachers" could be characterized as rigidly stereotyped: "Anyone who is a teacher also has to be good, kind, intelligent, just." Kelly calls such stereotypes *constellatory constructs* (1955, p. 155). The elements of the constellatory construct are dogmatically applied to anything and to anyone labeled "teacher." A whole "constellation" of persons who are expected to be no different from those with whom she has had experience is the result.

Fortunately, Jean-Mary's constellatory construct of "teacher" also has the characteristic of permeability. It will be recalled that a permeable construct is one that is susceptible to change through the addition of new elements to its range of convenience. Constellatory constructs, however, take a bit more prodding than some less rigid forms of thought before they can be modified. When confronted with a violation of her expectancy in the form of a teacher who was mean, unjust, and stupid, Jean-Mary experienced some confusion and anxiety: "*This* teacher is not at all like 'teachers' whose behavior I think I can anticipate."

The conflict induced by the discrepancy between her anticipation and her new experience can be resolved only by a restructuring of the construct "teacher" into a more relativistic prediction that admits of variation to the stereotype of "good, just, and intelligent." From start to finish, the change in Jean-Mary's construct system involves three phases, collectively termed by Kelly the *CPC cycle* (circumspection, preemption, and control).

Phase One: Circumspection

When confronted with a situation that required her to act in a way that violated several personal constructs, Jean-Mary was forced to view the elements that composed her "teacher" construct with *circumspection*. Circumspection, in Kelly's theory, is the opposite of the rigid, dogmatic thinking characteristic of constellatory constructs. Circumspection involves the use of *propositional constructs* that allow one to reason relativistically. "A teacher is good, just, kind and intelligent, but may *sometimes* also be cruel, stupid and unjust—and a lot of other incompatible things."

A propositional construct is a mode of thinking that avoids black/white pigeonholing and "nothing but" thinking. Propositional thinking is hypothetical, tentative, and relativistic. Fortunately, Jean-Mary's construct was becoming permeable and flexible. She was thus able to enter the first phase of the CPC cycle, circumspection, and survey the situation and the persons involved for possible alternative constructions.

Phase Two: Preemption

The circumspection phase must come to an end if one is to be able to act on the propositions evolved. If Jean-Mary stayed in the circumspection phase, her thinking would have been largely devoted to creating more and more alternative ways of construing those painful events and the people involved. Circumspection had the fortunate consequences of freeing her from the rigidity of her constellatory construct of "teacher" and providing her with a more propositional version. But unless she can leave the circumspection phase, she will be permanently caught up in "rehashing" the incident and attempting to decide among the various interpretations made possible by her propositional position.

Jean-Mary must consequently narrow her range of focus and begin thinking more preemptively, more decisively. She must choose the *relevant* elements from among her propositional alternatives, pick those issues she regards as crucial, and ignore the rest. Temporarily, she must *preempt one* issue as most important to her.

She did. The issue was loyalty to her sister, and prevention of needlessly inflicted hurt, despite the admonitions of her teacher to the contrary. Unfortunately, Jean-Mary took a bit longer than circumstances required in the circumspection phase to prevent that particular incident. Kelly described the preemptive phase in this way:

The preemption of issues characterizes the "man of action." He is likely to see things in what may appear to his associates to be an oversimplified manner. He consolidates all the possible perspectives in terms of one dichotomous issue and then makes his choice between the only two alternatives he allows himself to perceive. [1955, p. 516]

Jean-Mary finally preempted the issues to one dichotomous theme: *"defiance of a heretofore respected authority figure versus allegiance to my sister."*

Phase Three: Control

Having reduced the field to one dichotomous issue, the individual still has to make the choice between the opposing poles. In Jean-Mary's case, the choice was for loyalty and the prevention of gratuitous hurt. Unfortunately for her sister, the choice stage of her thinking was a little behind schedule. Yet, in the future, when confronted with similar situations, Jean-Mary would not hesitate to act on her new constructions of events. The futurity of her new constructions is an important aspect of this final phase of the CPC cycle, for Jean-Mary was now in *control* (the final "C") of possible future conflicts.

Had the cycle come to an abrupt halt at the preemption phase with Jean-Mary unable to make the choice, she would be thrown back to the beginning of the cycle to view the situation again with circumspection and redefine the issues. She would, in a sense, be destined to speculate forever.

Some Traditional Personality Variables as Kelly Construes Them

Kelly's willingness to engage in propositional constructions about personality led him to propose some unique formulations of traditional personality variables. Time-honored concepts like the unconscious, anxiety, hostility, and guilt were given systematic redefinitions. In effect, Kelly reconstrued them in terms of personal construct theory.

The Unconscious

For many years following the long-division classroom episode, neither Jean-Mary nor Robin was able to verbalize the change that took place in their relationship. If asked how they behaved differently, Jean-Mary could only reply that there *was* a perceptible difference, but one to which she could give no precise label. The important things were the way the relationship "felt" after the incident; the subtle nonverbal changes in communication; and the unvoiced hesitancy of both sisters in assuming that they could treat each other as they always had.

In Kelly's terms, both sisters had developed a preverbal or nonverbal construct. Jean-Mary and Robin construed events in ways that influenced their behavior, but to which they were unable to attach a verbal label or word symbol (Kelly, 1955, p. 459). The only cognitive representatives of their constructions of their changed relationship were behavioral, gestural, subtle impressionistic cues that defy word description.

The concept "unconscious" is partly subsumed under Kelly's notion of pre- and nonverbal constructs. His idea is similar to that of Freud himself. Freud had proposed that repression proper consisted of the preconscious system's removal of language "cathexes" from threatening ideas that have a relationship with content already primally repressed into the unconscious (cf. Chapter 3 of this book). Kelly, however, suggests that lack of a word label alone is not sufficient to prevent a construct from entering awareness. In order for a personal construct to be truly removed from consciousness it must be *submerged* along one of its two poles.

Recall that each construct has a "similarity" pole by which two or more elements are construed as alike, and a "contrast" pole by which at least one other element is seen as different. One or the other pole of the construct may be submerged so that, for example, the similarity elements are kept out of awareness. Thus, in Jean-Mary's case, the construct "I acted *similarly* to an unjust teacher" may be submerged, while the opposite end of the construct "I am *not* like that mean, stupid teacher," is all that remains to be verbalized.

The important question is, How does one pole of a construct become submerged? In effect, we are asking, How does repression occur according to Kelly's theory? The motivated forgetting of her perceived similarity to the disliked teacher occurs through a shifting of many constructs from the total system into a new arrangement of fewer units. The threatening end of the construct is "mislaid" in the shuffle because the construct in which it formerly resided as one pole has been "refiled" or subsumed under another superordinal construct that has no room for that pole. In short, "repression" involves a redefinition of the construct system to exclude some constructs.

Submergence of one pole of a construct implies the *suspension* of whole categories of constructs from the total system. In contrast with some notions of repression, suspension implies that the idea or element is forgotten simply because the person cannot tolerate any structure within which the idea would have meaning. Once he can entertain such a structure, the idea may again become available within it (Kelly, 1955, p. 473).

Thus, for Kelly, the unconscious is translated into the concepts of nonverbal constructs, submergence, and suspension.

Anxiety

The feelings of threat that Jean-Mary experienced when confronted with a violent discrepancy between her "teacher" construct and her experience of a particular teacher could be characterized as anxiety. What made the threat so damaging was the close connection it had with her self-concept. Forced complicity in the humiliation of her sister threatened to violate Jean-Mary's *core constructs.* Constructs that compose the central anticipations by which a person sets his life goals and construes *himself* in relation to these outcomes are called core constructs (Kelly, 1955, p. 482). In every way, Jean-Mary's core constructs were in danger of imminent change.

The feeling of anxiety that results from such threats is defined by Kelly as *"the recognition that the events with which one is confronted lie outside the range of convenience of one's construct system"* (1955, p. 495). In simpler language, Jean-Mary experienced anxiety because she felt that she had totally lost her ability to understand significant people in terms of her past expectations, and what was worse, she no longer understood herself.

An individual can tolerate some incompatibility between expectancy and experience, but the degree of conflict may not be very great before changed behavior results. In Jean-Mary's case, the discrepancy between her habitual mode of thinking teachers to be kind and just, and her experience with this stupid, unjust, and cruel one was too large. Furthermore, the enforced compliance with this outrageous person threatened to provoke an entire reconstruction of her construction of her self.

Similar ideas to those of Kelly have been emerging in recent years within cognitive dissonance theory (Festinger, 1957). The notion that perceptions which violate the self-concept are motivators for attitude change has received extensive empirical investigation (cf. Aronson, 1969). Rokeach (1973, esp. Chaps. 8 and 12) has even extended the analysis to the study of values in relation to self-consistent perceptions.

Guilt

Jean-Mary felt guilty long after the classroom episode because she had acted in a way that was inconsistent with her self-image. In Kelly's terms, guilt is defined as a *"Perception of one's apparent dislodgment from his core role structure"* (1955, p. 502). What differentiates guilt from anxiety in Kelly's theory is the concept of *core role structure.*

Core role structure is roughly similar to what the existentialists call being-for-the-other and to what Laing has termed metaidentity (cf. Chapter 8 of this book). The child's core role structure is his construction of who he is *in relation to significant people,* like parents. Thus, as Sechrest has concisely stated the experience of guilt from Kelly's perspective: "Guilt arises when the individual becomes aware that he is alienated from the roles by which he maintains his most important relationships to other persons" (1963, p. 228). Hence, it was alienation from her role of "loving sister" that evoked Jean-Mary's guilt.

Aggressiveness

Kelly defined aggressiveness in a way that is clearly different from the usual usage of the term. *"Aggressiveness is the active elaboration of one's perceptual field"* (1955, p. 508).

For Kelly, the individual who actively seeks to construct a greater number of alternative choices is acting "aggressively": "They are always precipitating themselves and others into situations which require decision and action" (1955, p. 508). Kelly's manner of construing aggressiveness, therefore, includes situations that normally would not be labeled aggressive, as well as those that anyone would agree display aggression.

For example, an individual actively pursuing his hobby of autograph collecting may continually place himself in situations in which he can confront celebrities to demand their autographs. In restaurants, on the street, at theaters, despite security guards, press agents, and milling mobs, the dedicated autograph hunter braves all manner of obstacle, insults all kinds of people, and pursues his prey aggressively. The aggressive person in Kelly's view may be a "social pusher" (1955, p. 509).

The Significance of Kelly's Theory

George A. Kelly's psychology of personal constructs has been construed by other psychologists in a variety of ways. It has been interpreted as everything from existential and phenomenological to Adlerian and Jungian. Kelly did not resent any of these labels. He resented such constructions only when they were applied preemptively as if personal construct theory were "nothing but" Adlerian psychology, or "nothing but" phenomenology.

In many ways, Kelly's insistence on the accurate measurement and description of experience anticipated some of the phenomenological theories current in psychology. And his hypothesis of Man the Scientist, his conception that every man creates and tests his own hypotheses about others, has only recently come to fruition in experimental psychology where shortly before it would have been blasphemy. The work of Martin Orne on demand characteristics (1962; 1969; 1973), Rosenthal and Jacobsen's study of "Pygmalion Effects" (1968a, 1968b), and even the implications of signal-detection theory as a decision model of behavior (cf. Monte, 1975, Chap. 4) seem to be delayed recognition that Kelly was correct. The whole area of artifact in behavioral research and the contaminating influences of subjects' hypotheses about the experimenter would profit from a consideration of Kelly's position (cf. Rosenthal & Rosnow, 1969).

Summary

George A. Kelly's theory of personal constructs is built upon his firm conviction that every man behaves "as if" he were a scientist. Each of us, out of the fundamental human need to understand the world, creates and tests hypotheses about the behavior of significant others. Kelly formulated a Fundamental Postulate to embody this concept: *"A person's processes are psychologically channelized by the ways in which he anticipates events"* (1955, p. 46).

Eleven corollaries expand this basic theme:

1. *Construction Corollary:* A person anticipates events by construing their replications.

2. *Individuality Corollary:* Persons differ from each other in their construction of events.

3. *Organization Corollary:* Each person characteristically evolves, for his convenience in anticipating events, a construction system embracing ordinal relationships between constructs.

4. *Dichotomy Corollary:* A person's construction system is composed of a finite number of dichotomous constructs.

5. *Choice Corollary:* A person chooses for himself that alternative in a dichotomized construct through which he anticipates the greater possibility for extension and definition of his system.

6. *Range Corollary:* A construct is convenient for the anticipation of a finite range of events only.

7. *Experience Corollary:* A person's construction system varies as he successively construes the replications of events.

8. *Modulation Corollary:* The variation in a person's construction system is limited by the permeability of the constructs within whose ranges of convenience the variants lie.

9. *Fragmentation Corollary:* A person may successively employ a variety of construction subsystems that are inferentially incompatible with each other.

10. *Commonality Corollary:* To the extent that one person employs a construction of experience which is similar to that employed by another, his psychological processes are similar to those of the other person.

11. *Sociality Corollary:* To the extent that one person construes the construction processes of another, he may play a role in a social process involving the other person.

Kelly's early experience as a professor of psychology in a small Kansas college in the Great Depression of the thirties harbored the roots of his philosophy of *constructive alternativism.* Through a variety of experiences with Freudian therapy and an overburdened schedule of clients, Kelly became convinced that man can construe events in different ways if only he is provided with the support to undertake the risk.

Kelly created on the basis of his theory an instrument of appraisal, the Role Construct Repertory Test (REP), and a therapeutic auxiliary technique called fixed-role therapy. The REP test requires the individual to systematically compare his personal interpretations of the roles of significant people. Such comparisons can then be analyzed impressionistically or objectively with the tools of correlation and factor analysis. Fixed-role therapy involves the psychologist's writing a personality sketch that differs in significant ways from those by which the client construes his life. The client is then invited to enact the role for two or more weeks. In many cases the alternative construction of events embodied in the fixed-role sketch is sufficient to aid the client in construing differently the events of his life and himself.

Personal constructs may be conceived as a person's means of making sense of life. Sometimes complex interactions among a person's constructions are necessitated by the demands of reality. Thus, for example, the circumspection-preemption-control cycle (CPC) involves the person in a restructuring of his construct system in three phases: (1) the circumspection phase, which involves propositional construction of events so that violations of old constructs or new evidence can be appraised and assimilated; (2) the preemption phase, during which the individual must narrow his constructions to one significant dichotomous construct that he interprets as most relevant; and (3) the control or choice phase, in which the individual commits himself to action on the basis of his decision to accept one or the other pole of the dichotomous construct seized upon in phase two.

Kelly's system has led to often novel formulations of basic personality constructs like the unconscious, anxiety, aggression, and guilt. Generally, each of these variables is defined in terms of the individual's capacity to modify and rearrange his system of constructs, and the emotional byproducts of those constructs that fail to predict events reliably.

FOR FURTHER READING

Kelly's influence as a personality theorist has waxed and waned with changing fashion in psychology. In consequence, the number of research studies or original theoretical works connected to personal construct theory is limited. Kelly's own comprehensive masterwork is the two-volume *Psychology of Personal Constructs* (New York: W. W. Norton, 1955). The first three chapters of vol. 1 of this work have been published as a self-contained paperback introduction to Kelly's theory under the title *A Theory of Personality: The Psychology of Personal Constructs* (New York: W. W. Norton, 1963).

Some of Kelly's theoretical papers have been organized by Brendan Maher into a single volume, *Clinical Psychology and Personality: Selected Papers of George Kelly* (New York: Wiley, 1969). Of particular significance among the papers in this volume is the one entitled "The Language of Hypothesis: Man's Psychological Instrument." Lee Sechrest, a student of Kelly's, provides an overview of Kelly's theory in his chapter "The Psychology of Personal Constructs," in Wepman and Heine (Eds.), *Concepts of Personality* (Chicago: Aldine, 1963), pp. 206–233.

The collection of research papers contained in D. Bannister and J. M. Mair's (Eds.) *The Evaluation of Personal Constructs* (New York: Academic Press, 1968; esp. chaps. 3, 4, and 10) will provide some indication of the investigations stimulated by Kelly's ideas. In a similar way, J. C. Bonarius' review, "Research in the Personal Construct Theory of George A. Kelly: Role Construct Repertory Test and Basic Theory," in vol. 2 of B. A. Maher (Ed.), *Progress in Experimental Personality Research* (New York: Academic Press, 1965), indicates the kinds of questions that have been asked with Kelly's concepts.

More recent research efforts can be surveyed in D. Bannister's (Ed.) collection of papers entitled *Perspectives in Personal Construct Theory* (New York: Academic Press, 1970). Bannister and F. Fransella have put together a paperback book summarizing Kelly's theory and surveying their own and others' research efforts on its behalf: *Inquiring Man: The Theory of Personal Constructs* (Baltimore: Penguin, 1971).

10 ERIK ERIKSON AND ERICH FROMM
Psychoanalytic Social Psychology

In youth you find out what you care to do and who you care to be. . . .
In young adulthood you learn whom you care to be with. . . . In adulthood,
however, you learn to know what and whom you can take care of.

ERIK ERIKSON, *Dimensions of a New Identity*

Love of life or love of the dead is the fundamental alternative that confronts
every human being.

ERICH FROMM, *The Anatomy of Human Destructiveness*

Erikson Constructs the Female: Inner Space

Ten-, eleven-, and twelve-year-old California boys and girls were invited
by Erik Erikson to construct on a table top with the available toy figures
and blocks an "imaginary moving picture" (Erikson, 1950, p. 98). Over the
course of a year and a half, 150 young people constructed nearly 450 such
scenes, although most of them failed to follow Erikson's instructions completely. Thus, only six or so of the youngsters constructed scenes based on
movies, and only a few of the toy figures were ever named after famous
actors.

Much to Erikson's surprise, "after a moment of thoughtfulness, the
children arranged their scenes as if guided by an inner design. . . ." (1950,
p. 98). For this and other reasons, Erikson regarded the play constructions
as significant personality revelations. In fact, Erikson detected quite early
in his sequence of observations certain *common elements* of design and
topography that distinguished boys' use of blocks and figures from the
girls' fabrications with these same materials. Figures 10–1 and 10–2 illustrate two representative constructions. With Freud's conception of psychosexual development in mind (see Chapter 2), even the most skeptical
student of personality will not find it difficult to predict which of these
drawings represents a boy's imaginary construction and which of them
depicts the girl's.

Inspection of Figures 10–1 and 10–2 will reveal that the materials Erikson
employed were quite ordinary: dolls representing family figures, some

FIGURE 10-1

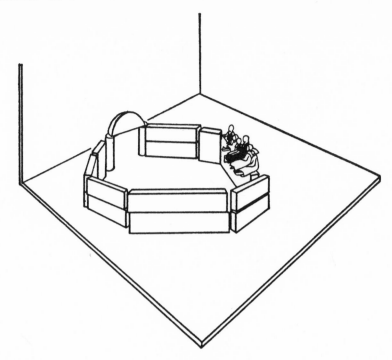

FIGURE 10-2

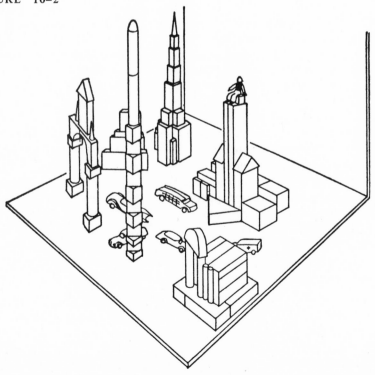

uniformed figures representing policemen, an Indian, monk, aviator, wild and domestic animals, furniture, automobiles, and a large assortment of wooden blocks. Yet the constructions of Figures 10–1 and 10–2 are vastly different. Figure 10–1 depicts a circular *enclosure* with an arched entranceway within which are seated several family figures. The design of the construction in Figure 10–1 is relatively *static,* exhibiting little movement and no real action. In fact, the dominant feeling of Figure 10–1 is "peacefulness."

By contrast, Figure 10–2 is characterized by tall *projections* and *dynamic* or stressful activity. The whole feeling of Figure 10–2 is one of controlled energy and potential danger. A figure balances precariously atop one of the elevated buildings. There are automobiles and trucks present in the "streets" of the scene, suggesting bustling city activities. The central and tallest construction, resembling a rocket, is built from a teetering and shaky selection of blocks. The dominant tone of Figure 10–2 is "excitement."

If, in true psychoanalytic spirit, you have made predictions about the sex of the persons who constructed the figures, you will, no doubt, not be surprised that the peaceful enclosure of Figure 10–1 was fabricated by a girl, whereas the tense array of skyward projections in Figure 10–2 was created by a boy. Erikson summarized his overall findings with 300 boys and girls:

> . . . the girl's scene is [typically] a house *interior,* represented either as a configuration of furniture without any surrounding walls or by a simple *enclosure* built with blocks. In the girl's scene, people and animals are mostly *within* such an interior or enclosure, and they are primarily people or animals in a *static* (sitting or standing) position. Girls' enclosures consist of low walls, i.e., only one block high, except for an occasional *elaborate doorway.* These interiors of houses with or without walls were, for the most part, expressly *peaceful.* Often, a little girl was playing the piano. In a number of cases, however, the interior was *intruded* by animals or dangerous men.
>
> Boys' scenes are either houses with elaborate walls or façades with *protrusions* such as cones or cylinders representing ornaments or cannons. There are *high towers,* and there are entirely *exterior* scenes. In boys' constructions more people and animals are *outside* enclosures or buildings, and there are more *automotive* objects and animals *moving* along streets and intersections. . . . While *high structures* are prevalent in the configurations of the boys, there is also much play with the danger of *collapse* or downfall; *ruins* were exclusively boys' constructions. [1968, pp. 270–271]

Erikson concluded from his study that a child's organization of play space parallels the morphology (structure) of his or her genital equipment. As Erikson put it in a statement that has drawn a great deal of criticism: ". . . in the male, an *external* organ, *erectable* and *intrusive* in character, serving the channelization of *mobile* sperm cells; in the female, *internal* organs, with vestibular *access,* leading to *statically expectant* ova" (1968, p. 271, italics added; cf. Erikson, 1950, p. 106). Erikson acknowledged that the differences in spatial organization of the play materials might also be indicative of the social expectations enforced by parents in rearing boys differently from girls. Thus, the boy's outward and upward projections may be his means of expressing his *learned* desire to achieve "high standing" and to be aggressive, mobile, and independent. Likewise, the girl's preoccupation with house interiors and enclosed, static space might be evidence of the social expectations modeled by parents to the effect that little girls eventually take care of a home, bear children, and rear them within its peaceful confines (Erikson, 1950, p. 106).

Biological, Cultural, and Psychological Components of Development

In a famous essay, "Womanhood and the Inner Space" (in Erikson, 1968), Erikson attempted to blend biological, cultural, and psychological interpretations of his findings. The purely *biological* interpretation asserts that preadolescents are overly concerned with their bodies and with their developing sexual equipment. Therefore, it is a natural consequence that play activities reflect in their structure the structure of the sexual equipment that is the object of the child's concern. The *social* interpretation restricts its explanation to the impact of learned attitudes and preferences. Thus, boys learn to enjoy the outdoors, girls the indoors; boys learn to seek adventure and excitement, girls learn to seek the tranquillity of family love and homemaking skills. The *psychological* (psychoanalytic) view emphasizes the unconsciously *symbolic* implications of the child's construction of play space. Hence, the psychological interpretation hinges on the boy's castration fear and on the girl's penis envy, an interpretation that will require some elaboration.

Following Freud's conception of psychosexual development, Erikson suggested that the girl experiences a genital trauma when she discovers that she does not have a penis. Again, following orthodox psychoanalytic doctrine, this early trauma causes the girl to turn from her mother to the father. She realizes that mother shares this lack and assumes that, indeed, it was mother who cheated her of the envied possession in the first place. Unlike Freud, however, Erikson shifted his focus of attention from this early "trauma" to the girl's growing sense of competence in being uniquely different from men. It is more important, Erikson argued, to understand the girl's transition from "a 'passive' renunciation of male activity to the purposeful and competent pursuit of activities consonant with the possession of ovaries, a uterus, and a vagina . . ." (1968, p. 275).

In essence, Erikson shifted psychoanalysis' traditional concern with abnormal, defensively motivated behaviors to a concern with the normal functioning of the healthy ego once the Oedipal and Electra complexes are resolved. Thus, rather than concentrate exclusively on the girl's defensive substitution of potential motherhood for the lost penis, Erikson preferred to focus attention on the girl's acceptance of the uniquely productive "inner spaces" of her own body. The issue, consequently, was changed from the girl's presumed resentment over not being a boy to her positive identification with womanhood, to her sense of solidarity with the femininely creative models at her disposal.

The differences, then, in spatial constructions evidenced by the boys and girls in the California study were to be interpreted as the result of *pervasive* and *combined* effects of one's sense of one's own body, one's social role, and one's psychosexual adjustments (Erikson, 1950, p. 108). In Erikson's view, significant differences in the way space is organized by boys and girls exist because "a profound difference exists between the sexes in the experience of the ground plan of the human body" (1968, p. 273).

Boys organize their play constructions in a way that parallels the anatomical construction and function of their genital equipment: *protrusive, extensive, intrusive,* and *mobile.* By contrast, because the biological ground plan of the girl's genital equipment revolves around internal, enclosing organs, girls organize their spatial constructions in a way that parallels the structure and function of their bodies: *enclosing, accessible, "expectant."*

Thus each child's play construction evidenced the *predisposing* effects of the individual's sense of his own body. But each play construction also evidenced the influence of social and psychological factors as they merged in the child's characteristic and personal way of dealing with a world that he himself creates. To some extent, Erikson was asserting that "anatomy is destiny," just as Freud had once paraphrased Napoleon's famous dictum that "history is destiny."

> Am I saying, then, that "anatomy is destiny"? Yes, it is destiny, insofar as it determines not only the range and configuration of physiological functioning and its limitations but also, to an extent, personality configurations. The basic modalities of woman's commitment and involvement naturally also reflect the ground plan of her body. . . . We may mention in passing woman's capacity on many levels of existence to actively *include,* to accept, "*to have and to hold*"—but also to *hold on,* and *hold in.* She may be protective with high selectivity and overprotective without discrimination. . . . So far I have only reiterated the physiological rock-bottom which must neither be denied nor given exclusive emphasis. For a human being, in addition to having a body, is *somebody,* which means an indivisible personality and a defined member of a group. . . . In other words, anatomy, history, and personality are our combined destiny. [Erikson, 1968, p. 285]

From his psychoanalytic perspective, Erikson identified the ego as the locus of the merging elements of biological, social, and psychosexual trends. The ego mediates between bodily and personal experiences, and between social and bodily experience:

> To do so, [the ego] uses psychological mechanisms common to both sexes—a fact which makes intelligent communication, mutual understanding, and social organization possible. . . . Here, then, the fact that a woman, whatever else she may also be, never is not-a-woman creates unique relations between her individuality, her somatic existence, and her social potentials and demands that the feminine identity be studied and defined in its own right. [Erikson, 1968, pp. 289–290]

Erikson thus emphasized that, although there are certainly commonalities across people in the way their egos function, substantial and real differences exist between the sexes that deserve special study and open acknowledgment.

"Inner Space" Reconsidered: The Critics

Erikson's approach to a psychoanalytic understanding of sex differences serves as a good model of his entire personality theory. His refocusing of psychoanalytic principles to understand the person's conscious reality functioning was instrumental in establishing contemporary psychoanalytic ego psychology. However, Erikson's early study of sex differences in ego function did not go uncriticized.

In an article entitled, "Psychology Constructs the Female, or the Fantasy Life of the Male Psychologist (with Some Attention to the Fantasies of His Friends, the Male Biologist and the Male Anthropologist)," Naomi Weisstein (1971) objected vigorously to Erikson's interpretations of femininity. Weisstein's objections ranged from a purely ideological dispute with Erikson to a critique of his (and others') methodology.

First, Weisstein argued that psychology does not know what women (or men) are really like because psychological theory routinely reflects only the cultural consensus or stereotypes of male and female personalities. Second, Weisstein suggested that personality research in general has failed to find any *innate* and reliably measured determinants that shape personality or sex differences. Third, and last, Weisstein feels that, contrary to Erikson's notion of a *biologically* determined body ground plan that predisposes a person's behavior to evidence sex-linked traits, people behave and interpret their own behavior in accord with *social* expectations. Thus, sex differences, if they exist, are likely to be a product of the environment's impact, and of male psychologists' prejudices.

Reactions like Weisstein's prodded Erikson to reconsider his concepts in the light of the feminist movement. In an essay entitled, "Once More the Inner Space" (1975), Erikson echoed Freud's early reaction to his own critics. Erikson suggested that the various liberation movements had taught him by their reaction to his concepts that even in the "post-Freudian era" people can be threatened by psychoanalytic findings. Furthermore, Erikson implied that at least some of his critics had found it necessary to repress or distort his findings. Like Freud's earlier revelations, these concepts provoked a painful conscious recognition of powerful unconscious forces and determinants (Erikson, 1975, p. 227). Thus, to begin with, Erikson's reconsideration of his position on sex differences took the form of a reaffirmation of his essential points.

Erikson reasserted that his concept of the biological ground plan of the body as the basis of behavioral differences was not proposed as the exclusive determinant. To reach a genuine understanding of sex differences in personality, biological, cultural, and psychoanalytic insights *in combination* must be brought to bear on the problem, a point that his critics sometimes chose to ignore. In particular, Erikson took issue with Elizabeth Janeway (1971), a critic who objected to his concept that a woman is "never-not-a-woman." Janeway felt that such a notion implies an absolutism or deterministic finality that denies the importance of free choice and independently undertaken action in shaping one's life. In effect, Janeway believed, Erikson had asserted that women were inescapably bound by their biology. Erikson responded:

> ... if the reiteration (by a man) of such a verity as "never-not-a-woman" appears to be shocking, one must consider that a man is never-not-a-man, either. If to this some may respond with conviction the corresponding fact "but that is what he wants to be!" it should be remembered that a boy, under certain cultural conditions, is not even permitted to *think* that he might ever *want* to be not-a-man or not-quite-a-man with all the proud trimmings of manhood in his culture. [1975, p. 235]

Erikson was here emphasizing what he perhaps should have emphasized from the beginning: namely, that cultural, biological, and psychological role limitations or determinants are equally enforced for both sexes. The point of contention is that the *male* role, that is, the cultural male stereotype, *seems* more desirable, is treated as more desirable, by the unthinking. Yet the male is as much locked into restrictive social requirements as is the female. True liberation, for both men and women, requires a productive cultural reevaluation, "for only a renewal of social creativity can liberate both men and women from reciprocal roles which, in fact, have exploited both" (Erikson, 1975, p. 237).

Erikson further clarified his conception of sex differences when, in a rather Jungian vein, he pointed to the existence of feminine components in the male's identity:

> ... to the boy and man, womanhood combines the highest as well as the lowest connotations, so that part of his own negative identity

—the "effeminate" traits he must suppress in himself as he becomes a man—is in stark conflict with the maternal ideals he received from and continues to seek in motherly persons. . . . If the little girl, then, feels inferior because of the boy's negative attitude to the woman in himself, she also knows that she is going to be assigned superior roles by a compensatory—if variably ambivalent—valuation given her traditionally in the roles of mother and sister, value giver and teacher, lady of the house, mistress, and playmate—all potentially confining roles and yet each endowed with a specific power which forces the man, in turn, to live up to his part. [1975, pp. 239–240]

Thus, Erikson's conception of sexual identity is based on the complementarity of the sexes. His critics continue to object to his essentially Freudian stance, to his "old-fashioned" conception of cultural roles, and, most potently, to his insistence on the shaping effects of biological and psychosexual limitations. Yet, in fairness, it must be pointed out that his observational studies of boys' and girls' play constructions did reveal substantial and reliable differences. Of course it is possible to believe that Erikson exaggerated the differences, misinterpreted them, or simply lied about their pervasiveness. Errors of misinterpretation or emphasis are, indeed, valid criticisms. But these confusions can only be cleared by further research and by controlled experimentation, a strategy not much favored by psychoanalytic theorists.

Psychoanalytic Ego Psychology: Erikson's Psychosocial Perspective

Although Erikson was trained as a psychoanalyst, indeed his training analyst was Anna Freud, it is clear that in his own theorizing he has emphasized personality dimensions rather different from those of classical psychoanalytic doctrine. Grounding his analysis of sex differences in Freud's psychosexual concepts, Erikson has worked to broaden Freud's emphasis on instinctual dynamics with a consideration of *psychosocial* dynamics.

For Erikson, the fundamental personality problem is to determine how an individual adjusts to the unique set of social and historical circumstances into which he is born. Consequently, Erikson's focus of attention is about equally divided among the id, ego, and superego. The process of adjustment to instinctual, cultural, and historical circumstance, and the development of one's *sense of self* in response to these determinants, are largely the tasks of the conscious ego.

"Where id was, there ego shall be." Freud employed this pithy, one-sentence summary to reaffirm his hard-won insight that the goal of psychoanalytic therapy is to strengthen and widen the patient's ego functioning (Freud, 1933, p. 80). By strengthening the ego's control, by freeing the ego from overwhelming assaults by the unconscious id, psychoanalysis empowers the individual personality with the capacity to master its own conflicts. Yet this conception of the ego as the reality executor of personality was a long time coming in psychoanalysis (Rapaport, 1959). The original emphasis of Freud's work was on the significance of *unconscious* instinctual conflict as the root of neurotic maladjustment. Only with slow and careful reconstruction of his theory was Freud able to conceptualize the ego as an independent group of personality processes worthy of the same attention as that so long accorded the id (cf. Chapters 2 and 3 of this book).

In 1923, when Freud published his final, structural model of the mind in *The Ego and the Id,* he assigned the individual's *conscious* interactions with the environment a more central place in the psychoanalytic scheme of things. The ego was now conceptualized as fighting a battle on two fronts: It must provide realistic and safe gratifications for the unconscious impulses of the id while at the same time it steers a course well within the moral and ethical limitations set by the superego. Despite the complexity of the tasks assigned to it, the ego was still viewed by Freud as largely dependent upon the seat of its origin, the id. In this structural model, Freud had conceptualized the ego as developing out of the id as a specialized portion of this unconscious reservoir with one clear goal: to serve the id, to provide appropriate and safe gratifications by scrutinizing reality and making the necessary adjustments that would assure survival. But, as Rapaport (1959, p. 9), pointed out, the ego was viewed by Freud as the "helpless rider of the id horse," forced to steer the id impulses only in directions already chosen by the id.

By 1926, with the publication of *Inhibitions, Symptoms and Anxiety,* the ego had taken on even more complex functions as the seat of several defense mechanisms, including repression. With this increased complexity of function came a subtle theoretical change in the ego's character. No longer completely ruled by the id horse, the ego was viewed as a semi-independent rider, autonomously pursuing its own ends to protect the integrity of the personality within the sphere of social and physical reality.

Because the ego is reality-oriented, judgmental rather than impulsive, Freud conceptualized the task of the therapist as the attempt to strengthen and free the patient's ego functioning from domination by the id. When the ego is free to perform its jobs correctly, the individual is able to master id impulses, satisfy the rigid demands of the idealistic and moralistic superego, and adjust the whole personality to the changing demands of life.

Many psychoanalysts, however, were reluctant to follow Freud's theoretical lead. As Anna Freud (1936) pointed out, some psychoanalysts viewed the study of conscious ego functioning as less important, less valuable than the study of the "deeper" unconscious process of the id. In fact, some orthodox Freudians held to the view that the term *psychoanalysis* should, by definition, "be reserved for the new discoveries relating to the unconscious psychic life, i.e., the study of repressed instinctual impulses, affects, and fantasies" (A. Freud, 1936, p. 3).

In contrast to this restrictive view of psychoanalytic theory, Anna Freud suggested that contemporary psychoanalysis aims to "acquire the fullest possible knowledge of all the three institutions [i.e., id, ego, superego] of which we believe the psychic personality to be constituted and to learn what are their relations to one another and to the outside world" (1936, pp. 4–5). Thus, in Anna Freud's view, psychoanalysis had always been concerned with the individual's conscious adjustment to life. Study of the id "was always only a means to an end. And the end was invariably the same: the correction of these abnormalities and the restoration of the ego to its integrity" (A. Freud, 1936, p. 4). As a therapeutic method, psychoanalysis had lavished attention on the unconscious because these latent impulses were the *source* of conflict that enmeshed the person's conscious self in a war with his own desires. But to achieve health, and to attain understanding of total personality functioning, the psychoanalytic therapist had always striven to liberate and strengthen the patient's conscious ego.

The publication of Anna Freud's *The Ego and the Mechanisms of Defense* (1936) sparked professional interest in the ego's complex roles in relation to the id, to the superego, and to reality. Consequently, the focus of attention within psychoanalysis gradually centered on the importance of the individual's relation to *external* physical and social reality. Ego psychology was thus born from the attempts of psychoanalysts to understand with their familiar theoretical concepts the "new" fields of *reality functioning* and *interpersonal* relationships (Rapaport, 1959, p. 11). We have already seen two psychoanalytic attempts to encompass social and interpersonal reality in the theories of Karen Horney (Chapter 6) and of Harry Stack Sullivan (Chapter 7). Yet neither of these theorists felt comfortable within the mainstream of orthodox psychoanalytic tradition because Horney and Sullivan found it necessary to modify extensively or to drop altogether chief psychoanalytic tenets. Thus, for example, neither Horney nor Sullivan accepted the validity of the Oedipus complex as a universal psychosexual phenomenon.

Other theorists, however, lying more directly within the realm of orthodox psychoanalytic theory, began to adopt the new emphasis on the ego as an independent personality entity. Heinz Hartmann (1939, 1964) attempted to conceptualize an area of human behavior left relatively unexplored by Freud. Stressing ego functions developed independently of the id through normal maturation and learning, Hartmann theorized about the *conflict-free* sphere of ego operations. The essence of Hartmann's contribution lay in his strategy of conceptualizing *some* ego functions as independent of the unconscious conflicts and id impulses that reside at the center of neurotic maladjustment. Hartmann proposed that healthy adaptation to life is dependent upon those ego capacities that are autonomous of the unconscious id impulses from which they may have originated. In short, some ego functions become freed of the unconscious roots that gave them birth. Gordon Allport's principle of functional autonomy of motives is a similar concept (cf. Chapter 12).

Hartmann further suggested that the individual ego's capacities for perception, reality appraisal, learning, and problem solving may all have arisen to bring safe satisfaction to the id, but these ego functions may be maintained independently thereafter as the person confronts and masters the changing circumstances of his life. With Hartmann, social and physical reality were given equal, if not superior, weight to instinctual impulses as determinants of personality functioning. The ego was no longer the "helpless rider of the id horse." It was now an autonomous steersman directing the healthy and conflict-free adjustment of the personality to his social situation, despite the demands of the id.

Ego psychology has continued to grow in scope and sophistication. The concept of "ego strength," that is, the ability of the ego successfully to negotiate the demands of reality, has proved of some value in understanding psychotic maladjustment (Bellak, Hurvich, & Gediman, 1973). Ego psychology has also been enriched by contributions of workers outside the scope of traditional psychoanalytic doctrine. Robert White, for example, has reconceptualized Freud's psychosexual stages within the broad framework of a drive for mastery or competence. White (1960, 1972) has thus extended ego psychology into the realm of interpersonal relationships and conscious, adaptive social functioning.

Erikson's Contribution to Psychoanalytic Ego Psychology

The selective history of psychoanalytic ego psychology we have just reviewed was a necessary preliminary to the task of understanding Erikson's position within psychoanalytic theory. Perhaps more than any other "ego theorist," Erikson has achieved wide recognition beyond psychoanalysis for his specification of the stages through which an individual ego develops. In response to the crises initiated by the biological and social givens of his life, the child's ego matures in an *epigenetic* sequence of combined psycho*sexual* and psycho*social* stages.

The term epigenetic is drawn from biology and means that the structure of an organism and its sequence of development are precisely laid down in that organism's genetic code. For the organism to reach full development of its potential structure, the environment must provide specific stimulation. The structure that thus develops was rigidly predetermined by the organism's genetic endowment, but its unfolding was governed by environmental variables. For Erikson, social demands influence the ways in which the biologically determined psychosexual characteristics of the infant develop. To Freud's oral, anal, phallic, and genital stages, Erikson couples eight interpersonal crises that guide the flowering of these biologically determined developments. In short, for Erikson, Freud's psychosexual stages are biological, inescapable givens of development. The child's interpersonal milieu, however, is the psychosocial half of the equation, an aspect that pre-ego psychologists neglected.

In somewhat simplified fashion it is now possible to capsulize the difference between classical psychoanalytic doctrine and psychoanalytic ego psychology: Where Freud interpreted human behavior as the result of a clash between the biological drives of the unconscious id and the conscious ego-superego, *the ego psychologist, like Erikson, interprets human behavior as the product of an interaction between the ego-id-superego apparatus and the external, social world.* The difference may, at first, appear not to be significant. An example may underscore its importance.

For Freud, the nursing relationship between mother and infant was of supreme and lasting importance in the development of personality. In supplying the infant with breast or bottle, the mother not only relieves his accumulated hunger tension, she also establishes a reliable sequence of pleasurable stimulation. The pleasurable activities of feeding, cuddling, touching, and sucking are all motivated, in Freud's scheme, by the same generalized sexual or pleasure drive: libido. As a result, hunger reduction becomes the prototype for all later libidinal (pleasurable-sexual) satisfactions. The importance of feeding, for Freud, was the light it shed on the interaction between the biological drives of the id (e.g., hunger) and the efforts of the ego to secure satisfaction and pleasure from the external world (e.g., from mother). But Freud's focus of attention was narrowly restricted to the effects *on the id* of the ego's interaction with reality.

Like Freud, Erikson regards the nursing relationship as crucial for personality development. But unlike Freud, Erikson does not restrict his theoretical considerations to id-ego interactions or to the result of id satisfactions by the ego. Instead, the feeding situation is for Erikson a model of *social* interaction between the infant and his interpersonal world. Hunger is certainly a biological (id) manifestation; but the consequences of its satisfaction by the mother transcend the immediate pleasurable id gains. Reliable and timely satisfactions of the infant's hunger establish for him a sense of *basic trust*, a sense that external reality is trustworthy. The infant learns from his feeding experiences to anticipate interaction with significant others in one of two ways: He either views person-to-person contacts with pleasurable eagerness and relish because in the past such interchanges have been safe and comforting; or he anticipates with anxious concern all such personal contacts because, in the past, people have proven to be frustrating and pain-provoking entities. Whereas Freud emphasized the consequences of biological drive reduction for the development of id-ego relations, Erikson emphasizes the personal, conscious impact of such interaction for the ego's adjustment to social reality. Once established, basic trust endures as an independent ego characteristic, free of the id drives from which it originated. Likewise, such ego functions as perception, problem solving, and the formation of an ego identity operate independently of the drives that gave them birth. Figure 10–3 illustrates the basic differences between orthodox, classical psychoanalysis and psychoanalytic ego psychology.

It thus becomes possible to discern within Erikson's work several trends that are uniquely characteristic of psychoanalytic ego psychology.

1. Erikson emphasizes the individual's conscious adjustments to social influences. Healthy maturation, rather than neurotic and conflicted maladjustment, is of central concern.

2. Erikson attempts to build upon the instinctual theoretical framework developed by Freud by adding his own epigenetic conception of personality development. Upon the psychosexual biological givens elucidated by Freud, psychosocial influences erect the structure of personality.

3. Erikson gives explicit recognition to the fact that motives may originate in unconscious or repressed id impulses, yet these motives may become freed of their id origins as the individual lives out his particular social and historical role.

4. Erikson has conceptualized the ego as the source of the person's self-awareness. During adjustment to reality, the ego develops a sense of its own continuity with the past and with the future. In brief, the ego comes to the realization that it is an "I."

FIGURE 10–3

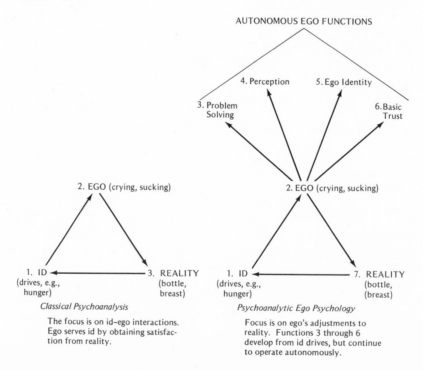

AUTONOMOUS EGO FUNCTIONS

4. Perception   5. Ego Identity

3. Problem Solving   6. Basic Trust

2. EGO (crying, sucking)   2. EGO (crying, sucking)

1. ID (drives, e.g., hunger) ← → 3. REALITY (bottle, breast)

1. ID (drives, e.g., hunger) ← → 7. REALITY (bottle, breast)

Classical Psychoanalysis

The focus is on id-ego interactions. Ego serves id by obtaining satisfaction from reality.

Psychoanalytic Ego Psychology

Focus is on ego's adjustments to reality. Functions 3 through 6 develop from id drives, but continue to operate autonomously.

Ego Identity: Sources of the Hypothesis

For life to be worthwhile, the individual must feel that his power to shape his own existence, his intention to be an autonomous self-provider, and his desires to be competently equal to life's tasks are all capacities that he himself has willingly nurtured. The healthy personality sees that the person he was, the person he is, and the person he is becoming are smooth continuations of the person he *must* be in the face of the realities that are his (Erikson, 1950, pp. 250, 269). As the executor of personality, the ego must master at the various stages of development certain important biological and social tasks to facilitate the healthy adaptation of the individual to his life circumstances.

Erikson proposed that the individual's ego progresses through a reliable sequence of stages in the development of personality from infancy to adulthood. Each successive stage in the epigenetic sequence sees the ego adding a new mode of competency for dealing with characteristic "crises" attending that phase of life. By adolescence, the central hurdle for the ego to mount is the crystallization of identity, of a sense, that is, of self-continuity. Knowing *who I am, who I am to become,* are crucial aspects of the ego's integrative task. Persons in whom the sense of self is tenuous and easily shaken are prone to a variety of pathological adaptations to life. The concept of ego-identity is complex and continually under refinement in Erikson's thinking. Thus, Erikson has wisely avoided providing any single restrictive definition of ego identity:

> I can attempt to make the subject matter of identity more explicit only by approaching it from a variety of angles. . . . At one time, then, it will appear to refer to a conscious *sense of individual identity;* at another, to an unconscious striving for a *continuity of personal character;* at a third, as a criterion for the silent doings of *ego synthesis;* and, finally, as a maintenance of an inner *solidarity* with a group's ideals and identity. [1959, p. 102]

A brief survey of Erikson's personal and clinical experiences that shaped his formulation of the concept of ego identity is in order.

Personal Sources of the Hypothesis

In 1970, Erikson published an autobiographical essay in which he traced some aspects of his own identity formation. In true psychoanalytic spirit, Erikson employed the facts of his own early life to illustrate the concept of *identity crisis* and the ultimate resolution of the crisis in the formation of an acceptable personal identity. Yet Erikson's account is somewhat less than completely candid. As one reviewer of *Life History and the Historical Moment* (1975), the book in which the autobiographical essay was reprinted, commented: "The immediately troubling thing about . . . [the autobiographical essay] is that the crises are wholly left out. . . . Our first impulse may be to feel envious, until we realize that no human being this serene can ever have lived" (Berman, 1975, p. 22). Despite the facade of serenity, Erikson provided glimpses into the motives that underlay his own intense interest in the concepts of identity and identity crisis.

As a child, Erikson was raised by his mother, Karla *née* Abrahamsen and her second husband, Theodor Homburger. Homburger, a physician, had married Erikson's mother after her first husband and his real father had abandoned her before Erikson's birth. Erikson's mother had been a resident of Denmark, and his father was apparently a native Dane. Throughout childhood, Erikson's mother and stepfather "kept secret from me the fact that my mother had been married previously. . . . They apparently thought that such secretiveness was not only workable (because children then were not held to know what they had not been told) but also advisable, so that I would feel thoroughly at home in their home" (1975, p. 27).

Nonetheless, Erikson developed a sense of "being different" from other children, and he entertained fantasies of being the son of "much better parents" who had abandoned him. Erikson's stepfather, however, did not fit the traditional image of stepfathers. Because Dr. Homburger was kindly and understanding, offering his name to the otherwise fatherless boy, Erikson has adopted Homburger as his adult middle name. But it is clear that Erikson's own choice of name—Erik Erikson—reflects his long-standing need to make his own identity,

Sometime after the age of three years, Erikson had developed the beginnings of his later identity crisis. Because his mother and stepfather, Dr. Homburger, were Jewish, Erikson's Scandinavian heritage of blue eyes, blond hair, and "flagrant tallness" enforced and intensified his feeling of somehow not belonging to his family. Further intensification of his identity crisis was produced when, as a schoolboy, Erikson was referred to as a "goy" in his stepfather's temple, whereas his schoolmates identified him as a Jew (1975, p. 27). Thus a conflicting family heritage, discordant social expectations and prejudices, and his own sense of not belonging to the family in which he grew up combined to create for Erikson an acute sense of identity confusion.

At puberty, having violated his stepfather's expectation that he, too, would become a doctor, Erikson consciously chose to be different. After graduation from a humanistic *Gymnasium,* the rough equivalent to high school, Erikson entered art school. Establishing for himself the identity of "artist," Erikson wandered through Europe, not completely aimless, but freely independent of socially enforced obligations to make something of himself: "I was a 'Bohemian' then" (1975, p. 28). At around this time, Erikson's identity crisis reached an apex of intensity, bordering on an "adolescent psychosis":

> . . . the choice of the occupational identity of "artist" meant, for many, a way of life rather than a specific occupation . . . and, as today,

it could mean primarily an anti-establishment way of life. Yet, the European establishment had created a well-institutionalized social niche for such idiosyncratic needs. A certain adolescent and neurotic shiftlessness could be contained in the custom of *Wanderschaft* [journey or excursion] . . . To be an artist, then, meant to have at least a passing identity, and I had enough talent to consider it for a while an occupational one. The trouble was, I often had a kind of work disturbance and needed time. *Wanderschaft* under those conditions meant neurotic drivenness as well as a deliberate search, even as today dropping out can be a time either of tuning in or of aimless negativism. . . . No doubt, my best friends will insist that I needed to name this crisis and to see it in everybody else in order to really come to terms with it in myself. [1975, pp. 25–26]

With the help of a youthful friend, Peter Blos, who later became a psychoanalytic expert on adolescence (e.g., 1962, 1970), Erikson overcame his crisis and learned to discipline himself to work regular hours. Joining the faculty of a school in Vienna founded by Dorothy Burlingham, Erikson met the circle around Anna Freud and, of course, her father, Sigmund Freud.

It must be obvious now what Freud came to mean to me, although, of course, I would not have had words for it at the time. Here was a mythical figure and, above all, a great doctor who had rebelled against the medical profession. Here also was a circle which admitted me to the kind of training that came as close to the role of a children's doctor as one could possibly come without going to medical school. What, in me, responded to this situation was, I think, some strong identification with my stepfather, the pediatrician, mixed with a search for my own mythical father. [Erikson, 1975, p. 29]

Much to his own surprise, Erikson was accepted by the psychoanalytic group surrounding Freud. Yet, he reports, he struggled to avoid being totally assimilated to the identity of "psychoanalyst," preferring to keep in touch with his previously formed identity of "artist." The fact that psychoanalysis then "collected at least a few men and women who did not quite belong elsewhere" admirably suited Erikson's unconsciously formed identity of "stepson" or "outsider." His professional training, therefore, was the outcome of a set of unique personal and historical circumstances. Psychoanalysis was at that period in its history when it was considered "outside" the medical establishment. Not quite belonging elsewhere, Erikson found in this group of outcasts a congenial compromise solution to the conflict between his "Bohemian" identity and his growing need for commitment to a productive cause. If medicine treated psychoanalysis as an unwanted stepson, psychoanalysis accepted Erikson as a long-lost son.

Except for his formal training under Anna Freud in psychoanalysis with children, and the possession of a Montessori diploma, Erikson neither sought nor obtained any other professional credentials. His eventual complete identification with the profession of "psychoanalyst" satisfied two important requirements: As a psychoanalyst, Erikson followed his stepfather's wish that he, too, enter medicine; yet, as a psychoanalyst, Erikson was able to remain aloof from medicine in accord with his own need to be an outsider while still practicing a clinical specialty. Erikson's need to identify himself as an outsider led not only to a successful resolution of his identity crisis, but also to nearly fifty years of productive clinical and theoretical work.

Clinical Sources of the Identity Hypothesis: War Veterans

When Erikson left Nazi-dominated Europe to seek citizenship in the United States, he worked for a time at the Mt. Zion Veterans' Rehabilitation Clinic in San Francisco. In treating military casualties, Erikson first coined his now famous phrase "identity crisis" to describe the chaotic, profoundly confused mental state of soldiers hospitalized for "battle neuroses." As Erikson described these soldiers, it was as if their egos had lost their shock-absorbing capacity (1968, p. 66).

> Anxiety and anger were provoked by anything too sudden or too intense, a sudden sensory impression from outside, an impulse, or a memory. A constantly "startled" sensory system was attacked by external stimuli as well as by somatic sensations: heat flashes, palpitation, cutting headaches. Insomnia hindered the nightly restoration of sensory screening by sleep and that of emotional rebinding by dreaming. . . . Above all, the men felt that they "did not know any more who they were": there was a distinct loss of ego identity. The sense of sameness and continuity and the belief in one's social role were gone. [1968, p. 67]

Erikson reported an illustrative case of a marine who had suffered loss of ego identity sometime after discharge from the service. The soldier told Erikson of a particular incident during an assault on a beachhead in the Pacific under enemy fire. Lying in the darkness, the soldier had experienced intense anger, rage, disgust, and fear at the failure of the "brass" to provide supportive air cover and naval reinforcements. It was as though he and his group of marines had to take the enemy's fire "lying down." As a medical officer, Erikson's patient was unarmed on that beachhead, and the mounting rage and panic he had experienced, and the similar feelings expressed by the men around him, seemed to have little to do with his medical duties. His memories of the remainder of the night on the beach were fogged and incomplete. The soldier claimed that medical corpsmen were ordered to unload ammunition instead of attending to medical duties. Sometime during the night, he recalled, somebody handed him a submachine gun—the remainder of what transpired was a blank. The following morning he found himself in an improvised field hospital, suffering from a severe intestinal fever.

That night, the enemy attacked from the air, and though all able-bodied men found shelter, he was unable to move or to help others. For the first time, he experienced real fear, a fear that, unlike the emotions he had felt on the beach, he knew to be his. After evacuation from the beach, he succumbed to raging headaches, chronic anxiety, and "jumpiness" to all sudden sounds and sensory impressions. In therapy with Erikson, the young ex-marine was able to trace his difficulties back to the night of the attack when somebody had forced him to take the submachine gun. He had observed his superior officer swearing and violently angry, and perhaps a little afraid. He told Erikson that the officer's behavior had disillusioned him because such an outpouring of rage and anger by an officer was shocking conduct. Erikson immediately saw the contradiction: Why was this soldier so outraged by anger in others; why was it necessary for him to see himself as a paragon of strength, insusceptible to anger or fear?

The soldier's free associations led back to his childhood and to an incident when his mother in a drunken rage had pointed a gun at him. Taking the gun from her, he broke it in half and threw it out the window. He left home for good, and, seeking the protection of a fatherly man (his school principal), he promised never to drink, swear, indulge sexually, or touch a gun (Erikson, 1950, p. 41). When his fatherly superior officer had exploded with violent oaths that night on the beachhead, and when someone had thrust a gun into his hands, his carefully formed sense of personal identity as a "good," moral, and benevolent person crumbled.

Thus, three factors conspired to provoke the battle neurosis to which this young man succumbed. First, his sense of shared identity with his group was threatened by the growing panic and anger of the men on the beachhead. Second, the constant assault on the soldier's bodily integrity by the real dangers of the battle, exploding bombs and the like, combined with his intestinal fever, led to a breakdown of his ego's capacity to ward off and control external stimuli. Third, the loss of his inner sense of personal continuity, or ego identity, in the face of his officer's anger and fear and his own possession of a gun served to undercut the remaining supports binding together his personality functioning. His lifelong rigidity and adherence to idealized moral values had served as a defensive bulwark against disturbing life circumstances. Now, in battle, these defenses were crumbling as he began to feel fear, rage, and panic (Erikson, 1950, p. 43). Erikson summarized his findings in this way:

> What impressed me most was the loss in these men [i.e., war veterans] of a sense of identity. They knew who they were; they had a

personal identity. But it was as if, subjectively, their lives no longer hung together—and never would again. There was a central disturbance of what I then started to call ego identity. At this point it is enough to say that this sense of identity provides the ability to experience one's self as something that has continuity and sameness, and to act accordingly. In many cases there was at the decisive time in the history of the breakdown a seemingly innocent item such as the gun in our medical soldier's unwilling hands: a symbol of evil, which endangered the principles by which the individual had attempted to safeguard personal integrity and social status in his life at home. [1950, p. 42]

Thus the concept of ego identity proved to be an indispensable tool in understanding the combined impact on personality of changes in the biological organism, changes in the ego, and changes in the social milieu (Erikson, 1950, p. 44).

Anthropological Sources of the Identity Hypothesis: Oglala Sioux

Erikson accepted an appointment with the Yale Institute of Human Relations within the Medical School. Under the leadership of John Dollard, Erikson was able to secure financial support for a field trip to South Dakota to study child-rearing practices among the Oglala subtribe of the Sioux at the Pine Ridge Indian Reservation.

The expressed purpose of the field trip was to "try to find out whence came the tragic apathy with which Sioux Indian children quietly accepted and then quietly discarded many of the values taught them in the immensely thoughtful and costly experiment of federal Indian education" (Erikson, 1950, p. 114). Teachers in the government-sponsored education program complained of a variety of character defects in the Indian children they taught.

Truancy was the most outstanding complaint: when in doubt Indian children simply ran home. The second complaint was stealing, or at any rate gross disregard of property rights as we understand them. This was followed by apathy, which included everything from lack of ambition and interest to a kind of bland passive resistance in the face of a question or of a request. Finally, there was too much sexual activity, a term used for a variety of suggestive situations ranging from excursions into the dark after dances to the mere huddling together of homesick girls in boarding-school beds. . . . The discussion was pervaded by the mystified complaint that no matter what you do to these children, they do not talk back. They are stoical and non-committal. [Erikson 1950, p. 125]

Erikson detected in his discussion with these teachers a deep and unconscious "fury" that even the most well-disciplined educators had allowed to affect their professional judgments. So disappointed, so discouraged, and so disillusioned were many of the teachers at their lack of success with these children that they had come to regard their failures as the fault of some inherent Indian personality flaw. Erikson, operating from his psychosocial perspective, felt that the difficulty lay elsewhere.

In order to understand the behaviors to which the teachers objected so strenuously, Erikson undertook a historical investigation of the Indians' tribal identity. The members of the Oglala tribe lived on land allotted to them by the federal government in a final act of political and economic subjugation. In times past, when the Sioux ranged over their land as masters of territory and of themselves, the buffalo was central to their lives. As a source of food, clothing, and fuel, the buffalo was the very nucleus around which the Sioux shaped their nomadic hunting existence. The early white settlers disturbed the hunting grounds with their homesteads and domesticated cattle, and they "playfully, stupidly, slaughtered buffalo by the hundred thousands" (Erikson, 1950, p. 116). When gold fever struck these early settlers, they invaded the Sioux's holy mountains, game preserves, and winter refuge. An appeal by the Sioux to the United States Army generals, warrior to warrior, was of little help in setting matters right.

The outcome of the resulting chronic warfare between settlers and Sioux could be capsulized in the tragedy of two massacres. General Custer's decisive defeat by Sioux was avenged years later at Wounded Knee by the Seventh Army cavalry's massacre of a small band of Indians they outnumbered by four to one. Erikson summarized this climax to the gradual erosion of the Indians' tribal identity:

> The young and seething American democracy lost the peace with the Indian when it failed to arrive at a clear design of either conquering or colonizing, converting or liberating, and instead left the making of history to an arbitrary succession of representatives who had one or another of these objectives in mind—thus demonstrating an inconsistency which the Indians interpreted as insecurity and bad conscience. [1950, p. 117]

Thus, the government policy of establishing reservations for the Indian, "guiding" the education of Indian children, and attempting to assimilate the Indian culture by foisting the larger society's values on this subculture resulted in the dissolution of the Indian's identity. Instead of fostering independence, enforced dependence of the Indian on the government was accomplished. In place of mutal trust, chronic suspicion and disappointment were engendered by the government's inconsistencies of policy. Where the Indian had a right to his sense of history as a "man wronged," the overcomplex government machinery regulating "Indian affairs" had substituted a sense of self as "one to whom something is owed" (Erikson, 1950, p. 119).

The crux of the problem, in Erikson's estimation, was the shock of contact between the two cultures. White, middle-class, competitive values modeled by the educators and government advisers were singularly inappropriate to the needs and traditions of the Indian. Teachers tried to alter age-old child-rearing practices, and the Indian family was forced to reconsider the meaning and the value of its existence. Erikson recounted many examples of the discordant effects of teachers' efforts and stoic Indian compliance, but one brief illustration will serve here:

> During school time the child is taught cleanliness, personal hygiene, and the standardized vanity of cosmetics. While having by no means fully assimilated other aspects of white female freedom of motion and of ambition which are presented to her with historically disastrous abruptness, the adolescent [Indian] girl returns home prettily dressed and clean. But the day soon comes when she is called a "dirty girl" by mothers and grandmothers. For a clean girl in the Indian sense is one who has learned to practice certain avoidances during menstruation; for example, she is not supposed to handle certain foods, which are said to spoil under her touch. Most girls are unable to accept again the status of a leper while menstruating. [1950, 131]

Thus, as in his clinical work, Erikson demonstrated that the concepts of identity and of identity crisis were essential for an understanding of "disturbed" behavior.

The Life Cycle: Eight Stages of Man

The very heart of Erikson's concept of personality is a sequence of eight stages of ego development. Each of the first five stages in Erikson's scheme builds on Freud's psychosexual stages, treating them as prerequisite and fundamental determinants of personality. Erikson feels that his own contribution in delineating the concept of ego identity has been to broaden rather than to revise or replace Freudian theory (Erikson, 1950, 1959, 1968). Thus, Erikson's clinical and personal experiences demonstrated to him the necessity for a concept of identity. But his psychoanalytic training convinced Erikson that one's sense of self always develops in unison with one's progress through the biological stages of Freud's psychosexual sequence.

Erikson's conception of the life cycle focuses on a series of sequential ego crises that begin in infancy and extend through life to old age. Successful resolution of each phase-specific crisis is the necessary preliminary to advancement through the entire sequence. Erikson describes the life cycle in terms of eight discrete crisis periods. However, his epigenetic scheme may be usefully previewed by grouping the ego crises into four broad life periods.

TABLE 10–1: LIFE CYCLE EGO CRISES

INFANCY	CHILDHOOD	ADOLESCENCE	ADULTHOOD
1. Trust versus Mistrust (Oral)	3. Initiative versus Guilt (Phallic)	5. Identity versus Role Confusion (early Genital)	6. Intimacy versus Isolation (Genital)
2. Autonomy versus Shame, Doubt (Anal)	4. Industry versus Inferiority (Latency)		7. Generativity versus Stagnation
			8. Ego Integrity versus Despair

Note: Corresponding Freudian psychosexual stages appear in parentheses.

The four divisions of Table 10–1 represent a condensation of Erikson's scheme in which he distinguishes between early and later childhood, and between young adulthood and adulthood proper (cf. Erikson, 1959, p. 120). Each of the eight psychosocial crises is to be viewed as having both positive and negative elements. Early misunderstanding of Erikson's proposals led many readers to assume that the negative and positive outcomes were mutually exclusive. Hence, in this mistaken view, a child who develops a sense of basic trust will not develop a sense of mistrust, and vice versa.

However, Erikson has been at pains in recent publications to point out that, for healthy development to proceed, it is necessary for the person to experience and to incorporate into his identity both negative and positive aspects of each crisis. Without a sense of mistrust, the child would be vulnerable to all manner of manipulation and to gross invasions of his personal integrity at the hands of his personal contacts. Each crisis is favorably resolved when the *ratio* of positive to negative elements incorporated into the person's identity leans toward the positive (Erikson, 1968, p. 105). A little bit of mistrust, of shame, of guilt, and so on, are good things in negotiating the demands of life and its people.

Acquiring a Sense of Trust versus a Sense of Mistrust

The earliest sense of identity that the infant may be said to harbor arises from his contact with mother in the feeding situation (Erikson, 1968, p. 105). Throughout the first year of life, the infant's most crucial contacts with reality are those mediated by the mother as she attends quickly, reliably, and calmly to his needs. From the repetitive handling, feeding, and love-motivated attentions of the mother, the infant acquires a fundamental attitude toward himself and toward his world. When mother's attentions have been given willingly, lovingly, reliably, and in quick response to the infant's cries, the infant develops the attitude of *basic trust* (Erikson, 1950, pp. 247 ff.; 1959, p. 56).

A sense of basic trust is first evidenced by the infant who shows a willingness to let mother out of sight without showing signs of intense anxiety or rage. Because the trusting infant's experiences have been marked by consistency, continuity, and sameness in the mother's responses to him, he develops a dim recognition that what he has learned to anticipate nearly always materializes.

> Such consistency, continuity, and sameness of experience provide a rudimentary sense of ego identity which depends, I think, on the recognition that there is an inner population of remembered and anticipated sensations and images which are firmly correlated with the outer population of familiar and predictable things and people. [Erikson, 1950, p. 247]

When the child begins to develop its first teeth, the parents' patience is likely to be tried to the limits. Seeking to bite and to grasp desirable objects and persons, the infant explores the boundaries of his capacity to trust and be trusted. Consequently, Erikson stressed that the sense of basic trust is not restricted to a perception of the outer world as trustworthy, "but also that one may trust oneself and the capacity of one's own organs to cope with urges; and that one is able to consider oneself trustworthy enough so that the providers will not need to be on guard lest they be nipped" (Erikson, 1950, p. 248).

It is important, too, in this context to understand that the infant's sense of trust is not damaged when the parents enforce restrictions or prohibitions. As long as the parental commands and prohibitions, "do's" and "don'ts," communicate to the infant a sense that the parent "knows what he's doing," minor frustrations and repeated "No's" engender no lasting adverse effects on identity. Because parents have to model the prevailing cultural standards of socialized behavior, only discipline that is administered without confidence and without consistency can result in damaged trust (Erikson, 1950, p. 249).

On the opposite side of the coin, the infant who has failed to experience reliability, continuity, and sameness, and who has therefore failed to develop a sense of basic trust, succumbs to an overwhelming sense of *basic mistrust*. In the extreme case, the schizophrenic child exemplifies the degree to which identity is damaged in the child who fails to trust himself and others. Withdrawal, bizarre behavior, and an inability to differentiate self from the environment, all characteristics of psychotic adjustment, may be traced to the missing sense of inner and outer "sameness."

Thus, the central crisis of the first year of life is the development of a larger proportion of basic trust than of basic mistrust. For the healthy trusting infant, continued life becomes not one hurdle after another, but one beckoning challenge after another arising from each past masterful effort. In this sense of healthy, reality-oriented personality strength, Erikson has proposed a developmental schedule of psychological virtues (1964, pp. 111 ff.). Successful resolution of each crisis throughout development leads to the attainment of a different virtue. Thus, the infant who has acquired a sense of basic trust that outweighs his sense of basic mistrust has also acquired one form of ego strength: namely, the capacity to *hope.*

The Latin root of the word "virtue" is *virilitas,* meaning "virility" or "strength." Coupled with this root is another Latin noun of the feminine gender, *virtus,* meaning "goodness." It is in the sense of these Latin roots that Erikson employs the term *virtue* and the specific virtues of *Hope, Will, Purpose, Competence, Fidelity, Love, Care, Wisdom.* At each of the eight developmental stages one of these virtues is added to the ego's changing and growing sense of continuity. Therefore, Erikson employs the term virtue to indicate the capacity of the ego for *strength, restraint,* and *courage* (Erikson, 1964, p. 113). In Erikson's own words, "I will call 'virtue,' then, certain human qualities of strength and I will relate them to that process by which ego strength may be developed from stage to stage and imparted from generation to generation" (1964, p. 113).

For the infant who finds himself and his world trustworthy, *"Hope is the enduring belief in the attainability of fervent wishes, in spite of the dark urges and rages which mark the beginning of existence"* (Erikson, 1964, p. 118; italics in original). Because at each stage of his development the trusting infant's desires and wishes have been reliably "verified" by the trustworthy environment in which he finds himself, he now dares to "hope" for an ever expanding array of achievements, masteries, possessions, and accomplishments. In short, the trusting infant has learned to dare, to risk, to gamble on disappointment of his desires. He trusts that failures, frustrations, losses will not be overwhelming; he hopes.

Acquiring a Sense of Autonomy versus a Sense of Shame and Doubt

Near the age of eighteen months, the infant gains more precise control over his muscles. Of prime importance to his eager parents is the fact that with increased voluntary muscular control comes the capacity for increased self-control. The child begins to experiment with two modes of muscular action: holding on and letting go (Erikson, 1950, pp. 251 ff.). Anyone who has stooped repeatedly to retrieve for the high-chaired child those treasured objects he endlessly delights in dropping to the floor knows what holding onto and letting go mean to the willful child.

In psychoanalytic terms, this period of muscular exertion and experimentation corresponds to the anal stage. Besides holding on to and letting go of tossable objects, the child also begins to learn how to hold on to feces and urine until the appropriate time and place is reached to let go of them with parental approval. Toilet training, consequently, is a battle of wills. Depending on the way the parents handle this important learning experience, the child either learns that holding on and letting go are powerful weapons to be employed against overly demanding parents, or he learns that elimination is "a relaxed 'to let pass' and 'to let be' " (Erikson, 1950, p. 251). Parental guidance at this stage must be firm, but protective of that sense of trust achieved during the previous oral stage:

> Firmness must protect him against the potential anarchy of his as yet untrained sense of discrimination, his inability to hold on and to let go with discretion. As his environment encourages him to "stand on his own feet," it must protect him against meaningless and arbitrary experiences of shame and of early doubt. [Erikson, 1950, p. 252]

The crisis of this stage of ego development, then, revolves around the necessity for the child to achieve a sense of independence or willful autonomy in the guidance of his body. His experiences with self-control will set the pattern for his later capacity to make free choices. If the child learns to overcontrol his impulses, it is likely that he has been needlessly and mercilessly shamed.

"Shame supposes that one is completely exposed and conscious of being looked at: in one word, self-conscious. One is visible and not yet ready to be visible . . ." (Erikson, 1950, p. 252). Thus, the child who has learned control over self by having been made to feel small or shameful for unavoidable lapses wins only a "hollow victory." Shamed beyond the limits of his trust, such a child learns to distrust the shamers. Instead of learning to regard the products of his body as dirty or evil, he learns to regard his tutors as evil.

There is a further negative consequence of harsh parental demands for self-control: Doubt. The child is made to feel that he is compelled by the will of others rather than by his own burgeoning sense of independence.

> Where shame is dependent on the consciousness of being upright and exposed, doubt . . . has much to do with a consciousness of having a front and a back—especially a "behind." For this reverse area of the body, with its aggressive and libidinal focus in the sphincters and in the buttocks, cannot be seen by the child, and yet it can be dominated by the will of others. The "behind" is the small being's dark continent, an area of the body which can be magically dominated and effectively invaded by those who would attack one's power of autonomy. [Erikson, 1950, p. 253]

Harry Stack Sullivan's concept of the Not-Me as the part of personality that lies outside of conscious reach, outside of self-acceptance, is similar in emotional flavor to what Erikson has here termed the "dark continent" of the child's being. His sense of ego identity—that feeling of sameness, continuity, and "me-ness"—is dependent upon the freedom accorded him by his parents to be the self that has been trusted.

The quality of ego strength that emerges during the establishment of a sense of autonomy corresponds to the virtue of *Will:* "*Will . . . is the unbroken determination to exercise free choice as well as self-restraint, in spite of the unavoidable experience of shame and doubt in infancy*" (Erikson, 1964, p. 119; italics in original). Thus, the child who attains a favorable ratio of autonomy to shame and doubt evidences a capacity for "free will," for "good will," and for willful self-control. Reasonable tolerance and realistic firmness shown to the child by his parents result in reasonable self-tolerance and realistic self-firmness (Erikson, 1959, p. 70).

Acquiring a Sense of Initiative versus a Sense of Guilt

Resolving the crisis of autonomy, the child of four or five years enters the next phase of ego development with the firm sense that he *is* a person (Erikson, 1959, p. 74). He must now discover what kind of person he is. In its most basic form, the crucial question for the child is to decide which of his parents will be the object of his identification. Freud characterized this stage of development as phallic, and the chief crisis as the solution of the Oedipus complex.

In addition to the Oedipal strivings, three important developments attend this stage and serve to bring the child closer to the point of crisis: (1) His range of movement is widened by the capacity to walk rather than crawl; (2) his use of language is more precise "to the point where he understands and can ask about many things just enough to misunderstand them thoroughly"; (3) language and locomotion combine to permit the child to expand his imagination, to create the impossible, to frighten himself with his own thoughts (Erikson, 1959, p. 75).

The key characteristic of this stage, therefore, is the child's growing capacity *to initiate* actions, thoughts, and fantasies. To the established hallmarks of trust and autonomy, the ego adds the capacity *to plan*. The child's increased capacity to anticipate or to reflect on the consequences of self-initiated activities can lead to jealous rage against siblings or against anyone who trespasses in what the child perceives to be his special area of privilege. For the male child, exclusive domination of mother's attention comes to a climax when he realizes that father is the stronger, more powerful competitor. To resolve these Oedipal strivings, the child internalizes those prohibitions that he imagines his father might enforce. These internalized standards become the basis of the superego or conscience (see the discussion of the superego in Chapter 3). With the formation of the superego, the child also solidifies his identification with the same sexed parent, taking on the sex-appropriate behaviors of that model.

During this stage, too, the child learns to cooperate with other children in planning mutual undertakings. He emulates desirable models like teachers, and he pursues idealistic goals and causes. Hence, the crisis for the ego in this stage is to establish a favorable balance between initiative and the residue of Oedipal guilt that was retained in the formation of the superego. In short, the child discovers what he *can* do and what he *may* do (Erikson, 1959, p. 75). Nowhere is this balance between ability and expectancy more apparent than in imaginative play:

> Play is to the child what thinking, planning, and blueprinting are to the adult, a trial universe in which conditions are simplified and methods exploratory, so that past failures can be thought through, expectations tested. [Erikson, 1964, p. 120]

The crucial increment to the ego's strength that results from a successful resolution of the crisis attending this stage is the virtue of *Purpose: "Purpose . . . is the courage to envisage and pursue valued goals uninhibited by the defeat of infantile fantasies, by guilt and by the foiling fear of punishment"* (Erikson, 1964, p. 122; italics in original). With the internalization of conscience, that is, with the adoption of external standards as his own moral and ethical guidelines, the child may be said to have his own purpose. His ego may now make judgments and plans that had in the past to be made for him.

Acquiring a Sense of Industry versus a Sense of Inferiority

In the first stage of basic *trust,* personality focused around the conviction, *"I am what I am given."* During the crisis of the second stage involving *autonomy,* personality was centered on the belief that, *"I am what I will."* At the third stage, when the sense of *initiative* reached critical proportions, the nucleus of personality was, *"I am what I can imagine I will be."* With the emergence of the fourth psychosocial crisis of industry versus inferiority, the central theme for personality development becomes *"I am what I learn"* (Erikson, 1959, p. 82). This fourth stage, consequently, coincides with the child's first school experiences.

With entrance into school and the enforced attention to the impersonal abstractions of the "three R's" that school brings, the child must forget past hopes and desires, taming his exuberant imagination in the service of productive learning (Erikson, 1950, p. 258). Corresponding to the Freudian latency period, this psychosocial stage finds the child leaving behind his efforts to win a place of privilege and mastery within the safety of his own family. He discovers, instead, that recognition outside the family is important. And that recognition is most easily obtained by producing—that is, by preparing for useful work.

The most important lesson that the child derives from his school experiences is the pleasure to be gained from completing a task by steady attention and persevering diligence (Erikson, 1950, p. 259). He learns to handle the implements of his culture, to acquire the rudiments of technology, or, in nontechnological cultures, the rudiments of survival. The key danger is that the child may despair of success; he may develop a sense of inadequacy and inferiority. When school life fails to maintain the accomplishments of the three previous ego crises, the child may fail to identify with the productive adult models that surround him.

A successful resolution of the crisis between industry and inferiority leads to the ego's development of a new strength, the virtue of *Competence:* "*Competence . . . is the free exercise of dexterity and intelligence in the completion of tasks, unimpaired by infantile inferiority*" (Erikson, 1964, p. 124). The child learns "by virtue of" his trust, autonomy, initiative, and industry that confident, independent, and active productivity is satisfying because it allows him to join and to effect changes in the adult human community.

Acquiring a Sense of Identity versus a Sense of Role Confusion

When the child's ego has assimilated an adultlike sense of industry, his childhood ends. In reaching this point in development, the adolescent has constructed a sense of his own sameness, a sense that, although he is changing, the "he" who changes is also fundamentally the same. This sense of continuity is the foundation of ego identity.

In adolescence, however, the four earlier crises are resurrected and the sense of sameness is requestioned.

> In their search for a new sense of continuity and sameness, adolescents have to refight many of the battles of earlier years, even though to do so they must artificially appoint perfectly well-meaning people to play the roles of adversaries; and they are ever ready to install lasting idols and ideals as guardians of a final identity. . . . The sense of ego identity then, is the accrued confidence that the inner sameness and continuity prepared in the past are matched by the sameness and continuity of one's meaning for others, as evidenced in the tangible promise of a "career." [Erikson, 1950, pp. 261–262]

The adolescent period is thus a socially sanctioned interval of role experimentation, of delay in making final choices. A full and healthy ego identity can emerge only when all previous identifications are integrated. The varying senses of one's identity in infancy, childhood, and in the school years must merge to become a comfortable and workable whole. The early stages of trust and autonomy were dominated by a sense of *bodily identity:* hunger and elimination. The later stages of initiative and industry were concerned chiefly with *social roles* modeled by important adult others. In adolescence the bodily and social identifications must coalesce to bridge the division between childhood and adulthood. "A lasting ego identity cannot begin to exist without the trust of the first oral stage; it cannot be completed without a promise of fulfillment which from the dominant image of adulthood reaches down into the baby's beginnings and which creates at every step an accruing sense of ego strength" (Erikson, 1959, p. 91).

The danger of this period has become a rather faddish label affixed indiscriminately to all sorts of behavior. "Identity crisis," the term coined by Erikson in the context of his theory, rightly applies to the potential of the adolescent to become role-confused. Because a wide variety of adult roles are modeled in our complex culture, the adolescent may turn the socially sanctioned period of temporary delay in choosing a role into a continued or semipermanent moratorium (Erikson, 1950, p. 262; 1963, p. 13).

In proper perspective, the *psychosocial moratorium* of adolescence permits the youth to explore a range of opportunities without the necessity of immediate commitment. For the adolescent who has failed to integrate all previous crisis solutions, the moratorium on final role choice permitted by society to its young is extended to a paralyzing and interminable era of confusion. Like Erikson's own youthful identity crisis as an "outsider," the confused adolescent cannot become what his life has prepared him to be.

> The prime danger of this age, therefore, is identity confusion, which can express itself in excessively prolonged moratoria . . .; in repeated impulsive attempts to end the moratorium with sudden choices, that is, to play with historical possibilities, and then to deny that some irreversible commitment has already taken place. . . . The dominant issue of this, as of any other stage, therefore, is that of the active, the selective, ego being in charge and being enabled to be in charge by a social structure which grants a given age group the place it needs —and in which it is needed. [Erikson, 1963, p. 13]

Thus, the sense of identity means "being at one with oneself," and harboring an affinity for one's community, both for its history and for its future (Erikson, 1974, p. 27). But with this positive sense of identity there is necessarily a negative aspect to one's sense of self. Each adolescent, consequently, harbors a *negative identity*. Healthy resolution of the identity crisis assures for the adolescent the means of discarding the dark identifications and troublesome conflicts that compose the negative identity. However, for the adolescent who succumbs to the crisis of establishing a positive ego identity, "The loss of a sense of identity often is expressed in a scornful and snobbish hostility toward the roles offered as proper and desirable in one's family or immediate community. Any part or aspect of the required role, or all parts, be it masculinity or femininity, nationality or class membership, can become the main focus of the young person's acid disdain" (Erikson, 1959, p. 129).

Negative identity choices are most easily discerned among the troubled or "disturbed" adolescents. Such young people willfully choose to become everything that parents and teachers had expressly indicated as undesirable. A negative identity is thus "an identity perversely based on all those identifications and roles which, at critical stages of development, had been presented to the individual as most undesirable or dangerous, and yet also as most real" (Erikson 1959, p. 131). For example:

> A mother who is filled with unconscious ambivalence toward a brother who disintegrated into alcoholism may again and again respond selectively only to those traits in her son which seem to point to a repetition of her brother's fate, in which case this "negative" identity may take on more reality for the son than all his natural attempts at being good: he may work hard on becoming a drunkard and, lacking the necessary ingredients, may end up in a state of stubborn paralysis of choice. [Erikson, 1959, p. 131]

"Vindictive choices" of negative roles around which to integrate one's sense of self represent a desperate attempt to regain some control over one's fate. Many adolescents faced with chronic identity diffusion would "rather be nobody or somebody bad, or indeed, dead—and this totally, and by free choice—than be not-quite somebody" (Erikson, 1959, p. 132).

Despite the dangers of adolescent identity diffusion, the majority of ego-integrated youth evidence attainment of another form of ego strength, the virtue of *Fidelity: "Fidelity is the ability to sustain loyalties freely pledged in spite of the inevitable contradictions of value systems"* (Erikson, 1964, p. 125; italics in original). The healthy youth, from his springboard of a firm self-identity and strong ego, develops a high sense of duty to the tasks of rendering reality faithfully to himself and to his culture. For the youth who has attained the strength of Fidelity, life becomes the living out of his established core identity. The roles he plays are the roles he is.

Like other theorists, Erikson employed the theatrical imagery of the actor and his mask of roles. The danger in the roles to which the adolescent turns in his experimentation with the multiple identities his life offers is that the role may become more real than the actor's core:

> But what if role-playing becomes an aim in itself, is rewarded with success and status, and seduces the person to repress what core-identity is potential in him? Even an actor is convincing in many roles only if and when there is in him an actor's core identity—and craftsmanship. [Erikson, 1974, p. 107]

Fidelity thus guarantees that the adolescent with a firm sense of self will match his inner necessities with outer demands. For the healthy "faithful" adolescent, the actor's mask is adjusted precisely to the actor's face.

Acquiring a Sense of Intimacy versus a Sense of Isolation

With entrance into young adulthood, the person becomes willing to risk his newly established identity by fusing it with the identities of others. "He is ready for intimacy, that is, the capacity to commit himself to concrete affiliations and partnerships and to develop ethical strength to abide by such commitments, even though they may call for significant sacrifices and compromises" (Erikson, 1950, p. 263).

A firm sense of personal integrity based on the fusion of past bodily and social identifications allows the young adult to face the fear of ego loss in situations and in unions that call for self-sacrifice. Thus, the young adult faces intimate social commitments ranging from intense friendships or physical combat to hesitant sexual experimentation.

The danger of this period is that the young adult may not be ready for the demands of intimacy. He may be unwilling to lend himself to intimate sharing with another, and thus retreat into personal isolation. Freud was once asked what he thought the healthy person should be able to do well. His curt answer was *"Lieben und arbeiten"* (to love and to work) (Erikson, 1950, p. 265). In the shift among combative, cooperative, and intimate interpersonal relationships, the new adult must learn not only to adopt a personal formula for intimate cooperation, but also his own unique mode of productivity.

True, healthy genital sexuality that marks this stage is characterized by:

1. mutuality of orgasm
2. with a loved partner
3. of the other sex
4. with whom one is able and willing to share a mutual trust
5. and with whom one is able and willing to regulate the cycles of
   a. work
   b. procreation
   c. recreation
6. so as to secure to the offspring, too, all the stages of a satisfactory development. [Erikson, 1950, p. 266]

Clearly, Freud's formula, "to love and to work," is more complicated than is at first apparent. Freud and Erikson mean to indicate that the healthy adult personality is able to absorb himself in intimate sexual fulfillment while *simultaneously* maintaining the independence of spirit necessary for productive and fulfilling work.

The key virtue attending the successful resolution of the conflict between intimacy and isolation in this stage is, of course, *Love:* "Love . . . *is mutuality of devotion forever subduing the antagonisms inherent in divided function"* (Erikson, 1964, p. 129; italics in original). Love is thus the strength of ego to share identity for "mutual verification" of chosen identity while taking from this supportive relationship the strength to be "self-ish."

Acquiring a Sense of Generativity versus a Sense of Stagnation

"Mature man needs to be needed, and maturity needs guidance as well as encouragement from what has been produced and must be taken care of" (Erikson, 1950, p. 267). The loving and working mature adults thus need to feel some concern for the next generation as exemplified in their own offspring. Because children are the products of the intimate fusion of bodily and personal identities of the parents, mother and father have a "libidinal investment" in their offspring.

Merely wanting children does not assure the attainment of a sense of generativity. The fundamental requirement is the ability to extend oneself, literally to give oneself to the future. Erikson chose the term *generativity* rather than synonyms like productivity or creativity because the key characteristic of the ego at this stage is its ability to transcend the immediate self-related interests of the person in favor of a view of generations to come (Erikson, 1968, p. 138).

The danger of this stage lies in the inability of some otherwise mature adults to find value in guiding and aiding the next generation. A pervasive sense of stagnation or boredom characterizes their approach to a variety of life tasks. There is present the feeling of living an adequate but unsatisfying life. A feeling exists that all accomplishments and all interpersonal intimacies are fundamentally impoverished because they lack relevance to one's diffuse sense of "Who I am."

The ego's strength in meeting the necessities of life is increased in the generative adult by the development of the virtue of *Care:* "*Care is the widening concern for what has been generated by love, necessity, or accident; it overcomes the ambivalence adhering to irreversible obligation*" (Erikson, 1964, p. 131; italics in original). By postulating the stage of generativity and the attainment of the virtue of Care, Erikson has extended the Freudian psychosexual stages beyond genital sexuality. Care assures for the mature ego the right to be needed and the privilege to need the young. Thus, care includes not only love for those persons whom one has created, but for all of man's created works as well.

Acquiring Ego Integrity versus Despair

The climax of the life cycle is reached when the foundations of infantile trust have made possible their adult counterpart: *integrity*. The adult who has been cared for, who has cared for others, can now care for himself. The fruit of the previous seven stages ripens in the adult whose ego can accept his life cycle "as something that had to be and that, by necessity, permitted of no substitutions: it thus means a new, a different love of one's parents" (Erikson, 1950, p. 268).

The adult in whom ego integrity has fully blossomed realizes that his individual life is but one life cycle in the flow of history. He is convinced that what had to be, was—and was satisfying. The danger is that the ego may have failed to integrate the crisis resolutions of the previous seven stages. The fear of death that emerges means that the individual is unable to accept his life cycle as the ultimate and one and only meaning that living embodies. *Despair* of what has been implies that what has been, has been in vain. Despair is the protest of a person who is not yet satisfied with a life that has never been satisfying. Despair indicates an unwillingness, paradoxical as it may be, to end a life that has failed to achieve fulfillment and that now culminates as the sum of a thousand little miseries.

The most important gift parents can provide their children is the strength, shown in their own example, to face ultimate concerns like death without the disintegrating effects of fear: "healthy children will not fear life if their elders have integrity enough not to fear death" (Erikson, 1950, p. 269). Thus, the virtue that serves as the hallmark of the climactic stage of the life cycle is *Wisdom:* "*Wisdom . . . is detached concern with life itself, in the face of death itself*" (Erikson, 1964, p. 133; italics in original). Adults who embody the kind of integrity that Erikson describes are wise in the sense that they view their limited lives as a totality that transcends petty disgust at the feeling of "being finished." They are able to transcend the despair "of facing the period of relative helplessness which marks the end as it marked the beginning" (Erikson, 1964, p. 134).

Some Concluding Remarks on Erikson

Erikson's psychosocial scheme of the life cycle has provided the conceptual tools for the analysis of the lives of significant historical figures. Erikson has thus examined the process of identity development in the lives of Martin Luther (1962) and of Mahatma Gandhi (1969). In both cases, Erikson sought to identify the historical, social, and psychological forces that uniquely combined with accidental circumstance to produce a human personality that changed the course of history.

Psychohistory, as this form of clinical investigation has come to be called, is gaining a wide foothold in a broad array of academic disciplines. It is not within the scope of this chapter to review this literature. But it is important to recognize the far-reaching acceptance Erikson's ideas have had. The concepts of identity, identity crisis, life cycle, ego-strength, and psychosocial development, all pioneered by Erikson, have found their way into quarters where orthodox psychoanalytic doctrine would be most unwelcome. Perhaps the reasons for the respectability of Erikson's concepts in the eyes of critics who would otherwise be hostile to psychoanalytic notions lie in some unique combination of Erikson's personal, social, and historical presence.

Erich Fromm: Freedom as Frightful

Like Erikson, Erich Fromm found in psychoanalysis a rich bed of concepts by which to understand man's behavior. Like Erikson, too, Fromm felt that classical or orthodox psychoanalytic doctrine was unnecessarily constraining. And, again, like Erikson, Fromm sought to broaden psychoanalytic instinct theory with a conceptualization of man as a social being in a world of interacting creatures. With the focus of psychoanalytic theory thus shifted from intrapsychic instinctual conflicts to the conflict between the individual and his culture, Fromm began his theorizing with an analysis of human freedom.

The rise of modern capitalism was paralleled by an expansion of man's personal freedom. Bounded by strict custom and rigidly enforced social roles, the medieval man remained relatively unconcerned with problems of individual rights and freedoms. Fromm described medieval society in this way:

> What characterizes medieval in contrast to modern society is its lack of individual freedom. Everybody in the earlier period was chained to his role in the social order. A man had little chance to move socially from one class to another. With few exceptions he had to stay where he was born. He was often not even free to dress as he pleased or to eat what he liked. The artisan had to sell at a certain price and the peasant at a certain place, the market of the town. ... Personal, economic, and social life was dominated by rules and obligations from which practically no sphere of activity was exempted. But although a person was not free in the modern sense, neither was he alone and isolated. In having a distinct, unchangeable, and unquestionable place in the social world from the moment of birth, man was rooted in a structuralized whole, and thus life had a meaning which left no place, and no need, for doubt. A person was identical with his role in society; he was a peasant, an artisan, a knight, and not *an individual* who *happened* to have this or that occupation. [1941, pp. 57–58]

Thus, medieval man had no need for individual freedom because he had yet no conception of himself as an *individual.* He was one with the structure of his society. With Martin Luther, in the period known as the Protestant Reformation, there came a revolutionized social and psychological milieu. Emphasis was placed on *independence* from smothering institutions like the Catholic Church, on *individual* decision making, and on *personal* achievement. In effect, when it came to political and social conduct, Luther and Calvin showed man that his fate was in his own hands. When it came to one's relation to God, however, Luther emphasized man's dependence and helplessness as well as man's worthlessness and need for absolute faith in God's mercy.

Upon this conception of man's material independence there soon followed the notion of personal responsibility. If personal effort, achievement, and independence of institutions were the basis of salvation, then personal moral responsibility was the price of this social liberation. Only upon God was man dependent; and only in the face of the Almighty was he helpless. Consequently as man's social freedom grew, there was a paradoxical growth in his feelings of personal helplessness and worthlessness (Fromm, 1941, p. 124). Freedom became a burden, and the chief element of that burden was the necessity for individual competition against one's fellows. For if man was to achieve his own salvation by establishing a personal dependent relationship with God, he must be secure in his belief that he merited God's largesse. By demonstrating his capacity to work, to achieve, to shoulder responsibility for his own economic and social survival, the free, independent man asserted his worthiness to be God's favored—and saved—creature. But in his attempts to demonstrate his individual merit, the new independence of spirit fostered a sense of competition: Some are more worthy than others.

Moneyed and prestigious classes of men arose, and this aristocracy of wealth and power was the foundation of the new capitalistic spirit. Less economically favored individuals felt a sense of uncertainty, fear, and helplessness in the face of such exaggerated power and conspicuous merit. Instead of fostering a brotherhood of man, independence fostered economic competition and alienation. The middle economic classes reacted to these pressures by fighting hard against their growing sense of powerlessness at the hands of the wealthy capitalists. "The luxury of the moneyed class increased their feeling of smallness and filled them with envy and indignation. As a whole, the middle class was more endangered by the collapse of the feudal order and by rising capitalism than it was helped" (Fromm, 1941, p. 99).

The predominant feeling pervading the consciousness of the middle classes was the sense of their own insignificance. Luther's conception of religion mirrored these critical social changes. Although his doctrine freed man from unthinking dependence on Church authority, it emphasized man's personal worthlessness and his dependence on God. "In psychological terms [Luther's] concept of faith means: if you completely submit, if you accept your individual insignificance, then the all powerful God may be willing to love you and save you" (Fromm, 1941, p. 100).

The Protestant Reformation thus evolved a painful dilemma for man: It permitted him to abandon reliance on institutional authority and social roles in order to be free and independent, but at the same time it made him more dependent on God and therefore more personally helpless. For contemporary man, the dilemma becomes more intense. The fact of the individual's insignificance in the face of powerful corporations, massive government bureaucracies, and transhuman technology has touched everyone's life.

The existence of contemporary man is marked by aloneness, fear, and bewilderment. His freedoms are not satisfying; they are frightful. Though he is totally an individual, contemporary man is also sometimes totally isolated. In short, contemporary man does not cherish his individuality, his independence. He flees from his own freedom.

The Mechanisms of Escape from Freedom

Clearly, Fromm's sketch of contemporary capitalistic society pictures man as a victim of his own works. The net effect of these conflicting trends toward independence and helplessness is impaired mental health. Following Freud's dictum: *"Lieben und arbeiten"* (to love and to work) Fromm characterized the normal or mentally healthy person as one who is able to work productively in the fashion demanded by his society, and who is able to participate in the perpetuation of that society. From the individual's own perspective, however, normalcy is defined as "the optimum of growth and happiness of the individual" (Fromm 1941, p. 159).

The difficulty with contemporary society is that the requirements it levels for normalcy often conflict with the individual's own needs for growth and happiness. Two courses of action are open to him as he tries to overcome his painful state of helplessness and aloneness. "By one course he can progress to 'positive freedom'; he can relate himself spontaneously to the world in love and work, in the genuine expression of his emotional, sensuous, and intellectual capacities; he can thus become one again with man, nature, and himself, without giving up the independence and integrity of his individual self" (Fromm, 1941, p. 161). This solution to the conflict between freedom and helplessness is essentially a healthy one.

The second course of action open to the individual involves the unhealthy strategy of relinquishing personal freedom completely. Seeking to merge himself with, or surrender his identity to, the conglomerate we call society, this individual strives to "escape freedom." Fromm distinguished among three such mechanisms of escape.

Authoritarianism

To attain the desired status of strength or power, the individual may seek to fuse himself with another—somebody or something lying outside of self (Fromm, 1941, p. 163). In extreme form, the individual becomes submissive, passive, even masochistic. Feeling insignificant, powerless, and inferior, the individual struggling to escape his own freedom succeeds in his struggle when he is able to submit to the power of others, to provoke self-humiliation, and even to intensify his worthlessness with self-belittling.

A nearly opposite authoritarian mechanism is sometimes seen in those who, rather than submit to authority, attempt to become the authority. In place of masochism, a strong sadistic desire to obtain absolute and unrestricted power over others becomes the means of escape. Such an authoritarian may desire to have others dependent on him, or to exploit others ruthlessly, or to cause others direct physical suffering and pain.

Both the masochistic and sadistic forms of authoritarianism solve the problem of the burden of freedom by annihilating the individual self. "Psychologically . . . [sadism and masochism] are the outcomes of one basic need, springing from the inability to bear the isolation and weakness of one's own self" (Fromm, 1941, p. 180). Fromm suggested that the unconscious foundation of both these strategies be called *symbiosis:* "Symbiosis, in the psychological sense, means the union of one individual self with another self (or any power outside of the own self) in such a way as to make each lose the integrity of its own self and to make them completely dependent on each other" (Fromm, 1941, p. 180). Thus for both the masochist and for the sadist, escape from freedom involves a flight from self. For the masochist, this end is accomplished when he is "swallowed up" by an outside force; for the sadistic personality the same end is accomplished when he "swallows up" others.

Destructiveness

Like authoritarianism, destructiveness is rooted in the individual's sense of overwhelming powerlessness and aloneness. Unlike the masochistic and sadistic strategies, the destructive individual does not seek union with an external object or power over it. The destructive strategy seeks to annihilate the object.

> I can escape the feeling of my own powerlessness in comparison with the world outside of myself by destroying it. To be sure, if I succeed in removing it, I remain alone and isolated, but mine is a splendid isolation in which I cannot be crushed by the overwhelming power of the objects outside of myself. The destruction of the world is the last, almost desperate attempt to save myself from being crushed by it. [Fromm, 1941, p. 202]

When the individual is blocked by external circumstance from directing his destructiveness outwardly, he may take the self as his target. Thus physical illness and suicide are regular outcomes of this strategy to escape from the burden of freedom.

Fromm modified Freud's notion of the death or destructive instinct by proposing a relationship between the degree to which the individual's growth strivings are thwarted and the amount of destructiveness such frustration engenders. "By this [thwarting] we do not refer to individual frustrations of this or that instinctive desire but to the thwarting of the whole of life, blockage of spontaneity of the growth and expression of man's sensuous, emotional, and intellectual capacities" (Fromm, 1941, p.

206). For this reason, Fromm proposed that the more the drive toward life is blocked, the stronger becomes the drive toward destruction: "*Destructiveness is the outcome of unlived life.*"

Those institutions and social roles that, by their very nature, frustrate the individual's striving for independence and growth, are precisely those societal conditions that most engender his destructiveness. In this regard, Fromm's thought bears a striking similarity to the self-actualization concepts of Maslow and Rogers (cf. Chapter 13), to Carl Jung's notion of individuation (cf. Chapter 4), and to Karen Horney's concepts of the real and ideal selves (cf. Chapter 6).

Automaton Conformity

The two previous mechanisms of escape from freedom revolve around unconscious strategies for relinquishing the integrity of the self or around the desire to destroy the world that threatens the self. Automaton conformity, by contrast, involves a strategy of escape by default. "To put it briefly, the individual ceases to be himself; he adopts entirely the kind of personality offered to him by cultural patterns; and he therefore becomes exactly as all others are and as they expect him to be" (Fromm, 1941, pp. 208–209).

Like the protective coloring of some animals, the individual who is a conforming automaton takes on the coloring, shading, and emotional texture of his surroundings. Because he mimics millions of other people, the automaton no longer feels alone. But for this reduction in his feelings of aloneness he pays the price of loss of selfhood. In his surrender of his true self to the facade of sameness with others, the individual does not achieve the security for which he hoped. Instead, he finds himself adopting a pseudo-self to compensate for the loss of his spontaneity.

Like R. D. Laing (Chapter 8), Fromm believes that the automaton conformist experiences a split between his genuine feelings or spontaneous urges and the face that he presents to the world.

> The loss of the self and its substitution by a pseudo self leave the individual in an intense state of insecurity. He is obsessed by doubt, since, being essentially a reflex of other people's expectation of him, he has in a measure lost his identity. In order to overcome the panic resulting from such loss of identity, he is compelled to conform, to seek his identity by continuous approval and recognition by others. Since he does not know who he is, at least the other will know—if he acts according to their expectation; if they know, he will know too, if he only takes their word for it. [1941, p. 230]

Thus, each of the three escape mechanisms "solves" the problem of freedom's burden only partially, only temporarily, only inadequately.

Fromm's Social Psychoanalytic Psychology: Sources of the Concept

Fromm (1962) has provided a uniquely revelatory account of the personal sources of his interest in the work of Sigmund Freud and of Karl Marx. It is clear from Fromm's notion of man's alienation from his own selfhood in the face of growing economic independence that he has attempted to blend modified Freudian concepts with Marxian economic ones. Although he credits Marx for being the more profound thinker, Fromm has found value in the complementary nature of the conceptual tools provided by Freud for understanding man's alienation from himself and those provided by Marx for understanding man's alienation from his fellows (Fromm, 1950, 1962, p. 12; 1970, 1959, and 1973).

An Adolescent Puzzle: Personal Interest in Psychoanalysis

Much as Erikson's concern with the crisis of identity arose from his own bewilderment and distress, Fromm's interest in psychology and social theory arose from a similar state of adolescent confusion. When Fromm was about twelve years old, an attractive young woman who was a friend of Fromm's family committed suicide:

> Maybe she was twenty-five years of age; she was beautiful, attractive and in addition a painter, the first painter I ever knew. I remember having heard that she had been engaged but after some time had broken the engagement; I remember that she was almost invariably in the company of her widowed father. As I remember him, he was an old, uninteresting, and rather unattractive-looking man, or so I thought (maybe my judgement was somewhat biased by jealousy). Then one day I heard the shocking news: her father had died, and immediately afterwards she had killed herself and left a will which stipulated that she wanted to be buried together with her father. [Fromm, 1962, p. 4]

At twelve, Fromm had not yet heard of the Oedipus complex or of incestuous fixations between children and parents. Yet the event deeply disturbed him. He had found the woman attractive and had developed quite a hatred for her father. "I was hit by the thought 'How is it possible?' How is it possible that a beautiful young woman should be so in love with her father, that she prefers to be buried with him to being alive to the pleasures of life and of painting?" (1962, p. 4.)

In his early twenties, the haunting question "How is it possible?" finally received an answer as Fromm delved into Freud's writings. What had been a frightening and confusing adolescent experience now took on dimensions as a crucial human character problem for which psychoanalysis seemed to provide appropriate investigative tools.

An Adolescent Model: Personal Interest in Marx's Social Theory

Fromm's family was strongly religious, and he was early exposed to Jewish tradition and custom. He reports that he was deeply affected by his study of the Old Testament, and in particular by the prophetic writings of Isaiah, Amos, and Hosea: "not so much by their warnings and their announcement of disaster, but by their promise of the 'end of days,' when nations 'shall beat their swords into plowshares and their spears into pruning hooks' " (1962, p. 5). Fromm suggests that the chief reason these prophets affected him so deeply was that as a Jewish boy in a Christian community he had experienced several episodes of anti-Semitism. The feelings of strangeness and of "clannishness" among Christians and Jews forced Fromm to an early dislike of isolation between men: ". . . what could be more exciting and beautiful to me than the prophetic vision of universal brotherhood and peace?"

The lessons to be learned from these experiences were intensified when Fromm was fourteen years old and the First World War broke out in the summer of 1914. Several of Fromm's schoolteachers expressed strongly nationalistic feelings about the war, and in one case, a Latin teacher expressed a genuine fondness for the whole concept of war. Fromm was thus provoked to ask his inevitable question: "How was it possible that a man who always seemed to have been so concerned with the preservation of peace should now be so jubilant about the war?" Another puzzle had been posed.

At around the same time, a wave of hatred was sweeping through Germany with the British people as its target. Suddenly a stereotype had been created that caricatured the British as cheap mercenaries, evil and unscrupulous destroyers of German heroes (Fromm, 1962, p. 6). This stereotype and its corresponding war hysteria that was paralyzing German thinking confused and frightened the young Fromm.

An English teacher proved to be the one exceptional model of sanity and reason amidst the onslaught of irrationality and hatred:

> I still see him standing in front of the class, answering our protests with an ironical smile, and saying calmly: "Don't kid yourselves; so far England has never lost a war!" Here was the voice of sanity and realism in the midst of insane hatred—and it was the voice of a respected and admired teacher! This one sentence and the calm, rational way in which it was said, was an enlightenment. It broke through the crazy pattern of hate and national self-glorification and made me wonder and think, "How is it possible?" [Fromm, 1962, p. 7]

The urgency of the question "How is it possible?" grew as the war drew on, seemingly without end. The propaganda battles launched by the embattled nations depicted men of each country as mindless butchers. Fromm was overwhelmed with the senseless killing, accusations, and pointless pain of war: "How is it possible that millions of men continue to stay in the trenches, to kill innocent men of other nations, and to be killed and thus to cause the deepest pain to parents, wives, friends? . . ." (1962, p. 8).

In 1918, at the end of the war, Fromm's insistent curiosity and abhorrence had been transformed into a desire to understand the irrationality of human mass behavior.

> My main interest was clearly mapped out. I wanted to understand the laws that govern the life of the individual man, and the laws of society—that is, of men in their social existence. I tried to see the lasting truth in Freud's concepts as against those assumptions which were in need of revision. I tried to do the same with Marx's theory, and finally I tried to arrive at a synthesis which followed from the understanding and the criticism of both thinkers. [1962, p. 9]

Fromm thus adopted from Freud the conviction that *most of what is real within ourselves is not conscious, and that most of what is conscious is not real* (Fromm, 1962, p. 89). From Marx, Fromm adopted the conviction that man is not free, and cannot be free, so long as he accepts uncritically external control by social custom or institutions. Thus, Freud pictured man as determined primarily by his biological instincts and the forces of repression exerted by his own ego; Marx depicted man as determined by the structure of his society and the forces of repression exerted by economic and political exigencies. Fromm profoundly modified both views into a social psychoanalytic theory of human character types.

Character Structure: The Nature of Human Nature

Fromm's concept of man struggling to escape his burden of self-created freedom can now be understood in a broader context. As contemporary society grew more complex, it became less human. Man sought not only to escape his growing sense of helplessness, he also struggled to regain mastery of the societal machinery that threatened to master him (Fromm, 1955a, pp. 309 ff.). In one stroke, man had created the means to subdue nature and mold it to his own needs, while at the same time he relinquished his ability to love himself and others. In brief, contemporary capitalistic society fosters both alienation of man from man and alienation of each individual from himself:

> People capable of love, under the present system, are necessarily the exceptions; love is by necessity a marginal phenomenon in present-day Western society. Not so much because many occupations would not permit of a loving attitude, but because the spirit of a production-centered commodity-greedy society is such that only the non-conformist can defend himself successfully against it. [Fromm, 1956, p. 111]

As Fromm has pointed out, the most pressing danger is not the sudden increase of cruelty or inhumanity that a consumer society breeds. The most potent danger is that future men will become feelingless, loveless, un-thinking robots (1955b, p. 105). Unable to be true to his nature, future man will be true to his "things." Acquisition, consumption, and material accu-mulation will claim man's loyalties. The most pressing question, therefore, that a truly humanized psychology can ask is: *What is man's true nature?*

Fromm has several times attempted to answer this question in his efforts to describe how society has forced distortions of human character into existence (1968, 1947, 1964, and 1973). Rejecting Freud's view that man's unalterable nature is to be found within his instinctual endowment for sexuality and aggression, Fromm has suggested that the most basic trait of human nature is a tendency toward self-actualization (1947, p. 29). Be-cause of this tendency to become fully functioning, to exercise completely his unique powers of reason and self-awareness, man's nature is not lim-ited by his inherited biological instincts. The single constraint governing man's existence is his need to be fully himself.

> Man is born as a freak of nature, being within nature and yet tran-scending it. He has to find principles of action and decision making which replace the principles of instinct. He has to have a frame of orientation which permits him to organize a consistent picture of the world as a condition for consistent actions. He has to fight not only against the dangers of dying, starving, and being hurt, but also against another danger which is specifically human: that of becoming insane. In other words, he has to protect himself not only against the danger of losing his life but also against the danger of losing his mind. [Fromm, 1968, 61]

Without a frame of reference, a consistent and reliable view of himself and his world, man soon succumbs to madness, that is, to a separation from himself. Because he has the capacity for self-awareness, man is never free of the prospect of his own death. He is a part of nature yet set apart by his ability to reflect on it. The fundamental dichotomy of man's existence is his vulnerability to the laws of nature, especially to the inevitability of death, and his painful awareness that in most other ways he has tran-scended his animal heritage (Fromm, 1947, p. 49). Evolution of the human brain in directions different from those of his animal cousins has lessened man's dependence on stereotyped instinctual responses. Man's superior cortical development has, furthermore, provided him with the power of reason and self-reflection (Fromm, 1973, p. 223). Taken together, the lessened dependence on instinct and the superior development of the brain's cortex have freed man from a mere survival-striving existence and have separated him from the rest of living creation. Alienated from himself and from others by the works his intelligence has made possible, man strives *to be himself,* master of his artifacts rather than mastered by them. He struggles to allow others to be fully themselves without himself succumbing to the extremes of apathy and nihilism.

To understand man's nature it is necessary to understand his predicament: He is both animal passion and human reason. His most important needs, as Maslow, too, asserted, are not biological. They are, instead, distinctly human—uniquely suprabiological, and founded in human character (Fromm, 1973, pp. 230 ff.). Fromm (1955a, 1973) has defined man's unique nature in terms of six peculiarly human, existential needs:

1. *The Need for Relatedness and Unity:* To overcome his feelings of aloneness and isolation from nature and from himself, man needs to love, to care for others. Love is a union with somebody or something outside of self (1955a, p. 37; 1973, p. 233).

2. *The Need for Transcendence and a Sense of Effectiveness:* Because man is aware of himself and his world, he sometimes recognizes how overpowering and frightening the vastness of the universe is. He may thus easily be overcome with a sense of his own helplessness and impotence (Fromm, 1973, p. 235). Man needs to surpass his own fear and uncertainty in the face of a hostile or indifferent universe. He may accomplish this end by actively striving to master his world and himself. Man needs to surpass his own potential passivity: "He is driven by the urge to transcend the role of the creature, the accidentalness and passivity of his existence, by becoming a 'creator'" (Fromm, 1955a, p. 41). In short, man must feel that he is *effective:* "I am because I effect." The similarity to Erikson's notion of a sense of industry and a sense of initiative is obvious.

3. *The Need for Rootedness:* Throughout his life man is torn from his roots. In birth, man is torn from the security and passivity of his womb existence. In late childhood, man is torn from the safety of mother's care. In adulthood, man faces the prospect of being torn from life itself as he faces death. Thus, throughout life, man has need for roots, for a sense of stability, permanency, and secure sameness similar to the security he experienced in the mother-child relationship (Fromm, 1955a, p. 43; 1973, p. 232). Erikson's notion of ego identity as a sense of continuity is similar.

4. *The Need for a Sense of Identity:* "Man may be defined as the animal that can say 'I,' that can be aware of himself as a separate entity" (Fromm, 1955a, p. 62). Man must feel in control of his fate. He must be able to say

"I am I." In short, he must make decisions, reflect on them, and feel that his life is truly his own.

5. *The Need for a Frame of Orientation and an Object of Devotion:* "Man needs a map of his natural and social world, without which he would be confused and unable to act purposefully and consistently" (Fromm, 1973, p. 230). Because he is enveloped in a universe of puzzling phenomena and frightening realities, man has the need to make sense of his life. He needs to be able to predict the complexities of his existence. A *frame of orientation* is a set of beliefs about the ultimate course of his destiny. A frame of orientation is, therefore, an absolute necessity for the maintenance of sanity (Fromm, 1955a, p. 64 ff.).

Man needs not only a frame of orientation but also an *object of devotion,* a goal or God to which he can attach meaning, to whom he can attribute the meaning of his life. Where the frame of orientation provides a map of existence, the object of devotion is the goal toward which that map directs man's search (Fromm, 1973, p. 231).

6. *The Need for Excitation and Stimulation:* In his most recent work, Fromm (1973, p. 237) has added a sixth basic need characteristic of man's healthy functioning. Surveying neurological and behavioral evidence, he concludes that the human brain is constantly active, continually functioning even in the presence of reduced external stimulation. He infers from the evidence that man needs a constantly stimulating, interest-provoking environment. Fromm does not mean that man requires a chronic succession of novel stimuli. Rather, he needs stimulation that induces him to *actively* construe his world, to *actively* participate in life.

Fromm thus proposed a distinction between a *simple stimulus* and an *activating stimulus:* "The simple stimulus produces a *drive*—i.e., the person is driven by it [e.g., hunger, pain]; the activating stimulus results in a striving—i.e., the person is actively striving for a goal" (Fromm, 1973, p. 240). Simple stimulation that does not engage man's reason results in simple passive reactions. To avoid boredom, simple stimuli must constantly change or continually increase in intensity.

Contemporary technological society provides many simple stimuli that foster passivity and boredom. One consequence of continuous simple stimulation is that contemporary man is driven to seek methods of boredom escape. Thus, alcohol, drugs, television, and sexual promiscuity can all be means of avoiding an overwhelming sense of boredom in the face of the continual barrage of simple stimuli. The trouble with these escape mechanisms is that in themselves they are further sources of simple, boredom-producing stimulation that provide only temporary and superficial relief.

Another more pathological consequence of contemporary man's boredom is *malignant aggression.* Unlike the animal who practices aggression for defense, man is unique in his capacity to be violent, cruel, and destructive for no rational defensive purpose. To escape the ready-made patterns of behavior and the chronically unengaging entertainments offered by his technological culture, man resorts to active aggression and violence. In a life without meaning, violence and destructiveness provide man with some measure of distorted mastery. Such aggression is malignant because it subverts the very essence of man's character; it solves man's sense of despair at the meaninglessness of his life by allowing him malignant control over the life of another. In short, boredom provokes malignant aggression.

Distortions in Human Character Enforced by Society

In Fromm's view human nature is intimately bound up with self-awareness. The social form of man's existence, however, is a potent shaper of that self-awareness. Nowhere is Fromm's attempt to blend Freudian and Marxian concepts more apparent than in his treatment of this point. The content and the breadth of the individual's self-awareness are powerfully molded by the customs, taboos, and traditions of the society that engulfs him. To concretize this concept, Fromm proposed that each society establishes in each of its members a shared *social unconscious* (1962, pp. 88 ff.).

The social unconscious is composed of those thoughts and feelings that the society will not permit an individual to harbor in awareness. Thus, Fromm combined Freud's concept of repression with Marx's concept of social illusion. Society's customs, prohibitions, and conventions enforce a kind of social repression by establishing specific cognitive categories by which every individual is expected to order his conception of the world. The social unconscious, therefore, is a product of a kind of *socially conditioned filtering* process that allows some thoughts to be consciously entertained and some thoughts to be forced out of awareness.

The socially conditioned filter operates through three cultural mechanisms. First, the common *language* of a culture employs a set of grammatical and syntactical rules that powerfully shape the way reality is labeled. "The whole language contains an attitude of life, is a frozen expression of experiencing life in a certain way" (Fromm, 1962, p. 118).

Second, shared *rules of logic* determine what is regarded by members of a culture as "natural" or reasonable. Thus, cultures differ in the degree to which cause-and-effect, "scientific" thinking is regarded as the only appropriate way to understand the world. A good example of a vastly different view of the "proper" way to construe and relate to "reality" can be gleaned from Carlos Casteneda's fascinating accounts of the magical or mystical techniques of perception practiced by a Yaqui Indian sorcerer (e.g., Casteneda, 1968, 1971). Don Juan, the sorcerer under whom Casteneda studied, was able to manipulate situations and social cues so effectively that Casteneda was forced to concede that "reality" was not so very real. Cause and effect in the Yaqui Indian tradition do not serve as cognitive categories by which to order one's experience. Experience is structured by a more intuitive, direct contact with unseen, untouchable, unexplainable "reality." The culture shock engendered by Casteneda's apprenticeship to Don Juan nearly cost Casteneda his sanity.

The third mechanism by which the social filter shapes social character and the social unconscious is the use of taboos or *explicit prohibitions.* Certain ideas, feelings, or attitudes are treated as improper, dangerous, or forbidden to the extent that they are simply not consciously experienced.

Consequently, the social unconscious and the individual unconscious are constantly interacting, for at least part of the individual unconscious is determined or shaped by social filtering processes. Societies function in such a way that the individual is made to feel that he *willingly* acts the way he *ought* to act. The individual who successfully adapts to his culture is convinced that *he wants* to behave as his culture demands because such conformity is physically and spiritually satisfying (Fromm, 1955a, p. 77). The difficulty, of course, is that the society may be pathological—that is, overtly inimical to the essence of human nature as defined by the six previously discussed needs: *relatedness, transcendence, rootedness, identity, activating stimulation,* and a *frame of orientation.* Pathological societies subvert or block the gratification of these needs. In consequence, pathological societies create pathological human character types, for only a distorted version of human nature could adapt to the distorted demands of a pathological, need-depriving culture.

Fromm has described several varieties of character type. Generally he groups them into two classes of *productive* (healthy) and *nonproductive* (unhealthy, pathological) types. In his first work on this theme he described four nonproductive character types as contrasted with a fifth, productive personality. None of these types exists in pure form because productive and nonproductive elements combine in differing proportions in particular persons. Thus the ultimate mental health or illness of a given character type depends upon the ratio of positive to negative traits embodied in that individual.

The Receptive Orientation: Passivity and Dependence

It must be remembered that each of the character types to be discussed represents a particular solution to the problem of adapting to social demands. Such adaptation, it will be recalled, is motivated by man's need to solve the fundamental dichotomy of his existence, namely, the clash between his feelings of aloneness and alienation and his feelings of shared creaturehood.

The receptive personality solves this dilemma by adopting the belief that all good, all satisfactions, all worthwhile comforts and values are received from sources outside self (Fromm, 1947, p. 70.) Thus, the receptive type feels that his central task in life is *to be loved,* not loving. He tends to be indiscriminate in his choice of love objects, desiring from nearly everyone a continual income of attention, devotion, and help. Unable to offend anyone, the receptive type continuously says "yes" to everyone as if his critical faculties were paralyzed.

The receptive type may be described by the key negative trait labels of *passive, opinionless, submissive, unrealistic, cowardly, wishful, gullible,* and *sentimental* (Fromm, 1947, p. 120). On the positive side, however, the receptive type may embody enough health and productive motivation to transmute these negative traits into positive characteristics. Thus, for the receptive type who harbors some productivity, passivity may become *acceptance,* opinionlessness may lead to *responsiveness,* submissiveness becomes changed into *devotion,* unrealistic perceptions may be altered to *idealistic* ones, cowardice becomes *sensitivity,* wishful thinking grows into *optimism,* and so on.

In summary, the orientation of the nonproductive receptive type is chiefly marked by his passivity and by his expectancy that someone will provide.

The Hoarding Orientation: Never Let Go

The hoarding personality solves the dilemma of aloneness and the need for others in a way that is directly opposite to the receptive type. The hoarder strives to accumulate possessions, power, and love, and he struggles to avoid dispensing any of his hoard. Acting as if he had built a protective fortress around himself, the hoarding type strives to bring within its protective boundaries all that he might ever want or need. Even love is treated as a possession. To obtain love, the beloved other must be totally possessed.

The hoarding type is "tight" in nearly every physical respect: tight-lipped, tight-boweled, tight-stomached, tight-eyed—that is, he says nothing, is constipated, cramped and ulcered, and squinty. Above all else, he desires his sense of order, neatness, and cleanliness to be shared by those around him. He thus resembles closely Freud's anal retentive (erotic) character type (cf. Chapter 2).

Key traits to describe the hoarding type include *unimaginative, stingy, suspicious, cold, stubborn, obsessional, possessive* (Fromm, 1947, p. 120). In the hoarding type who possesses some degree of productivity and health, these negative traits may be changed. Thus, unimaginative is changed to *practical,* stingy to *economical,* suspicious is changed to *careful,* cold to *reserved,* stubborn becomes *steadfast,* obsessional becomes *methodical,* and possessive is changed to *loyal.*

The Exploitative Orientation: Aggressive and Conceited

The exploitative personality solves the problem of aloneness by taking from others. Unlike the receptive type who *expects to receive* or the hoarder who *expects to keep,* the exploiter *expects to take, to grab, to snatch away from others* that which he needs or desires. He thus feels attracted only to people from whom he can steal love, or to people who themselves have to be taken from others. Intellectually, the exploiter does not create ideas, he steals them, plagiarizes them. In short, for the exploiter things that can be taken from someone else always seem better or more desirable than things they themselves can produce (Fromm, 1947, p. 72).

The exploiter can be described by the following key trait labels: *aggressive, egocentric, conceited, rash, arrogant, seducing.* In the exploitative character who embodies some measure of health and productivity these negative traits may be changed to more positive qualities: Agressive thus becomes *taking the initiative,* egocentric becomes *able to make claims,* conceited is changed to *proud,* rash to *impulsive,* arrogant to *self-confident,* and seducing becomes altered to *captivating* (Fromm, 1947, p. 120).

A somewhat analogous character type has been studied by Christie and his colleagues under the descriptive label of *Machiavellian* (Christie & Geis, 1968, 1970). A Machiavellian personality is well described by most of the traits Fromm uses to define the exploitative personality. Furthermore Fromm's last nonproductive type, the marketing personality, to be described shortly, also shares some characteristics of Christie and Geis's Machiavellian personality. It is interesting that Christie and Geis's work is based on empirical measurements of personality that closely correspond to Fromm's theoretical type.

The Marketing Orientation: Selling Oneself

The marketing personality is peculiarly a product of modern industrial society. Success is measured for the marketing personality by how well he sells himself, by how well, that is, he packages his personality in desirable qualities. Thus his family background, the clubs to which he belongs, the schools he attended all have to be "right." When his personality package fulfills the socially expected conditions of "rightness," the marketing type's skills, knowledge, or services will be in demand.

> Since modern man experiences himself both as the seller and as the commodity to be sold on the market, self-esteem depends on conditions beyond his control. If he is "successful," he is valuable; if he is not, he is worthless. [Fromm, 1947, p. 79]

The marketing personality represents the ultimate in alienation. To solve the problem of aloneness, the marketing type literally becomes a product that will attract customers. He sells himself without ever knowing himself. He knows only *what* will sell, not the price *he* will pay for the transaction.

Key descriptive traits for the marketing type include *opportunistic, inconsistent, childish, aimless, tactless,* and *indifferent* (Fromm, 1947, p. 121). Christie and Geis's Machiavellian type shares the traits of opportunism and indifference. When, however, the marketing type possesses some positive or productive qualities, these negative traits may undergo transformation into healthy characteristics: Opportunistic may become *purposeful,* inconsistent is modified to *able to change,* childish is changed to *youthful,* aimless is modified to become *experimenting,* tactless is changed to *curious,* and indifferent becomes *tolerant.*

The Productive Type: Personality without a Mask

In contrast to the nonproductive orientations, the productive personality solves the problem of aloneness by becoming more fully himself. He dons no masks, erects no facades, attempts to manipulate no one. "Productiveness is man's ability to use his powers and to realize the potentialities inherent in him. . . . Productiveness means that he experiences himself as the embodiment of his powers and as the 'actor'; that he feels himself one with his powers and at the same time that they are not masked and alienated from him" (Fromm, 1947, p. 91).

Thus, Fromm, too, employed the terminology of the actor and his mask to describe the ungenuineness, the hollowness, and the artificiality that the productive personality *avoids.* The productive person is independent, autonomous, integrated, spontaneous, loving, creative, and, in a word similar to Erikson's, *generative* (Fromm, 1947, pp. 93 ff.). The productive person is one who is able *to love* and *to work.* He feels at one with himself, with his fellows, with the universe. In brief, he is *related, transcendent, rooted;* and he has a strong sense of *identity* with a stable *frame of orientation* toward his life. This description of the healthy personality is quite similar to Abraham Maslow's notion of the self-actualizing personality and to Carl Rogers' notion of the newly emerging person discussed in Chapter 13. For all three theorists, and to a lesser extent for Erikson, the healthy personality is one who finds himself sufficiently acceptable and worthy as he really is without a protective mask.

Man's Potential for Destruction: Love of Death versus Love of Life

In recent years Fromm has sought to sharpen his hypothesis that human character types may be either productive or nonproductive. It will be recalled that Fromm rejects the instinctivist thesis of Freud, which states that man's capacity for aggression and for love are strictly biological potentials. It will also be recalled that one of the mechanisms of man's escape from freedom is destructiveness. Fromm had suggested in his first major work (1947) that when the individual's self-actualizing or growth tendencies are thwarted, his destructive urges are intensified. The more his drive to live, to grow, to become fully what his nature promises is blocked, the greater the intensification of his destructive or aggressive tendency.

Fromm has expanded and modified this fundamental tenet of the opposition of life and death strivings into a hypothesis about the essence of human evil. Fromm has proposed that certain personalities are essentially evil because they are *necrophilous,* literally, "lovers of death and decay" (1964, 1973). The opposite, healthy personality is termed *biophilous,* meaning literally "lover of life and growth." For Fromm, the necrophilous orientation is the "quintessence of evil," a truly malignant form of human existence. The malignant aggression evidenced by the necrophile is uniquely human, having no counterpart among the lower animal orders. Malignant aggression is truly destructiveness pursued for its own sake, undertaken for the enjoyment that devastation brings, practiced not for defense, but for perverse satisfaction.

The Necrophilous Character Type

The majority of people are a blend of biophilous and necrophilous traits. In extreme form, however, the necrophilous character type is defined as *"the passionate attraction to all that is dead, decayed, putrid, sickly; it is the passion to transform that which is alive into something unalive; to destroy for the sake of destruction; the exclusive interest in all that is purely mechanical. It is the passion 'to tear apart living structures' "* (Fromm, 1973, p. 332).

One easily discernible trait of the necrophilous personality is his concern with putrid or filthy aspects of his own and others' life habits. A predominant phrase in his vocabulary is "this is shitty," or "life is shitty, people are shitty," and so on (Fromm, 1973, p. 341). For the necrophile, all of life is excrement. The necrophile clearly exaggerates those traits found in the personality type that Freud called the anal sadistic.

Another observable trait of the necrophilous personality is his concern with mechanical, nonhuman gadgetry. The necrophile who is interested in photography takes pictures of people, but his interest is directed to the quality and sophistication of his *camera;* he listens to music, but his love is for experimentation with his complicated stereophonic receiver; he loves time-saving appliances, but even the simplest addition is done on a calculator, even the shortest walk to a grocery store is reason to drive there by car. In effect, the necrophilous character substitutes an affinity for *technique* and for *technology* in place of the biophilous person's affinity for life, for people, for beauty (Fromm, 1973, p. 343).

Within the stream of the necrophile's life, there is a marked concern with the processes of elimination, with fecal products, and with human filth. Fromm suggests that the necrophilous person is a malignant form of the classically described Freudian anal sadistic character. Thus, the distortion of development responsible for the emergence of the malignant necrophilous personality proceeds as follows: normal anal character ⟶ sadistic character ⟶ necrophilous character (Fromm, 1973, p. 349). The supreme difference between the sadistic anal type described by Freud and the necrophilous type is the latter's profound sense of alienation and detachment from everything human and alive.

Each of the previously discussed four nonproductive personality types (receptive, exploitative, hoarding, and marketing) solves the problem of his own sense of aloneness by establishing some kind of relationship to life. The relationship may be distorted, nonproductive, and manipulative, but at least each of these orientations remains focused on life. Each of them struggles to derive satisfaction from living people, however immoral and unethical his strategy may be. The necrophile, by contrast, is not interested in life, in people. His interest is in death, in nonliving technology, in destroying the life in others.

> [The necrophile] turns his interest away from life, persons, nature, ideas—in short from everything that is alive; he transforms all life into things, including himself and the manifestations of his human faculties of reason, seeing, hearing, tasting, loving. . . . The world becomes a sum of lifeless artifacts; from synthetic food to synthetic organs, the whole man becomes part of the total machinery that he controls and is simultaneously controlled by. . . . He aspires to make robots as one of the greatest achievements of his technical mind, and some specialists assure us that the robot will hardly be distinguished from living men. This achievement will not seem so astonishing when man himself is hardly distinguishable from a robot. . . . Death is no longer symbolically expressed by unpleasant-smelling feces or corpses. Its symbols are now clean, shining machines; men are not attracted to smelly toilets, but to structures of aluminum and glass. [Fromm, 1973, p. 350]

The lifeless world of twentieth-century technology is a world of death, and it is a world that creates necrophilous men just as alienated man fabricated from his aloneness an equally dehumanizing culture.

It is important to note that Fromm's conception of the necrophilous character type is the logical extension of his early concern with the mechanisms of escape from freedom. The necrophilous man is the ultimate development of schizophrenic separation of genuine feelings from public behavior. He behaves in a routinized, stereotyped, and unspontaneous way —a cluster of mannerisms that suggests necrophilia originates from early unbearable experiences of distrust, disinterest, and emotional coldness at the hands of the mothering one.

The Origins of Necrophilia

Fromm has hypothesized that the roots of adult necrophilia are to be found in childhood. Some children are unable to establish the normal Oedipal relationship to mother in all of its typical sexual and pleasurable manifestations. "It would seem that such infants never develop warm, erotic, and later, sexual feelings toward mother, or that they never have a desire to be near her. Nor do they later fall in love with mother substitutes. For them mother is a symbol: a phantom rather than a real person" (Fromm, 1973, p. 363).

Instead of the usual perception of mother as a symbol of earth, home, warmth, safety, life, she is to the unattached child a representation of chaos and death: "she is not the life-giving mother, but the death-giving mother; her embrace is death, her womb is a tomb" (Fromm, 1973, p. 363). What are the causes of this malignant transformation of the Oedipal situation? Fromm suggests that a definitive answer is yet unavailable, but that three factors are worth considering.

The first possibility is that some genetically determined factor that regulates the child's innate capacity to form affectional bonds is lacking or malfunctioning. Such a factor might be similar to that which operates in cases of autism. The autistic child is uncommunicative, uninterested in human contact, and fascinated with repetitive mechanical processes. Such a biologically determined factor might be physically expressed in damage to the child's central nervous system, to, for example, the ascending reticular activating system of the brain stem. Damage to this network of fibers might hinder the child's ability to form lasting memories so that his world is constantly chaotic and frightening. Emotional attachments are therefore impossible.

The second possibility is that the mother herself is a cold, rejecting, or inconsistent caretaker. As a potential necrophilous personality herself, the mother's interactions with a cold or detached infant would only intensify and further exaggerate his human alienation. The result would be a child unable to attach himself emotionally to mother, to father, to friends, to anyone. With time, the consequence of this early emotional abrasion or deprivation would be a defensively malignant interest in nonliving, non-reactive *things:* in short, necrophilia.

Fromm also suggests a third, and perhaps more tenuous, hypothesis. Traumatic experiences in the first years of the child's life that involve frustration of his needs for affection and safety might cause the buildup of malignant rage and hate. In effect, a child damaged in this way would have experienced outright abuse or clearly discernible rejection or hate at the hands of his caretakers. His own resulting defensive hate and resentment eventually fester into the malignant aggression and destructive intent so characteristic of the necrophile (Fromm, 1973, p. 365).

Fromm summarized the distinction between the necrophilous personality and his opposite, the biophilous personality, in this way:

I have tried to give a picture of the necrophilic and the biophilic orientations in their pure forms. These pure forms are, of course, rare. The pure necrophile is insane; the pure biophile is saintly. Most people are a particular blend of the necrophilous and the biophilous orientations, and what matters is which of the two trends is dominant. Those in whom the necrophilous orientation gains dominance will slowly kill the biophilic side in themselves; usually they are not aware of their death-loving orientation; they will harden their hearts; they will act in such a way that their love of death seems to be the logical and rational response to what they experience. On the other hand, those in whom love for life still dominates, will be shocked when they discover how close they are to the "valley of the shadow of death," and this shock might awaken them to life. [1964, p. 48]

Comparative Summary

Erik Erikson and Erich Fromm each took from psychoanalysis a conviction that unconscious motives shape the direction of the individual's life history. But each of these theorists modified this psychoanalytic tenet with a consideration of the social side of human enterprise.

Erikson, unlike Fromm, identified himself closely with orthodox psychoanalysis, viewing his own theorizing as an extension of the bedrock principles elucidated by Freud. Perhaps the identification with traditional psychoanalytic doctrine and the desire to preserve its essential elements were fostered in Erikson's approach by his own gratefulness for his early acceptance into the psychoanalytic mainstream. His adolescent role confusion, the culmination of his development as an "outsider," was greatly reduced by his commitment to the role of psychoanalytic therapist. Neither completely Jewish nor completely Scandinavian, the young Erikson had long wondered who his real father was, why he was "Jew" to his school chums and "goy" to his stepfather's relatives, and how he would ever be somebody.

From his interests in resolving his personal adolescent crisis, Erikson drew an especial sensitivity to the difficulties of being young. From his rather different adolescent confusions, Fromm developed a profound curiosity about man's motives. The suicide of a beautiful young painter to whom Fromm had been attracted, and her apparent motive of desiring to join her deceased father, posed for Fromm a life-long interest: "How is it possible—how is it possible that people behave against their own best interests?" As Erikson had found personal answers in psychoanalysis, Fromm, too, found that Freud's concepts helped to dispel his puzzlement.

Erikson's interest in the development of the individual's reality functioning was spurred on by his early researches with California boys and girls' fantasy productions. He found that basic biological and anatomical differences in bodily equipment were paralleled in a child's play constructions: Boys built high, tottering, exterior, protrusive scenes from play materials. Girls constructed enclosing, static, interior scenes. From these findings Erikson proposed that Freud's psychosexual stages of development were indicative of the shaping effect that anatomy exerts on the developing child's self-awareness and on his awareness of others' expectations for him. Thus, for Erikson, psychoanalytic theory had to be supplemented with social and historical concepts in order to understand how the child develops a sense of his own identity. In this way, Erikson joined the ranks of, and greatly enriched, psychoanalytic ego psychology.

Fromm, by comparison, found value in Freud's work, but he also found a greater significance in the work of Karl Marx. Where Freud had clearly shown the means by which man becomes alienated from himself, Marx had demonstrated the social consequences of man's alienation from his fellows. As industrial and capitalistic growth proceeded, man found himself increasingly alienated from himself and from others. The more his freedom from institutions and from mere survival efforts grew, the more such freedom became a burden. Dehumanized and alienated, contemporary man seeks to return to a more satisfying state of oneness with nature, with himself and with his fellow man. Escape mechanisms like authoritarian submission or domination, destructiveness, and automation conformity all have one goal in common: the unconscious desire to relinquish individuality, to default selfhood in the panic-activated striving to be secure. Without a genuine self, one cannot be alienated. One becomes an unfeeling, and therefore unhurt, robot.

Like Fromm, Erikson conceptualizes the healthy personality as one who, in Freud's words, is able to work and to love. That is, healthy functioning involves the capacities to share intimacy with another and to work fruitfully and with personal satisfaction. The healthy society, for both Erikson and Fromm, aids the individual in accepting the inexorability of his own development. Erikson calls such acceptance—that what one has lived *had* to be—a "sense of ego integrity." Fromm employs Marxian terminology toward the same end, calling the acceptance of one's life the escape from illusion. Both theorists feel, therefore, that healthy development involves the flowering of all that a person is, the full actualization of his capacities, and the complete acceptance of self, for better or worse.

Erikson has proposed that such integrity or ego strength is achieved in an unalterable sequence of psychosocial stages. Beginning in infancy, the child's ego must first learn to trust himself and others in order to become autonomous and self-sufficient. With trust and autonomy come the virtues of hope and will. The child becomes secure enough to risk the potential disappointment that hope entails, and independent enough to dare to willfully initiate his own adaptations to his world. Once these fundamental ego strengths are acquired, the child is able to acquire, in sequence, a sense of initiative (purpose), a sense of industry (competence), a sense of identity (fidelity), a sense of intimacy (love), a sense of generativity (care), and, finally, a sense of integrity (wisdom).

Fromm has tackled the same problem, namely, that of the individual's self-fulfillment in a society of individuals, from a different perspective. Fromm has proposed a distinction between productive and nonproductive orientations, and more fundamentally, between the biophilous and necrophilous personalities. In both cases, the second-named personality type is a product of distorted and damaging "solutions" to the problem of aloneness. Of the nonproductive strategies, the receptive and hoarding types represent opposite coping modes. The receptive type is passive and dependent, expecting all "good" to come from an external source, whereas the hoarding type struggles to acquire "goods" and to accumulate them behind a protective fortress of stinginess. The exploitative and marketing personalities, on the other hand, represent solutions to the unbearable sense of aloneness that require the direct manipulation of others. For the exploitative type, the essence of life is the control he exerts over others, the opportunities that life presents for him to "grab" and to steal from others. The marketing type steals, too, but he does so by packaging his own personality as a commodity to steal favors and win success.

More fundamental is Fromm's distinction between the lovers of death and the lovers of life. The necrophilous personality is a malignant anal sadistic character type who prefers things to people, death to life, filth to beauty. Perhaps because of a biological malfunction, or through early rejecting and traumatic childhood experiences, the necrophile is unable to attach himself to anyone, to have any shared intimacy, unable to pursue any truly productive orientation. The biophilous personality, on the other hand, corresponds to what other theorists call the self-actualized personality or, in Erikson's terminology, the individual who has achieved ego integrity. He is one who can live by loving and working.

Both Erikson and Fromm have expanded Freud's instinctual emphasis to include interactions with social reality. For in the end, a people-world requires the people in it to adjust their desires and regulate their passions by mutual consent.

FOR FURTHER READING

Erikson's most comprehensive treatment of both his early and later theorizing is contained in *Childhood and Society* (New York: W. W. Norton, 1963), rev. ed. His recently published *Life History and the Historical Moment* (New York: W. W. Norton, 1975) contains several essays concerning his views on woman's liberation, the abuse of the term *identity crisis,* and the significance of his own adolescent identity crisis. In *Insight and Responsibility* (New York: W. W. Norton, 1964) Erikson considers the various "virtues" that may arise through healthy resolution of the eight psychosocial developmental crises.

Robert Coles has provided a detailed account of the personal and historical influences that shaped Erikson's ideas in *Erik Erikson: The Growth of His Work*

(Boston: Little, Brown, 1970). Richard I. Evans, in vol. 8 of his famous "Dialogs" series, interviews Erikson and provides commentary on his work. This interview may be had in the full-length version of *Dialog with Erik Erikson* (New York: Harper & Row, 1967) or in moderately condensed form in R. I. Evans' *The Making of Psychology* (New York: Knopf, 1976).

J. Marcia has provided some confirmatory empirical evidence for Erikson's concept of ego identity in "Development and Validation of Ego-Identity Status," *Journal of Personality and Social Psychology* (1966), *3,* 551–558, and N. L. Toder and J. Marcia provided further support in "Ego Identity Status and Response to Conformity Pressure in College Women," *Journal of Personality and Social Psychology* (1973), *26,* 287–294.

Erich Fromm's views are nowhere, except in textbooks, completely summarized in one volume. The place to start is with Fromm's *Escape from Freedom* (New York: Holt, Rinehart & Winston, 1941; also available in paperback from Fawcett, Greenwich, Conn.). Fromm's debts to Marx and Freud are lucidly set forth in his *Beyond the Chains of Illusion: My Encounter with Marx and Freud* (New York: Simon and Schuster, 1962). His critical attitude toward psychoanalysis may be discerned in two of his works: *The Crisis of Psychoanalysis* (New York: Holt, Rinehart & Winston, 1970) and *Sigmund Freud's Mission: An Analysis of His Personality and Influence* (New York: Harper & Row, 1959).

Fromm's *The Anatomy of Human Destructiveness* (New York: Holt, Rinehart & Winston, 1973) contains his views on necrophilia, and an attempt to organize ethological, biological, and psychological insights on human aggression. Richard I. Evans provides another illuminating interview in his *Dialog with Erich Fromm* (New York: Harper & Row, 1966), or in condensed form in *The Making of Psychology* (New York: Knopf, 1976).

Richard Christie and Florence Geis' work on a type of personality they call the Machiavellian has some remarkable similarity to Fromm's exploitative character type. Christie and Geis' work may be had in their *Studies in Machiavellianism* (New York: Academic Press, 1970). Similarly, William H. Whyte, Jr.'s classic *The Organization Man* (New York: Simon and Schuster, 1956) deserves scrutiny for its similarity to Fromm's marketing character type.

11 KURT LEWIN
Field Theory

Instead of saying that all behaviour is a search for pleasure, it seems better to say that all behaviour is the riddance (or avoidance) of painful tension, encouraged perhaps by pleasure-evoking images of expected goals.

HENRY MURRAY, *Explorations in Personality*

A Throw of the Darts: Bull's Eyes Are Not Always Goals

An adult subject is invited to play a game of darts. Left to himself, he tosses darts at a target of numbered concentric circles. The outermost and largest circle has an arbitrary value of 1, and the values of the increasingly smaller rings correspondingly increase to 10, the bull's eye.

After fifteen or twenty minutes of dart throwing, the subject has a pretty good idea of his *best performance.* His last few throws have all centered in the circle marked "7" and despite repeated attempts, he can do no better. Because he is alone, unobserved, and unscored, he feels no real disappointment. In fact, he is quite content that more times than not he achieves a "7."

The experiment begins in earnest. A psychologist enters the room and instructs the subject that he is to continue playing darts as before, but with a minor modification. Before each of his throws, *the subject is to announce his goal* for that throw by calling out the number of the target circle at which he is aiming. For each throw of the darts, the psychologist records whether the subject achieved his announced goal, exceeded it by landing the dart in a more difficult zone of the target, or failed altogether to attain it.

Recall that this subject's *immediate past performance* has averaged around a "7." It would be expected that a purely rational man would therefore announce that he aspired to what he knew he could reasonably achieve, namely a "7." The subject, however, announces that his goal for the next shot is an "8." (Some subjects in the same situation with the same past performance level might announce a less difficult aspiration, say a "6.") The subject misses his announced toss of "8," and the dart lands in "4." He is greatly disappointed and somewhat embarrassed. Because the psychologist is taking down his score, he feels a bit pressured.

For his next throw, he announces that he will aim for a "5," a bit of a comedown from his previous attempt, but still above his immediate past performance of "4." The dart again lands in "4." On his third toss, the man, contrary to all reasonable expectation, announces that he will attempt to hit the bull's eye, a "10!"

PROBLEM: *What motivates the subject to behave in ways that violate common sense?* And, *Why has failure motivated him to aim higher, at more difficult tasks?*

The answers to both problems may be partially indicated by rephrasing them into one question: Is the man drawn to the difficult bull's eye, or is he repelled *away from* some more noxious goal that only he can sense?

Level of Aspiration and the Fear of Failure

A subject's goal-setting behavior in situations involving various levels of difficulty is called *level of aspiration* performance, a term coined by Tamara Dembo (1931, cited in Lewin et al., 1944, p. 333). F. Hoppe (1930), another of Lewin's associates, performed the first experimental studies of level of aspiration phenomena. A variety of tasks was employed, including dart throws, ring tosses over a stake, and target shooting, but subjects' behavior in these diverse situations can be conceptualized as progressing through a set sequence (Lewin et al., 1944, p. 334):

1. *Immediate past performance* (e.g., subject scored a "7")
2. *Setting level of aspiration* (deciding the level of difficulty for the next throw: "try for an '8' ")
3. *Acting on the level of aspiration* (new performance, achieved only a "4")
4. *Reaction to achievement* (disappointment, setting new level of aspiration higher or lower: "try for a '5,' " or "try for a bull's eye")

This sequence has been summarized as a series of events over time in Figure 11–1.

FIGURE 11-1:   TYPICAL TIME SEQUENCE OF LEVEL OF ASPIRATION EXPERIMENT

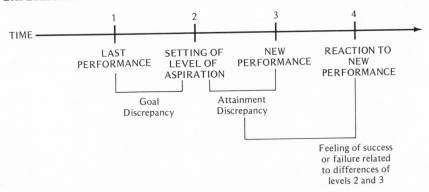

Modified from Lewin et al., 1944, p. 334.

Figure 11–1 illustrates some of the terminology employed in level of aspiration studies. The difference, if any, between what a subject was actually able to do in his immediate past throw and what he tries to do on the next is his *goal discrepancy*. If he sets his sights on a more difficult goal than his last achievement, the goal discrepancy is described as *positive;* conversely, if he sets his level of aspiration lower than his past achievement, the goal discrepancy is *negative.* For example, a subject who has just scored a "7" and who now announces he will try for an "8" has set a positive goal discrepancy of +1.

Similarly, the difference between a subject's actual next achievement after trying out his new aspiration and the level that he had announced is called the *attainment discrepancy.* Attainment discrepancy can, of course, also be positive or negative, depending upon its relationship to the level of aspiration that the subject had announced. If, for example, the subject had announced that he was "trying for an '8'," but actually attained only a "6," his attainment discrepancy would be a –2.

Some Typical Outcomes of Level of Aspiration Experiments

Lewin and his colleagues (1944, pp. 338–354) found that subjects generally set a moderately positive level of aspiration in the beginning of an experiment. With increasing degrees of experience in the presence of the experimenter, success and failure play important roles: Success induces most subjects to raise their aspiration level, while repeated failure compels them to lower it.

Jucknat (1937) conducted similar experiments with children, in which they were required to solve ten mazes of increasing difficulty. When the maze series led to success, defined as the attainment of the level of difficulty *set by the subject,* 51% of them raised their level of aspiration; 41% kept their aspiration level the same; and only 8% lowered it (Festinger, 1942, analyzed Jucknat's data).

Subjects may interpret their own performance on tasks of varying difficulty in terms of a group with which they identify or to which they aspire for membership. When high-school subjects are led to believe that their scores are different from those of college graduates, they tend to shift their level of aspiration upward to conform to that reported for the college norm group (Lewin et al., 1944, p. 343).

Habitual success or failure on similar achievement-oriented tasks like schoolwork affects subjects' performance in the experimental task. Jucknat (1937) found that children who were relatively good school performers with a history of success set high levels of aspiration in the initial experimental task. Children who were poor students and had experienced minimal success at educational tasks tended to show wide variability in their levels of aspiration. Such children set their level either unrealistically high, or extremely low to an equally unrealistic degree.

Jucknat's findings indicate a crucial problem for any theory of aspiration level: *What accounts for subject's variability of aspiration level?* Why should it be possible for a history of failure to be responsible for one child setting his goals unrealistically low and another similar child setting them unrealistically high?

Lewin's Model of Level of Aspiration: Balance of Forces

The operational meaning of level of aspiration is clearly discernible in the nature of the task. Lewin accepted Frank's (1935) definition of level of aspiration as "the level of future performance in a familiar task which an individual, knowing his level of past performance in that task, explicitly undertakes to reach" (quoted in Lewin et al., 1944, p. 335). The crucial questions remain: *Under what conditions will a subject set his level of aspiration above* (positive to) *his last performance?* And, *What influences the subject to set his level of aspiration below* (negative to) *his past performance?*

To answer these questions Lewin and his colleagues devised a conceptual model of the person as subject to *forces* that impel him in various directions. In a sense, Lewin created a spatial or topographical analogy of personality whereby locomotion in space from region to region represents the dynamics of personality. The various levels of task difficulty could thus be represented as different *regions* in space. A subject's varying decisions about the level of difficulty to which he aspires could likewise be represented as *locomotion* between regions. The attractiveness or repulsiveness of the levels of difficulty as the subject succeeds or fails might be represented as positive or negative goal regions.

Lewin conceptualized the individual as buffeted by the forces emanating from positive-attractive goals and from repellent-negative goals. Borrowing the concept of *valence* from chemistry, Lewin employed the term to indicate the *value,* positive or negative, that a task may have in the individual's estimation. Figure 11–2, Part i illustrates a field of forces (f) for a positive goal (G+) in the person's life space. *Life space* is a term that has rather precise meaning for Lewin and consideration of it will be undertaken at a later point. For now, life space may be viewed as the totality of the individual's personal and physical environment *for a particular moment in time.* Figure 11–2, Part ii illustrates the individual's life space with a central negative-repellent goal (G–). Note that in Figure 11–2, Part i, all forces (f) in the life space tend *toward* the positive goal region (G+). Each lettered region is marked by *a force toward the goal:* [$(f_{A,G})$; $(f_{B,G})$; $(f_{D,G})$]. Taking the first notation as an example, the symbols in parentheses are read "force in region A toward goal." It follows that the central goal region has a positive valence (Va) that is greater than zero: $Va_G > 0$. If no other valences (goals) existed in the life space *at that moment,* a person in any region, A, B, or D, would attempt to locomote to the goal region.

FIGURE 11-2: FORCES ON THE PERSON DIRECTED TOWARD AND AWAY FROM VALENCES IN THE LIFE SPACE

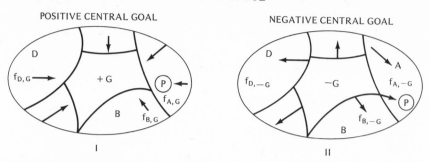

After Lewin, 1946, p. 929.

Conversely, in Figure 11–2, Part ii, the central goal region is negative, and all forces in the life space are directed *away from* the goal. This repellent nature of the goal is indicated by inserting a minus sign before the goal in the notation for the forces of each lettered region: [$(f_A$ -G); $(f_B$ -G); $(f_D$ -G)]. Taking the first notation as an example, these symbols are read "the force in region A *away from* the goal." The strength of the forces in both cases, of course, is dependent on the strength of the goal's valence and the psychological distance of the person from the goal. The stronger the valence and the closer the person feels to that region, the greater the magnitude of the force, positive or negative, exerted upon him:

$$[fP_{,G} = F (Va(G), e_{P,G})]$$

This notation is read: *"the force on the person toward the goal is a function* (F) *of the valence of the goal, and the psychological distance* ($e_{P,G}$) *of the person from the goal"* (Lewin, 1944, p. 933).

Lewin thus conceived of the person behaving in a field of forces, steered by situational and personal factors. In terms of the level of aspiration experiment, the critical moment in the subject's experience occurs when he has to decide on the difficulty level for his next throw. A variety of forces enters into his decision. Some of these forces are clearly more potent than strictly common-sense considerations for his immediate past skill at the task. He sets his level of aspiration as if he were behaving on the basis of the outcome of a mental equation that he intuitively and with lightning speed solves on the spot.

Some of the factors that enter into his equation are (1) *valence of the goal,* that is, the value he places on success or failure. Valence in this context refers to the subjective strength of the force that positive success and negative failure exert upon the subject; (2) *subjective probability of success,* that is, his estimate of how confident he can be that in his task he will succeed; and (3) *subjective probability of failure,* that is, his estimate of his chances that on this task he will fail.

Subjective probability of success and failure can be thought of as similar to psychological distance from the goal, because success or failure determines subject's attainment of satisfaction or endurance of discomfort.

Forces Toward Success and Away from Failure

Lewin conceptualized the person in the level of aspiration task as balancing two competing forces: a *tendency to approach success* and to enjoy the feelings of competence that success brings; and a *tendency to avoid failure* and the feelings of anxiety or embarrassment that failure brings.

There are obviously individual differences in the strength of these motives. Some individuals exhibit a balance of these tendencies such that their approach toward success is stronger than their fear of failure:

$$fP_{,suc} > fP_{,-fai}$$

By contrast, other individuals harbor such intense anxieties over the prospect of failure that for them the equation is balanced in the other direction: Their fear of failure is considerably greater than any anticipated pleasure in success:

$$fP_{,-fai} > fP_{,suc}$$

Lewin consequently assumed that a person's behavior may be represented as the outcome of an equation that balances the *valence of success* [Va(Suc)] on a particular activity (A) at a specific level of difficulty (n) against the *valence of failure* [Va(Fai)] on the same activity at the same difficulty level. The equation yields the net or *resultant force* operating for a given task, after success has been subjectively weighed against failure:

$$Va(SucA^n) + Va(FaiA^n) = Va(A^n)$$

The equation is read: *"the valence of success on an activity at n level of difficulty plus the valence of failure on that activity equals the overall valence of that activity."* Since the valence of failure is negative, that is, the individual wishes to *avoid* it, the sum of success and failure valences is derived algebraically with Va(FaiA^n) as some *negative* value (e.g., $10 + -6 = 4$).

The second assumption that Lewin and his colleagues made was that success at an easy task has a lower valence (the person enjoys it less) than success at a difficult task (Lewin et al., 1944, p. 360). Everyone knows that it is "better" to earn an A in a physics course than in a physical education course, or that it is more satisfying to hit a target from 100 feet than from 20 feet. Conversely, the negative effects of failure, the pain or embarrassment of falling short of expectation, is always greater when a task is perceived as easy. Thus, the negative valence of failure *increases* with decreases in task difficulty. Or to put it another way, the negative valence of failure *decreases* as tasks grow more difficult. For example, missing the stake with a horseshoe from 60 feet is a lot less embarrassing than missing it from 10 feet.

Lewin, et al. represented these assumptions about task difficulty and valence with these notations (1944, p. 361):

$$pos\ Va\ (Suc\ A^{high}) > pos\ Va\ (Suc\ A^{low})$$

which may be read: *"positive valence for success at a task of high difficulty is greater than the positive valence of success at a task of low difficulty."* Similarly, for the pain of failure:

$$neg\ Va\ (Fai\ A^{high}) < neg\ Va\ (Fai\ A^{low})$$

which may be read: *"negative valence for failure at a task of high difficulty is less than the negative valence of failure at a task of low difficulty."*

A further theoretical assumption is necessary to account for the relationship between feelings of success and failure as they combine at the moment of decision, at the very instant when the person chooses the level at which to set his aspiration. If the positive valence of success increases with difficulty and the negative valence of failure decreases, then the total valence of a given task will always be greater at a high level of difficulty than at a low level. More simply, the resultant magnitude of valence will always be greater at the upper levels of difficulty. For this reason, people in Western culture generally seek more difficult tasks, set their aspirations in the positive direction, because the stakes are higher:

$$Va\ (A^{high}) = Va\ (Suc\ A^{high}) + Va\ (Fai\ A^{high}) >$$
$$Va\ (Suc\ A^{low}) + Va\ (Fai^{low}) = Va\ (A^{low})$$

[After Lewin et al., 1944, p. 361]

Resultant Valence Theory

The assumptions previously outlined were first proposed by Sybille Escalona (1940) and later expanded by Festinger (1942) as a set of explicit postulates that Lewin adopted for his theory. Lewin referred to Escalona and Festinger's account as the *resultant valence theory* because its main conclusion is that a person's decision to act is a product of complementary and competing forces that combine and subtract from each other until a net resultant force is left.

In Lewin's model, following resultant valence theory, a person's behavior is not a direct outcome of the valence (value) of success or failure considered by themselves. Rather, as we have seen, another set of factors must be considered to modify the individual's perception of success and failure. A subject's subjective probability of success or failure, his personal estimate of his chances on a given task, must be assumed to "weight" the valences of success and failure (Lewin, et al., 1944, p. 362).

Festinger (1942) had pointed out that an individual's estimate of success and failure are generally reciprocal: the higher the probability of success, the lower the estimate of failure, and vice versa. For example, if an individual feels that his chances of success are 60% (6 out of 10), then he simultaneously must feel that his probability of failure is 40% (4 out of 10). Likewise, if an individual feels that his chances of failing are 90% on a difficult task, then his estimate of success on that task must be 10%.

The probabilities of success and failure are presumed to "weight" the valences of success and failure, respectively. Escalona assumed that the simplest relationship between a person's value for success [Va(Suc)] and his subjective probability of attaining it was multiplicative (Lewin et al., 1944, p. 362):

$$^o Va(SucA^n) = Va(SucA^n) \times Po(SucA^n)$$

The equation may be read: *"Weighted valence of success on a task at n level of difficulty* [$^o Va(SucA^n)$] *equals the valence of success on that task times the person's subjective probability of success* [$Po(SucA^n)$] *for that task."*

Weighted valence of success [$^o Va(SucA^n)$] is a *resultant force* of the variables involved in anticipation of success. Similarly, a weighted or resultant negative valence of failure may be symbolized as the product of a person's subjective probability of failure [$Po(FaiA^n)$] on a task at some level of difficulty and the valence of failure for him on that task [$Va(FaiA^n)$]:

$$^o Va(FaiA^n) = Va(FaiA^n) \times Po(FaiA^n)$$

It is important to remember that the valence of failure is negative and therefore that the above equation represents the weighted valence of failure [$^o Va(FaiA^n)$] as a force to *avoid* the task. As an avoidance force, it would always be entered, were the exact values known, as a negative number into the equation.

In order to determine the individual's actual decision on any given task, the weighted valence for success and the weighted valence for failure must be algebraically combined. For example, using purely arbitrary values, suppose that a person's immediate past performance on the dart board has been to hit the "7"circle. His value for this success [$Va(SucA^7)$] is 5. His subjective probability of success for hitting the seventh circle [$Po(SucA^7)$] is 50 percent, and his probability of failing to hit the seventh circle is, therefore, 50 percent [$Po(FaiA^7)$]. The person's valence for failure, the negative value he subjectively assigns to his feelings of discomfort at the thought of failure [Va(FaiA⁷)], is –3. Following Lewin's formula for weighted valence of success:

$$Va(SucA^7) \times Po(SucA^7) = {}^oVa(SucA^7)$$
$$5 \quad \times \quad 50 \quad = \quad 250$$

and for weighted valence of failure:

$$Va(FaiA^7) \times Po(FaiA^7) = {}^oVa(FaiA^7)$$
$$-3 \quad \times \quad 50 \quad = \quad -150$$

Finally, the weighted valences for success and failure (250 and –150) are summed to determine the resultant valence or net attraction of that task for that person:

$$^oVa(SucA^7) + {}^oVa(FaiA^7) = {}^oVa(A^7)$$
$$250 \quad + \quad -150 \quad = \quad 100$$

Considered by itself, this outcome is meaningless. It serves only to illustrate the use of Lewin's concepts. To understand the implications of these concepts, it is necessary to compare the resultant valences for a whole series of tasks graded in difficulty level from very easy to very difficult. To these possibilities, we turn next.

Realistic and Unrealistic Levels of Aspiration

Lewin's and others' research showed that most subjects behave realistically. That is to say, while they aspire to a higher level of achievement than their immediate last effort, the level of their aspiration hovers realistically close to their demonstrated ability. A small minority of subjects, however, behave "atypically." These subjects set their aspiration levels unrealistically high, relative to their past performance, or unrealistically low. Lewin's model of combined forces should, in principle, be able to account for both the "typical," realistic performer, and the "atypical," unrealistic one.

Typical Subject: Realistic Goal Discrepancy

The first example to be examined begins with the premise of our last illustration, namely, that the person in the dart-throw situation has just thrown a "7." However, in order for the scale of values to be broad enough to illustrate the principles involved, the range of possible circles in this dart board is not ten but fifteen. Following Atkinson (1964, pp. 101–102), the columns of Lewin et al.'s (1944, p. 358) original table of values have been rearranged in Table 11–1 to conform to the order of operations in the sequence of equations presented thus far.

TABLE 11–1: ILLUSTRATION OF LEVELS OF ASPIRATION WITH ARBITRARY VALUES

LEVELS OF DIFFICULTY	ATTRACTION TO TASK $[°Va(SucA^n)] =$ $Va(SucA^n) \times Po(SucA^n)$	AVOIDANCE OF TASK $[°Va(FaiA^n)] =$ $Va(FaiA^n) \times Po(FaiA^n)$	RESULTANT VALENCE $[°Va(A^n)] =$ $°Va(SucA^n) + °Va(FaiA^n)$
15	$10 \times 0 = 0$	$0 \times 100 = 0$	0
14	$10 \times 0 = 0$	$0 \times 100 = 0$	0
13	$10 \times 0 = 0$	$0 \times 100 = 0$	0
12	$10 \times 0 = 0$	$0 \times 100 = 0$	0
11	$10 \times 5 = 50$	$0 \times 95 = 0$	50
10	$9 \times 10 = 90$	$0 \times 90 = 0$	90
9	$7 \times 25 = 175$	$-1 \times 75 = -75$	100
8	$6 \times 40 = 240$	$-2 \times 60 = -120$	120 Level of Aspiration
7*	$5 \times 50 = 250$	$-3 \times 50 = -150$	100 Past Performance
6	$3 \times 60 = 180$	$-5 \times 40 = -200$	-20
5	$2 \times 75 = 150$	$-7 \times 25 = -175$	-25
4	$1 \times 90 = 90$	$-9 \times 10 = -90$	0
3	$0 \times 95 = 0$	$-10 \times 5 = -50$	-50
2	$0 \times 100 = 0$	$-10 \times 0 = 0$	0
1	$0 \times 100 = 0$	$-10 \times 0 = 0$	0

Too Difficult

+1

Goal Discrepancy

Too Easy

*Immediate past performance on dart toss. Note that task with the largest magnitude of resultant valence in last column (120) is one level of difficulty higher than past performance. Goal discrepancy is therefore 1 in the positive direction. (Modified from Lewin et al., 1944, p. 388.)

The first column of Table 11–1 may be conceptualized as the levels of difficulty on a dart-throwing task. To obtain an initial orientation, consult the central horizontal row of the table, which contains the relationships already derived in the previous example of the individual who has achieved a "7" on his last throw.

Returning to the first column, it can be seen that the individual views the possibility of landing a dart in circles from the twelfth level upward as "Too Difficult" even to attempt. These extremely difficult levels do not engage his motivation at all. On the other hand, the zone of difficulty from about the fourth circle down to the first is viewed as so "easy" as not to be worth the effort. Therefore, these four levels of difficulty also do not engage his motivation. His immediate past experience was the feat of landing a dart in the seventh circle of the board, and this achievement is indicated in the table's central horizontal row.

The remainder of Table 11–1 is divided into three large units, one for each determinant of level of aspiration: $^0Va(SucA^n)$; $^0Va(FaiA^n)$; and $^0Va(A^n)$. The first large column, *Attraction to Task,* lists arbitrary numbers for the individual's value for success $[Va(SucA^n)]$ for each level of difficulty; values of his subjective probability of being successful at each level $[Po(SucA^n)]$; and the product of their multiplication. The values are arbitrary, but they conform to Lewin's conceptualization that *the more difficult the task, the greater the valence of success* and *the lower the probability of attaining it.* Hence, while valence for success $[Va(SucA^n)]$ increases upward from his past performance level (7), his probability of success $[Po(SucA^n)]$ decreases in the same direction. In fact, his probability of success drops to 0 for tasks 12 through 15. Even though these tasks are most valued $[Va(SucA^{12-15})=10]$, the product of these values is zero because the individual feels little hope of ever attaining them. Consequently, the *resultant valence of success* for tasks above 12 is zero; they are highly valued, but unattainable. Therefore they exert no force on the individual.

His last performance at task 7 is assigned a 50% probability of success because, having actually achieved it, he reasons that he has a 50/50 chance of attaining it each time he tries. This outlook is essentially realistic since there are only two possibilities: success or failure. His past experience has shown that this level of achievement is *possible,* but not certain, because at least sometimes he fails to achieve it. Thus, realistically speaking, level 7 represents his average best performance in the past.

Although the highest magnitude of valence for success is at task 7 $[^0Va(SucA^7)=250]$, we have to take account not only of the attractive forces represented in this section of the table, but of the repellent ones of failure at this task. The second large unit of Table 11–1, *Avoidance of Task,* lists values for the valence of failure $[Va(FaiA^n)]$; for the probability of failure $[Po(FaiA^n)]$; and for their product $[^0Va(FaiA^n)]$, the resultant valence of failure. In this section of the table, the reverse relationship has been maintained so that the value of avoiding failure *increases* as task difficulty grows easier, and the probability of failure increases to certainty (100 percent) as tasks become more difficult.

If we confine our attention for the moment to the past performance (7) segment of this second large column, we can see that Lewin and his colleagues assigned a negative value (–3) to the individual's valence of failure on this task. His probability of failing [$Po(FaiA^7)$] is, of course, 50% since his probability of success was 50%. The product of his valence of failure and probability of failure [$Va(FaiA^7) \times Po(FaiA^7)$] is therefore –150 (–3 X 50). This figure is the resultant negative valence, the overall tendency to *avoid* the seventh-level task. This value, as we have seen, must be added to the attractive value of the task: 250 + –150 = 100, so that the resultant overall valence for task 7 is ascertained. Column 3 of Table 1 lists the overall Resultant Valences for all 15 levels of difficulty, and task 7 can now be compared to them.

Scanning the last large column of Table 11–1, the resultant values for the 15 levels of difficulty reach their greatest magnitude at task 8, with a value of 120. Thus, task 8 has the greatest overall attractive value for the individual who has just completed task 7 successfully, *and, therefore, it is this task to which he aspires.* His goal discrepancy is +1, a realistic aspiration because he desires to move upward from task 7 to task 8, a difference of only one level.

This individual is behaving realistically because he sets his goals well within the boundary of his ability as demonstrated by past performance. Lewin's formulation correctly predicts that his immediate past performance of 7 will not be the highest valence for him, because he has already mastered it. Yet he does not aspire so far above his past success that attainment would be impossible.

But what of the individual for whom the fear of failure is so intense that he will do anything to avoid failing? To say it another way, what happens to the type of personality who is not *attracted* to any task so much as he is *repelled* by the thought of *possible* failure?

"Atypical" Subject: Unrealistic Goal Discrepancy

The question can be answered by reference to Table 11–2. All of the Attraction to Task (Column 2) values in this table are the same as those in Table 11–1. There is a key difference, however, between the two tables. The valence of failure values [$Va(FaiA^n)$] in column 3 of Table 11–2 have been *doubled*. Thus, Table 11–2 illustrates the case of the individual for whom the fear of failure is paramount. The result is clearly discernible: He shifts his level of aspiration *upward* toward the level 10 task, for an unrealistic goal discrepancy of +3.

To understand this paradoxical outcome for the atypical subject, a glance at the last column, Resultant Valence, is sufficient. Tasks from level 6 downward have such high negative (avoidance) valences that failure at any task below his past performance level of 7 provokes intense discomfort. Such tasks are interpreted as "easy" and therefore as intensely embarrassing.

TABLE 11–2: VALENCE OF FAILURE $[Va(FaiA^n)]$ VALUES DOUBLED FROM TABLE 11–1

LEVELS OF DIFFICULTY	ATTRACTION TO TASK $[{}^\circ Va(SucA^n)]$ = $Va(SucA^n) \times Po(SucA^n)$	AVOIDANCE OF TASK $[{}^\circ Va(FaiA^n)]$ = $Va(FaiA^n) \times Po(Fai^n)$	RESULTANT VALENCE $[{}^\circ Va(A^n)]$ = ${}^\circ Va(SucA^n) + {}^\circ Va(FaiA^n)$
15	$10 \times 0 = 0$	$0 \times 100 = 0$	0
14	$10 \times 0 = 0$	$0 \times 100 = 0$	0
Too 13	$10 \times 0 = 0$	$0 \times 100 = 0$	0
Difficult 12	$10 \times 0 = 0$	$0 \times 100 = 0$	0
11	$10 \times 5 = 50$	$0 \times 95 = 0$	50
Goal + 3 → 10	$9 \times 10 = 90$	$0 \times 90 = 0$	90 Level of Aspiration
Discrepancy 9	$7 \times 25 = 175$	$-2 \times 75 = -150$	25
8	$6 \times 40 = 240$	$-2 \times 60 = -240$	0
7*	$5 \times 50 = 250$	$-6 \times 50 = -300$	–50 Past Performance
6	$3 \times 60 = 180$	$-10 \times 40 = -400$	–220
5	$2 \times 75 = 150$	$-14 \times 25 = -350$	–200
Too 4	$1 \times 90 = 90$	$-18 \times 10 = -180$	–90
Easy 3	$0 \times 95 = 0$	$-20 \times 5 = -100$	–100
2	$0 \times 100 = 0$	$-20 \times 0 = 0$	0
1	$0 \times 100 = 0$	$-20 \times 0 = 0$	0

Doubled Values

*Immediate past performance on dart toss. Note that the task with the largest magnitude of Positive resultant valence with these *doubled values* is now 90, in last column. Goal discrepancy is *increased* to 3 in the positive direction. Because this person fears failure more strongly than person in Table 1, resultant Positive valence is highest at Level 10. (Modified from Lewin et al., 1944, p. 365.)

His immediate past performance on the task at level 7 is likewise negative because the avoidance valences have been doubled. Going upward from his past performance level, the combination of valences that yields the greatest resultant *attractive* valence [$^{o}VaA^{n}$)] is 90 at level 10, a task three steps higher in difficulty than his past successful effort. He is consequently driven by his fear of failure to seek a task that is three steps more difficult than the task on which he has 50% of the time been successful in the past.

This individual is behaving *unrealistically*. He is acting to *avoid failure*, not just to attain success. The task at level 10 is just difficult enough so that its negative valence for failure is at the 0 level, and the resultant overall valence based on its value for success is high enough to exceed any other task in attractive value. The question arises: Why shouldn't even more difficult tasks, say 13 or 14, be *more attractive* since they are even less negative? Recall that as the level of difficulty *increases*, the negative valence of failure decreases. But for tasks above level 12, the degree of difficulty is so great that the individual views them as impossible. Therefore, they are valueless in attractive power.

Behavior as a Function of Person and Environment

Lewin conceived of level of aspiration as a phenomenon with complex, interrelated determinants. Not only is the behavior of individuals governed by inherent personality factors like striving for success and avoidance of failure, but also by the immediate situation and by immediate past performance. The balance achieved between an individual's tendency to approach success and his avoidance of failure is a good model of Lewin's entire approach to personality and motivation, for Lewin conceived of personality as a *dynamic balance or equilibrium of forces* acting outwardly from the person on his environment, and inwardly upon the person from his situation.

Individual personality factors do not of themselves explain behavior, any more than a description of the situation by itself is sufficient to account for a person's activities. Only when the person is conceived of as operating within an entire *field of forces* can his behavior at the moment be understood. Lewin put this conceptualization into the form of an equation:

$$B = F (P,E)$$

which may be read: *"Behavior is a function of the person and his immediate environment"* (1946, pp. 918–919; 1935, p. 79; 1936, p. 11). These two sets of factors, state of the person and his environment at the moment, were postulated by Lewin to be parts of the same *whole*. Thus, environment is as much dependent on the person as the person is dependent on his environment:

> In other words, to understand or to predict behavior, the person and his environment have to be considered as *one* constellation of inter-dependent factors. We call the totality of these factors the life space (LSp) of that individual, and write B = F(P,E) = F(LSp). [Lewin, 1946, p. 919]

To Lewin, the task of psychology was to specify the nature of the function (F) that relates behavior to the life space. In short, he was attempting to create for psychology a description of the *laws* that regulate behavior.

Aristotelian and Galilean Thinking: Lewin's Scientific Strategy

There are two ways in which the behavior of the individual who sets his level of aspiration unrealistically can be understood. The first, and historically oldest strategy, is to consider him a special, unique, or "atypical" case in a class apart from the majority of "normal" or typical individuals. In this conceptual strategy, the individual behaves as he does *because* he is exceptional, *because* he is immune to the laws of behavior set by the majority. More important, his behavior is caused by factors uniquely inherent in him, variables that are purely products of his special character. It is, after all, he who differs from the behavior observed most frequently for others in a situation that is the same for them as it is for him. To repeat, the unrealistic individual is conceptualized as occupying a class apart from the normal, a class characterized by principles different from those underlying the behavior of the majority. His behavior is different because the class to which he belongs is different.

The second and more sophisticated strategy for conceptualizing the "atypical" cases or the uniqueness of the individual with variable aspiration level is to interpret his anomalous behavior as one part of an *event structure*. An event structure is the total combination of person and situation variables that interact at one moment in time, creating thereby a unique whole. Out of their interaction emerges the specific behavior in question. The focus of this strategy is on attempting to explain exceptionality as a product of unique combinations of known principles or laws. *The same laws that govern the most frequently observed behavior of the majority govern the atypical case when they combine in a unique way.* The general laws are not violated by the unique case; they are just as applicable once the different interrelationship of this unique person's state with the state of the situation at that moment is made explicit.

The first of these conceptual strategies that identifies lawfulness with frequency of occurrence is the *Aristotelian mode of thought,* characteristic of medieval physics (Lewin, 1936, pp. 8, 19). Medieval physics slowly evolved away from Aristotelian class explanations of phenomena in its transition toward *Galilean* "dynamic" physics. Galilean conceptualization characterizes the second mode of representing the atypical level of aspiration-subject as a total event structure, obeying a unique combination of known laws.

For Aristotle, phenomena could be described as lawful when they occurred with regularity. The more frequent the occurrence, the stronger the law governing it (Lewin, 1935, p. 8). Exceptional occurrences are not lawful and cannot be explained by any application of the principles they seemingly violate. Indeed, the very fact that some events *can* violate a law is strong support for the existence of laws that operate with general regularity. In Aristotelian thinking, the "exception proves the rule."

Aristotelian thinking and its contrast to Galilean thought occupied Lewin at some length, for psychology in his view was still in the throes of Aristotelian thinking (1935, pp. 3, 35). Lewin elucidated some of the general characteristics of Aristotelian thinking. First, Aristotelian concepts are evaluative and normative. The scientist anthropomorphically assigns values of good and bad to the phenomena he observes. For example, in Aristotelian physics there was a distinction between the "higher" heavenly movement of stars and the "lower" earthly movement of terrestrial objects. The laws of motion for heavenly bodies like stars could not be employed to understand the behavior of objects falling on earth.

Second, Aristotelian physics classified objects into categories on the basis of their presumed inherent properties, as observed by the scientist. For Aristotle, membership in a particular class was of paramount importance because the class defined the essence of the object and determined its behavior. Aristotelian classification took the form of paired opposites like cold-warm, dry-moist. Such classes were rigidly conceived to be mutually exclusive and exhaustive.

As an analogous phenomenon, were we to conceive of normal and neurotic behavior as two opposite classes of human personality, mutually exclusive categories, we would be very Aristotelian in style. Fortunately, with the advent of Freud, among others, neurotic behavior was seen as one end of a varying continuum of behavior that ranges through *degrees* of normality. In place of the normal-abnormal dichotomy, Freud conceptualized all behavior as evidencing various degrees of anxiety and defensiveness. Similarly, so-called normal phenomena like dreams and slips of the tongue are governed by the same principles that shape neurotic symptom formation. The difference is a matter of degree and combination of events. In this sense, Freud was a Galilean thinker who *homogenized* what were once diverse categories.

Third, Aristotelian thought emphasized historical causes in understanding phenomena, and thus was limited to the investigation of events as they occurred. What has most often happened in the past is true of the future if the object belongs to the same class:

> A crude example will make this clearer: light objects, under the conditions of everyday life, *relatively frequently* go up; heavy objects go down. The flame of the fire, at any rate under the conditions known to Aristotle, almost always goes upward. It is these *frequency rules,* within the limits of the climate, mode of life, etc., *familiar to Aristotle, that determine the nature and tendency to be ascribed to each class of objects* and lead in the present instance to the conclusion that flames and light bodies have a tendency upward. [Lewin, 1935, p. 7; italics added]

Flames are classified with light bodies, and the observed regular occurrence of their past behavior in motion upward defines the essence of the class "light body."

Fourth, the really crucial difference between Aristotelian and Galilean thinking as Lewin interpreted it for psychology lay in the example of the modern physicist's attempts to understand the diversity of the universe as *gradations of fundamental uniformity:*

> The outlook of a Bruno, a Kepler, or a Galileo is determined by the idea of a comprehensive, *all embracing unity of the physical world.* The same law governs the course of the stars, the falling of stones, and the flight of birds. This *homogenization* of the physical world with respect to the validity of law deprives the division of physical objects into rigid abstractly defined classes of the critical significance it had for Aristotelian physics, in which membership in a certain conceptual class was considered to determine the physical nature of an object. [Lewin, 1935, p. 7; italics added]

Lewin's conceptualization of aspiration level is a case of *homogenization* of subject matter. The concepts of rational decision making and the apparently irrational behavior of the atypical subject are explained by one uniform set of principles. Both realistic and unrealistic goal discrepancies are incorporated under one set of laws, the differences between them handled by differing combinations of valences and subjective probability, not by different principles.

Fifth, in contrast to Aristotelian thought, the Galilean thinker conceptualizes a phenomenon as a relationship of a concrete individual to a concrete situation. The Galilean scientist creates a concrete situation that is abstracted from the stream of events that occurs spontaneously. The situation he creates is one in which he can control the conditions and manipulate them. Instead of asking "What has most often happened in the past?" the Galilean asks: "Given that this event has happened, *what would happen if* I changed the conditions in this specific way?" The "what would happen if" type of question is the essential mode of thought of the Galilean conceptualization. Unlike the Aristotelian who observes what happens as it happens spontaneously, the Galilean actively intervenes in events, restructures them according to imaginative hypothesis ("what would happen if?"), and observes what his alteration of relationship among the variables produces.

The Galilean is concerned to construct experiments in imagination and to test them in reality. The creation of a "pure" or concrete situation in which to manipulate conditions was exemplified by Galileo's studies of falling bodies. He rejected the observation of free falling bodies because he felt that the situation could not be controlled and the movements were too rapid to be measured. Unlike Aristotle, Galileo was unwilling to accept the *unquestioned* evidence of direct observation. Instead, he constructed a "pure" concrete case with inclined planes and slower moving objects. The situational factors, namely, the slope of the plane and the weight of the moving body could be varied at will. Thus the characteristics of the body and the situation in which it behaves were the subjects of Galileo's scrutiny and manipulations.

A systematic comparative summary of Aristotelian and Galilean thinking as interpreted by Lewin (1936) is given in Table 11–3.

The Person Conceptualized as Buffeted by Forces in a Field of Valences

Conjure up and reflect upon the images evoked by Kurt Koffka's beautifully lucid example of the mutual influence of a person and his immediate environment. Koffka was clearly a Galilean thinker:

> Think of yourselves as basking in the sun on a mountain meadow or on a beach, completely relaxed and at peace with the world. You are doing nothing, and your environment is not much more than a soft cloak that envelops you and gives you rest and shelter. And now suddenly you hear a scream, "Help! Help!" How different you feel and how different your environment becomes. Let us describe the two situations in field terms. At first your field was, to all intents and purposes, homogeneous and you were in equilibrium with it. No action, no tension. As a matter of fact, in such a condition even the differentiation of the Ego and its environment tends to become blurred; I am part of the landscape, the landscape is part of me. And then, when the shrill and pregnant sound pierces the lulling stillness, everything is changed. Whereas all directions were dynamically equal before, now there is one direction that stands out, one direction

TABLE 11–3: ARISTOTELIAN AND GALILEAN THINKING COMPARED

STRATEGY	ARISTOTELIAN	GALILEAN
1. Goal	To discover the essence of things and the causes behind all occurrences.	To discover laws. To predict individual cases.
2. Concept Formation	Division into classes, rigid and opposite.	Homogenization of phenomena; psychological phenomena treated as one field continuum governed by same laws.
3. Nature of Lawfulness	Lawfulness exists only where there is regularity of occurrence; individual case is not lawful. A law is a rule.	All events are lawful, even those that occur only once. Each occurrence is part of total event structure.
4. Proof of Lawfulness	Demonstration of the frequency of similar events, disregarding individual differences. The rule is more certain the greater the number of cases. "Exception proves the rule."	Investigation of individual "pure" cases created in imagination to be manipulated in reality. The asking of "what would happen if?" questions. Systematic variation of factors in controlled situation.
5. Causation or Dynamics	Essence of a thing or its inherent character determines its behavior or movement or tendency; behavior is determined by the past or by the future (teleology).	Every event depends upon the totality of the contemporary situation. Only relations among several facts can be the cause of events.

Based on Lewin, 1936, pp. 9–10.

into which you are being pulled. This direction is charged with force, the environment seems to contract, it is as though a groove had formed in a plane surface and you were being forced down that groove. At the same time there takes place a sharp differentiation between your Ego and the voice, and a high degree of tension arises in the whole field. [Koffka, 1935, p. 43]

Kurt Koffka, one of the pioneers of Gestalt psychology, along with the movement's founder, Max Wertheimer, and Wolfgang Köhler, another member of the pioneering triumvirate, adapted the concept of "field" in physics for use in psychology. Revolutionized by field concepts, physics replaced the earlier notion of the emptiness of space as mere nothingness with the conceptualization of invisible space as a system of stresses, strains, and lines of force. Maxwell and Faraday, and later Einstein, construed the behavior of a local object as subject to the stress, strain, and lines of force spread out into the infinity of the field (cf. Koffka, 1935, pp. 43 ff.; Einstein & Infeld, 1938).

The key word is "system," for the concept of field is nothing without a conceptualization of the interrelationship of the parts to make the whole. A field conception demands that the characteristics of an observed moving object, together with the characteristics of the surrounding forces, be specified in order to predict the object's local motion. Thus, it was a configuration of forces and object that became the focus of modern physics. The Gestalt psychologists sought to capitalize on this conceptual revolution and to apply the fruits of its strategy to the formation of a similar conceptual scheme for psychology. Indeed, the word "Gestalt" can be translated into English as "configuration" or as "whole."

In many ways Lewin followed closely in the tradition of the Gestalt psychologists and their field concepts. He adopted from them his underlying conviction that only by considering the "wholeness" or Gestalt of person and situation as they operate on each other can behavior be understood. Recall Lewin's programmatic formula:

$$B = F(P,E) = F(LSp)$$

Lewin's approach to motivation and personality is often characterized as a field theory because fundamental to Lewin's thinking was the concept of the life space as a field of forces, marked by differentiated regions through which the person moves. The network of motives, forces, and regions is a Gestalt of person and situation, truly a Galilean mode of understanding behavior.

Life Space as Field: Topology

The life space of the individual is a Gestalt of lines of force with differing degrees of differentiation or compartmentalization. It is marked by continually changing location of boundaries, obstacles, and competing forces. In terms of the level of aspiration studies, the individual in that situation may be thought of as behaving in compliance with the net result of complementary forces toward and away from specific goals and valences (tasks). As each task is undertaken or avoided, the whole field of factors, including the person himself, is changed. For once having failed on a given task, one can never behave quite the same way toward that task or toward other tasks higher or lower in the hierarchy of difficulty. Similarly, once having successfully attained some level of achievement, the individual can never again view levels above or below it with the same eyes he had before success intervened.

In order to represent the individual personality within the life space, Lewin had to borrow and reshape several concepts from a branch of geometry known as *topology.* Topology is that form of mathematics that is concerned with space and spatial relationships in geometric patterns and configurations. However, topology pictures such relationships in non-numerical ways. No computations with numbers are possible within its scope.

Space is represented in topology with structural symbols like circles which depict the boundaries of enclosed areas. Such circular closed spaces are called Jordan curves in topology. The term "circle" is used only in the sense that a Jordan curve is a closed figure. A Jordan curve may take any shape as long as no part of the "circle" intersects itself. Thus, an odd-shaped puddle of water could be represented as a Jordan curve, while a figure eight could not.

Lewin adapted many concepts from topology and from vector mathematics in physics to the task of conceptualizing the person in his life space. In fact, life space diagrams may be considered adaptions of Jordan curves and vectors. *Vectors* are lines of force represented by arrows whose length indicates the strength of the force and whose point indicates the region of application. The longer the line, the greater the force of the vector.

Barriers in the Life Space: The Detour Problem

Behavior is always the outcome of the balance of forces operating in the field at a given moment. Life spaces may also include barriers or obstacles to locomotion. Barriers may be real physical entities or symbolic obstacles that stand in the way of desired goals. Consider the situation diagrammed in Figure 11–3.

A child of one year stands behind a U-shaped barrier in region A of the field. The barrier separates him from the goal (+), a piece of candy. Since he cannot climb directly over the barrier because of its height, pathway $W_{A,G}$, the direct route to the candy, is outside the limits of his climbing ability. If he wants to solve the problem without help, he must make a detour that requires him *to turn away from the goal* and proceed in the opposite direction, a pathway represented by $W_{A,D}$. Following pathway $W_{A,D}$ around the barrier eventually would bring him back to the goal. But because he is only one year old, and because he has no experience with such round-about solutions, he is unable to see that a detour is necessary. The diagram in Figure 11–3 indicates that the child's life space is *less extensive* than the situation. In other words, the child's whole psychological world at that moment consists of the barrier and goal without the open

FIGURE 11-3: THE DETOUR PROBLEM

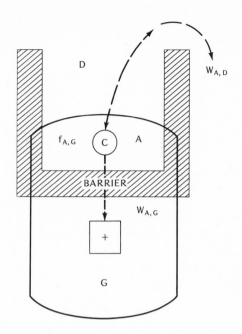

Modified from Lewin, 1946, p. 933.

FIGURE 11-4. THE DETOUR PROBLEM FOR AN OLDER CHILD

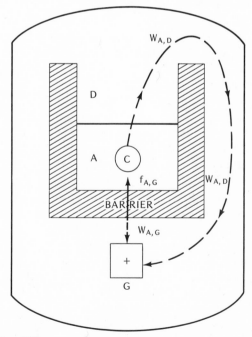

After Lewin, 1946, p. 930.

space at the rear (D) being part of his psychological field. The detour route simply does not exist for him.

For the one-year-old child, the force toward the goal from region A ($F_{A,G}$) is equivalent to path $W_{A,G}$ and to no other pathway (Lewin, 1946, p. 931). Thus, there is not only a physical obstacle preventing the child from reaching the goal, but also an "experience barrier," a lack of insight.

A child of five years, on the other hand, has a much broader, more differentiated view of the situation. Figure 11–4 represents this older child's perspective of the problem. His life space encompasses the entire field of goal, barrier, and detour route. Consequently, he is able to see that the only appropriate solution is the round-about path $W_{A,D}$. Even though this route will take him away from the goal momentarily, he is able to foresee the eventual consequences of the detour. For this child the forces of the field are more complex because the tendency to locomote toward the goal from region A is equivalent to both paths: $W_{A,G}$ and $W_{A,D}$. What makes him decide on the detour path rather than the direct and unachievable route is his greater degree of insight based on his accumulated experience. In Lewinian terminology, the life space of the older child is more "differentiated," that is, contains more regions, more interconnections between regions, and a greater number of alternative pathways.

Characteristics of the Life Space: Explanatory Principles

Lewin distinguished between the psychological world and the physical world. Both are present within the life space. From the psychological perspective, the conditions of the life space represent the person's entire universe at that moment. Theoretically, therefore, it should be possible to derive any behavior from the content of the person's life space. Yet, even if it were possible to delineate the entire content of a person's life space *for one moment in time,* the influence of events that lie outside the life space at that moment, but which may enter in the next instant, obsolete any prediction almost as it is made.

For example, a person alone in his room busy writing a letter may be suddenly interrupted by the appearance of a friend in the doorway. He makes a mistake in his writing. Even if the complete content of the life space and all of the possible interrelationships up to the moment that friend appeared were completely known, a prediction of the letter writer's mistake could not have been derived from that knowledge. The outside influence, a friend who *psychologically* did not exist in the person's life-space situation of "writing a letter alone in a room" is responsible for the mistake (Lewin, 1936, p. 70).

In consequence, Lewin concluded that the psychological world is not dynamically closed. An individual's life space is open at its boundary points to outside physical influences. These influences are not, strictly speaking, a part of the individual's psychological world until they are incorporated within the life space events at a particular moment. Yet, psychologically, such "alien" influences are immeasurably important to an understanding of a person's behavior. Lewin illustrated these concepts with the diagram in Figure 11–5.

FIGURE 11–5

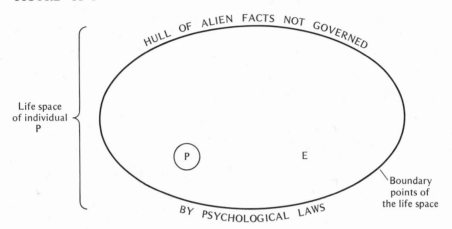

P = Person
E = Psychological Environment

After Lewin, 1936, p. 73.

Figure 11–5 depicts how Lewin conceptualized the separation between the physical world and the psychological world of the individual. The physical world may become significant within the psychological world at any moment. The "hull of alien facts" refers to those influences in the physical world, including other people, who may become subject to the psychological laws governing the person in his life space, but who at the time of observation are not yet within the hull.

> This does not mean that we have to include within the psychological life space the whole physical world with its "objective" characteristics in terms of physics. *These facts are to be included in the representation of the psychological life space only to the extent and in the manner in which they affect the individual in his momentary state.* We can express this by calling them quasi-physical facts. [Lewin, 1936, p. 24; italics added]

In a similar manner, Lewin suggested that social reality should be considered a group of "quasi-social facts," and the individual's personal education and intellectual skills are likewise "quasi-conceptual facts" (1936, pp. 25–26). Thus, the objective physical world has significant effects only to the extent that it is "real" for the person at some particular moment. To this extent, all facts are "quasi-facts."

Lewin formulated three basic principles founded on this conception of the immediacy of events in the life space:

The Principle of Concreteness

Sometimes in their enthusiasm for theory, psychologists confuse a principle of explanation with the phenomenon to be explained. Thus, resort to the concept of "drive" or to the abstraction of "development" does not by itself explain the outcome of behavior. To say that the person did such and such as part of his "developmental trend" is to say nothing. "Effects can be produced only by what is 'concrete,' i.e., by something that has the position of an individual fact which exists at a certain moment . . ." (Lewin, 1936, p. 33). Principles cannot be represented in the life space; only real objects and events can influence behavior.

The Principle of Relational Character

Aristotelian thinking tends to derive an event from the nature of a single object and its presumed inherent nature. For example, personality might be "explained" in Aristotelian form by reliance on the concept of inner drive, or by the concept of inherited traits. The point is that the Aristotelian would seize upon one or the other concept and use it exclusively to explain personality. Lewin, on the other hand, felt that behavior could be explained only as the product of several related facts operating together: "The transition to the Galilean thinking involved a recognition of the general validity of the thesis: An event is always the result of the interaction of several facts" (1936, p. 33). Thus, it is always the dynamic balance of several forces that result in a net force to direct behavior.

The Principle of "Contemporaneity"

Recalling Lewin's formula $B = F(P,E)$, a precise question can be formulated. What is the temporal relationship of behavior (B) to the two factors that make up the situation, Person (P) and environment (E)? In Lewin's conceptualization, neither the past nor the future can influence present events. Only "facts" immediately present in the life space can direct the outcome of a behavioral sequence (Lewin, 1936, p. 34).

> Since neither the past nor the future exists at the present moment it cannot have effects at the present. In representing the life space therefore we take into account only what is contemporary. [Lewin, 1936, p. 35]

The three principles, concreteness, relatedness, and contemporaneity, emphasize the immediacy of psychological reality. For it is only what is real and present to the person that will influence his behavior.

Characteristics of the Person: Specialized Region of the Life Space

Lewin depicted the person as one specialized region of the life space. Within this region, Lewin distinguished the "inner personal" (I) regions from the motor and perceptual region (M). The motor-perceptual region is a kind of boundary between the inner personal region and the environment of the life space.

The inner personal region is itself compartmentalized into peripheral (P) and central (C) segments. The relationships of these person components are shown in Figure 11–6.

Needs and other psychological processes like dreams and fantasies can only influence the environment of the life space by action through the perceptual and motor apparatus, that is, through bodily activity. The parts of the person that are strictly perceptual (eyes, ears, etc.) are partly linked with the motor (muscle) apparatus, and partly differentiated. In a sense—the way we colloquially say that the body is the boundary between a person and his world—Lewin depicted the motor region as part of the body

FIGURE 11–6: THE PERSON

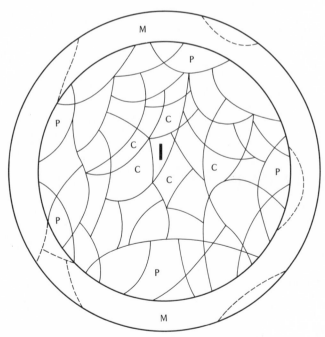

M = Motor–Perceptual Region
P = Peripheral Region of Inner Person
C = Central Region of Inner Person
I = Inner Person

After Lewin, 1936, p. 177.

that serves as a boundary between the "inner person" and the outer world of the life space (1936, p. 177).

The most important function of the motor region is speech because it is the means of communication between the person and his social environment. For that matter, gestural communications like smiling, blinking, and waving are also under the control of the motor region. The purpose of these bodily expressions is, of course, to bring about changes in the environment demanded by changes (e.g., needs) in the inner personal region.

The essential point about Lewin's conceptualization of the person is the relationships among the various subregions. Central and peripheral cells of the inner person are stratified, that is, layered in three dimensions. Peripheral strata (P) are nearer the surface of the boundary between the inner personal region and the environment of the life space. The central strata (C) are more deeply located and only rarely is their expression seen on the surface. For example, there is a difference between superficial anger and intense personal rage. Almost always, a person is able to verbalize concerns that are of only peripheral importance to his inner self. But deep, inner concerns of the central strata are difficult to express. As Lewin stated it, "... it is difficult to touch the real core of the person. ... With some persons it seems to be easy to touch certain central places and to injure them like an 'open wound' " (1936, pp. 180–181).

Though Lewin did not employ the analogy of the actor and his mask, his distinction between inner central and peripheral regions certainly follows in this tradition.

Differentiation, Reality, and Time as Dimensions of the Life Space

The compartmentalization into peripheral and central strata brings up the question of psychological differentiation. Children and adults differ in their degree of experience, in the complexity with which they approach the tasks of life. Lewin represented the difference as *degree of differentiation* of the life space. Children, therefore, are, on the whole, less differentiated into interconnecting regions than adults. Lewin, however, was most careful to point out that the total number of regions was not the most important consideration for determining degree of differentiation. What is more important is the degree of intercommunication between regions, or, as Lewin termed it, *dynamic unity*. Figure 11–7 illustrates the relationship between dynamic unity and complexity of structure.

While the two life spaces in Figure 11–7, A and B, are equally differentiated into compartments, the barriers in person B's life space are more rigid and less permeable. Thus, a change in one region, say region 5, is more likely to affect the whole person represented in A than in B. System B is said to possess less dynamic unity. As a concrete example, system B might

FIGURE 11-7: DYNAMIC UNITY OF THE LIFE SPACE

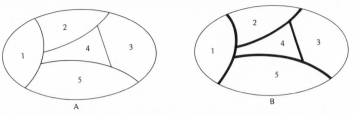

The degree of differentiation in persons A and B differs only in the rigidity of the boundaries, not in the number of regions. Yet Person A is "more differentiated" because intercommunication between regions is more easily accomplished.

After Lewin, 1936, p. 184.

represent the cognitive functioning of a particularly rigid, close-minded individual who is unable to change his opinions or attitudes easily, even in the face of contradictory evidence (cf., for example, Rokeach, 1960; or Witkin et al., 1962).

As development progresses, the child, a relatively plastic creature, is capable of creating new compartments and thus increasing his differentiation. But the original boundaries, those that are older and more practiced because they are present from the beginning, are likely to be the strongest and least permeable. Consider the two persons, A & B, represented in Figure 11–8. The child represented by A is relatively undifferentiated, but the basic boundaries of his cognitive "inner personal" region are set. We might think of these inner personal boundaries as basic moral values and fundamental attitudes toward significant people in his life.

In Figure 11–8, the same basic boundaries are present for child B, but each of the regions, A, B, C, D, has become more differentiated into segments. Thus, there is increased complexity with maturity, but the complexity is organized about basic boundaries.

There is one further characteristic of the person as a differentiated region of the life space that bears exploration. Lewin specified several subdimensions of time as "psychological present," "psychological past," and "psychological future." For the child, the psychological present and future are most significant because his sense of psychological past is relatively shallow. There are, furthermore, various levels of reality that interact with the time dimension. The child, for example, is more governed by fantasy or wishfulness than by the immediate concreteness before him. A child is often less able than an adult to distinguish between fantasy, or wishfulness, and reality (Lewin, 1936, 1939).

In Lewinian terms there is a distinction to be made between a "reality" dimension and an "irreality" dimension. To represent these time and reality-irreality perspectives, Lewin devised three-dimensional representations of the person as a region of the life space. Figure 11–9 illustrates the differences between the child and the adult with regard to the dimensions of reality and irreality.

FIGURE 11-8:   DEVELOPMENT OF DIFFERENTIATED REGIONS

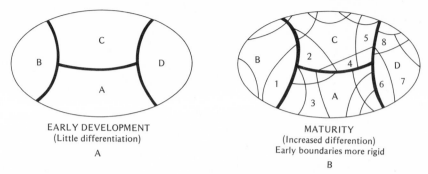

EARLY DEVELOPMENT
(Little differentiation)

A

MATURITY
(Increased differention)
Early boundaries more rigid

B

After Lewin, 1936, p. 190.

FIGURE 11-9:   REALITY-IRREALITY LEVELS IN THE CHILD AND ADULT

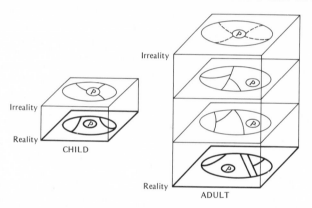

The degree of reality–irreality separation in the child corresponds to the intermediate level of the adult.

After Lewin, 1936, p. 204.

The number of layers along the reality(R)-irreality(I) dimension in Figure 11–9 is greater for the adult. The adult is thus able to make finer discriminations among various levels of imagination and fantasy.

The Person Buffeted by Conflicting Forces: Decision Theory

Lewin's conceptualization of the person as a differentiated region of the life space buffeted by forces of the field leads to a significant representation of psychological conflict. Using Lewin's field model, the psychologist in Galilean fashion can ask: *What would happen if* the person were subjected to two valences exerting *equal* force in *opposite* directions?

Approach-Approach Conflict

Consider as a concrete example the case of the child who must choose between going on a picnic with his family and playing with his friends at home. He can engage in only one of these desirable activities and must relinquish one. Essentially, he is buffeted in his life space by two positive valences exerting equal attraction. His conflict is the difficulty that he has in deciding which goal to approach. This kind of conflict has been appropriately termed an approach-approach conflict (cf. Miller, 1944; Dollard and Miller, 1950), though Lewin himself referred to it by number as a Type I conflict (1935, p. 89).

An approach-approach conflict is relatively easy to resolve because no matter which of the two goals the individual finally approaches, he suffers no really intense negative effects. The situation of the field in an approach-approach conflict is not particularly stable because even the slightest nudge in one or the other direction is sufficient to get the child off dead center. Lewin illustrated a Type I, approach-approach conflict as a person caught between two positive valences, each exerting force on him, as shown in Figure 11–10.

FIGURE 11-10: APPROACH-APPROACH CONFLICT

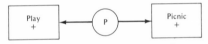

The two positive valences exert equally attractive forces on the person (P).

After Lewin, 1935, p. 89.

Conflicts are thus conceptualized as decision processes in Lewinian field theory (1946, p. 943; 1936, pp. 137–138). The person is pictured as caught between two overlapping fields in which the forces for each goal are nearly matched in intensity. He alternates between seeing himself in some future situation in which one of the goals (G1) is adopted at the cost of the other (G2); and imagining himself having chosen in the opposite direction, approaching Goal 2 and relinquishing Goal 1. The final decision, that is, the direction his behavior will actually take, as in the level of aspiration studies, will be determined by the goal whose force the individual feels is the strongest. This decision will, of course, be influenced by how close the person comes to one or the other goal.

Decision in a conflict situation is represented in Figure 11–11 as two overlapping life spaces. The overlap and the near equivalence of the two goal's attractive forces ($F_{P,G}1$) and ($F_{P,G}2$) are represented by equal length vectors (arrows). Note that the person is in region D, the region of overlap.

Approach-Avoidance Conflict

A conflict situation may also arise when the driving forces of a *single* goal are both positive and negative at the same time. For example, a child may want to climb a tree at the same time that he is afraid of falling. Hence, the tree has both positive and negative valences simultaneously. Lewin depicted this kind of conflict, an approach-avoidance or Type II conflict, as two opposing valences exerting contradictory forces on the person from a single region, as illustrated in Figure 11-12.

An approach-avoidance conflict is difficult to resolve because the strength of the negative avoidance forces and positive attractive forces vary with distance from the goal to different degrees. At some point from the goal, an equilibrium of attractive and repellent forces is established. The strength of the valence to approach exactly matches the strength of the tendency to retreat. Paralysis of behavior results. An assumption of Lewin's conceptualization of approach-avoidance conflict is that the *strength of the avoidance tendency is greater than the strength of the approach tendency at distances close to the goal.* To say it another way, the more the child backs off from the tree, the faster the avoidance tendency diminishes, relative to the approach tendency. This relationship is graphed in Figure 11–13. Note that the curve for the negative valence drops to zero strength at some distance from the goal, while the approach tendency continues to operate. Yet, as the child approaches closer to the goal, the avoidance tendency rises more sharply, causing him to retreat again to a safe distance, and so on. The farther he withdraws, the less strength the avoidance valence has, and consequently the more attractive the goal now seems. The child begins to approach the tree again, until the valence for avoidance again increases in strength. This vacillation between approach and avoidance is characteristic of the Type II conflict.

FIGURE 11-11: CONFLICT AS OVERLAPPING SITUATIONS

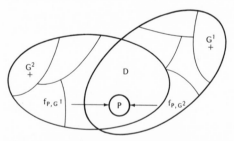

Person (P) is in the region of intersection (D) of two situations that contain equally attractive valences (G+). The forces (f^P, G^1) of the two goals are represented as equal–length vectors.

After Lewin, 1946, p. 943.

FIGURE 11-12: APPROACH-AVOIDANCE CONFLICT

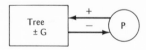

A single goal exerts both positive and negative force on the individual.

Modified from Lewin, 1935, p. 89.

Avoidance-Avoidance Conflict

The last situation in which incompatible field forces cause psychological conflict concerns the situation in which a person must decide between two equally *negative* goals. He is repelled by both, but must decide to endure one or suffer the consequences of the other. For example, a mother may say to her child, "If you don't do your arithmetic homework, you will be spanked." The child is confronted with two equally unpalatable alternatives (Lewin, 1935, p. 121). He desires neither to undertake homework, nor to suffer the consequences of avoiding it, as illustrated in Figure 11–14

As first glance, it might seem that an avoidance-avoidance conflict is not essentially different from a Type I, approach-approach conflict. The diagrams are essentially similar, except for the change from two positive to two negative valences. In order to understand the real difference between them, it is necessary to consider the field of forces involved in each type. In the Type I, approach-approach conflict, the forces acting on the child

FIGURE 11-13: RELATIONSHIP BETWEEN DISTANCE AND STRENGTH OF FORCE FOR CONFLICTING TENDENCIES IN AN APPROACH-AVOIDANCE CONFLICT

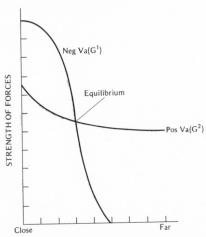

Positive valence (desire to climb tree) continues to exert attraction some distance from tree, while negative valence (fear of falling) drops off to zero.

FIGURE 11-14: AVOIDANCE-AVOIDANCE CONFLICT

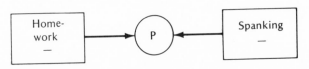

The person is caught between two negative valences, one of which he must endure. After Lewin, 1935, p. 122.

lead to a stable equilibrium within the field. In other words, the forces are *task directed* in an approach-approach conflict. Like the approach-avoidance conflict, there is at some point a balance of forces in the approach-approach situation such that the strength of both goals' attractiveness is equal. Until a decision is reached to value one goal more than the other, behavior is stabilized within the field and directed toward the goals. In common parlance, there is nothing else to do but decide between them. The field forces of the approach-approach conflict are illustrated in the first diagram in Figure 11–15.

In field terms, all of the vectors of the approach-approach conflict tend in the same direction, toward the goals. But the second diagram in Figure 11–15 shows that this unity of direction is not the case in an avoidance-avoidance conflict. Here, all the field forces are directed away from the goals. No stable equilibrium is reached in an avoidance-avoidance conflict because there are some forces from both goals that direct the person to *leave the field* entirely. Thus, in an avoidance-avoidance conflict there *is* something else a person can do other than pay attention to the tasks at hand. He can concentrate on escaping both goals.

FIGURE 11-15: FIELD FORCES IN APPROACH-APPROACH AND AVOIDANCE-AVOIDANCE CONFLICTS

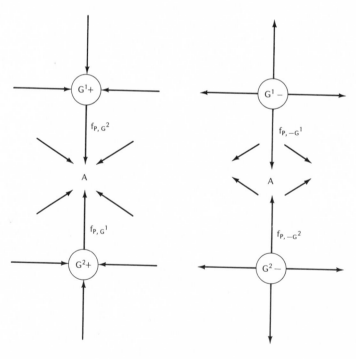

The person is in region A.

After Lewin, 1946, p. 937.

Leaving the Field

To "leave the field" does not necessarily mean a physical locomotion out of the region of the conflict, although this behavior toward escape is certainly one possibility. One can leave the field by *psychological withdrawal* without setting foot outside the situation. Such withdrawal often takes the form of directing attention to other activities and ignoring the elements of the conflict. Thus, for example, a child burdened by the choice between a spanking and homework may start to clean up his room because this substitute activity is one that his mother also finds satisfactory. In effect, the child hopes to avoid the unpalatable choice and to distract his mother's interest at the same time. He has effectively left the field by changing it.

Lewin described three ways in which leaving the field may be accomplished: *physical flight; substitution* of another task that satisfies the authority figure, as just described; or outright *deception,* whereby the person caught in the dilemma lies to create the illusion that he has complied with the demands of the situation.

Transcending the Spatial Analogy: The Zeigarnik Effect

With Lewin's emphasis on locomotion within and between regions of the life space, there comes the danger of losing sight of the fact that we are dealing only with an analogy. The concept of the person's locomotion through the field, buffeted by attracting and repelling forces, is of course meant to represent *psychological dynamics.* In true Galilean spirit, Lewin and his students were able to create "pure" situations in which the conceptual model was subject to tests of its explanatory power.

Among the elegant and precise experiments designed and executed by Lewin and his group of graduate students were those of Bluma Zeigarnik (1927, in Ellis, 1967) on forces involved in remembering finished and unfinished tasks. To understand the significance of Zeigarnik's work, recall that Lewin's conceptual scheme focuses attention on the resultant strength of forces acting on the person relative to all competing forces in the field at that moment. The effect of the forces is to create within the individual states of tension corresponding roughly to needs or "quasi-needs." Could the process of memory be conceptualized in terms of forces and states of tension? Zeigarnik, and later Ovsiankina (1928), developed a means to test the model and answer the question.

Fantastic Memory of the Berlin Waiters

The story is sometimes told that Zeigarnik's interest in the problem of memory as a tension system within the individual was sparked by her observations of the fantastic feats of memory performed by waiters in Berlin sidewalk cafés (cf. Morgan & King, 1966, p. 146; Atkinson, 1964, p. 83). Though each waiter was responsible for several tables and the orders of several parties at each table, none of the waiters ever wrote down the orders. Nor did any of them forget "who got what" up to the moment the order was served. After each customer's bill was tallied in the waiter's head, and his task was therefore complete, he quickly forgot that customer and his order. This persistency of memory until *completion of the task* suggested to Zeigarnik that a tension system was operating up to the point of carrying out the intention.

Though the Berlin waiter story may be merely apocryphal, Zeigarnik did devise some elegant experiments to test hypotheses drawn from Lewin's field theory. She reasoned that the phenomenon of memory might be related systematically to the subject's *intention* to complete a task. If a comparison were to be made between a subject's recall of tasks that had been completed and tasks on which the subject had been interrupted before completion, the subject should evidence greater recall of the uncompleted tasks (U). Uncompleted tasks represent an unspent amount of tension, tension that must be released only by completion. Consequently, the tension corresponding to the subject's intention to complete the interrupted task would be evidenced by more efficient recall of the tasks he still intended to work to completion.

Zeigarnik gave 164 subjects, drawn from students, teachers, and children, simple problem-solving tasks to perform. Such activities as mental arithmetic problems, puzzles, and manual tasks like constructing a cardboard box or modeling a figure from clay were employed. No time limit was set, but subjects generally averaged three to five minutes for eighteen to twenty-two such activities. Without the subject's knowledge, the group of tasks was randomly divided into two subgroups so that one-half of the total number of tasks were interrupted before completion. After the subject had attempted the tasks, and all materials were put out of sight, Zeigarnik asked them to "please tell me what the tasks were upon which you worked during this experiment" (1927, p. 300).

Zeigarnik's results showed that *subjects recalled almost twice as many uncompleted tasks as completed ones.* She expressed her results in the form of a ratio of uncompleted recalled (UR) to completed recalled (CR) tasks:

$$\frac{UR}{CR}$$

In actuality, Zeigarnik found that the ratio of uncompleted to completed tasks recalled was on average 1.9. This finding supports the hypothesis that uncompleted tasks enjoy a clear advantage in the subject's memory. When subjects were then allowed to complete *some* of the interrupted activities, memory for the tasks that remained uncompleted was again better than for those completed:

$$\frac{UR}{CR} = 1.85$$

The only time the near two-to-one superiority of the uncompleted tasks was reduced was when the subject understood before the experiment began that *the activities were to be used as a test of memory.* Under these conditions, the subject functioned to recall as many tasks as possible, regardless of the state of completion, because he perceived the task to be a challenge to his mental skills. Only when the subject was asked in an informal way, after the experiment was over, to recall what he had done, did the "Zeigarnik effect" of the two-to-one superiority of uncompleted tasks become manifest.

Application of Galilean Strategy to a Theory of Recall

Aristotelian conceptualization, it will be recalled, sees the factors that cause behavior as inherent to the organism, as located within and explained by the structure of its personality variables, to the exclusion of its situation. Thus an Aristotelian theorist might explain the need to recall the interrupted tasks as the result of an inherent drive to avoid anxiety over failure (cf. Rapaport, 1971, pp. 94–103). Lewin disdained such one-sided formulations, preferring instead, the concept of *field forces:* situational plus person forces.

The advantage of the field force conceptualization of the Zeigarnik effect, which we shall momentarily survey, has been most lucidly stated by Henle (1957) working in the Gestalt tradition. Henle distinguished between motivational forces arising within the individual, *ego-referent forces,* and forces arising from other parts of the psychological field, that is, *field-referent forces.*

In terms of the Zeigarnik experiments, therefore, a fully adequate Galilean conceptualization requires an accounting for the distinction between forces arising from the *person's* need to recall more interrupted tasks than completed ones, and the forces arising from the nature of the *task* situation itself:

> Not only does the *task* need to be done (a field force); the *individual* needs to do it (an ego force). With the interrupted task technique, for example, the subject both perceives the interrupted activity—perceives the demands of the task have not been met—and is himself interrupted. [Henle, 1957, p. 289]

To ascertain whether ego-referent forces alone are sufficient to explain the Zeigarnik effect, as an Aristotelian conceptualization would have it, it is possible in Galilean fashion to ask some "what would happen if?" questions: *What would happen if the Zeigarnik situation were created with the ego forces eliminated? Would the subject still spontaneously recall more interrupted activities? Would he spontaneously resume more interrupted than completed tasks?*

If the answers are yes, then clearly ego forces alone are not sufficient to explain the effect. Henle reported the results of an unpublished experiment (Baltimore et al., cited in Henle, 1957, p. 290) which created this "what if" situation.

An observer watches a subject perform the Zeigarnik tasks, *but does not himself participate.* He therefore is not personally involved, ego-engaged, as it were. The only forces thus operating for the observer are field forces, not his own needs to complete tasks. The results of such procedure show that the observer recalls the incomplete tasks better; that is, he remembers more of the tasks on which the participating subject was interrupted. Furthermore, the observer will spontaneously choose to work on tasks like those on which the subject was interrupted. The force operating on the observer must therefore arise from the nature of the field forces, not merely from his own needs.[1]

Lewin's great achievement in incorporating the Zeigarnik effect into his theory of field forces was his Galilean persistence in postulating an interaction of field and ego forces to account for the recall of interrupted tasks.

Conceptualization of the Zeigarnik Effect as a Balance of Forces

Another of Lewin's students, Ovsiankina (1928), repeated Zeigarnik's work, but allowed subjects voluntary access to the materials of the tasks, both completed and uncompleted, after the experiment was apparently over. Spontaneously, subjects resumed more of the interrupted tasks than those they had successfully completed. Ovsiankina's experiment demonstrates not only a superiority of recall for interrupted tasks, but also pro-

[1]It can be argued that the results of this experiment do not demonstrate the effects of field forces but only of ego-referent forces, if we assume that the observer *identifies* with the subject. According to this explanation, the observer's ego-needs are vicariously aroused as he unconsciously imagines himself in the place of the subject. As Henle (1957) points out, however, this alternative explanation is a very unlikely possibility in the light of the steps taken to minimize observer-subject identification. For one thing, obvious subject failures were eliminated from the data tabulation to insure against the effects of vicarious observer humiliation and anxiety. Furthermore, observers and subject were total strangers, a fact that argues for minimal identification of observer with subject, though it does not eliminate the possibility. Finally, even if the observer did experience minimal arousal of his ego needs, it must be remembered that *as an observer,* his performance of interrupted tasks still requires an explanation in terms different from those applied to the actual subject. Some *interaction* of field and ego-referent forces is required to account for the observer's resumption of tasks that he himself did not perform because he could not have derived the *same* ego tensions from them as did the subject who directly participated.

vides an overt, behavioral index of the force of the tension created within the individual by interruption of the task. In fact, subjects resumed about 80 percent of the interrupted activities.

Lewin conceptualized these experimental findings in Galilean fashion within his scheme of quasi-mathematical formulation.

Assumption One

Lewin's initial assumption was that the intention to reach a goal (G) corresponds to a tension (t) within some system (S^G) in the person. The amount of such tension will be greater than zero (Lewin, 1951, p. 9):

$$t(S^G) > 0$$

Assumption Two

The tension within the person [$t(S^G)$] is released if the goal (G) is attained (i.e., if the task is completed):

$$t(S^G) = 0 \text{ if } P \subset G$$

This notation is read: "*The tension within the person is equal to zero if Person (P) attains goal region.*"

Assumption Three

Lewin proceeded to coordinate the notion of goal tension with the concept of force in the life space: "To a need for G [tension to complete task] corresponds a force $F_{P,G}$ acting on the person and causing a tendency of locomotion toward G" (1951, p. 10). Specifically:

$$\text{if } t(S^G) > 0 \text{ [then] } F_{P,G} > 0$$

Assumption three implies that when a state of tension exists, it provokes a corresponding change in the individual's location within the life space. It is only a short step from here to the assumption that the force on the person to recall the task ($F_{P,G}$) varies with the amount of tension within the person (Lewin, 1951, p. 16):

$$F_{P,G} = f\,[t(S^G)]$$

This formulation is read: "*Force on the person to recall task* (or reach goal) *is a function (f) of the goal tension system* [$t(S^G)$]."

Assumption Three-A

Besides actual locomotion within the life space, a need or $t(S^G)$ leads to mental activity, to thinking about the task: ". . . in other words, the force $F_{P,G}$ exists not only on the level of doing (reality) but also on the level of thinking (irreality) . . ." (Lewin, 1951, p. 10). The tension will be channeled into an effort to recall:

$$\text{If } t(S^G) > 0 \text{ [then] } F_{PR} > 0$$

which may be read: *"If the tension within the person is greater than zero, then the force on the person to recall* (F_{PR}) *is greater than zero."*

Derivation: Tendency to Recall Uncompleted Tasks

It follows from these four assumptions that the tendency to recall an interrupted or uncompleted task is greater than the tendency to recall a completed one: "This derivation can be made as follows. We indicate the completed task by C, the unfinished one by U, and the corresponding systems [within the person] as S^c and S^u, respectively. We can then state

(a) $t(S^u) > 0$ according to [assumption one]
(b) $t(S^c) = 0$ according to [assumption two]."

(Lewin, 1951, p. 10)

The logical consequence is easily deduced: *If the tension of an uncompleted task is greater than the tension of a completed one, then the corresponding force on the person for uncompleted tasks is greater than for completed ones:*

$$F_{PU} > F_{PC}$$

Implications

Recall that the Zeigarnik ratio $\dfrac{UR}{CR}$ is reduced from 1.9 when the subject is made aware that he is participating in a memory experiment. In other words, the experimenter's instructions induce an additional force in the subject to recall all tasks equally because the purpose of the experiment is a challenge to memory. Lewin called this artificially created tension "induced force" (if_P). Obviously, there are two kinds of induced force because there are two kinds of recall that are enhanced by it: induced force to recall uncompleted tasks ($if_{P,RU}$), and induced force to recall completed tasks ($if_{P,RC}$). Since Lewin's model of the field suggests that behavior is always determined by the total forces acting in the life space at any given moment, we must take account not only of the spontaneous tendency of the person to recall completed and uncompleted tasks ($f_{P,RU}$ and $f_{P,RC}$) but also of those forces induced in him by the experimenter.

Generally, it must hold that when the induced forces are weak, the total resultant force on the person to recall uncompleted tasks is greater than the total resultant force to recall completed tasks, as Zeigarnik showed. The resultant force is always the sum of the induced forces provoked by the experimenter's instructions plus the subject's own spontaneous tendencies: if$_{P,UR}$ + f$_{P,UR}$ = resultant force to recall uncompleted tasks. Similarly, the resultant force to recall completed tasks is given by: if$_{P,RC}$ + f$_{P,RC}$.

Induced forces tend to *decrease* the effects of the subject's own spontaneous need to recall uncompleted tasks more often. Induced forces operate to make him "need" to recall *all* tasks. Since the induced forces are non-specific, that is, they operate equally on complete and uncompleted tasks, we can assume that:

$$if_{P,RU} = if_{P,RC}$$

It can then be predicted that the stronger the induced forces, the closer the $\frac{UR}{CR}$ ratio will be to 1. To say it another way, if the experimenter's instructions to the subject to consider this a task of memory are emphasized, the superiority of the uncompleted tasks in recall will be reduced. In effect, the induced forces are subtracted from the subject's natural tendency to recall more uncompleted tasks.

But as we know, the person spontaneously feels more force to recall uncompleted tasks:

$$f_{P,RU} > 0 \text{ [while] } f_{P,RC} = 0$$

Hence, when the subject is unaware of the purpose of the experiment, *the sum of the induced and spontaneous forces to recall uncompleted tasks is greater than the sum of the induced and spontaneous forces to recall completed ones:*

$$[if_{P,RU} + f_{P,RU}] > [if_{P,RC} + f_{P,RC}]$$

Lewin expressed the implication of this formulation as follows: "The more the recall loses its spontaneity, and becomes a result of the experimenter's instructions, the more the Zeigarnik quotient approaches 1" (1951, p. 19). Consequently, the complete equation for the Zeigarnik effect, taking account of the balance of induced and spontaneous forces, is:

$$\frac{RU}{RC} = F \frac{if_{P,RU} + f_{P,RU}}{if_{P,RC} + f_{P,RC}}, \text{ where F means function.}$$

[Lewin, 1951, p. 19]

The Zeigarnik effect is thus a ratio of combined induced and spontaneous forces.

The Significance of Lewin's Conceptualizations

The significance of the Zeigarnik effect, as well as the importance of the level of aspiration studies, can easily be lost in the welter of symbolic notations. Lewin was attempting to accomplish three very specific goals by his conceptualizations:

1. The creation of a broad, universally applicable set of "laws" or functions to account for the relationship between changes in situation and changes in behavior. Such laws would be independent of any particular brand of psychology. They would stand neutral and apart from particular theoretical content.

2. The application of Galilean thinking to individual cases in the attempt to uncover in the "pure case" of experimentally manipulated situations, the techniques that would best illustrate the interaction of person and situation, behavior and field.

3. The sharpening of vaguely stated psychological hypotheses by the judicious application of mathematical and quasi-mathematical tools to concretely constructed and imaginatively conceived field situations.

In each of these attempts, Lewin achieved different degrees of success. His conceptual system fell somewhat short of the establishment of universal laws of behavior, but it did indicate the usefulness of a conceptual scheme to coordinate research. Lewin's experimental undertakings were innovative and truly Galilean. He and his students demonstrated elegantly the application of Galilean thinking by their design and execution of experiments that yield not only data to confirm the immediate hypothesis, but *relationships* to test the logic of theory. Lewin's development of a conceptual scheme, as, for example, in the Zeigarnik effect and in the level of aspiration studies, had the character of homogenizing diverse subject matter. The persistence of memory and the study of task choice, as well as the decision in a conflict situation, all boil down to one principle: the *balance* of competing forces operating at that moment in the field. For example:

LEVEL OF
ASPIRATION: *strength of the tendency to succeed* versus *strength of the tendency to avoid failure.*

ZEIGARNIK EFFECT: *strength of the tendency to recall complete tasks* versus *strength of the tendency to recall uncompleted tasks.*

CONFLICT: *strength of the tendency to approach* versus *strength of the tendency to avoid.*

Lewin's mathematics laid bare the logic of each situation and homogenized, under the rubric of force, all of those diverse behavioral phenomena.

Summary

Lewin's programmatic formula, $B = F(P,E) = F(LSp)$, established the basic scheme by which he hoped to discover the fundamental laws governing behavior. Beginning with a study of levels of aspiration, Lewin conceptualized the person as surrounded by a field of competing forces. In deciding the level of difficulty to try for, the individual balances his tendency to approach success against his tendency to avoid failure, and he weights the valences of each with his subjective estimate of his chances for success and failure.

The concept of the life space, for Lewin, is similar to the concept of field in physics. The person locomotes through various regions of his life space, buffeted by forces that both attract and repel him. The important point is that no single variable drawn from the subject's personality or from his situation is fully adequate by itself to account for his behavior. Only the totality of the field forces and his momentary psychological state are sufficient explanatory principles.

Lewin specified three principles that emphasize the immediacy of experience within the field:

1. *Concreteness:* Only events that are real and concretely present to the person can affect his behavior.
2. *Contemporaneity:* Only the present moment can be studied. Future and past have significance only in terms of the effects they produce in the present.
3. *Relatedness:* No single "fact" by itself can explain behavior; only combinations of events are sufficient.

With these three principles, Lewin embarked on a Galilean investigation of psychology. Aristotelian thinking, characterized by a concern for naturally occurring events and class descriptions of phenomena, was abandoned by Lewin in favor of the Galilean strategy of creating "pure" cases and asking "what would happen if?" questions.

Lewin conceptualized the person as a differentiated region of the life space. Though he did not employ the imagery of the actor and his mask, he did use a similar distinction between an inner personal region, composed of central or core cells, and peripheral regions nearer the surface. The person is essentially a network of compartments, divided into motor and perceptual regions, and into central and peripheral "personal" regions. The degree of differentiation of the person is a measure of his fund of experience. With maturity, the person and his life space undergo increased compartmentalization into regions that allow for greater complexity of intercommunication among the various subsystems. Additionally, the life space must be understood as a three-dimensional entity, harboring both reality-irreality dimensions and time perspectives of psychological past, present, and future.

Lewin's model of forces allows for a conceptualization of conflict in terms of decision processes. The conflicted individual is caught between two or more overlapping situations, each exerting force. Three types of conflict are presented in terms of the combination of valences and forces acting on the person: approach-approach (++); approach-avoidance (+-); and avoidance-avoidance (- -).

Lewin's field model fostered the design and execution of many empirical investigations. Notable among these were the experiments of Bluma Zeigarnik on the persistence of memory for incomplete tasks. Subjects were found to remember interrupted activities about twice as well as completed ones. Lewin conceptualized Zeigarnik's results in true Galilean fashion as a balance of competing tensions that exert force on the individual to attain the goal—that is, to remember that which he intends to work to completion.

FOR FURTHER READING

Kurt Lewin's most important papers concerning personality theory have been collected into two volumes: *A Dynamic Theory of Personality* (New York: McGraw-Hill, 1935) and *Principles of Topological Psychology* (New York: McGraw-Hill, 1936). Lewin's important work in the area of aspiration level is well summarized by Lewin, Dembo, Festinger, and Sears in "Level of Aspiration," in J. McV. Hunt (Ed.), *Personality and the Behavior Disorders* (New York: Ronald Press, 1944), vol. 1. An overview of Lewin's work in the area of developmental psychology was provided by him in "Behavior and Development as a Function of the Total Situation," in L. Carmichael (Ed.), *Manual of Child Psychology* (New York: Wiley, 1946).

Lewin's theorizing about level of aspiration performance has been expanded and modified by J. W. Atkinson into a theory of achievement motivation. Atkinson's most readable presentation of his own theory is to be found in his *An Introduction to Motivation* (Princeton, N.J.: Van Nostrand, 1964), Chaps. 4, 9, and 10. Another worker in the area of achievement motivation, David McClelland, has written extensively about the conditions under which individuals aspire to success and the societal origins of these motives in *The Achieving Society* (Princeton, N.J.: Van Nostrand, 1961). A collection of readings on the historically important earlier work in the area of achievement motivation is to be found in J. W. Atkinson's (Ed.) *Motives in Fantasy, Action, and Society* (Princeton, N.J.: Van Nostrand, 1958).

Applications of Lewin's work to the area of social interaction may be observed in Lewin's *Resolving Social Conflicts* (New York: Harper & Row, 1951). An important and by now classic study of leadership styles is Lewin, Lippitt, and White's "Patterns of Aggressive Behavior in Experimentally Created 'Social Climates'," in *Journal of Social Psychology* (1939), 10, 271–299.

The Gestalt psychology tradition to which Lewin owed several debts is most comprehensively set forth in Kurt Koffka's *Principles of Gestalt Psychology* (New York: Harcourt, Brace and World, 1935). In a much briefer way, Wolfgang Köhler discussed the philosophical underpinnings and goals of Gestalt psychology in *The Task of Gestalt Psychology* (Princeton, N.J.: Princeton University Press, 1969). In a similar vein, Köhler again tackled the meaning of Gestalt theory for the whole of psychology in *Dynamics in Psychology* (New York: Liveright, 1940).

Desmond Cartwright's "Lewinian Theory as a Contemporary Systematic Framework," in S. Kock (Ed.), *Psychology: A Study of a Science* (New York: McGraw-Hill, 1959), vol. 2, pp. 7–91, is perhaps the best single source for evaluating the significance of Lewin's field theory.

12 GORDON W. ALLPORT
Trait and Self Theory

To the S-R colleague the [eclectic] intuitionist says, "You consider the reflex (e.g., the patellar [knee-jerk]) as a basic model. Fine, but where would you locate in it the laughter of the self-transcending subject who feels silly as he watches his patella respond to the hammer?"

GORDON W. ALLPORT, "The Fruits of Eclecticism: Bitter or Sweet?"

"How Shall a Psychological Life History Be Written?"

Within a year of his graduation from college, at the age of twenty-two, Gordon Allport sent to Sigmund Freud a note announcing that while he, Allport, was visiting Vienna, Freud would no doubt be glad to make his acquaintance. In response to what Allport afterward labeled his "callow forwardness," Freud invited the brash young traveler to his office. The visit proved to be of lasting consequence for Allport's subsequent career as a personality theorist.

Soon after I had entered the famous red burlap room with pictures of dreams on the wall, he summoned me to his inner office. He did not speak to me but sat in expectant silence for me to state my mission. I was not prepared for silence and had to think fast to find a suitable conversational gambit. I told him of an episode on the tram car on my way to his office. A small boy about four years of age had displayed a conspicuous dirt phobia. He kept saying to his mother, "I don't want to sit there . . . don't let that dirty man sit beside me." To him everything was *schmutzig* [filthy]. His mother was a well-starched *Hausfrau*, so dominant and purposive looking that I thought the cause and effect apparent.

When I finished my story Freud fixed his kindly therapeutic eyes upon me and said, "And was that little boy you?" Flabbergasted and feeling a bit guilty, I contrived to change the subject. While Freud's misunderstanding of my motivation was amusing, it also started a deep train of thought. I realized that he was accustomed to neurotic defenses and that my manifest motivation (a sort of rude curiosity and youthful ambition) escaped him. For therapeutic progress he would have to cut through my defenses, but it so happened that therapeutic progress was not here an issue. [1968, pp. 383–384]

Allport further commented that the experience with Freud provided a significant insight into the pitfalls of "depth" psychology: "This experience taught me that depth psychology, for all its merits, may plunge too deep, and that psychologists would do well to give full recognition to manifest motives before probing the unconscious" (1968, p. 384). It is difficult not to see in Allport's midadventure the roots of a personal distaste for psychoanalytic assessment.

Often, in later years, Allport championed research and assessment strategies that emphasized exploration of the "psychic surface" of life (1960, p. 96). A direct question directly put frequently elicits as much, if not more, information about a person's motives than hours of projective testing and psychoanalytic interviewing. Commenting on the prevailing trend of motivational theory in the 1950's, Allport pointed out that psychologists often acted as if the individual's conscious verbal reports about himself were untrustworthy. Indeed, psychologists were all too interested in indirect assessments of the patient's past when at least some significance should have been attributed to his present strivings. Allport bluntly stated his own contrary position on the matter of direct motivational assessment. It is possible to detect in his statement some residue of disappointment and anger dating from his ill-fated interview with Freud:

> When we set out to study a person's motives, we are seeking to find out what that person is trying to do in this life—including, of course, what he is trying to avoid and what he is trying to be. I see no reason why we should not start our investigation by asking him to tell us the answers as he sees them. [1960, p. 101]

It was not Allport's intention to deny the existence or significance of unconscious motives or the importance of infantile experiences. Rather, he was concerned to supplement any such one-sided emphasis on hidden, past motives with an equal emphasis on the person's conscious and contemporary self-evaluation. In the same spirit in which Harry Stack Sullivan had suggested that every scientist is a man, Allport assumed that every man was entitled to be heard. In the same way that George Kelly had concluded that every man was a personality scientist, Allport chose to believe that every personality scientist wants to comprehend the whole man. That comprehension must, in part, rest on an understanding of what the person himself believes he is trying to do.

Allport lucidly stated the guiding questions that shaped his work in personality: "How shall a psychological life history be written? What processes and what structures must a full-bodied account of personality include? How can one detect unifying threads in a life, if they exist?"

(1968, p. 377). Although these were the abiding questions that governed Allport's theorizing and research, he was forced to confess toward the end of his life: "I still do not know how a psychological life history should be written" (1968, p. 377). But Allport had learned—and taught—the important lesson that rigid reliance on abstract theories of personality should be tempered with a willingness to admit one's dogmatism, with a readiness to accept the facts however unpalatable they may prove to be, and with a firm conviction that whole persons are more complex than our explanations of them. Allport admonished psychologists to abide by two principles (1968, p. 23):

1. *"Do not forget what you have decided to neglect."* If a theory seemingly accounts for a small piece of reality, never lose sight of the fact that it does not account for all realities.

2. *"Theorize in such a way that what is true in any region of mental life can be verified to be so."* The goal of psychological science is to seek the truth, in so far as it can be known. However, the "whole truth will always be the product of many workers' efforts." Therefore, "no psychologist has the right to interpret his results in such a way as to block the solution of related problems."

In his own work, Allport sought to blend a scientific strategy that would yield generalizable data about human nature with a philosophic commitment to the significance of the unique individual. To achieve these complementary goals Allport postulated some very definite criteria by which to construct a theory of personality.

Criteria for a Full-Bodied Personality Theory: Personalism

Like Kurt Lewin (see Chapter 11), Allport found difficulty in merging science's traditional interest in universal laws with psychology's presumed focus on the uniqueness of the individual. In *Personality: A Psychological Interpretation* (1937), his first systematic treatment of the field, Allport wrote:

The outstanding characteristic of man is his individuality. He is a unique creation of the forces of nature. Separated spatially from all other men he behaves throughout his own particular span of life in his own distinctive fashion. It is not upon the cell nor upon the single organ, nor upon the group, nor upon the species that nature has centered her most lavish concern, but rather upon the integral organization of life processes into the amazingly stable and self-contained system of the individual creature. [1937, p. 3]

Nevertheless, Allport pointed out, science seems to be embarrassed by the individual case. In its attempts to seek uniformities and regularities in nature, science has focused all of its efforts on whole classes of phenomena. From this perspective, the individual is regarded only as an instance or an example of a universal principle. For the scientist, processes like intelligence, perception, and learning are regulated by general laws, and it is his job to discover how these laws apply despite particular individual differences among the subjects with whom he works (cf. Chapter 1 for a discussion of Cronbach's concept of experimental versus individual difference psychology [1957, 1975]).

In opposition to the classic scientific strategy, Allport identified himself with the rationale and methods of *personalistic* psychology. Personalism focuses on psychological processes as they are embodied in individuals:

> The chief tenet of [personalistic psychology] is that every mental function is embedded in a personal life. In no concrete sense is there such a thing as intelligence, space perception, color discrimination or choice reaction; there are only *people* who are capable of performing such activities and of having such experiences. . . . Nor can motives ever be studied apart from their personal setting, they represent always the striving of a total organism toward its objective [Allport, 1937, p. 18]

The distinction between the investigation of general or universal laws, and the application of such laws to the individual case occupied Allport's attention throughout his career. He adopted from the philosopher W. Windelband (in Allport, 1937, p. 22) the terms *nomothetic* and *idiographic* to describe the differences between a concern for the general principle and an interest in particular individuals.

Idiographic and Nomothetic Disciplines

As a psychologist, Allport asserted that his chief interest must by definition be the construction of methods and concepts that encompass the complexity of the individual case. As a personalistic psychologist, or personologist as Murray (1938) termed this strategy, Allport argued that idiographic (particular) and nomothetic (general) methods and concepts should be blended. "[The psychological study of individuality] will not be content with the discovery of laws pertaining to mind-in-general, but will seek also to understand the lawful tendencies of minds-in-particular. But there is no need for two disciplines. Psychology can treat both types of subjects" (Allport, 1937, p. 23).

The clear implication of Allport's argument that idiographic and nomothetic strategies can be merged is that the personologist believes: "Personality . . . is a pattern that exists 'out there.' We boldly ask what a person is like in his essential nature (not merely how he affects other people, or how he behaves in different situations). Of course, his behavior is variable, but always within the limits and ranges set by the [person's] structure itself" (Allport, 1961, p. 572). Thus, the personologist seeks to understand *individual consistency:* personal uniformities and the regularities in behavior evidenced by the individual over time. In this sense, the personologist is concerned with "laws" of behavior. But this concern is always for the whole of personality as it exists in real people who show an endless variety of unique, novel, and matchless combinations of personality variables (Allport, 1960, pp. 146–7). Consequently, for the personologist, only laws that are applicable to the unique individual case are worth his attention (cf. Lewin, Chapter 11, especially his concept of Galilean science). If there is some measure of logical inconsistency in the concept of laws with both idiographic and nomothetic import, the personologist prefers the study of individual regularity to the investigation of a fictional "average" person.

The Meaning of Personality: Suggestions for an Adequate Theory

Allport's emphasis on the importance of the individual case, and the necessity to understand the whole person, led him to formulate five criteria by which to judge the adequacy of any personality theory (1960, pp. 20 ff.).

First, a truly satisfactory theory will *construe the human personality as integumented*—that is, as centered within the functioning organism. Personality, for Allport, is not explainable exclusively in situational terms, nor in terms of others' opinions of the person. Interpersonal theories and theories that emphasize the variability of behavior across different situations tend to confuse a person's *reputation* with the person himself. An adequate personality theory recognizes that *persons* are the locus of personality, that personality is *biophysical,* having both psychological and physiological components, and that persons have their own inner congruence or consistency (Allport, 1960, p. 21).

Second, the adequate personality theory will *regard the organism as replete, not empty.* Behavioristic formulations of the person tend to restrict their conceptualizations to only those aspects that are observable, measurable. Events that occur between the observable stimulus and the observable response of the organism are inadmissible to some behavioristic, positivistic theories. The result is a formulation of the human person as an "empty organism." Allport argued that the full-bodied personality theory "must assume from the outset that there is nothing scientifically shameful about postulating a well-furnished personality that *is* something and *does* something—a personality that has internal structures and substructures which 'cause,' or partially cause, behavior" (1960, p. 25).

Third, an adequate personality theory will *regard motivation "as normally a fact of present structure and function,* not merely as an outgrowth of earlier forces" (Allport, 1960, p. 20; italics added). Allport directed, once again, his criticism to psychoanalytic theories that tend to regard all motivation as a product of the organism's past. Such formulations pay scant attention to the uniqueness and comtemporaneity of human motives. Furthermore, some formulations of personality attempt to reduce the multiplicity of human motives to a few basic drives, needs, wishes, or vectors with the implication that all personalities can be accounted for by proper application of these dimensions. Allport suggested that such formulations accomplish little that is of use in the task of understanding any single full-bodied personality: Drives, needs, wishes, and so forth merely summate to an abstraction of genuine human personality (1960, p. 27).

Fourth, the satisfactory personality theory will *employ units of analysis "capable of living synthesis"* (Allport, 1960, p. 20; italics added). Allport criticized the tendency prevalent among psychologists to reduce personality to a set of measurable variables without the foresight to plan such analytic reductions around the basic goal of resynthesizing the measurements into a whole picture: "To say that John Brown scores in the eightieth percentile of the 'masculinity-femininity' variable, in the thirtieth percentile on 'need for achievement' and at average on 'introversion-extroversion' is only moderately enlightening. Even with a more numerous set of dimensions, with an avalanche of psychometric scores, patterned personality seems to elude the psychodiagnostician" (1960, p. 30).

Fifth, the full-bodied personality theory will *"allow adequately for, but not rely exclusively upon, the phenomenon of self-consciousness"* (Allport 1960, p. 20). While it is true that self-awareness may be transient and ephemeral, it is equally true that "all sensing, acting and willing are, at bottom, *owned* and that selfhood is the central presupposition we must hold in examining the psychological states of human beings" (Allport, 1960, pp. 34–35). In short, as William James stated the matter, "Whatever I may be thinking of, I am always at the same time more or less aware of *myself,* of my *personal existence*" (1963, p. 166). The adequate theory of personality will devote suitable attention to the person's capacity for self-attention.

The most important implication of Allport's requirements for an adequate personality theory is his insistence that no "law" of behavior is as inevitable in its application as a law of physics. The organism's active participation in life, his capacity for self-initiated organization of his life, always make the inexorability of psychological "laws" suspect. Allport, therefore, advocated what he called an "open system" in personality theory (1960, Chap. 3).

An "open" personality theory, as contrasted with a "closed" one, stresses with equal emphasis past and present motives, and it includes the possibility that organisms are future-oriented. The open personality theory regards the person not only as "re-active" but as "pro-active," as well. Organisms change. The open personality theorist recognizes that his concepts must incorporate the fact of change as a fundamental tenet. Furthermore, while the closed-system formulation of personality regards the person as striving to achieve homeostasis in the face of environmental

changes, the open-system approach acknowledges that organisms sometimes strive for more than mere preservation of the status quo.

As Allport succinctly stated, most closed-system personality theories
are limited by their emphasis on *"being* rather than *becoming"* (1960, p. 44).
Like Rogers and Maslow (see Chapter 13), Allport preferred the view that
persons strive toward self-enhancement, *for* increased growth, rather than
from a sensed deficiency, toward a state of increased appreciation of self.
"If I argue for the open system," Allport stressed, "I plead more strongly
for the open mind" (1960, p. 53).

The Person: Traits and Dispositions

Allport's emphasis on a full-bodied and open-system personality theory
was a natural outgrowth of his earliest conceptualization of personality
(1937, p. 48):

> Personality is the dynamic organization within the individual of
> those psychophysical systems that determine his unique adjustments
> to his environment.

In devising his definition, Allport devoted a good deal of effort to synthe-
sizing the varied usages of the term personality into a coherent and workable construct. Characteristically, Allport's definition emphasizes four of
the five criteria that, as we have seen, he regarded as essential to a full-
bodied view of personality. The first emphasis involves the usage of the
term *dynamic organization.* Allport meant to stress that personality is always an organized whole, but a whole that is constantly changing (dynamic). Personality is thus self-regulating and continually evolving (1937,
p. 48).

Second, the term *within the individual* was intended to indicate that
personality is something "real"—something that resides within the skin.
For Allport, as previously discussed, a personality theory or definition
must imply its acceptance of the view that personality is integumented,
residing as a real, though perhaps not directly observable, entity *in* people.
Personality is not an abstraction, nor is it a scientifically convenient fiction.
Personality *is,* and it is *in* persons.

Third, the term *psychophysical systems* was meant to convey a recognition
of the fact that personality has roots in the physical, chemical processes
of the body's glands and nervous system. "The term 'psychophysical'
reminds us that personality is neither exclusively mental nor exclusively
neural. The organization entails the operation of both body and mind,
inextricably fused into a personal unity" (Allport, 1937, p. 48; italics added).

Fourth, and last, the phrase *unique adjustments to his environment* emphasizes both Allport's conviction that psychology must attend to the individ-

ual personality in all of its singularity and Allport's concern that psychological generalizations be understood as subject to change. Personality is a mode of survival, in Allport's view, and thus the individual adjusts not merely to his geographical environment but to those aspects of his life situation that he alone construes as meaningful (1937, p. 50). To repeat Allport's apt phrase, personality is becoming, not merely being.

In his 1961 revision of his major work, Allport somewhat modified his personality definition by substituting a new phrase for the previous "unique adjustments to his environment." The modified definition now ended with the phrase, *"characteristic behavior and thought"* (1961, p. 28). It is remarkable that in the twenty-four years intervening between his first and second definitions of personality, Allport found so little to alter. The alteration was designed to broaden the conceptualization of personality as involving more than "adjustment" to personal and physical environments, as the first definition had implied. Thus Allport recast his definition in 1961: "We not only adjust to our environment but we reflect on it. Also, we strive to master it, and sometimes succeed. Behavior and thought, therefore, make both for survival and for growth."

Allport's definition was clearly intended to provide a definite framework for the researcher of personality phenomena. The definition implicitly suggests that persons may be studied by investigating their unique organization of psychophysical systems, that is, by investigation of their measurable *traits.*

The Concept of Traits: Personal Consistency

Allport and Odbert (1936; cf. Allport, 1961, Chap. 14) estimated that there are nearly 18,000 words, mostly adjectives, in the English language that may be used to designate traits of personality. In fact, the language may harbor even more trait labels than this awesome number suggests, for Allport and Odbert excluded from their estimate all compound words like *nature-lover,* or *hater-of-affectation.* The problem for the psychologist lies in the embarrassment of riches that this myriad of trait names represents. Of the 18,000-plus traits indicated in the language, how many are veridical (i.e., really exist)? Allport and Odbert estimated that approximately 25 percent of the 18,000 trait names actually indicate real person characteristics if clearly evaluative items like *adorable, disgusting,* and *evil* are excluded (see 1961, p. 355).

A further limitation needs to be imposed on the wide range of possible trait names. Some of the labels embodied in the English language to indicate personality characteristics refer to transient or temporary states of mood or activity: for example, *abashed, frantic, rejoicing.* When these items are excluded, the total number of trait names indicating veridical and relatively stable personality characteristics is reduced to approximately 4,000 or 5,000 items. Of course, even this reduction does not impose limits on the number of possible combinations of trait labels that may be employed to describe various personalities. The important point, however, is that the concept of trait is clearly embedded quite firmly in our language and, therefore, in our thinking. Indeed, it is nearly impossible to think of any specific person without simultaneously calling to mind a host of characteristic traits.

For the psychologist, the concept of personality trait requires precise specification, and more important, the way trait is defined will determine the psychologist's mode of investigation. Allport, a strong advocate of the trait approach, defined the concept in this way:

> A trait is . . . a *neuropsychic structure having the capacity to render many stimuli functionally equivalent, and to initiate and guide equivalent (meaningfully consistent) forms of adaptive and expressive behavior.* [1961, p. 347]

Allport thus asserted that traits are indeed real, that they are rooted in nervous system functioning, and that in combination they serve as the steersmen of behavior. A trait lends consistency to personality by allowing the person to respond similarly to a wide array of situations, that is, it renders diverse stimuli "functionally equivalent." For Allport, traits are rather complex enduring dispositions to respond to one's environment in particular ways. A trait is always established within the personality through a combination of innate physical attributes and acquired environmental habits (1937, p. 292). Allport illustrated his conception of trait development and function with the following example:

> A young child finding that his mother is nearly always present to satisfy his wants, develops for her an early affective attachment (conditioning). But later other social contacts likewise prove to be conducive to this child's happy and successful adjustment: playmates, for example, or family gatherings, or crowds at the circus. . . . the child gradually comes to seek people, rather than to avoid them. A trait (not an instinct) of gregariousness develops. The child grows eager for social intercourse; he enjoys being with people. When isolated from them for some time, he misses them and becomes restless. The older he grows the more ways he finds of expressing this gregarious interest. He seeks to ally himself with groups of people at the lodge, at the theater, at church; he makes friends and keeps in touch with them, often entertains them, and corresponds with them. . . . Sociability has become a deep and characteristic quality of this individual's personality. Its expression is variable; a wide range of equivalent stimuli arouse it. [1937, pp. 292–293]

Thus, the child's trait of gregariousness or sociability renders many stimuli equivalent and guides many behaviors into equivalent forms of expression. In short, the trait develops motivational properties that characterize the *personal style* of the individual. The way in which Allport conceptualized a trait's mediation between diverse stimuli and the individual's characteristically uniform responses to them is illustrated in Figure 12–1.

As Figure 12–1 indicates, the child's trait of *gregariousness* allows diverse situations like theater going, church going, letter writing, and family gatherings to be treated by the individual as opportunities to express his fundamental and pervasive enjoyment of the company of others. The behaviors that constitute his personal style are all somewhat varied because they are particular responses to the specific characteristics of each social situation. But each of these behaviors shares the common denominator of gregariousness or sociability as the guiding motive. Thus, the trait of gregariousness unifies an individual's "characteristic behavior and thought" in the face of diverse environmental circumstances. In common-sense terms, we often say that John or Jane did something "typical" of them. To be able to make that judgment, it was first necessary to have observed John or Jane behaving over a period of time in some *consistent* fashion despite changing situational factors. Traits are the basis of this personal consistency.

Individual and Common Traits

Allport further distinguished between *individual* and *common* traits. In theory, it is logically impossible for any two individuals to possess precisely the same trait (1937, p. 297). Because each individual is a product of a unique genetic endowment, a singular history of personally meaningful experiences, and a never-repeated developmental progression, the to-

FIGURE 12-1: TRAIT AS MEDIATOR BETWEEN STIMULI AND RESPONSES

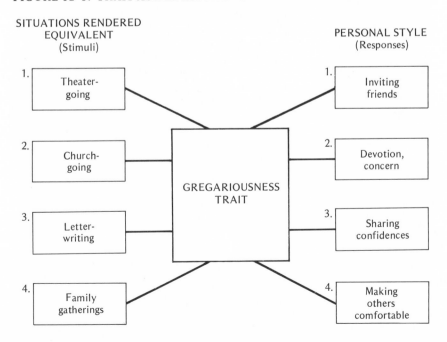

SITUATIONS RENDERED
EQUIVALENT
(Stimuli)

PERSONAL STYLE
(Responses)

1. Theater-going
2. Church-going
3. Letter-writing
4. Family gatherings

GREGARIOUSNESS TRAIT

1. Inviting friends
2. Devotion, concern
3. Sharing confidences
4. Making others comfortable

tality of his personhood must be unique. Thus, even though two individuals may be said to possess the trait of aggressiveness, the personal style with which this common trait will be translated into behavior is different in each person. In this extreme sense, then, every trait is individualistic, for total identity across individuals is nonexistent. Yet, for all practical purposes, individuals do share some similarities. It is possible to speak of *generally* aggressive personalities. That is to say, it is possible to visualize several persons who are characterized by possession of a roughly similar tendency to behave aggressively. In this more nearly common-sense meaning, traits may be described as *common*.

> The original endowment of most human beings, their stages of growth, and the demands of their particular society, are sufficiently standard and comparable to lead to some basic modes of adjustment that from individual to individual are *approximately* the same. To take an example: the nature of the struggle for survival in a competitive society tends to force every individual to seek his own most suitable level of aggression. As the saying goes, everyone *must* be either a boot or a door-mat. [Allport, 1937, p. 298]

It is clear from Allport's emphasis that only with reluctance was he willing to acknowledge the nomothetic aspects of traits. Traits may be thought of as common, but, Allport insisted, the psychologist must recognize that in measuring shared traits he is assessing only some common *aspect* of the trait. A true trait is always individual in the strict sense of its role within the context of an entire personality's unique organization of many traits. Context is everything.

Cardinal, Central, and Secondary Traits

Allport allowed that, within the context of an entire network of traits that compose a personality, some traits play major directing roles and some play minor roles. In rare cases, a particular trait is so outstanding, so pervasive that nearly all of an individual's activities can be traced to its operation. A trait of this significance in the economy of a personality is apparent to even the most casual observer. Such pervasive, dominantly influential traits are termed *cardinal traits* (Allport, 1937, pp. 337 ff.). Characters drawn from the world's literature illustrate both the rarity and the uniqueness of cardinal traits. Our language has been enriched by trait names derived from outstanding fictional and historical personalities (1937, pp. 302–303):

Boswellian	Homeric	Puckish
Byronic	Lesbian	Quixotic
Christ-like	Machiavellian	Rabelaisian
Dionysian	Narcissistic	Sadistic
Falstaffian	Napoleonic	Sapphic
Faustian	Pickwickian	Shylock

A cardinal trait like *Christ-like* or *Machiavellian* is so potent and singular that all other traits embodied in the same personality seem secondary and subservient to the strength of this master steersman.

At a level of influence somewhat less than that of a cardinal trait are the *central traits.* "Central traits are those usually mentioned in careful letters of recommendation, in rating scales where the rater stars the outstanding characteristics of the individual, or in brief verbal descriptions of a person" (Allport, 1937, p. 338).

Somewhat less conspicuous, less generalized, less consistent, and frequently less influential in the overall guidance of behavior are the lowest level traits called *secondary traits.* Secondary traits are evoked by a narrower range of equivalent stimuli and direct a more restricted range of equivalent responses (1937, p. 338).

Individual Traits as Personal Dispositions (p.d.'s)

In 1961, Allport introduced some terminological changes into his theory of traits. To emphasize his fundamental distinction between individual and common (aspects of) traits, Allport chose to rechristen the individual trait as a *personal disposition (p.d.)* (1961, p. 358). *Personal dispositions* followed the classification scheme of *cardinal, central,* and *secondary* traits. In fact, Allport employed a definition of p.d.'s nearly identical to his definition for individual traits:

> *A personal disposition is a generalized neuropsychic structure (peculiar to the individual), with the capacity to render many stimuli functionally equivalent, and to initiate and guide consistent (equivalent) forms of adaptive and stylistic behavior.* [1961, p. 373]

Allport did not adhere to any precise distinction between his concept of individual trait and personal disposition. He did, however, suggest that the term *personal disposition* was meant to carry the supplementary meaning of "personality *form,*" and he thus offered as a synonym the term *morphogenic trait* (1961, p. 358). In all, it is clear that Allport meant to emphasize that individual traits, or p.d.'s, or morphogenic traits are the fundamental, objective, stable units of individual consistency.

The Study of Personal Dispositions: Single-Case Strategy

"How shall a psychological life history be written?" This abiding question in Allport's approach to personality is clearly an idiographic query. It represents Allport's overriding concern—indeed, his own cardinal trait as a

psychologist—to comprehend the complexity and novelty of the individual person fully, with satisfying attention to detail. To some of his critics, as we shall later see, the question represents at best an unanswerable paradox, and at worst, an absurdity.

Allport, perhaps sharing a professional trait with men like Jung, Maslow, and Rogers, relished paradoxes and delighted in transcending absurdities. He suggested that every psychologist is confronted with six persistent riddles. Each psychologist will linger long over different riddles, propose different solutions or means of detouring around the riddle, but more often than not he will be forced to admit that he has come face to face with a paradox. Here are Allport's six persistent psychological riddles (1968, p. 300):

1. How is the mind you study related to its body? The *psychophysical* riddle.

2. Are the objective methods you by preference employ suited to the subjective facts that are your ultimate data? The riddle of *positivism.*

3. How do you account for such integration and unity as the human personality manifests? The riddle of the *self.*

4. Why is it that, in spite of your postulate of strict determinism, you half-believe, and nearly always act on a hypothesis of indeterminism? The riddle of *free will.*

5. Why is it that the old laws of mental connection, going back to Aristotle, seem sometimes adequate and sometimes inadequate in accounting for the organization of higher mental processes? The riddle of *association.*

6. Why is it that, after making your analyses of mental states, you are unable to find in the sum total of them any close approximation of the way mental life is uniquely and individually presented in nature? The riddle of *individuality.*

Allport proposed these riddles as part of an essay honoring the centenary of William James's birth. It was Allport's contention that James had lingered long over each of these riddles and therein lay his unique contribution to philosophy and psychology. But of course Allport wished to point up the significance of James's attitude toward these riddles for all of contemporary psychology:

> The message of James for psychology today is this: narrow consistency can neither bring salvation to your science, nor help to mankind. Let your approaches be diverse, but let them in the aggregate do full justice to the heroic qualities in man. If you find yourselves tangled in paradoxes, what of that? Who can say that the universe shall not contain paradoxes simply because he himself finds them unpalatable? [Allport, 1968, p. 323]

Allport's abiding concern: *"How shall a psychological life history be written?"* can be seen as his personal strategy for dealing with these paradoxes. Each of the six paradoxes (psychophysicalism, positivism, self, free will, association, and individuality) is reducible to that key question: *"How shall a psychological life history be written?"* For in writing the individual's life history, the psychologist attempts to answer the most fundamental riddle of them all: To what extent are any of these riddles pertinent to real persons? Or, in slightly rephrased form: Is a scientific theory of personality compatible with attempts to understand the personality of a single real person? Allport phrased it this way:

> Now the goals of science are to understand, predict, and control events. How, in dealing with a concrete person, can we expect to understand, predict, control, unless we know the individual pattern and not merely the universal tendencies of the human mind-in-general? [1965, p. 159]

Thus, Allport implied that the first five of the six riddles are answerable when the sixth, the riddle of individuality, is the psychologist's predominant concern. Indeed, for Allport, the first five are riddles only because the sixth is sometimes rejected as a suitable problem for science (cf. Allport, 1960, pp. 117 ff.). "How shall a psychological life history be written?" First and foremost it should be written from the self-revealing, though not necessarily intentionally so, evidence fabricated by the person himself.

Personal Documents: A Morphogenic Approach to Life History

Individuals create self-revealing personal documents out of a variety of motives. For example, adolescents often keep detailed diaries or personal journals recounting their innermost thoughts, feelings, and aspirations. Such a document is often so revealing that the most grievous sin a parent can commit is to violate its secrecy. Personal documents may take many forms: autobiographies, diaries, letters, interviews, even literary productions (Allport, 1942; 1961). "The personal document may be defined as *any self-revealing record that intentionally or unintentionally yields information regarding the structure, dynamics, and functioning of the author's mental life*" (Allport, 1942, p. xii).

The motives that impel individuals to create self-revealing productions are varied. Allport described thirteen motives that might underlie such productions (1942, pp. 69–75):

1. *Special Pleading:* to argue in a convincing way some self-serving or self-justifying premise.

2. *Exhibitionism:* a single-minded desire to display one's virtues and vices.

3. *Desire for Order:* compulsive need to record the circumstances of one's day.

4. *Literary Appeal:* desire for aesthetic and artistic satisfaction.

5. *Securing Personal Perspective:* a personal "taking stock" of one's life, achievements, failures, and so on.

6. *Catharsis:* a need to secure relief from tension and anxiety by writing when relief through direct action is unattainable.

7. *Monetary Gain:* personal revelations for prize competition, for payment in an experimental investigation, and so forth. Payment does not rule out, however, the validity of the self-revelations.

8. *Assignment:* school task imposed for some educational or therapeutic reason.

9. *Assisting in Therapy:* production of personal document for therapist to assist in one's own cure.

10. *Redemption and Social Reincorporation:* "confessions" of an ex-criminal, spy, alcoholic, etc. Generally such confessions are motivated by a genuine desire for forgiveness and acceptance.

11. *Public Service:* desire to achieve public or social reform.

12. *Desire for Immortality:* "battle against oblivion," or a desire not to be forgotten after death.

13. *Scientific Interest:* though not necessarily created for this reason, personal documents sometimes are donated to psychologists with the intention of furthering science.

This diverse array of motives suggests the methodological problems that the historian, sociologist, anthropologist, or psychologist faces when he decides to study evidence of this sort. All of these personal documents suffer from varying degrees of lack of candor, defective recollection on the part of the writer, and from conscious or unconscious self-concealment. Nonetheless, it was Allport's conviction that personal documents were a valuable source of answers to the question: "How shall a psychological life history be written?"

To assess the value of a personal document, the psychologist must ask how useful it is in meeting the three goals of science: understanding, prediction, and control beyond the level of unaided common sense (1942, p. 148). It was Allport's judgment, after a thorough survey of the literature relating to research on personal documents, that their use was well justified:

> Personal documents are good if they serve the comparison of lives, one with another, leading to statistical generalizations and to an understanding of uniformities of behavior. But they are good also if standing one by one they provide concrete evidence of the nature of

single personal lives from which all psychological science is derived; if they yield evidence of pluralistic causation; if they give clinicians and practitioners a sounder basis for work; and if they enhance the understanding, prediction, and control of individual lives (which is all that science ultimately demands). [Allport, 1942, p. 59]

Allport's evaluation suggests that personal documents may be treated in research with a variety of conceptualizations and methods. Analyses ranging from impressionistic characterizations, psychoanalytic hypothesizing, and direct content analysis to sophisticated statistical and factorial assessments are, in principle, possible. But two significant points about Allport's advocacy of personal document research bear mention: First, by definition, the study of personal documents is the *idiographic* strategy of assessing the unity, uniqueness, and consistency of the individual. Second, this single-case approach treats personality investigation as an attempt to comprehend the organism from the *subjective* or phenomenal perspective. In effect, the single-case approach solves the riddle of individuality by an appeal to the person's own solution.

An Illustrative Case: Jenny Gove Masterson's Letters

Within four years of the publication of his monograph on the use of personal documents in psychology, Allport published a series of letters that reveal in dramatic detail the story of a mother-son relationship from the mother's point of view (Allport, 1946). The letters were presented to Allport by a young couple, identified as Glenn and Isabel, because they felt there might be some psychological value in the rather complete series of self-revelations produced by a very remarkable woman named "Jenny Gove Masterson." The correspondence between Glenn and Isabel and Jenny began in March 1926, when Jenny was fifty-eight years old, and ran its course of 301 letters over the next eleven and a half years. In October 1937, the remarkable correspondence ended with Jenny's death at the age of seventy.

In 1965, Allport made the "Jenny Masterson" letters more widely available by publishing some of them in book form along with several varieties of analyses of Jenny's personality. Allport posed the following challenges to psychologists:

To me the principal fascination of the Letters lies in their challenge to the reader (whether psychologist or layman) to "explain" Jenny— if he can. Why does an intelligent lady behave so persistently in a self-defeating manner? When and how might she have averted the tragedy of her life? Could proper guidance or therapy at an appropriate time have helped alter the rigid course of her conduct? Was the root of her trouble some wholly unconscious mechanism? [Allport, 1965, p. viii]

Some brief details about Jenny's life are in order here. Jenny Gove Masterson was born in Ireland of Protestant parentage in 1868. Migrating to Canada when Jenny was five years old, the Gove family took up residence in Montreal, but the mother worked hard to preserve the family's sense of Irish culture and tradition. Jenny was one of seven children, five younger sisters and one younger brother in all. When Jenny was eighteen her father died, and to support her family, Jenny became a telegrapher. Unfortunately, Jenny and her siblings did not get along well, so by the time Jenny was twenty seven years old, bitter quarrels and disputes resulted in disintegration of the family. Jenny married an American railway inspector, Henry Masterson, a marriage that further outraged the family because of Masterson's previous marriage.

Jenny and Henry Masterson moved to Chicago, where Jenny found herself bored with an enforced idle existence. "She complained that she was being 'kept' by a man. She quarreled more than once with her husband over this issue, but he, like most men of his day, was firmly set against a wife seeking employment" (Allport, 1965, p. 3). The issue was not resolved at the time of Henry Masterson's death in 1897, when Jenny was twenty nine years old. A month after her husband's death, Jenny gave birth to her only child, a son named Ross.

Returning to work as a telegrapher to support herself and Ross, she devoted herself entirely to caring for Ross with "undivided affection." When Ross was five years old, Jenny vacationed with him in Montreal and spent some time with her sisters. Ross stayed on with Jenny's sisters for several months and "outgrew many of his 'spoiled' ways." However, when Jenny returned to Montreal, she accused her sisters of neglecting Ross; they accused her of spoiling him. The quarrel ended with another bitter separation.

Until Ross was seventeen he and Jenny were closest companions, a relationship that ended when Ross left for college "back East" at Princeton. Jenny continued to work to support Ross's education and entertainment expenses. In his sophomore year, the United States entered World War I, and Ross enlisted in the ambulance corps. At his departure for France, Jenny visited Ross and met his college friends, including Glenn and Isabel, her later correspondents.

When Ross returned from France in 1919, he found himself disoriented, disatisfied with his old ambitions and habits. For the next few years, with the exception of obtaining his college degree, Ross embarked on a series of failures in business and personal achievements. In consequence, Ross and Jenny had many grave quarrels, including one rageful encounter when Jenny learned of his secret marriage. "On his first visit to her following her discovery she drove him out of her room with violent denunciations and a threat to have him arrested if he ever tried to see her again" (Allport, 1965, p. 6).

Jenny renewed her contacts with Ross's college friends, Glenn and his wife Isabel, and requested permission to "keep in touch" with them. Her motives for this renewed acquaintance with Glenn and Isabel seem to have been a mixture of nostalgia for the days when "Ross was all hers," and a need to maintain a source of information about Ross's whereabouts.

Jenny's Personality: Samples of Her Letters

Writing to Glenn and Isabel on the occasion of Ross's visit to her room with his new wife, Jenny described the scene as follows:

> Ross brought this same woman and her brat to my house one Sunday evening and I was angry and told him that if he ever brought any more prostitutes to my house I would have them both arrested. Anyone, short of a fool, would know what she was at one glance. [Allport, 1965, p. 9]

In her letter of January 5, 1927, Jenny recalled her childhood:

> My father dropped dead one day, and had no provision made for his family—7 of them, all under 18. Not one in the house capable of earning a penny. It was my salary that kept the house going. . . . No one ever denied it, or pretended to think otherwise, and when I dared to marry the man I had been in love with for years, but dreaded to take my money out of their house . . . why, they said I was like the cow that gave the milk and then kicked the pail. [Allport, 1965, p. 27]

In June 1928, Jenny gave vent to one of her characteristic outbursts of pessimism and martyrdom:

> Anyway I am firmly convinced that I am "through" and ought to step out. I have done all, of any use, that it is possible for me to do in this world. Whether it was for good or bad it is over and done and nothing can change it now, "The moving finger writes, and having writ moves on" and my days for possible usefulness are past. I should step out, but am a coward. To suppose that Ross needs me would be indeed a joke. [Allport, 1965, p. 50]

In 1929, Ross underwent surgery for a tumor on his inner ear and for an "abscess on the outer covering of the brain." During his convalescence, he stayed with "one of his women." About two months after the operation, Jenny received word that Ross had died in a sudden relapse. She was to outlive her son by eight years. Glenn was summoned to attend the funeral and cremation of Ross's body. After the ceremony, Glenn accompanied Jenny back to her room. Ending an hour of respectful silence, Jenny spoke: "The body is consumed, now we'll have a good steak dinner" (recollection of Isabel, in Allport, 1965, p. 153). Jenny wrote to Glenn and Isabel, following Ross's death:

> After a while I shall count up all my riches—after the horror of this loss becomes blunted a bit—you know "the years roll by and on their wings bear healing"—wounds do not remain open for always—and then I shall count up my riches—such wonderful friends—*such* friends—the glory of the sun and the stars—the sigh of the sea—the laughter of little children. [Allport, 1965, p. 73]

An Analysis of Jenny's Personal Dispositions

Allport's perennial question: "How shall a psychological life history be written?" can, as always, be answered on two levels. A psychologist may decide to analyze the letters with regard to nomothetic (general-universal) results. His preferred method might be a statistical content analysis of the frequency with which Jenny used particular phrases or word combinations, or the statistical relationship between various classes of emotional response and the people mentioned in her writings. A somewhat different approach might be taken by the psychologist who wished to form an impressionistic portrait of Jenny as a unique person. This psychologist might ask a series of judges to read the Masterson letters and to record in their own words Jenny's outstanding traits. Then, eliminating items on which the judges fail to agree, a "trait portrait" might be formed.

Allport reported the results of the latter type of investigation undertaken by himself with thirty-six judges. These thirty-six people used a total of 198 trait names to characterize Jenny. Loosely clustered, the 198 items fell into nine categories:

1. *Quarrelsome-Suspicious* (e.g., distrustful, paranoid, opinionated)
2. *Self-Centered* (e.g., selfish, jealous, possessive, martyr complex)
3. *Independent-Autonomous* (e.g., hardworking, stubborn, calculating)
4. *Dramatic-Intense* (e.g., emotional, rigid, serious, violent)
5. *Aesthetic-Artistic* (e.g., intuitive, fastidious, expressive)
6. *Aggressive* (e.g., ascendant, domineering, self-assertive)
7. *Cynical-Morbid* (e.g., pessimistic, sarcastic, despondent)
8. *Sentimental* (e.g., loyal, affectionate, maternal)
9. *Unclassified* (e.g., intelligent, witty, whimsical)

(Based on Allport, 1965, pp. 193–194.)

Clearly, some of the categories are contradictory, and some overlap. Yet nearly all the judges agreed that prominent traits or p.d.'s in Jenny's personality were *suspiciousness, self-centeredness, autonomy, a dramatic nature, aggressiveness, morbidity,* and *sentimentality.*

Allport reported a more elaborate study of Jenny's letters by one of his students. Jeffrey Paige (in Allport, 1965, pp. 199 ff.) employed a computer lexicon of social science terms to analyze Jenny's letters. Containing nearly three thousand items, the coding system used by Paige reduced Jenny's letters to a small number of "tag" words that summarized large classes of phrase usage in Jenny's writing. For example, Jenny employed many phrases to express her aggression, hostility, open rage, and opposition to Ross and his women. All of these phrases were coded into computer language under the tag *ATTACK*. Once programmed in this way, the computer might be asked to sort out several kinds of data from Jenny's letters.

Paige found, using the first fifty-six letters up to the death of Ross, eight factors that embodied Jenny's most prominent traits. Listed in order of decreasing frequency of expression, these traits were:

1. aggression
2. possessiveness
3. need for affiliation
4. need for autonomy
5. need for familial acceptance
6. sexuality
7. sentience (love of art, literature, natural beauty)
8. martyrdom   (1965, pp. 200–201)

There is clearly much overlap between the judge's impressionistic analyses of Jenny's letters and the computer-derived traits.

Close analysis of other computer-derived data reveals interesting emotional reactions to the people of her life. Jenny expresses more affection for Glenn than for Isabel; she makes more requests of Glenn for advice than of Isabel. But the computer had some trouble with items tagged "Good" and "Bad." For example, the statement: "I have a truly noble son, an honor to his college, his friends, his family"—a sarcastic comment—is labeled "Good" by the computer. Apparently sarcasm is lost on computers.

It is easy to see why Allport insisted that very little is gained by sophisticated statistical and factorial analyses of individual persons. The impressionistic judgments of Jenny's personality provide as much information on most issues as the computer-derived traits. Furthermore, commonsense analysis provides some of the ineffable "flavor" of Jenny's personal dispositions, a quality not likely to be present in computer printout. Yet, the more sophisticated computer analysis does accomplish tasks that are impossible for the human investigator.

Large-scale correlations of selected subclasses of statements, analysis of Jenny's attitudes toward the significant figures in her life on a comparative basis, and an assessment of Jenny's most frequently used categories of self-understanding are all possible only with the computer's help. But of course, neither common sense nor the computer can answer the ultimate question: "Are we satisfied that Jenny's life history has been adequately written?" The question can be answered only by a first-hand reading of Jenny's personal documents.

Difficulties with the Trait Strategy and Single-Case Approach

Allport's insistence that an adequate personality psychology must be based on attempts to understand the individual case evoked a great deal of criticism. The main issues in the controversy centered on Allport's distinctions between the idiographic and nomothetic scientific strategies. Part of the controversy, too, concerned Allport's conceptualization of traits as the fundamental units of study.

Falk (1956), anticipating later criticisms, suggested that there is no real dispute between nomothetic and idiographic goals in science. Study of *unique* events, while admissible to scientific scrutiny, is not essential to the formulation of scientific theory. Furthermore, Falk argued, the idiographic approach is a necessary *preliminary* method to the development of generalizations, for the observation of single events always precedes the construction of laws. But, Falk suggested, general laws are adequate, when properly applied, to the task of understanding the unique personality.

Robert Holt (1962) extended the objections to the idiographic-nomothetic distinction on the basis of logic. Labeling Allport's point of view a "romantic personology," Holt voiced four objections to traits and to single-case studies. First, Holt suggested that Allport had confused art and science in his attempts to achieve *comprehensive* "understanding" of single persons. The feeling of fully understanding a person is more suitable to the artist; the scientist, by contrast, is satisfied when he can reliably predict and control the events he studies. The intuitively satisfying "thrill of recognition" that accompanies the feeling of understanding the unique individual lies solely in art's domain. Science seeks to derive general propositions (nomothetic laws) from the study of individuals and a pure idiographic study of personality is, at best, an adjunct to this effort.

Second, Holt objected to Allport's characterization of traditional science as unconcerned with imaginative and creative accounts of phenomena. All scientists employ intuition, creativity, and imagination in choosing what to study, how to study it, and how to verify hypotheses.

Third, Holt pointed out that, strictly speaking, it is impossible to conceptualize a truly unique event. If a given personality were unique, heretofore never experienced, a totally unique trait name would have to be coined or some unique combination of existing trait names would have to be employed. In either case, personology would be a confusing Babel, although the second approach would in effect be nomothetic. Unfortunately, a combination of trait names would hardly satisfy Allport because it would fail to capture the personal element in personality.

Fourth, Holt voiced a suspicion prevalent among many scientists. The full richness of reality may be impossible to capture either artistically or scientifically. To attempt to achieve full understanding is to seek to completely identify with the observed, an act that even the most skilled phenomenologist is unable to achieve. In short, if uniqueness is to be the proper object of personology's study, then either personology will have to be a mute science without an adequate language or it will have to forego all forms of abstraction. In all, Holt concluded that there was no logical basis for establishing a special branch of natural science for the study of the unique personality because such a study is, by definition, not scientific.

The concept of traits as the fundamental units of personality has also come in for a share of criticism. B. F. Skinner (e.g., 1953, 1974, 1975), in the tradition of radical behaviorism, objects to postulating inner mechanisms to explain observable behaviors. Traits, unconscious ids, or instincts are all equally irrelevant to explain observed responses once the environmental stimuli controlling those responses are identified.

> When we say that a man eats *because* he is hungry, smokes a great deal *because* he has the tobacco habit, fights *because* of the instinct of pugnacity, behaves brilliantly *because* of his intelligence, or plays the piano well *because* of his musical ability, we seem to be referring to causes. But on analysis these phrases proved to be merely redundant descriptions. A single set of facts is described by the two statements: "He eats" and "He is hungry." A single set of facts is described by the two statements: "He smokes a great deal" and "he has the smoking habit." [Skinner, 1953, p. 31]

Thus, from the behaviorist's point of view, postulating traits of personality is merely a redundant statement of the behavior that has already been observed.

More recently, the concept of traits has come under fire for methodological reasons that involve a failure to find the reliable consistencies in personal behaviors implied by the concept. Walter Mischel surveyed the literature related to trait investigations and concluded: "With the possible exception of intelligence, highly generalized behavioral consistencies have not been demonstrated, and the concept of personality traits as broad response predispositions is thus untenable" (1968, p. 146). Mischel argued that a large proportion of studies purporting to demonstrate the existence of personality traits in the observed person actually show the contaminating effects of the observer's preconceived categories (1968, p. 70). When the reliability of a group of personality raters' judgments is high, it may spuriously suggest that the labels they have used actually indicate the existence of corresponding traits or states in the person so labeled. In short, Mischel feels that the concept of trait is not particularly useful for any scientific account of personality. His survey of the literature failed to turn up any significant evidence that adequate predictive power accrues to the psychologist who embraces trait theory. In effect, individuals show less cross-situational consistency than the concept of enduring personality traits demands.

With the exception of Mischel's commentary, Allport was aware of the criticisms directed against his theorizing. In a significant restatement and modification of his position, Allport reported that in the years intervening between his first proposal of traits as fundamental units of personality and the criticisms that followed he had come to the conclusion that ". . . my earlier views seemed to neglect the variability induced by ecological, social, and situational factors. This oversight needs to be repaired through an adequate theory that will relate the inside and outside systems more accurately" (1966, in 1968, p. 63).

"Traits Revisited": A Heuristic Realism

In his 1966 restatement of trait theory, Allport altered his position on the existence and research value of traits very little. While he acknowledged the value of the criticisms that had been made, Allport reaffirmed his belief that:

> Whatever tendencies exist reside in a person, for a person is the sole possessor of the energy that leads to action. Admittedly different situations elicit differing tendencies from my repertoire. I do not perspire except in the heat, nor shiver except in the cold; but the outside temperature is not the mechanism of perspiring or shivering. My capacities and my tendencies lie within. [1968, p. 47]

However, Allport conceded that trait theory would have to be made more sophisticated, more predictive, and more empirically testable if it was to survive as a useful construct in contemporary psychology. To further this aim, he proposed a safeguard for trait theory construction called *heuristic realism.*

Heuristic realism is a twofold guiding assumption. First, knowing full well that he may be wrong, the personologist *chooses* to believe that "the person who confronts us possesses inside his skin generalized action tendencies (or traits) and that it is our job scientifically to discover what they are" (1968, p. 49). Thus, the personologist postulates that traits are *real,* but realizes the tentative nature of this assumption.

Second, heuristic realism asserts that owing to the complexity of the objects or events observed, and because present methods are not completely adequate, the goal of scientifically conceptualizing personality's realness cannot be fully successful. Yet, the heuristic realist proceeds "as if" success were possible, for only by making the attempt will any progress toward knowledge of the person be attained. In short, Allport's revised position was more restrained, somewhat less enthusiastic.

Allport's emphasis on idiographic or morphogenic method thus became less unbending. He was more willing to concede that statistical and general concepts were valid ways of approaching personality. Yet, as always, Allport refused to abandon the fundamental tenet that it is the individual, the unique personality, which beckons most strongly to the personologist's curiosity.

The Self: Personality Development

Early in his career Allport tackled at some length the third of his proposed riddles, the riddle of the self. In his 1937 statement of his position, Allport upbraided psychology's lack of interest in the mature or healthy personality.

In Allport's view, the mature personality was distinguished by three attributes that made apparent the need for some concept of personality unification. The self, as the locus of all active adaptation to life, would serve this theoretical need. First of the attributes of the healthy, mature personality is his capacity to defer momentary needs, pains, or desires in favor of reaching a long-term goal. Able to lose himself in some activity he regards as important, the mature personality is not deterred by temporary setbacks or defeats. In short, the pursuit of personally meaningful goals represents an *extension of the self* (1937, p. 213). In effect, the person is going beyond self to invest his energies in causes and goal-seeking that transcend his individual life.

The second attribute of the mature personality is what Allport called *self-objectification* (1937, p. 214). Self-objectification is "that peculiar detachment of the mature person when he surveys his own pretensions in relation to his abilities, his present objectives in relation to possible objectives for himself, his own equipment in comparison with the equipment of others, and his opinion of himself in relation to the opinion others hold of him" (1937, p. 214). The capacity for self-objectification is always tied to insight and to a sense of humor (see the quote that opens this chapter). In simplest terms, the mature person is capable of taking a hard look at self and accurately interpreting what he sees.

The third attribute of the mature personality is his evolvement of a *unifying philosophy of life.* Although his philosophy may not be expressed in words, the mature person nevertheless lives his life by some dominant guiding principles by which he places himself in the scheme of things.

Allport's statement of these three attributes bears remarkable resemblance to Maslow's notion of self-actualizing people and to Carl Rogers' concept of the newly emerging person (cf. Chapter 13). All three of these theorists expressed an interest in understanding how the healthy personality conducts his life.

For Allport, the three attributes of the mature personality, self-objectification, extension of self, and a unifying philosophy of life, require that the personality theorist be able to account for their development in some personalities and for their failure to develop in the damaged personality. In order to achieve this aim, Allport developed an explanatory scheme to account for the emergence of the healthy self.

Emergence of the Self in Infancy

The infant, as Piaget suggested (see Chapter 7), is certainly unaware of himself as self, that is, as an active and efficacious agent. In a word, the infant lacks *self-consciousness* (Allport, 1961, p. 111). Self-consciousness is a gradual attainment during the first six years of life.

The first sense of one's self to evolve, according to Allport, is the *bodily self.* To illustrate, consider the infant of five or six months who manages to get his foot into his mouth for a two- or three-toothed bite: "If he hurts his foot he cries but has no idea at all that *he* has hurt *him*" (1961, p. 112). But with the passing of time, many such bodily sensations are experienced as recurrent and reliable aspects of *me.* Combined with these sensations are the frustrations of desires and wants that originate in external agents, like mother. "A child who cannot eat when he wants to, who bumps his head, soon learns the limitations of his too, too solid flesh" (1961, p. 112).

But bodily self is only the most basic and preliminary sense of the evolving self. By the end of the first year of life, a new aspect of selfhood begins to emerge. "Today I remember some of my thoughts of yesterday, and tomorrow I shall remember some of my thoughts of both yesterday and today; *and I am certain that they are the thoughts of the same person*—of myself" (Allport, 1961, p. 114; italics added). This emerging certainty that I am the *same me* as time passes is what Allport calls *self-identity.* Self-identity depends intimately on the child's developing capacity for language. For with the possibility of employing words to think and to communicate, the regularity, the solidity, and the sameness of existence become apparent. The most important aspect of the child's language use is the capacity to label himself with a name. "He hears constantly 'Where is Johnny's nose?' 'Where are Johnny's eyes?' 'Good Johnny,' 'John naughty' " (1961, p. 115). With the repetition of his name in various contexts, the child becomes aware of the continuity of self, and by the second year of life he understands his status as an independent agent in his family group.

The third aspect of developing selfhood to emerge is the child's feeling that he can successfully manipulate his world. He develops what Robert White (1960) calls a sense of competence and an income of *self-esteem.* Self-esteem, as an essential aspect of selfhood, begins to acquire importance near the end of the second year of life and becomes critical for healthy development in the third year. Parents often have difficulty with the two-and-a-half-year-old because he resents anyone taking over his prerogatives:

> A two-year-old went to the bathroom with his father to have his face washed. Saying, "Let me," he struggled to turn on the faucet. He persisted without success. For a time the father waited patiently, but finally "helped" the child. Bursting into screams of protest the child ran from the bathroom and refused to be washed. His father had spoiled everything. [Allport, 1961, p. 118]

Thus, by the third year of life a child develops a strong need for autonomy and for feelings of esteem when he tackles the tasks of living. At the same time the child undergoes what parents call negativism, saying "No!" to nearly every important demand that the parents make. In effect, the child regards every adult proposal or demand as a threat to his integrity. "To him it seems safer to resist any adult proposal in advance, as a protection to dawning self-esteem" (Allport, 1961, p. 119). So, by the end of the third year of life, three aspects of self have emerged: the bodily self, self-identity, and self-esteem or pride.

Emergence of Self in Later Childhood

From four to six years of age, the child consolidates and refines the three aspects of self that have already emerged. Additionally, the child's egocentric orientation to the world reaches full expression. He believes that the world exists for his benefit. As Piaget described, the child believes that the sun follows him, "that God, or Santa Claus is a Being whose primary duty is to serve his interests" (Allport, 1961, p. 122). In short, the child is unable to escape his own thought boundaries; only his own viewpoint exists. Slowly, however, the child experiences the fourth aspect of selfhood, the *extension of self*. He discovers that his particular likes and dislikes are an important part of what he himself is. He understands the meaning of possession: "This ball is *mine*," "He is *my* Daddy," and so on. Each of these things is seen as an extension of self.

Important during this period, too, is the developing awareness of the child that his parents want him to be a certain kind of self. The child's *self-image* begins to loom large as, at first, an uncertain, then as a more definite aspect of getting along with important others. Although conscience has not yet developed fully, the child of five or six years begins to realize the difference between being "good" and "naughty."

From ages six to twelve, the child's sense of an extended self and his self-image are enhanced by his experiences with peers in the school setting. He learns what is expected of him in regions beyond the security of the family situation. It becomes important for the child to be able to shift gears as he moves from family to outside situations so that, for example, his rough-and-ready talk with peers is restrained to a more polite form of conversation at home. At this time, the child's sixth aspect of selfhood emerges, namely a conception of himself as a "rational coper" (1961, p. 124).

The *self-as-rational-coper* corresponds in Allport's view to what Freud termed the ego. The self, like the Freudian ego, attempts to mediate between the demands of one's impulses and the restraints of society (parents, teachers). In this sense, not all of the self-as-rational-coper's activities are conscious. Some of its attempts to mediate between need and reality may be unconscious and defensively oriented in its striving to maintain self-esteem. By the twelfth year, furthermore, the child is capable of reflective thought and hypothetical or "as if" reasoning, and this achievement also marks the child's realization that self is a thinker and a judger—in short, a rational coper.

Emergence of Self in Adolescence: The Actor and His Masks

The period of adolescence (beginning near the age of twelve or thirteen) is marked by what Erikson calls an "identity crisis" (Erikson, 1950, 1959). The central question for the adolescent is: "Just who am I?" or "Am I a child or an adult?"

Parents may exacerbate the crisis by treating the adolescent as a dependent child, or by going to the opposite extreme and forcing overly mature responsibility onto his shoulders. Physically and sexually mature enough to play adult roles, the adolescent may vacillate between adult and childhood attitudes. In his attempts to discover his identity, he plays various roles, trying on each for size and comfort and discarding those with which his emerging sense of self-identity clashes.

> The search for identity is revealed in the way an adolescent tries on different masks. He first develops one line of chatter, then another, one style of hairdress and then another (always within the range permitted by the peer group). He imitates one hero and then another. He is still searching for a garb that will fit. What he really wants is not yet fully present—his adult personality. [Allport, 1961, p. 125]

The problems of adolescence eventually become focused around one central issue, the last of the emerging aspects of selfhood. *Planning for the future, choosing to direct one's life into realistic and appropriate channels,* become the central concerns of the person entering adulthood. "Paring down the self-image and aspirations to life-size is a task for his adult years" (1961, p. 126). Thus, the last aspect to emerge within the slowly evolving self is what Allport calls *propriate striving,* meaning literally "self-governing motivations." In its role as the hub of conscious existence, the self is the proprietor or governor that senses "ownership" and responsibility for the outcome of one's life. Propriate striving, therefore, is the culmination of a long line of development that began with the infant's realization that he *is*. The central theme of a life, the dominant and distant goals of a life history, are the essence of propriate striving. Thus, propriate strivings are embodied in feelings of knowing what *I* want, who *I* want to become, and why *I* must be and have these qualities.

From the realization that one is to the development of a sense of self as rational coper, the maturing person who will achieve healthy selfhood accepts life's circumstances on its own terms. The unitary bond underlying the seven aspects of self is the person's continuous recognition that all of these selves are "me:" "*I am the proprietor of my life.*"

Personality as a Process of Becoming: The Proprium

Because each of the seven emerging aspects of self is experienced as relevant, as personal, as "owned," Allport suggested substituting for the term self or ego, the term *proprium* (1955, p. 40). Thus the proprium is the embodiment of the bodily self, the self-identity, self-esteem, extended-self, self-image, self as rational coper, and self-as-proprietor.

> Personality includes these habits and skills, frames of reference, matters of fact and cultural values, that seldom or never seem warm and important. But personality includes what is warm and important also —all the regions of our life that we regard as peculiarly ours, and which for the time being I suggest we call the *proprium.* The proprium includes all aspects of personality that make for inward unity. [Allport, 1955, p. 40]

The key characteristic of the proprium, according to Allport, is its warm or intimate quality, the feeling of being really a part of *me.* Recall from Chapter 8 Allport's example of the intimacy of bodily function:

> Think first of swallowing the saliva in your mouth, or do so. Then imagine expectorating it into a tumbler and drinking it! What seemed natural and "mine" suddenly becomes disgusting and alien.... What I perceive as belonging intimately to my body is warm and welcome; what I perceive as separate from my body becomes, in the twinkling of an eye, cold and foreign. [1955, p. 43]

Thus another key characteristic of the proprium is that its various aspects lie within the realm of personal awareness. To the degree that we accept these aspects of self as "me" it is conscious. Yet, there is an aspect of selfhood that is far more active, far less a focal point of awareness. This aspect is the *self-as-knower*.

> This puzzling problem arises when we ask, "Who is the I who knows the bodily me, who has an image of myself and sense of identity over time, who knows that I have propriate strivings?" I know all these things and, what is more, I know that I know them. But who is it who has this perspectival grasp? [Allport, 1961, p. 128]

Recognizing the danger of creating a personality within the personality, Allport nonetheless argued that the self-as-knower is inherent to the structure of the person. The self-as-knower was not to be conceptualized as a "little man" inside the person, but rather as the *totality of the person as process,* as an entity that is *becoming* (1961, p. 130; 1955, p. 53). Yet Allport was forced to admit that this conception did not really solve the riddle of the Self:

> It seems on the whole sounder to regard the propriate functions of wanting, striving, willing as interlocked with the total personality structure. They are felt as self-relevant, but are not caused by a separate agent within the personality. As for the knower, whether it is simply an inference we make at a high level of complexity . . . or whether it is necessary to postulate a pure knower, a continuing transcendental self . . . is a riddle we have not solved. [1961, p. 138]

Consequently, Allport reserved the term *proprium* to indicate the unity of the eight aspects of self. The last of these aspects, self-as-knower, seemingly transcends and unifies the remaining seven. Table 12–1 summarizes the developmental history of the proprium.

Deficit and Growth Motives: Functional Autonomy

Allport's belief that the concept of Self or Proprium is necessary in psychology combined with one of his earlier conceptions to provoke considerable controversy. The earlier conception was Allport's contention that with many repetitions, a particular motive becomes autonomous or independent of the stimulation that first aroused it. This principle, termed *functional autonomy,* underwent several modifications in Allport's thinking.

As we have already seen, Allport objected to prevailing trends in motivational theory, particularly Freudian explanations, that rely almost exclusively on the person's past unconscious needs to account for his present status (1960, Chapters 6, 9). Allport preferred, in keeping with his emphasis on individuality, to view adult motives in terms of the person's contem-

TABLE 12–1: ASPECTS OF THE PROPRIUM

DEVELOPMENTAL PERIOD	PROPRIUM CHARACTERISTIC	PERSONALITY FUNCTION
First year	Bodily-self	Sensation-perception of physical pains, pleasures, and limitations.
Second year	Self-identity	Continuity of experience made possible through language.
Third year	Self-esteem	Pride in accomplishment; independence and negativism.
Four to six years	Self-extension	Abstract concept of possession: "mine."
Four to six years	Self-image	"Good" and "naughty" selves; sensitivity to praise and blame.
Six to twelve years	Self-as-rational-coper	Realistic solving of life's tasks; mediator between needs and reality.
Twelve years through adolescence	Propriate strivings	Ownership and acceptance of feelings, needs, thoughts; self-defined life goals.
Adulthood	Self-as-knower	The totality of all previous aspects of the proprium.

porary situation and feelings. Postulating an abstract scheme of a limited range of past motives that are responsible for all future behaviors, desires, and feelings was merely absurd to Allport:

> "Science must generalize." Perhaps it must, but what the objectors [to the study of uniqueness] forget is that *a general law may be a law that tells how uniqueness comes about.* It is a manifest error to assume that a general principle of motivation must involve the postulation of abstract or general motives. The principle of functional autonomy . . . is general enough to meet the needs of science, but particularized enough in its operation to account for the uniqueness of personal conduct. [1937, p. 194]

In Allport's original proposal of functional autonomy he pointed to a variety of everyday examples of motives that have been freed of their initial sources but continue to function as ends in themselves. "An ex-sailor has a craving for the sea, a musician longs to return to his instrument after an enforced absence, a city-dweller yearns for his native hills, and a miser continues to amass his useless horde" (1937, p. 196). While the sailor may have first gone to sea to earn a living, his current status as a wealthy banker precludes any need to return to the sea. Yet, he continues to desire to do so. Similarly, the miser has amassed sufficient wealth, struggling perhaps against great early deprivations, but he continues to amass money though no longer under the press of survival need.

Allport adduced a variety of experimentally studied behaviors that signified to him the perseveration of motives in the absence of their originating stimuli. To take one example with which we are already familiar from Chapter 11, the Zeigarnik effect is a demonstration that subjects will spontaneously resume tasks that they failed to complete during an experiment. Despite the fact that the experiment is over, that the experimenter does not criticize their inability to finish the tasks, subjects desire of their own accord to return to these unfinished, and sometimes trivial, tasks to work them to completion. Working the task to its conclusion has become functionally autonomous of the original experimental requirements.

Allport's conception of functionally autonomous motives was heavily criticized by Bertocci (1940) for its all-inclusiveness. Bertocci questioned the logic of Allport's concept because it seemed to imply that *any* motive could become autonomous if repeated often enough. Furthermore, Bertocci suggested that even if motives could become functionally autonomous with repetition, there was no limiting principle to prevent the creation of a chaos of completely independent, competing motives.

In the light of these criticisms, Allport was forced to restate his concept and bring it into line with the other developments of his theory. In 1961, he defined functional autonomy more broadly:

> *Functional autonomy ... refers to any acquired system of motivation in which the tensions involved are not of the same kind as the antecedent tensions from which the acquired system developed.* [1961, p. 229]

To modify his original conception further Allport proposed two levels of functional autonomy and a guiding or limiting principle by which to judge whether a motive was indeed autonomous.

In the most primitive form of functional autonomy, a motive becomes *perseverative* or self-repeating because of its roots in some biochemical or neurological process. For example, a rat fed reliably at one time of the day will become most active each day just before feeding time. But if the experimenter puts the rat on a starvation regimen, the fact that the rat is hungry all of the time does not prevent him from becoming most active at the time of day when he was fed in the past. In effect, an autonomous rhythm has been established that persists for some time, (Allport, 1961, p. 230).

Other forms of *perseverative functional autonomy* include addictions to drugs, alcohol, or tobacco, the tension induced by the Zeigarnik effect, and a child's circular activities like dropping a spoon repeatedly as long as mother returns it to his grasp. Each of these behaviors qualifies as functionally autonomous only in the sense specified by Allport's 1961 definition cited previously. In each of these cases, the original source of the tension under which the motive was acquired is different from the tension that maintains the motive.

Propriate functional autonomy, by contrast, does not depend directly on any feedback mechanism or biochemical processes. Propriate functional autonomy is best illustrated by somewhat more complex situations: The student who originally undertakes a field of study because it is required continues to study it beyond the externally enforced requirements; creative activities that benefit mankind earn the creative person tangible rewards, but we do not believe he works passionately at his tasks *for* the rewards; and the miser who hoards and amasses a huge fortune continues to do so in the absence of need. Each of these cases is governed by the propriate strivings of the self. Thus, the self is the guiding principle that determines which motives will become functionally autonomous. In this sense, Allport was proposing a similar distinction to Maslow's notion of the difference between deficiency and growth motivation (cf. Chapter 13). Functionally autonomous motives are growth motives.

Functionally autonomous motives come about, according to Allport, "because it is the essence or core of the purposive nature of man" (1961, p. 250). Three principles govern the development of such motives:

1. *Principle of organizing the energy level:* There must be motives to consume one's available energies. If existing motives have been satisfied, new ones will develop. This idea is, in principle, similar to Maslow's notion that self-actualizing people are those in whom all basic biological needs are fulfilled. Self-actualizers must then turn to higher motives to achieve fulfillment. Allport cites the example of the man, well fed and rested, who looks for new worlds to conquer; or the woman whose children have all grown and who now looks "for something to do."

2. *Principle of mastery and competence:* Man has motivational energies that transcend the simple need to react to his environment. He has the need to master it, to feel a sense of competence in tackling the tasks of life.

3. *Principle of propriate patterning:* Allport directly addressed the issue of whether functionally autonomous motives were totally independent of all personality moorings and limits in this principle. The source of the anchorage for all functionally autonomous motives is the self. "Indeed, to a large extent they constitute the self" (1961; p. 252). A young man who becomes a physician, a politician, or a hermit does not do so because he is responding to innate ambitions or to remote reinforcements of his past. These ambitions exist because "a self-image, gradually formed demands this particular motivational focus" (1961, p. 252). Thus, the self or proprium is the pattern or template against which functionally autonomous motives are shaped, directed, and unified.

> We prefer to say that the essential nature of man is such that it presses toward a relative unification of life (never fully achieved). In

this trend toward unification we can identify many central psychological characteristics. Among them are man's search for answers to
the "tragic trio" of problems: suffering, guilt, death. We identify also
his effort to relate himself to his fellow men and to the universe at
large. We see that he is trying to discover his peculiar place in the
world, to establish his "identity." As a consequence of this quest—
which is the very essence of human nature—we note that man's
conduct is to a large degree proactive, intentional, and unique to
himself. [Allport, 1961, p. 252]

Like Jung, Allport, too, believed in the self as the ultimate reconciler of
opposites. Within this scheme, even the religious sentiment has its place:
"A man's religion is the audacious bid he makes to bind himself to creation
and to the Creator. It is his ultimate attempt to enlarge and to complete
his own personality by finding the supreme context in which he rightly
belongs" (Allport, 1950, p. 142).

Summary

Allport's early experience in an interview with Freud that he himself had
engineered seemingly had lasting effects on Allport's conceptualization of
the person and his motives. Refusing to accept the Freudian thesis that all
motives can be reduced to a few basic unconscious drives, Allport
proposed that motivational research should at least begin with an assessment of the individual's own estimates of his motives. *"How shall a psychological life history be written?"* became, for Allport, the abiding focus of his
personality theory. Perhaps the single most important advice Allport had
for psychologists was "Do not forget what you have decided to neglect."
 Allport's emphasis on individuality led him to adopt from the philosopher Windelband the distinction between idiographic and nomothetic
strategies of acquiring knowledge. Allport argued that the two strategies
should be blended in order to achieve what he called full-bodied understanding of personality. Yet, Allport's emphasis was always on the idiographic (particular) method. His definition of personality was designed to
organize the various usages prevalent in psychology at the same time that
it allowed for a study of the dynamic organization of psychophysical
systems that constitute the individual, unique personality.
 Traits were conceptualized by Allport as the fundamental units of individual consistency. Distinguishing between common traits and individual
traits, Allport stressed that any individual possesses a unique organization
of these personal dispositions to characteristic behavior and thought. A
trait functions to mediate between larger classes of stimuli and equally
large classes of response. The trait of sociability, for example, serves to

render many diverse situations functionally equivalent by initiating a range of meaningfully consistent behaviors. Allport was careful to stress that traits are conceptualized as neuropsychic structures, that is, as real biophysical processes existing within persons.

The concept of traits was further organized into a hierarchy of cardinal, central, and secondary traits. Cardinal traits are the master dispositions of personality, so pervasive and influential that they seem to influence every activity of the person. Central traits are somewhat less pervasive and influential, but nevertheless exert strong directive influences on the person's characteristic ways of behaving. Secondary traits are the least influential forms of personal disposition. Allport proposed a synonym for individual traits: morphogenic trait. The important aspect of the concept of traits, however, is that the psychologist's main goal is to understand the individual's unique combination of psychological and physical endowment that is the basis of his traits.

Allport's abiding concern with the individual (idiographic) approach and with the concept of trait was heavily criticized. The main points of this criticism were that uniqueness probably lies within the range of nomothetic (general) laws and that little evidence exists for the concept of enduring dispositions to characteristic response (Holt, 1962; Mischel, 1968).

The study of personal documents occupied Allport at some length as he attempted to answer his own fundamental question: *"How shall a psychological life history be written?"* His *Letters from Jenny* reproduced an edited and abridged sample of 301 letters written by Jenny Gove Masterson over a span of eleven years. The letters reveal in intimate detail the story of a mother-son relationship through the eyes of the mother. Allport's and his students' various analyses showed a great deal of agreement that Jenny was a suspicious, self-dramatizing, possessive woman. Allport questioned the usefulness of sophisticated statistical and computer strategies for understanding the uniqueness and the flavor of the individual personality. Yet, Allport conceded, the computer analysis by Jeffrey Paige did allow for exact and precise comparisons of emotional responses at a level of complexity not possible for the unaided investigator.

Allport's restatement of his trait concepts stressed the need for a heuristic realism in conducting research of individual personality. The heuristic realist, first, recognizes that though he may be wrong, it is better to proceed as if traits were real entities residing in real, unique personalities. Second, though it is always a matter of approximation, and success is never certain, the heuristic realist realizes that it is better to make the attempt to understand individuals than to dismiss the idea as absurd.

Allport's personality theory also stressed the importance of individual personality unity and the fact that the person is always becoming, not just being. The sense of self that characterizes the mature, healthy individual is a gradual acquisition that proceeds through seven stages:

> Sense of bodily-self
> Sense of self-identity
> Sense of self-esteem
> Extension of self
> Self-image
> Self-as-rational-coper
> Propriate striving

The proprium, for Allport, is the final sense of self that develops, in which the individual is capable of knowing and capable of knowing that he knows. In short, the self-as-knower poses the ultimate riddle of personality: How does the individual recognize that *he* is the person who is?

Closely connected with his concept of proprium was Allport's motivational theory of functional autonomy. Functional autonomy asserts that motives may continue to operate even when the original tensions on which they were based no longer operate. To modify the construct in the light of its subsequent criticism, Allport distinguished between two kinds of functional autonomy: perseverative and propriate. Perseverative functional autonomy involves biochemical or neurophysical processes that continue to operate through their own momentum or rhythm in the absence of the original deficit need that provoked them. Propriate functionally autonomous motives are those activities that serve some function of the self in its active striving for fulfillment. These motives arise from the proprium's innate essence according to three principles: organizing the energy level, mastery and competence, and propriate patterning.

FOR FURTHER READING

Allport's most comprehensive work in personality theory is to be found in two successive editions of the same work: *Personality: A Psychological Interpretation* (New York: Henry Holt, 1937) was his first major contribution and continues to be valuable as an introduction to his early ideas; and *Pattern and Growth in Personality* (New York: Holt, Rinehart & Winston, 1961), which is a revision of the former work, reflects Allport's changing conceptions of such important concepts as functional autonomy and individual traits.

A collection of Allport's midcareer papers may be found in *The Person in Psychology* (Boston: Beacon Press, 1968). Allport's small volume, *Becoming: Basic Considerations for a Psychology of Personality* (New Haven, Conn.: Yale University Press, 1955), contains an historical survey of the use of the concept of self and Allport's recommendations for adopting the analogous concept of the proprium.

Allport's publication of Jenny Masterson's letters provided psychologists with raw data on a unique personality that deserves the reader's careful attention to *Letters from Jenny* (New York: Harcourt, Brace & World, 1965). In a similar vein, Allport presents the benefits and limitations of personal documents in psychological research in *The Use of Personal Documents in Psychological Science* (New York: Social Science Research Council Bulletin, No. 49, 1942).

Allport's work in the area of social psychology and the study of rumor transmission may be had in his and Leo Postman's *The Psychology of Rumor* (New York: Holt, Rinehart & Winston, 1947). Allport's views on the crucial function of religion in the mature, healthy personality may be gleaned from his *The Individual and His Religion* (New York: Macmillan, 1962).

Criticisms of Allport's concepts abound. Walter Mischel's *Personality and Assessment* (New York: Wiley, 1968) is a thorough review of the research allegedly supporting the concept of trait. Allport's concept of uniqueness receives devastating blows at the hands of Robert Holt in "Individuality and Generalization in the Psychology of Personality," *Journal of Personality* (1962), **30**, 377–402. B. F. Skinner's *Science and Human Behavior* (New York: Free Press, 1953) may be read in part as a resounding rebuttal of Allport's trait concepts. Peter Bertocci's "Critique of Gordon W. Allport's Theory of Motivation," *Psychological Review* (1940), **47**, 501–532, cogently attacks the concept of functional autonomy.

An interview of Allport is to be found in R. I. Evans' (Ed.) *Gordon Allport: The Man and His Ideas* (New York: Dutton, 1971), or in condensed form in Evans' *The Making of Psychology* (New York: Knopf, 1976). Individual case studies in the tradition of Allport by one of his students can be had in Robert White's *Lives in Progress* (New York: Holt, Rinehart & Winston, 1966).

13 ABRAHAM MASLOW AND CARL ROGERS
Self-Actualization Theory

and i(being at a window
in this midnight)
            for no reason feel
deeply completely conscious of the rain or rather
Somebody who uses roofs and streets skillfully to make a
possible and beautiful sound . . .

e. e. cummings, "take for example this"

Even if human nature and man's behaviour are absolutely determined, man's
belief in his free will, ability to choose and individual responsibility would
still be his "psychology" and the real object of human psychology. . . .
    . . . psychotherapy can only be based on an individualistic psychology,
that is, should strive to adjust the individual to himself, which means enable
him to accept himself.

OTTO RANK, Beyond Psychology

The Paradox of Normality

The person who has achieved complete psychological health probably does not exist. Indeed, persons who merely approximate total personality integration are very rare. The vast majority of people in the world, however, must be considered to have established for themselves a balance of personality health and abnormality that leans toward health. Yet, personality theories are, for the most part, about deviant persons, about ill-conceived adaptions to life circumstances, and about major and minor personality flaws.

In consequence the student of personality is bound to run headlong into an enduring paradox inherent in the field. While by implication all theorists are interested in the factors that underlie the healthy functioning of the normal personality, the observational clarity—real or imagined—lent by extreme exaggeration of mental functioning in the abnormal personality presents an irresistible lure to the investigator.

The paradox is clear:

a. The majority of people are assumed to be relatively healthy.

b. Personality theorists center their studies on the abnormal personality.

c. Knowledge derived from this nonrepresentative sample of the human population serves as a pool of principles for application to the entire species.

Have we nothing to learn from direct study of the healthy personality?

Abraham Maslow, the first theorist to be considered in this chapter, has in recent years focused his attention on those rare persons who are on the verge of, or who have already achieved, psychological health. Maslow prefers to think of this state of exemplary personality integration as *self-actualization*. Of course, Maslow's concern with such atypical individuals establishes an equally nonrepresentative sample of personalities as the basis of psychological generalizations, but this sample may serve as a much needed corrective to a long history of concern with deviance. Maslow's intention was to establish the conditions under which all humans can attain their fullest degree of selfhood or health:

> Health is not simply the absence of disease or even the opposite of it. Any theory of motivation that is worthy of attention must deal with the highest capacities of the healthy and strong man as well as with the defensive maneuvers of crippled spirits. [1970, p. 33]

Like Carl Rogers, the second theorist to be treated in this chapter, Maslow regards the truly healthy personality as one that possesses sufficient personal fortitude and creativity to be innocent. "Innocence," in the sense that Maslow uses the term, refers to the healthy personality's capacity to live without pretense, to be genuinely bereft of guile in thought, in word, and in action. The creative, innocent, and healthy person is able to devote himself completely to whatever task is at hand. He is able to free himself from the distractions, fears, and petty influences imposed by other people, for he is in the process of becoming completely himself, becoming more real, authentic, and less influenced by a need to placate others. Maslow employed the metaphor of the actor, his mask, and his audience to portray this state of being:

> This [freedom from the influence of others] means dropping masks, dropping out efforts to influence, to impress, to please, to be lovable, to win applause. It could be said so: If we have no audience to play to, we cease to be actors. With no need to act we can devote ourselves, self-forgetfully, to the problem. [1971, p. 65]

In becoming more our real selves and less the persons we expect others want us to be, we approach closer to psychological health.

The Origin of Maslow's Interest in Psychological Health and Strength

Maslow's original training was in experimental psychology, and he completed his doctoral thesis under Harry Harlow at the University of Wisconsin. Harlow was then (circa 1933) just beginning to set up his primate laboratory for the study of monkey behavior. Maslow's research involved a great many observational investigations of animal interaction and group affiliations. In fact, his doctoral study was concerned with the establishment of dominance hierarchies in a colony of monkeys.

Maslow noted throughout his early researches (e.g., 1936a, 1936b, 1937, in Maslow 1973) that dominance of one animal over others was only rarely established through overt physical aggression. To Maslow it seemed rather that the dominant animal exhibited a kind of internal "confidence" or "dominance–feeling" that communicated to his less assertive cage mates that his will would prevail (1936b, p. 45).

When Maslow later applied his animal research findings and methods to the investigation of human behavior, he again employed the notion of "dominance-feeling": "If we were forced to choose a single synonym or definition for dominance-feeling, we should say that it was chiefly the evaluation of, or confidence in, the personality (self-confidence)" (1937, p. 53). Maslow extended his analysis in an Adlerian vein to suggest that a need for dominance may exist in some personalities as either a compensation for inferiority feelings, or as an inherent need in itself, or:

> ... it is possible that the most parsimonious way of treating this concept is to think of it in specific, rather than general terms. It may be possible and even desirable to speak *not* of a craving for dominance, but of craving for health *per se*. ... Or one may crave to be free of timidity, not because of an attempt to increase self-evaluation, but simply for vocational efficiency; e.g., in order to be a better teacher or a more efficient physician. [1937, p. 64]

Dominance-Feeling in Humans

Maslow adapted his observational infrahuman primate strategies to the study of human dominance-feeling. He created a method he called "conversational probing." Conversational probing is intensive interviewing of a subject after a satisfactory rapport is established: "This meant mostly a frank, trusting, friendly relationship, resembling somewhat the transference of the psychoanalysts" (Maslow, 1939, p. 75). Maslow studied approximately 130 women and a few men in this fashion. Of these, the majority of subjects were college students between the ages of twenty and twenty-eight; 75 percent were Protestant, 20 percent were Jewish, and 5 percent were Catholic.

The interview data were organized around a basic premise: *What personality variables correlate with dominance-feeling?* Dominance-feeling was now redefined in human terms as a form of self-evaluation:

> High dominance-feeling empirically involves good self-confidence, self-assurance, high evaluation of the self, feelings of general capability or superiority, and lack of shyness, timidity, self-consciousness or embarrassment. [Maslow, 1939, p. 74]

In addition to the traits Maslow listed in defining high dominance, he also found evidence among his subjects that they were unconventional, less religious, extroverted, and, surprisingly, more hypnotizable than low-dominance subjects (1942, pp. 108 ff.). Furthermore, Maslow discovered a number of variables that were uncorrelated with high dominance. If a subject was high in dominance-feeling it was unlikely that she was "nervous," anxious, jealous, or neurotic. The high-dominance subjects began to look like the picture of psychological health.

Sexual Behavior and Attitudes of High-Dominance Women

In a later study Maslow focused attention on the sexual behavior of his subjects. He reported a wide range of impressionistic and statistical data about his high-dominance subjects' sexual preferences, but one particular phenomenon deserves a brief description.

Women of high dominance-feeling had very specific ideas about the "ideal man" and about the "ideal lovemaking situation." For the high-dominance woman, only a high-dominance man is attractive. Preferably, he should be even more dominant than she. This paragon of masculinity was described as: "highly masculine, self-confident, fairly aggressive, sure of what he wants and able to get it, generally superior in most things" (Maslow, 1942, p. 126).

In contrast, women of medium to low dominance-feeling stressed qualities like kindness, amiability, and love for children, along with gentleness and faithfulness as desirable masculine traits.

Ideal lovemaking for the high-dominance woman involves a preference for:

> ... straightforward, unsentimental, rather violent, animal, pagan, passionate, even sometimes brutal lovemaking. It must come quickly, rather than after a long period of wooing. She wishes to be suddenly swept off her feet, not courted. She wishes her favors to be taken,

rather than asked for. In other words she must be dominated, must be forced into subordinate status. [Maslow, 1942, p. 127]

At this point in the discussion, most male students are occupied with the crucial decision of whether to devote their lives to personality psychology. Maslow, however, was also interested in the preferences of the middle- and low-dominance woman. He found that women lower in dominance-feeling were repelled by the kind of "ideal man" that attracted high-dominance subjects. Middle-dominance women preferred an "adequate" rather than a superior man, "a comfortable and 'homey' man rather than a man who might inspire slight fear and feelings of inferiority" (Maslow, 1942, p. 126). In short, high-dominance women seek a good lover; middle- and low-dominance women are more interested in a good husband and father.

The Good Specimen Strategy: "Exceptional" Primates

Maslow's distinction between high dominance and low dominance may be conceptualized as the difference between relatively secure and relatively insecure personalities (1942, p. 133). He later developed from these distinctions an interest in extreme cases of the secure personality, the personality totally actualized and completely acceptant of self. People in whom dominance-feeling has come to complete fruition were later conceptualized as "most fully human," for these people share as their common trait a trust in self that is describable as general personality strength.

Maslow eventually came to describe his strategy of research with these exceptionally healthy or strong personalities as the study of the "good specimen":

> I propose for discussion and eventually for research the use of selected good specimens (superior specimens) as biological assays for studying the best capability that the human species has. . . . What I am frankly espousing here is what I have been calling "growing-tip statistics," taking my title from the fact that it is at the growing tip of a plant that the greatest genetic action takes place. [1971, pp. 5,6,7]

Thus Maslow initiated the study of the "best" that human nature has to offer, the most "saintly," the wisest, most actualized human personality. He turned to a group of selected historical and contemporary figures who seemed to embody the traits he associated with this "good specimen." What is interesting, as we shall see, is that the observational data Maslow collected tended to be similar, in some cases identical to, the early data on dominance-feeling.

Personal Sources of the Hypothesis:
Informal Study of Personal Acquaintances

In a rather candid statement, Maslow (1971) reported the personal sources of his interest in the self-actualizing personality (SA). Devotion to and admiration for two of his teachers, Max Wertheimer, the founder of Gestalt psychology, and Ruth Benedict, the eminent cultural anthropologist, sparked the young Maslow's interest in the exceptional person. They had impressed him with their calm acceptance of life and with their special capacity to take delight in intellectual and cultural pursuits. Yet, at the same time, Benedict and Wertheimer were something of an enigma to Maslow. In trying to ferret out the sources of Benedict and Wertheimer's approach to life and its people, Maslow embarked on a private and informal investigation of self-actualization:

> [My investigations on self-actualization . . .] started out as the effort of a young intellectual to try to understand two of his teachers whom he loved, adored, and admired and who were very, very wonderful people. It was a kind of high-IQ devotion. I could not be content simply to adore, but sought to understand why these two people were so different from the run-of-the-mill people in the world. These two people were Ruth Benedict and Max Wertheimer. They were my teachers . . . and they were most remarkable human beings. My training in psychology equipped me not at all for understanding them. It was as if they were not quite people but something more than people. My own investigation began as a prescientific or nonscientific activity. I made descriptions and notes on Max Wertheimer, and I made notes on Ruth Benedict. When I tried to understand them, think about them, and write about them in my journal and my notes, I realized in one wonderful moment that their two patterns could be generalized. I was talking about a kind of person, not about two noncomparable individuals. . . . I tried to see whether this pattern could be found elsewhere, and I did find it elsewhere, in one person after another. [1971, pp. 41–42]

Begun as a private and informal undertaking, Maslow's interest in psychologically healthy, self-actualized people soon became a serious professional interest. It is clear that this concern with the exceptional organism, "the good specimen," was an extension of Maslow's early work with the exceptionally dominant personalities he had studied in and out of the animal laboratory.

Consequently, Maslow began to develop criteria of normality or health. From his observations of personal acquaintances who might embody such qualities, Maslow was able to develop an impressionistic sketch of the exceptionally healthy person. Using biographical information on historical figures, and on some contemporary public ones, Maslow discovered nine individuals in whom he felt "fairly sure" self-actualization was well under way. Though Maslow's "fairly sure" personal acquaintances had necessarily to remain anonymous in his report of the research (except for Wertheimer and Benedict), the historical figures he chose as SA subjects were Abraham Lincoln in his last years and Thomas Jefferson. Additionally, Maslow discovered seven "highly probable" figures: Albert Einstein, Eleanor Roosevelt, Jane Addams, William James, Albert Schweitzer, Aldous Huxley, and Spinoza. Ultimately, a whole array of public and historical figures were selected as "potential cases" of SA. Among these figures were Adlai Stevenson, Ralph Waldo Emerson, George Washington, Walt Whitman, Martin Buber, and Goethe; in all a total of thirty-seven potential cases (Maslow, 1970, p. 152).

Maslow's analysis of the personalities with whom he was directly familiar was rather different from the usual clinical-experimental investigation. Because subjects tend to freeze up when informed they are being studied as examples of exceptional psychological health, most of Maslow's observations had to be surreptitious (1970, p. 152). Therefore, the data took the form of impressionistic analyses of informal conversations and easily observable behaviors. With time, Maslow developed a definition of the self-actualizing person (SA) as one who *is* what he can be (1970, p. 46):

> ... [self-actualization] may be loosely described as the full use and exploitation of talents, capacities, potentialities, etc. Such people seem to be fulfilling themselves and to be doing the best that they are capable of doing, reminding us of Nietzsche's exhortation, "Become what thou art!" [Maslow, 1970, p. 150]

In the course of his work, Maslow interviewed and studied over three thousand individuals, of whom only a "handful" were discovered to have potential for self-actualization. In fact, only one individual who was self-actualized in the fullest sense was found.

Characteristics of Self-Actualizers

From his observations, interviews, and partial test results, Maslow developed a schematic picture of the self-actualizing personality. Maslow's propensity for lists of things in his writing is well known, and his description of the SA syndrome is no exception. The SA pattern consists of fifteen characteristics that are positive or favorable and five negative (from the viewpoint of other people) traits. All twenty items have been summarized in Table 13–1 with a brief description of the meaning of each item. In addition, the twenty separate items have been grouped into seven classes where overlap and similarity permit such redistribution. To preserve the essence of continuity in Maslow's original list, the number of the item in that list is indicated in parentheses (see Maslow, 1970, Chap. 11; see also the earlier version in Moustakas, 1956, pp. 160 ff.).

From Table 13–1 it can be seen that SA people are generally characterized by independence and self-trust. They are accepting of others and self, and most important, accepting of what life holds in store for them. They are people in whom basic needs for food, shelter, and intimacy with an opposite-sex partner have been satisfactorily met. Self-actualizers, consequently, are functioning in response to "higher" needs, needs for the classic "Goods" of the well-lived life. Beauty, Truth, Justice, and many other capitalized virtues are the very core of the self-actualizer's existence. In this sense, therefore, SA people taught Maslow an important lesson: Man strives not merely for survival, not merely out of deficiencies, but *for* meaningful existence out of an innate need to be whole. The question that now occupied Maslow was, *How do such higher motivations develop to engage the self-actualizer's being?*

The Hierarchy of Motives: From Deficiency to Being Motivation

Maslow conceptualized human needs in a hierarchy of potency. Needs lowest in the scale are prepotent to needs lying above them. Prepotency means that higher needs cannot emerge until lower ones have first been satisfied. Thus, lower needs exert potency in shaping an individual's behavior *before* the higher needs, and continue to be potent until satisfied.

For example, a man whose every biological need is satisfied—hunger, thirst, and sex to be specific—is likely to turn to poetry, photography, art, or music to have some meaningful way of spending his energies and occupying his time.

> It is quite true that man lives by bread alone—when there is no bread. *But what happens to man's desires when there is bread and when his belly is chronically filled?* [Maslow, 1943, in 1973, p. 157; cf. 1970, p. 38; italics added]

The answer, of course, is that the "higher" needs emerge to exert potency in shaping man's strivings. The cycle continues, however, for once "higher" needs for beauty, truth, justice, and so on are fulfilled, even "higher" needs emerge. The highest of the needs in the hierarchy are the *B-values* (Being-values), or metaneeds as Maslow termed them. The metaneeds will be considered shortly, but it is important to note that the fifteen metaneeds are *not* hierarchically arranged. Having reached the self-actualization step in the hierarchy, the individual experiences needs for the B-values like Beauty, Truth, and Justice more or less simultaneously, though

TABLE 13–1: MASLOW'S SELF-ACTUALIZATION PATTERN

SELF-ACTUALIZATION CHARACTERISTIC	DESCRIPTION
Reality (1) and Problem Centered (4)	More efficient and accurate perception of reality; unusual ability to detect the fake, phony, and dishonest; focus on problems external to self; invests energies in "causes."
Acceptance of self and others (2); Spontaneity and simplicity (3)	Accepts own nature in stoic style; accepts what cannot be changed; is spontaneous and always natural; prefers simplicity to pretense and artificiality—in self and others; conventional on surface to avoid hurting others.
Need privacy (5); Independence of culture and environment (6); Resists enculturation (15)	Relies on own judgment; trusts in self; resists pressure from others and social norms; able to "weather hard knocks" with calm; resists identification with cultural stereotypes; has autonomous values carefully considered.
Freshness of appreciation (7); Creativeness (14)	Maintains constancy for awe and wonder; ability to marvel at and enjoy the good things of life: food, sex, sports, travel; thousandth baby seen is as wonderful as first; creative in daily tasks of living; inventive and original in child-like way.
Unhostile sense of humor (13); Democratic (11); *Gemeinschaftsgefühl* (9); Intimate personal relations (10)	Does not enjoy jokes at expense of others; prefers a philosophic humor that pokes fun at the human condition; enjoys company of all people regardless of social or racial origins; Adler's *Gemeinschaftsgefühl* means "fellow-feeling" or social interest; strong interest in others' welfare; small number of intense and intimate friendships.

Peak (mystical) experiences (8); Discrimination between means and ends (12)

Has experienced mystic states characterized by feelings of limitless horizons opening, being more powerful and more helpless simultaneously, with loss of time sense; strong ethical-moral sense but not in conventional ways; discriminates between moral means and ends differently from average person; means can be ends.

IMPERFECTIONS: Unexpected ruthlessness; occasional absentmindedness; overkindliness; nonneurotic guilt and anxiety

"There are no perfect people"; SA individuals can display surgical coldness when called for in situations of betrayal; overkindliness gets them into trouble by letting others impose on them; uninterested in social "chatting" or party going; anxiety and guilt present, but from realistic not neurotic sources; sometimes philosophical concerns cause a loss of sense of humor.

Based on Maslow, 1970, pp. 153—176.

not with equal intensity. The basic hierarchy may be schematized as on page 491 (based on Maslow, 1970, pp. 35–46).

When a lower-order need predominates—for example, hunger in the physiological step—then all behavior is directed to the fulfillment of that need. If its satisfaction is a chronic problem, then the next highest need in the hierarchy will fail to develop full potency.

When all four levels in the hierarchy, the basic needs, are satisfied, the highest needs for self-actualization emerge. Collateral with self-actualization needs are the uniquely human desires to know, to understand the world, and to enjoy its beauty. Although Maslow was not particularly clear on the matter, he seems in the final revision of his definitive work (1970) to have intended the aesthetic and knowledge needs to be grouped with self-actualization as equal potency motives.

The term "self-actualization" was first coined by Kurt Goldstein (1939) and adopted by Maslow to indicate the healthy, well-lived life previously described by the fifteen characteristics attributed to self-actualizing people. In any event, it seems clear that in Maslow's scheme *satisfaction striving*, rather than deficiency motivation, is the motor of personality. Maslow construes the organism not as pushed by drives, but as pulled by the need to be fulfilled.

Beyond Self-Actualization: The B-Values

The rare individual who achieves the stage of self-actualization enters on a course of what Maslow called "growth motivation." In the language of needs, the self-actualized person develops Being-needs or B-values. He is no longer engaged on the road to "becoming" self-actualized, for he has successfully progressed through the hierarchy of basic needs. He now embarks on the growth processes of living to *enhance his being, to expand his knowledge of self and others,* and *to operationalize his personality* in any activity that he undertakes.

In this sense, Maslow proposed the further set of Being-needs that emerge at the point of self-actualization in the basic hierarchy. To these B-values Maslow often assigned the name "metamotives": "Self-actualizing people are not primarily motivated (i.e., by basic needs); they are primarily metamotivated (i.e., by metaneeds = B-values)" (1971, p. 311).

With the proposal of the B-values, Maslow recognized the possibility that some individuals may satisfy all their basic needs through to the esteem levels in the hierarchy and yet not be self-actualized. In a sense, some people suffer the neuroses of the rich, the "existential" neuroses of being affluent and directionless. To truly be self-actualizing, one must be committed to long-reaching goals: the B-values. Thus Maslow revised his definition of the self-actualizing personality:

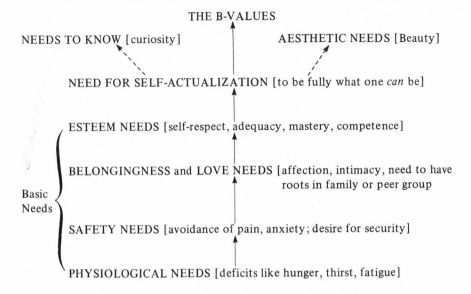

THE B-VALUES

NEEDS TO KNOW [curiosity]   AESTHETIC NEEDS [Beauty]

NEED FOR SELF-ACTUALIZATION [to be fully what one *can* be]

ESTEEM NEEDS [self-respect, adequacy, mastery, competence]

BELONGINGNESS and LOVE NEEDS [affection, intimacy, need to have
                                      roots in family or peer group

Basic
Needs

SAFETY NEEDS [avoidance of pain, anxiety; desire for security]

PHYSIOLOGICAL NEEDS [deficits like hunger, thirst, fatigue]

> ... it may turn out to be useful to add to the definition of the
> self-actualizing person, not only [a] that he be sufficiently free of
> illness, [b] that he be sufficiently gratified in his basic needs, and [c]
> that he be positively using his capacities, but also [d] that *he be*
> *motivated by some values which he strives for or gropes for and to which he*
> *is loyal.* [1971, p. 301; italics added]

Originally Maslow proposed a list of fourteen B-values (1962, p. 78), only
later to add a fifteenth (1971, pp. 318–319). The fifteen B-values are listed
in Table 13–2 along with the "deficiency diseases" or metapathologies that
result when one of the B-values is unsatisfied. Thus, Maslow felt that the
B-values were as necessary to human existence as vitamins or foods or
water.

The B-values in Table 13–2 overlap to some degree. In Maslow's opinion the overlap is an essential characteristic of Being-needs:

> It is my (uncertain) impression that any B-value is fully and ade-
> quately defined by the total of the other B-Values. That is, truth, to
> be fully and completely defined, must be beautiful, good, perfect,
> just, simple, orderly, lawful, alive, comprehensive, unitary, dichoto-
> my-transcending, effortless, and amusing. . . . *It is as if all the B-Values*
> *have some kind of unity, with each single value being something like a facet*
> *of this whole.* [Maslow, 1971, p. 324; italics added]

Maslow regarded the values and diseases in Table 13–2 as a kind of "psychological periodic table" that offered the possibility of discovering psychological diseases not yet observed and classified.

TABLE 13-2: B-VALUES AND METAPATHOLOGIES

B-VALUE or METANEED	PATHOGENIC DEPRIVATION	SPECIFIC METAPATHOLOGIES (MOTIVATION DISEASE)
1. Truth	Dishonesty	Disbelief; mistrust; cynicism.
2. Goodness	Evil	Utter selfishness; hatred; reliance only on self; disgust; nihilism
3. Beauty	Ugliness	Vulgarity; loss of taste; tension; fatigue
4. Unity-Wholeness	Chaos, atomism	Disintegration; arbitrariness
4A. Dichotomy-Transcendence	Black/White dichotomies; forced choices	Either/or thinking; seeing everything as dualistic; a simplistic view of life
5. Aliveness; Process	Deadness; mechanizing of life	Robotizing; feeling totally determined; loss of zest in life
6. Uniqueness	Sameness; uniformity	Loss of feeling of individuality or being needed
7. Perfection	Imperfection; sloppiness	Discouragement (?); hopelessness
7A. Necessity	Accident; occasionalism; inconsistency	Loss of safety; unpredictability
8. Completion; Finality	Incompleteness	Cessation of striving; no use trying.
9. Justice	Injustice	Insecurity; anger; cynicism; mistrust
9A. Order	Lawlessness, chaos	Insecurity; wariness; loss of safety
10. Simplicity	Confusing complexity	Overcomplexity; confusion; loss of orientation
11. Richness; Totality	Poverty	Depression; uneasiness; loss of interest
12. Effortlessness	Effortful	Fatigue; strain; clumsiness
13. Playfulness	Humorlessness	Grimness; depression; paranoid humorlessness
14. Self-Sufficiency	Accident; occasionalism	Dependence upon the perceiver and others
15. Meaningfulness	Meaninglessness	Despair; senselessness of life

Condensed from Maslow, 1971, pp. 318–319.

Maslow commented on the metapathologies to be found in everyday life: "I have used the world of television and especially of television advertising as a rich source of metapathologies of all types, i.e., of the vulgarization or destruction of all intrinsic values ..." (1971, p. 319). A moment's thought about television commercials will confirm Maslow's opinion. Bad breath, body odor, loose dentures, psoriasis, warts, gastritis, hemmorrhoids, "feminine freshness," and foot odor constitute only a partial list of television advertising's critical concerns. If this civilization is ever buried by atomic holocaust, future anthropologists who resurrect the video tapes of major network commercials are certain to conclude that as a society we were offensive to each other in a degree never before reached on earth.

Peak Experiences as Momentarily Intense B-Value States

In 1902, William James published his Gifford Lectures under the title *The Varieties of Religious Experience*. In a series of twenty lectures, James surveyed from a variety of poetic, theological, and biographical writings the diversity of ways in which individuals reported experiencing God. One particular subclass of such experiences called the "mystical state" occupied James at some length. From his researches, James was able to distinguish four characteristics of the mystical experience that separated it from states of normal consciousness. Maslow accepted James's descriptive criteria as adequate characterization of *peak experiences* undergone by self-actualizing people (see Maslow, 1964; 1970, p. 164). James listed the following characteristics of the mystical experience (1902, pp. 371–373):

1. *Ineffability:* "The subject of [a mystical experience] immediately says that it defies expression, that no adequate report of its contents can be given in words. It follows from this that its quality must be directly experienced; it cannot be imparted or transferred to others."
2. *Noetic Quality:* The word "noetic" is based on a Greek root meaning "mind" or "intellect." James employed the term to indicate the essentially intellectual, "truth-finding" quality of a mystic experience.
3. *Transiency:* "Mystical states cannot be sustained for long. Except in rare instances, half an hour, or at most an hour or two, seems to be the limit beyond which they fade into the light of common day."
4. *Passivity:* "... the mystic feels as if his own will were in abeyance, and indeed sometimes as if he were grasped and held by a superior power."

Because of the generally unearthly, surreal quality of mystical experiences (peak experiences), Maslow initially felt that only self-actualizing people underwent them with any appreciable regularity (1964, p. 22). But as he became more skilled in interviewing subjects and in phrasing questions to elicit the information, Maslow discovered that most "average" people have had some peak experiences. The difficulty lay in the fact that some persons tend to react with defensive escape strategies rather than with "openness" or acceptance. Maslow found that individuals who hold particularly materialistic, mechanistic views of life are those individuals who try to ward off and forget peak experiences. These "nonpeakers" thus deliberately cut themselves off from an important spiritual part of life.

At the other extreme, however, Maslow cautioned that contemporary cultural mores among youth tend to foster an impatience or over-eager readiness to undergo the transcendent moments of a peak experience. Drugs, meditation rituals, and shortcuts of all kinds cheapen the peak experience: "The sudden insight becomes 'all' and the patient and disciplined 'working through' is postponed or devalued" (1971, p. 345). When peak experiences are sought, actively induced, or otherwise treated as a commodity to be acquired, the total value of the experience is lost. Maslow suggested that the resulting disappointment leads to an attitude of apathy or superficiality, a tendency to desanctify or *desacralize* life.

The Defense of Desacralizing

Desacralizing, a term adopted from Eliade (1961; see also 1958), was employed by Maslow to indicate a defensive strategy some individuals use to cope with the demands of living. Desacralizing means to deny the awesome, marvelous, beautiful, sublime aspects of people and the universe. In effect, the desacralizer has learned to "reduce the person to the concrete object and to refuse to see what he might be or to refuse to see him in his symbolic values or to refuse to see him or her eternally" (Maslow, 1971, p. 49). Maslow has suggested that one characteristic of the self-actualizing personality that separates him from the "average" person is his ability to "resacralize" people and things. The self-actualizing person has learned to be awe-inspired by others, to marvel at and enjoy the good things of life, to accept the spiritual as well as the material.

Extending his criticism of desacralization to the domain of the sciences, Maslow found the social sciences in particular to be wanting in their treatment of persons:

> Briefly put, it appears to me that science and everything scientific can be and often is used as a tool in the service of a distorted, narrowed, humorless, de-eroticized, de-emotionalized, desacralized, and de-sanctified *Weltanschauung*. This desacralization can be used as a defense against being flooded by emotion, especially the emotions of humility, reverence, mystery, wonder, and awe. [1966, p. 139]

For some scientists, particularly those who work in the "personal" sciences of psychology, sociology, and anthropology, classical scientific method may serve the function of a defense mechanism. By abstracting, objectifying, and generally dehumanizing their human subjects, these scientific workers unconsciously seek to isolate themselves from the all-too-human failings, emotions, anxieties, and confusions they investigate in others (Maslow, 1966, p. 33).

> More than any other kind of knowledge we fear knowledge of ourselves, knowledge that might transform our self-esteem and our self-image. . . . While human beings love knowledge and seek it—they are curious—they also fear it. The closer to the personal it is, the more they fear it. So human knowledge is apt to be a kind of dialectic between this love and this fear. Thus knowledge includes the defenses against itself, the repressions, the sugar-coatings, the inattentions, the forgettings. [Maslow, 1966, p. 16]

Maslow suggested that, at least for some scientific workers, the acquisition of scientific knowledge about human persons is anxiety-instigated and therefore amounts to a "cognitive pathology." For example, when the need to know is based on a compulsive seeking after certainty rather than on enjoyment of discovery, it is pathological. Or, when an individual compulsively denies his doubts, his ignorance, and his mistakes, not from a position of knowledge but from a fear of confessing human fallibility, his scientific skills and knowledge are serving pathological ends. Or, when the individual feels that knowledge makes him "tough-minded," "hard-nosed," and "scientifically rigorous," he may defensively close himself off to the tender, romantic, poetic, and spiritual aspects of the people he studies.

Maslow summarized his view of the "desacralizing" tendency of some contemporary scientific efforts by indicating the directions a new and more humanistic scientific enterprise should pursue:

> If humanistic science may be said to have any goals beyond sheer fascination with the human mystery and enjoyment of it, these would be to release the person from external controls and to make him *less* predictable to the observer (to make him freer, more creative, more inner-determined) even though perhaps more predictable to himself. [1966, p. 40]

Hence, for Maslow, the sciences, and psychology in particular, are value-laden enterprises in which the worth of the investigator becomes mingled with the virtue of the investigated.

The Effects of Peak Experiences

The B-values—Truth, Beauty, Goodness, Unity, and so on—that assume such significance for the self-actualized person, are intensified in states of peak experience. The individual who has undergone such moments comes away from them feeling that the world "looks different." Maslow isolated sixteen aftereffects of the peak experience. The person who has undergone a peak experience feels (based on Maslow, 1962, pp. 97–107):

1. more integrated, whole, and unified;
2. more at one with the world;
3. as if he were at the peak of his powers, most fully himself;
4. graceful, without strain, effortless;
5. creative, active, responsible, self-controlled;
6. free of inhibitions, blocks, doubts, self-criticisms;
7. spontaneous, expressive, innocent;
8. creative, self-confident, flexible;
9. unique, individualistic;
10. free of past and future limits;
11. free of the world, free to be;
12. undriven, unmotivated, nonwishing, beyond needs;
13. rhapsodic, poetic;
14. consumed, finished, closed, complete, subjectively final;
15. playful, good-humored, childlike;
16. lucky, fortunate, grateful.

In short, the peak experience is evidence that:

> Man has a higher and transcendent nature, and this is part of his essence, i.e., his biological nature as a member of a species which has evolved. [Maslow, 1971, p. 349]

Humanistic Psychology: The Third Force

Both Maslow, and the second theorist to be considered in this chapter, Carl Rogers, considered themselves to be *humanistic psychologists.* Humanistic psychology emphasizes man's capacity for goodness, creativity, and freedom. Unlike the strictly deterministic and somewhat mechanistic views of man to be found in Freud's psychoanalysis and in contemporary behaviorism, humanistic psychology construes man as a spiritual and rational, purposeful and autonomous creature. Maslow expressed this view in the Preface to his definitive work:

> If I had to condense the thesis of this book into a single sentence, I would have said that *in addition* to what the psychologists of the time had to say about human nature, man also had a higher nature and that this was instinctoid, i.e., part of his essence. And if I could have had a second sentence, I would have stressed the profoundly holistic

nature of human nature in contradiction to the analytic—dissecting —atomistic—Newtonian approach of the behaviorisms and of Freudian psychoanalysis. [1970, p. ix]

Thus Maslow's theory represents an alternative to the two major shaping forces of contemporary psychology found in behaviorism and in Freudian psychoanalysis. For this reason, the work of Maslow and Rogers, and many others, has been christened "third force" psychology to emphasize its stature as a viable and equally comprehensive viewpoint. Toward the end of his life, Maslow emphasized that he had not intended a "sophomoric" two-valued orientation of being either pro-Freudian or anti-Freudian, or probehaviorist and antibehaviorist. He felt, rather, that he had embodied the best of both of these viewpoints and had gone beyond them to a psychology of transcendence (1971, pp. 3–4).

One evidence of his transcendent thinking was his vision of a psychological Utopia in which healthy, self-actualized people would live and work in harmony. Called *Eupsychia,* this Utopia would represent an attempt to blend what is godlike in man's nature to what is most fully human, to actualize what Maslow saw as man's inherently good being.

For Maslow, Eupsychia would attempt to provide the environment in which man could become totally what he is (1970, p. 277).

Carl Rogers: Psychotherapist as Self-Actualization Facilitator

Unlike Maslow, Rogers began his study of human nature with troubled personalities. As a clinical psychologist, Rogers explored the human's potential for change in the therapeutic relationship. In the knotted, defensive, and anxious verbal stream of his patients, Rogers, too, found that psychological disability results when persons are prevented from being what they truly are.

Rogers' personality theory emerged slowly from his careful and exacting psychotherapeutic studies. He was among the first therapist-researchers to capture the cloistered conversation of the psychotherapeutic relationship on wire recordings in immutable and repeatably observable form. (Recording sound on a thin thread of wire was the antecedent of the modern metallic-oxide-coated recording tape.) Along with the willingness to commit the processes of therapy to scientific scrutiny, Rogers pioneered a pervasive change in the way the clinical relationship could be used to induce personality change and in the ways personality data could be derived from the relationship.

Consider the following fragments of two recorded counseling interviews with college students. They are printed side by side to facilitate direct comparisons. The left-hand transcript is of a client and therapist who view the therapeutic situation as structured, problem-centered, and under the direct control of the therapist. The right-hand column contains the transcript of a similar client-therapist interview in a situation with a counselor who recognizes that therapeutic processes are very much person-centered.

DIRECTIVE COUNSELING TRANSCRIPT

Counselor: I noticed that you stated you enrolled in Psychology 411 [study-habits course] because you didn't know how to study well enough—uh—and then I checked over the problem list, and I saw that you went rather heavy on —you worried about low grades and poor memory and so on. How well did you do in high school?

Student: Well, I was just an average student.

C: And what major did you have there?

S: Ah, you mean—

C: In high school, you took college preparatory or commercial?

S: It was an academic course. I took languages and English and history.

C: What course did you like the best? [Student presumably answers; later in session counselor summarizes:]

C: It seems to me that your problem is that you want to learn more about yourself. We'll be getting all these tests back, and there are those [study] projects, and the way we do, I see you each week at this time and you'll begin to get a little better picture—and then I'll help you check it and I'll tell you if it's right— (Laugh)

S: Mm-hm.

C: So we can work it out. I would suggest—I would more or less work this project out because you say you are having difficulties concentrating. . . .

(From Rogers, 1942, pp. 116–117)

NONDIRECTIVE COUNSELING TRANSCRIPT

Student: I haven't written to my parents about this at all. In the past they haven't been of any help to me in this respect, and if I can keep it away from them as much as possible, I'll do so. But there's a slight matter of grades to explain, and they're not good, and I don't know how I'm going to explain without telling them about this. Would you advise me to tell them about it?

Counselor: Suppose you tell me a little more about what you had thought about it.

S: Well, I think I'm compelled to, because—

C: It's a situation you've really got to face.

S: Yes, there's no use getting around it, even if they can't take it the way they should, because I've already flunked my gym course. I just haven't come. . . .

C: It will be fairly hard for you to tell them.

S: Yes. Oh, I don't know if they're going to sort of condemn me. I think so, because that's what they've done in the past. . . .

C: You feel that they'll be unsympathetic and they'll condemn you for your failures.

S: Well my—I'm pretty sure my father will. My mother might not. He hasn't been—he doesn't experience these things; he just doesn't know what it's like. . . .

C: You feel that he could never understand you?

(From Rogers, 1942, pp. 135–136)

The Key Difference: Focus on Feelings

There are significant and easily discernible differences between the two counseling interviews. The essence of the directive counselor's effort is information gathering and dispensing. The flow of communication between counselor and client tends to be one way: from counselor to client. Responsibility for the direction and outcome of the relationship implicitly lies with the authoritarian counselor. Restricted to the role of question answerer, the client is led through a series of diagnostic queries and away from any confrontation with his feelings, confusions, anxieties. To the degree that client feelings are mentioned at all, they are *talked about* rather than genuinely experienced or forthrightly made the focus of concern. The counselor goes so far as to summarize by assuming the "wise knower" role: "It seems to me that your problem is you want to learn more about yourself." It is a rational, perhaps even correct, statement. But it is the counselor's statement; the client is reduced to a series of noncommunicative "Mm-hm's."

The second counseling transcript is immediately striking by its different emotional flavor. Most outstanding of these differences is the sheer wealth of feelings that the client is encouraged to express. In all replies, with different degrees of success, the counselor attempts to respond to the emotional content of the client's statements rather than to the cognitive or informational aspects of the situation. The nondirective counselor tried to respond to the troubled *person* by helping him to clarify his feelings: "It's a situation you've really got to face"; or, "It'll be fairly hard for you to tell them." When the counselor is successful in detecting the emotional meaning of a client remark, these rephrasings of the client's statements allow the client to examine his feelings "out in the open." When the counselor is unsuccessful at mirroring the emotional tone of the client's statements, the client sometimes feels that the counselor is "putting words into my mouth," or that he missed the boat completely. But even when mistaken, the counselor's attitude communicates to the client a genuine, if fallible, concern to understand the world as the client sees it.

The differences between these two counseling interviews are only a small sample of the insights about the counseling relationship systematized by Rogers. His development of a personality theory is so inextricably interwoven with his clinical therapeutic work that some consideration must be given to the slow development of what Rogers came eventually to call *client-centered counseling and theory* as a replacement for the original "nondirective" label.

Development of the Nondirective Viewpoint: Clients Are People

In 1974, as part of his address to the American Psychological Association on the occasion of receiving its Distinguished Professional Contribution

Award, Rogers traced his impact on psychology. In particular, he formulated from his perspective of nearly half a century of therapeutic work the
kernel of the central hypothesis that had initiated and guided his theoretical development:

> . . . the gradually formed and tested hypothesis [was] that the indi-
> vidual has within himself vast resources for self-understanding, for
> altering his self-concept, his attitudes, and his self-directed behavior
> —and that these resources can be tapped if only a definable climate
> of facilitative psychological attitudes can be provided. [1974a, p. 116]

The similarity with Maslow's conception of human nature is obvious. Both
theorists regard man as inherently good, as self-directed, and as striving
toward increased autonomy. Rogers' theory, then, can be understood as
the attempt to discover the conditions that foster the individual's utiliza-
tion of *his own* powers for health and understanding.

Early Pragmatism: "If It Works, Do It"

Rogers began his career as a clinical psychologist trained in the hard-nosed
empiricism of Columbia University. He was granted an internship at the
newly founded Institute for Child Guidance while in doctoral training, and
in the atmosphere of this clinic Rogers was exposed to a multiplicity of
theoretical viewpoints. Members of the staff at the guidance clinic were
largely Freudian and psychodynamic in their orientation, and the contrast
to the statistical, objective atmosphere of Columbia made Rogers feel ". . .
I was functioning in two completely different worlds, 'and never the twain
shall meet' " (1961, p. 9; cf. 1974c, p. 7).

The conflict of intellectual traditions was an important learning experience for Rogers, opening him to the possibility that experts differ drastically in their interpretations. Before completion of his doctorate, Rogers
obtained a position in the Child Study Department of the Society for the
Prevention of Cruelty to Children in Rochester, New York (1961, p. 9). For
the next twelve years, Rogers was engaged in the application of psychological services to delinquent and underprivileged children. Many of the staff
of the Rochester facility were trained in the Philadelphia School of Social
Work and operated from the neopsychoanalytic viewpoint developed by
Otto Rank. For some indication of Rank's theoretical orientation, the second epigraph at the beginning of this chapter on Rogers' theory will be
helpful, as well as this representative statement of Rank's views:

> I conceive of human help for the individual not as a planned method
> of psycho-therapeutic techniques with respect to a control of his
> stimuli and responses but as *his experiencing of the irrational forces
> within himself* which he has not heretofore dared to express spontane-
> ously. [1941, p. 47; italics added]

Rogers later commented in a conversation with J. T. Hart that his own early emphasis on responding to the feelings of the client sprang from the influence of Rank and his followers at the Rochester facility (Rogers, 1966 in Hart & Tomlinson, 1970, p. 515). Most important of all, however, was the lesson to be learned from his colleagues' attitude toward therapeutic technique: "There was only one criterion in regard to any method of dealing with these children and their parents, and that was, "Does it work?" (1961, p. 10).

The lesson on pragmatism was reinforced for Rogers when his careful dynamic prodding and questioning to uncover the sexual conflicts of a young delinquent client did not prevent the boy from getting into the same difficulty with the law. On probation after therapy with Rogers, the boy again succumbed to his "propensity to set fires" (1961, p. 10). Rogers' trust in expert opinion thus received another damaging blow.

Insight into the Dignity of the Individual Person: A "Failure"

Another influence which shaped Rogers' slowly developing theoretical formulations occurred during an interview with a client's mother. The boy was something of a "hellion," and Rogers could clearly see that the mother's early rejection of the boy was responsible. Despite repeated attempts at directing her flow of conversation toward the attainment of this insight, he could not accomplish a successful breakthrough. His report of the experience is particularly instructive:

> Finally I gave up. I told her that it seemed we had both tried, but we had failed. . . . She agreed. So we concluded the interview, shook hands, and she walked to the door of the office. Then she turned and asked, "Do you ever take adults for counseling here?" When I replied in the affirmative, she said, "Well then, I would like some help." She came to the chair she had left, and began to pour out her despair about her marriage, her troubled relationship with her husband, her sense of failure and confusion, all very different from the sterile "case history" she had given before. Real therapy began then. . . . [Rogers, 1961, p. 11]

From this experience of "failure" Rogers learned an important lesson about the nature of the ideal psychotherapeutic experience and about the dignity of the person: ". . . it is the *client* who knows what hurts, what directions to go, what problems are crucial, "what experiences have been deeply buried" (1961, pp. 11–12). Thus, Rogers slowly came to the viewpoint that authoritative, directive, and diagnostically oriented psychological service was far less important than allowing the client to speak freely, feel freely, and think freely. Freud had come to much the same conclusion when

Fraülein Elisabeth objected to his constant probing. But Freud developed a rather different conception of the person and his motives than Rogers was now developing (cf. Chapter 2).

Early Nondirective View: Too Much Freedom

In 1940, Rogers accepted a position with Ohio State University to teach graduate students about counseling. As he taught, he was forced to focus his views more sharply, in the process forming a perspective of psychotherapy that was unique. Up to this point, Rogers had felt that he was simply writing and teaching about clinical techniques that all clinicians were using (1959, p. 187). But when invited to deliver a lecture to the Psi Chi chapter at the University of Minnesota entitled "Newer Concepts in Psychotherapy," Rogers soon discovered from the furor and controversy the lecture aroused that he was indeed saying something new (1974c, p. 8).

From the Minnesota lecture, Rogers derived the second chapter of his book on counseling from the nondirective viewpoint. In *Counseling and Psychotherapy* (1942), Rogers emphasized four important principles of the "new" psychotherapy:

1. The newer therapy "relies much more heavily on the individual drive toward growth, health, and adjustment. Therapy is not a matter of doing something *to* the individual, or of inducing him to do something about himself. It is instead a matter of freeing him for normal growth and development . . ." (1942, p. 29).

2. ". . . this newer therapy places greater stress upon the emotional elements, the feeling aspects of the situation, than upon the intellectual aspects" (1942, p. 29).

3. ". . . this newer therapy places greater stress upon the immediate situation than upon the individual's past" (1942, p. 29).

4. The newer approach ". . . lays great stress upon the therapeutic relationship itself as a growth experience. . . . Here the individual learns to understand himself; to make significant independent choices, to relate himself successfully to another person in a more adult fashion" (1942, p. 30).

Thus the central concept in Rogers' first formulation of his views was that the person has within himself the capacity to solve his own problems, as previously pointed out. The task of the therapist is to establish the conditions that allow the person to attain this insight himself: *Attainment of insight* was, therefore, one of the key goals of nondirective therapy in the 1940's. To enable the client to achieve self-insight, the counselor's chief tool was the *clarification of feelings* through rephrasing the emotional content of the client's statements. (Cf. Hart, 1970, pp. 6 ff.) Rogers summarized his early view of the counselor's role in this way:

> *Effective counseling consists of a definitely structured, permissive relationship which allows the client to gain an understanding of himself to a degree which enables him to take positive steps in the light of his new orientation.* [Rogers, 1942, p. 18]

Though controversial, Rogers' techniques and philosophy were widely adopted by practitioners who failed to sort out the philosophy from the techniques. The problems that followed in the application of nondirective therapy were due in part to two crucial aspects of this early formulation: (1) Little or no *explicit* theory had been developed to guide the counselor's efforts. (2) In the hands of an unskilled or inadequately trained therapist, the permissive and accepting attitude was construed by his clients as a threatening "don't care" attitude or as a directionless, disorganized relationship. Rogers felt that the difficulty lay in the tendency of some counselors to interpret his formulations too literally (1951, p. 26). In effect, some counselors supposed that their role was to be merely passive and to adopt a laissez-faire policy: "the passivity and seeming lack of interest . . . is experienced by the client as a rejection, since indifference is in no real way the same as acceptance" (Rogers, 1951, p. 27).

Client-Centered Therapy: Empathic Understanding

The first phase of Rogers' development of his position emphasized the warmth and acceptance of the counseling relationship. Too much acceptance, too much freedom for the client had proved to be a problem. In 1951, however, Rogers published a second major work on counseling more carefully delineating his views. The book's title, *Client-Centered Therapy,* was meant to emphasize the new rationale of his approach: "The client, as the term has acquired its meaning, is one who comes actively and voluntarily to gain help on a problem, but *without any notion of surrendering his own responsibility for the situation*" (Rogers, 1951, p. 7n.; italics added).

Thus, the publication of *Client-Centered Therapy* marked the beginning of a second phase in Rogers' thinking (cf. Hart, 1970). The focus had shifted to the counselor's efforts to be *empathic* in his understanding of the client's world, and to the *communication* of that understanding to the client. The technique of reflection of feelings, though present from the first nondirective period, now assumed more importance. Reflection of feelings was not merely to be employed to help the client attain insight and clarification of his emotions, but also as an important tool to communicate the counselor's understanding of the client's inner world. In mirroring back the client's feelings, the counselor simultaneously transmits his desire to perceive the world as the client perceives it. In effect, the goal of the counselor is to achieve the *internal frame-of-reference* of his client:

> . . . it is the counselor's aim to perceive as sensitively and accurately as possible all of the perceptual field as it is being experienced by the client . . . ; and having thus perceived this internal frame of reference of the other as completely as possible, to indicate to the client the extent to which he is seeing through the client's eyes. [Rogers, 1951, p. 34]

Thus, by 1951, two of the three major elements that characterize Rogers' view of personality were present to his thinking. First was the necessity for the counselor to provide a warm and permissive relationship; second was the necessity for the counselor to assume the internal frame of reference of the client and to communicate his empathic understanding of the client's world.

Experiential Therapy: The Conditions of Personality Change

The third element characteristic of Rogers' view of personality emerged during the most recent, third aspect of the development of client-centered theory. Hart (1970) and Gendlin (1964, 1968, 1970) have characterized this phase of Rogers' and their own work as the "experiencing" phase or as *experiential therapy.*

The focus had again shifted by 1957 to a *mutual expression of feelings* by client *and* counselor. *Experiencing* became the technical term to describe the internal, directly felt emotional processes that the client and counselor struggle to put into words. Because tangled and latent feelings are the core of psychological maladjustment in Rogers' view, the tasks of learning to experience one's own distorted and trapped emotions and of learning to communicate them to oneself and to the counselor became the central goals of experiential therapy.

One of the key causes of this shift in emphasis from pure verbal transactions to direct emotional experience can be found in a research effort undertaken by Rogers and his colleagues at the University of Wisconsin. Working with nonverbal, often uncooperative, schizophrenic patients in a state hospital required the radical shift in therapeutic strategy (see Rogers, 1967; Gendlin 1966). If psychotherapy from the client-centered framework had been a verbal interchange between a willing client and a warmly accepting therapist, it now had to be something more direct, less verbal, and increasingly experiential.

Along these lines Rogers had already provided a theoretical rationale for personality change in therapy that implied that constructive alterations in personality could occur regardless of the specific verbal techniques employed by the counselor. If six operationally defined conditions of relationship were met, then *any* person-to-person contact embodying them could promote positive personality growth. The six conditions postulated by Rogers (1957) were:

1. *Two persons are in psychological contact* so that each of them is aware, even if in only the dimmest fashion, that the other's presence makes a difference.

2. *The first person, the client, is in a state of incongruence,* being vulnerable or anxious. Incongruence means that a discrepancy exists between his self-image and his ongoing experiences, between the actor and his mask. Any experience that threatens his self-picture will be defensively distorted.

3. *The second person, or therapist, is congruent* or integrated in the relationship. Congruence means that the therapist is genuinely himself, totally free to express what he actually feels, positive or negative, in the situation with his client. He is not, however, a paragon of virtue. It is only necessary that he be congruent or spontaneously real in the therapeutic relationship, including the ability to express feelings that are not particularly pleasing: "I am afraid of this client"; or "I am bored with him."

4. *The therapist experiences unconditional positive regard for the client.* Unconditional positive regard means that the counselor warmly accepts the client in all of his "human facets." It is unconditional: no feelings of "I like you *if* you are thus and so." Rather, the counselor "prizes" the person without evaluation, recognizing that the client is an independent human being capable of his own valid experiences.

5. *The therapist experiences an empathic understanding of the client's internal frame of reference and endeavors to communicate this experience to the client.* In short, the counselor tries to see the world as the client sees it and to communicate that he does so. The counselor does not *experience* the client's feelings; he *understands* them. For the counselor, it is an "as if" cognitive act, not an emotionally involving one. He understands the client's emotions "as if" they were his own without ever losing sight of the "as if" quality.

6. *The communication to the client of the therapist's empathic understanding and unconditional positive regard must be minimally achieved.* If the client does not perceive acceptance and understanding, they do not exist for him.

When these six conditions are fulfilled in *any* relationship, intentionally therapeutic or otherwise, personality change in a positive, healthy direction will occur. The client who experiences these conditions will be more able to accept his feelings and perceptions freely as his own; he will grow to become that idealized image that he has never before dared to strive for overtly; he will become more autonomous in his decision making. The emphasis is clearly not on the counselor's technique, nor on the specifics of verbal interchange. Crucial to personality change is the quality of the directly experienced relationship.

Personality Changes Evoked by the Therapeutic Relationship

Rogers and his colleagues formulated a conceptualization of the specific process of personality change that occurs when these six conditions exist between two persons. From hundreds of recorded therapeutic sessions and from his own experiences, Rogers was able to discern the basic similarities of the client's progressive changes in experience within the therapeutic relationship. Rogers proposed that such personality changes may be thought of as a seven-stranded process or continuum of experience. One end of the continuum is personality or experiential *rigidity;* the opposite end is *fluidity* or psychological flow (Rogers, 1958; 1961). Clients with differing degrees of personality difficulty may be conceptualized as initially occupying different positions between the two extremes. As therapy progresses, the client progresses toward the fluidity end of the spectrum.

The first three phases through which the client passes involve his initial inability to see his difficulty, a gradual dim recognition that some problem exists, and a tendency once a problem is recognized to speak of himself as an object without real feeling. Thus the first three stages of personality change may be identified as:

1. *Rigidity of Self-Perception:* no recognition of need to change self
2. *Dim Recognition of Problem:* problem exists in others
3. *Self Treated as Object:* does not own his feelings

In the fourth stage, there is some movement in the direction of greater flexibility. But the client continues to discuss emotions out of his past life rather than as feelings he *now* experiences. Some questioning of his own interpretations also occurs and consequently anxiety and distrust of his own perceptions begins to develop. This fourth or middle phase may be identified as:

4. *Partial Recognition of Feelings:* tendency to treat feelings as colorless objects

In the last three phases of the process of personality change, the client progressively approaches accurate recognition and ownership of feelings, acceptance of self with reevaluation of personal interpretations, and finally, in the seventh phase, genuine experiencing of feelings with richness and clarity. These last three phases of the process of personality change may be identified as:

5. *Improved Recognition of Feelings:* feelings of wanting to be the "real me"
6. *Acceptance of Feeling with Richness:* self is free to "own" feelings
7. *New Feelings Experienced Freely:* self is totally flexible, trustworthy, and capable of change and growth

The seven phases outlined here provide an instructive scheme by which to understand Rogers' developing conception of personality. It is easy to see that Rogers views the psychologically maladjusted personality as one who is defensively rigidified, constricted in his experiencing of self, and conflicted in his willingness to "own" his feelings. To describe this phenomenon, Rogers, too, employed the metaphor of the actor and his mask, for the rigid, defensive person is adopting a series of false fronts or masks to deceive others and himself. In the warm and accepting empathic relationship of psychotherapy, the person:

> . . . begins to drop the false fronts, or the masks, or the roles, with which he has faced life. He appears to be trying to discover something more basic, something more truly himself. [Rogers, 1961, p. 109]

The task that remains is to explore how Rogers systematized these discoveries into an explicit theory of personality.

Self-Actualization: Phenomenal World of the Self

It is clear from Rogers' view of the psychotherapeutic relationship that he regards the individual's subjectively felt and interpreted experience as the fundamental psychological reality. As Rogers stated this proposition: *"Every individual exists in a continually changing world of experience of which he is the center"* (1951, p. 483). The individual's experience is his reality (1959, p. 222). Of course it is equally true that experience is private, restricted to the person's phenomenal world. For this reason, as we shall see, Rogers and his colleagues employed a variety of indirect measures to assess the individual's private world.

The Infant's Phenomenal World: Self-Actualization

The most basic, innate tendency of the human infant is a drive toward "actualizing his organism." Instead of postulating a long list of needs or drives, Rogers chose to hypothesize that most biological functions and psychological urges could be subsumed under one major heading: a need to maintain and to enhance one's life (1951, p. 488). For Rogers, as for Maslow, self-actualization is a rather inclusive concept:

> We are talking here about the tendency of the organism to maintain itself—to assimilate food, to behave defensively in the face of threat, to achieve the goal of self-maintenance even when the usual pathway to that goal is blocked. We are speaking of the tendency of the organism to move in the direction of maturation, as maturation is defined for each species. . . . [The organism] moves in the direction of limited expansion through growth, expansion through extending itself by means of its tools, and expansion through reproduction. It moves in the direction of greater independence or self-responsibility. [1951, p. 488]

In Rogers' description of self-actualization, we recognize the same basic processes of movement toward greater autonomy and self-trust that he had described for the microcosm of psychotherapy.

Like psychotherapy process, self-actualization is a directional concept in Rogers' scheme, for the person tends to behave in ways that enhance his actualization tendencies and in ways designed to avoid situations that threaten self-actualization.

As the infant develops biologically, his psychological maturation tends to keep pace through his increasing self-awareness. Gradually, a part of the infant's phenomenal world becomes differentiated and recognized as "me," "I," or "myself." From the total global mass of perceptual stimuli, the infant learns slowly and cautiously to identify himself as an independent agent. Piaget's observations and Sullivan's concept of prototaxic experience considered in Chapter 7 are similar formulations (Rogers, 1951, p. 497; 1959, p. 233).

The Development of the Self-Structure: Threat

The infant develops his picture of "me" through his interactions with significant others. Much as Sullivan had described, Rogers indicated the importance of the child's sensitivity to the praise and blame of the adults in his world. These evaluations of his behavior are assimilated to the infant's self-structure, and as socialization continues, the perceptual field continues to grow in complexity. Many behaviors consistent with his parents' conception of what he should be will be praised; a variety of behaviors that are disapproved of by his parents will be punished or responded to by them with emotionally abrasive communications.

> [The child] . . . experiences words and actions of his parents in regard to these satisfying behaviors, and the words and actions add up to

the feeling "You are bad, the behavior is bad, and you are not loved or lovable when you behave in this way." This constitutes a deep threat to the nascent structure of the self. The child's dilemma might be schematized in these terms: "If I admit to awareness the satisfactions of these behaviors and values I apprehend in these experiences, then this is inconsistent with my self as being loved or lovable." [1951, p. 500]

Thus, in order to preserve the continuity of parental love in his world, the child must fend off threats of withdrawal of that affection. In effect, much as Sullivan had postulated the Bad-Me and the Not-Me personifications of self, Rogers hypothesized that the infant must deal with those of his behaviors that arouse parental disapproval by removing both the threat and the motive for the behavior from his awareness. For example, the infant may distort his experience of the situation: "The accurate symbolization would be: 'I perceive my parents as experiencing this behavior as unsatisfying to them.' The distorted symbolization, distorted to preserve the threatened concept of self, is: '*I* perceive this behavior as unsatisfying' " (Rogers, 1951, p. 500).

In short, the child learns to experience reality secondhand. He adopts not his spontaneous feelings and perceptions as guides to his behavior, but the defensively safe feelings that maintain parental love and approval. Experience is thus distorted in the service of "self" survival. The self structure becomes "an organized configuration of perceptions of self which are admissible to awareness" (Rogers, 1951, p. 501). Threatening self-perceptions are excluded.

Healthy Self-Structure Development

How is it possible for any infant ever to develop a healthy, spontaneously natural, self-concept? Rogers suggested that three parental characteristics fostered healthy self-structure formation: (1) ability to accept the child's feelings and strivings; (2) ability to accept own feelings that certain of child's behaviors are undesirable; (3) and communication of acceptance of the child as a person. (Based on Rogers, 1951, p. 502.) The child who experiences a relationship with his parents based on the three previously listed qualities experiences no threat to himself as a loved or lovable person.

The Need for Positive Regard

As the self-structure develops, a need for positive regard grows in intensity. Positive regard is, of course, the experience of feeling accepted, loved, "prized." The source of the infant's income of positive regard is located in others' evaluations of him.

Rogers added an important corollary to this fundamental tenet: The need for positive regard is reciprocal, for "when an individual discriminates himself as satisfying another's need for *positive regard,* he necessarily experiences satisfaction of his own need for positive regard" (1959, p. 223). Satisfying another's need for love and acceptance is in itself satisfying. Rogers' concept of the reciprocity of positive regard is similar to Sullivan's notion of the empathic linkage between mother and child (cf. Chapter 7). Rogers' description of the infant's developing need for positive regard bears quoting:

> The infant learns to need love. Love is very satisfying, but to know whether he is receiving it or not he must observe his mother's face, gestures, and other ambiguous signs. He develops a total gestalt as to the way he is regarded by his mother and *each new experience of love or rejection tends to alter the whole gestalt.* Consequently, *each behavior on his mother's part such as a specific disapproval of a specific behavior tends to be experienced as disapproval in general.* So important is this to the infant that he comes to be guided in his behavior not by the degree to which an experience maintains or enhances the organism, but by the likelihood of receiving maternal love. [1959, p. 225; italics added]

As Sullivan had suggested, a kind of emotional "hot and cold" game ensues. When the infant learns to steer his behavior in relation to his tendencies to maintain others' positive regard, he is simultaneously learning another important lesson: He discovers that he must treat himself in the same ways as he is treated by others. In more technical language, he must "introject" or internalize the evaluations of significant others. In so doing, he develops a capacity for *self-regard* (1959, p. 224).

The infant gradually acquires *conditions of worth.* That is to say, he "understands"—however dimly at first—that only under certain conditions is he positively esteemed by others, by himself in response to others, and most important, by his parents. Conditions of worth are thus the conditions (behaviors) that provide acceptance or provoke rejection.

Incongruence between Self and Experience

As Laing had emphasized the significance of a divided self in which experience and behavior are widely separated, Rogers, too, developed a notion of *self-incongruence.*

> Because of the need for self-regard, the individual *perceives* his *experience* selectively, in terms of the *conditions of worth* which have come to exist in him.

a) Experiences which are in accord with his *conditions of worth* are *perceived* and *symbolized* accurately in *awareness*.

b) Experiences which run contrary to the *conditions of worth* are *perceived* selectively and distortedly as if in accord with the conditions of worth, or are in part or whole, *denied to awareness*. [1959, p. 226]

In a way similar to Sullivan's proposal of a mechanism of selective inattention, Rogers suggested that the conditions of worth by which the individual has learned to navigate his world serve as selective filters in screening new experiences. Those experiences that are denied access to awareness because they violate the self-structure form the foundation of potential psychological maladjustment. For once the core of experience is discrepant with the self-picture and denied to awareness, the individual is vulnerable to anxiety every time a fresh experience threatens to trigger perception of the discrepancy.

Experiences that are threatening to one's self-structure are said to be "subceived." *Subception* means that the individual perceives the threat but does not admit it to full awareness in the higher cognitive brain centers (Rogers, 1959, p. 200; see also McLeary & Lazarus, 1949). Subception of threatening discrepancies between self-structure and new experiences begins the process of defensive personality disorganization.

Personality Disorganization

When for some persons the discrepancy between self structure and experience becomes so great that subception no longer functions with complete success, the result is personality disorganization (Rogers, 1959, pp. 228–229). Such a contingency may arise if the perception of a threatening experience arises suddenly and so forcefully that denial is impossible. Because the perception is accurately symbolized in awareness, the gestalt of the self-structure is broken by the intrusion of discrepant data (Rogers, 1959, p. 229).

Rogers offered an example of this kind of maladjustment:

> ... take the familiar picture of a mother whom the diagnostician would term rejecting. She has as part of her concept of self a whole constellation which may be summed up by saying, "I am a good and loving mother. ..." With this concept of self she can accept and assimilate those organic sensations of affection which she feels toward her child. But the organic experience of dislike, distaste, or hatred toward her child is something which is denied to her conscious self. The experience exists, but it is not permitted accurate symbolization. ... Since the good mother could be aggressive toward her child only if he merited punishment, *she perceives much of his behavior as being bad, deserving punishment, and therefore the aggressive acts can be*

> carried through, without being contrary to the values organized in her picture
> of self. [1951, pp. 511–512; italics added]

At times of great provocation, such a mother might scream at her child, "I hate you." But almost in the same breath she would rush to explain that "she was not herself."

Sometimes the individual experiences psychological maladjustment when the total self structure is founded on the evaluations of others. Since these alien values have no genuine connection with the person's own experiences, he may perceive himself as a "nothing," as a "zero" (Rogers, 1951, p. 512). Laing's concept of *implosion* and Horney's concept of extreme *detachment* are similar (cf. Chapter 8 and Chapter 6).

Operationalizing the Concept of Self: Q-Sort Methodology

Rogers' reliance on the concepts of self, self incongruence, and ideal self emerged from his experiences with patients in therapy. Often, when he had allowed clients to express their problems in their own fashion, without guidance or interpretation, they would refer to the *self* as the core of their experience: "I feel I'm not being my real self"; "I never had a chance to be myself"; or, "It feels good to let myself go and just *be* myself here" (1959, p. 201).

As a consequence of their therapeutic efforts, Rogers and several of his students and colleagues mounted an early research project to investigate the individual's changing conception of self in therapy (Rogers & Dymond, 1954). The process of psychotherapeutic change seemed to be directly expressible in terms of changes in the individual's *perceived self* and his movement toward his *ideal self.*

At about the time that Rogers had begun to conceptualize the self as the key element in any description of the person's experience, a colleague at the University of Chicago, William Stephenson, developed a rationale and a statistical method uniquely applicable to a study of the phenomenal world of the self. Called a *Q-sort* technique, Stephenson's procedures were applied to a variety of social and personal processes (1953). Rogers and his research team adopted Q-sort methods to operationalize the concept of self.

Essentially, the Q-sort technique involves providing a person with a large number of written statements and asking him to sort them into a deliberately determined number of piles. The array of categories into which the subject places his statements are purposefully constructed to approximate a statistically normal distribution. Printed on cards, the statements describe various aspects of a person's self. In the most widely used version, the subject is asked to sort one hundred statements into nine piles ranging from "least like me" to "most like me." Other variations involve the inclusion of additional categories: "what I most would like to become," or "what I most dislike about me." A typical arrangement of a Q-sort distribution looks like this (based on Dymond, in Rogers & Dymond, 1954, p. 77):

	Least Like Me			Undecided			Most Like Me		
Pile No.	0	1	2	3	4	5	6	7	8
No. of Cards (Total: 100)	1	4	11	21	26	21	11	4	1

The criteria by which the self-statement cards may be sorted are nearly limitless. One very instructive example of a subject's card sorting responses before and after therapy is provided in Table 13–3.

In the left-hand column of Table 13–3 is a small sample of "Mrs. Oak's" statements chosen as most characteristic of herself before therapy. In the right-hand column are her statements describing self after therapy. The bottom half of the table contains an additional sample of Q-sort statements that were chosen before and after therapy by Mrs. Oak as least characteristic of herself.

The items of Table 13–3 show that before therapy, Mrs. Oak regarded herself as driven, insecure, and disorganized. After therapy, by the time of the five-month follow-up interview, she viewed herself as more in control and more secure. The items that Mrs. Oak felt were least characteristic of herself before therapy included an ability to be independent and comfortable with others. After therapy, Mrs. Oak perceived herself to be less helpless and less guilty.

TABLE 13–3: MRS. OAK'S CHANGES IN PERCEIVED SELF IN TERMS OF Q-SORT STATEMENTS

BEFORE THERAPY	"Most Characteristic"	AFTER THERAPY
I usually feel driven.		I express my emotions freely.
I am responsible for my troubles.		I feel emotionally mature.
I am really self-centered.		I am self-reliant.
I am liked by most people who know me.		I understand myself.
I am intelligent.		I feel adequate.

BEFORE THERAPY	"Least Characteristic"	AFTER THERAPY
I feel comfortable while talking with someone.		I have few standards and values of my own.
I make strong demands on myself.		I feel helpless.
I am optimistic.		I often feel guilty.

From Rogers, in Rogers & Dymond, 1954, p. 275.

The correlation between the perceived self before and after therapy was low: .30. In another Q-sort, Mrs. Oak was asked to sort the items in order of importance to her for the *person she would like to be,* thus providing an estimate of her ideal self. After therapy, Mrs. Oak again sorted the items in relation to her ideal self. The before self-ideal included: "I feel emotionally mature"; "I can live comfortably with people around me"; "I am a rational person." The after self-ideal included the following items: "I understand myself"; "I express my emotions freely"; and, "I am poised" (Rogers, 1954, p. 274). The degree of similarity for Mrs. Oak's self-ideal before and after therapy was great: The correlation for before and after ideal selves was .72. The key question is whether Mrs. Oak perceived her actual self to have become more like her ideal self after therapy. The correlation between her perceived self and ideal self before therapy was .21, a very low degree of relationship. Thus, before therapy Mrs. Oak perceived a large discrepancy between what she was and what she would like to be. After therapy, the correlation between her ideal self and her actual self—that is, the self she felt she had become—was .69 at termination, and .79 within several months after therapy (1954, p. 282). Thus, the Q-sort method had shown that Mrs. Oak felt herself to be more like her ideal self after therapy than before.

Rogers and his colleagues employed a variety of other assessment techniques; but in all cases the client's consistent movement in the direction of greater freedom, more independence, and more congruence between perceived self and ideal self was measurably real.

The New Emerging Person

Rogers' self-actualization theory of personality originally emerged from the context of understanding personality change in psychotherapy. He has extended the theory to education (1969), to a model of the fully functioning person (1961, 1969, 1959), and to group conflict (1959).

Most recently, in a paper originally intended only for private circulation (1974b; see also Evans, 1975, pp. 151 ff.), Rogers has suggested that a new, more fully human person has begun to emerge in American society. After reviewing a variety of alienating and destructive cultural trends, Rogers concluded:

> So we have every reason to doubt whether our culture can survive. Sometimes it seems the only question is whether we will commit world suicide with the bomb, or simply decay until world leadership is taken over by other hands. It is not a pretty picture. [1974b, p. 3]

In a more hopeful vein, Rogers went on to suggest that within the decaying culture there are the dim outlines of a new growth or revolution of values exemplified in the emergence of a new person. This "Homo novus," as he might be called, is to be found almost everywhere: among corporation executives who abandon the rat race to live simpler lives; among long-haired young men and women who defy cultural values to form counter-cultures; among nuns and priests who leave their institutions and dogma for more independent lives; and so on.

A core of common personality characteristics can be discerned in these newly emerging, more humanistic persons. Among these characteristics: distaste for phoniness and corruption; desire for authenticity; recognition that institutions are for the people who compose them; relative unconcern with material possessions; nonmoralistic caring evidenced in desire to help others; a wish for intimacy and closeness with others; and a healthy skepticism about science and technology. This person desires to explore "inner space," to look within himself through a variety of pathways like drugs, meditation, religious ritual. Finally, the new person is comfortable with nature, enjoying its beauty and bounty. In sum, he is a "process person": "aware that he is continually in process—always changing. In this process he is spontaneous, vitally alive, willing to risk. His likes and dislikes, his joys and his sorrows are passionate and are passionately expressed" (Rogers, 1974b, p. 19).

The similarity of description between Rogers' "newly emerging person" and Maslow's self-actualizing person is unmistakable. Both these theorists have found that man can be happy only when he is most fully himself.

Summary

Carl Rogers and Abraham Maslow developed rather similar self-actualization conceptions of personality. Maslow's interests in psychological health seem to have emerged from his early work on dominance-feeling in infrahuman primates and from his interview research of dominant women. Rogers, on the other hand, developed his conceptualization of the self-actualizing nature of human motivation from his experiences in psychotherapy.

Maslow's central concept is the growth or health striving character of human personality. Proceeding through a hierarchy of basic needs, the individual progresses toward ultimate health and fully spontaneous expression of the self. At the lowest level of the hierarchy are the physiological needs like hunger and thirst. Having satisfied these, the individual's behavior becomes directed by his needs for safety; then by his needs for love and esteem. Finally, when these basic motives have been fulfilled, the need for self-actualization—to be fully what one can be—emerges.

Rogers discovered essentially the same rule of human growth from his observations of clients in therapy. In the earliest stages of his work, Rogers' central concern was to allow the client to feel warmly accepted and fully free to express himself. Slowly, Rogers developed this nondirective orientation to include the necessity for the counselor to enter the client's phenomenal world or internal frame of reference. In order for constructive personality change to occur, the counselor must communicate his understanding of the client's internal frame of reference to the client. In the final stage of Rogers' theoretical development, the emphasis shifted to the direct experiential aspects of the client's world. The therapist's role was conceptualized to include the empathic understanding of the client's experience.

Maslow's conceptualization of the self-actualizing person as independent, creative, and growth-motivated corresponds to Rogers' notion of the person who emerges from a successful psychotherapeutic relationship. Maslow has gone further than Rogers in one respect. Specifically, Maslow has postulated that the self-actualizing person embarks on a further course of metamotives. These Being-values, as Maslow termed them, include the classic virtues like beauty, truth, justice, honesty, and freedom. When deprived or frustrated, these B-values show evidence of being innate, for the frustrated individual succumbs to metapathologies. Rogers has most recently elaborated the concept of a newly emerging person in American culture. This Homo novus is largely motivated by the same classic virtues or "goods" that Maslow described as B-values.

In Maslow's theory, the motor of personality is the drive toward self-actualization, toward psychological health, toward fully accepted humanness. In Rogers' theory, the same innate striving toward enhancement and expression of one's spontaneous urges and feelings constitutes the fundamental layer of personality. In both theories, psychological maladjustment is the product of learned tendencies to subvert or block the inner self core, the spontaneous and natural expression of self.

For Rogers and Maslow, human nature is inherently good. Man's most fundamental striving is to be completely himself. When his self structure is dominated by others' evaluations, he is no longer free. He is vulnerable, anxious, and imprisoned behind his own defenses.

FOR FURTHER READING

Maslow's definitive statement of his position is to be had in *Motivation and Personality* (Harper & Row, 1970), 2d ed. His early papers on dominance-feeling with primates have been collected into a single volume by J. Lowry and entitled *Dominance, Self-Esteem, Self-Actualization: Germinal Papers of A. H. Maslow* (Monterey, Calif.: Brooks-Cole, 1973). A collection of Maslow's later papers, including a semi-autobiographical account of the sources of his interest in self-actualization, is *The Farther Reaches of Human Nature* (New York: Viking, 1971). Sometimes bitter, sometimes ironic, Maslow's criticism of classical scientific method in application to persons may be found in his *The Psychology of Science: A Reconnaissance* (New York: Harper & Row, 1966).

William James' lectures on mystical experience bear a strong similarity to Maslow's views on peak experiences. James' very readable lectures are to be found in *The Varieties of Religious Experience* (New York: Random House, 1902). Maslow's own account of peak experiences is to be had in *Religions, Values and Peak-Experiences* (New York: Viking, 1964). The collection of papers in R. May, E. Angel, and H. F. Ellenberger's (Eds.) *Existence: A New Dimension in Psychiatry and Psychology* (New York: Basic Books, 1958) retains its value as a thorough grounding in the history and current practice of existential psychology. A rather novel and somewhat critical view of humanistic psychology is provided by Hans Eysenck in "Reason with Compassion," *The Humanist* (March/April, 1971), 24–25.

Two of Rogers' early works adequately set forth his initial strategy and philosophy: *Counseling and Psychotherapy* (Boston: Houghton Mifflin, 1942) and *Client-Centered Therapy* (Boston: Houghton Mifflin, 1951; available in paperback). To bring Rogers' perspective on theory and therapy up to date, two recent volumes should be consulted. The first of these is a collection of research and theory papers edited by J. T. Hart and T. M. Tomlinson under the title *New Directions in Client-Centered Therapy* (Boston: Houghton Mifflin, 1970) and is, perhaps, the better of the two. The second collection of papers is to be found in David Wexler and Laura North Rice's (Eds.) *Innovations in Client-Centered Therapy* (New York: Wiley, 1974).

Rogers' definitive statement of his position is given by him in "A Theory of Therapy, Personality and Inter–Personal Relationships as Developed in the Client-Centered Framework," in S. Koch (Ed.), *Psychology: A Study of a Science,* Vol. III, *Formulations of the Person in the Social Context* (New York: McGraw-Hill, 1959). A more up-to-date survey of Rogerian method and philosophy is provided by Betty Meador (with Rogers' collaboration) in "Client-Centered Therapy," in Raymond Corsini (Ed.), *Current Psychotherapies* (Itasca, Ill.: Peacock, 1973), Chap. 4. A personally revealing account of Rogers' early career may be had in *On Becoming a Person* (Boston: Houghton Mifflin, 1961).

Rogers' own expansion of his ideas to the field of marriage and to other two-person intimate relationships may be found in his *Becoming Partners: Marriage and Its Alternatives* (New York: Dell, 1972). The efficacy and process of encounter groups are treated to a sympathetic examination by Rogers in *Carl Rogers on Encounter Groups* (New York: Harper & Row, 1970). An interview with Rogers, along with a reprint of his ongoing debate with B. F. Skinner and one of his previously unpublished papers, are to be had in R. I. Evans' *Carl Rogers: The Man and His Ideas* (New York: Dutton, 1975). The interview in condensed version may also be found in Evans' *The Making of Psychology* (New York: Knopf, 1976).

14

JOHN DOLLARD AND NEAL MILLER/ALBERT BANDURA AND RICHARD H. WALTERS
Social Learning Theory

One afternoon a visiting British student [at Yale] asked [Neal] Miller why he did not hedge the issue in his writing; why was he always so dogmatic about the principle that stimulus reduction was the only mechanism of reinforcement? Miller replied in his wonderful Washington twang, "There is only one thing you find in the middle of the road."

JEROME KAGAN, "A Psychologist's Account at Mid-Career"

At a recent cocktail party . . . [I] was cornered by an inquiring lady who expressed considerable puzzlement over adolescents' fascination for unusual and bizarre styles. The lady herself was draped with a sack, wearing a preposterous object on her head, and spiked high heel shoes that are more likely to land one in an orthopedic clinic, than to transport one across the room to the olives.

ALBERT BANDURA, "The Stormy Decade: Fact or Fiction?"

The Lynching of Arthur Stevens: A Social Learning Analysis

A continually growing mob of southern white townsmen of McCord County tortured, lynched, and then mutilated the corpse of Arthur Stevens on June 20, 1933. Arthur Stevens was a twenty-three-year-old black man accused of brutally murdering Iona Durfee, a neighboring white farm girl. The young man had been arrested after the Durfee girl's body was discovered because it was rumored that Arthur Stevens and she had recently ended a lengthy sexual relationship. Upon interrogation, Arthur Stevens allegedly confessed his guilt. Although the names of persons and places connected with this event are fictitious, the narrative details are drawn from an actual investigative report of the National Association for the Advancement of Colored People (Miller & Dollard, 1941, pp. 235 ff.).

Sheriff R. E. Ingle, sensing the hostile mood of the dead girl's neighbors, moved Stevens from jailhouse to jailhouse throughout the county, finally settling for an out-of-state location some two hundred and ten miles from McCord County. The angry neighbors and acquaintances of the murdered girl were nevertheless able to discover the new location, and it was not long before they drove the distance to storm the jail and take Arthur Stevens captive.

Returning to a spot within a short distance of the murder, this nuclear mob of Iona Durfee's neighbors tortured and killed their prisoner. Stevens' mutilated body was then hung from a tree in the neighboring county seat where this grisly display would attract the largest number of onlookers.

The barbarity did not end with the lynching. For a whole day the lynch mob, attracting new recruits, wreaked havoc on the town's black population. Black men, women, and children were indiscriminately attacked and chased out of town in plain view of the local authorities:

> In general, people in [the town] seemed to approve of the lynching as the best way "to keep the nigger in his place." Deputy Sheriff T. V. Brown stated in the local newspaper on the day of the lynching that "the mob will not be bothered [i.e., interfered with], either before or after the lynching." Widespread, if not complete, community connivance in the crime was indicated. [Miller & Dollard, 1941, pp. 236–237]

The riot was halted only when troops were sent to the town on June 21, the day following the lynching.

Although it might seem callous or even flippant, this incident of mob violence may serve as an especially suitable case study of social learning and imitation. The lynching of Arthur Stevens exaggerates and exposes clearly some behavioral processes that ordinarily occur in less extreme and less malignant form. The lynching also serves as an example of the real-life situations that engage the interest of the social learning theorist.

The Social Conditions of Learning: Modification of Hullian Theory

The uninhibited brutality of the lynch mob poses a crucial question for the behavioral scientist: "Would a person who had heard about the murder of the Durfee girl and perhaps seen her corpse have reacted with the extreme outburst of aggression against Stevens which was characteristic of the nuclear mob?" (Miller & Dollard, 1941, p. 237). Put another way, is the behavior of a crowd different from the behavior of a lone individual in the same situation? If, as Miller and Dollard assumed, behavior is shaped by social conditions, then the answer must be a definite yes. The object of a social learning analysis, then, must be to describe how the individuals who composed the nuclear mob were influenced both by the event itself and by the presence of like-minded individuals.

To perform such analysis, Miller and Dollard adapted and simplified concepts from Clark L. Hull's 1943 theory of learning (Hull had not yet published this first complete statement of his theory, but Miller and Dollard had access to manuscript copies). Although Hull had created the theory on the basis of laboratory experimentation with animals, Miller and Dollard saw the possibility of extending the theory to complex human endeavors. (See Chapter 15 of this book for a brief account of Hull's major concepts; see also Hull, 1943, 1951, 1952.)

It is important to understand that, in this undertaking, Miller and Dollard were embarking on a journey seldom made by psychologists who identified themselves with the behaviorist or neobehaviorist traditions. With his strict commitment to scientific method, Hull had begun his work with infrahuman primates because these "simpler" organisms could provide the kind of easily interpreted data so necessary to a beginning scientific enterprise. As it turned out, experimental work with these "simpler" creatures produced a theory far from the clear-cut and indisputable propositions that Hull had initially envisioned. Hull did, however, formulate precise and experimentally testable deductions about the learning behavior of the organisms he studied. And such formulations, even when they did not withstand the criticism and counterexperiments of his critics, served to spur new research and continuing theoretical reformulations.

The important point in the present context of social learning theory is that Miller and Dollard, along with their colleagues at Yale, had set out to expand the scope of Hullian neobehaviorism into a scientifically respectable form of *sociobehaviorism*. The conceptual tools and intellectual strategy would be largely the same, but the focus of their operation would be widened to encompass the conditions under which humans interact and learn from one another. The historical development of stimulus-response (S-R) theory must not tempt us away from our more immediate goal of understanding the basic concepts of Miller and Dollard's social learning theory (see Berlyne, 1968, and Atkinson, 1964, Chaps. 5, 6, 7, for excellent historical summaries of S-R theory).

At the outset of their 1941 statement (p. 1), Miller and Dollard clearly set forth the goals of their social learning theory:

Human behavior is learned; precisely that behavior which is widely felt to characterize man as a rational being, or as a member of a particular nation or social class, is acquired rather than innate. *To understand thoroughly any item of human behavior*—either in the social group or in the individual life—*one must know the psychological principles involved in its learning and the social conditions under which this learning took place. It is not enough to know either principles or conditions of learning; in order to predict behavior both must be known.* [Italics added]

For Miller and Dollard, principles of learning established by experimentalists in the laboratory were to be supplemented with the facts and data of those social sciences that had studied human behavior in the culture at large. Such an interdisciplinary analysis, however, was to be firmly founded on the premise that all important social behaviors are nonetheless understandable with familiar psychological principles of learning.

A scientific account of learning and conditioning had already been provided in the work of Ivan Pavlov, E. L. Thorndike, John B. Watson—the founder of behaviorism—and Clark L. Hull, among many others. But such laboratory work had dealt with a very narrow range of contrived animal responses and was guided by an equally constricted conception of human capability. As Bandura (1974) has pointed out, these early workers had treated human behavior as merely a special case of laboratory animal learning—albeit a complex special case. As the dog's, rat's, or cat's behavior had *automatically* and *without awareness* been altered by the conditioning procedures, so too could human behavior be shaped mechanically and unconsciously. Proper and speedy application of the reinforcing stimulus guaranteed the occurrence of the preselected response. Workers in the field of learning have only slowly recognized the importance of human expectations and awareness in conditioning and have finally acknowledged that the "laws" of learning are something less than universal and absolute (see, for example, Dulany, 1961; Farber, 1963; Breger & McGaugh, 1965; Spielberger & DeNike, 1966; London, 1972).

Humans learn better if *told* what behaviors are to be rewarded, punished, or ignored. They learn well, too, from watching another perform, from observing a model's actions. For humans, imitation and copying, along with verbal transmission of information, constitute important aspects of their learning behavior. These aspects were left largely neglected by early workers, who preferred the mechanistic model of learning that had grown out of their animal work. To remedy this neglect, Miller and Dollard turned their combined resources to the study of human social learning and imitation.

The Lynching Analyzed: Drive, Cue, Response, and Reward

The lynching of Arthur Stevens is an example of the kind of complex human social behavior that cannot be studied in the laboratory. It can, however, be analyzed with concepts drawn from laboratory studies of learning and with specially modified principles from anthropology and sociology. To begin, we need some familiarity with four fundamental principles drawn by Miller and Dollard from Hullian learning theory. *Drive, cue, response,* and *reward* comprise the most basic conceptual tools to understand learning, and they will be exemplified in the context of the lynching.

Drive: The Mob's Anger and Fear

What provokes the crowd to violence? What stimulates the crowd to behave barbarically? What *drives* them? These questions are directed to the matter of motivation, to the springs of action or to the "go" of behavior. In Hullian theory, the fundamental instigator to action is *drive,* a deficit state of the organism's tissues conceptualized along the model of hunger and thirst. The hunger drive, for example, may vary in intensity in correspondence to the number of hours since the last feeding. Thus the "go" of behavior is some biological need that requires satisfaction.

Miller and Dollard modified the Hullian notion somewhat by broadening the concept of drive to include any strong stimulus that impinges upon an organism:

> A drive is a strong stimulus which impels action. Any stimulus can become a drive if it is made strong enough. The stronger the stimulus, the more drive function it possesses. The faint murmur of distant music has but little primary drive function; the infernal blare of the neighbor's radio has considerably more. [1941, p. 18]

Strong stimuli impel the organism to action. Such motivating stimuli may be divided into two groups: primary and secondary drives.

Primary drives are innate, biologically based states similar to Hull's notion of drive. Pain, hunger, thirst, and fatigue are all primary drives. A person goaded by the experience of any of these states is said to be motivated to take action to reduce the uncomfortable drive. Note that by itself, a drive is a nondirectional concept. An organism may be in pain, may be intensely hungry, or profoundly fatigued and so on without having the vaguest idea about how to reduce the discomfort. The specific action that the drive impels the person to undertake, the particular form or direction that his behavior will take, are not contained in the notion of initiating drive. Another concept is required to account for behavioral direction, and it will be considered in the next section.

Secondary drives are acquired, learned, social needs. Culture, technology, and the trappings of social life tend to reduce the full intensity at which primary drives are ordinarily experienced. Only in times of war, riot, or natural disaster is the typical citizen likely to experience any of his primary drives at the full "agonizing height" such motives may reach. Thus social living, with its more or less efficient distribution of goods and services, becomes a need in itself, an acquired or secondary drive. Money, for example, cannot be eaten, drunk, or seduced. But money can purchase satisfiers of each of these primary drives and therefore be itself a secondary drive stimulus.

Secondary drives, then, are elaborations of and dependent upon one or more primary drives. "Thus hunger may take the form of an appetite for particular foods; sex, that of an attraction to beautiful women; thirst, that of a desire for a specific type of drink" (Miller & Dollard, 1941, p. 19).

The drive mobilizing the lynch mob is fear. To be more precise, the fear drive in this case was a composite of several specific fears. The first of these arose from long-standing social tradition in the South. Lower- and middle-class whites had experienced increasing economic competition with blacks as the number of jobs decreased. Because of his socially enforced inferior caste, the black had been willing to accept lower wages and poorer working conditions than whites competing for the same jobs. Consequently, Arthur Stevens became the highly visible embodiment of all those factors attributed by whites to blacks in general. In essence, although Arthur Stevens was responsible for none of these social inequities, he was a black, the easily discernible target of long-standing racial strife and economic rivalry. He was the human symbol of man's most ancient fears: the fear of starvation, of exposure to illness, cold, and pain. The first fear, then, was based on primary drives but was itself an acquired, secondary drive.

The second fear driving the crowd was the threat of sex relations with, or rape of, white women by black men. As Miller and Dollard put it:

> Sexual jealousy is a painful drive everywhere in our society . . . Sexual equality is, after all, a step toward social equality. If Negroes were allowed sexual privileges with white women, it would be difficult to exclude them from the family group; and, if the Negro were included in the family group, it would be impossible to maintain his subordinated status. [1941, p. 239]

Because rumors had circulated in the community about Stevens' ongoing sexual relationship with Iona Durfee, the murder became the triggering incident in an explosion of long-term resentment and fear.

The third fear comprising the mob's total drive was the fear of physical assault upon whites by blacks. A detailed and gruesome account of the victim's state, as described by her father, was published in the local newspaper: "She had been 'choked so hard her eyes were coming out of their sockets.' Her head had been violently bashed in, her arms had been broken, and she was otherwise lacerated" (Miller & Dollard, 1941, p. 239). In effect, the entire community had become a witness to the murder as filtered through the father's eyes. To make matters worse, Iona's sister was quoted as saying that no form of punishment could be bad enough for the murderer.

In summary, three primary and/or secondary fears provoked the crowd to action: fear of economic nonsurvival, fear of interracial sexual equality, and fear of direct physical attack by blacks. There can be little doubt that fear is a potent drive.

Cue: Choice of Response and Response Target

Drive impels the organism to respond. However, as we have already seen, drive is nondirectional. What governs the selection of a particular response once the organism is activated by drive? What determines the selection of the specific object toward which responses will be directed? In terms of our case study, why were torture, mutilation, and murder the particular responses of the mob toward Arthur Stevens? Why were not less violent actions taken? Why were the townsmen unwilling to let normal criminal justice punish the offender?

We already know why Arthur Stevens was the object of such unbridled fury: He was the highly visible symbol of an already despised ethnic group, an ethnic group that provoked the drive of fear. In short, by virtue of his skin color, Arthur Stevens was distinctive. He had also distinguished himself in other important ways: He had committed brutal murder and rape of a white girl, or so the crowd believed. In Miller and Dollard's stimulus-response terminology, Stevens' behavior evidenced several particularly potent cues.

A cue is a highly distinct stimulus possessing some characteristic of quality, quantity, or intensity that causes it to be easily discriminated from other stimuli (Miller & Dollard, 1941, p. 22). Because of their attention-getting value, cues direct the selection of responses by determining how, when, and where an individual will respond. The cue and drive functions of a stimulus are closely related:

> Thus a drive stimulus such as hunger may have a selective or cue function as well as its impelling or drive function. In fact, hunger is a part of the stimulus pattern involved in determining the response to a restaurant sign. An individual standing between a restaurant sign to the right and a hotel sign to the left will respond to the stimulus pattern of drive plus signs by turning to the right if he is hungry and to the left if he is tired. [Miller & Dollard, 1941, p. 23]

Cues may be thought of as stimuli that are not strong enough to possess drive properties but which are nevertheless sufficiently distinctive to govern the direction that motivated behavior will take.

The cues of rape and murder triggered in these southern townsmen a long-standing tradition of behavior toward such acts. "Death of a kind more horrible than that stipulated by the law is believed to be necessary to keep men like Stevens in line" (Miller & Dollard, 1941, p. 241). Added to the distinctively brutal quality of Stevens' alleged acts were the cue properties of the mob situation itself. Powerful aggressive impulses like those brought into daylight by the lynch mob ordinarily engender personal moral inhibitions and scruples. Furthermore, lynching is clearly an illegal act, a form of behavior at least as grave as the murder and rape it is meant to redress. But, as we have seen, local authorities signaled in a variety of ways that nothing would be done to the participants.

Widespread community involvement provided a protective cloak under which "the most deadly of angry phantasies may be acted out" (Miller & Dollard, 1941, p. 243). Incredibly, the local radio station broadcast news of "a lynching party to which all white people are invited." Obviously the community picked up these official cues that any and all violence would be tolerated, indeed, condoned.

Thus, the two most important sources of cues directing the mob's violent aggression were Stevens' skin color and his alleged brutal acts against a white girl, and the official signals that no punishment would ensue. To look at the situation in another way, when all normal prohibitive cues are removed, the most intense primary drives are unleashed.

Response: Suiting the Punishment to the Crime

Drive impels the person to respond in particular ways by forcing attention to the available cues signaling which responses are appropriate or tolerable. The drive of fear impelled the crowd to seize, torture, and kill the highly distinctive symbol of their long-term hatred and frustration. Stevens' acts were distinctive and brutal enough to arouse the mob further to nearly unspeakable violence. The particular form that those aggressive responses assumed almost defy belief. Miller and Dollard described the mob's response:

> The nuclear mobsters decided on a protracted torture for Stevens. This is said to have lasted for some ten hours during Friday, June 20. It is amazing that Stevens could have lived through so many hours of pain. To make the punishment fit the crime, Stevens was castrated, and to add horror, he was compelled to eat his own genitals. Red hot irons were plunged into his body at various points. To make his suffering more intense, he was several times promised a swift death; each time he was given a simulated hanging in which life was almost choked out of him, but he was then cut down and tortured more. [1941, p. 246]

The problem confronting the social learning theorist is to explain how such barbaric "responses" came to be attached to the cues of rape and murder. Drive impels the person to respond. Cues function to direct the drive into particular behavioral forms. But those behavioral forms must exist in the repertoire of the responder prior to activation by drive. There must be some *initial hierarchy* of possible responses in the person's repertoire from which particular responses are selected on the basis of current cues and past performances.

At first, one or more responses in the hierarchy are dominant, that is, they are most likely to be made in the presence of particular cues. If these dominant responses meet with punishment or with lack of success, their probability of occurrence in the presence of those cues decreases. Other responses in the hierarchy are tried until one or more meets with success. Success is defined as the reduction or satisfaction of the operative drives —in the present case, anger and fear. These successful, that is, drive-reducing, responses alter the initial hierarchy by assuming dominance. The *resultant hierarchy* of responses that emerges is evidence that the person has attached new responses to the available cues. In a word, he has learned. Henceforward response and cue are bound together in such a way that appearance of the cue evokes the newly dominant response (Miller & Dollard, 1941, p. 1). Learning, then, is the attachment of responses to cues under conditions of drive arousal.[1]

Reward: The Drive-Reducing Consequences of Response

What strengthens the connection between cue and response? To ask the same question in another way: What guarantees that the cue will call forth the response on each subsequent occasion?

In Miller and Dollard's learning model the response becomes attached to the cue because it is rewarded or *reinforced.* That is to say, the response leads to a reduction in the drive's intensity. The organism is thus led to expect that responses that have in the past reduced the drive's intensity will do so again. Reduction in drive intensity is generally a pleasurable experience. Consequently, following Clark L. Hull's model of learning, Miller and Dollard defined a reinforcer (reward) as anything that reduces (satisfies) a drive. Food reduces the hunger drive and, therefore, food is a reinforcer. Water satisfies the thirst drive and, of course, water is a reinforcer. When an organism feels the mounting tension of hunger, responses that have led to food consumption in the past are likely to be called forth again. Such responses—say, entering a restaurant—have been rewarded in the past by a reduction in the hunger drive.

It must be remembered that Miller and Dollard, quite unlike Hull, do not limit the organism's number of operative drives to biological needs like hunger and thirst. For Miller and Dollard any strong stimulus may operate as a drive. Thus any response that terminates or reduces strong stimulation

[1]It is important to note that Miller and Dollard were among the first psychological theorists in the tradition of neobehaviorism to emphasize verbal processes as mediators of learning. Thus, as Miller pointed out in a personal communication to the author, he and Dollard regarded verbal instructions as one means by which responses can be elicited and rewarded (see Miller and Dollard, 1941, pp. 26–27; Dollard and Miller, 1950, pp. 37 ff.). Therefore, the resultant hierarchy of responses that emerges need not depend solely on tedious trial and error. Verbal communications, observation of another's responses, and covert verbal responses like reasoning—all can contribute to producing a new response that will ultimately be rewarded or punished.

may be a reinforcer. The form that such motivating stimulation may take is infinitely variable. It is safe to assume, therefore, that appropriate drive reducers (reinforcers) exist in equally wide variety.

The *drive-stimulus-reduction hypothesis,* as Miller (1959) later labeled this explanation of reinforcement, generated a great deal of research and controversy. A variety of exceptions to the view that stimulus or drive reduction is rewarding were reported in the literature. Olds and Milner (1954), for example, showed that rats could learn a lever-pressing response for the "reinforcement" of small amounts of electric current delivered directly to the septal area of their brains (see also Olds and Olds, 1965). Although such brain stimulation may be pleasurable, it is difficult to interpret this phenomenon as a *reduction* in drive. Yet electrical stimulation to particular brain areas serves as a powerful reinforcer.

Other experimenters (Sheffield, 1954; 1960) devised alternative explanations of reinforcement based on the assumption that *increases* in drive could also be rewarding. For example, a male rat who had never before been in contact with female rats would repeatedly perform a response to reach a female in heat even though his every attempt to mount her and copulate was frustrated by the experimenters (Sheffield, Wulff, & Backer, 1951). Because there was no way in which the rat's sex drive could be *reduced* in such a situation, it is difficult to understand from the drive-reduction point of view why he continued to perform the response. Apparently increases in sexual tension may operate as reinforcers. It was Freud, incidentally, who had come to a similar view of sexual stimulation when he modified his pleasure principle to accommodate his new concept of the compulsion to repeat (see Chapter 3; Freud, 1920a).

Miller was therefore led to introduce some interpretative distinctions into the drive-reduction hypothesis:

> In its weak form, [the drive-reduction hypothesis] states that the sudden reduction in the strength of any strong motivational stimulus always serves as a reward, or in other words, is a *sufficient* condition for reinforcement. In its strong form, it states that all reward is produced in this way, or in other words, that drive reduction is not only a sufficient but also a *necessary* condition for reinforcement. [1959, p. 256]

The weak form of the drive-reduction hypothesis is the more liberal of the two, for it allows that drive reducers can be reinforcers without specifying that *only* drive reducers are reinforcing. The strong form of the hypothesis, by contrast, asserts that the absolutely *necessary* quality of a reinforcer is that it be a drive reducer. By postulating that any strong stimulation may serve as a drive, Miller and Dollard had sharpened the drive-reduction hypothesis to an appreciable degree. Even the more liberal weak form, however, is violated by the exceptions previously discussed. Miller summarized his position in this way:

Although I believe that [the drive-stimulus-reduction] hypothesis has a considerably less than 50 per cent chance of being correct, especially in the strong form, I do believe it is better at the present moment than any other single hypothesis. Therefore, I feel that it is worthwhile to try out applying it consistently, if only to highlight the obstacles and infuriate others into devising superior hypotheses and the experimental programs to support them.

When one systematically explores a given hypothesis and points out the weaknesses of various theoretical and experimental attacks on this hypothesis, however, it is difficult to avoid the reputation (and after that, the fact) of being emotionally fixated on the hypothesis. Furthermore, the very controversial nature of the drive-stimulus-reduction hypothesis makes it conspicuous, so that it seems to be the cornerstone of one's whole theoretical thinking.

Let me try to destroy both illusions. The stimulus-reduction hypothesis of reinforcement could be discarded without having an appreciable effect on the rest of my theoretical formulations. I take this occasion to urge attempts to formulate and rigorously test competing hypotheses, and time permitting, may even join in that activity myself. *However unsatisfactory, the drive-reduction hypothesis is not likely to be abandoned as long as it is the best thing of its kind that we have. The decisive way to kill it is with a superior alternative.* [Miller, 1959, pp. 256–257; italics added]

A more succinct statement of Miller's feelings on the drive-reduction hypothesis is given in the epigraph at the opening of this chapter.

All the brutal acts perpetrated against Arthur Stevens by the lynch mob, though shocking and repugnant, nevertheless exist within the human repertoire. Ordinarily such responses have an extremely low probability of occurrence. Torture, mutilation, and murder, while certainly, and sadly, within the capability of humans, are acts that rarely are contemplated and even more infrequently enacted. Yet, in the lynching of Arthur Stevens such responses were called forth from the mob members for the reasons already mentioned in our discussion of cues. The operative drives were fear and anger. Thus, these violent and murderous responses were reinforced by reductions in the fear and anger drives of mob members.

Considered from an opposite point of view, the rewarding consequences of these brutal responses were enhanced by the singular lack of cues signaling punishment or retribution.

Violent acts against Arthur Stevens clearly received potent reinforcement because the drives provoking these responses are powerful, if unpleasant, human motives. By having observed the aggressive responses of the nuclear mob toward Stevens, and from the undeniable evidence of unhindered and unpunished aggression provided by the condition of Stevens' mutilated body hung for display, the larger community understood that aggressive responses were successful when performed in a group.

Viewed in this way, the violence of each individual served as an additional cue to all other mob members that atrocities performed in concert would provoke no legal, social, or personal retaliation. In effect, the mob fed off its own successful acts of cruelty.

The mob's violent responses were thus a product of the joint effect of two circumstances: the reinforcement that accrued from a reduction in their fear and anger drives; and the removal of social, legal, and personal restraints normally operating on individuals who act alone.

Intensity of Violence: The Frustration-Aggression Hypothesis

It is unlikely that any lone individual could act as sadistically as had the mob. Although some individuals might act alone to kill Stevens upon hearing of his crime, and although another few persons might imagine all sorts of sadistic tortures for him, only the entire crowd acting as a mob unit could perpetrate the full range of atrocities actually carried out.

Consequently, it is necessary to conclude that the mob served a function as a unit or entity in its own right that would not otherwise be embodied in any single person. Floyd Allport, in his classic work on social psychology, had argued that the essence of a crowd's intense response was to be sought in the thwarting of each of its individual member's "elemental drives" of hunger, sex, and the need for protection:

> The participants in a lynching mob exhibit responses of *struggle* against the thwarting of certain fundamental individual drives. If *our own* kin are done violence, our prepotent habits of love (family and sexual responses) are violated or imperiled. Hence the primitive wrathful struggle reaction is evoked. [1924, p. 293]

Floyd Allport's explanation of the violence of some mobs bears a strong similarity to Miller and Dollard's account:

> Crowds, then, are struggle groups of an elementary and violent character. With the exception of a few varieties, such as panics and religious revivals, the reactions of struggling, fighting, and destroying are their universal phenomena. The menacing of the drives of a large number of individuals simultaneously both draws them together and incites them to common action. The struggle and the anger may take a mild form such as the rivalry for supremacy in a football match; or it may be as violent as that of the lynching party. *But it is always a struggle of some sort against limitation, oppression, and opposition to the free satisfaction of some original or derived drives.* . . . The formation of the crowd springs from the collective struggle responses of individuals.

> The mob members do not demand a victim merely in order to shed blood, but *to restore their thwarted responses to their normal operation.* [Allport, 1924, p. 294; italics added]

Allport's explanation of mob violence hinges on two principles: First, the mob members share a *common interest in the satisfaction of powerful drives,* namely, the drives of sex, need for protection, and hunger. Thwarting or frustrating these drives unleashes equally potent aggressive responses toward the person or object perceived to be the cause of frustration. Secondly, *the crowd is an entity unto itself.* As a mob member, each individual's personal aggressive responses are intensified, augmented, excited by the observable emotional reactions of those who surround him. The individual's violent intentions are socially facilitated by the presence of similarly aroused individuals:

> In the crowd it is the emotional reaction which is facilitated by the expressive behavior (facial expression, gestures, shouts, hisses, murmurs) of the others ... The pressure of elbows and bodies as the crowd surges forward effects the individual in a powerful manner. It serves not only as a social facilitation, but as a suggestion of the vast size and strength of the mob and the necessity for placing one's self at its disposal. [F. Allport, 1924, p. 296]

It will be recalled that the lynch mob that tortured and killed Arthur Stevens had available to them a number of cues that signaled the social "legitimacy" and power of their group. The deputy sheriff's remarks that the lynch mob would not be bothered before or after the lynching, the radio announcement inviting "all white people" to the lynching party, and the nuclear mob's unhampered violence against Stevens had served to communicate: (1) increasing violent excitement; (2) decreased expectation of punishment (Miller & Dollard, 1941, p. 248). In this sense, the lynching of Arthur Stevens is a case study of violence by contagion. The two factors isolated by Allport—thwarting of fundamental drives and social facilitation—are the very heart of Miller and Dollard's social learning analysis. It must immediately be pointed out, however, that Miller and Dollard's drive-cue-response-reward model lends the kinds of scientific precision lacking in Allport's descriptive account. Yet Allport's basic idea that the thwarting of an organism's fundamental drive satisfactions evokes aggressive responses found a parallel concept in the frustration-aggression hypothesis put forward by Miller, Dollard, and their colleagues at Yale fifteen years later.

Social Learning Version of the Thwarting Hypothesis

The principles of social learning outlined thus far were not the first collaborative effort of Miller and Dollard. Joining with Leonard Doob, O.

Hobart Mowrer, and Robert Sears, Miller and Dollard had published an extremely influential analysis of aggression in 1939, two years before their book on social learning and imitation reached the bookshelves. The "Yale group," as the five-man team came to be known, framed their own version of Allport's thwarting hypothesis of aggression:

> This study takes as its point of departure the assumption that *aggression is always a consequence of frustration.* More specifically, the proposition is that the occurrence of aggressive behavior always pre-supposes the existence of frustration and, contrariwise, that the exis-tence of frustration always leads to some form of aggression. [Dollard, Doob, Miller, Mowrer, & Sears, 1939, p. 1]

The scientific attractiveness of the hypothesis lies in its simplicity and precision. Unfortunately, both of these virtues proved to be liabilities as well. Yet the value of any scientific hypothesis lies not in its ultimate truth, but in its capacity to generate research and spark the formulation of new hypotheses. Like the drive-reduction formulation, the frustration-aggres-sion hypothesis was initially stated in its strongest, boldest form, a state-ment, consequently, that generated controversy—and research.

Frustration was defined as *"that condition which exists when a goal-response suffers interference."* *Aggression* was defined as *"an act whose goal-response is injury to an organism (or organism-surrogate)"* (Dollard et al., 1939, p. 11).

To illustrate, consider what transpires when a young boy hears an ice-cream truck's bell outside his home. He appeals to his mother, pulls her toward the door, looks at her with puckered, pleading lips, and so on. His mother, having gone through this ritual many times, and having ruined many a carefully prepared supper, decides not to allow her son the ice cream (Dollard et al., 1939, pp. 3 ff.). A firm "No!" and a decisive turn to her normal routine leave her son's goal-directed pursuits frustrated. She has interfered with the satisfaction of his hunger drive for ice cream and has disappointed his expectations in the success of his familiar strategies. The little boy cries, kicks, and screams, shouting "I hate you!" to his mother, the source of frustration.

This example illustrates fundamental concepts employed by the Yale group. The young boy is *instigated* to wheedle his mother into buying him ice cream. An *instigator* is "some antecedent condition of which the pre-dicted response is a consequence" (Dollard et al., 1939, p. 3). In plainer terms, an *instigator* is the immediate trigger stimulus for the response sequence that leads ultimately to frustration. For the little boy, the directly observable instigators are the sound of the bell and the presence of an ice-cream vendor. The concept of instigator is not limited to observable antecedent conditions. Neither the sound of the ice-cream truck nor the presence of the vendor might be known to an observer, yet the boy's pleading and puckering might indicate that some instigator had initiated his behavior. Internal instigators like the boy's memory that at 3 P.M. every day an ice-cream truck is parked on his street might be responsible for his behavior. Past observations of the boy's responses would be sufficient for an observer to infer the presence of these internal instigators.

Several instigators may combine to provoke a response. Thus the strength of instigation to a particular response may vary. A measure of this strength may be the degree to which the instigated response is pursued when incompatible or competing responses are simultaneously elicited. If the little boy, for example, is willing to run through a lawn sprinkler blocking his path to the ice-cream truck, it can be inferred that the lawn sprinkler's instigation to avoid getting wet is weaker than the ice-cream truck's instigation to obtain a cone. It follows that the boy's tendency to respond aggressively to frustration of his attempts to obtain a cone will vary with the strength of the instigation to obtain that cone. In more colloquial terms, *the more powerful his desire to have an ice-cream, the more likely will frustration of that desire produce aggression* (Dollard et al., 1939, p. 28).

If the strength of the instigation to make a response affects the degree of aggression that follows frustration, it is possible to deduce a further prediction. *The amount of aggression elicited by frustration of a response will vary with the degree of frustration.* This relationship, of course, implies that the greater the degree of frustration or interference with an instigated response, the greater will be the degree of resultant aggression (Dollard et al., 1939, p. 30). For example, Hovland and Sears (1940) assumed that poor economic conditions indicate a great degree of interference with or frustration of goal-directed activities of a given social group's members. It should follow, therefore, that during periods of economic austerity the amount of aggression in response to this frustration will be greater than during periods of economic prosperity. Hovland and Sears computed the per acre value of cotton for fourteen southern states for the years 1882 to 1930. As a measure of violence and aggression, these investigators employed the number of reported lynchings in these fourteen states for the same period. The correlation between the value of cotton and the number of lynchings was –.67, demonstrating that as the price of cotton decreased, the number of lynchings increased. As one wit reviewing this investigation put it: "when the cotton price went down, the victims went up" (Geiwitz, 1969, p. 62).

A third and final relationship between frustration and aggression can be postulated. *The amount of aggression provoked by a given frustration will be affected by the number of past or simultaneous frustrations endured* (Dollard et al., 1939, p. 31). A series of minor frustrations may summate to produce a greater aggressive response than would be evoked by any one frustration endured alone. There is always one final straw that breaks the camel's back.

Thus, three factors regulate the intensity of aggression produced by frustration: (1) the strength of the initial instigation to make the frustrated response; (2) the degree of frustration of or interference with the instigated response; (3) the number of past or simultaneous frustrations of similar responses. It may be noted that a fourth factor, operating subtractively, can also affect the expression of aggression. The fear of punishment or retaliation often inhibits a person from acting out anger that he nevertheless strongly feels. This fourth factor may thus be considered a negative influence on the expression of aggressive responses: (4) the stronger the threat of punishment, the less aggression will be expressed.

A return look at the earlier example of Arthur Stevens' lynching will place these four conditions in perspective. From the nuclear mob's viewpoint, the instigation to aggression (postulate 1) was overwhelmingly strong: Stevens had committed the most heinous of crimes in his alleged rape-murder of a white girl. Stevens had also carried on a prior sexual relationship with the girl and thereby had threatened to equalize white-black social status. The implied threat to the economic and social superiority of whites embodied in Stevens' sexual relationship with Iona Durfee was therefore itself a very intense source of frustration (postulate 2). Moreover, Stevens was merely the tangible symbol of a long series of "frustrations" (postulate 3) represented by every black person in the community. The mob's violence was further intensified by their belief (postulate 4) that no punishing consequences would follow from their acts.

Direct and Indirect Aggression: Translation of Freudian Theory

According to the fourth assumption of the Yale group, the direct expression of aggression can be inhibited by a strong expectation that punishment will ensue. Ordinarily, the strongest instigation to aggression that can be aroused by frustration will be acts of aggression against the perceived source of the frustration (Dollard et al., 1939, p. 39). "A man who has just had his vacation plans disrupted by his employer will be expected ... to be most angry at his employer but also somewhat more irritable toward the world in general" (Dollard et al., 1939, p. 39).

His expectation that punishment (e.g., getting fired) will follow upon direct expression of anger toward his boss is likely to inhibit the thwarted vacationer's aggression. But, as Freud suggested, blocked anger will nevertheless find expression in more devious ways against "safer" targets. Forced by his fear of punishment to displace the anger onto less appropriate targets, the man receives some satisfaction, but he also engenders some new frustration. Because his original impulse to aggression is blocked, the man is likely to perceive the blocking agent as a new frustrator. This new frustration will heighten the aggressive tendencies already evoked and intensify the instigation to other less direct forms of aggression.

A vicious cycle is begun. The initial frustration (ruined vacation) induces aggression that cannot be expressed (fear of punishment). This secondary frustration, in turn, provokes more aggression that likewise must be displaced. "From this it follows that *the greater the degree of inhibition specific to a more direct act of aggression, the more probable will be the occurrence of less direct acts of aggression*" (Dollard et al., 1939, p. 40). These less direct acts may involve *displacement of the aggression* (e.g., kicking a chair instead of the boss) or a *change in the form* of aggression against the original target (i.e., making sarcastic jokes at the boss's expense).

The formulation of the relationship between frustration and aggression devised by Dollard, Miller, and their colleagues was primarily inspired by certain tenets of Freudian theory. Freud's influence is most clearly seen in the displacement corollaries to the basic hypothesis. Dollard had drawn the basic frustration-aggression hypothesis along lines originally established by Freud in his early, pre-death-instinct days (cf. Freud, 1916, 1917b). Freud had hypothesized that certain severe forms of depression represent an effort by the depressed person's ego to turn hostile impulses against the self. For example, the recent widow who castigates and disparages herself for a myriad of faults and character defects may appear to friends and relatives as singularly hypocritical and ungenuine if before the death of her spouse such self-reproaches were never in evidence. The suspicion is easily aroused that all these self-reproaches are really accusations against the deceased husband whose departure frustrated an intense love relationship. As Freud theorized:

> If one listens patiently to a melancholic's many and various self-accusations, one cannot in the end avoid the impression that often the most violent of them are hardly at all applicable to the patient himself, but that with insignificant modifications they do fit someone else, someone whom the patient loves or has loved or should love. . . . So we find the key to the clinical picture: we perceive that the self-reproaches are reproaches against a loved object which have been shifted away from it on to the patient's own ego. . . . If the love for the object—a love which cannot be given up though the object itself is given up—takes refuge in narcissistic identification, then the hate comes into operation on this substitute object [i.e., the self], abusing it, debasing it, making it suffer and deriving sadistic satisfaction from its suffering. [1917b, pp. 250–251]

In effect, the widow who intensely mourns the loss of her husband simultaneously experiences feelings of hostility and resentment at being deprived of a love-object. Freud's analysis, which we need not examine in detail here, extended to the processes by which the ego identifies with the lost love-object. By becoming like the lost love-object, the ego attempts to mitigate the loss and frustration. But in so doing, the person's own ego becomes the target of the frustration-aroused aggressive feelings, feelings that would more properly be directed to the departed husband.

The frustration-aggression hypothesis was the Yale group's attempt to translate the fertile but untestable Freudian hypotheses into stimulus-response constructs. Although the translation modified the original Freudian ideas to a significant degree, the resultant S-R hypothesis allowed empirically minded psychologists to capitalize on the extraordinary range of creative ideas contained in psychoanalysis. The Freudian notion that instincts or drives are malleable and subject to continual modification in the light of experience served as another important source of theoretical borrowing. If, as Freud held, drives may combine or transfer energy from one to another, then it should follow that satisfaction denied to one form of aggression may nevertheless be obtained through a different aggressive avenue.

The Yale group adopted this notion of the *equivalence of drive forms* by framing it in their own terminology:

> It has been assumed that the inhibition of any act of aggression is a frustration which increases the instigation to aggression. Conversely, *the occurrence of any act of aggression is assumed to reduce the instigation to aggression.* In psychoanalytic terminology, such a release is called *catharsis.* [Dollard et al., 1939, p. 50]

For example, a man whose characteristic way of handling hostile impulses was to direct them against himself, was able to engage in more productive activities after an explosive argument with his wife. The man's wife had frustrated his attempts to save money by withdrawing sums from their savings account for household expenses. Only by denying himself small luxuries had the husband been able to save the money. He expressed no direct anger or hostility toward his wife, saying instead: "I don't blame you for not paying any attention to my wishes; they aren't worth worrying about. I'm no good to anybody anyway."

When his wife tried to apologize, she succeeded merely in provoking more self-recriminations and pitiful sobbing. But when she said a few angry words to him, he exploded with "an avalanche of vituperation," apparently for the first time releasing long-pent-up hostility. The wife's few angry words, under ordinary circumstances, would not have been sufficient to trigger such intense outwardly directed anger. But in this instance, even the small degree of additional frustration and provocation represented by her remarks was enough to spark an overdue angry outburst. Soon after he had vented his rage against her, the husband was able cheerfully to plan new ways to restore his savings account (Dollard et al., 1939, pp. 50 ff.).

The man's expression of anger against his wife served as a needed form of catharsis to reduce his customary self-directed aggression. The "avalanche of vituperation" directed against the wife served to lessen the instigation to self-aggression. It logically follows that with the strength of the original frustration held constant, the expression of aggression in one form decreases the instigation to other forms of aggression.

Criticisms and Limitations of the
Frustration-Aggression Hypothesis

Because the Yale group had specified an unvarying law-like relationship between frustration and aggression, the hypothesis was left open to criticisms that question the reliability of the relationship. Does frustration *always* evoke aggression? Cannot frustration induce the organism to other than aggressive responses? Some critics suggested that frustration does evoke a whole range of responses other than aggression toward the agent of frustration, namely: fantasy, flight, identification, and fixation. Furthermore, a sizable proportion of the opponents to the frustration-aggression hypothesis found the Yale group's definition of terms ambiguous and misleading. What is perceived by one person as frustrating may be interpreted by another as only mildly annoying. A brief review of some of these criticisms is in order.

Buss (1966) argued that a very large part of daily living involves obstacles to desired ends. Yet aggression does not follow every frustration of every important motive. In fact, "frustration" is so much a part of contemporary life that it is difficult to find situations that would not fit the Yale group's definition.

Erich Fromm (1973) has also criticized the frustration-aggression hypothesis on the grounds that frustration is not adequately defined. Depending upon the way "frustration" is defined, the Yale group's hypothesis may sorely miss the beneficial aspects that sometimes accrue to temporary frustrations:

> ... we might consider a basic fact of life: that nothing important is achieved without accepting frustration. The idea that one can learn without effort, i.e., without frustration, may be good as an advertising slogan, but is certainly not true in the acquisition of major skills. Without the capacity to accept frustration man would hardly have developed at all. And does not everyday observation show that many times people suffer frustrations without having an aggressive response? People waiting in line in order to obtain a theater ticket, religious people who fast, people in war who have to do without adequate food—in these and hundreds of other cases frustration does not produce aggression. What can, and often does, produce aggression is what the frustration means to the person, and the psychological meaning of frustration differs according to the total constellation in which the frustration occurs. [Fromm, 1973, pp. 67–68]

For Fromm, then, frustration can be given precise meaning only in terms of the individual's total character structure and social situation. Without the necessary personality and situational information, the prediction of aggression from knowledge of alleged "frustrations" is pointless.

Sargent (1948) anticipated Fromm's criticism by arguing that the two most important determinants of whether frustration will evoke aggression are the individual's past experiences and the way he perceives or defines his present situation. In Sargent's view, the most immediate consequence of frustration is not aggression. Rather, frustration first arouses a pronounced emotional reaction that may range from generalized anger through inferiority to jealousy. Once a particular emotional state is evoked, the individual's past experiences with such feelings determine the form his overt responses will assume. The individual may *withdraw* from the frustrating stimulus, *regress* to more primitive behaviors, *rationalize* the situation's true meaning into one more acceptable or less provocative, or he may *inhibit* overt reaction altogether. His overt responses thus may take a variety of forms including bullying, showing off, daydreaming, flight, excusing, and apologizing. Direct aggression against the agent of frustration is, therefore, not always the necessary consequence of thwarted goal-seeking. Sargent's expansion of the frustration-aggression hypothesis is summarized in Figure 14–1.

Bandura and Walters (1963), two theorists to be considered in the second part of the present chapter, also criticized the frustration-aggression formulation on the grounds that prior learning and other social mediating factors are largely excluded from the hypothesis. Bandura and Walters proposed an alternative formulation that emphasized the effects of social reinforcement for aggression and the influence of aggressive models who receive rewards for violent acts. In Bandura and Walters' alternative explanation, frustration serves not as a direct impetus to aggressive behavior, but as an intensifier of more neutral responses in the individual's repertoire which are then interpreted as "aggressive" because of their increased vigor (Bandura & Walters, 1963, pp. 133 ff.).

Bandura (1973) has extended his initial criticism of the frustration-aggression hypothesis to one of its corollaries. It will be recalled that the Yale group had deduced from the basic formulation the implication that venting one's anger in any particular form reduces the intensity of the instigation to aggression in other forms. This view implies that the expression of aggression has a "cathartic" effect on the individual's global tendency to be aggressive. Bandura reviewed evidence that demonstrates aggressive responding under some conditions may not purge the individual of anger, but rather reinforces continued aggressive responding (Bandura, 1973).

Contemporary Status of the Frustration-Aggression Hypothesis

Although we have reviewed only a few of the more cogent criticisms to emerge in the years following publication of the frustration-aggression hypothesis, it became apparent to the Yale group shortly after publication

FIGURE 14–1: EXPANSION OF FRUSTRATION-AGGRESSION HYPOTHESIS

FRUSTRATED MOTIVE	POSSIBLE EMOTIONS	PAST EXPERIENCES Habitual Responses	OVERT BEHAVIOR
Hunger Thirst Affection Prestige Affiliation Etc.	When cause is unclear = *Generalized Anger*	Inhibition of response from mild suppression to full unconscious repression	Tenseness, physical symptoms, e.g., becoming pale, headache.
	Known person is perceived as agent = *Hostility*	Overt expression	Throwing things, kicking things, profanity, attack on agent, criticism of agent.
	Rival achieves a desired goal = *Jealousy*	Displacement	Scolding wife, spanking children, kicking dog, scapegoating.

Regression ──────▶ Tantrums, running to mother, bursting into tears, thumb-sucking.

Situational cues confused = *Generalized Anxiety*

Rationalization ──────▶ "Explaining" to self, to others.

Withdrawal or flight ──────▶ Fantasy, daydreams, isolation.

Others seen as superior = *Feelings of Inferiority*

Compensation ──────▶ Bullying, showing off, making friends.

Modified from Sargent, 1948.

that modifications and clarifications would have to be introduced into the original statement. Miller (1941) issued the first acknowledgment of the prevailing criticisms by declaring that aggression is but one of many consequences of frustration. As Miller indicated, this point had actually been made in the Yale group's 1939 publication, but their strong statement of the general hypothesis obscured the more conservatively stated limitations. Miller (1941), with the endorsement of the other Yale group members, now emphasized that prior rewards and punishments can shape a variety of responses to the frustrating agent.

Sears (1941), another member of the Yale group, also modified the original statement by emphasizing the possibility that other unlearned patterns of response could be evoked by frustration. On the whole, however, both Miller (1941) and Sears (1941) implied that aggression was likely to be the dominant response in the organism's total repertoire of reactions to frustration.

In its broadened version, the frustration-aggression hypothesis has tended to be accepted by contemporary psychologists as a useful statement to guide further naturalistic and experimental research. They recognize that the hypothesis is not an absolute statement of universal and immutable psychological law, but is, instead, a limited, empirically testable account of at least one of the antecedents of aggression (cf. Janis, Mahl, Kagan, & Holt, 1969; Berkowitz, 1969; Feshbach, 1970; and Miller, 1976). Berkowitz has lucidly summarized the contemporary view:

> Basically, I believe a frustrating event increases the probability that the thwarted organism will act aggressively soon afterward, and that this relationship exists in many different animal species, including man. This acceptance of the central thesis of the frustration-aggression hypothesis does not mean complete agreement with the version formulated by Dollard, Doob, Miller, Mowrer, and Sears in their classic monograph, *Frustration and Aggression* (1939). Almost thirty years have gone by, and additional information has been acquired. There is now good reason to believe . . . that their major proposition is at once too simple and too sweeping. Contrary to their original argument, the existence of frustration *does not* always lead to some form of aggression, and the occurrence of aggressive behavior *does not necessarily* presuppose the existence of frustration. [1969, p. 2]

Stimulus-Response Motivation Theory: Learned Fears (Anxiety)

Freud had struggled with the concept of anxiety from the very beginning of his theoretical pursuits. A brief review of the steps leading up to Freud's final conceptualization of the role of anxiety in neurotic behavior was undertaken in Chapter 3. The central idea of Freud's theory (1926) was that anxiety functions as a signal to the ego of impending danger. The danger may arise from overwhelming id desires for satisfaction of unacceptable impulses, from external situations that threaten to overpower the ego's resources and reduce it to infantile helplessness, or from the moralistic censure of the superego. Once initiated, the unpleasant state of anxiety provokes the ego to undertake defensive maneuvers like repression.

O. Hobart Mowrer (1939), a member of the Yale group, saw the significance of Freud's notion that anxiety is a signal of danger that has acquired its motivating properties from previous experiences with painful stimulation. Mowrer argued that Freud's concept could be understood as a case of stimulus-response avoidance conditioning. Mowrer's translation of the Freudian concept into S-R terminology assumed this form:

> A so-called "traumatic" ("painful") stimulus (arising either from external injury, of whatever kind, or from severe organic need) impinges upon the organism and produces a more or less violent defense (striving) reaction. Furthermore, such a stimulus-response sequence is usually preceded or accompanied by originally "indifferent" stimuli which, however, after one or more temporally contiguous associations with the traumatic stimulus, begin to be perceived as "danger signals," i.e., acquire the capacity to elicit an "anxiety" reaction. [1939, p. 554]

Mowrer was thus hypothesizing that anxiety is a *learned* reaction to physical pain. The learning sequence involves the following steps: Noxious stimuli that cause pain provoke an unlearned withdrawal or defense response. An infant who out of curiosity grasps a hot radiator rapidly withdraws the burned hand and cries. After a number of such experiences with different radiators in different rooms, the infant develops a *conditioned avoidance reaction* to hot radiators. Stimuli that were present on each occasion that he burned his hand become conditioned *signals* to avoid the radiator. Thus, for example, the sound of hissing steam from a hot radiator's valve may eventually provoke the same withdrawal and fright reactions that the original pain evoked. The difference, of course, is that the sound of steam signals impending pain without the actual experience of a burned hand.

The child is said to have learned to anticipate pain from the presence of the conditioned stimulus (i.e., from the sound of hissing steam). Mowrer suggested that these conditioned "danger signals" have two outstanding characteristics: (1) danger signals create or intensify the organism's state of tension and attention; (2) the state of heightened tension itself is uncomfortable and therefore impels the organism to escape from the danger situation. Any responses that reduce the discomfort of anxiety tension are thus powerfully reinforced and are likely to be repeated in future similar situations.

> In short, *anxiety (fear) is the conditioned form of the pain reaction,* which has the highly useful function of motivating and reinforcing behavior that tends to avoid or prevent the recurrence of the pain producing (unconditioned) stimulus. [Mowrer, 1939, p. 554]

In Mowrer's view, therefore, *anxiety is the anticipation of actual physical injury or pain,* an anticipation that is learned by Pavlovian conditioning.

Experimental Demonstration of an Acquired Fear Drive

Nine years after Mowrer published his translation of Freudian theory into stimulus-response concepts, Miller (1948) was able to demonstrate that an acquired fear could function as a powerful drive. Miller's experiment quickly became a classic of S-R psychology because it provided the link between theory and observed behavior.

Miller (1948) employed the two-compartment shuttle box illustrated in Figure 14–2 to condition white rats to fear one of the compartments. The left compartment of the apparatus illustrated in Figure 14–2 is painted white and has an electrified grid floor. Painted black, the right compart-

FIGURE 14-2: MILLER'S ACQUIRED FEAR APPARATUS

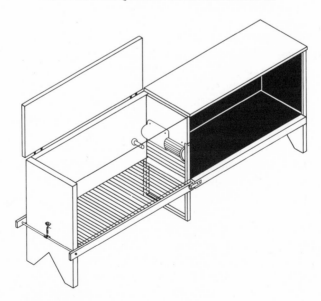

Modified from Miller, 1948.

ment has a wooden floor. Once an animal is placed in the white compartment, escape may be accomplished by pressing the bar in the rear wall of the enclosure or by turning the wheellike device in the wall separating the white and black compartments. In either case, the response causes the black striped door below the wheel to drop, allowing the animal to flee into the safety of the nonelectrified black compartment. The animal presumably learns that white means pain, black means safety.

On the first trial, the animal is placed in the white, grid-floored compartment for one minute and allowed to explore it freely without shock. At the end of the minute, electric shocks are delivered to the animal's feet through the floor grid at five-second intervals for the duration of this second minute. At the end of the second minute, the experimenter drops the black-striped door by remote control and allows the animal to escape into the black compartment. During the period of time it takes the animal to discover the escape route, continuous shock is delivered through the floor grid. The entire procedure is designed to elicit as much fear as possible in the presence of the white compartment and its associated cues. Ten of these experimenter-controlled escape trials are provided for each animal.

All twenty-five of the animals soon acquired the response of running through the opened striped doorway. On subsequent trials, when shock was *not* delivered through the grid, all animals continued to run through the open doorway to escape the white compartment. Clearly they had acquired a conditioned fear of the white compartment.

For the next sixteen trials, the rules of the game are changed so that the experimenter no longer automatically opens the door to the black compartment. The animals must now learn that, to escape, the wheellike device in the wall above the door must be turned a fraction of an inch to drop the door. During these trials *no shock is administered through the grid.* The key questions, therefore, are whether the acquired drive of fear of the white compartment will motivate the learning of this new response, and whether escape into the black compartment will reinforce the response of turning the wheel. Most of the animals tended to concentrate their attention on the region of the doorway. Some crouched and cowered, urinated and defecated, and some stood on their hind legs to place their paws on the wheel above the door. Some of the animals eventually poked their noses into the bars of the wheel and turned it a fraction of an inch. Fortunately for these nose pokers, that slight turn activated the door release. The majority of them ran immediately into the black compartment.

Within this successful group of animals, however, a small number of rats were startled by the door's sudden opening, and they drew back in increased fear. Such animals tended to avoid the door and wheel in later trials. The remainder of the animals who did not learn to operate the escape door tended to freeze and crouch, and they had to be removed by the experimenter after 100 seconds had elapsed. It must be kept in mind, however, that the successful animals had demonstrated that fear of the white compartment could be acquired (conditioned) and that such acquired fear could motivate the learning of a new response that provided the same reinforcement as the original escape response (i.e., the reduction of fear).

Another question arises: Can animals who learned to operate the wheel also learn another new response to effect escape when the wheel is rendered nonfunctional? In more technical language, when the wheel no longer leads to reinforcement, will that response *extinguish* and a new, reinforced response be acquired? To find out, Miller again changed the rules of the game so that the animal could escape the white compartment only by pressing the bar in the back wall. On subsequent trials, the number of turns on the wheel gradually decreased as the animals discovered that this activity no longer provided an escape route. Without the reinforcement of escape, wheel turning soon extinguished. Slowly, during the trial-and-error responses that emerged, the animals discovered that pressing the bar would drop the door. Within ten trials, successful animals switched to this new response apparently for the reinforcement of escaping the feared white compartment. Note, moreover, that *no shock* was administered during these new learning trials. The acquired fear of the white compartment (not the original shock pain) motivated the new learning. Reduction of this same acquired fear reinforced the learning of the new bar-pressing response.

Miller had thus confirmed Mowrer's (and Freud's) hypothesis that fear (anxiety) may serve the function of an *acquired* drive that motivates the organism to anticipate pain (shock) and to respond defensively (escape). Miller summarized his results in this way:

> The general pattern of the fear response and its capacity to produce a strong stimulus is determined by the innate [i.e., biological] structure of the animal. The connection between the pain and the fear is also presumably innate. But the connection between the cues in the white compartment and the fear was learned. Therefore the fear of the white compartment may be called an acquired drive. Because the fear can be learned, it may be called acquirable; because it can motivate new learning, it may be called a drive. [Miller, 1948, p. 97]

The demonstration that fear can be learned and that such fear can motivate new learning took S-R theory another giant step toward its goal of accounting for complex human motives (see also Miller & Myers, 1954; Miller, 1950; and Miller & Novin, 1962). The fact that theorists like Miller, Dollard, Mowrer, and other Yale group members found Freudian theory a fruitful source of ideas is an important lesson for contemporary theorists who advocate total abandonment of psychoanalytic concepts. As we shall see, Miller and Dollard carried the translation of Freudian theory into S-R language several steps further.

Acquired Drives as a Social Mask

Along with their translation of Freudian concepts into S-R language, Miller and Dollard adopted Freud's distinction between surface and depth personality phenomena. The analogy of the actor and his mask was not used by Miller and Dollard, yet they employed a similar stimulus-response distinction between the innate primary drives and the facade of acquired secondary drives:

> The conditions of society tend, besides obscuring the rôle of certain primary drives, to emphasize certain secondary or acquired drives. These secondary drives are acquired on the basis of the primary drives, represent elaborations of them, and serve as a façade behind which the functions of the underlying innate drives are hidden. . . . Such acquired drives or appetites vary according to the social conditions under which they are learned and often impart a cultural coloring to the innate drives. . . . In short, acquired drives may assume the aspect of social needs. [1941, p. 19]

Anxiety or specific learned fear is, as we have seen, one of the most powerful acquired drives. The needs for approval, for money, and for prestige are also learned drives or acquired social motives. In each case, the acquired need is based on several combined biological needs. The need for approval, for example, is a learned motive based on the unlearned drives of hunger, thirst, and pain-avoidance. Because in infancy each of these primary drives can be satisfied only with the cooperation of powerful adult caretakers, the child quickly learns to adopt patterns of drive expression that evoke parental approval. In this way, as Freud, too, suggested, the child assures himself of continued adult indulgence of his needs.

The biological, unlearned cravings of the actor's body are thus expressed through the social mask of acquired drives. Social living necessitates adoption of socially acceptable patterns of satisfaction. Society enforces drive expressions that it approves, and these acceptable masking drives are the only channels through which primary drive reduction is permitted. Thus, in Miller and Dollard's view, an adequate explanation of human behavior must focus on the ways innate drives are shaped and reshaped by the prevailing social standards.

S-R Conflict Theory: Operationalizing Freudian Hypotheses

Freud spent a considerable number of years wrestling with the problem of how best to depict the combining, competing, conflicting forces that underlie neurotic behavior. It will be recalled from our discussion in Chapter 3 that in his final model of the mind, Freud pictured the neurotic personality as one who is torn between the insistent demands of the id and the continual restraint-censorship of the ego-superego. At a slightly different level of analysis, Freud also depicted neurotic conflict in terms of the perpetual war between the life and death instincts.

Kurt Lewin, it will be remembered from Chapter 11, employed the conceptual framework of field theory to specify three types of conflict: *approach-approach* conflict, in which the individual locomotes between two nearly equally attractive goals; *avoidance-avoidance* conflict, in which the individual struggles to withdraw from two nearly equally repellent goals; and *approach-avoidance* conflict, in which the person is simultaneously attracted and repelled by a single goal.

Miller (1944, 1959, and 1964) borrowed, modified, and elaborated upon the concepts of Freud and Lewin in devising a stimulus-response model of conflict. As we shall see, Dollard and Miller (1950) applied the emerging theory of conflict to the problems of accounting in stimulus-response terms for neurotic symptoms and for classic Freudian defense mechanisms like repression and displacement.

Basic Assumptions of S-R Conflict Theory

The first step in Miller's analysis was to focus on the most complex of the three types of conflict, approach-avoidance conflict, and to specify as precisely as possible the assumptions that would guide research. In an early statement of the theory Miller (1944) listed four guiding principles and later (1959) added two postulates:

1. *The tendency to approach a goal is stronger the nearer the subject is to it.* For example, a small boy who avidly desires a puppy in a pet shop window, will become more excited, more elated, more desirous the closer he gets to actually touching the dog. In other words, there is an *approach gradient* that may, for experimental purposes, be conceptualized as actual physical distance from the goal. For purposes of general personality theory, the approach gradient may be translated into psychological distance from a goal.

2. *The tendency to avoid a feared stimulus is stronger the nearer the subject is to it.* To extend the previous example, consider the plight of the boy outside the pet shop window with this additional piece of knowledge: a year ago, the boy was badly bitten by a vicious dog. Consequently, although he desires, as most children do, to possess, to touch, and to pet the dog in the window, he simultaneously feels a surge of anxiety the closer he actually comes to physical contact with the puppy. Thus, there is also a *gradient of avoidance*. It is the tension between these approach and avoidance urges that lies at the heart of the conflict. The question therefore arises: Which gradient, approach or avoidance, increases more rapidly with

nearness? Will approach win out with increasing nearness, or will avoidance prove to be the stronger tendency?

3. *The strength of the avoidance tendency increases more rapidly with nearness to the goal than the strength of the approach tendency.* Preliminary experimental work suggested that the behavioral paralysis that usually characterizes someone caught between approaching and avoiding a goal could be explained by assuming that the avoidance gradient is steeper or increases more sharply as the person comes near the goal. In our example of the boy and puppy, the closer he gets to actually touching the dog, the more his anxiety grows and outweighs his desire. He approaches just so far, and he will move toward the puppy not one step more. The steepness of the avoidance gradient relative to the approach gradient refers to their graphic characteristics, as illustrated in Figure 14–3.

It can be seen from the graph in Figure 14–3 that the avoidance gradient (broken line) rises much more rapidly in intensity than the approach gradient as the subject approaches closer to the goal. Another way of saying the same thing is to point out that at distances far from the goal the discrepancy between approach and avoidance tendencies is not so exaggerated. It might be helpful to return to Figure 11–13 in Chapter 11, where Lewin's conceptualization of the same phenomenon is illustrated.

Judson Brown (1940, 1948), one of Miller's students, employed an apparatus designed by Miller to test this assumption. A group of rats were trained to run down a short, straight alley to a point where they obtained food. The goal zone was made very distinctive by the presence of a light.

FIGURE 14-3:   GRADIENTS OF APPROACH AND VOIDANCE

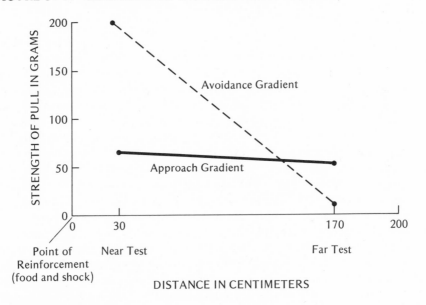

From Miller, 1944, p. 434.

On each trial, the animals wore a harness attached through a cord to a calibrated spring marker that recorded the average strength of their pulls down the alley. Another group of rats similarly harnessed were given electric shocks in the goal zone. After the first group of animals had learned to approach the food, they were restrained for one second at a point distant from the goal or at a point near the goal so that measurements could be made of the force they exerted against the restraint. The solid line in Figure 14–3 represents the average force of the animals' pull thirty centimeters from the goal (Near) and 170 centimeters from it (Far). It can be seen that animals restrained near the goal pulled harder than those restrained at some distance, thus confirming the assumption of an approach gradient.

Brown's study also included a measurement of the strength of the tendency to *avoid* the goal region for those rats who had received an electric shock in the goal zone. The broken line in Figure 14–3 represents the pulling force *away from* the shock region exerted by rats restrained near (30 centimeters) and far from the goal (170 centimeters). It can clearly be seen that the force of pull away from the goal is much greater for those rats restrained near the place where they had been shocked. It can also be seen that the gradient of avoidance is much steeper than the gradient of approach. Thus Brown had confirmed both the avoidance gradient assumption, and the assumption that the avoidance gradient is steeper than the approach gradient. An interesting question now poses itself: Would the amount of pull toward (or away from) the goal region change if the rats were made more or less hungry or given more or less intense shock?

4. *The strength of the tendencies to approach or avoid varies with the strength of the drive upon which they are based.* In other words, the obvious answer to our question is yes. Increased hunger and increased fear intensify their respective goal responses. In our previous example of the boy and puppy, we would naturally expect the child to be much more greatly frightened of the puppy if his previous injury at the fangs of the vicious dog had been severe enough to require hospitalization. A glancing nip of the dog's teeth would hardly produce as much avoidance of puppies as a skin-tearing gash.

Brown's (1940, 1948) study also confirmed this fourth assumption. Groups of rats who had been deprived of food for forty-eight hours evidenced stronger pull forces toward the goal region than rats deprived of food for only one hour. Thus, a decrease in the hunger drive served to lessen the approach tendency. Likewise, rats given a strong electric shock pulled away from the goal with more force than rats given only mild shock. These results are illustrated in Figure 14–4, where the weak and strong avoidance gradients are indicated by broken lines. Figure 14–4 also illustrates the principle that the avoidance gradients (even the weak avoidance gradient) are usually steeper than the approach gradients.

The four assumptions thus far considered received substantial experimental support, but an open question about assumption number three (i.e., the avoidance gradient is steeper than the approach gradient) remained.

FIGURE 14-4: WEAK AND STRONG GRADIENTS OF APPROACH AND AVOIDANCE

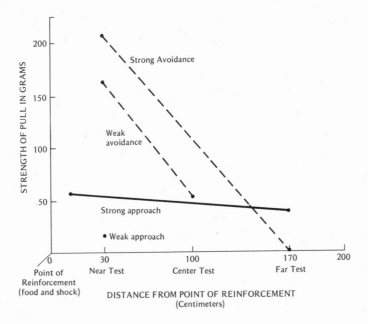

From Miller, 1944, p. 435.

Miller reported (1959) that he and Judson Brown had begun to speculate that the reason the avoidance gradient was steeper might lie in the fundamental difference between the *learned* drive of fear and the innate, *physiological* drive of hunger. In all of the conflict experiments conducted by Miller and his students, the approach gradients had been calculated on the basis of the animal's hunger drive, an innate physiological need. The responses of approaching the distinctively lit goal region were, of course, learned. Such approach responses, precisely because they are learned, should vary in strength as the situational cues are changed. If the goal zone is somehow made distinctively different, the animal's learned response tendencies to approach it should decrease. But the *drive* that underlies these approach responses, hunger, does not depend on environmental cues; hunger increases and decreases primarily in response to *internal*, physiological factors (Miller, 1959, p. 213). Thus, approach tendencies based on the physiological drive of hunger should be significantly less variable than avoidance tendencies based on a learned drive of fear. The animal's fear drive and avoidance responses, related as they are to learned, environmental cues, should both vary greatly with moves toward and away from the shock zone.

Another way to understand these same deductions is to say that because fear is a learned drive, it will decrease more rapidly than hunger as the animal moves away from the learned cues of the shock region. At the same distance, the animal's unlearned—physiological—hunger drive will be relatively unaffected. Consequently, the gradient of avoidance rises more steeply (or decreases more sharply, from the other point of view) than the gradient of approach. Miller and one of his students, Edward J. Murray (Miller & Murray, 1952a, 1952b), were able to confirm these deductions in modified conflict situations with white rats.

In one study (Miller & Murray, 1952b), white rats were trained to escape electric shock by running down a wide white alley to an elevated "island of safety." Following the learning trials, half the animals were tested with the shock turned off so that they were performing only in response to the learned fear drive, not to the unlearned drive of pain. The other half of the group were tested with the shock turned on so that they were driven by pain, and perhaps a little fear.

Each of these two subgroups was further divided into halves. One half of the pain group and one half of the fear group were tested in new alleys somewhat different in appearance from the alley in which they had originally learned the escape response. In this way, the hypothesis that learned cues are more easily affected by environmental changes than unlearned cues (i.e., pain) could be tested. As usual, the gradients of avoidance were measured by the animal's strength of pull away from the shock region. The results showed that animals tested with the *shock on* (unlearned pain drive) in both the original and the new alley varied significantly *less* in their strength of pull than animals tested only with the learned drive of fear. The gradients of avoidance for the learned-drive rats were considerably steeper because they pulled far more strongly in the original alley than in the new alley.

5. *Below the asymptote of learning, increasing the number of reinforced trials will increase the strength of the response tendency that is reinforced* (Miller, 1959, p. 206). This assumption says that the greater the number of trials on which the animal has been shocked or given food, the stronger will be his approach or avoidance responses. This relatively straightforward assumption was confirmed in a study by Kaufman and Miller (1949) in which rats given 81 food-reinforced trials to run down a maze alley ran faster than rats given only 1, 3, 9, or 27 reinforced trials. Furthermore, each of these groups was also given a shock trial during which consumption of the food pellet was paired with an unpleasant electric shock. Even after shock, animals given the largest number of food-reinforced trials continued to run down the alley faster than animals given successively fewer numbers of reinforcements.

Kaufman and Miller (1949) also showed that when each of the subgroups was given three increasingly intense shock trials, the animals that had been given the larger number of food reinforcements were more likely than their less fortunate comrades to run the full length of the alley. Bower and Miller (1960), in a similar experimental procedure, were able to demonstrate that increasing the *size* of the reward (number of food pellets available on a given trial) increases the strength of the approach tendency.

In fact, as in the Kaufman and Miller experiment, stronger shocks were required to deter animals given large rewards than rats given small rewards.

6. *When two incompatible responses are in conflict, the stronger one will occur* (Miller, 1959, p. 206). This last deduction is again a relatively straightforward one that predicts how approach-avoidance conflicts may sometimes be solved. Those responses based on the stronger of two drives, or responses with the longest series of reinforcements, will ultimately win out.

Dollard and Miller (1950) were able to extend parts of the stimulus-response conflict model to neurotic conflict and to the therapist's attempts at reducing such conflicts. To these applications of the model we turn next.

Applications of S-R Conflict Theory: Neurosis

Freud had convincingly argued that the core of neurotic behavior was unconscious conflict between warring impulses. Moreover, Freud had shown that it was typical of his patients that such conflicts had been acquired in childhood. In their second collaborative effort, Dollard and Miller (1951) borrowed these two Freudian tenets as the starting point for their own stimulus-response analysis of neurotic behavior. The bridge between the precisely controlled laboratory rat studies and the clinically observed misery of neurotic patients was to be constructed from Freudian hypotheses that had been carefully translated into stimulus-response concepts.

Dollard and Miller (1950), as they had done in their earlier work (Miller and Dollard, 1941), began their analysis with the social conditions responsible for the learning of unconscious conflicts. They identified four critical child-rearing situations in which the parents as mediators of cultural standards provide opportunities for the learning of conflict. These four critical learning situations are feeding, cleanliness training, sex training, and reactions to the child's anger.

The Feeding Situation

Because the hunger of the infant is intense and because he cannot deal with it by himself, he is dependent upon his caretakers for satisfaction and relief. He is also dependent upon them for learning how to cope with his primary drives. From the way his parents treat his needs he learns whether his cries, his pains, his urgent expressions of his need to be comforted matter to these important providers. When his cries of hunger are not consistently met with immediate attention, the child learns that his needs are eminently ignorable. He learns that the world is a place in which sometimes needs are met and sometimes one has to cry oneself to sleep.

Eventually, he acquires the attitude of apathy and social indifference. Other people do not matter, for I do not matter to them.

As Erik Erikson (see Chapter 10) has pointed out, the parents' manner of satisfying the child's needs may lead to the formation of an attitude of basic trust in other and in self, or to an attitude of basic mistrust in others and in one's own capacity to cope with the world. More important, Dollard and Miller theorized, is the fact that the attitudes the child acquires toward self and toward others in the first year of life are learned without the aid of verbal labels:

> The young child does not notice or label the experiences which it is having at this time. It cannot give a description of character traits acquired during the first year of life nor yet of its hardships, fears, or deep satisfactions. What was not verbalized at the time cannot well be reported later. An important piece of history is lost and cannot be elicited by questionnaire or interview. Nevertheless, the behavioral record survives. The responses learned occur and may indeed recur in analogous situations throughout life. They are elicited by unlabeled cues and are mutely interwoven into the fabric of conscious life. [1950, p. 136]

Thus, as Freud too had asserted, the critical early acquisitions of life are unconscious because they are nonverbal.

Cleanliness Training

The demands of the culture for the acquisition of bladder and bowel control are rigid and unyielding. Equally intense are the child's spontaneous urges to urinate immediately and without shame when the bladder is full and to defecate when the bowel becomes full. Cultural demands necessitate the breaking of the innate connection between these internal urge cues and their natural immediate responses. The child must learn a new sequence between the experience of his bladder or bowel urges and appropriate times and places to satisfy them.

Parents devise and use a variety of techniques to teach their children this important aspect of cleanliness, and the usual result is frustrated and anxious children along with frustrated and angry parents. The child is caught in the conflict between its spontaneous urges and the demands of the parents for appropriate toilet habits. Depending upon the severity of punishment used, the child may learn to fear the parents, to fear its own urges, or to be excessively conforming to the demands of others. Furthermore, it is possible for the child to acquire an exaggerated loathing for dirt or disarray. He may even be unable to distinguish between parental disapproval of badly timed defecations and disapproval of himself:

> ... the child may not be able to discriminate between parental loathing for its excreta and loathing for the whole child himself. If the

child learns to adopt these reactions, feelings of unworthiness, insignificance, and hopeless sinfulness will be created—feelings which sometimes so mysteriously reappear in the psychotic manifestations of guilt. [Dollard & Miller, 1950, p. 140]

Early Sex Training

The first sexual conflict that the child is likely to acquire concerns the social taboo over masturbation. As Freud had suggested, infants soon discover the pleasurable experience of exploring their own genital areas. When the parent first observes this behavior the most usual reaction is intense anxiety, for the parents too are the products of the culture. They therefore react to the child's exploratory self-manipulation with either direct or indirect threats. The parents may, if the child has acquired language, label the response "nasty" or use some equivalent negative tag, so that ultimately the child learns the same feelings of anxiety over masturbation and for parts of his own body that he learned in toilet training.

Another important aspect of early sex training is to be found in the way the child acquires his sexual identity. Practically from birth, the child is exposed to cultural, and therefore parental, pressures to assume the role of boy or girl. Male and female names, particular types of clothing, specific play objects for each sex, and particular vocational aspirations are all enforced and pressed upon the developing child. Moreover, the parents usually convey to the child that important rewards are to be gained from interaction with members of the opposite sex. Thus taboos against homosexuality are also enforced. In all of these ways the child is exposed to anxiety and specific learned fears as part of his educational program in the art of becoming a socialized human being. He has also been exposed, consequently, to important sources of sexual conflict.

Reactions to the Child's Anger

As the frustration-aggression hypothesis suggested, anger may be induced in the child from a wide variety of daily frustrations. How this resultant anger is treated by the parents provides a new and powerful source of conflict learning. Parents generally act with firm disapproval of angry outbursts by their children. Yet, in the very early years of childhood, parents are inclined to ignore or at least to tolerate anger.

It is possible that the severity of parental punishment for angry responses may be responsible for the attachment of anxiety feelings to cues that would normally elicit only anger. When the child has been consistently and severely punished for angry outbursts or for what parents interpret as stubbornness, the resultant fear may in future situations be elicited in place of anger. "The person can thus be made helpless to use his anger even in those situations where the culture does permit it. He is viewed as abnormally meek or long suffering. Robbing a person of his anger completely may be a dangerous thing since some capacity for anger seems to be needed in the affirmative personality" (Dollard & Miller, 1950, p. 149).

These four training situations, then, may be thought of as the potential kernels of later personality traits, or as the possible core of an adult neurosis. *The common characteristic in each of these critical learning experiences is the acquisition of learned fears or anxiety in connection with spontaneous impulses of anger, sexuality, hunger, and elimination.* Conflict by itself, however, is not unique to the neurotic personality. Emotional dilemmas are endured by nearly everyone at one or another times in their lives. Dollard and Miller acknowledged their inability to specify completely the conditions that must exist for conflict between drives to generate a neurosis (1950, pp. 155 ff.). However, the most important conditions seemed to be the capacity of some conflicts to be acquired without verbal labeling and the strength of the drives that may thus compete unconsciously.

The Neurosis of Mrs. A.: Conflict, Repression, and Displacement

Whereas the conflict underlying an adult neurosis has its origins in the powerful and discordant learnings of childhood, the actual *symptoms* of adult neurosis may be acquired through current acts of learning how to reduce anxiety. The important prerequisite for the acquisition of a neurotic symptom, therefore, is the presence of unrelieved childhood anxiety over the expression of some unverbalized impulse like sex or aggression. Symptoms are patterns of behavior that have proved effective in reducing this anxiety. Therefore neurotic symptoms may be thought of as acquired responses for dealing with the conflict between the impulse and the learned fear of its satisfaction. A brief excursion into the life of Mrs. A. will clarify these points.

Mrs. A.'s Two Basic Conflicts

Mrs. A. was twenty-three years old when she first sought the services of a therapist to help her overcome an especially strong fear that had been growing in intensity for about five months. Dollard and Miller gathered the facts of the case through the cooperation of this New York specialist (Dollard & Miller, 1950, pp. 16 ff.). Her chief difficulty seemed to be that she frequently became obsessed by the irrational fear that her heart would stop beating if she did not concentrate on counting each of its beats. Her fear of heart failure was greatly intensified whenever she went out alone for a walk, or to a movie, or shopping. Her life had become greatly constricted and her daily activities had been narrowed to little more than those of a recluse.

Mrs. A.'s first attack of uncontrollable and irrational fear had occurred while shopping. Feeling faint and terrified for no apparent reason, she had telephoned her husband at his office to ask him to come and get her. Though vague, her fear centered on the idea that should something happen to her, "no one would know where I was" (Dollard & Miller, 1950, p. 17). From that day, Mrs. A. became afraid to go out alone. The symptom was altered somewhat after a conversation with an aunt who had a neurotic fear of heart trouble. The vague fear of being out alone was thus changed to an intense concern about her own heart, a focused but no less overpowering dread.

Mrs. A.'s family history held the key to the origins of her symptom. Born of unknown parents in a city in the South, Mrs. A. had spent the first few months of life in an orphanage before being placed with foster parents. There were already three children in the family, all of them older than Mrs. A. The foster mother is described by Dollard and Miller as working class with a "coarse and vulgar demeanor." "Swearing continually," the foster mother punished her foster child for the slightest offense: "She whipped me all the time—whether I'd done anything or not." Added to this picture of inconsistent love and discipline, Mrs. A.'s foster mother imposed extremely severe sex training on the children, forcing them to feel that sex was dirty and wrong. Dollard and Miller elaborate:

> Despite the repressive sex training she received, Mrs. A. had developed strong sexual appetites. In early childhood, she had overheard parental intercourse, had masturbated, and had witnessed animal copulation. When she was ten or twelve, her foster brother seduced her. During the years before her marriage a dozen men tried to seduce her and most of them succeeded. [1950, p. 18]

Parental attitudes, however, had taken their toll, for Mrs. A., in spite of her strong sexual appetites, was disgusted by the thought of sex, found sexual topics painful to contemplate, and was extremely reserved in her relations with her husband. This marriage had been a stroke of good fortune because despite her lack of education and her coarse manners, Mrs. A.'s natural beauty had enabled her to marry an army officer. Yet in some ways the marriage proved painful. She was awkward about entertaining friends and made obvious errors in grammar and pronunciation. Her husband's family rejected her and attempted to dominate her relations with her husband.

By the time Mrs. A. visited the therapist, her heart phobia and assorted other anxieties threatened to overwhelm her completely. Her husband threatened to leave her; friends and other relatives were almost totally alienated by her chronic complaints. She was understandably hurt, anxious, and fearful that she might be "going crazy." Surprisingly, however, Mrs. A. was completely baffled by her own fears, and she showed little insight into the meaning or origins of her fears. Clearly repression of her conflicts was operating.

Mrs. A. was suffering the effects of two conflicts. On the one hand, it is clear that her early childhood experiences in sexual matters had engendered a powerful negative attitude toward activities which she simultaneously found pleasurable. In briefest terms, Mrs. A. had been taught to attach feelings of anxiety to her spontaneous feelings of sexual interest and pleasure. She saw no connection, however, between her foster mother's attitude and training and the current difficulties she was facing.

Mrs. A.'s second conflict, though less severe, was similarly connected with competing drives. Badly treated by her mother-in-law, she felt bitterly resentful. Whenever she felt the impulse to voice her anger and resentment she was seized with fear lest she damage her marriage or provoke greater mistreatment at the hands of her husband's relatives. She became tormented by feelings of helplessness and worthlessness. In short, Mrs. A.'s conflicts might be characterized as a sex-fear conflict and as an anger-fear conflict.

The Drive-Reducing Functions of Symptoms

Mrs. A. frequently did rather stupid things, acts that would surely endanger her marriage further or at the very least intensify her own fears. For example, when out alone, despite her sexual loathings, she would place herself in situations that courted sexual seduction by strange men. She would attempt to hitchhike rides with truck drivers, or go on drinking sprees with single girls. This apparent stupidity indicates the effects of repression and of the competing drives for sexual pleasure inhibited by anxiety.

In analysis, her heart phobia became understandable as a means of controlling her impulses to seek sexual pleasure while holding her learned anxiety and guilt at bay.

> When on the streets alone, her fear of sex temptation was increased. Someone might speak to her, wink at her, make an approach to her. Such an approach would increase her sex desire and make her more vulnerable to seduction. Increased sex desire, however, touched off both anxiety and guilt, and this intensified her conflict when she was on the street. . . . When sexy thoughts came to mind or other sex stimuli tended to occur, these stimuli elicited anxiety. . . . Since [heart-beat] counting is a highly preoccupying kind of response, no other thoughts could enter her mind during this time. While counting, the sexy thoughts which excited fear dropped out. Mrs. A. "felt better" immediately when she started counting, and the counting habit was reinforced by the drop in anxiety. [Dollard & Miller, 1950, p. 21]

Of course, the heart-beat counting symptom does not resolve the basic conflict, the desire for sex and the fear of obtaining it, but it does act to relieve the anguish momentarily and to prevent further guilt. The important point is that the symptom is acquired through reinforcement—the reduction in anxiety and guilt—and is maintained by the chronically high drive level of the underlying, unverbalized conflict. Another question immediately poses itself: How does repression operate to keep the individual from the obvious self-insight that would alleviate much of the misery?

Repression: A Learned "Not-Thinking" Response

According to Dollard and Miller's hypothesis, drives, cues, and responses that have not been verbally labeled will be unconscious (1950, p. 198). The largest category of unverbalized material will be drawn from these years of childhood when language was absent or only primitively developed. Mrs. A.'s attitudes toward sex fall into this category, along with her innately strong sexual desires.

After language is acquired, however, anxiety-provoking thoughts and perceptions may still be repressed by an analogous mechanism. Freud had proposed that repression occurs in two varieties: *primal repressions* during the early years of life when unverbalized impulses are stored in the unconscious; and *repression proper* during later years when a symbolic or verbal derivative of primal repressions threatens to provoke recall of this material. Such derivatives are deprived of their language labels by the preconscious censor system (cf. Chapter 3). Repression proper, therefore, is a mechanism by which verbal labels are severed from their referents. Without words properly connected to the ideas they are meant to represent, recall and conscious processing of these thoughts are impossible. Miller and Dollard provided a stimulus-response equivalent to this mechanism to explain how thoughts may be kept from awareness.

In Dollard and Miller's terms, *repression* involves the automatic, nonverbal avoiding of certain thoughts. When a thought that is anxiety arousing enters awareness, anything, any activity, or any other thought that can push the threatening idea from the center of awareness will be reinforcing, that is, anxiety reducing. Like Mrs. A.'s heart-beat counting symptom, anxiety-arousing ideas can be avoided by concentrating on an equally powerful distractor. At first, the individual must exert some conscious effort to avoid the anxiety-laden thought, but rather quickly the act of mental avoidance becomes automatic. He does not label the act: "I am going to avoid this thought"; he merely commences the distracting activity or initiates the distracting chain of thought. Because the relief that such activities bring is immediate and immense, the act of "stopping thinking" is a powerful reinforcer.

Repression, in Dollard and Miller's view, is a *learned avoidance response.* The objects of avoidance are the words with which thoughts can be expressed. In effect, fear or disgust or pain may be attached through conditioning to a word that represents an idea or an impulse. Fear of the word eventually generalizes to the idea or impulse that it represents. An incident from the life of Mrs. A. provides a clear example of how words (and their underlying thoughts) may become objects of avoidance:

> With my mother I could never discuss anybody's being pregnant. She wouldn't say they were pregnant. She'd say, "Oh, she is *so big*"—and she'd say it as though she were hitting me. It felt to me like she was hitting me. The way mother would talk about pregnancy was sickening. It was something wrong—can I use the word—it was something *dirty*. Once when a girl had a miscarriage, she talked about it—I didn't want to listen to it! [Dollard & Miller, 1950, pp. 204–205]

Years later, Mrs. A. was still pained by these thoughts, and, more important, was angered by them. The language labels associated with pregnancy and the implied theme of sexuality are what Dollard and Miller call *cue-producing responses* (1950, p. 100). Words may increase the distinctiveness of the stimuli to which they are attached. Then the word becomes the person's cue for a further response. For example, in Mrs. A.'s experience the word *pregnancy* became the cue-producing response that led to anxiety and disgust for the ideas of sexuality and bearing a child. The word, rather than a pregnant woman, became the signal (cue) for the responses of anxiety and disgust.

Because the anxiety attached to the word generalizes to the thoughts represented by the word, the individual greatly decreases his anxiety by the simple expedient of "not thinking" the word. As part of his doctoral dissertation at Yale (reported in Miller, 1950), Miller demonstrated how this anxiety-mediating function of language could be acquired. In random order, a subject was shown the letter "T" and the number "4," and he was required to say them aloud at each presentation. After every occurrence of "T" the subject received an electric shock, but he never received one for presentations of "4." Recordings of his galvanic skin response (GSR) showed that he rapidly learned to respond with anticipatory fear to "T" as evidenced in a large peak in the continuously recorded GSR tracings (see Figure 14–5). The symbol "4" elicited no comparable GSR changes.

Once this discrimination between "T" and "4" had been reliably established, the subject was instructed in a modified procedure involving the presentation of dots instead of symbols. The subject was now required to *think* "t" to the first dot presented, to *think* "4" to the second dot, and so on in alternating sequence. As illustrated in Figure 14–5, dots to which he thought "T" elicited large GSR peaks as compared with GSR changes for dots representing "4." Figure 14–5 shows three blocks of trials to the dots: trials 1 to 5, in which the GSR changes are at maximum; trials 11 to 15 in which there is some decline as the response begins to extinguish; and trials 21 to 25, in which "T-dots" continue to elicit larger GSR changes than "4-dots," though the absolute magnitude of GSR changes is considerably reduced.

Miller's conditioning experiment demonstrates that there is a functional

FIGURE 14-5: GSR RESPONSES TO THOUGHT OF LETTER PREVIOUSLY SHOCKED

GSR RESPONSES on TRIALS 1 to 5

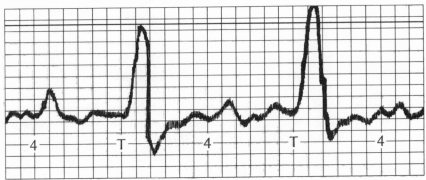

GSR RESPONSES on TRIALS 11 to 15

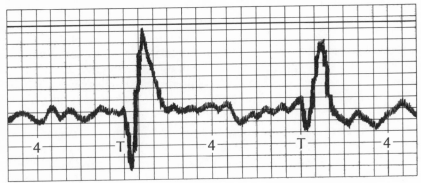

GSR RESPONSES on TRIALS 21 to 25

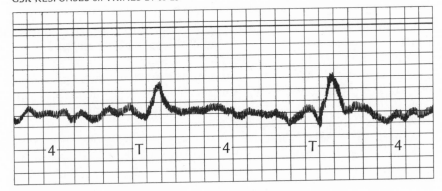

From Miller, 1950, p. 464.

equivalence between *saying* a word aloud and *thinking* it. The anxiety that had been learned in response to the shocked "T" was generalized to the thought of "T" in the absence of continued shock. Fear can also be attached to the thought of performing a response if that response has been punished severely. When a child is scolded or spanked for some misdeed, *thoughts* of future similar misdeeds will evoke the same feelings of anxiety that were attached to the act. In such situations, the parents usually tell the child precisely what he is being punished for so that the child may verbally rehearse the sequence that led to punishment. Moreover:

> Sometimes parents, with their superior intelligence and experience, can tell what a child is likely to do before he says or does anything obvious. Thus they may warn the child when he has an evil thought before he has made any gross overt response. *Such warnings attach fear to the thought and help to break down the discrimination between thoughts on the one hand and spoken words and acts on the other.* To the small child it is as if the parents could read his mind. [Dollard & Miller, 1950, p. 207; italics added]

Thus, the avoidance of certain thoughts is sometimes equivalent to the avoidance of certain acts. And by "not thinking," that is, by "forgetting," the individual reduces the discomfort of anxiety that the thoughts evoke. Viewed in this way, repression (not-thinking) of thoughts or impulses makes them "unconscious" because it deprives the impulse or thought of its verbal cues. Repression may therefore operate in one of three ways:

1. *Prevention of verbal labeling of a drive:* For example, a person may experience sexual arousal, but not attach the word (or meaning) "sexual" to his experience. He has learned that "sexual" arousal provokes anxiety; unlabeled arousal does not (Dollard & Miller, 1950, p. 211). He may even mislabel the arousal as "nervousness" or "boredom." Part A of Figure 14–6 summarizes this form of repression.

2. *Prevention of responses producing a drive:* An individual may learn to avoid making an anxiety-arousing response and to substitute a more neutral distracting response. For example, a person in a sexually arousing situation will detect his own bodily arousal. A man may experience an erection in the presence of a sexually attractive woman. Ordinarily perception of one's own physical response (i.e., the erection) increases sexual arousal. If such arousal simultaneously evokes anxiety, the person may turn to an incompatible activity that can distract his attention from the anxiety-provoking bodily response. He may, for example, declare that he is hungry and avidly devote himself to preparing or to eating a meal. Substitution of the distracting eating response for the act of perceiving one's own sexual response decreases the sexual arousal. Part B of Figure 14–6 summarizes this form of repression.

FIGURE 14–6: THREE FORMS OF REPRESSION OR "NOT THINKING" AVOIDANCE RESPONSES

A. NOT LABELING OR MISLABELING A DRIVE

Conflicted Drive ⟶ Repression by Mislabeling ⟶ Anxiety Reduction (Reinforcement)
(Sexual arousal)   (Calls arousal "nervousness")   (No conflict because there is no "sexual" arousal)

B. INHIBITION OR SUBSTITUTION OF DRIVE RESPONSES

Conflicted Drive ⟶ Repression by Response Substitution ⟶ Anxiety Reduction (Reinforcement)
(Bodily sexual   (Turns attention to incompatible   (No conflict because disturbing bodily
arousal: erection)   responses; e.g., eating)   response is ignored; attention on new
                                                                        response)

C. INHIBITION OF VERBAL MEDIATING DRIVE RESPONSES

Conflicted Drive ⟶ Immediate Response ⟶ Repression by ⟶ Anxiety Reduction (Reinforcement)
(Anger caused by   (Suppression of anger)   "Not Thinking"   (No conflict because insult
insulting remark)   (Turns thoughts   is not thought about)
                                                          away from
                                                          remembered insult)

Based on Dollard and Miller, 1950.

561

3. *Inhibition of responses mediating the drive:* A person may be made angry by someone's insulting remark, for example, but he has learned not to express his anger because such responses always evoke anxiety. Therefore, at the moment of the insult, the individual holds his anger in check. But the thought of the insult may, at some later time, evoke the feeling of anger that was never expressed. Anxiety, of course, is simultaneously evoked. The person can now control his anxiety only by not thinking about the original insult. It is not the insult, but the *thought* of it that must be avoided. Consequently, to continue to inhibit his anger (and the accompanying anxiety), he must "stop thinking" about the insult. "Stopping thinking" about the insult prevents the experience of anxiety in a way that is similar to the original suppression of the anger response at the moment of insult. Part C of Figure 14–6 summarizes this form of repression.

Generalization (Displacement) of Repression

Repression is caused by conflict. A strong acquired fear drive competes with some unlearned drive like sex or anger. The neurotic is one who has acquired extremely strong avoidance tendencies that prevent him from approaching a variety of goals whose possession would cause him anxiety. Fear-reducing symptoms (e.g., Mrs. A.'s heart-beat counting) and fear-reducing repressions (verbal avoidance responses) eventually restrict the neurotic's capacity to undertake even the most mundane tasks. Inhibitions, anxiety, and misery are his lot.

On the basis of Miller's conflict theory, it might be supposed that the psychotherapist's task is relatively straightforward and simple. All the therapist has to do is to increase the neurotic's approach tendencies and decrease his avoidance tendencies by appropriate verbal interchange. In this way, the conflict underlying the neurotic's misery and symptoms will be reduced, he will be able to conduct his life more adaptively, and the need for repressions and avoidance responses will be reduced. Unfortunately, even these limited goals are unbelievably complex and difficult to achieve.

For one thing, anxiety is not limited to the particular drive or response to which it was originally attached. Anxiety may generalize to similar drives and to similar responses, ever widening the neurotic's focus of misery. Consider the graphic representation of Mrs. A.'s sex-fear conflict in Figure 14–7. It will be recalled that Mrs. A. had unusually strong sexual desires and that these had been coupled through learning with particularly strong anxiety and disgust responses. The broken line labeled "strong avoidance" indicates Mrs. A.'s frame of mind about sexual impulses before seeking therapeutic relief. Her approach tendencies, that is, her desire for sexual experiences, are indicated by the less steep approach gradient. It will be noted that the approach and avoidance gradients intersect at a point far from the feared goal. When the avoidance gradient is steep, as in Mrs. A.'s anxiety over sex, or in the case of rats given strong shock in the goal zone,

FIGURE 14-7: FEAR ELICITED BY WEAK AND STRONG AVOIDANCE GRADIENTS

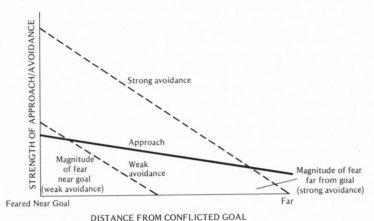

From Dollard and Miller, 1950, p. 361.

the avoidance gradient's point of intersection with the approach gradient will always be farther away from the goal than when it is less intense. Another fact about strong (or steep) avoidance gradients is obvious from Figure 14-7. The point of intersection with the approach gradient is not only far from the goal, but it is relatively low in intensity at that distance. If the gradient were less steep, the point of intersection would occur closer to the goal; *but it would also intensify the avoidance tendency.* Thus, paradoxically, a steep avoidance gradient assures that the person will remain "far" from the threatening goal, where the "dangerousness" of it is less intensely felt. A less steep avoidance gradient, crossing the approach gradient at a point closer to the dangerous goal, implies that the person will approach closer, but will feel the danger of the goal more acutely.

In terms of Mrs. A.'s conflict, if the therapist were successful in reducing the strength of her avoidance tendencies toward sex, he would paradoxically succeed in increasing her conflict and fear. She would more closely approach the conflicted goal by being more strongly tempted to do things that frighten her (Dollard & Miller, 1950, p. 361). The weak avoidance gradient in Figure 14-7 crosses the approach gradient at a point closer to the conflicted goal. It also crosses the approach gradient at a point of higher intensity.

Translated into the facts of Mrs. A.'s case, the reassuring and permissive attitude of her therapist initially reduced the amount of anxiety she experienced. She became more sexually responsive toward her husband and was even able to become a more assertive, aggressive person. But the nearer to these goals she became, the more she practiced her assertiveness and sexuality, the more she began to experience a resurgence of symptoms and fear.

Thus, as Figure 14-7 implies, for therapy to be successful the patient must be supported through the period of conflict intensification until the avoidance gradient can be lowered below that of the approach gradient. If this reduction can be achieved, the two gradients no longer intersect, and the patient can be expected to approach without fear the previously conflicted goals. In behavioral terms, this achievement means that avoidance responses like repression and symptom formation will no longer be necessary. Of course, these accomplishments depend upon the therapist's skill in helping the patient to unlearn fears and to learn new, more adaptive ways of dealing with his drives. There is a further complication in the fact that the neurotic personality is rarely conflicted over one drive, or over one set of incompatible responses. More typical is the case of multiple conflicts which conflict with each other.

If the conflicted response, say sexual intercourse, is strongly inhibited from occurring, it is reasonable to expect the next most similar response in the person's repertoire to replace it. Thus, Mrs. A. engaged in flirtations with truck drivers by hitchhiking rides with them. In effect, though she would not engage in intercourse, which she desired, she placed herself in situations in which she could "go through the motions" of seduction.

Miller and Kraeling (1952) were able to show that the steeper avoidance gradient in conflicts generalizes to new situations *less* than the approach gradient does. In Miller and Kraeling's experiment white rats were trained in a distinctively wide, white alley to approach food in the lit goal zone. Subsequently, each rat was given three trials in the same alley with electric shock administered in the place where food was to be found. The resulting approach-avoidance conflict was tested for generalization to a succession of alleys that differed in varying degrees from the training alley in appearance. First, animals were tested in the training alley without shock, and only 23 percent of them would now approach the food. When animals were tested in a second kind of alley that differed from the original to a moderate degree (painted gray), the number of rats who would approach the lit goal zone close enough to touch the food increased to 37 percent. In the final test, animals were placed in an alley that differed greatly from the original (narrow and painted black), and fully 70 percent of the rats approached the food closely enough to touch it. In other words, with increasingly different stimuli, the tendency to approach generalized more strongly than the tendency to avoid the goal. As the critical cues became more different, the animals apparently felt less afraid to approach the conflicted goal zone.

Stimulus Generalization as the Equivalent of Freud's Displacement

In matters directly concerning personality, the concepts of approach and avoidance gradients have to be translated from their physical distance referents into more psychologically meaningful terms. Thus, the distance a rat is willing to travel down an alleyway to approach food when fear-provoking cues are minimized can be converted in human terms to a gradient of generalization. Stimuli that are perceived as similar to desired goals may evoke from the conflicted person similar responses. It also follows from this line of reasoning that stimuli that are perceived as similar to feared goals will evoke similar avoidance responses. From the psychotherapist's point of view, these deductions resemble Freud's concept of displacement.

Freud had pointed out that when an instinct is frustrated, the person will seek an alternate, perhaps safer, target from which to obtain satisfaction. In devising the frustration-aggression hypothesis, as we have seen, the Yale group followed the same displacement principle to predict how a thwarted anger response will be redirected to a more available target when the prime target is out of reach or too dangerous.

Dollard and Miller (1950; see also Miller, 1960) applied exactly this reasoning to a further proposal about what happens in therapy when a patient's fears are moderately reduced. The paradoxical therapeutic effect of reducing Mrs. A.'s avoidance tendencies only to have her experience increased anxiety when she moved closer to the feared goal may be accompanied by yet another paradox. When the avoidance gradient is reduced (patient's fear lessened), she will generalize her responses to situations that are similar to the ones eliciting the conflict. This response generalization (displacement) phenomenon is analogous to the behavior of the rats in Miller and Kraeling's study. Removed to an alley that differed significantly from the one in which they had been shocked, these less fearful animals approached the food closely enough to touch it. They had generalized their approach responses more than their avoidance tendencies.

The reverse effect may be expected when the avoidance gradient is increased (made steeper): Generalization of responses to similar stimuli will be lessened. Or, put another way, *the individual will make his approach responses only to stimuli that are perceived as significantly different from the original conflicted goal.*

Figure 14-8 illustrates both of these displacement principles. Graph I in Figure 14-8 shows the point of strongest generalization of response with a weak conflict (moderately steep avoidance gradient). The point of strongest displacement (generalization) along an axis marked in arbitrary "dissimilarity" units instead of physical distance is at C. Point C evokes the strongest tendency to make an alternate response because the avoidance gradient (broken line) is at its lowest intensity at precisely this place. Note also that Point C is two dissimilarity steps removed from the original goal at Point A. The solid line in the graph represents the approach gradient or the response that is normally inhibited by the conflicting fear of the goal.

In Graph II of Figure 14-8, the avoidance gradient is steeper and consequently crosses the approach gradient at a point farther away from goal A. Therefore, the point of strongest displacement is also farther away from the original goal at A. In terms of the dimension of perceived "dissimilarity," the point of strongest displacement is now between C and D, where cues resembling the original goal have *less* similarity to it. That is

FIGURE 14-8:   DISPLACEMENT OF RESPONSES IN WEAK AND STRONG CONFLICTS

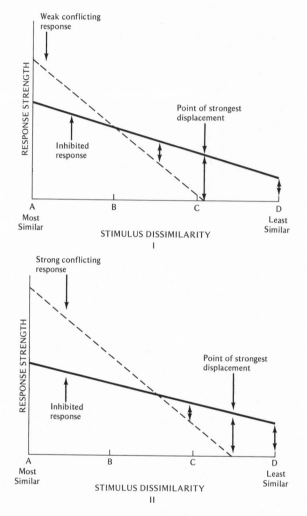

Note that the gradient of avoidance in Graph I is less steep than in Graph II. The point of greatest displacement of responses in Graph I is at C; but in Graph II the strongest point of displacement occurs at a point between C and D. A steeper gradient of avoidance, therefore, leads to displacement of responses to stimuli which are less similar to the original goal and stimuli.

From Miller, 1960.

to say, the person will displace his responses to goal objects that resemble the original feared goal significantly *less*—when the avoidance gradient is steep. Like the animals in the Kraeling and Miller experiment, the original alley where shock had actually been administered induced only 23 percent of the rats to approach the goal. But an alley that differed significantly from the original induced 70 percent of the animals to generalize their approach responses, for these animals apparently experienced a lessening of their fear in this less similar situation.

It can be deduced from these graphs that if the avoidance gradient were increased (made steeper), a point would be reached at which all generalization (displacement) of responses would be inhibited. Thus, increasing a patient's fears will decrease his tendency to make responses to similar feared objects. Conversely, decreasing a patient's fears (avoidance tendencies) will increase his tendency to displace inhibited responses onto similar situations or persons. In plainer terms, Mrs. A. will be motivated by the therapist's successful attempts to alleviate her anxiety to place herself even more frequently into seduction situations. Moreover, these seduction situations will elicit increased conflict because they will greatly resemble the original feared goal.

Paradoxically, therefore, a moderate decrease in Mrs. A.'s fears will increase the possibility of displacement of response to similar situations and persons. But of course the result is a vicious circle of mounting conflict and anxiety. The more her original fears are reduced, the more she succumbs to similarly fear-provoking stimuli. In certain cases, therefore, as in the case of the alcoholic who drinks to lessen his fears, therapy will be counterproductive if it merely reduces the fear enough to trigger a new round of similar anxieties. It may be of benefit, therefore, with certain patients for the therapist to increase the patient's awareness of realistic dangers in order to reduce the number of cues that can call forth his self-defeating responses (Miller, 1964).

It should be pointed out, however, that these paradoxical effects will hold as long as the decrease in the patient's anxiety is only moderate. Complete removal of the avoidance tendencies obviously removes the conflict altogether. The problem is to help the patient through the rough period of initially moderate lessening of anxiety until the underlying conflict can be completely resolved.

Conclusion: The Productivity of Miller and Dollard's Work

Only the part of Miller and Dollard's work that is directly relevant to personality theory has been surveyed. Neal Miller has continued to explore behavioral variables in the stimulus-response tradition by shifting his focus to the physiological level of analysis. His most recent work has been on instrumental conditioning of so-called involuntary responses like heart-beat rate, blood pressure, and urinary output (Miller & Carmona, 1967; Miller & DiCara, 1967, 1968a, 1968b; and Miller, 1975). This new line of work holds great promise as an adjunct therapeutic technique for cases of high blood pressure and intractable pain. Miller has been very cautious in promulgating his results because some difficulties have developed in replicating the early experiments. Concentrated effort by Miller and his colleagues at Rockefeller University to bring the phenomenon under more precise control is presently underway.

Miller and Dollard's social learning theory stands as a milestone in the history of stimulus-response psychology and, more broadly, as a turning point in the development of empirically sound psychological theory. Their work has demonstrated that social analysis can be combined with experimental method to yield precise predictions about the nature of personality.

We move next to a brief consideration of a somewhat different social learning approach to personality begun by Albert Bandura and Richard Walters, and carried forward in recent years by Bandura alone.

Bandura and Walters: Learning by Imitation

The lynching and mutilation of Arthur Stevens, it will be recalled, provided an example of how social analysis may be combined with psychological principles like drive reduction, frustration-aggression, and reinforcement to create a truly *social* learning theory. Miller and Dollard had focused attention on the unique properties of a crowd. They concluded that no individual would have enacted these vicious and inhumane crimes against Stevens. The mob, acting as a self-stimulating entity, increased the level of violence in each of its members, reinforced the escalation of successive atrocities, and promulgated the belief that no punishment would ensue. In short, the lynch mob had provided the classroom in which each of its students could learn from the others how best to satisfy his need to vent aggression.

With the publication of *Social Learning and Imitation* (1941), Miller and Dollard reintroduced into psychology a series of problems long neglected by specialists in learning theory. The concept that an organism may acquire or modify a response by watching another perform had not been given much attention by workers interested in Pavlovian conditioning or in instrumental learning. But Miller and Dollard's efforts to combine social and psychological principles into a unified theoretical framework forced some psychologists to reconsider the whole issue of learning by imitation. The prime implication of the drive, cue, response, reward model developed by Miller and Dollard was that imitation of another's actions is a *learned* motive. Miller (1976, pp. 170–171) has recently modified this early view to include the possibility that people and other primates have a strong *innate* motive to imitate the behavior of others. Therefore, the drive to imitate another's behavior may be a product of primate evolution; but in any case, the imitation response is modifiable through learning.

Types of Imitation Learning:
Same-Behavior, Matched-Dependent, Copying

The term imitation, as used by Miller and Dollard, is only a broad heading for three different kinds of behavior. The simplest form of apparent imitation is *same-behavior,* by which two independent individuals perform the same response to the same stimulus. Two individuals, for example, may board the same bus because both of them have read the destination marker indicating the bus's route (Miller & Dollard, 1941, p. 92). Similarly, two motorists driving parallel on the same street may stop simultaneously for a red light that they independently observe. *Same-behavior* clearly does not require one respondent to observe the responses of the other. Therefore same-behavior is not genuine imitation learning, but only mimics its appearance to the careless observer.

Copying is a true form of imitation, for the learner must match his responses to those of an observed model. The copier must have a crucial piece of knowledge: To what degree does his own behavior successfully reproduce the model's responses? Typically, the ability to copy is acquired with the help of an independent critic who rewards successful imitations and ignores or punishes mismatches. Miller and Dollard provide an example of copying in the case of a young man who was singularly awful at singing. Because his friends often engaged in group singing at parties, the man was particularly well motivated to learn how to participate without the usual complaints of "You're off key!" or "You sound terrible!" The only response that his friends consistently reinforced was that of ceasing to sing.

When offered help in the form of singing lessons, the man readily agreed. His "teacher" modeled the correct response by singing a note and requesting that the learner attempt to copy it. The model's note was thus a *cue* guiding the learner's responses. This young man proved to be a very poor imitator, but with a good deal of patience and some carefully worded criticisms, the copier gradually learned to match the model's notes. A combination of anxiety evoked by the teacher's verbal criticisms and the occasional harmonious sound of teacher and student singing the same note reinforced the gradual acquisition of the ability to "sing on key." Several performances with friends who generously praised his burgeoning skill strengthened the young man's motivation to increase his skill by copying the more proficient model. The important point is that constant knowledge of success and failure at matching the model's responses served to regulate the acquisition of this response.

The third kind of imitation learning is called *matched-dependent* learning. Matched-dependent behavior tends to arise in social situations where one person is older, more skilled, shrewder, or more experienced than another (Miller & Dollard, 1941, p. 92). In this case, the younger or less intelligent learner not only matches his behavior to that of the model, but is also dependent on the model's presence for knowledge of when or where to make the matching response. For example, two brothers, aged six and three, were playing in different parts of the house when the older child, Jim, heard the sound of his father coming home. Jim began running toward the kitchen to greet his father because he had detected the critical cue of his father's footfalls. The younger brother, Bobby, had not heard this cue, but happened to be running in the direction of the kitchen during the course of his play. Upon reaching the kitchen, the father greeted both boys with a surprise of candy. This reinforcement had rather different consequences for the two brothers. For Jim, it reinforced his response of attentiveness to cues signaling the return of his father. For Bobby, however, the candy reinforced his attentiveness to the actions of his brother.

On subsequent nights, Bobby ran to whatever part of the house he saw Jim running to, for matching Jim's behavior was proving to be a source of reward. Because their father now made it his custom to greet his running sons with some small token of affection, Bobby made it his business to follow Jim whenever Jim began to run. This matching response soon generalized to other situations, so that Bobby ran whenever he saw Jim run. Bobby had learned to imitate his brother, but not to detect the sound of his father coming home. Therefore, Bobby's behavior was dependent upon the cues provided by Jim.

Miller and Dollard analyze the matched-dependent behavior of Bobby with their customary drive, cue, response and reward model. From Bobby's point of view as imitator, the drive is an appetite for candy, the cue directing expression of the drive is the sight of Jim running, the response to be made to this cue is running in the same direction as Jim, and, of course, the reward is eating the candy (Miller & Dollard, 1941, p. 95).

From Jim's point of view as leader, the drive is, as for Bobby, an appetite for candy. But the critical cue for Jim is father's footfalls. Response and reward are, of course, the same as Bobby's: running and eating the candy, respectively. The difference between the imitator's learning and the leader's learning is in the cues that elicit the response. For Bobby, running to father for a reward is dependent upon Jim's detection of father's presence and Jim's response of running. The complete model of matched-dependent imitation is summarized in Figure 14-9.

Social Conditions Underlying Imitation

Miller and Dollard (1941) designed and executed several experimental studies with children in situations in which they were rewarded for imitating the behavior of a model. The details of these studies need not concern us; but their major conclusions concerning the conditions that affect learning by imitation are of some importance in the light of Bandura and Walters' subsequent work.

Miller and Dollard concluded that there are at least four types of models. The first type includes models who are superior by virtue of the status

FIGURE 14–9: MILLER AND DOLLARD'S MODEL OF MATCHED-DEPENDENT BEHAVIOR

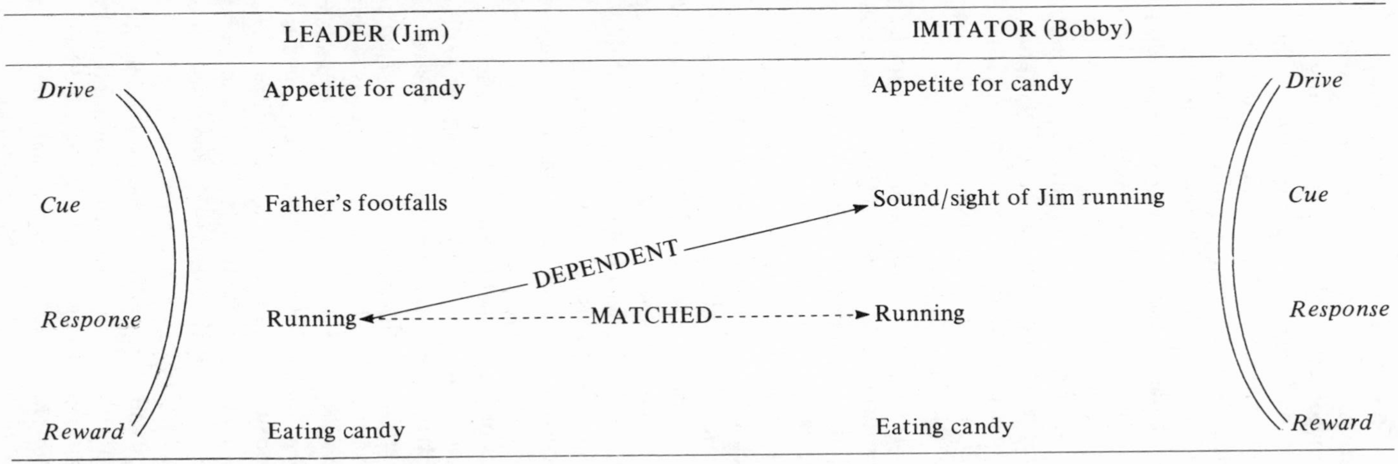

LEADER (Jim)   IMITATOR (Bobby)

Drive   Appetite for candy   Appetite for candy   *Drive*

Cue   Father's footfalls   Sound/sight of Jim running *Cue*

Response   Running   Running   *Response*

DEPENDENT ......MATCHED......

Reward   Eating candy   Eating candy   *Reward*

Modified from Miller & Dollard, 1941, p. 96.

they acquire through "age-grading." Culturally meaningful terms like *infant, child, adolescent, college student, grown man,* and *old man* are used to designate the kind of behavior that may be expected from the person so labeled. In effect, such age-grading constitutes a hierarchy of skill and prestige, for with increasing age, a person is usually accorded increased privilege and authority. Children rapidly learn to copy the behavior or dress of their older siblings or acquaintances because such behaviors are perceived by the child as the road to greater freedom or independence. Thus age-grade superiors are copied because they are cues to the rewarding effects of mature status.

The second class of persons who are likely to be imitated includes those individuals perceived to be superior in social status. For example, it is socially agreed that persons who use correct English, who are clean and well dressed, and who are self-controlled and polite are generally of superior social rank. The indefinable entity known as social class may be based on the acquisition of superior or more plentiful material goods. Wealth and power are easily discernible cues that greatly motivate the less socially powerful individual to imitate the behavior of those who possess these desirable attributes.

The third class of persons who are probable candidates for imitation are those individuals who appear to be especially intelligent or shrewd. As Miller and Dollard define intelligence, the trait indicates "the ability to read rapidly the environmental cues [that lead to reward], and to produce or improvise (by recombination of response units) adaptive responses to them" (1941, p. 193). The less intelligent, like Bobby in the matched-dependent example, fail to learn how to read environmental cues leading to success and reward. Like Bobby, they learn, instead, to copy the behavior of those who can.

The final class of persons who may serve as distinctive models are the technicians or specialists who have knowledge or skills by virtue of their special training that the nonspecialist does not possess. Scientists, doctors, plumbers, lawyers, psychologists, carpenters, and artists, among others, may serve as the layman's interpreter of reality within the area of the special skill. The layman is dependent on the specialist to indicate the adaptive response that is required under the special circumstances for which he has consulted this interpreter of reality.

Obviously, not each of these four types of models can be copied by all would-be imitators to the same degree. In the case of the socially superior, for example, an individual of low social status may provoke punishing consequences instead of rewarding ones by his imitation. His peers may accuse him of "putting on airs," or of "acting high and mighty." Another way punishment rather than reward may result from imitation is in the case of the less intellectually able person who tries to perform a difficult or dangerous response modeled by a person of superior intelligence. Shameful failure or physically punishing effects may dull the imitator's ardor. Miller and Dollard summarized their view of imitation in this way:

> The conditions of life of our own society, and perhaps of many others, conspire to reward an acquired drive to match and copy. Such a drive seems to be a common American attitude. It probably derives strength from the fact that doing the same as others is rewarded in a multitude of situations, whereas the perception of being different is a signal for punishment. In the course of the socialization of the child, he soon learns that the safest line of behavior is that which is being carried out, or can be carried out, by someone else of the same age-grade status. It is safe in one environment to shout "Wop!" at another child, or to fight the teacher, or to eat with one's knife, because age- and classmates are seen carrying out the same behavior. [1941, p. 200]

To be different from those one admires or has learned to feel safe with is a very strong inducement to anxiety. To reduce the unpleasant feeling, copying—or when that is not possible, matched-dependent responding— is the dominant mode of adaptation to life's circumstances.

Bandura and Walters' Concept of Imitation Learning

Unlike Miller and Dollard, the work of Bandura and Walters is not based on Hull's model of learning, and it owes even less to Freud's conception of disturbed behavior. The jumping-off point for Bandura and Walters' development of their own social learning theory was in fact a critique of Miller and Dollard's model. Bandura has acknowledged that Miller and Dollard's work was influential in capturing his interest in imitation learning, but he has also stressed that both he and Walters set out to expand the notion of imitative learning beyond the restrictions of the drive, cue, response, reward paradigm adopted by their predecessors (Bandura, 1969; 1971c, 1976).

Criticism of Miller and Dollard's Learning Theory

We have already seen that Bandura and Walters were critical of the Yale group's frustration-aggression formulation on the grounds that the aggressive response may be modified or increased through reinforcement. Bandura and Walters (1963) and, more recently, Bandura (1969, 1971c) have criticized Miller and Dollard's approach to imitation learning. In the Miller-Dollard model, the imitator must be motivated (drive arousal), must attend to relevant cues of the model's behavior, and he must be positively reinforced for correct responses during a series of trial-and-error attempts to match the model. In this theory the subject must perform the correct response before he can learn it, for only by successfully matching the model will he receive the same reinforcement.

Bandura and Walters (1963, p. 55) point out that their predecessors' theory does not account for cases of learning by imitation when the imitator *acquires* the model's response but does not *perform* it at the moment of acquisition. Miller and Dollard's theory puts a severe limitation on the range of behavioral changes that can be induced by a model. Thus, a child watching television may be learning how to talk like a cowboy, walk bowlegged like one, and to spit tobacco juice like his favorite western hero. But he *learns* how to make all these responses by merely observing the model perform, without himself performing or experiencing rewards for the performance of these responses until some time later when he plays cowboys and Indians with his friends. The responses have already been acquired; it is only their *performance* that remains to be shaped by social reward.

Another fundamental criticism advanced by Bandura and Walters was directed to the difficulty of making precise predictions about the targets of displaced responses from Miller's conflict model. In Miller's model, it will be recalled, displaced responses are thought to be made on the basis of the relative strengths of the approach and avoidance gradients, and the degree of similarity of a new situation to the conflicted goal. For example, Miller's model predicts that when a person is frustrated by a highly feared individual, he will displace his aggression onto a less threatening (less similar) person. Called "scapegoating," displacement of this sort is very difficult to predict with precision.

Bandura and Walters suggest that Miller's description of the similarity continuum lacks the precision to predict exactly who or what the scapegoat may be. Only an understanding of the conflicted individual's life circumstances can permit this foreknowledge. Bandura and Walters (1959), for example, had shown that boys who are highly aggressive outside the home tend to have parents who reprimand or strongly punish them for aggression enacted in the home. It is possible to interpret this finding as a case of aggression displaced from the parents onto less similar outsiders; but Bandura and Walters found that these same parents reward aggressive responding outside the home (see also Bandura, 1973). Thus "displacement" may actually be a case of *discrimination* learning. The aggressive boys have simply been taught by reward and punishment the places where aggression is most likely to produce approval. Consequently, these youngsters have merely learned to differentiate between stop and go signals rather than to displace aggression out of fear.

Bandura and Walters' criticism of Miller and Dollard's approach to social learning thus calls attention to the fact that their theoretical machinery underemphasizes the social variables:

> One reason for the inadequacy of Miller's displacement model is that it adopts a basically nonsocial approach to a problem in social learning. . . . The theory thus ignores the influence of the original agents of frustration and punishment in determining responses toward

stimulus objects other than themselves. In fact, *parents often through precept, example, and control of reinforcement contingencies determine rather precisely the kind of displaced responses that a child will or will not exhibit.* Displaced aggression is further modified by the responses it elicits from other socializing agents and from the objects of aggression themselves. *Miller's generalization gradients thus become relatively meaningless for a human-learning situation in which the patterns of reward-punishment contingencies displayed by parents and other agents of socialization have no consistent relationship to the similarity of the parents to possible objects of aggression.* [Bandura and Walters, 1963, pp. 19–20; italics added]

Bandura and Walters thus fault Miller and Dollard's learning theory on two counts: It does not account for the acquisition of modeled responses that are not immediately performed and rewarded; the conflict model fails properly to credit the impact of the individual's social environment. Overall, Bandura and Walters seem to feel that Miller and Dollard's theory is more appropriate to the animal laboratory than to human social interaction.

In a personal communication to the author, Neal Miller has pointed out that in some respects these criticisms are unfair because they largely neglect the modifications and additions to conflict theory that have been directed to the influences of prior learning. Specifically, Miller notes, Bandura and Walters falsely charge that his generalization gradients become "relatively meaningless" because, in their view, the conflict theory ignores the influences of agents of socialization and other sources of learned punishment. Miller continues:

In fact, with specific respect to displacement, in my 1948 [1960, in Miller, 1971] article on Theory and Experiment Relating Psychoanalytic Displacement to Stimulus Response Generalization, I say, "Experiments on discrimination show that the steepness of gradients of generalization can be modified by learning. If aggression against a scapegoat is not punished, this will extinguish the generalized inhibition and steepen the gradient. Similarly, if the expression of aggression against a scapegoat is rewarded, this will strengthen the generalized aggression and flatten the gradient. Under these conditions, the greater steepness of the gradient of inhibition could be the result of a learned discrimination. ..." [Personal communication, 1976]

Thus Miller feels that his work on conflict theory had already taken account of the influences on displacement of punishment and reward. Furthermore, Miller feels that Bandura and Walters' assertion that he and Dollard developed an essentially nonsocial approach to social phenomena simply ignores the facts:

Since we were the first ones to place heavy emphasis upon the *social conditions* of learning, it is a bit ironic that Bandura and Walters criticize us for having a theoretical machinery that underemphasizes the social variables. This is an example of the well-known technique of ignoring a part of a predecessor's work (and/or refusing to develop implications that are clearly inherent in it) in order to set up a straw man and then demolish him to make one's own contributions seem more original. [Miller, personal communication, 1976]

Criticism of Miller and Dollard's Psychoanalytic Assumptions

Miller and Dollard had attempted to translate Freudian psychoanalytic theory into stimulus-response equivalents. In most of these borrowings Miller and Dollard had to modify the original Freudian concept so that its observable referents could be manipulated experimentally. Yet, the underlying assumptions of Freudian theory with respect to the hidden sources of conflict, competing sexual and aggressive strivings that operate to produce symptoms, and the neurotic's disturbed behaviors as signs of more fundamental unconscious disorder remained at the heart of Miller and Dollard's work. Bandura and Walters, totally unsympathetic to psychoanalysis, rejected Freudian assumptions and the medical model of disease on which they were based:

> In accordance with [Freudian psychodynamic] models, behavior deviations are frequently considered to be derivatives or symptoms of underlying disease processes which disrupt social functioning in a manner analogous to that in which toxic substances affect the functioning of the body. This symptom-underlying disease analogy is reflected in the use of terms such as "mental health," "mental disease," and "emotional disorder," and in the labeling of persons exhibiting atypical behavior as "sick" and as "patients" and even of cultural and subcultural patterns as "sick," "healthy," and "unhealthy". . . . General medicine has progressed from the demonology that dominated it during the dark ages; as scientific knowledge has increased, magical explanations have been replaced by scientific ones. In contrast, theories of psychopathology in which demons reappear in the guise of "psychodynamic forces," still reflect the mystical thinking that once predominated in science (Reider, 1955). These demonic agents are typically "ego-alien," buried under layers of personality, and held in check by counter-agents or lines of defenses. [1963, pp. 29–30]

The psychodynamic model of behavior directs the psychologist's attention to inner causes of disturbed behavior. Internal agents like the ego and the id, dammed-up emotional energy, or systems like the unconscious are presumed to direct observable behaviors. But each of these internal agencies must itself be inferred from observable responses; no inner psychic agency can be directly observed.

In contrast, Bandura and Walters prefer a social learning theory that posits as causal agents relationships between observable responses and their environmental consequences. Inferences about the organism's internal states may, of course, be made; but predictions about behavioral change are devised on the basis of manipulable and observable stimulus conditions. Bandura has succinctly summarized the key difference between his social learning theory and psychodynamic theory:

> ... social-learning approaches treat internal processes as covert events that are manipulable and measurable. These mediating processes are extensively controlled by external stimulus events and in turn regulate overt responsiveness. By contrast, psychodynamic theories tend to regard internal events as relatively autonomous. These hypothetical causal agents generally bear only a tenuous relationship to external stimuli, or even to the "symptoms" that they supposedly produce. [1969, pp. 10–11]

Thus, while Bandura and Walters are willing to make inferences about the internal cognitive and emotional states of the individual, they see these internal conditions as directly under the influence of observable stimulus events. Internal states are not autonomous and not frozen in time as Freud had suggested.

To be fair, it should be pointed out that Miller and Dollard also attempted to modify Freudian theory so that only observable stimulus conditions would be postulated as the controlling agents of behavior. But, in the end, Miller and Dollard found it necessary to assume that neurotic conflict had its unconscious (nonverbal) determinants. Symptoms were traceable to early childhood critical learning experiences that had continued to operate relatively autonomously and isolated from change at the nonverbal level. Bandura and Walters preferred to conceptualize neurotic symptoms as products of past learning that are *currently* regulated, maintained or modified by ongoing environmental rewards and punishments (cf. Bandura, 1961, 1967, 1971c, 1974; Mischel, 1973).

The Range of Modeling Effects: Novel Responses, Disinhibition, Facilitation

In their 1963 collaboration, Bandura and Walters employed the terms *observational learning* and *imitation* as roughly equivalent. In more recent statements of the theory (Bandura, 1969, 1971a, 1971c), the term *modeling* has tended to replace the earlier terminology in order to avoid the restricted and simplistic meanings usually associated by the layman with imitation learning. The vast amount of experimental research connected with this theory has demonstrated at least three major forms of learning that may be induced through observation of a model.

The first kind of learning that may be acquired through observation of a model is the acquisition of patterns of behavior that did not previously exist in the learner's repertoire (Bandura and Walters, 1963, p. 60; Bandura, 1971a, p. 6). In his recent statement of social learning theory, Bandura refers to this phenomenon as the *observational learning effect.*

The second influence of modeling is to increase or decrease the intensity of a previously learned inhibition. These *inhibitory and disinhibitory effects* are usually the result of observing a model being rewarded or punished for some specific response. Thus a child may act aggressively, a response he had previously learned to inhibit, when he observes a model receive a reward for some specific aggressive response. The child is said to be disinhibited. The reverse, of course, can also be modeled, in which case the label inhibitory effect is appropriate.

Response facilitation effects constitute the third class of modeling influences. "People applaud when others clap; they look up when they see others gazing skyward; they adopt fads that others display; and in countless other situations their behavior is prompted and channeled by the actions of others" (Bandura, 1971a, p. 6). In response facilitation, no new responses are acquired and no previously inhibited behaviors are released from restraint. In many ways, response facilitation effects resemble what Dollard and Miller called "matched-dependent" behavior.

The acquisition of new patterns of behavior by observing a model was demonstrated by Bandura, Ross, and Ross (1963a) with nearly 100 children enrolled in the Stanford University Nursery School. Subjects were divided into various subgroups and one control group and then further divided into male and female categories within a group. Subjects assigned to the "Real-Life Aggressive" condition were taken to a room in which an adult model could be observed behaving aggressively toward an inflated Bobo doll. Using responses that were highly unlikely to be in the child's repertoire, the adult model sat on the Bobo doll, punched it repeatedly in the nose, pummeled it on the head with a mallet, and tossed it into the air, terminating the sequence by kicking the doll around the room. The entire sequence was repeated three times.

Subjects assigned to the "Human Film-Aggression" condition watched a color movie of the same models as in the real-life condition enacting the same sequence of aggression toward the Bobo doll. The key difference, of course, was the fact that these children were not exposed to living adult models.

Subjects assigned to the "Cartoon Film-Aggression" condition watched a different film, in which the model wore a cat costume, cavorted in a specially designed setting, and aggressed toward the Bobo doll in a manner identical to the actions of the models in the other two conditions. Following exposure to one of these conditions, children were taken to another room containing some very attractive toys. After allowing the children to play with the toys briefly, the experimenter explained that "these were her very best toys" and she had decided to reserve them for other children. This mild frustration was sufficient to instigate aggression when these children were removed to another room containing new toys, some of which were conducive to aggressive play. A mallet, a three-foot Bobo doll, two dart guns, and a tether ball were among the items to be found in the experimental room.

Results showed that children exposed to aggressive models, whether on film or in real-life conditions, significantly increased their aggressive responding compared to control subjects. However, a slight difference in the total amount of aggression was found between subjects who were exposed to the real-life model and those who watched the cartoon model. Real-life models induced a slightly greater number of aggressive responses from their observers. Sex differences were also found. Boys exhibited significantly more aggression than girls across conditions, more precisely imitative aggressive responses than girls, and more nonimitative aggressive behavior. The sex of the model also influenced the aggression of the observers. Male models induced more aggression from both boys and girls; and male models with male observers induced the highest level of imitative aggression overall.

The disinhibitory effects of modeling were also demonstrated in the Bandura, Ross, and Ross (1963a) study in the extra-aggressive responses of boys who not only performed the exact behaviors of the model, but added several novel aggressive responses of their own. The effect of the aggressive model was thus not only to shape a particular pattern of aggressive activity, but to release from normal restraint a whole host of other aggressive behaviors. Bandura and Walters (1959) also obtained interview data from adolescent boys that suggest disinhibition may affect sexual responses. These boys reported that they were more likely to engage in sexual intercourse during a double or triple dating evening than if they were alone with their own date. It can be assumed that inhibitions are progressively lessened as boys watch one another in sexual play with their dates.

Response facilitation effects of modeling may be demonstrated in a number of ways in which one person imitates the actions of another out of curiosity or to receive a reward similar to the model's. A high-prestige model like the president of the United States is shown on television visiting a church on Sunday. Admirers of the president soon follow his lead. Most street beggars know that it is a wise policy to have a dollar bill or two in the pot to suggest to passersby the magnitude of other people's generosity. Charity telethons on television are often conducted in such a way that the continually rising total of contributions is frequently brought to viewers' attention on the premise that they, too, will feel the urgings of their charitable selves.

Clearly the range of behavioral change that can be induced by modeling is very broad. This brief survey merely touches on the vast literature that has arisen surrounding the ways in which modeling affects behavior. The obvious question of *how* modeling exerts its effects will occupy us next.

The Determinants of Learning through Modeling

Bandura and Walters (1963) and more recently Bandura (1969, 1971c) have summarized the variables that govern modeling phenomena. The basic assumption of Bandura and Walters' social learning theory is that the observer acquires from the model chiefly symbolic representations of the behaviors demonstrated, not stimulus-response connections. Thus Bandura and Walters focus their attention on the uniquely human capacity to form cognitive images, ideas, and judgments about the stimuli they observe. Unlike previous stimulus-response theories of learning, Bandura and Walters' theory attempts to correct the myopic view of the typical psychological textbook account of human learning by allowing for the human's capacity to become aware and to interpret the reality of which he is a part. Bandura made the point well:

> The marked discrepancy between textbook and social reality is largely attributable to the fact that certain critical conditions present in natural situations are rarely, if ever, reproduced in laboratory studies of learning. In laboratory investigations experimenters arrange comparatively benign environments in which errors do not create fatal consequences for the organism. By contrast, natural environments are loaded with potentially lethal consequences for those unfortunate enough to perform hazardous errors. For this reason it would be exceedingly injudicious to rely on differential reinforcement of trial-and-error performances in teaching children to swim, adolescents to drive automobiles, medical students to conduct surgical operations, or adults to develop complex occupational and social competencies. Had experimental situations been made more realistic so that animals toiling in Skinner boxes and various mazes were drowned, electrocuted, dismembered, or extensively bruised for the errors that invariably occur during early phases of unguided learning, the limitations of instrumental conditioning would have been forcefully revealed. [Bandura, 1971a, pp. 2–3]

The most complex human behaviors are learned not through trial and error, but through verbal transmission of information and through observation of a skilled model. Thus, a surgical resident does not continuously perform surgical procedures on patients until he gets one right; he observes and receives information from his teachers about the nature of surgery until, with constant supervision and criticism, he participates in a small way in several surgical procedures. The major processes in this kind of learning through modeling may be divided into four categories: *attention, retention, reproduction,* and *motivation.*

Attentional Processes: Knowing Who and What to Observe

Mere exposure to a model does not assure learning. The learner must attentively observe the relevant events in the total modeling situation and accurately perceive those cues to which his attention has been directed (Bandura, 1969; 1971c). The variables that control whether the observer will be attentive to the model include the distinctiveness of the model, the psychological and motivational state of the learner, the likability of the model, the observers' past history of reinforcements for attending to similar models, and the complexity of the modeled events.

Retention Processes: Long-Term Memory for What Was Observed

Without the capacity to recall what the model did, the observer is unlikely to demonstrate any behavioral change. The model's responses must be coded into some symbolic form (e.g., words) that may later be recalled to duplicate the performance. Once the modeled event has been coded into symbols (words or images), it may be covertly rehearsed to strengthen retention of the performance.

Reproduction Processes: Using Memory to Guide Imitation

The symbolically coded memories may now be employed to guide an actual performance by the learner. A person learning to dance may, for example, silently recite "One—two—three" to keep rhythm with the music. Or he may actually recite to himself the exact pattern of steps he wishes to execute: "One foot out, one foot forward, then back. . . ." Obviously, even if the learner has correctly acquired and retained the symbolic representation of the dance he desires to do, he may not be a skillful performer. He may be physically handicapped, or be unable to observe himself make errors, or his partner may be too polite to point out that, although he has all the right moves, he makes them like a Sherman tank.

Thus, physical ability, self-observation, and feedback are essential guiding processes.

Motivational Processes: Rewards and Punishments for Performance

Even if a person acquires and retains the modeled performance, he himself will rarely translate it into actual behavior if the consequences of such translation are punishing. Thus, our dancer friend may find that executing what he has learned leads to ridicule on the dance floor, and he resumes his life as a wallflower.

Reinforcement may also operate a step farther back in the learning sequence. Prior reinforcements, or reinforcements that the model receives, may determine the cues to which the learner will direct his attention.

In Bandura and Walters' theory, reinforcement may operate directly on the learner's behavior, as in the case of the dancer who is punished for poor performance. But reinforcement may also operate vicariously: What the learner observes happening to the model will affect his own performance. Most people have had the experience of attending a live stage performance and observing one of the actors forget his lines. People in the audience begin to experience the anxiety and tension that the actor himself is feeling. It is said that we identify with the actor's plight, for we feel emotions that are appropriate to him. Vicariously (literally: "in place of another") we experience what stage performers call "flop sweat."

Vicarious Reinforcement: Identification with the Model

It was part of Freud's theory that sexual identification of the boy with his father involved the boy's perception of the father as a more powerful person than himself. The boy sees the father possess the mother, and because of his own rivalrous desires, he both envies and fears the father. Ultimately, in the attempt to resolve the conflict, the boy resolves his Oedipus complex by becoming more like the father, by taking on some of the father's characteristics. In Bandura's terms, the child is said to have identified with the model. Thus, in Bandura's view, Freud's explanation of learning by imitation hinges on "status envy." Actually this extension of Freud's ideas was developed by Whiting (1959, 1960).

Bandura, Ross, and Ross (1963b) set out to test this explanation of learning-by-identifying with the model's rewards, along with two other explanations of identification. One of these, the social power theory (Macoby, 1959, Parsons, 1955), assumes that a child identifies with an adult because he is the controller of desirable resources rather than the consumer of them. The other theory of identification tested by Bandura, Ross, and Ross is the secondary reinforcement theory (Mowrer, 1950), which asserts that adult models are the mediators of the child's biological and social rewards. Because the model is repeatedly paired with acquisition of positive rewards, the model attains status as a secondary reinforcer in his own right. Through stimulus generalization, responses that are similar to those of the model are likely to be adopted by the child so that he can administer positive reinforcers to himself.

Thus, in the Bandura, Ross, and Ross (1963b) investigation, the question of which of these explanations of identification with a model is correct resolves itself into three possibilities: (1) the child identifies only with the *consumer* of desirable goods (status envy theory); (2) the child identifies only with the adult *controller* of desirable goods (social power theory); (3) the child identifies with the adult who *dispenses* desirable goods (secondary reinforcement theory).

Bandura, Ross, and Ross (1963b) set up two kinds of three-person experimental groups representing the nuclear family constellation. In the first group, an adult assumed the role of controller of resources, another adult was the recipient of the resources, and the child was essentially ignored. In the second group, an adult controlled the resources, but the child was the recipient. The other adult in this triad assumed a powerless, subordinate role. Within each of these experimental conditions, the sex of the adult model who controlled the rewards was varied, simulating either the male-dominated home or the female-dominated home. Following the dispensing of rewards, the two adult models in each group performed a complex series of responses designed to determine which of the adults the child would imitate.

During a twenty-minute play session, the child or adult who was the consumer was offered by the adult controller a variety of attractive toys, including pinball machines, mechanical sparkling toys, dolls, and drinks from a toy soda-fountain dispenser. After this social interaction session, a surprise game was announced. Each adult in the group modeled various responses in playing a two-box discrimination game. Two small boxes with hinged lids, identical in color and size, were placed on stools four feet apart and eight feet from the starting line. The lid of each box held a rubber doll. The controller explained that a sticker–picture would be hidden in one of the two boxes and the object of the game was to guess which box. The adults were to have the first turns.

From a rack of hats, the controller then selected his "thinking cap," a green-feathered sailor cap. He remarked aloud "Feather in front," and, of course, wore the feather facing forward. The other adult model selected a yellow-feathered cap, commenting, "Feather in the back." The child then made his own choice of hats, and it was carefully noted whether he matched his selection to the controller's or to the other adult's.

The game involved each adult's exhibiting a novel set of verbal and motor responses in "guessing" the box in which the sticker–picture had been hidden. Thus, for example, the controller marched slowly toward the boxes repeating, "March, march, march." Reaching the boxes, he said "Sock him," whereupon he hit the rubber doll aggressively off the box lid. Of course he had chosen the correct box, and as he reached in to obtain the sticker he said, "Lickit-sticket." The other adult model performed an equally bizarre set of responses; when, for example, she started toward the box, she said, "Get set, go," walking stiffly all the while. Upon finding the sticker, she exclaimed: "A stickeroo," and "Wetto-smacko." Each model performed on four alternate trials to allow the children to become familiar with each adult's routine. Then the children were allowed to play the game and three independent raters scored their responses in terms of the number of imitative elements of posture and speech each child demonstrated.

Bandura, Ross, and Ross's results overwhelmingly support the social power theory of identification. In both experimental groups, regardless of whether the adult or the child received the rewards, the children more often identified with (imitated) the controller of the resources. Interestingly, in the experimental condition in which the recipient was the adult, the experimenters had introduced an element of competition. After the social interaction session in which the child was ignored and the adult received the rewards, the controller informed this adult consumer that he was taking a trip to San Francisco and would gladly buy the adult anything she would like. The consumer adult requested an expensive two-wheel bicycle, and the controller promised to obtain it. Even in this competitive, frustrating situation, the child imitated the controller more frequently than the recipient of such lavish rewards. The extension of Freud's identification theory thus received a telling rebuttal because the children failed to identify with the consuming adult whose status was presumably enviable.

Secondary reinforcement theory, however, did receive some support. Children did not identify exclusively with the controller; in some cases, children adopted a few elements of behavior of the adult who assumed a subordinate role in the experimental groups where the child was the recipient. The highest preference for the noncontrolling adult was found in those cases where the ignored adult was the male and the recipient child was also a male. Yet, even for girls, the occasional tendency to identify with the ignored adult was greater when that adult was a male. Children apparently learn the reinforcing effects of the male role in society at large, and adoption of the male's behaviors is preferred because of this secondary association with his observed rewards outside the experimental situation.

Conditions Governing Vicarious Reinforcement

Vicarious positive reinforcement (or vicarious punishment) is merely a statement of the observed effects of seeing a model rewarded or punished. *How* vicarious reward and punishment operate to suppress or instigate behavior in the observer is a more profound question.

Bandura (1971a, 1971c) has proposed six mechanisms that regulate the effects of observed reward and punishment. The first possibility is that observation of the model's rewards and punishments serves an *informative function*. The observational learner discovers through the model's consequences how to do things that will be rewarded and to avoid things that will evoke punishment. The informative function of the model's behavioral consequences is thus similar to what Miller and Dollard term a cue.

The second mechanism that may be involved in vicarious reinforcement is *incentive motivational effects.* "Seeing others reinforced can function as a motivator by arousing in observers expectations that they will be similarly rewarded for analogous performances" (Bandura, 1971c, p. 26). Thus, individuals not only learn what leads to punishment and reward, but the model's successes may arouse in them an expectancy or a desire to obtain those rewards.

The third mechanism by which vicarious reinforcement may function also involves *emotional arousal,* but in this case the arousal refers to a general heightening of responsiveness. Observations of a model being punished arouse fright; the fear, in turn, suppresses not only the specific responses the model made, but also all responding of the observer. He turns his attention elsewhere or attempts to escape the situation.

The fourth mechanism may be thought of as vicarious reinforcement's power to *increase the observer's susceptibility to direct reinforcements.* In effect, observation of the model's pattern of rewards and punishments may increase the observer's accuracy of imitation in order to later obtain actual reinforcements in a situation similar to the model's.

Fifth, when a model is reinforced for some behavior, his social status may be increased; likewise, when the model is punished his social status may be decreased. Thus, *modification of social status* may be an additional cue provided by watching a model rewarded and punished.

Sixth, and last, reinforcements applied to the model may reflect on the reinforcer. *Valuation of the reinforcing agents* may be altered when they are perceived as abusing their power, or employing it beneficently. Thus, an observer may be provoked to aggressiveness by watching what he believes is an unjust application of punishment to a model.

Application of Vicarious Reinforcement to Neurotic Behavior

Modeling may be an especially effective means of eliminating unreasonable fears during the course of psychotherapy (Bandura, 1965a, 1971b). In fact, modeling may be most useful where neither operant shaping techniques nor Pavlovian conditioning is feasible. As Bandura (1965b, p. 339) points out, most applications of learning theory to psychotherapy involve a conceptualization of the therapist as a source of reinforcements. Bandura and Walters, and most recently Bandura alone, have turned their attention

to the possibility of therapeutic models as the source of behavioral repertoires.

Bandura, Blanchard, and Ritter (1969) used a specially adapted modeling procedure to aid a group of people with a strong phobia for snakes.
Some of the participants in this research project were so phobic for snakes
that they were unable to perform their jobs in situations where even the
most remote possibility existed that contact with a snake might occur.
Other participants were restricted from leisure activities like hiking and
camping, or from purchasing homes in rural areas.

One group of subjects was given exposure to filmed models engaging
in successively more threatening activities with snakes. Two other behavioral procedures were simultaneously employed. First, participants were
taught deep muscle relaxation exercises and other anxiety-neutralizing
techniques to employ while watching the filmed models. Second, each
participant was given complete control over the rate at which the scenes
in the film were presented. By remote control the projector could be
stopped or reversed, and subjects were instructed to make use of the
control whenever the filmed sequence became too anxiety-provoking to
bear. Subjects thus viewed a threatening scene repeatedly until it had been
completely neutralized.

A second group of subjects received a somewhat different treatment
procedure involving the use of live models and gradual active participation. For example, the therapist (model) performed feared responses with
a snake, slowly guiding the subject to pet, stroke, and hold the snake's
body with a gloved hand. As the subject became less fearful, the therapist
gradually reduced his participation. Subjects thus gradually assumed complete control over the snake and were even able to let it loose in the room
or to allow it to roam over their bodies.

A third group of subjects were given another form of behavioral psychotherapy that did not involve modeling at all. In this procedure, called
systematic desensitization (Wolpe, 1958, 1973), mental images of the feared
stimuli are paired with incompatible relaxation exercises until the most
feared *thought* can be tolerated without anxiety.

One of the assessment measures employed after the various forms of
treatment were completed involved the subjects' approaching, looking,
touching, and holding live snakes to within five inches of their faces.
Subjects given either the filmed modeling treatment or systematic desensitization showed considerable improvement over their own pretreatment
responses, as shown in Figure 14–10. But, most important, subjects who
had participated in the live modeling procedure demonstrated almost total
neutralization of snake phobia. Nearly every subject (92 percent) in this
condition was able to approach and handle closely a live snake.

The modeling procedures also effected substantial changes in the subjects' attitudes toward snakes. Both the film-mediated modeling groups
and the desensitization groups showed a change in attitude in the favor-

FIGURE 14-10: COMPARISON OF METHODS OF TREATMENT FOR SNAKE PHOBIA

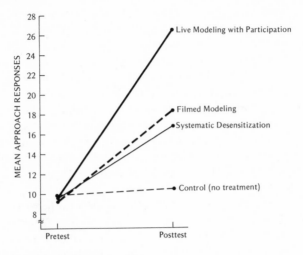

From Bandura, Blanchard, and Ritter, 1969.

able direction toward snakes over their own pretreatment attitude measures. The live-modeling subjects again showed the greatest improvement in attitude.

Thus modeling may be used to extinguish fear responses vicariously, as in the case of the subjects who viewed the film. Additionally, live modeling with participation by the subjects not only extinguished their fears, but taught them a series of responses for dealing with real snakes that had not existed in their imaginations or in their behavioral repertoires.

Conclusion: The Social Learning Viewpoint

It is impossible to capture within the scope of this chapter all of the diverse elements and laboratory investigations that constitute Bandura and Walters' social learning theory. Unlike Miller and Dollard's formulation, Bandura and Walters draw exclusively upon a series of empirical studies, and general principles or deductive strategies are uncommon.

Bandura and Walters share another difference from Miller and Dollard in their view of how human personality evolves within the individual. The actor-and-mask analogy would find great disfavor with Bandura and Walters, for these investigators are convinced that the actor's behavior is the actor. While they are not unwilling to make inferences about the person's internal cognitive states, they adamantly refuse to make these inferential variables into a class of personality phenomena apart from the behavior that they instigate.

Summary

Miller and Dollard attempted to combine the principles of social analysis of behavior with principles of learning drawn from the animal laboratory. Adopting a drive, cue, response, reward model of learning from Clark Hull, and a psychodynamic sexual and aggressive-drive theory from Freud, Miller and Dollard and their colleagues at Yale were able to develop and test a series of intriguing stimulus-response hypotheses.

The lynching of Arthur Stevens illustrated Miller and Dollard's social learning theory application of laboratory learning principles. Driven by fear of economic and sexual competition, directed by the cues of Stevens' skin color and alleged heinous crimes against a white girl, the lynch mob responded with unspeakable violence in an attempt to reduce these unpleasant drives.

The notion that thwarted drives lead to aggression had been suggested by Freud and by Floyd Allport, in different contexts. The Yale group of Dollard, Miller, Mowrer, Doob and Sears developed an S-R equivalent, the frustration-aggression hypothesis. Though initially stated in its most extreme form, the Yale group eventually moderated its statement to include the possibility that frustration may arouse other than directly aggressive consequences. In a similar way, conflicting evidence forced Miller to restate the drive-reduction hypothesis of reinforcement.

Miller and Dollard's analysis of neurotic behavior drew heavily on Miller's conflict theory and on Freud's concepts of displacement, repression, and the unconscious. In a series of fruitful experiments with rats, Miller translated Freudian theory into observable responses of approach and avoidance to positively and negatively reinforced goals. He was able to show that with a few basic assumptions about the strength of these tendencies, a whole range of personality phenomena could be deduced. The explanation hinged on his earlier demonstration that the drive of fear could be acquired or learned by instrumental conditioning procedures. Thus, acquired fear drives connected to critical social learning experiences in childhood were postulated as the basis of later adult neurosis.

The critical childhood experiences in which fear could be attached to spontaneous impulses included feeding, cleanliness care, the expression of anger, and sex training. Because the fear attached to cues in these situations tends to be acquired before the development of language, symbolic coding is not possible. Such fears then may operate unconsciously (nonverbally) through to adulthood. Adult neurotic symptoms, therefore, are learned responses for coping with intensely experienced anxieties whose origin is forgotten (repressed).

Bandura and Walters, unlike Miller and Dollard, eschew psychodynamic theories of personality and abnormal behavior. Beginning with a critique of Miller and Dollard's theory, Bandura and Walters developed their own social learning theory, with the emphasis on the acquisition of responses through modeling. They point out that nearly the whole range of learned behaviors can be acquired or modified through observational learning. Observational learning involves four basic processes: attention to the model, retention of the relevant model cues, reproduction of the model's performance, and motivational incentive to perform (reinforcement).

In Bandura and Walter's theory, reinforcement may be direct or it may be vicarious. Vicarious reinforcement means that the imitator feels the effects of the model's rewards and punishments, and modifies his own performance accordingly.

With the death of Richard Walters, Bandura has gone on to restate and elaborate their theory of social learning. Applications to psychotherapy, investigations of modeled aggression, and tests of competing theories of model-identification have been performed by Bandura and his colleagues at Stanford University. Basing their work on established empirical laboratory principles, Bandura and his coworkers have struggled to extend behavior theory beyond its stimulus-response-reinforcement boundaries to encompass what is truly human about human beings: their capacity to interpret reality and to be aware of themselves as interpreters.

FOR FURTHER READING

The essence of Dollard and Miller's social learning theory may be obtained from two very readable books: *Social Learning and Imitation* (New Haven, Conn.: Yale University Press, 1941, with Miller as senior author) and *Personality and Psychotherapy* (New York: McGraw-Hill, 1950, with Dollard as senior author). The first of these publications contains their work on imitation learning, whereas the latter book emphasizes stimulus-response principles in application to neurosis and psychotherapy.

Much of Neal Miller's experimental work and theorizing has been collected into the one-volume *Neal Miller: Selected Papers on Conflict, Displacement, Learned Drives and Theory* (Chicago: Aldine-Atherton, 1971; also available in a two-volume paperback edition). Miller's definitive summary of stimulus-response theory is contained in "Liberalization of Basic S-R Concepts: Extensions to Conflict Behavior, Motivation, and Social Learning," in S. Koch (Ed.), *Psychology: A Study of a Science* (New York: McGraw-Hill, 1959), Study I, vol. 2.

Miller's more recent physiological work on the instrumental conditioning of "involuntary" responses is concisely summarized in "Applications of Learning and Biofeedback to Psychiatry and Medicine," in A. M. Freeman, H. I. Kaplan, and B. J. Sadock (Eds.), *Comprehensive Textbook of Psychiatry, II* (Baltimore: Williams and Wilkins, 1975). An interview with Neal Miller, in which he reassesses his and Dollard's contribution to the field, is to be had in R. I. Evans' *The Making of Psychology* (New York: Knopf, 1976).

Leonard Berkowitz's volume *Roots of Aggression: A Re-Examination of the Frustration-Aggression Hypothesis* (New York: Atherton, 1969) amply fulfills the promise of its title.

Bandura and Walters' social learning theory has undergone much expansion and modification since the publication of their initial monograph, *Social Learning and Personality Development* (New York: Holt, Rinehart & Winston, 1963). The scope of these changes and expansions can be gleaned from Bandura's relatively brief module *Social Learning Theory* (Morristown, N.J.: General Learning Press, 1971) and from his comprehensive survey of experimental literature, *Principles of Behavior Modification* (New York: Holt, Rinehart & Winston, 1969).

Extensions of Bandura's social learning theory to psychotherapy can be surveyed from his brief "Behavioral Psychotherapy," *Scientific American* (March, 1967) or from the more comprehensive literature review in "Psychotherapy Based upon Modeling Principles," in E. Bergin and S. L. Garfield (Eds.), *Handbook of Psychotherapy Research* (New York: Wiley, 1971).

An interview with Bandura, in which he discusses his debt to Miller and Dollard, may be read in R. I. Evans' *The Making of Psychology* (New York: Knopf, 1976). Bandura's analysis of the human propensity for aggression and the variables that control its expression (e.g., television) may be found in his *Aggression: A Social Learning Analysis* (Englewood Cliffs, N.J.: Prentice-Hall, 1973). An earlier analysis of adolescent aggression by Bandura and Walters may be of interest for comparison purposes: *Adolescent Aggression* (New York: Ronald Press, 1959).

The comparison between the philosophies of radical behaviorists, such as B. F. Skinner, and the men considered in this chapter can be instructive. Skinner's *About Behaviorism* (New York: Knopf, 1974) or his article, "The Steep and Thorny Way to a Science of Behavior," *American Psychologist* (1975), **30**, 42–49, can be contrasted with any of the works cited above.

15 HANS EYSENCK
Biological S-R Theory

Most people of course, whatever they may say, do not in fact want a scientific account of human nature and personality at all. . . . Hence they much prefer the great story-teller, S. Freud, or the brilliant myth-creator, C. G. Jung, to those who, like Cattell or Guilford, expect them to learn matrix algebra, study physiological details of the nervous system, and actually carry out experiments, rather than rely on interesting anecdotes, sex-ridden case histories, and ingenious speculation.

HANS EYSENCK, *Psychology Is About People*

Behaviorist as Irritant, as Scientist, as Philosopher

When the young Hans Eysenck, freshly graduated from the University of London, obtained his first job as research psychologist in the wartime Mill Hill Emergency Hospital, he proceeded to alienate, shock, and generally embarrass his immediate superiors. The Mill Hill Hospital received war casualties who had succumbed to a variety of mental disturbances. Eysenck was curious to discover the reliability of the psychiatric diagnoses by which incoming airmen and soldiers were classified. If two or more psychiatrists examined the same patient, would their diagnoses agree? Furthermore, if they did agree, would the prescribed treatments correspond? It seemed to Eysenck a simple matter to decide because all a research psychologist had to do was collect a sample of cases and perform the necessary statistical correlations. Eysenck's account of what transpired in the office of the Hospital Superintendent when he attempted to solicit permission to carry out this piece of research is quite revealing:

> [The Superintendent] received me in a fatherly fashion, and listened patiently to my plan. Then, to my surprise, he suggested that there were so many more interesting things that could be done, it would be a pity to waste my time in this fashion. After all, did not everyone know that these psychiatrists had been well-trained, had medical degrees, and could therefore (almost by definition) do no wrong? When I cheerfully suggested that even such supermen might welcome definitive proof of the reliability of their judgments he became

more serious. . . . And when I answered that I was not throwing doubt on anything or anybody, but just wanted to know with some precision how accurate these difficult and complex judgments could be, he told me in no uncertain terms that I was at liberty to collect these data, but I was also at liberty to look for another job. This argument seemed a winner, and I acknowledged its superior force by withdrawing from the unequal contest. I did, to be sure, collect my data but kept rather quiet about it. [1972, pp. 357–358]

Eysenck's apparently innocent desire "to know with some precision" whether traditionally accepted ideas were sound is rather characteristic of his entire approach to personality. His surreptitious research into psychiatric diagnoses, incidentally, showed such professional judgments to have very little similarity from one psychiatrist to another—even when the second psychiatrist already knew of the first psychiatrist's diagnosis. But, of course, that finding held no surprise for Eysenck.

Eysenck's philosophical position may be described as a commitment to the *hypothetico-deductive* method of classical physics (1952, p. 16; 1957a, p. 264). Beginning with basic observational data, the scientist who employs this method formulates a hypothesis or tentative explanation of the events he has observed. Controlled conditions are then established to test the validity of his hypothesis. To devise precisely the right kind of experimental situation to test the hypothesis requires that the scientist deduce the logical, preferably quantitative, implications of his prediction.

Although a given hypothesis is derived logically from an initial set of uncontrolled observations, conclusions are never accepted solely on the basis of logic. The final criterion of acceptability for any conclusion is whether it conforms to the new observations made under the controlled conditions of the experimental test situation.

The hypothetico-deductive strategy really comes into its own when the predictions or deductions from the original observations involve the proposal of new, heretofore unexpected, propositions. To some extent these kinds of hypotheses transcend what could have been predicted on the basis of common sense. It is to this more surprising and exciting kind of prediction that Eysenck's personality formulations are directed.

As a behaviorist concerned with the measurable, quantitative aspects of personality, Eysenck has frequently criticized what he considers to be less empirical, less factual, and less scientific approaches to personality investigation. One of the chief targets of his critical attacks has been Freudian psychoanalysis, which he regards as primarily fictional and, at best, untestable (Eysenck, 1953a, 1957b, 1960, 1963b, 1965; Eysenck & Wilson, 1973; cf. Rachman, 1963, and Eysenck & Rachman, 1965). For Eysenck, the most important aspects of any psychological formulation are that it be empirical, observationally testable, and a fertile source of new hypotheses (Eysenck, 1957a, pp. 250 ff.). His own efforts are exemplary in all these qualities.

Early Descriptive Researches:
Introversion-Extroversion and Neuroticism

Despite the criticism and the occasional open incredulity of the psychiatric profession, Eysenck pursued his elusive quarry of an empirical, experimentally based model of personality. One of his earliest studies involved the administration of a large number of personality, psychomotor, and performance tests to a sizable sample of neurotic and normal airmen and soldiers (Eysenck, 1947). In a kind of dragnet approach to personality assessment, Eysenck and his colleagues gathered a huge quantity of statistical data on nearly ten thousand subjects. The resulting mass of information was factor analyzed. Factor analysis allows the researcher to correlate a group of individuals' scores on one measure with their scores on all other measures to arrive at a more limited number of factors that embody clusters of the original measurements. The clusters of associated variables that emerge from the correlation matrix are sometimes suggestive of personality trends or dimensions. Procedures for extraction of the factors are mathematically complex and need not concern us here.

What is important about Eysenck's elaborate measurement procedures in the present context is that the collection of data was undertaken to test a particular personality hypothesis.

Jung's Typology and Dimensional Hypothesis

It will be recalled from Chapter 4 that Carl Jung, having broken with Freud, established his own analytic theory of personality. As part of his system, Jung proposed a *typological model* of personality organized around the attitude types of introversion and extroversion, and subdivided according to functional type. In addition, Jung had proposed that the two fundamental attitude types, introversion and extroversion, were associated with different forms of mental illness.

The introvert, in Jung's view, when and if he succumbs to a mental illness, will likely suffer from *psychasthenia* (Jung 1921, p. 379). Psychasthenia was the classical psychiatric label for a syndrome characterized by extreme nervousness, anxiety, and fatigue. Today, psychasthenia would include more specific diagnoses of *phobia* (*irrational* fears of persons, places, things), or *obsessive-compulsive neurosis* (intrusion into consciousness of threatening sexual and aggressive ideas which are defended against by the performance of a compulsive series of ritual acts or magical verbalizations like repetitive handwashing or the recitation of a particular phrase in moments of anxiety), or *anxiety state* (the experience of intense physical and mental symptoms of fear without conscious knowledge of the cause of the fear).

On the other hand, Jung felt that the extrovert, when and if he suc-

cumbs to mental illness, is likely to suffer from *hysterical* disorders (para-
lyses, anesthesias or loss of feeling, blindness, tunnel vision—all without
organic cause. Cf. Chapter 2, Freud's early cases; Jung, 1921, p. 336). Thus,
while the introvert is vulnerable to intense anxiety symptoms, the extrovert develops a more "primitive" and impulsive form of neurosis based on
converting the anxiety into bodily symptoms.

To understand how Jung came to these conclusions, it will be helpful
to refresh our memory of Jung's descriptions of the two personality types
of introversion and extroversion:

> I have . . . finally, on the basis of numerous observations and experi-
> ences, come to postulate two fundamental attitudes, namely *introver-*
> *sion* and *extraversion.* The first atttitude is normally characterized by
> a hesitant, reflective, retiring nature that keeps to itself, shrinks from
> objects, is always slightly on the defensive and prefers to hide behind
> mistrustful scrutiny. The second is normally characterized by an
> outgoing, candid, and accommodating nature that adapts easily to a
> given situation, quickly forms attachments, and, setting aside any
> possible misgivings, will often venture forth with careless confidence
> into unknown situations. In the first case obviously the subject [that
> is, the person himself], and in the second the object [that is, external
> reality], is all-important. [1917, pp. 44–45]

It was thus Jung's opinion that the extrovert is "captured" by external
events and objects, and that he is ruled by prevailing social opinion that
surrounds him. The introvert, much to the contrary, gives greatest weight
to his own subjective reactions to external events; he devalues and deem-
phasizes the significance of the objective world by elevating his own emotions, evaluations, and personal reactions to dominance (Jung, 1921, p.
500). Consequently, the introvert is likely to succumb to the strength of
his own all-important emotions with an outbreak of neurosis whose dominant characteristic is the experience of anxiety.

The extrovert, ruled by the external world, succumbs to hysterical neuroses more easily because he seeks to divest himself of his emotional pain;
he favors the repression of unacceptable thoughts and the externalization
or conversion of threatening impulses into "objectified" bodily symptoms.
With the achievement of these readily observable afflictions, the hysteric
extrovert is in a position to profit with an income of sympathy from the
social environment to which he is so sensitive. This "secondary gain," the
income of sympathy and the concern of his intimates, is an important part
of the hysteric's childlike impulsivity and egocentric demands for attention.

In an initial test of Jung's scheme, Eysenck and his colleagues selected
a sample of seven hundred neurotically maladjusted patients at the Mill
Hill Emergency Hospital for whom comprehensive case histories and clinical observational data were available. The psychiatrist in charge of each

case prepared an "item sheet" on which the patient's familial and personal history, symptoms, diagnosis, treatment, and various social data were recorded. Eysenck selected thirty-nine items from each of seven hundred such data sheets and submitted the information to a factor analysis. The resulting matrix of intercorrelations yielded two bipolar factors consisting of a number of traits.

One factor was associated with a cluster of traits that seemed to be best described as "general neuroticism." Specifically, the items that tended to be correlated on this factor were badly organized personality, dependency, abnormality before illness, narrow interests, dismissal from military service, abnormality in parents, unsatisfactory home, and poor muscular tone (Eysenck, 1947, p. 36). It must be remembered that these trait descriptions originated in the attending psychiatrist's ratings of the patient.

The second major factor that emerged from the factor analysis seemed partially to confirm Jung's hypothesis. Individuals high in the general neuroticism factor could be divided into two groups. One group was neurotically maladjusted by virtue of possessing symptoms associated with high anxiety: obsessional tendencies, headache, tremor, irritability, among others. The second group of individuals tended to have somewhat different symptoms characteristic of hysterical disorder: bodily symptoms with no organic basis, little energy, narrow interests, hypochondriasis, poor work history, sexual difficulties.

Eysenck's analysis of the item-sheet data thus demonstrated that a general factor or dimension of neuroticism-normality could be used to categorize psychologically disabled patients, and that the group high in neuroticism could be further subdivided into anxiety neurotics and hysterical neurotics. The important question was whether empirical evidence could be found for a second dimension of introversion-extroversion that would cut across the two neurotic groups as Jung had suggested.

Empirical Evidence for a Dimension of Introversion-Extroversion

Starting from the premise that Jung's hypothesis was correct, Eysenck surveyed the available experimental literature on the issue of introversion-extroversion. He generally found support from a wide variety of sources that introversion was associated with anxiety, obsessive-compulsive symptoms, and reactive-depression neuroses. Similarly, the extroverted personality type seemed to be associated in a variety of investigations with the symptoms characteristic of hysterical neuroses (Eysenck, 1947, Chaps. 2, 7).

In his own researches with the sample of neurotic soldiers, Eysenck found direct empirical evidence on a variety of performance, metabolic, and personality measures that a dimension of extroversion-introversion could be used to distinguish between the two groups of neurotic illnesses.

Coining a new term to cover the first group of neurotic symptoms (anxiety, phobia, depression, obsessive-compulsive disorders), Eysenck classified them under the heading *dysthymia* (1947, p. 37n). Dysthymics thus corresponded to Jung's *psychasthenics* and to his introvert personality types. Eysenck retained the label *hysteric* for the second group, as Jung had proposed, and he found that hysterics tended to be extroverted in accordance with Jung's hypothesis. Eysenck's conclusions were based on a variety of experimental and questionnaire evidence that is best summarized in Eysenck's own terms:

> ... *(neurotic) introverts* show a tendency to develop anxiety and depression symptoms, ... they are characterized by obsessional tendencies, irritability, apathy, and ... they suffer from a lability of the autonomic system. According to their own statement, their feelings are easily hurt, they are self-conscious, nervous, given to feelings of inferiority, moody, day-dream easily, keep in the background on social occasions, and suffer from sleeplessness. In their body-build vertical growth predominates over horizontal growth; their effort response is poor, and their choline esterase activity is high. Salivary secretion is inhibited. Their intelligence is comparatively high, their vocabulary excellent, and they tend to be persistent. They are generally accurate, but slow; they excel at finicking work (Tweezers test). Their level of aspiration is unduly high, but they tend to under-rate their own performance. Withal, they are rather rigid, and show little interpersonal variability. Their aesthetic preferences are towards the quiet, old-fashioned type of picture. ... They do not appreciate jokes very much, and sex jokes in particular are not much favoured. Their handwriting is distinctive. [1947, pp. 246–247]

The thirty traits that cluster together into the pattern of the neurotic introvert, as stated here by Eysenck, are characteristic of his early descriptive research. More probing investigation into the causes underlying the clustering of traits for the neurotic introvert would eventually follow. At this stage of the research, however, Eysenck was limited to specification of descriptive traits. Thus, in contrast to the neurotic introvert:

> ... *(neurotic) extraverts* show a tendency to develop hysterical conversion symptoms, and a hysterical attitude to their symptoms. Furthermore, they show little energy, narrow interests, have a bad work-history, and are hypochondriacal. According to their own statement, they are troubled by stammer or stutter, are accident prone, frequently off work through illness, disgruntled, and troubled by aches and pains. In their body-build, horizontal growth predominates over vertical growth; their effort response is quite good, and their choline esterase activity low. Salivary secretion is not inhibited. Their intelligence is comparatively low, their vocabulary poor, and

they show extreme lack of persistence. They tend to be quick but inaccurate; they are bad at finicking work (Tweezers test). Their level of aspiration is low, but they tend to over-rate their own performance. They are not very rigid, and show great interpersonal variability. Their aesthetic preferences are towards the colourful, modern type of picture. In aesthetic creation, they produce scattered designs, often having abstract subjects. They appreciate jokes, and are particularly fond of sex jokes. Their handwriting is distinctive. [Eysenck, 1947, p. 247]

Neurotic introverts and extroverts share some traits, but on the whole their patterns of responses to Eysenck's various tests and measurements are quite distinguishable. More important, the pattern of measurements for introverts and extroverts *who are neurotic* tend to resemble the two hypothetical classes of dysthymic (anxiety) neuroticism and hysterical disorder.

Historical Antecedents of Introversion-Extroversion Dimensions

Eysenck's early descriptive and correlational researches had established in a general way the validity of Jung's hypothesis. The direction that Eysenck's investigations were taking seemed to many psychiatrists and psychologists uninteresting, irrelevant, and, at worst, unnecessarily troublesome:

> To many, if not most, psychologists interested in personality it seemed as if I had attempted to resurrect a corpse—equivalent, perhaps, to trying to reintroduce into physics the notions of phlogiston, or aether, or a geocentric planetary system. This had many disadvantages, which will be only too obvious; no one wanted to read about extraversion, no one wanted to support research into this field, no one wanted to reconsider problems which were thought to be closed once and for all. [Eysenck, 1970, p. 3]

The concepts of introversion-extroversion were, in most psychologists' minds, associated with Carl Jung's typology. But aside from Jung's basic premise of an association between psychasthenia (dysthymia) and introversion, and between extroversion and hysteria, Eysenck accepted none of Jung's formulation. In fact, Eysenck went to great length to point out that the concepts of introversion-extroversion were not originated by Jung, but instead had a 2000-year history in philosophy, medicine, and psychology (1947, 1953, 1967, 1970). Although it would be of some interest to trace all the roots of dimensional personality theories and speculations, the discussion will be limited to the three antecedents that seem to have most influenced Eysenck. In historical order of development, we will consider the influence on Eysenck's formulations exerted by Hippocrates' and Galen's classical temperament theory, by Pavlov's conception of nervous system types, and by Clark L. Hull's drive X habit theory of learning.

Galen's and Hippocrates' Theory of Temperaments

Two ancient Greek physicians, Hippocrates (460?–377? B.C.) and Galen (A.D. 130–200?), devised a *temperament theory* of personality and human conduct. Galen, however, is usually given credit for systematizing the previously vague notions of biological constitution and psychological character types into a coherent fourfold typology of temperaments (see Chapter 5 for a brief description of classical temperament theory in terms of Alfred Adler's typology).

In Galen's sytem, personality was related to four body fluids or *humors:* blood, black bile, yellow bile, and phlegm. An excess of one of the four humors was thought to determine the emotional temperament of the individual. When blood predominates, the temperament is *Sanguine* (warm-hearted, volatile, optimistic, easy-going); a predominance of black bile results in a *Melancholic* temperament (sad, depressed, anxious); yellow bile produces the *Choleric* temperament (quick to action, angry, assertive); and, finally, when phlegm predominates, the resulting temperament is, of course, *Phlegmatic* (slow to action, lethargic, calm) (cf. R. I. Watson, 1963, p. 80; Allport, 1937; Eysenck, 1964a, 1967 and 1972).

The German philosopher, Immanuel Kant (1724–1804), amplified the classical temperament theory by proposing separate groups of verbal trait descriptions for each of the four temperaments. For example, Kant described the Sanguine personality as one who is carefree and full of hope, good natured and sociable, but capricious and given to pranks (Eysenck and Eysenck, 1969, p. 12). Kant's verbal descriptions for the remaining three types of temperament may be gleaned from Figure 15–2. The important point about Kant's verbal labels was that he attempted to demonstrate how various discrete traits cluster together in a given type of temperament. The correlation among the various characteristics for a given type was thought to be high so that knowledge of any one trait would be a reliable indication of the presence of the others. Unfortunately, Kant's verbal scheme, like temperament theory itself, was of a *categorical* nature, whereby any individual was classified into one of only four possible personality types. Little or no allowance was made for overlap between types or for different *degrees* of temperamental expression in different individuals belonging to the same type. A moment's thought will indicate the obvious flaw in such a conception of personality. The four discrete, independent categories of temperament theory are clearly suitable only for classification of pure or extreme personality types—if such people exist.

Most people do not fall cleanly into only one compartment. Personalities generally possess some unique *combination* of qualities from a broader spectrum of traits than those represented by the notion of four mutually exclusive categories. To rectify the errors inherent in this system, a variety of nineteenth century philosophers and psychologists sought to reconceptualize temperament theory into a more logically defensible form. They devised a series of *dimensions* or *continua* that would represent each temperament type as varying in the degree to which it possessed specific traits along some theoretical spectrum ranging from low to high.

One such dimensional modification of temperament theory was proposed by Wilhelm Wundt (1832–1920), the founding father of experimental psychology. The key to Wundt's scheme lay in his attempt to reorganize the four types according to the degree to which they each possessed two variable characteristics: degree of emotionality and degree of changeableness (Eysenck and Eysenck, 1969). Wundt suggested that the four personalities differ in the strength of their emotions and in the rate at which they change their opinions and feelings. He therefore suggested that these two continuously variable dimensions of *emotionality* and *changeability* be employed to describe subtle variations in each of the four temperaments. In Wundt's dimensional scheme, each of the two dimensions was anchored at its end points with extreme opposite types of personality. The distance between each of these bi-polar extremes was conceptualized by Wundt as containing a series of continuously varying gradations. Hence, the midpoint of each dimension represented the individual who possesses traits of both extremes in equal proportions.

The first of Wundt's dimensions can be termed *Non-Emotional* at one pole and *Emotional* at the opposite extreme. Similarly, the second dimension running crosswise to the first is anchored at one end with the *Unchangeable* personality type and at the other end with the *Changeable* type. (Actually, the precise terminology that Wundt employed was *Weak* versus *Strong* emotional types, and *Slow* versus *Quick* reaction types. Eysenck employed the changed terminology used here in recounting Wundt's system because it makes Wundt's meaning more understandable.) The exact arrangement of Wundt's two dimensions and the position of the four classic temperaments within them can be seen in Figure 15–1. Figure 15–1 shows that Wundt regarded the Phlegmatic and Sanguine personalities as having essentially weak emotions (Non-emotional). At the opposite end of the emotionality dimension are the strongly emotional temperaments of the Melancholic and Choleric personalities.

The second dimension in Figure 15–1, *Unchangeable* versus *Changeable*, is orthogonal to or independent of the first dimension. That is to say, a person's position on the *Emotionality* dimension does not determine his position on the *Changeable* dimension. Consequently, according to Wundt, the melancholic and phlegmatic personalities are extreme types of the *Unchangeable* personality, whereas the choleric and sanguine personalities are extreme samples of the *Changeable* type, as illustrated in Figure 15–1.

FIGURE 15-1: DIMENSIONAL CLASSIFICATION OF TEMPERAMENT

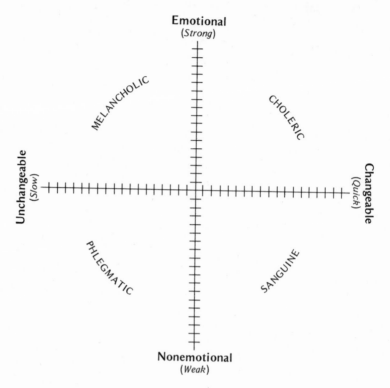

Based on Eysenck, 1953 and 1967.

For each of the four types of temperament in this scheme, two continuously variable characteristics are postulated, and each of these characteristics is presumed to be independent of the other.

Eysenck realized that these early physicians, philosophers, and psychologists were essentially correct in their descriptions of personality. They attempted to order personalities on the basis of the traits they observed frequently clustering together in people who came under their scrutiny. Eysenck's own work on the introversion-extroversion and neuroticism-normality dimensions produced a comparable picture of human character types. Although the labels were changed in accordance with contemporary psychological vocabulary, Eysenck's two dimensions agreed quite closely with the dimensions introduced into classical temperament theory by Wundt. Eysenck's neuroticism-normality dimension shares a strong conceptual similarity to Wundt's emotional-nonemotional dimension; and his introversion-extroversion dimension is, in most respects, descriptively similar to Wundt's unchangeable–changeable dimension. Figure 15–2 shows these correspondences. The differences between a categorical conception of personality classification and a dimensional scheme can also be discerned in Figure 15–2.

FIGURE 15-2: DIMENSIONAL AND CATEGORICAL PERSONALITY CLASSIFICATION

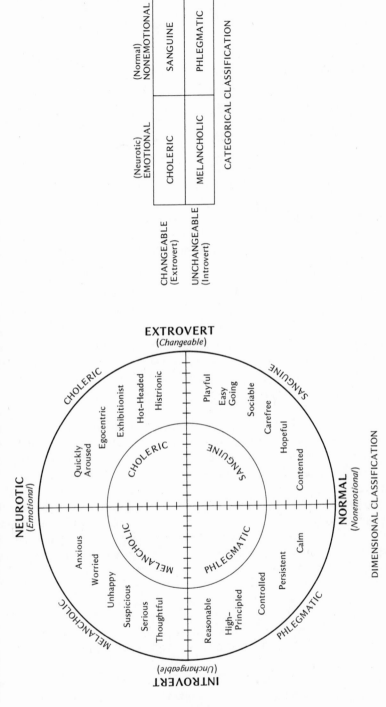

Adapted from Eysenck, 1953, p. 17; 1967, p. 35.

It is important to keep in mind when comparing Eysenck's concepts with the early views of personality classification that these "classical" conceptions were subjective, speculative, and informal. Eysenck made this point well:

> ... what these various philosophers, physicians, and psychologists were doing was to look for uniformities of conduct in the lives of the people whom they were able to observe, and reduce these uniformities to a description of a categorical or continuous type. They made no attempt to formulate specific theories about the formal structure which was so well described in their word pictures, and they made no attempt to demonstrate by experimental or statistical means the accuracy or otherwise of their hypotheses. [1967, pp. 34–35]

The problem confronting Eysenck, therefore, was to discover and confirm the essence of truth contained in these early views while simultaneously expanding them to include causal explanations for the observations they embodied. Neither the categorical nor the dimensional scheme of personality classification by itself provides an explanation for the observed consistencies in behavior. To answer the question of *why* a particular personality's traits cluster together, or *why* an introvert differs from an extrovert requires that the investigator turn away from the readily observable or *phenotypical* aspects of personality. Instead, the more fundamental *genotypical* factors that produce the observed uniformities must in themselves become objects of investigation.

The problem of the actor and his mask is thus encountered, though in radically different form, once again. In the observations of the ancients, Wundt, Kant, and Jung, Eysenck found a provocative but incomplete tradition of personality investigation. Eysenck was pleased to extend this tradition into contemporary psychology by providing the experimental and statistical tests required to convert a tradition into a scientifically respectable theory. But to do so, he would have to penetrate the mask of descriptive observables through to the actor's living core of personality organization, the central nervous system. The crucial ideas that provided the key to this more fundamental genotypical aspect of personality came, surprisingly, from Ivan Pavlov's efforts with dogs to provide a physiological explanation for the classical temperaments.

Pavlov's Peculiar Dogs: Excitation/Inhibition Temperaments

At the turn of the century, the Russian physiologist, Ivan Petrovitch Pavlov (1849–1936), devised an experimental situation in which to measure the secretion of digestive hormones in dogs. In the course of his work, he developed a theory of nervous system processes that greatly amplified the classical theory of temperaments.

By a careful surgical preparation, Pavlov was able to divert one of the dog's salivary ducts to an external portion of the jaw where drops of saliva could be collected and measured. Experimental dogs were also subjected to a second surgical procedure whereby the upper portion of the digestive tract was severed from the stomach and then rerouted to an external fistula or opening. Food taken into the mouth, chewed and swallowed never reached the dog's stomach. It was returned instead to a collection dish near the fistula so that Pavlov could precisely measure the quantity of meat powder consumed in proportion to the saliva secreted.

Pavlov discovered that even when food did not reach the stomach, gastric secretions were still produced at a rate nearly half that of normal digestive activity. "Sham feeding" thus led Pavlov to conclude that some central brain processes were responsible for triggering of digestive activity even in the absence of real food in the stomach (Pavlov, 1927, 1928). True to his rigorous scientific and physiological training, Pavlov decided to study the problem of "psychically controlled secretions" revealed by sham feeding with the same precision of measurement and control employed in his previous investigations.

A basic experimental groundplan was followed. Dogs were isolated from distracting visual and auditory stimuli by securing them in a harness stand in a sound–deadened chamber. The experimenter, in an adjoining room, presented to the dog remotely controlled stimuli that were previously unassociated in the dog's experience with food or salivation. The sound of a ticking metronome, flashing lights of controlled intensities, and bell or buzzer sounds were employed as neutral stimuli.

By presenting the neutral stimulus immediately *before* forcing meat powder into the dog's mouth, the two stimuli—buzzer and meat—became associated in the dog's central nervous system processes. The buzzer came to signal the subsequent occurrence of the event that the dog experienced as "meat-powder-in-the-mouth." After a suitable number of pairings, the unconditioned reflex of salivation-to-meat-powder was supplemented by a conditioned reflex of salivation-to-buzzer (Pavlov, 1927, Lectures II, III).

Excitation and Inhibition Processes in the Cortex

After pairing with meat powder, the buzzer had acquired the capacity to evoke salivation, although with less force than the normal stimulus. Pavlov's problem was to explain the formation of this new pathway by inferring from the dog's observable behavior the unobservable corresponding nervous processes.

Pavlov thus postulated that the cortex of the brain is composed of two types of cells or neurons. When incoming stimuli are detected by the dog's sensory receptors, the excitation is passed along to the brain where *excitatory* cortical cells begin firing in response. When a given sequence of paired stimuli has often enough been repeated, a definite corresponding pattern of excitatory cell firing is established. This cortical process is reliably evoked each time the same stimulus pattern is repeated, allowing the dog to show the benefit of his experience by being able to anticipate one stimulus from the presence of the other. In short, excitatory cell firings are the basis of positive conditioned reflexes.

Pavlov also postulated the existence of *inhibitory* cortical cells. Inhibitory centers of the cortex function to dampen or retard the excitatory cells. In some cases, inhibitory cells even compete with excitatory processes. For example, the common-sense notion of distraction or diversion of attention corresponds to one kind of inhibition that Pavlov termed *external inhibition* (1927, p. 48). A dog thoroughly conditioned to salivate at the sound of a buzzer will cease salivation altogether if a novel stimulus like a loud bang or an unfamiliar person is suddenly introduced into the situation. The dog is said to be momentarily distracted or surprised. His conditioned reflex is *inhibited* until the novelty of the distracting stimulus diminishes.

A second type of inhibition was postulated by Pavlov. Called *internal inhibition,* this cortical process involves a slow or gradual development of a competing conditioned response (Pavlov, 1927, Lecture IV). For example, the continual presentation of the conditioned stimulus without the unconditioned stimulus ever again being presented leads to a gradual termination of the conditioned response. In more concrete terms, the experimenter continues to present the buzzer without ever following it with meat powder. The dog eventually ceases to salivate at the buzzer sound. In effect, he has "unlearned" the conditioned reflex. More precisely, he has learned to inhibit his former conditioned response to the buzzer. This process is called *extinction* of a conditioned reflex, but it is more properly thought of as learning a new inhibitory response (Pavlov, 1927, p. 48).

Individual Differences in Excitation and Inhibition

Not all dogs were alike in their ability to form and maintain conditioned reflexes. Moreover, there seemed to be a correlation between a dog's innate temperament and his conditioning ability. Dogs who were most sociable, affable, and active when left to themselves proved to be the worst subjects for the establishment of positive conditioned reflexes like salivation to a buzzer. Strapped into the conditioning harness in the isolated experimental chamber, such normally active dogs soon became drowsy and fell asleep! By contrast, dogs who were quiet and "stolid" outside the experimental situation and who, therefore, Pavlov initially assumed would be poor conditioning subjects, proved to be under certain circumstances the most easily conditionable dogs (1928, p. 306).

To explain this diversity of reactions to the conditioning procedures, Pavlov initially postulated two "extreme types" of nervous system and two "balanced types." In the first extreme type of dog, excitatory cortical processes predominate, and inhibitory processes are weak or nearly absent in normal behavioral activities. Unrestrained by inhibitory cortical processes, such dogs are the affable, outgoing, always curious, sociable animals who therefore seem likely candidates for rapid conditioning. Yet, it was precisely this kind of dog who gave Pavlov the most trouble in the conditioning situation. Affable and outgoing outside the experimental chamber, the dog would paradoxically become drowsy and fall asleep during the monotony of conditioning. Pavlov initially assumed that because this dog was a "specialist in excitation," his excitatory cells were quickly exhausted. Inhibitory processes would than take over, causing the paradoxical effect of drowsiness and sleep. For such "specialists in excitation," the repetition of the same constant sequence of stimuli in conditioning rapidly depletes the easily aroused excitatory cells. Pavlov found that such dogs were good conditioning subjects if the conditioning procedure was varied so that a constant succession of novel stimuli was available (Teplov, 1964, p. 14; Pavlov, 1927, pp. 287 ff.).

The second extreme type of nervous temperament is predominantly inhibitory in normal behavioral activities. Outwardly, this dog appears "cowardly," cringing in corners and slinking along the floor as if afraid of everything and everyone. However this kind of dog, contrary to expectation, conditions well in the monotonous experimental situation once he is sufficiently used to the experimenter and the equipment. But his positive conditioned reflexes are easily disrupted and extinguished. Only inhibitory reflexes (e.g., learning *not* to respond to one of a pair of stimuli that is not reinforced by meat powder) are stable and strongly established (Pavlov, 1927).

Between these two extremes of excitatory and inhibitory specialists, Pavlov found dogs who were "equilibrated" or *balanced* in their degree of inhibition and excitation (1928, p. 374 ff.). This central or balanced type of dog is found in two distinct varieties. In the first type, the balance between excitation and inhibition is well established so that the dog conditions well in both positive and inhibitory reflexes. This first balanced type tends to *behaviorally* resemble the extreme excitatory dog in his lively, outgoing manner. In the second balanced type of nervous system, excitatory and inhibitory processes reach an equilibrium but only with difficulty is this balance maintained. The balance is continually threatened with disruption at the slightest provocation or distraction (Pavlov, 1928, p. 375). Behaviorally, this second balanced type resembles the extreme inhibitory animal in his quiet, stolid, and calm temperament.

Thus Pavlov proposed four types of nervous systems to correspond with Classical temperament theory's four humoral types:

Extreme Excitatory Type: Choleric (Poor conditionability)

Extreme Inhibitory Type: Melancholic (Good inhibitory conditionability)
Balanced (Excitatory) Type: Sanguine (Good conditionability)
Balanced (Inhibitory) Type: Phlegmatic (Good but easily distracted)

Experimental Neurosis: Breakdown of the Inhibition/Excitation Balance

One of the chief distinguishing features of the four nervous system types was the individual's degree of susceptibility to experimentally induced neurotic behavior. Such neurosis may be induced, for example, if a conditioning procedure is established in which *both* excitatory and inhibitory cortical processes are made to alternate rapidly so that they "collide" in the dog's nervous system. Each of the *extreme* nervous types will succumb to a different form of "nervous breakdown."

Using a mechanical vibrator applied to the dog's skin, Pavlov conditioned an *extreme excitatory* dog to salivate at 30 vibrations a minute. When the vibrator was set to oscillate at only 15 vibrations per minute, no food was presented. In this way, the dog learned to discriminate between 30 and 15 vibrations. He salivated to 30 vibrations, an excitatory response, and withheld salivation to 15 vibrations, an inhibitory response. When, however, Pavlov employed 15 and 30 vibrations in close succession, dogs of the excitatory type suffered an extreme disorganization of behavior. Their weak inhibitory processes completely failed to keep pace with the rapid alternation between 15 and 30 vibrations. Their stronger excitatory processes assumed dominance in this collision with inhibitory processes. The animal became uncontrollably excited, straining and struggling to escape the harness and bite the experimenter. In short order, the extreme excitatory type of dog showed every sign of an anxiety attack. The effect was long lasting, often requiring months of treatment with tranquilizing drugs to effect a "cure."

Pavlov felt that this form of experimentally produced neurotic behavior in the excitatory dog was analogous to the human neurosis of psychasthenia (Pavlov, 1928, p. 375). Thus, Pavlov, too, identified excitatory processes with anxiety neurosis (dysthymia), as did Eysenck working many years later in the tradition of Jung and the classical Greek physicians. But, unlike Eysenck, Pavlov identified the extreme excitatory neurotic animal first with the sanguine temperament, then later with the choleric temperament (Teplov, 1964, p. 16). According to Eysenck's analysis of the classical temperaments, such an extreme excitatory animal would be classed as melancholic (see Figure 15–2).

To return to Pavlov's peculiar dogs, the inhibitory type of animal at the opposite extreme succumbed to a different type of "neurosis" when exposed to the same alternation of excitatory and inhibitory stimuli. Because the discrimination between the food-reinforced 30 vibrations and the non-reinforced 15 vibrations was made difficult as excitatory and inhibitory processes "collided," this type of animal succumbed to his stronger inhibitory tendency not to respond. Inhibiting all response, these dogs became rigid, drowsy, nearly hypnotized. Outside the conditioning chamber, they became withdrawn and nonreactive, easily frightened and sometimes physically ill.

Pavlov identified this pattern of "nervous breakdown" in the inhibitory dog as similar to the human hysterical disorders. He further suggested that the inhibitory neurotic animal corresponded to the melancholic temperament (1928, p. 377). In Eysenck's terms, however, such an animal would correspond to the choleric temperament, at the extreme extroverted end of the dimension.

Dogs of the two central or balanced types, although superficially resembling the two extreme types, do not succumb readily, if at all, to experimentally induced neuroses (Pavlov, 1928, p. 375). Pavlov later changed his system of classification and his opinion about the formation of experimental neuroses, but the details of this story go far beyond what is practical in the present context (see Teplov, 1964, for the detailed history). At this point in his work, however, Pavlov identified the two balanced types of dog as corresponding to the sanguine (stable balance) and phlegmatic (unstable balance) personalities.

Inconsistencies in Pavlov's Scheme

Eysenck (1957a, pp. 111 ff.) has pointed to a variety of inconsistencies in Pavlov's descriptions of the four nervous types. Pavlov had tried to create a typology that would coordinate observable behavioral traits with underlying nervous system processes of inhibition and excitation. He then further attempted to coordinate classical temperament theory with his data on individual differences in conditioning and with susceptibility to different types of experimentally induced neuroses. It was an ambitious undertaking that was fraught with discrepancies at both the behavioral and neurological levels of explanation.

For example, Pavlov identified the extreme excitatory nervous type as a choleric personality. Presumably, in making this classification, Pavlov was focusing his attention on the dog's behavior *in the conditioning situation,* where the tedious experimental procedures made the animal drowsy and difficult to condition. But the animal's personality traits at liberty are more accurately described in temperament theory as a sanguine personality, the outgoing, friendly, emotionally demonstrative type. Yet, in Pavlov's system, this dog is classed as a choleric type. Under appropriate conditions, furthermore, the "choleric" dog succumbs to a psychasthenic (anxiety) neurosis that is more characteristic of the melancholic type. Which type is he? Is he the *sanguine* personality because he is normally outgoing and affable? Or is he *choleric* because he becomes hard to handle in the conditioning situation? Or is he *melancholic* because he succumbs to anxiety neurosis?

Because such inconsistencies exist in Pavlov's system, Eysenck was unable to adopt the classification scheme without major revision. However, Pavlov's contribution to personality was to point to the inhibition and excitation basis that underlies observable personality type and neurotic predisposition. The problem for Eysenck was to apply the conditioning data accurately and consistently to the task of personality classification. With his dimensions of introversion-extroversion and emotionality-stability, Eysenck was able to solve the problem.

Eysenck's first step in untangling the Pavlovian scheme was an assumption that Pavlov had been essentially correct in his biological strategy: Observable differences in the four personalities have their source in less observable inhibition-excitation processes of the nervous system. Eysenck adopted these concepts, but he applied them to human temperaments in a drastically different way.

For Eysenck, *the essence of the melancholic and phlegmatic temperaments is their withdrawal from social and physical stimulation,* as described by the ancients. Thus, contrary to Pavlov, Eysenck assumed that the melancholic and phlegmatic personalities are characterized by extremely sensitive excitation processes. In the melancholic, this extreme cortical arousal is coupled with high emotional reactivity so that the melancholic feels intellectually and emotionally overwhelmed by even mild social and physical stimulation. He succumbs to emotional despair, anxiety, and to a protective tendency to retreat from his surroundings. In the phlegmatic personality, however, this same high cortical excitation and sensitivity leads to withdrawal behaviors designed to escape overwhelming stimulation in the form of a protective "I don't care" apathy. Yet the phlegmatic lacks the melancholic's high emotional reactivity, and he thus remains free of neurotic anxiety and despair. Eysenck therefore classified both the melancholic and the phlegmatic as introverts but only the melancholic as neurotic. Because both personality types have highly aroused cortical processes, the defining property of introversion in Eysenck's scheme, the melancholic and phlegmatic should, in principle, form conditioned reflexes easily and strongly.

At the other extreme, *the essence of the choleric and sanguine personalities in Eysenck's view is their responsivity and rapt attention to the social and physical environment.* The sanguine personality is fundamentally outgoing, sociable and emotionally tranquil. He delights in a constant succession of novel experiences. The choleric personality is also attentive to the social environment, but he finds no delight in it. He is more emotional, more irritable and more prone to become irascible. The choleric may even turn mean, taking delight in manipulating or hurting others. Eysenck thus classed the choleric and sanguine personalities as extroverts but only the choleric as neurotic. He assumed that their cortical processes were far less sensitive, far less aroused, and considerably more inhibitory than those of introverts. In a sense, their strong inhibitory processes force the extrovert types to seek constant stimulation from the social environment to overcome their own cortical inertia. Because both personality types have strong inhibitory processes, the defining property of extroversion in Eysenck's scheme, the sanguine and choleric personalities should, in principle, form positive conditioned reflexes poorly or weakly. The similarities and differences between Pavlov's and Eysenck's explanations of temperaments are summarized in Table 15–1 (pp. 610–11).

The notion that nervous systems may differ in their tolerance to stimulation has been taken up by some contemporary Russian workers whose investigations bear some resemblance to Eysenck's concepts. We turn next to a brief consideration of these efforts.

Because the melancholic and phlegmatic personalities both condition well, a fact that indicates sensitive excitatory processes, and because both are socially withdrawn, Eysenck classed them as introverts. Because both personalities differ in their emotional disposition, Eysenck classed the withdrawn but anxious melancholic as neurotic and the withdrawn but calm phlegmatic as normal. Thus, the melancholic is introverted and neurotic, whereas the phlegmatic is introverted and normal.

Similarly, because the choleric and sanguine personalities show poor conditioning of positive reflexes, a trait that suggests strong inhibitory processes, and because both are socially outgoing and responsive, Eysenck classed them as extroverts. The emotional difference between them consists of the choleric's high neuroticism and the sanguine's essentially normal emotional reactivity. Thus the choleric is an extroverted neurotic personality, whereas the sanguine is extroverted and normal. To summarize some of the similarities and differences between Pavlov and Eysenck, their respective types and dimensions are compared in Table 15–1. (pp. 610–11).

Weak and Strong Nervous Systems: The Work of B. M. Teplov

Pavlov developed a number of criteria by which to describe the action of the cerebral cortex in conditioning. The one criterion that has significance for an understanding of Eysenck's conception of personality dimensions is what Pavlov termed "strength of the nervous system" (Gray, 1964, Teplov, 1964)

A modern Russian worker, B. M. Teplov (1964), adopted Pavlov's concept of strength of the nervous system, restricting its meaning to the *intensity of excitatory process* in the cortex. Thus, Teplov defined the *strong nervous system* as one with a large capacity to tolerate intense stimulation. A *weak nervous system,* therefore, is conceptualized as one with a small capacity to tolerate stimulation. In terms of excitation and inhibition processes, the concept of strength has particularly precise meaning. The strong nervous system is less sensitive than the weak nervous system. It is strong in the sense that it can operate with stimulus intensities of far larger

TABLE 15–1: PAVLOV'S TYPES AND EYSENCK'S DIMENSIONS CONTRASTED

CLASSICAL TEMPERAMENTS	PAVLOV'S TYPES	BEHAVIORAL TRAITS (Pavlov)	EYSENCK'S DIMENSIONS	CLASSICAL TEMPERAMENTS
Choleric →	Extreme Excitatory	Outgoing, affable friendly at liberty, but becomes drowsy in monotony of experimental chamber. Conditions well only when stimuli are varied and novel. Neurosis caused by failure of inhibition and resembles human *psychasthenia*.	Extreme Emotional Introvert (Neurotic) →	Melancholic
Melancholic →	Extreme Inhibitory	Cowardly, cringing, nervous, this dog conditions well in the monotony of the experiment. But positive reflexes (e.g., salivation to reinforced stimulus) are poorer than negative conditioned reflexes (e.g., withholding response, or discrimination). Neurosis caused by failure of excitatory cells and resembles human *hysteria*.	Extreme Emotional Extrovert (Neurotic) →	Choleric

Sanguine ◄——— Balanced Excitatory

Conditions well in both positive and negative responses. Outgoing, affable, like extreme excitatory type. Resists experimental neurosis.

Stable Introvert ———► Phlegmatic

Phlegmatic ◄——— Balanced Inhibitory

Conditions well, but positive responses disrupted easily. Quiet, stolid, and alert, like inhibitory animal when calm. Resists experimental neurosis.

Stable Extrovert ———► Sanguine

Note reversal of classical temperaments between Eysenck's and Pavlov's schemes. Furthermore, the behavioral descriptions are Pavlov's, *not* Eysenck's, and in fact contradict Eysenck's trait descriptions of introverted and extroverted personalities.

Based on Pavlov, 1928, p. 377; Pavlov, 1927, p. 286; Eysenck, 1957a; Teplov, 1964, pp. 13, 18.

magnitude than a weak nervous system before it must act to protectively inhibit further increases in intensity. But, for precisely this reason, the strong nervous system is insensitive to low-intensity stimulation. At low intensities, the strong nervous system's inhibitory processes overwhelm the excitation, causing such an animal to become drowsy and fall asleep.

The weak nervous system is weak only in the sense that it is operating almost continuously at its maximum excitatory strength. Therefore, any excitatory stimulus almost immediately pushes the weak nervous system beyond its excitatory capacity. To protect itself against overexcitation, it "shuts down" its excitatory centers at levels of stimulus intensity that for the strong nervous system would be only mildly arousing. Thus, as paradoxical as it may sound, the weak nervous system responds with stronger excitation to low-excitation level stimuli than the strong nervous system. Conversely, the strong nervous system, because it operates with greater levels of inhibition, is able to tolerate stronger stimuli. But these two relationships between inhibition-excitation and stimulus intensity must be kept in mind: *The strong nervous system is a specialist in inhibition;* it has a higher excitatory threshold, that is, it can endure more stimulation or more intense stimulation without protecting itself. *The weak nervous system is a specialist in excitation;* it has a low excitatory threshold, that is, it reaches and exhausts its full excitation capacity rather quickly, at relatively low levels of stimulation.

To operationalize the concept of weak and strong nervous types, Teplov and his coworkers have employed another one of Pavlov's concepts called *transmarginal inhibition.* Transmarginal inhibition literally means "beyond the boundary" inhibition. The basic premise underlying this concept is called the "law of strength" (Gray, 1964, p. 276). The law of strength asserts that a subject's conditioned response will increase in magnitude as the intensity of the conditioned stimulus increases. In concrete terms, a subject conditioned to blink at the sound of a tone will blink all the more sharply or more quickly if the loudness of the tone is increased. As the tone is made even louder, the conditioned response—blinking—will also increase in intensity *up to some limiting point.* At this particular point in the loudness continuum, the subject's blink response will decrease or cease altogether. The louder the tone is made beyond the point where the response has been increasing, the more response magnitude tends to decrease. This point is called the protective threshold or *threshold of transmarginal inhibition.* Pavlov thought of the transmarginal inhibition threshold as protective because the nervous system was damping itself down by inhibition before increasing-stimulus intensities overworked the cortical excitatory cells (Gray, 1964, p. 161).

The key point about transmarginal inhibition is that *the weak nervous system reaches this threshold sooner than the strong nervous system.* In more precise terms, the weak nervous system shows signs of lessening response-intensity at lower stimulation-intensity levels than the strong nervous system. The difference between transmarginal inhibition thresholds for the weak and strong nervous systems is graphed in an idealized form in Figure 15–3.

Eysenck's introversion-extroversion dimension closely parallels Pavlov's and Teplov's weak-strong dimension. Specifically, the introvert is said to have a weak (sensitive) nervous system dominated by excitatory processes *under low levels of stimulation;* the extrovert is conceptualized by Eysenck as having a strong (stable) nervous system dominated by inhibitory processes *under moderate-intensity stimulation.* Under strong or intense stimulation, the introvert's nervous system responds with transmarginal or protective inhibition, whereas the extrovert's nervous system responds with increasing excitation. Thus, in Eysenck's view the introvert is "stimulus-shy," and the extrovert is "stimulus-hungry." The introvert withdraws from social contacts, from prolonged interaction with the physical environment, and from all arousing stimulation because he is so sensitive to such excitation. The extrovert seeks social stimulation, physical arousal, and excitement to feed his never-satiated cortical lethargy.

It is possible with these conceptual tools to derive a variety of behavioral phenomena concerning the conditionability of extreme (excitatory) introverts and extreme (inhibitory) extroverts. A direct application of the notion that introverts have weaker or more sensitive nervous systems would lead to the prediction that extreme introverts condition more rapidly than extreme extroverts. Yet such a formulation would fail to take account of important conditioning variables that might be expected to change the outcome. Variables like intensity of unconditioned and conditioned stimuli and their rate of presentation should be expected to differ-

FIGURE 15-3: TRANSMARGINAL INHIBITION (TMI) THRESHOLDS FOR "WEAK" AND "STRONG" NERVOUS SYSTEMS

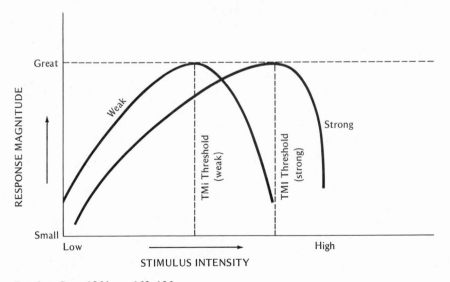

Based on Gray, 1964, pp. 162, 186.

entially affect the strong and the weak nervous system. Under certain conditions, extroverts should condition more easily or more rapidly than introverts.

In consequence, Eysenck turned to a more fully developed behavior theory that included among its concepts a more precise set of relationships between inhibition and excitation. With some modifications, Eysenck was able to adapt Clark L. Hull's *drive X habit* theory of learning to the task of individual personality prediction.

Hull's Drive Theory: Individual Differences in Performance

Clark L. Hull (1884–1952) developed an influential hypothetico-deductive theory of learning and performance that incorporated basic concepts similar to excitation and inhibition. The advantage of Hull's formulation from Eysenck's point of view was its relative precision in describing the interaction of inhibition and excitation.

Hull's theory (1943, 1951, 1952) was formulated to account for a different kind of conditioning from that of Pavlov's work with dogs. Instead of involuntary reflex conditioning, Hull was more concerned with instrumental conditioning. In this variety of learning, a voluntary response of the organism like pressing a bar or making right and left turns in a maze is rewarded or reinforced to increase the likelihood that the organism will repeat the response.

The basic premise underlying Hull's formulation was that reinforcers are stimuli that reduce or satisfy an organism's biological drives. For instrumental learning to occur, an organism must first be in a state of high drive arousal (e.g., very hungry). Then, those responses that the organism employs to obtain satisfaction for the drive will become associated with the stimuli on which the drive is based. In common-sense terms, if a hungry rat discovers through trial and error that turning right into a particular alley of a maze brings him reliably into contact with food, then right turns will become habitual whenever he is hungry in that maze.

To indicate the learned connection between the stimuli of the maze's choice points and the response of turning right, Hull employed a "habit" symbol: $_SH_R$. If the rat is not in a state of drive arousal (i.e., not hungry) when placed in the maze, then his habit of turning right at a particular choice point will have a low probability of being translated into actual behavior. As the hunger drive begins to mount in intensity, it will activate the previously reinforced habit of turning right at the appropriate choice point. Hull indicated this relationship between drive and habits with a simple symbolic notation:

$D \times {}_sH_R = {}_sE_R$, where ${}_sE_R$ indicates observable performance.

In words, the formulation states that observable performance is evoked when drive (D) multiplies previously learned stimulus-response connections or habits (${}_sH_R$). Clearly this simple formulation must be modified to take account of variables that would add to or subtract from the organism's drive arousal and past habit strengths. Hull suggested two competing forms of variables, *reactive inhibition* (I_R) and *conditioned inhibition* (${}_sI_R$).

Reactive and Conditioned Inhibition

Reactive inhibition (I_R) in Hull's formulation is similar to Pavlov's concept of internal inhibition. In Hull's theory, reactive inhibition is a kind of neural fatigue that develops gradually as responses are repetitively made. Serving as a negative drive state, I_R continues to increase until the amount of nervous system fatigue is great enough to cancel the animal's positive drive to respond.

A second kind of inhibition develops as a direct consequence of I_R. As I_R increases, the animal suffers a general feeling of fatigue and discomfort associated with continued responding. When he ceases to respond as a consequence of I_R, the fatigue of this "reactive inhibition" state is allowed to dissipate. Dissipation of I_R is experienced as satisfying or rewarding. But note what is being reinforced: the act of *not responding*. Thus there develops a conditioned negative habit, a tendency to not-respond. This second kind of inhibition is a *learned* inhibitory response reinforced by the reduction in I_R that rest produces. Hull referred to this kind of inhibition as *conditioned inhibition* (${}_sI_R$).

Hull entered the two kinds of inhibition into his general formula for learned performance in such a way that combined I_R and ${}_sI_R$ would *subtract* from drive's activation of habit:

$$S^{\overline{E}}R = (D \times {}_sH_R) - (I_R + {}_sI_R),$$

where ${}_s\overline{E}_R$ indicates resultant performance—that is, performance after total inhibition has been subtracted. It is important to emphasize that the two kinds of inhibition not only originate differently, but function differently. Whereas reactive inhibition (I_R) dissipates with time, conditioned inhibition (${}_sI_R$) is relatively enduring. Reactive inhibition is conceptualized as a negative, innate drive; conditioned inhibition is a *learned* negative habit.

Eysenck's Formulation of Drive, Habit, and Inhibition

The exact restructuring of Hull's formula that Eysenck adopted for his 1957 model of personality is somewhat complex and concerned with theoretical issues in learning theory that may be omitted here.[1] For present purposes it is sufficient to understand that Eysenck adopted the general Hullian notion that drive multiplies habits and that inhibition reduces the effects of positive drive. Eysenck provided a clear example of the relationship among these variables in the analogy of a person playing tennis:

> Clearly the excellence of his [tennis] performance will depend upon two things. It will depend, in the first place, on his drive; the more highly motivated he is to play well, the better his performance will be, on the whole. It also depends, of course, on his experience and on the amount of practice that he has previously put into the task, on the length of time he has been playing, and so on. In other words, it will depend on the system of bodily habits which he has built up during the past [$_sH_R$]. ... His actual performance will be a function of both these variables; *the stronger the drive, and the more highly developed the habits which are necessary for carrying out his task, the better his performance will be.* Where does inhibition fit into this picture?
>
> The answer of course is this. If a person is carrying out a task, particularly under conditions of massed practice, then inhibition will continue to accumulate. Being a negative drive, it will subtract from the positive drive under which the organism is working. And, finally, when inhibition builds up to such an extent that it is equal to positive drive under which the person is working, he will simply cease to work altogether because now drive is equal to inhibition, and drive minus inhibition equals zero. If we put this into our general formula it will read: performance equals habit X zero. Habit X zero—or indeed, anything multiplied by zero—is, of course, zero and, therefore, performance will cease. [1964a, p. 73; italics added]

The logical deduction to be made from this conceptualization of the effects of inhibition on drive is that continued performance leads ultimately to a

---

[1]For readers with a strong interest in Hullian theory it may be of some benefit to record Eysenck's modified performance formula (Eysenck, 1957a, p. 58):

$$_sE_R = f \ (D_+ \times {}_sH_R) + f \ (D_+ \times {}_sI_R) + f \ (D_- \times {}_sH_R) + f \ (D_- \times {}_sI_R)$$

The important consideration about Eysenck's adaptation of Hull's formulation is that each of the components in the above notation involves a habit component ($_sH_R$ or $_sI_R$) multiplied by either a positive (D_+) or a negative drive (D_-) component. In this way, even the simplest performance is conceptualized as having complex determinants of drive, inhibition, and habit strength. The last term of the formula [$D_- \times {}_sI_R$] involves the multiplication of two negative components, that is, the multiplication of negative drive (originally called I_R) and conditioned inhibition. Such a multiplication would produce, paradoxically, a positive effect on performance. The first term of the formula [$D_+ \times {}_sH_R$] also produces a positive effect on performance. The second and third terms, however, result in a negative influence, a tendency *not* to respond.

cessation of activity. Such a cessation may be only momentary, but if the prediction is correct, the performer will experience a fleeting block to further action. There is a good deal of experimental evidence that such blocks to performance occur. For a firsthand experience of what is sometimes termed an *involuntary rest pause* (IRP), try the following demonstration:

> Simply tap, as fast as you can, with the index fingers of your right and left hands, on the edge of the table, trying to maintain a rhythm. After a very short time, you will find that one or the other of your fingers will cease to obey your will; it will suddenly take an involuntary rest pause on its own, disrupting your performance and making it impossible for you to continue. This involuntary rest pause is quite brief. It is not a question of muscular fatigue, because the amount of muscular energy expended is minimal. Nevertheless, you will find that you are quite incapable, for a period of perhaps half a second to a second, of bringing the behaviour of your fingers under your voluntary control. [Eysenck, 1964a, p. 74]

During the period of the IRP, inhibition will dissipate. Performance may then again continue at the rapid rate attained before inhibition reached the critical level. As we shall see, important predictions about introverts' and extroverts' performances can be made.

The Theoretical Yield: Hippocrates, Pavlov, Jung, and Hull

The contributions of the early Greek physicians, Pavlov, Jung, and Hull provided Eysenck with the conceptual tools to formulate a *causal* explanation of the differences between introverts and extroverts. The early temperament theory of Hippocrates and Galen suggested the basic dimensions along which individual personalities may be arranged. Pavlov's excitation-inhibition hypothesis of cortical functioning provided the first clues to the physiological basis of these personality dimensions. In addition, Pavlov's work partly confirmed Jung's clinical insight into the relationships between introversion and anxiety neuroses, and between extroversion and hysterical disorder. Hull's *drive* X *habit – inhibition* formulation of learning contributed the necessary theoretical relationships to bridge the gap between physiological speculation and observable performance.

With these conceptual tools at his disposal, Eysenck was able to formulate a pair of personality postulates that would combine these various antecedent theories into a coherent, yet tentative, experimental model of why introverts differ from extroverts.

Individual Differences and Typological Postulates: An Experimental Theory

To span the distance between the theory of excitation-inhibition and personality types, Eysenck postulated that people differ in their *balance* of excitation to inhibition processes:

The Postulate of Individual Differences

Human beings differ with respect to the speed with which excitation and inhibition are produced, the strength of the excitation and inhibition produced, and the speed with which inhibition is dissipated. These differences are properties of the physical structures involved in making stimulus-response connections. [1957a, p. 114]

With the postulate of individual differences Eysenck was proposing that personality psychologists and experimental psychologists join forces in investigating a variable that had often been interpreted as having interest only for the experimentalist. Excitation and inhibition were now to be conceptualized as fundamental to any understanding of personality differences.

To extend the logic of his position, Eysenck also proposed a relatively precise specification of these personality differences in relation to excitation and inhibition processes:

The Typological Postulate

Individuals in whom *excitatory* potential is generated *slowly* and in whom *excitatory potentials* so generated are relatively *weak,* are thereby predisposed to develop *extraverted* patterns of behaviour and to develop *hysterical-psychopathic* disorders in cases of neurotic breakdown; individuals in whom *excitatory* potential is generated *quickly* and in whom *excitatory* potentials so generated are *strong,* are thereby predisposed to develop *introverted* patterns of behaviour and to develop *dysthymic* disorders [anxiety, phobias, obsessive-compulsive symptoms] in case of neurotic breakdown. Similarly, individuals in whom *reactive inhibition* is developed *quickly,* in whom *strong* reactive inhibitions are generated, and in whom reactive inhibition is *dissipated slowly,* are thereby predisposed to develop *hysterical-psychopathic* disorders in case of neurotic breakdown; conversely, individuals in whom *reactive inhibition* is developed *slowly,* in whom *weak* reactive inhibitions are generated, and in whom reactive inhibition is *dissipated quickly,* are thereby predisposed to develop *introverted* patterns of behaviour and to develop dysthymic disorders in case of neurotic breakdown. [1957a, p. 114; italics added.]

With the typological postulate, Eysenck laid the groundwork for a truly hypothetico-deductive model of personality. Introverts were conceptualized as having stronger and more easily aroused excitatory processes, coupled with their rapid dissipation of inhibition. Extroverts, on the other hand, were conceptualized as having relatively weak excitatory processes and slow dissipation of inhibition. Taking only the *extreme* extrovert and the *extreme* introvert as models, the typological postulate can be summarized in the form of a table. When reading Table 15–2 it must be remembered that Eysenck's typology is dimensional, allowing for degree of expression of inhibition and excitation, whereas the summary in Table 15–2 is essentially categorical.

On the basis of the typological postulate, a number of hypotheses can be deduced about introverts' and extroverts' performance in laboratory situations. For example, if introverts do have stronger excitatory cortical processes and relatively weak inhibitory effects, they should condition more quickly than extroverts in laboratory tasks like eye-blink conditioning. Other deductions can be made along these same lines. For any task that requires strong excitatory processes and the rapid dissipation of inhibition, introverts should evidence superior performance. Three representative areas of study will illustrate this deduction.

Eye-Blink Conditioning: Introverts Are Not Always Superior

Evidence drawn from human classical conditioning experiments contains some element of confusion. An early study of the conditioned eye-blink response by Cyril Franks (1956) was explicitly designed to test Eysenck's hypothesis of the superior conditionability of introverts. Using a precisely measured blast of air delivered through a specially prepared pair of eyeglasses, Franks conditioned sixty dysthymic, hysteric, and normal subjects to blink to the sound of a tone. Franks' procedure resembled Pavlov's work with the conditioned salivary response: the *unconditioned stimulus* (UCS) was the puff of air, the *unconditioned response* (UCR) was an electrically measured eye blink, and the *conditioned response* (CR) was, of course, the new eye-blink response to the *conditioned stimulus* (CS), a tone presented over the subject's earphones.

TABLE 15–2:   **SUMMARY OF TYPOLOGICAL POSTULATE AS EXTREME TYPES**

	EXCITATION	INHIBITION	NEUROTIC PREDISPOSITION
Introverts	High (Rapid)	Low (Slow)	Dysthymia
Extroverts	Low (Slow)	High (Rapid)	Hysteria-Psychopathy

Based on Eysenck, 1957a.

Twenty subjects composed each of the three groups. Assignment to dysthymic, hysteric, or normal classification was made on the basis of psychiatric diagnoses, paper-and-pencil measures of personality, and direct observation of symptoms. Subjects in the dysthymic and hysteric groups were selected to represent extreme cases of each disorder. All subjects were presented with thirty reinforced (paired CS and UCS) trials, interspersed with eighteen test trials (CS alone). The subject's participation in the experiment ended with ten consecutive extinction trials (CS alone). Franks also measured each subject's psychogalvanic skin response (PGR), on the assumption that differences in conditionability would be reflected even in this autonomic nervous system sweat response.

The results of Franks' experiment seemed to provide evidence that dysthymics acquire a greater number of conditioned eye blinks to the tone than either normals or hysterics. Hysterics tended to resemble normals in conditioning rate. The one measure that separated dysthymics, normals, and hysterics at a statistically significant level was their measured degree of introversion/extroversion, not their type of neurosis. Dysthymics, extremely introverted, had conditioned "better" than either normals or extroverts (i.e., the hysterics). Franks' experiment thus supported Eysenck's hypothesis.

A later study by Franks (1957) confirmed his early finding that neuroticism of itself was not the basis of differing performance in the conditioning task for dysthymics and hysterics. Franks' study was considered crucial for Eysenck's theory because a variety of other workers had suggested that all neurotic subjects, having heightened emotional drive, would condition faster than normals. Franks' studies showed that introversion/extroversion, not neuroticism (or emotional drive), differentiated easily conditioned from poorly conditioned subjects.

A problem arose for Eysenck's hypothesis when Franks himself (1963) and several independent investigators were unable to replicate his original findings. Eysenck reviewed the literature reporting no differences between introverts and extroverts in conditionability and drew an important conclusion. Those investigators who had failed to establish exactly identical conditions of reinforcement rate and conditioned and unconditioned stimulus intensities were the ones who had failed to find any conditioning differences between introverts and extroverts.

Specifically, Eysenck argued that his 1957 statement of the typological postulate had specified that inhibition would rise during nonreinforced trials (CS alone). Trials on which the unconditioned stimulus is present (i.e., the air puff) provide strong excitation that prevents or disrupts the development of inhibition. Thus, in Franks' procedure of interspersing test and reinforcement trials, extroverts had been provided with an opportunity to develop strong inhibitory effects. *Partial reinforcement* of this sort favors the introvert because he has the capacity to dissipate quickly the small amount of inhibition he develops; the extrovert, on the other hand, slowly dissipates the large amount of inhibition he has developed. Thus, in Franks' (1956) investigation extroverts conditioned more poorly than introverts because the conditioning parameters favored the introverts.

Eysenck was led to specify more carefully the theoretical assumptions from which predictions were to be made. In concrete terms, Eysenck (1967, 1966) now delineated three parameters that would favor introverts and, consequently, three opposite parameters under which extroverts would be expected to condition more rapidly. First, *partial reinforcement* procedures would favor introverts for the reasons already specified.

Second, the *strength of the unconditioned stimulus* (e.g., air puff) might be expected to act differentially on introverts and extroverts. Low-strength UCS would be expected to foster the growth of inhibition, whereas relatively strong UCS should favor the development of excitation. However, as we have seen, Teplov had shown that increasing the strength of the UCS increases the intensity of the conditioned response only up to some limiting point, beyond which the response intensity decreases as transmarginal (protective) inhibition sets in. For introverts TMI is reached sooner. Thus, at levels near the transmarginal inhibition point, strong unconditioned stimuli should favor extroverts because their strong inhibitory nervous systems profit most from stimuli intensities that are disorganizing for the more sensitive introvert nervous systems.

Third, the *interval between the CS and the UCS* (i.e., between tone and puff of air) should be assumed to affect the rates of conditioning for introverts and extroverts. A short interval between CS and UCS favors the introvert because his more sensitive nervous system is able to respond to this rapid rate of presentation, whereas the extrovert's more inhibitory nervous system cannot keep pace. Furthermore, the more rapid the rate at which the UCS follows the CS, the more rapidly will reactive inhibition (fatigue) build in the extrovert's nervous system, thus causing poorer conditioning performance.

Eysenck (1966, pp. 503 ff.) cited an unpublished study by A. Levey in which all three parameters were manipulated with introvert, extrovert, and ambivert (equally introverted and extroverted) subjects. Levey employed partial reinforcement (67 percent) versus continuous reinforcement (100 percent); long CS-UCS interval (800 milliseconds) versus short CS-UCS interval (400 milliseconds); and strong UCS (6 pounds of pressure per square inch) versus weak UCS (3 pounds of pressure per square inch). Levey's results were something less than completely confirmatory of Eysenck's hypotheses. Yet, on the whole, when conditions were arranged to favor the introverts, they tended to condition more rapidly than extroverts; conversely, when the three parameters were arranged to favor the extroverts, their performance was superior to introverts' performance. Figures 15–4 and 15–5 show the conditioning rates for introverts and extroverts under favorable and unfavorable conditions. Eysenck summarized the general results of Levey's study in this way:

FIGURE   15–4

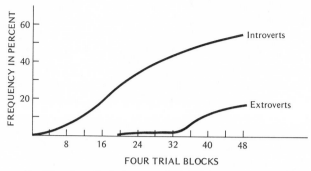

Conditions favorable for introverts: Partial reinforcement, weak UCS, and short CS–USC interval.

From A. Levey, as reported by Eysenck, 1966, p. 507; curves are somewhat idealized and fitted to data points.

If the results of this experiment can be taken as representative, we might conclude that strength of the UCS was the most important parameter [separating extroverts and introverts], followed by CS-UCS interval, with reinforcement schedule last. [1966, p. 504]

Motor Movements and Involuntary Rest Pauses

Using a behavioral phenomenon with which we are already familiar, Spiel-mann (1936) was able to demonstrate that extroverts develop more fre-quent involuntary rest pauses (IRP) than introverts on a task involving massed practice. As usual, this prediction was made on the theoretical assumption that during unrelieved responding, the extrovert's more rapid

FIGURE   15–5

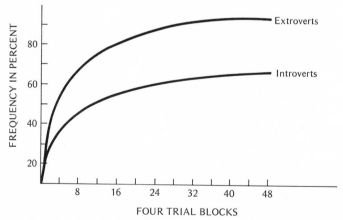

Conditions favorable for extroverts: 100 percent reinforcement, strong UCS, and long CS–UCS interval.

buildup of inhibitory cortical effects causes him to experience many of these involuntary "time-outs."

Subjects in Spielmann's investigation were required to tap repeatedly with a metal stylus on a metal plate. The time the metal stylus was in contact with the metal plate was automatically recorded, and each gap between contacts was likewise registered. From ninety working-class participants, the five most introverted and the five most extroverted were selected on the basis of personality questionnaire scores.

As expected, the average IRP scores showed that the extrovert subjects paused nearly fifteen times as often as the introverts. Careful analysis of the data also demonstrated that the onset of IRPs was significantly earlier in the task for the extrovert group than for the introverts (Eysenck, 1953, p. 432; cf. Eysenck, 1963a, 1964a, pp. 76 ff., and 1964b).

Auditory Vigilance: Gaps in Attention

Another laboratory task on which extroverts and introverts may be expected to differ in performance is the vigilance or "watch-keeping" perceptual problem (Mackworth, 1950, 1957, Bakan, 1959). Vigilance tasks may take many forms, but they all have in common that the subject is required to detect in a long series of stimuli a particular sudden change or discrepancy in the sequence. Thus, for example, a subject may listen to a lengthy recording of someone pronouncing a seemingly endless series of digits. His task is to detect three successive odd digits—when they occur. A vigilance task may also be performed in the visual mode. A subject sits facing an electric clock device whose hands jump at one second intervals. His goal is to detect an irregular double jump of the sweep hand—when it occurs.

On theoretical grounds it may be expected that introverts will perform better—detect more of the required stimuli—than extroverts. Because inhibition builds rapidly in extroverts and because a vigilance task is monotonous, the extrovert will experience more IRPs than the introvert. When an IRP happens to coincide with the occurrence of the stimulus that is to be detected, the extrovert will miss it. Introverts, on the other hand, experiencing fewer IRPs and having greater stimulus sensitivity, should miss fewer of the designated stimuli.

Claridge (1967) employed an auditory vigilance task involving the detection of three consecutive odd digits with fifty-seven dysthymics, forty-eight hysterics, and fifty-five normal subjects. Dysthymics (introverts) were predicted to perform better than the hysterics. Besides a score for the vigilance task, Claridge also monitored subjects' physiological arousal with measurements of galvanic skin response and heart rate. Results showed that, as predicted, dysthymics were superior in total vigilance scores to hysterics and to normals. On the physiological measures, dysthymics showed a higher level of arousal (heart rate and GSR) than either normals or extroverts throughout the duration of the task.

The Biological Basis of Personality: Arousability and the ARAS

The clear implication of Eysenck's proposal that individuals differ in their excitation/inhibition balance is that this difference is mediated by something in the central nervous system. Fundamentally, Eysenck's theory is biological, though of necessity most tests of the theory are behavioral. In 1967, Eysenck revised and extended his basic introversion-extroversion theory by postulating specific relationships between these personality dimensions and the *ascending reticular activating system* (ARAS) of the brain. He also now rooted the dimension of normality-neuroticism (dysthymia and hysteria) in central nervous system structures. A group of functionally related subcortical structures, including the hypothalamus, the gyrus cinguli, the hippocampus, and their interconnections, had been conceptualized by James W. Papez (1937) as mediators of bodily arousal associated with emotion. Producing their effects by activating the involuntary branch of the nervous system, these structures are responsible for changes in heart rate, respiration, blood pressure, and other signs of emotional activation. To the entire group of structures the names *visceral brain* and *limbic system* are often applied.

The relationships that Eysenck proposed can be summarized succinctly in two word equations:

Introversion/Extroversion = Differences in ARAS Arousal
Normality/Neuroticism = Differences in Visceral Brain Activation

ARAS and Cortical Arousal

The ascending reticular activating system is a network of fibers extending from the spinal cord to the thalamus of the brain at a level below the cortex. Figure 15–6 illustrates the basic location and boundaries of the ARAS. (It might be helpful for readers unfamiliar with basic neuroanatomy to consult an introductory physiological psychology text. Thompson's [1967] is a particularly good one.)

Figure 15–6 also shows the general location of the visceral brain (VB) structures, though in reality these structures are more widely separated. The ascending arrows indicate the direction of influence of the ARAS on the cortex. Descending arrows, from the cortex toward the ARAS, indicate the reciprocal influence of the cortex on the ARAS. Generally, the ARAS serves to stimulate the cortex, to activate its cells to a state of excitability. The cortex may in turn "feed back" on the ARAS either to further increase its excitatory input or to damp it down.

Physiological interest in this arousal network or reticulum of fibers began when it was discovered in 1935 by Bremer that cutting through the brain stem at midbrain level caused cats to become almost permanently

FIGURE 15-6: ANATOMICAL LOCATIONS OF ARAS AND VB

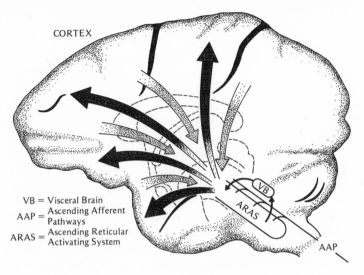

CORTEX

VB = Visceral Brain
AAP = Ascending Afferent Pathways
ARAS = Ascending Reticular Activating System

From Eysenck, 1967, p. 231.

sleeping animals. The electrical activity of such cats' brains showed a characteristic "sleeping wave" on the electroencephalograph (EEG). In a normally sleeping cat, it is possible to induce an arousal EEG pattern by simply waking the animal or doing something to engage his attention. But in cats with transected brain stems it was possible to produce an arousal EEG pattern only for short periods lasting as long as the stimulus used to arouse the cat.

In 1949, Moruzzi and Magoun, instead of shutting down the ARAS by cutting into the brain stem, set out to stimulate it electrically. Records of EEG tracings from the cortex of stimulated cats showed that stimulation of the ARAS evokes cortical arousal.

The ARAS seems also to be involved in states of attention and concentration. Fuster (1958) was able to improve rhesus monkeys' performance on a visual discrimination task by stimulating their ARAS. This finding suggests that part of the ARAS's function may be to mediate information processing in humans (cf. French, 1957). The evidence, however, is somewhat contradictory (Eysenck, 1967; Thompson, 1967). Generally it seems safe to say that the ARAS is responsible for cortical efficiency in learning, conditioning, wakefulness, and attention. The ARAS seems to mediate states of arousal, ranging from sleep to extreme behavioral excitation.

There is, however, another portion of the ARAS that seems to have an inhibitory effect on the cortex. Known as the "recruiting system," this portion of the ARAS serves to damp down cortical excitation. Thus, in the ARAS Eysenck seems to have found the physiological causes of excitation and inhibition and, therefore, the basis of introversion-extroversion. The specific relationships between ARAS arousal thresholds and introversion-extroversion will be discussed shortly. It is possible, however, to recognize at this point that introverts are assumed to have higher levels of ARAS arousal (lower ARAS thresholds) than extroverts.

Visceral Brain and Emotional Activation

The second personality dimension exemplified by the extreme criterion groups of dysthymics and hysterics compared to normals is the dimension of normality-neuroticism. Eysenck assumes that this dimension consists largely of differences in emotional activation such that neurotics are more highly emotionally reactive than normals. In this sense, the structures of the visceral brain (VB) are conceptualized as the mediators of this reactivity.

Though we cannot review the relevant research relating the structures of the VB (hypothalamus and limbic system) to states of emotion, it is perhaps sufficient to point out that the hypothalamus and other visceral brain units exert their effects through the autonomic or involuntary nervous system. The range of neural effect extends from activation of glands and muscles to heart rate, respiration, and perspiration. Individuals in whom there is a low threshold of visceral brain activation (i.e., behaviorally high emotional activation) are presumed to be susceptible to neurotic disorder. Thus, in short, the visceral brain's level of activation ranges from low (normal) to chronically high (neurotic).

There is a complicating factor connected with the visceral brain and neuroticism. In states of extreme emotional activation (e.g., intense rage, or profound sadness, or extreme fear), the normal separation of functioning between the ARAS's arousal of the cortex and the VB's emotional activation of the autonomic nervous system breaks down. In effect, the dimensions of introversion-extroversion and neuroticism-normality lose their independence when the individual is emotionally active (Eysenck, 1967, p. 232). Thus, while it is possible to be intellectually aroused without emotional activation, it is impossible to be emotionally activated without simultaneous intellectual or cortical arousal.

In the first case, that of cortical arousal without VB (emotional) activation, problem-solving activity dominates the individual. For example, Eysenck cites the case of the scientist sitting quite immobile and to all appearances fast asleep. But subjectively, his mind is hard at work tackling unsolved and intricate professional problems (Eysenck 1967, p. 232). His cortex is aroused, but his emotions are not.

In the second kind of arousal, the visceral brain and the autonomic nervous system become involved. This type of "activation" might be illustrated by the scientist sitting quietly in his bath when suddenly the long-sought solution to his "impossible" problem dawns on him. He has been *intellectually* aroused all the while that he sat in the bath. He runs screaming from the bath, shouting "Eureka!" with mad abandon, while a euphoric sense of ecstasy wells within him. Heart pounding, short of breath, profusely perspiring, this scientist now presents a clear picture of emotional activation *and* intellectual arousal.

In cases where the level of emotional activation is intense, cortical arousal must also have occurred. Thus, in Eysenck's dimensional system, the separation of intellectual arousal from emotional activation holds only for normal individuals. *Neurotics evidence a capacity for emotional arousal to stimuli that would be only cortically arousing to a normal individual* (Eysenck, 1967, p. 233). In more technical terms, the neurotic individual is reaching maximum cortical and emotional arousal nearly simultaneously because the hypothalamus and other structures in the limbic system (visceral brain) are bombarding the ARAS with stimulation. At the same time, the ARAS is arousing the cortex.

Translation of Excitation/Inhibition into Arousal Concepts

With the proposal that biological bases might be found for the dimensions of introversion-extroversion and for normality-neuroticism, Eysenck sharpened the causal level of his personality theory.

To make clear the transition from the 1957 theory of excitation/inhibition to the 1967 theory of biological functions, it is necessary to distinguish among four extreme types of personality. Individuals may be said to be normal or neurotic, introverted or extroverted, with of course various degrees in between these absolutes. It follows that an individual may be a normal introvert or a neurotic introvert, just as he may be a normal extrovert or a neurotic extrovert. The hypothetical nervous system states of ARAS arousal and VB activation that correspond to these four extreme types are indicated in Table 15–3.

TABLE 15–3: BIOLOGICAL BASIS OF PERSONALITY

DIMENSIONAL POSITION	LEVEL OF ARAS AROUSAL	LEVEL OF VB ACTIVATION
Normal Introvert	High	Low
Normal Extrovert	Low	Low
Neurotic Introvert (Dysthymic)	High	High
Neurotic Extrovert (Hysteric)	Low[*]	High

[*]Note that the *neurotic* extrovert's ARAS arousal is higher than the normal extrovert's ARAS arousal because of the breakdown of separation between ARAS and VB functioning in states of high (neurotic) emotion. But the extrovert's characteristic ARAS arousal level is always lower than the introvert's level, and is therefore simply listed as "low."

Based on Eysenck, 1967.

It is obvious that the emphasis in this biological version of Eysenck's theory is on differences in arousal level (excitation) rather than on inhibition-level differences. In Eysenck's previous model of these personality dimensions, most of the experimental tests were directed to the hypothesized effects of inhibition (e.g., IRPs, vigilance). Experimental tests of the biological theory, however, usually spring from hypotheses about the effects of the introvert's higher cortical ARAS arousal. With this shift in theoretical emphasis came several complications. The one of immediate interest in the present context concerns a general law of motivation proposed in 1908 by Yerkes and Dodson.

The Yerkes-Dodson Law: Inverted-U Hypothesis

Yerkes and Dodson proposed a principle of motivation and performance that, with some modifications, has been widely accepted in contemporary psychology by theorists interested in states of arousal. In briefest form, Yerkes and Dodson's law states that motivation or arousal may be conceptualized as a continuum ranging from very low levels through very high levels of excitation. At the low end of the continuum, the organism is so underaroused (undermotivated) that it falls asleep. At the high end, the organism is so aroused that its behavior is disorganized, fragmented, or frenzied. Yerkes and Dodson proposed that between these two extremes lies a state of moderate arousal in which the organism is sufficiently motivated to perform well, but not so aroused as to be disorganized or distracted.

Modern theorists (e.g., Malmo, 1959; Hebb, 1955; Lindsley, 1951; Broadhurst, 1959) refer to this hypothesis as the "inverted-U hypothesis" for reasons that will be obvious after inspecting Figure 15–7.

FIGURE 15-7: INVERTED-U LAW OF MOTIVATION AND PERFORMANCE

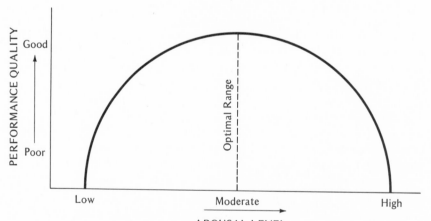

Performance is optimal at moderate levels of arousal.

Figure 15–7 shows in idealized form the relationship between arousal level and quality of performance. As arousal increases, performance improves until it reaches a maximum at the height of the inverted-U curve. From that point onward, increases in arousal lead to decreases in performance. This hypothesis clearly has direct relationship to Teplov's strength-of-the-nervous-system concept and the effects of transmarginal inhibition previously illustrated in Figure 15–3. A complication must be added to the inverted-U hypothesis. What happens, we might ask, when the task that the individual is performing can vary in difficulty or complexity? Will tasks of different difficulty levels require different levels of optimal arousal? The answer is a definite yes. If we confine our consideration of task difficulty to three arbitrary levels, low, medium, and high difficulty, then we can plot motivation-performance curves for each task level. Figure 15–8 illustrates the theoretical relationships among task-difficulty level, performance, and arousal level.

FIGURE 15-8: YERKES-DODSON LAW FOR INTERACTION OF AROUSAL LEVEL, PERFORMANCE, AND TASK DIFFICULTY

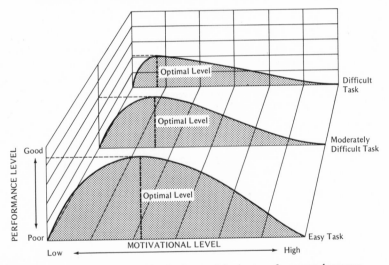

As task difficulty increases, optimal level of arousal for best performance decreases. From Eysenck, 1963, p. 131.

The three curves in Figure 15–8 are designed to indicate that the optimal level of arousal for best performance changes as task-difficulty level increases. For tasks of low difficulty, a somewhat higher level of arousal or motivation is optimal than for tasks of moderate difficulty. Tasks of greatest difficulty require the lowest level of arousal. The general rule is: *The more difficult the task, the lower the optimum arousal.*

With the Yerkes-Dodson law in mind, predictions from Eysenck's biological model of personality cannot only be more precise, but can also take account of the interaction between cortical arousal and emotional activation. Levey's results with variations of the three conditioning parameters of partial reinforcement, CS-UCS interval, and UCS intensity are more easily explained by this refined model than by the earlier excitation/inhibition account. It will be recalled that Levey's results showed that the most important parameter manipulation separating introverts from extroverts was stimulus intensity. Extroverts conditioned better with strong UCS (air puff), and introverts were superior with the weak UCS. If UCS intensity is conceptualized as a form of arousal, the Yerkes-Dodson law predicts that introverts, having a higher level of initial arousal, will perform poorly with the additional arousal provided by a strong UCS. Extroverts, on the other hand, profit from the arousal increment because their initial cortical arousal is low.

A Test of the Yerkes-Dodson Law

An interesting question now poses itself. The four extreme types of individual (normal and neurotic introverts, and normal and neurotic extroverts) should, in principle, possess differing levels of combined cortical and emotional arousal. Presumably, neurotic introverts, in whom ARAS and VB excitation are both chronically high, should be placed at the top rank of a hierarchy of arousal. Normal extroverts, having low ARAS arousal and low VB activation, should fall at the bottom of the hierarchy of arousal. In between these extremes, normal introverts and neurotic extroverts, each having *one* form of high arousal, should evidence moderate degrees of excitation. The theory, however, does not specify whether the normal introvert is more highly aroused than the neurotic extrovert. Consequently, only an empirical investigation can provide rankings for these two personality types (cf. Eysenck, 1953b, pp. 436 ff., and 1967, pp. 182 ff.). It might, however, be supposed that a very neurotic extrovert would surpass a normal introvert in absolute drive level because the neurotic extrovert's emotional reactivity acts as a multiplier of habits in Hull's sense of the term.

To illustrate this kind of experimental test of the theory, McLaughlin and Eysenck (1967) had the four different types of criterion personalities learn lists of paired nonsense syllables. One list was difficult to learn, and the other relatively easy. Results were tabulated in terms of the number of errors a subject made in reaching a specified criterion of learning. In addition to determining the optimum level of arousal for learning, the experiment was also designed to test a hypothesis about a phenomenon called "reminiscence."

Experimental psychologists have known for a long time that memory for a learned response improves if time intervenes between the acquisition of the response and its performance. Thus, when studying for an exam in psychology, recitation of what has been learned will be better the following day when compared to immediate recitation. During the period of rest, the memory is consolidated, or made more permanent in specific neural circuits. However, while the process of consolidation is in progress, performance of the learned response is impeded. Thus, memory seems to improve with rest, for rest allows consolidation to reach completion.

Eysenck hypothesized that the process of consolidation is most facilitated in individuals having high initial cortical arousal, that is, in introverts. Thus, introverts should show poorest performance on memory tasks that require immediate postacquisition performance, whereas extroverts, who have low arousal and poor consolidation, will perform best immediately after acquisition (cf. McLaughlin & Eysenck, 1967, pp. 574 ff.).

In the experiment conducted by McLaughlin and Eysenck (1967), tests of memory for the learned lists were conducted immediately after acquisition, and thus favored extroverts. But, as we already know, the Yerkes-Dodson law also governs performance on tasks of varying difficulty. It can be presumed that the difficult list of paired nonsense syllables would present a task requiring a moderately low level of arousal for optimal performance. Thus, taking the two effects together, the reminiscence evidence indicates that extroverts should perform better with immediate recall, whereas the Yerkes-Dodson law suggests that on the difficult list the low-arousal normal extroverts will show superior performance to neurotic extroverts, and to all highly aroused introvert personalities. Conversely, learning the easy list should require a higher level of arousal than learning the difficult list to produce optimal performance. The prediction for the easy list thus must be that neurotic extroverts will evidence best performance because they have slightly higher arousal than normal extroverts. Neurotic introverts, having the highest level of combined ARAS and VB arousal, should, in principle, be too highly aroused to perform well on either list under conditions of immediate recall.

Figures 15–9 and 15–10 show the outcome of McLaughlin and Eysenck's investigation. The major predictions about the superiority of extroverts' performance were confirmed. Moreover, when a line is drawn through the plotted error scores for all subjects, the resulting curves resemble the inverted-U motivation-performance curve. As expected, the optimal level of arousal is shifted to the left (i.e., toward lower optimal arousal) for the difficult list.

One prediction, however, received no support. On the difficult list, neurotic introverts, while performing more poorly than normal extroverts as predicted, had fewer errors than normal introverts. The difference between neurotic and normal introverts was not significantly different. Yet it is difficult to understand why the less highly aroused normal introverts scored more poorly than neurotic introverts. A further unanswered question remains: If performance tests were administered *after* a rest period, would introverts then show superior recall? The elegance of Eysenck's theory is that it allows such questions to be asked.

FIGURE 15-9: **EASY LIST**

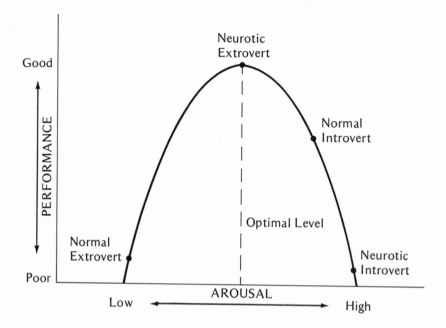

Based on McLaughlin & Eysenck, 1967.

FIGURE 15-10: **DIFFICULT LIST**

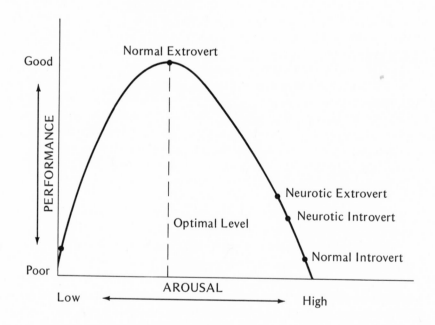

Based on McLaughlin & Eysenck, 1967.

Direct Tests of the Arousal Theory:
Stimulant and Depressant Drugs

The translation of the excitation/inhibition hypothesis into its biological equivalent of ARAS arousal levels led to testable hypotheses of a somewhat different sort than those based on the usual laboratory tasks.

If ARAS bombardment of the cortex is really the basis of the introversion/extroversion dimension of personality, then stimulant and depressant drugs should produce behavioral effects similar to those produced by excitation and inhibition. Furthermore, stimulants and depressants should produce different effects in introverts and extroverts. "In general, the prediction would be that stimulant drugs lead to greater arousal and hence to more introverted behavior, while depressant drugs lead to greater inhibition and hence to more extroverted behavior" (Eysenck, 1967, p. 265).

The preexisting state of arousal in a particular experimental subject would, of course, have to be taken into account to allow for the fact that introverts begin any task with a higher arousal level than extroverts. Therefore, the general hypothesis can be refined: *introverts require less of a stimulant drug to reach a specified criterion of behavioral arousal than extroverts.* In a similar vein, it can be hypothesized that *introverts require a larger dose of a depressant drug to reach a specified criterion of inhibition than extroverts.*

A variety of research studies supports these predictions (e.g., Claridge, 1967; Laverty, 1958; Shagass & Kerenyi, 1958). Such studies generally employ a measurement of "sedation threshold." A particular drug, say, a depressant, is injected intravenously at a known rate until slurred speech and specific EEG changes are noted. The amount of the drug required to reach this criterion is a measure of sedation threshold (Shagass & Kerenyi, 1958). Shagass and Kerenyi showed that subjects classified as introverts by psychiatric diagnosis and by paper-and-pencil measures had higher sedation thresholds (i.e., required a larger dosage) than extrovert subjects, thus confirming Eysenck's theory. Furthermore, subjects classified as obsessional (belonging to the dysthymic group in Eysenck's terminology) also had higher sedation thresholds than subjects classified as hysterics.

Environmental Influences: Socialization
of Introverts and Extroverts

Eysenck's work, it will be recalled, began with an ill-omened investigation of psychiatric diagnostic reliability. He has never abandoned his interest in providing a laboratory-based and empirically testable foundation for the treatment of neurotics. Such treatment should be founded, in Ey-

senck's view, on the measurable differences between introverts and extroverts. Dysthymic disorders, characteristic of the highly aroused
introvert personality, may be conceptualized as *conditioned maladaptive responses,* acquired, of course, through Pavlovian-like processes (Eysenck,
1960). Hysterical disorders, characteristic of the less-aroused extrovert
personality, are conceptualized as failures to acquire certain essential responses for successful living. Eysenck and Rachman state the matter in this
way:

> Reinforcing events occur more or less at random in the histories of
> the people who constitute the population of a particular country.
> Those who are biologically predisposed to form conditioned re-
> sponses quickly, strongly and lastingly [i.e., introverts with high
> ARAS arousal] will easily develop dysthymic disorders because these
> are by hypothesis simply conditioned autonomic reactions. On the
> other hand, those who are biologically predisposed to form condi-
> tioned responses only weakly, poorly, and with great difficulty will
> fail to form very readily those conditioned responses which underlie
> the process of socialization. [1965, p. 40]

Eysenck has several times reviewed the evidence for the possible genetic
basis of the dimensions of introversion/extroversion and normality/-
neuroticism (1957a; 1967; 1973). His general conclusion has been that both
of these dimensions have strong dependence on genetic components, and
thus, to some as yet unspecified degree, both dimensions represent factors
that are inherited. The introvert inherits a nervous system easily able to
form conditioned responses, and if the introvert also inherits an emotionally reactive autonomic nervous system (high neuroticism), he will be in
a position to acquire strong anxiety responses. Such responses, so easily
acquired, almost certainly guarantee that the introvert will be inhibited,
sensitive to stimulation, and fearful in the presence of a demanding or
complex social environment. In short, the introvert is oversocialized.

The extrovert, by contrast, inherits the type of nervous system that is
not easily conditionable, not particularly sensitive to stimulation, and not
especially fearful in demanding or complex social situations. In fact, the
extrovert is a "stimulus seeker" because his relatively high levels of inhibitory cortical processes demand constant novel and potent input of external
excitation. Some evidence suggests that extroverts may be of two types.
In the first, sociability, or out-going, stimulus-seeking behavior predominates. In the second type of extrovert, impulsivity and an inability to keep
antisocial urges and behaviors in check predominate. The first type resembles the normal personality but may succumb to hysterical disorder. The
second type approaches the criminal or psychopathic personality (Eysenck,
1964a; Eysenck & Eysenck, 1969). Instead of exhibiting hysterical neurosis,
this second type of extrovert personality succumbs to criminal or antisocial

behaviors because he has failed to acquire the necessary socialization essential to ethical and moral control.

Some research suggests that neuroticism and extroversion/introversion are not orthogonal (e.g., Claridge, 1967; cf. Eysenck & Eysenck, 1969). It would appear that introversion is more closely related to neuroticism than is extroversion. Eysenck's original personality questionnaire for measuring introversion/extroversion, The Maudsley Personality Inventory, sometimes provided results that showed (introvert) dysthymics to be closely related to high neuroticism, whereas (extrovert) hysterics resembled normals on the neuroticism dimension. Eysenck has argued that this partial breakdown of orthogonality between neuroticism and introversion was an artifact of the Maudsley Personality Inventory's overinclusion of biased items (Eysenck & Eysenck, 1969). To obviate this difficulty, a new form of this instrument was devised that purports to demonstrate that the two dimensions are in fact independent as hypothesized. Called the Eysenck Personality Inventory (Eysenck & Eysenck, 1968), this test more or less confirmed the independence of the neuroticism and introversion dimensions. Yet, there still remains a substantial block of test and experimental evidence to suggest that extreme introversion is by its very nature a substantially more neurotic personality type than extroversion.

Later work by Eysenck resulted in yet a third personality assessment test. Called the Eysenck Personality Questionnaire (Eysenck & Eysenck, 1975a), this most recent version incorporates items to measure a third dimension of personality. *Psychoticism* has entered Eysenck's recent thinking as an additional dimension of disordered personality that, like neuroticism and introversion/extroversion, is inheritable. The psychoticism dimension is conceptualized as orthogonal to or independent of both neuroticism and introversion/extroversion. An individual who scores high in psychoticism is described by the Eysencks as a "loner" who cares very little for the company of other people. He shows overt hostility to others, even to close relations, and he tends to disregard dangers. He enjoys making fools of other individuals, and this trait may be carried to an extreme of cruelty. The high *P* scorer tends to find enjoyment in "unusual things," and often stands out as peculiar (Eysenck & Eysenck, 1975b, p. 5).

Taken together, the three dimensions indicate Eysenck's overall conception of personality. Each of the dimensions has both environmental and biological components. Eysenck has summarized his position on the relative importance of biological and environmental factors in shaping personality:

> Human behaviour is rightly said to be bio-social in nature, i.e., to have both biological and social causes; it is time the pendulum started swinging back from an exclusive preoccupation with social causes to an appropriate appreciation and understanding of biological causes. . . . Biological causes act in such a way as to predispose an

individual to respond in certain ways to stimulation; this stimulation may or may not occur, depending on circumstances which are entirely under environmental control. [1967, pp. 221–222]

Eysenck's theory, therefore, may be understood as an attempt to bridge two very wide gulfs: the gulf between a study of individual differences in personality and the experimental investigation of conditioning, learning, and perceptual phenomena; and the gulf between observable phenotype and inferred causal genotype of an organism. If Eysenck has not been completely successful, he has at the least demonstrated what the successful strategy will be.

Summary

Eysenck's theory of personality may best be described as a hierarchical model having a minimum of three levels. At the first phenotypic or observable level, personality types of introversion and extroversion are described in terms of measurable traits like sociability, shyness, impulsiveness, and activity. These traits are usually measured with paper-and-pencil instruments like the Maudsley Personality Inventory, the Eysenck Personality Inventory, or the Eysenck Personality Questionnaire. Eysenck's early research with soldiers and airmen at the Mill Hill Emergency Hospital involved this essentially descriptive approach.

At the second level of the hierarchy, performance on laboratory tasks like motor movements, conditioning, and vigilance is used to define the dimensions of introversion and extroversion. Specific predictions for differential performance on a variety of these tasks are made on the basis of the hypothetical third level.

The third level is the fundamental, causal basis of the upper two divisions. Conceptualized as an excitation/inhibition balance (or ARAS arousal and inhibition of the cortex), this causal level may be classed as the genotypical basis of personality. As an inheritable dimension, excitation/inhibition (or ARAS functioning) may be thought of as the biological roots of personality. Figure 15–11 illustrates these three levels of Eysenck's theory.

Eysenck's original factorial study of personality performance and physiological data derived from a large group of subjects demonstrated that two orthogonal (independent) dimensions could be used to describe their personalities. A dimension of introversion/extroversion and a dimension of normality/neuroticism were conceptualized as independent and continuous axes along which individuals could be arranged by degree. The typical extrovert may be described as one who likes people, is sociable, strongly attracted to novel and exciting stimuli, easygoing and optimistic. He is fond of practical jokes and sometimes becomes aggressive and impulsive,

FIGURE 15-11: THREE LEVELS OF EYSENCK'S THEORY

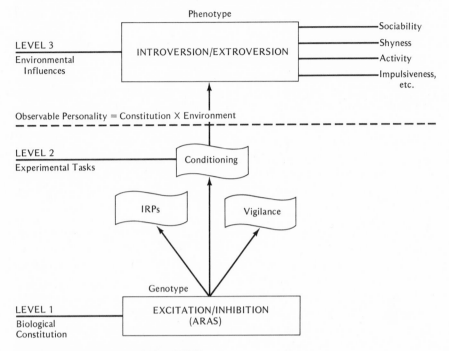

Simplified from Eysenck, 1964 and 1967.

unable to inhibit or control his anger. The typical introvert, by contrast, may be characterized as shy, quiet, withdrawn, and somewhat detached from the social environment. He is a planner, always looking ahead to anticipate problems before they arise. He avoids overt and intense stimulation and excitement, keeping his emotions under strict control. Generally pessimistic, the introvert behaves as if a well-ordered and quiet life were his chief desire (Eysenck & Eysenck, 1975b).

The individual who scores high in neuroticism may be characterized as emotionally reactive, anxious, moody, depressed. His sleep is disturbed, he experiences chronic fatigue and assorted bodily pains. "His main characteristic is a constant preoccupation with things that might go wrong, and a strong emotional reaction of anxiety to these thoughts" (Eysenck & Eysenck, 1975b p. 5).

Following Carl Jung's clinical insights that introverts succumb to dysthymic (psychasthenic or anxiety) disorders, and that extroverts succumb to hysterical neuroses, Eysenck was able to show that a long tradition stemming from Hippocrates and Galen through Pavlov and Hull had confirmed and refined Jung's hunches.

Pavlov's conditioning investigations established the existence of excitation and inhibition as fundamental cortical processes underlying types of temperament. Pavlov's concepts of the "strength of the nervous system" and of "transmarginal inhibition" were later elaborated by B. M. Teplov to account for personality dimensions similar to Eysenck's notion of introversion/extroversion.

Clark L. Hull's concepts of drive and habit, along with his notions of reactive and conditioned inhibition, provided Eysenck with key conceptual tools to begin devising a biological and causal account of the introversion/extroversion dimension. Introverts are individuals in whom the excitation/inhibition balance is tipped in the direction of excitation, giving them "weak" or sensitive nervous systems. Thus they condition more easily than extroverts, are more easily pained by excessive stimulation, and generally perform in a superior way on laboratory tasks requiring sustained attentiveness. Extroverts, by contrast, are individuals in whom the balance is tipped in the direction of greater inhibitory cortical functioning. For this reason, extroverts are said to have a "strong" nervous system not easily aroused by excessive stimulation, but one which is easily overcome with boredom by repetitious or monotonous tasks that rapidly build inhibition.

Eysenck has recently provided a biological translation and refinement of his excitation/inhibition theory. The ascending reticular activating system (ARAS) has been conceptualized as the basis of cortical arousal and inhibition. In this role, the ARAS is also the basis of introversion/extroversion. Introverts have more highly aroused ARAS functioning than extroverts. The dimension of neuroticism has been conceptualized as related to the functioning of the autonomic nervous system. Subcortical brain structures of the limbic system and the hypothalamus, known collectively as the "visceral brain" (VB), have been postulated by Eysenck to underlie the dimension of emotionality or neuroticism. Neurotics have a higher level of chronic VB activation than do stable or normal individuals. Under conditions of extreme emotional arousal, the separation between the introversion/extroversion dimension and the normality/neuroticism dimension breaks down. The visceral brain can thus supplement ARAS arousal of the cortex, evoking in the neurotic personality an even higher level of arousal than would otherwise be possible.

In terms of socialization, Eysenck has postulated that introverts are more socialized (inhibited, ethical, anxious) than extroverts because of their greater ease of conditioning. Extroverts are less socialized and may be divided into two extreme groups. Some extroverts are characterized essentially by a trait of extreme sociability, and these individuals tend to resemble the normal personality on measures of neuroticism. On the other hand, some extroverts are characterized by a trait of extreme impulsiveness and by a lack of ethical and moral inhibitions. These individuals are generally described as criminal or psychopathic personalities.

The advantage of Eysenck's theoretical strategy is that it allows for concrete predictions and tests of its validity. Furthermore, Eysenck's theory may eventually provide the basis for more rational and scientifically precise diagnosis and treatment of disordered behavior. The possibility of altering an individual's position on the introversion/extroversion dimension by means of depressant and stimulant drugs in order to alter his disordered behaviors may soon be feasible.

FOR FURTHER READING

The development of Eysenck's continually more biological formulations may be gleaned from successive reading of three of his works: *The Scientific Study of Personality* (London: Routledge & Kegan Paul, 1952), which concerns his early descriptive measurements of introversion-extroversion; *The Dynamics of Anxiety and Hysteria* (London: Routledge & Kegan Paul, 1957), which presents his more causal inhibition theory; and *The Biological Basis of Personality* (Springfield, Ill.: Charles C Thomas, 1967), which presents the definitive statement of his cortical hypotheses of arousal.

All three of the above-mentioned books are difficult reading. A more readable, though less comprehensive, overview of Eysenck's system may be had in his *Crime and Personality* (London: Routledge & Kegan Paul, 1964). At a popular level of presentation, Eysenck's *Psychology Is About People.* (New York: Library Press, 1972) not only provides a short account of his introversion-extroversion concepts but also surveys some of his wartime research on humor and aesthetic preferences. Another aspect of Eysenck's theory may be observed in *The Inequality of Man* (London: Temple Smith, 1973; also available from Robert Knapp, San Diego, Calif.), where Eysenck enters the current controversy surrounding the nature of IQ measurements.

A three-volume collection of research papers connected to his theory was edited by Eysenck under the title *Readings in Extraversion-Intraversion* (London: Staples, 1970–1971). Eysenck's low opinion of psychoanalytic theory and method may be sampled from his *Uses and Abuses of Psychology* (Baltimore: Penguin, 1953) and from his essay "Psychoanalysis: Myth or Science?" in S. Rachman (Ed.), *Critical Essays on Psychoanalysis* (New York: Pergamon Press, 1960).

Eysenck's position on behavior therapy for the neuroses is lucidly presented in *The Causes and Cures of Neurosis* (San Diego: Robert Knapp, 1965), which he co-authored with Stanley Rachman. Eysenck also edited a collection of research papers on the various forms of conditioning therapy, published as *Behavior Therapy and the Neuroses* (New York: Pergamon Press, 1960).

An interview with Eysenck, in which he discusses the implications of his work for psychotherapy and for unifying the whole of psychology, is contained in R. I. Evans' *The Making of Psychology* (New York: Knopf, 1976).

Background reading on Pavlov's changing conceptions of personality and neuroses is best begun with Pavlov's own *Conditioned Reflexes: An Investigation into the Physiological Activity of the Cortex* (New York: Dover, 1927) and his *Lectures on Conditioned Reflexes* (New York: International Publishers, 1928). The wealth of historical information and the attempt to place Pavlov's ideas into contemporary perspective are well worth the reader's attention to J. A. Gray's (Ed.) *Pavlov's Typology* (New York: Macmillan, 1964).

Bibliography

Adler, Alfred [1907]. "The Study of Organ Inferiority and Its Psychical Compensation." In H. L. Ansbacher and R. R. Ansbacher (Eds.), *The Individual Psychology of Alfred Adler*. New York: Harper, 1956.

Adler, Alfred [1908]. "The Aggression Drive in Life and Neurosis." In H. L. Ansbacher and R. R. Ansbacher (Eds.), *The Individual Psychology of Alfred Adler*. New York: Harper, 1956.

Adler, Alfred [1910]. "The Psychology of Hermaphroditism in Life and in Neurosis." In H. L. Ansbacher and R. R. Ansbacher (Eds.), *The Individual Psychology of Alfred Adler*. New York: Harper, 1956.

Adler, Alfred [1912]. "The Neurotic Character." In H. L. Ansbacher and R. R. Ansbacher (Eds.), *The Individual Psychology of Alfred Adler*. New York: Harper, 1956.

Adler, Alfred [1913a]. "Individual-Psychological Treatment of Neurosis." In Alfred Adler, *The Practice and Theory of Individual Psychology*. Totowa, N.J.: Littlefield-Adams, 1959.

Adler, Alfred [1913b]. "Individual-Psychological Treatment of Neurosis." In H. L. Ansbacher and R. R. Ansbacher (Eds.), *The Individual Psychology of Alfred Adler*. New York: Harper, 1956.

Adler, Alfred. *Understanding Human Nature*. Greenwich, Conn.: Fawcett, 1927.

Adler, Alfred [1929a]. *The Science of Living*. New York: Doubleday, 1969.

Adler, Alfred [1929b]. *Problems of Neurosis*, Philip Mairet (Ed.). New York: Harper, 1929.

Adler, Alfred [1930a]. *The Problem Child*. New York: Putnam, 1963.

Adler, Alfred [1930b]. *The Science of Living*. London: Allen & Unwin, 1930.

Adler, Alfred [1930c]. *The Education of Children*. Chicago: Henry Regnery, 1970.

Adler, Alfred. *What Life Should Mean to You*. New York: Putnam, 1931.

Adler, Alfred [1933]. "The Meaning of Life." In H. L. Ansbacher and R. R. Ansbacher (Eds.), *The Individual Psychology of Alfred Adler*. New York: Harper, 1956.

Adler, Alfred [1935]. "The Fundamental Views of Individual Psychology." In H. L. Ansbacher and R. R. Ansbacher (Eds.), *The Individual Psychology of Alfred Adler*. New York: Harper, 1956.

Adler, Alfred. *The Individual Psychology of Alfred Adler: A Systematic Presentation in Selections from His Writings*. H. L. Ansbacher and R. R. Ansbacher (Eds.). New York: Harper, 1956.

Adler, Alfred. *The Practice and Theory of Individual Psychology*. Totowa, N.J.: Littlefield Adams, 1959.

Adler, Alfred. *Social Interest: A Challenge to Mankind*. New York: Putnam, 1964.

Adler, Alfred. *Superiority and Social Interest: A Collection of Later Writings*. H. L. Ansbacher and R. R. Ansbacher (Eds.). New York: Viking Press, 1973.

Allport, Floyd. *Social Psychology*. Boston: Houghton Mifflin, 1924.

Allport, Gordon. *Personality: A Psychological Interpretation.* New York: Henry Holt, 1937.

Allport, Gordon. *The Use of Personal Documents in Psychological Science.* New York: Social Science Research Council Bulletin (No. 49), 1942.

Allport, Gordon [Ed.]. "Letters from Jenny" (published anonymously in this edition). *Journal of Abnormal and Social Psychology,* 1946, **41,** 315–350 and 449–480.

Allport, Gordon. *The Individual and His Religion.* New York: Macmillan, 1950.

Allport, Gordon. *Becoming: Basic Considerations for a Psychology of Personality.* New Haven: Yale University Press, 1955.

Allport, Gordon. *Personality and Social Encounter: Selected Essays.* Boston: Beacon Press, 1960.

Allport, Gordon. *Pattern and Growth in Personality.* New York: Holt, Rinehart & Winston, 1961.

Allport, Gordon [1964]. "The Fruits of Eclecticism: Bitter or Sweet?" In G. Allport, *The Person in Psychology.* Boston: Beacon Press, 1968 (paper originally published: *Acta Psychologica,* 1964, **23,** 27–44).

Allport, Gordon [1966]. "Traits Revisited." In G. Allport, *The Person in Psychology.* Boston: Beacon Press, 1968 (paper originally published: *American Psychologist,* 1966, **21,** 1–10).

Allport, Gordon [Ed.]. *Letters from Jenny.* New York: Harcourt, Brace & World, 1965 (see also: Allport, 1946).

Allport, Gordon. *The Person in Psychology: Selected Essays.* Boston: Beacon Press, 1968.

Allport, Gordon, and H. S. Odbert. "Trait Names: A Psycho-Lexical Study." *Psychological Monographs,* 1936, **47,** No. 211, 1–171.

Angyal, Andras. *Foundations for a Science of Personality.* New York: Viking Press, 1941.

Angyal, Andras. *Neurosis and Treatment: A Holistic Theory.* New York: Viking Press, 1965.

Ansbacher, Heinz L., and Rowena R. Ansbacher. *The Individual Psychology of Alfred Adler: A Systematic Presentation in Selections from His Writings.* New York: Harper, 1956.

Ansbacher, Heinz, and Rowena Ansbacher (Eds.). *Superiority and Social Interest: A Collection of Alfred Adler's Later Writings.* New York: Viking, 1973.

Aronson, Eliot. "The Theory of Cognitive Dissonance: A Current Perspective." In Leonard Berkowitz (Ed.), *Advances in Experimental Social Psychology,* Vol. 4. New York: Academic Press, 1969.

Asch, Solomon E. "Forming Impressions of Personality." *Journal of Abnormal and Social Psychology,* 1946, **41,** 258–290.

Atkinson, J. W. *An Introduction to Motivation.* New York: Van Nostrand, 1964.

Bakan, Paul [1959]. "Extraversion-Intraversion and Improvement in an Auditory Vigilance Task." In H. J. Eysenck (Ed.), *Readings in Extraversion-Intraversion,* Vol. 3: *Bearings on Basic Psychological Processes.* London: Staples Press, 1971b (paper originally published: *British Journal of Psychology,* 1959, **50,** 325–332).

Bandura, Albert. "Psychotherapy as a Learning Process." *Psychological Bulletin,* 1961, **58,** 143–159.

Bandura, Albert [1964]. "The Stormy Decade: Fact or Fiction?" In D. Rogers (Ed.), *Issues in Adolescent Psychology.* New York: Appleton-Century, 1972 (paper originally published: *Psychology in the Schools,* 1964, **1,** 224–231).

Bandura, Albert [1965a]. "Influence of Models' Reinforcement Contingencies on the Acquisition of Imitative Responses." In A. Bandura (Ed.), *Psychological Modeling: Conflicting Theories.* Chicago: Aldine-Atherton, 1971 (paper originally published: *Journal of Personality and Social Psychology,* 1965, **1**, 589–595).

Bandura, Albert [1965b]. "Behavioral Modifications through Modeling Procedures." In Leonard Krasner and Leonard Ullman (Eds.), *Research in Behavior Modification.* New York: Holt, Rinehart & Winston, 1965.

Bandura, Albert. "Behavioral Psychotherapy." *Scientific American,* March, 1967.

Bandura, Albert. *Principles of Behavior Modification.* New York: Holt, Rinehart & Winston, 1969.

Bandura, Albert [1971a]. "Analysis of Modeling Processes." In A. Bandura (Ed.), *Psychological Modeling: Conflicting Theories.* Chicago: Aldine-Atherton, 1971.

Bandura, Albert [1971b]. "Psychotherapy Based upon Modeling Principles." In E. Bergin and S. L. Garfield (Eds.), *Handbook of Psychotherapy Research.* New York: John Wiley, 1971, pp. 653–708.

Bandura, Albert [1971c]. *Social Learning Theory.* Morristown, N. J.: General Learning Press, 1971.

Bandura, Albert. *Aggression: A Social Learning Analysis.* Englewood Cliffs, N.J.: Prentice-Hall, 1973.

Bandura, Albert."Behavior Theory and the Models of Man." *American Psychologist,* 1974, **29**, 859–869.

Bandura, Albert. "Conversation with Richard I. Evans." In R. I. Evans (Ed.), *The Making of Psychology.* New York: Knopf, 1976.

Bandura, Albert, E. B. Blanchard, and B. Ritter. "The Relative Efficacy of Desensitization and Modeling Approaches for Inducing Behavioral, Affective, and Attitudinal Changes." *Journal of Personality and Social Psychology,* 1969, **13**, 173–199.

Bandura, Albert, Dorothea Ross, and Sheila A. Ross [1963a]. "Imitation of Film-Mediated Aggressive Models." *Journal of Abnormal and Social Psychology,* 1963, **66**, 3–11.

Bandura, Albert, Dorothea Ross, and Sheila A. Ross [1963b]. "A Comparative Test of the Status-Envy, Social Power, and Secondary Reinforcement Theories of Identificatory Learning." *Journal of Abnormal and Social Psychology,* 1963, **67**, 527–534.

Bandura, Albert, and Richard H. Walters. *Adolescent Aggression.* New York: Ronald Press, 1959.

Bandura, Albert, and Richard H. Walters. *Social Learning and Personality Development.* New York: Holt, Rinehart & Winston, 1963.

Bateson, Gregory. "Double Bind, 1969." In Gregory Bateson, *Steps to an Ecology of the Mind.* New York: Ballantine Books, 1972 (paper originally delivered at Symposium on the Double Bind, American Psychological Association, 1969).

Bateson, Gregory, Don D. Jackson, Jay Haley, and John Weakland [1956]. "Toward a Theory of Schizophrenia." In Gregory Bateson, *Steps to an Ecology of the Mind.* New York: Ballantine Books, 1972 (paper originally published: *Behavioral Science,* 1956, **1**, 251–264).

Bellak, Leopold, M. Hurvich, and H. Gediman. *Ego Functions in Schizophrenics, Neurotics and Normals.* New York: John Wiley, 1973.

Berkowitz, Leonard. "The Frustration-Aggression Hypothesis Revisited." In L.

Berkowitz (Ed.), *Roots of Aggression: A Re-Examination of the Frustration-Aggression Hypothesis.* New York: Atherton, 1969.

Berlyne, Daniel E. "Behavior Theory as Personality Theory." In Edgar F. Borgatta and William A. Lambert (Eds.), *Handbook of Personality Theory and Research.* Chicago: Rand McNally, 1968.

Berman, Marshall. "Review of *Life History and the Historical Moment* by Erik Erikson." In *The New York Times Book Review,* March 30, 1975.

Bertocci, Peter A. "Critique of Gordon W. Allport's Theory of Motivation." *Psychological Review,* 1950, **47,** 501–532.

Binswanger, Ludwig. "The Existential Analysis School of Thought." In Rollo May, et al. (Eds.), *Existence: A New Dimension in Psychiatry and Psychology.* New York: Basic Books, 1958.

Blos, Peter. *On Adolescence: A Psychoanalytic Interpretation.* New York: Macmillan (Free Press), 1962.

Blos, Peter. *The Young Adolescent: Clinical Studies.* New York: Macmillan (Free Press), 1970.

Bottome, Phyllis. *Alfred Adler: A Portrait from Life.* New York: Vanguard, 1957.

Bower, Gordon H., and Neal Miller. "Effects of Amount of Reward on Strength of Approach in an Approach-Avoidance Conflict." *Journal of Comparative and Physiological Psychology,* 1960, **53,** 59–62.

Breger, Louis, and James L. McGaugh. "Critique and Reformulation of 'Learning-Theory' Approaches to Psychotherapy and Neurosis." *Psychological Bulletin,* 1965, **63,** 338–358.

Breuer, Josef, and Sigmund Freud [1893]. "On the Psychical Mechanism of Hysterical Phenomena: A Preliminary Communication." In Josef Breuer and Sigmund Freud, *Studies on Hysteria,* Vol. II of *The Standard Edition of the Complete Psychological Works of Sigmund Freud.* James Strachey (Ed.). London: Hogarth Press, 1955.

Breuer, Josef, and Sigmund Freud [1893–1895]. *Studies on Hysteria,* Vol. II of *The Standard Edition of the Complete Psychological Works of Sigmund Freud.* London: Hogarth Press, 1955.

Broadhurst, P. L. "The Interaction of Task Difficulty and Motivation: The Yerkes-Dodson Law Revived." *Acta Psychologica,* 1959, **16,** 321–338.

Brown, Judson S. [1940]. "Generalized Approach and Avoidance Responses in Relation to Conflict Behavior" (unpublished doctoral dissertation, Yale University; cited by Neal Miller, 1944).

Brown, Judson S. "Gradients of Approach and Avoidance Responses and Their Relation to Level of Motivation." *Journal of Comparative and Physiological Psychology,* 1948, **41,** 450–465.

Brown, Roger. *Social Psychology.* New York: Macmillan (Free Press), 1965.

Bruner, Jerome S., David Shapiro, and Renato Tagiuri. "The Meaning of Traits in Isolation and in Combination." In Renato Tagiuri and Luigi Petrullo (Eds.), *Person Perception and Interpersonal Behavior.* Stanford, Calif.: Stanford University Press, 1958.

Buber, Martin. *Good and Evil.* New York: Scribner, 1952.

Buss, Arnold H. "Instrumentality of Aggression, Feedback, and Frustration as Determinants of Physical Aggression." *Journal of Personality and Social Psychology,* 1966, **3,** 153–162.

Campbell, Donald T. "Prospective: Artifact and Control." In Robert Rosenthal and Ralph Rosnow (Eds.), *Artifact in Behavioral Research.* New York: Academic Press, 1969.

Carlson, Rae. "Where Is the Person in Personality Research?" *Psychological Bulletin,* 1971, **75**, 203–219.

Castenada, Carlos. *The Teachings of Don Juan: A Yaqui Way of Knowledge.* New York: Ballantine Books, 1968.

Castenada, Carlos. *A Separate Reality: Further Conversations with Don Juan.* New York: Simon and Schuster, 1971.

Christie, Richard, and Florence Geis. "Some Consequences of Taking Machiavelli Seriously." In E. Borgatta and W. Lambert (Eds.), *Handbook of Personality Theory and Research.* Chicago: Rand McNally, 1968.

Christie, Richard, and Florence Geis. *Studies in Machiavellianism.* New York: Academic Press, 1970.

Claridge, Gordon S. *Personality and Arousal.* New York: Pergamon Press, 1967.

Cooper, David. *Psychiatry and Anti-Psychiatry.* London: Paladin and Tavistock Publications, 1967.

Cooper, David. *The Death of the Family.* New York: Random House (Vintage), 1970.

Coopersmith, Stanley. *The Antecedents of Self-Esteem.* San Francisco: W. H. Freeman, 1967.

Coopersmith, Stanley. "Studies in Self-Esteem." *Scientific American,* February 1968.

Cronbach, Lee J. "The Two Disciplines of Scientific Psychology." *American Psychologist,* 1957, **12**, 671–684.

Cronbach, Lee J. *Essentials of Psychological Testing* (2d ed.). New York: Harper, 1960.

Cronbach, Lee J. "Beyond the Two Disciplines of Scientific Psychology." *American Psychologist,* 1975, **30**, 116–127.

Dembo, Tamara [1931]. "Der arger als dynamisches problem." *Psychologische Forschung,* 1931, **15**, 1–44.

Dollard, John, Leonard Doob, Neal Miller, O. H. Mowrer, and Robert Sears. *Frustration and Aggression.* New Haven: Yale University Press, 1939.

Dollard, John, and Neal Miller. *Personality and Psychotherapy: An Analysis in Terms of Learning, Thinking and Culture.* New York: McGraw-Hill, 1950.

Dreikurs, Rudolf. "Individual Psychology: The Adlerian Point of View." In J. M. Wepman and R. W. Heine (Eds.), *Concepts of Personality.* Chicago: Aldine, 1963.

Dulany, D. E. "Hypotheses and Habits in Verbal 'Operant Conditioning.' " *Journal of Abnormal and Social Psychology,* 1961, **63**, 251–263.

Dymond, Rosalind. "Adjustment Changes over Therapy from Self-Sorts." In Carl R. Rogers and Rosalind F. Dymond (Eds.), *Psychotherapy and Personality Change.* Chicago: University of Chicago Press, 1954, pp. 77–84.

Einstein, Albert, and Leopold Infeld. *The Evolution of Physics: From Early Concepts to Relativity and Quanta.* New York: Simon and Schuster, 1938.

Eliade, Mircea. *Rites and Symbols of Initiation.* New York: Harper, 1958 (originally published as *Birth and Rebirth*).

Eliade, Mircea. *The Sacred and the Profane.* New York: Harper and Row, 1961.

Eriksen, Charles W., and Jan Pierce. "Defense Mechanisms." In E. Borgatta and W. Lambert (Eds.), *Handbook of Personality Theory and Research.* Chicago: Rand McNally, 1968.

Erikson, Erik H. [1950]. *Childhood and Society* (2d ed.). New York: W. W. Norton, 1963.

Erikson, Erik H. *Identity and the Life Cycle: Selected Papers. Psychological Issues,* Monograph No. 1, Vol. 1. New York: International Universities Press, 1959.

Erikson, Erik H. *Young Man Luther: A Study in Psychoanalysis and History.* New York: W. W. Norton, 1962.

Erikson, Erik H. "Youth: Fidelity and Diversity." In Erik H. Erikson (Ed.), *The Challenge of Youth.* New York: Doubleday, 1963.

Erikson, Erik H. *Insight and Responsibility.* New York: W. W. Norton, 1964.

Erikson, Erik H. (Ed.) *Identity: Youth and Crisis.* New York: W. W. Norton, 1968.

Erikson, Erik H. *Gandhi's Truth: On the Origins of Militant Nonviolence.* New York: W. W. Norton, 1969.

Erikson, Erik H. *Dimensions of a New Identity: Jefferson Lectures, 1973.* New York: W. W. Norton, 1974.

Erikson, Erik H. "Once More the Inner Space." In Erik H. Erikson, *Life History and the Historical Moment.* New York: W. W. Norton, 1975.

Erikson, Erik H. *Life History and the Historical Moment.* New York: W. W. Norton, 1975.

Escalona, Sybille. "The Effect of Success and Failure upon the Level of Aspiration and Behavior in Manic-Depressive Psychoses." *University of Iowa Studies in Child Welfare,* 1940, **16**, 199–302.

Esterson, Aaron. *The Leaves of Spring.* Baltimore: Penguin (Pelican ed.), 1970.

Evans, Richard I. *Carl Rogers: The Man and His Ideas: A Dialogue.* New York: Dutton, 1975.

Eysenck, Hans J. *Dimensions of Personality.* London: Routledge & Kegan Paul, 1947.

Eysenck, Hans J. *The Scientific Study of Personality.* London: Routledge & Kegan Paul, 1952.

Eysenck, Hans J. [1953a]. *Uses and Abuses of Psychology.* Baltimore: Penguin (Pelican ed.), 1953.

Eysenck, Hans J. [1953b]. *The Structure of Human Personality* (Rev. ed.). London: Methuen, 1970.

Eysenck, Hans J. [1957a]. *The Dynamics of Anxiety and Hysteria: An Experimental Application of Modern Learning Theory to Psychiatry.* London: Routledge & Kegan Paul, 1957 (American edition: Praeger).

Eysenck, Hans J. [1957b]. *Sense and Nonsense in Psychology.* Baltimore: Penguin, 1957.

Eysenck, Hans J. *The Maudsley Personality Inventory.* San Diego, Calif.: Educational and Industrial Testing Service, 1959.

Eysenck, Hans J. "Learning Theory and Behavior Therapy." In H. J. Eysenck (Ed.), *Behavior Therapy and the Neuroses.* New York: Pergamon Press, 1960.

Eysenck, Hans J. [1963a]. "The Measurement of Motivation." *Scientific American,* May 1963, 130–140.

Eysenck, Hans J. [1963b]. "Psychoanalysis: Myth or Science?" In Stanley Rachman (Ed.), *Critical Essays on Psychoanalysis.* New York: Macmillan, 1963.

Eysenck, Hans J. [1964a]. *Crime and Personality.* London: Routledge & Kegan Paul, 1964 (American edition: Houghton Mifflin).

Eysenck, Hans J. [1964b]. "Involuntary Rest Pauses in Tapping as a Function of Drive and Personality." In H. J. Eysenck (Ed.), *Readings in Extraversion-Intraversion,* Vol. 3: *Bearings on Basic Psychological Processes.* London: Staples, 1971 (paper originally published: *Perceptual and Motor Skills,* 1964, **18**, 173–174).

Eysenck, Hans J. *Fact and Fiction in Psychology.* Baltimore: Penguin, 1965.

Eysenck, Hans J. [1966]. "Conditioning, Introversion-Extroversion and The Strength of the Nervous System." In H. J. Eysenck (Ed.), *Readings in Extraversion-Intraversion,* Vol. 3: *Bearings on Basic Psychological Processes.* London:

Staples, 1971 (paper originally published: Proceedings of the 18th International Congress of Psychology, 9th Symposium, 1966).

Eysenck, Hans J. *The Biological Basis of Personality.* Springfield, Ill.: Charles C Thomas, 1967.

Eysenck, Hans J. "Historical Introduction." In H. J. Eysenck (Ed.), *Readings in Extraversion-Intraversion,* Vol. 1: *Theoretical and Methodological Issues.* London: Staples, 1970.

Eysenck, Hans J. *Psychology Is About People.* New York: The Library Press, 1972.

Eysenck, Hans J. *The Inequality of Man.* London: Temple Smith, 1973 (American edition: Robert R. Knapp, San Diego, Calif.).

Eysenck, Hans J., and Sybil B. G. Eysenck. *The Eysenck Personality Inventory.* San Diego, Calif.: Educational and Industrial Testing Service, 1968.

Eysenck, Hans J., and Sybil B. G. Eysenck. *Personality Structure and Measurement.* San Diego, Calif.: Robert R. Knapp, 1969.

Eysenck,Hans J., and Sybil B. G. Eysenck [1975a]. *Eysenck Personality Questionnaire.* San Diego, Calif.: Educational and Industrial Testing Service, 1975.

Eysenck, Hans J., and Sybil B. G. Eysenck [1975b]. *The Manual of the Eysenck Personality Questionnaire.* San Diego, Calif.: Educational and Industrial Testing Service, 1975.

Eysenck, Hans J., and Stanley Rachman. *The Causes and Cures of Neurosis.* London: Routledge & Kegan Paul, 1965 (American edition: Robert R. Knapp, San Diego, Calif.).

Eysenck, Hans J., and Glenn D. Wilson. *The Experimental Study of Freudian Theories.* London: Methuen, 1973 (American edition: Harper & Row).

Falk, John L. "Issues Distinguishing Idiographic from Nomothetic Approaches to Personality." *Psychological Review,* 1956, **63**, 53–62.

Farber, I. E. "The Things People Say to Themselves." *American Psychologist,* 1963, **18**, 185–197.

Fenichel, Otto. *The Psychoanalytic Theory of Neurosis.* New York: W. W. Norton, 1945.

Feshbach, Seymour. "Aggression." In Paul H. Mussen (Ed.), *Carmichael's Manual of Child Psychology,* Vol. 2 (3d ed.). New York: John Wiley, 1970, pp. 159–259.

Festinger, Leon. "A Theoretical Interpretation of Shifts in Level of Aspiration." *Psychological Review,* 1942, **49**, 235–250.

Festinger, Leon. *A Theory of Cognitive Dissonance.* New York: Row, Peterson, 1957.

Frank, J. D. "Individual Differences in Certain Aspects of the Level of Aspiration." *American Journal of Psychology,* 1935, **47**, 119–128.

Franks, Cyril [1956]. "Conditioning and Personality: A Study of Normal and Neurotic Subjects." In H. J. Eysenck (Ed.), *Readings in Extraversion-Intraversion,* Vol. 3: *Bearings on Basic Psychological Processes.* London: Staples, 1971 (paper originally published: *Journal of Abnormal and Social Psychology,* 1956, **52**, 143–150).

Franks, Cyril [1957]. "Personality Factors and the Rate of Conditioning." In H. J. Eysenck (Ed.), *Readings in Extraversion-Intraversion,* Vol. 3: *Bearings on Basic Psychological Processes.* London: Staples, 1971 (paper originally published: *British Journal of Psychology,* 1957, **48**, 119–126).

Franks, Cyril. "Personality and Eyeblink Conditioning Seven Years Later." *Acta Psychologica,* 1963, **21**, 295–312.

Frazer, James George. *The Golden Bough.* New York: Macmillan, 1963.

French, J. D. "The Reticular Formation." *Scientific American,* May 1957 (reprinted in R. F. Thompson [Ed.], *Physiological Psychology: Readings from Scientific American*. San Francisco: W. H. Freeman, 1972).

Freud, Anna [1936]. *The Ego and the Mechanisms of Defense* (Rev. ed.). New York: International Universities Press, 1966.

Freud, Sigmund [1894]. "The Neuro-Psychoses of Defence." In Vol. III of *The Standard Edition of the Complete Psychological Works of Sigmund Freud*. James Strachey (Ed.). London: Hogarth Press, 1962.

Freud, Sigmund [1895]. "Project for a Scientific Psychology." In Vol. I of *The Standard Edition*. London: Hogarth Press, 1966.

Freud, Sigmund [1896a]. "Heredity and the Aetiology of the Neuroses." In Vol. III of *The Standard Edition*. London: Hogarth, 1962.

Freud, Sigmund [1896b]. "Further Remarks on the Neuro-Psychoses of Defence." In Vol. III of *The Standard Edition*. London: Hogarth, 1962.

Freud, Sigmund [1896c]. "The Aetiology of Hysteria." In Vol. III of *The Standard Edition*. London: Hogarth Press, 1962.

Freud, Sigmund [1897]. "Extracts from the Fliess Papers." In Vol. I of *The Standard Edition*. London: Hogarth Press, 1966.

Freud, Sigmund [1898]. "Sexuality in the Aetiology of the Neuroses." In Vol. III of *The Standard Edition*. London: Hogarth Press, 1962.

Freud, Sigmund [1900]. *The Interpretation of Dreams*. Volumes IV and V of *The Standard Edition*. London: Hogarth Press, 1953.

Freud, Sigmund [1901]. *The Psychopathology of Everyday Life*. In Vol. VI of *The Standard Edition*. London: Hogarth Press, 1960.

Freud, Sigmund [1905]. "Three Essays on the Theory of Sexuality." In Vol. VII of *The Standard Edition*. London: Hogarth Press, 1953.

Freud, Sigmund [1908a]. "On The Sexual Theories of Children." In Vol. IX of *The Standard Edition*. London: Hogarth Press, 1959.

Freud, Sigmund [1908b]. "Character and Anal Eroticism." In Vol. IX of *The Standard Edition*. London: Hogarth Press, 1959.

Freud, Sigmund [1910a]. *Five Lectures on Psychoanalysis*. In Vol. XI of *The Standard Edition*. London: Hogarth Press, 1957.

Freud, Sigmund [1910b]. "The Psychoanalytic View of Psychogenic Disturbance of Vision." In Vol. XI of *The Standard Edition*. London: Hogarth, 1957.

Freud, Sigmund [1911]. "Formulations on the Two Principles of Mental Functioning." In Vol. XII of *The Standard Edition*. London: Hogarth Press, 1958.

Freud, Sigmund [1912]. "A Note on the Unconscious in Psychoanalysis." In Vol. XII of *The Standard Edition*. London: Hogarth Press, 1958.

Freud, Sigmund [1913]. "On Beginning the Treatment." In Vol. XII of *The Standard Edition*. London: Hogarth Press, 1958.

Freud, Sigmund [1914a]. "On Narcissism: An Introduction." In Vol. XIV of *The Standard Edition*. London: Hogarth Press, 1957.

Freud, Sigmund [1914b]. "On the History of the Psychoanalytic Movement." In Vol. XIV of *The Standard Edition*. London: Hogarth Press, 1957.

Freud, Sigmund [1915a]. "Instincts and Their Vicissitudes." In Vol. XIV of *The Standard Edition*. London: Hogarth Press, 1957.

Freud, Sigmund [1915b]. "Repression." In Vol. XIV of *The Standard Edition*. London: Hogarth Press, 1957.

Freud, Sigmund [1915c]. "The Unconscious." In Vol. XIV of *The Standard Edition*. London: Hogarth Press, 1957.

Freud, Sigmund [1916]. *Introductory Lectures on Psychoanalysis*. Volumes XV and XVI of *The Standard Edition*. London: Hogarth Press, 1961 and 1963.

Freud, Sigmund [1917a]. "A Difficulty in the Path of Psychoanalysis." In Vol. XVII of *The Standard Edition*. London: Hogarth Press, 1955.

Freud, Sigmund [1917b]. "Mourning and Melancholia." In Vol. XIV of *The Standard Edition*. London: Hogarth Press, 1957.

Freud, Sigmund [1920a]. *Beyond the Pleasure Principle*. In Vol. XVIII of *The Standard Edition*. London: Hogarth Press, 1955.

Freud, Sigmund [1920b]. "A Note on the Prehistory of the Technique of Analysis." In Vol. XVIII of *The Standard Edition*. London: Hogarth Press, 1955.

Freud, Sigmund [1923a]. *The Ego and the Id*. In Vol. XIX of *The Standard Edition*. London: Hogarth Press, 1961.

Freud, Sigmund [1923b]. "The Infantile Genital Organization: An Interpolation into the Theory of Sexuality." In Vol. XIX of *The Standard Edition*. London: Hogarth Press, 1961.

Freud, Sigmund [1924a]. "A Note Upon the Mystic Writing Pad." In Vol. XIX of *The Standard Edition*. London: Hogarth Press, 1961.

Freud, Sigmund [1924b]. "The Dissolution of the Oedipal Complex." In Vol. XIX of *The Standard Edition*. London: Hogarth Press, 1961.

Freud, Sigmund [1925a]. *An Autobiographical Study*. In Vol. XX of *The Standard Edition*. London: Hogarth Press, 1959.

Freud, Sigmund [1925b] "Some Psychical Consequences of the Anatomical Distinction between the Sexes." In Vol. XIX of *The Standard Edition*. London: Hogarth Press, 1961.

Freud, Sigmund [1925c]. "Some Additional Notes on Dream-Interpretation as a Whole." In Vol. XIX of *The Standard Edition*. London: Hogarth Press, 1961.

Freud, Sigmund [1926]. *Inhibitions, Symptoms and Anxiety*. In Vol. XX of *The Standard Edition*. London: Hogarth Press, 1959.

Freud, Sigmund [1930]. *Civilization and Its Discontents*. In Vol. XXI of *The Standard Edition*. London: Hogarth Press, 1961.

Freud, Sigmund [1931]. "Female Sexuality." In Vol. XXI of *The Standard Edition*. London: Hogarth Press, 1961.

Freud, Sigmund [1933]. *New Introductory Lectures*. In Vol. XXII of *The Standard Edition*. London: Hogarth Press, 1964.

Freud, Sigmund [1940]. *An Outline of Psychoanalysis*. In Vol. XXIII of *The Standard Edition*. London: Hogarth Press, 1964.

Freud, Sigmund. *The Origin of Psychoanalysis: Letters to Wilhelm Fliess, Drafts and Notes, 1897–1902*. Marie Bonaparte, Anna Freud, and Ernst Kris (Eds.). New York: Basic Books, 1954.

Freud, Sigmund, and C. G. Jung. *The Freud/Jung Letters*. William McGuire (Ed.). Princeton, N.J.: Princeton University Press, 1974.

Fromm, Erich. *Escape from Freedom*. New York: Avon Books, 1941 (also published by Holt, Rinehart & Winston).

Fromm, Erich. "Individual and Social Origins of Neurosis." In *American Sociological Review*, 1944, **9**, 380–384.

Fromm, Erich. *Man for Himself*. Greenwich, Conn.: Fawcett Books, 1947 (originally published by Holt, Rinehart & Winston).

Fromm, Erich. *Psychoanalysis and Religion*. New Haven: Yale University Press, 1950.

Fromm, Erich. *The Forgotten Language: An Introduction to the Understanding of Dreams, Fairy Tales and Myths*. New York: Grove Press, 1951 (also published by Holt, Rinehart & Winston).

Fromm, Erich [1955a]. *The Sane Society*. Greenwich, Conn.: Fawcett Books, 1955 (also published by Holt, Rinehart & Winston).

Fromm, Erich [1955b]. *The Dogma of Christ.* Garden City, N.Y.: Doubleday, 1955 (also published by Holt, Rinehart & Winston).

Fromm, Erich. *The Art of Loving.* New York: Bantam Books, 1956 (also published by Harper).

Fromm, Erich. *Sigmund Freud's Mission: An Analysis of His Personality and Influence.* New York: Simon and Schuster, 1962.

Fromm, Erich. *The Heart of Man: Its Genius for Good and Evil.* New York: Harper & Row, 1964.

Fromm, Erich. *The Revolution of Hope: Toward a Humanized Technology.* New York: Holt, Rinehart & Winston, 1968.

Fromm, Erich. *The Crisis of Psychoanalysis.* Greenwich, Conn.: Fawcett Books, 1970 (also published by Holt, Rinehart & Winston).

Fromm, Erich. *The Anatomy of Human Destructiveness.* New York: Holt, Rinehart & Winston, 1973.

Furtmüller, Carl. "Alfred Adler: A Biographical Essay." In H. L. Ansbacher and R. Ansbacher (Eds.), *Superiority and Social Interest.* New York: Viking Press, 1973.

Fuster, Joaquin M. "Effects of Stimulation of Brain Stem on Tachistoscopic Perception." *Science,* 1958, **127,** 150.

Geiwitz, P. J. *Non-Freudian Personality Theories.* Monterey, Calif.: Brooks-Cole, 1969.

Gendlin, Eugene T. "A Theory of Personality Change." In Philip Worschel and Donn Byrne (Eds.), *Personality Change.* New York: John Wiley, 1964.

Gendlin, Eugene T. [1966]. "Research in Psychotherapy with Schizophrenic Patients and the Nature of That Illness." In J. T. Hart and T. M. Tomlinson (Eds.), *New Directions in Client-Centered Therapy.* Boston: Houghton Mifflin, 1970 (paper originally published: *American Journal of Psychotherapy,* 1966, **20,** 4–16).

Gendlin, Eugene T. "Focusing Ability in Psychotherapy, Personality, and Creativity." In John M. Shlien (Ed.), *Research in Psychotherapy,* Vol. III. Washington, D.C.: American Psychological Association, 1968.

Gendlin, Eugene T. "Existentialism and Experiential Psychotherapy." In J. T. Hart and T. M. Tomlinson (Eds.), *New Directions in Client-Centered Therapy.* Boston: Houghton Mifflin, 1970.

Goffman, Erving. *The Presentation of Self in Everyday Life.* New York: Doubleday, 1959.

Goffman, Erving. *Asylums.* New York: Doubleday, 1961.

Goldstein, Kurt. *The Organism.* New York: American Book Co. (Van Nostrand), 1939.

Gray, J. A. "Strength of the Nervous System as a Dimension of Personality in Man." In J. A. Gray (Ed. and Trans.), *Pavlov's Typology.* New York: Macmillan, 1964.

Groddeck, Georg [1922]. *The Book of the It.* New York: New American Library, 1961.

Hart, Joseph. "The Development of Client-Centered Therapy." In J. T. Hart and T. M. Tomlinson (Eds.), *New Directions in Client-Centered Therapy.* Boston: Houghton Mifflin, 1970.

Hart, J. T., and T. M. Tomlinson (Eds.). *New Directions in Client-Centered Therapy.* Boston: Houghton Mifflin, 1970.

Hartmann, Heinz [1939]. *Ego Psychology and the Problem of Adaptation.* New York: International Universities Press, 1958.

Hartmann, Heinz. *Essays on Ego Psychology: Selected Problems in Psychoanalytic Theory.* New York: International Universities Press, 1964.

Hebb, Donald O. "Drives and the C. N. S. (Conceptual Nervous System)." *Psychological Review,* 1955, **62,** 243–254.

Heider, Fritz. *The Psychology of Interpersonal Relations.* New York: John Wiley, 1958.

Henle, Mary [1957]. "On Field Forces." In Mary Henle (Ed.), *Documents of Gestalt Psychology.* Berkeley: University of California Press, 1961 (paper originally published: *Journal of Psychology,* 1957, **43**).

Holt, Robert R. "Individuality and Generalization in the Psychology of Personality." *Journal of Personality,* 1962, **30,** 377–402.

Hoppe, F. "Untersuchungen zur Handlungs—und affeckt—Psychologie, IX. Erflog und Musserflog [Investigations in the Psychology of Action and Emotion, IX. Success and Failure]." *Psychologische Forschung,* 1930, **14,** 1–63.

Horney, Karen. *The Neurotic Personality of Our Time.* New York: W. W. Norton, 1937.

Horney, Karen. *New Ways in Psychoanalysis.* New York: W. W. Norton, 1939.

Horney, Karen. *Self-Analysis.* New York: W. W. Norton, 1942.

Horney, Karen. *Our Inner Conflicts.* New York: W. W. Norton, 1945.

Horney, Karen. *Are You Considering Psychoanalysis?* New York: W. W. Norton, 1946.

Horney, Karen. *Neurosis and Human Growth.* New York: W. W. Norton, 1950.

Horney, Karen. *Feminine Psychology.* New York: W. W. Norton, 1967.

Hovland, Carl, and Robert Sears. "Minor Studies of Aggression, IV: Correlations of Lynchings with Economic Indices." *Journal of Psychology,* 1940, **9,** 301–310.

Hull, Clark L. *Principles of Behavior.* New York: Appleton-Century-Crofts, 1943.

Hull, Clark L. *Essentials of Behavior.* New Haven: Yale University Press, 1951.

Hull, Clark L. *A Behavior System.* New Haven: Yale University Press, 1952.

Jaffé, Aniela. *From the Life and Work of C. G. Jung.* New York: Harper & Row, 1971.

James, William. *The Varieties of Religious Experience.* New York: Modern Library (Random House), 1902.

James, William. *Principles of Psychology.* Greenwich, Conn.: Fawcett, 1963.

Janeway, Elizabeth. *Man's World, Woman's Place.* New York: William Morrow, 1971.

Janis, Irving L., George F. Mahl, Jerome Kagan, and Robert G. Holt. *Personality: Dynamics, Development, and Assessment.* New York: Harcourt, Brace & World, 1969.

Jones, Ernest. *The Life and Work of Sigmund Freud: The Formative Years and the Great Discoveries,* Vol. 1. New York: Basic Books, 1953.

Jones, Ernest. *The Life and Work of Sigmund Freud: Years of Maturity,* Vol. 2. New York: Basic Books, 1955.

Jones, Ernest. *The Life and Work of Sigmund Freud: The Last Phase,* Vol. 3. New York: Basic Books, 1957.

Jourard, Sidney M. [1971a]. *The Transparent Self.* (Rev. ed.) New York: Van Nostrand, 1971.

Jourard, Sidney M. [1971b]. *Self-Disclosure: An Experimental Analysis of the Transparent Self.* New York: John Wiley, 1971.

Jucknat, M. "Performance, Level of Aspiration and Self-Consciousness." *Psychologische Forschung,* 1937, **22,** 89–179.

Jung, Carl G. [1905]. "The Reaction Time Ratio in the Association Experiment." In Vol. 2 of *The Collected Works of C. G. Jung.* R. F. C. Hull (Trans.). Princeton, N.J.: Princeton University Press, 1973.

Jung, Carl G. [1907]. *The Psychology of Dementia Praecox.* In Vol. 3 of *The Collected Works of C. G. Jung.* Princeton, N.J.: Princeton University Press, 1960.

Jung, Carl G. [1908]. "The Content of the Psychoses." In Vol. 3 of *The Collected Works of C. G. Jung.* Princeton, N.J.: Princeton University Press, 1960.

Jung, Carl G. [1909a]. "The Psychological Diagnosis of Evidence." In Vol. 2 of *The Collected Works of C. G. Jung.* Princeton, N.J.: Princeton University Press, 1973.

Jung, Carl G. [1909b]. "The Psychological Diagnosis of Evidence." In Vol. 2 of *The Collected Works of C. G. Jung.* Princeton, N.J.: Princeton University Press, 1973.

Jung, Carl G. [1912]. *Symbols of Transformation.* (2d ed.) Vol. 5 of *The Collected Works of C. G. Jung.* Princeton, N.J.: Princeton University Press, 1956.

Jung, Carl G. [1913]. "On the Doctrine of Complexes." In Vol. 2 of *The Collected Works of C. G. Jung.* Princeton, N.J.: Princeton University Press, 1973.

Jung, Carl G. [1914]. "On Psychological Understanding." In Vol. 3 of *The Collected Works of C. G. Jung.* Princeton, N.J.: Princeton University Press, 1960.

Jung, Carl G. [1916]. "General Aspects of Dream Psychology." In Vol. 8 of *The Collected Works of C. G. Jung.* Princeton, N.J.: Princeton University Press, 1969.

Jung, Carl G. [1917]. *Two Essays on Analytical Psychology.* In Vol. 7 of *The Collected Works of C. G. Jung.* Princeton, N.J.: Princeton University Press, 1953 and 1966.

Jung, Carl G. [1921]. *Psychological Types.* Vol. 6 of *The Collected Works of C. G. Jung.* Princeton, N.J.: Princeton University Press, 1971.

Jung, Carl G. [1931]. "The Structure of the Psyche." In Vol. 8 of *The Collected Works of C. G. Jung.* Princeton, N.J.: Princeton University Press, 1969.

Jung, Carl G. [1935]. *The Relations between the Ego and the Unconscious.* In Vol. 7 of *The Collected Works of C. G. Jung.* Princeton, N.J.: Princeton University Press, 1953.

Jung, Carl G. [1936]. *The Archetypes and the Collective Unconscious.* In Vol. 9i of *The Collected Works of C. G. Jung.* Princeton, N.J.: Princeton University Press, 1959 and 1969.

Jung, Carl G. [1938]. "Psychological Aspects of the Mother Archetype." In Vol. 9i of *The Collected Works of C. G. Jung.* Princeton, N.J.: Princeton University Press, 1959 and 1969.

Jung, Carl G. [1939]. "Conscious, Unconscious and Individuation." In Vol. 9i of *The Collected Works of C. G. Jung.* Princeton, N.J.: Princeton University Press, 1959 and 1969.

Jung, Carl G. [1940]. "The Psychology of the Child Archetype." In Vol. 9i of *The Collected Works of C. G. Jung.* Princeton, N.J.: Princeton University Press, 1959 and 1969.

Jung, Carl G. [1948]. "On Psychic Energy." In Vol. 8 of *The Collected Works of C. G. Jung.* Princeton, N.J.: Princeton University Press, 1969.

Jung, Carl G. [1950]. *Aion: Researches into the Phenomenology of the Self.* Volume 9ii of *The Collected Works of C. G. Jung.* Princeton, N.J.: Princeton University Press, 1959.

Jung, Carl G. [1952]. "Synchronicity: An Acausal Connecting Principle." In Vol. 8 of *The Collected Works of C. G. Jung.* Princeton, N.J.: Princeton University Press, 1969.

Jung, Carl G. [1954]. "On the Psychology of the Trickster Figure." In Vol. 9i of

The Collected Works of C. G. Jung. Princeton, N.J.: Princeton University Press, 1959 and 1969.

Jung, Carl G. [1957]. *The Undiscovered Self: Present and Future.* In Vol. 10 of *The Collected Works of C. G. Jung.* Princeton, N.J.: Princeton University Press, 1970.

Jung, Carl G. *Memories, Dreams, Reflections.* Aniela Jaffé (Ed.). New York: Pantheon Books (Random House), 1961.

Jung, Carl G. *Analytical Psychology: Its Theory and Practice.* (The Tavistock Lectures.) New York: Pantheon Press (Random House), 1968.

Kagan, Jerome. "A Psychologist's Account at Mid-Career." In T. S. Krawiec (Ed.), *The Psychologists,* Vol. 1. New York: Oxford University Press, 1972.

Kaufman, Edna, and Neal Miller. "Effect of Number of Reinforcements on Strength of Approach in an Approach-Avoidance Conflict." *Journal of Comparative and Physiological Psychology,* 1949, **42,** 529–532.

Kelly, George A. *The Psychology of Personal Constructs,* Vols. 1 and 2. New York: W. W. Norton, 1955.

Kelly, George A. [1958a]. "Man's Construction of His Alternatives." In Brenden Maher (Ed.), *Clinical Psychology and Personality: Selected Papers of George Kelly.* New York: John Wiley, 1969 (paper originally published: Gardner Lindzey (Ed.), *The Assessment of Human Motives.* New York: Holt, Rinehart & Winston, 1958).

Kelly, George A. [1958b]. "Personal Construct Theory and the Psychotherapeutic Interview." In Brenden Maher (Ed.), *Clinical Psychology and Personality: Selected Papers of George Kelly.* New York: John Wiley, 1969.

Kelly, George A. [1963]. "The Autobiography of a Theory." In Brenden Maher (Ed.), *Clinical Psychology and Personality: Selected Papers of George Kelly.* New York: John Wiley, 1969.

Kelly, George A. [1964]. "The Language of Hypothesis: Man's Psychological Instrument." In Brenden Maher (Ed.), *Clinical Psychology and Personality: Selected Papers of George Kelly.* New York: John Wiley, 1969 (paper originally published: *Journal of Individual Psychology,* 1964, **20,** 137–152).

Kline, Paul. *Fact and Fantasy in Freudian Theory.* London: Methuen, 1972 (American ed. published by Harper & Row).

Koffka, Kurt. *Principles of Gestalt Psychology.* New York: Harcourt, Brace, 1935.

Kraeplin, Emil. *Lectures on Clinical Psychiatry* (2d, rev. ed.) London: Baillere, Tindall and Cox, 1905 (as cited by R. D. Laing, 1959).

Kris, Ernst. "Editor's Introduction." In M. Bonaparte, E. Kris, and A. Freud (Eds.), *The Origins of Psychoanalysis: Letters of Sigmund Freud to Wilhelm Fliess, Drafts and Notes, 1897–1902.* New York: Basic Books, 1954.

Laing, R. D. *The Divided Self.* Baltimore: Penguin (Pelican ed.), 1959.

Laing, R. D. *The Politics of Experience.* New York: Ballantine Books, 1967 (originally published by Pantheon Books, 1967).

Laing, R. D. [1969a]. *The Politics of the Family.* New York: Vintage (Random House), 1969.

Laing, R. D. [1969b]. *Self and Others.* New York: Pantheon (Random House), 1969.

Laing, R. D. *Knots.* New York: Vintage (Random House), 1970.

Laing, R. D. [1976a]. *The Facts of Life.* New York: Pantheon (Random House), 1976.

Laing, R. D. [1976b]. "Conversation with R. I. Evans." In R. I. Evans (Ed.), *R. D. Laing: The Man and His Ideas.* New York: Dutton, 1976.

Laing, R. D., and D. G. Cooper. *Reason and Violence: A Decade of Sartre's Philosophy, 1950–1960*. New York: Vintage (Random House), 1971.

Laing, R. D., and Aaron Esterson. *Sanity, Madness and the Family*. Baltimore: Penguin (Pelican ed.), 1964.

Laing, R. D., H. Phillipson, and A. R. Lee. *Interpersonal Perception: A Theory and a Method of Research*. New York: Springer, 1966 [This edition also includes the IPM test].

Laverty, S. G. [1958] "Sodium Amytal and Extraversion." In H. J. Eysenck (Ed.), *Readings in Extraversion-Intraversion*, Vol. 3: *Bearings on Basic Psychological Processes*. London: Staples, 1971 (paper originally published: *Journal of Neurology and Neurosurgery and Psychiatry*, 1958, **21**, 50–54).

Lewin, Kurt. *A Dynamic Theory of Personality*. New York: McGraw-Hill, 1935.

Kewin, Kurt. *Principles of Topological Psychology*. New York: McGraw-Hill, 1936.

Lewin, Kurt. "Field Theory and Experiment in Social Psychology." *American Journal of Sociology*, 1939, **44**, 868–897.

Lewin, Kurt. "Behavior and Development as a Function of the Total Situation." In Leonard Carmichael (Ed.), *Manual of Child Psychology*. New York: John Wiley, 1946.

Lewin, Kurt. *Field Theory in Social Science*. D. Cartright (Ed.). New York: Harper, 1951.

Lewin, Kurt, Tamara Dembo, Leon Festinger, and Pauline S. Sears. "Level of Aspiration." In J. McV. Hunt (Ed.), *Personality and the Behavior Disorders*, Vol. 1. New York: Ronald Press, 1944, pp. 333–378.

Lindsley, Donald B. "Emotion." In S. S. Stevens (Ed.), *Handbook of Experimental Psychology*. New York: John Wiley, 1951, pp. 473–516.

London, Perry. "The End of Ideology in Behavior Modification." *American Psychologist*, 1972, **27**, 913–920.

Lundin, Robert W. "Personality Theory in Behavioristic Psychology." In Joseph M. Wepman and Ralph W. Heine (Eds.), *Concepts of Personality*. Chicago: Aldine, 1963.

Mackinnon, D. W., and W. F. Dukes. "Repression." In Leo Postman (Ed.), *Psychology in the Making: Histories of Selected Research Problems*. New York: Knopf, 1962.

Mackworth, H. N. *Researches on the Measurement of Human Performance*. Medical Research Council Special Report, No. 268. London: Her Majesty's Stationery Office, 1950.

Mackworth, H. N. "Some Factors Affecting Vigilance." *The Advancement of Science*, 1957, **53**, 389–393.

McLeary, R. A., and R. S. Lazarus. "Autonomic Discrimination without Awareness." *Journal of Personality*, 1949, **18**, 171–179.

McLaughlin, R. J., and Hans J. Eysenck [1967]. "Extraversion, Neuroticism and Paired-Associate Learning." In H. J. Eysenck (Ed.) *Readings in Extraversion-Intraversion*, Vol. 3: *Bearings on Basic Psychological Processes*. London: Staples, 1971 (paper originally published: *Journal of Experimental Research in Personality*, 1967, **2**, 128–132).

Macleod, Robert B. "Phenomenology: A Challenge to Experimental Psychology." In T. W. Wann (Ed.), *Behaviorism and Phenomenology: Contrasting Bases for Modern Psychology*. Chicago: University of Chicago Press, 1964.

Macoby, Eleanor E. "Role-Taking in Childhood and Its Consequences for Social Learning." *Child Development*, 1959, **30**, 239–252.

Maier, N. R. F. "Frustration Theory: Restatement and Extension." *Psychological Review,* 1956, **63,** 370–388.

Malmo, R. B. "Activation: A Neurophysiological Dimension." *Psychological Review,* 1959, **66,** 367–386.

Maslow, Abraham H. [1936a]. "The Role of Dominance in the Social and Sexual Behavior of Infra-Human Primates: I. Observations at Vilas Park Zoo." In Richard J. Lowry (Ed.), *Dominance, Self-Esteem, Self-Actualization; Germinal Papers of A. H. Maslow.* Monterey, Calif.: Brooks-Cole, 1973 (paper originally published: *Journal of Genetic Psychology,* 1936, **48,** 261–277).

Maslow, Abraham H. [1936b]. "The Role of Dominance in the Social and Sexual Behavior of Infra-Human Primates: II. An Experimental Determination of the Behavior Syndrome of Dominance." In Richard J. Lowry (Ed.), *Dominance, Self-Esteem, Self-Actualization: Germinal Papers of A. H. Maslow.* Monterey, Calif.: Brooks-Cole, 1973 (paper originally published: *Journal of Genetic Psychology,* 1936, **48,** 278–309).

Maslow, A. H. [1937]. "Dominance-Feeling, Behavior and Status." In Richard J. Lowry (Ed.), *Dominance, Self-esteem, Self-Actualization: Germinal Papers of A. H. Maslow.* Monterey, Calif.:Brooks-Cole, 1973 (paper originally published: *Psychological Review,* 1937, **44,** 404–429).

Maslow, Abraham H. [1939]. "Dominance, Personality and Social Behavior in Women." In Richard J. Lowry (Ed.), *Dominance, Self-Esteem, Self-Actualization: Germinal Papers of A. H. Maslow.* Monterey, Calif.: Brooks-Cole, 1973 (paper originally published: *Journal of Social Psychology,* 1939, **10,** 3–39).

Maslow, Abraham H. [1942]. "Self-Esteem (Dominance-Feeling) and Sexuality in Women." In Richard J. Lowry (Ed.), *Dominance, Self-Esteem, Self-Actualization: Germinal Papers of A. H. Maslow.* Monterey, Calif.: Brooks-Cole, 1973 (paper originally published: *Journal of Social Psychology,* 1942, **16,** 259–294).

Maslow, Abraham H. [1943]. "A Theory of Human Motivation." In Richard J. Lowry (Ed.), *Dominance, Self-Esteem, Self-Actualization: Germinal Papers of A. H. Maslow..*Monterey, Calif.: Brooks-Cole, 1973 (paper originally published: *Psychological Review,* 1943, **50,** 370–396).

Maslow, Abraham H. *Toward a Psychology of Being.* New York: Van Nostrand, 1962.

Maslow, Abraham H. *Religions, Values and Peak-Experiences.* New York: Viking Press, 1964.

Maslow, Abraham H. *The Psychology of Science: A Reconnaissance.* New York: Harper & Row, 1966.

Maslow, Abraham H. *Motivation and Personality* (2d ed.) New York: Harper & Row, 1970.

Maslow, Abraham H. *The Farther Reaches of Human Nature.* New York: Viking Press, 1971.

May, Rollo. "The Origins and Significance of the Existential Movement in Psychology." In R. May, E. Angel, and H. F. Ellenberger (Eds.), *Existence: A New Dimension in Psychiatry and Psychology.* New York: Basic Books, 1958.

May, Rollo. "The Emergence of Existential Psychology." In R. May (Ed.), *Existential Psychology.* New York: Random House, 1961.

Mead, George Herbert. *Mind, Self and Society from the Standpoint of a Social Behaviorist.* Charles W. Morris (Ed.), *The Works of George Herbert Mead,* Vol. 1. Chicago: University of Chicago Press, 1934.

Miller, Neal. "The Frustration-Aggression Hypothesis." *Psychological Review,* 1941, **48,** 337–342.

Miller, Neal. "Experimental Studies of Conflict." In J. M. Hunt (Ed.), *Personality and the Behavior Disorders,* Vol. 1. New York: Ronald Press, 1944, pp. 431–465.

Miller, Neal. "Studies of Fear as an Acquirable Drive: I, Fear as Motivation and Fear Reduction as Reinforcement in the Learning of New Responses." *Journal of Experimental Psychology,* 1948, **38,** 89–101.

Miller, Neal. "Learnable Drives and Rewards." In S. S. Stevens (Ed.), *Handbook of Experimental Psychology.* New York: John Wiley, 1950, pp. 435–472.

Miller, Neal. "Liberalization of Basic S-R Concepts: Extensions to Conflict Behavior, Motivation, and Social Learning." In Sigmund Koch (Ed.), *Psychology: A Study of a Science, Study I,* Vol. 2. New York: McGraw-Hill, 1959, pp. 196–292.

Miller, Neal. "Theory and Experiment Relating Psychoanalytic Displacement to Stimulus-Response Generalization." *Journal of Abnormal and Social Psychology,* 1960, **43,** 155–178.

Miller, Neal. "Some Implications of Modern Behavior Theory for Personality Change and Psychotherapy." In Philip Worchel and Donn Byrne (Eds.), *Personality Change.* New York: John Wiley, 1964, pp. 149–175.

Miller, Neal. *Selected Papers on Conflict, Displacement, Learned Drives and Theory.* Chicago: Aldine-Atherton, 1971.

Miller, Neal. "Applications of Learning and Biofeedback to Psychiatry and Medicine." In A. M. Freeman, H. I. Kaplan, and B. J. Sadock (Eds.), *Comprehensive Textbook of Psychiatry, II.* Baltimore: Williams and Wilkins, 1975, pp. 349–365.

Miller, Neal. "Conversation with Richard I. Evans." In R. I. Evans (Ed.), *The Making of Psychology.* New York: Knopf, 1976.

Miller, Neal, and Alfredo Carmona. "Modification of a Visceral Response, Salivation in Thirsty Dogs, by Instrumental Training with Water Reward." *Journal of Comparative and Physiological Psychology,* 1967, **63,** 1–6.

Miller, Neal, and Leo Dicara. "Instrumental Learning of Heart Rate Changes in Curarized Rats: Shaping, and Specificity to Discriminative Stimulus." *Journal of Comparative and Physiological Psychology,* 1967, **63,** 12–19.

Miller, Neal and Leo Dicara [1968a]. "Changes in Heart Rate Instrumentally Learned by Curarized Rats as Avoidance Responses." *Journal of Comparative and Physiological Psychology,* 1968, **65,** 8–12.

Miller, Neal, and Leo Dicara [1968b]. "Long Term Retention of Instrumentally Learned Heart-Rate Changes in the Curarized Rat." In Neal Miller, *The Selected Papers of Neal Miller,* Vol. II. Chicago: Aldine-Atherton, 1971, pp. 776–781 (paper originally published: *Communications in Behavioral Biology,* Part A, **2,** pp. 19–23. New York: Academic Press, 1968).

Miller, Neal, and John Dollard. *Social Learning and Imitation.* New Haven: Yale University Press, 1941.

Miller, Neal, and Doris Kraeling. "Displacement: Greater Generalization of Approach than Avoidance in a Generalized Approach-Avoidance Conflict." *Journal of Experimental Psychology,* 1952, **43,** 217–221.

Miller, Neal, and Edward Murray [1952a]. "Displacement: Steeper Gradient of Generalization of Avoidance than of Approach with Age of Habit Controlled." *Journal of Experimental Psychology,* 1952, **43,** 222–226.

Miller, Neal, and Edward Murray [1952b]. "Displacement and Conflict: Learnable Drive as a Basis for the Steeper Gradient of Avoidance than of Approach." *Journal of Experimental Psychology,* 1952, **43,** 227–231.

Miller, Neal, and Arlo K. Myers. "Failure to Find a Learned Drive Based on Hunger; Evidence for Learning Motivated by 'Exploration.'" *Journal of Comparative and Physiological Psychology,* 1954, **47,** 428–436.

Miller, Neal, and Donald Novin. "Failure to Condition Thirst Induced by Feeding Dry Food to Hungry Rats." *Journal of Comparative and Physiological Psychology,* 1962, **55,** 373–374.

Milne, A. A. *Winnie-the-Pooh.* New York: Dutton, 1926.

Mischel, Walter. *Personality and Assessment.* New York: John Wiley, 1968.

Mischel, Walter. "On the Empirical Dilemmas of Psychodynamic Approaches: Issues and Alternatives." *Journal of Abnormal Psychology,* 1973, **82,** 335–344.

Monte, Christopher F. *Psychology's Scientific Endeavor.* New York: Praeger, 1975.

Morgan, Clifford, and Richard A. King. *Introduction to Psychology* (3d ed.). New York: McGraw-Hill, 1966.

Moruzzi, G., and H. W. Magoun [1949]. "Brain Stem Reticular Formation and Activation of the EEG." In R. L. Isaacson (Ed.), *Basic Readings in Neuropsychology.* New York: Harper & Row, 1964 (paper originally published: *Electroencephalography and Clinical Neurophysiology,* 1949, **1,** 455–473).

Mosak, Harold, H. "Early Recollections as a Projective Technique." *Journal of Projective Techniques,* 1958, **22,** 302–311.

Mosak, Harold, H., and Richard R. Kopp. "The Early Recollections of Adler, Freud, and Jung." *Journal of Individual Psychology,* 1973, **29,** 157–166.

Moustakas, Clark E. (Ed.). *The Self: Explorations in Personal Growth.* New York: Harper, 1956.

Mowrer, O. Hobart. "A Stimulus-Response Analysis of Anxiety and Its Role as a Reinforcing Agent." *Psychological Review,* 1939, **46,** 553–565.

Mowrer, O. Hobart. "Identification: A Link between Learning Theory and Psychotherapy." In O. H. Mowrer, *Learning Theory and Personality Dynamics.* New York: Ronald Press, 1950, pp. 69–94.

Murphy, Gardner, and Joseph K. Kovach. *Historical Introduction to Modern Psychology* (3d ed.). New York: Harcourt Brace Jovanovich, 1972.

Murray, Henry A. *Explorations in Personality.* New York: Oxford University Press, 1938.

Olds, James, and Peter Milner. "Positive Reinforcement Produced by Electrical Stimulation of Septal Area and Other Regions of Rat Brain." *Journal of Comparative and Physiological Psychology,* 1954, **47,** 419–427.

Olds, James, and Marianne Olds. "Drives, Rewards and the Brain." In Theodore M. Newcomb (Ed.), *New Directions in Psychology,* Vol. 2. New York: Holt, Rinehart & Winston, 1965.

Orgler, Hertha. *Alfred Adler: The Man and His Work.* New York: Capricorn (Putnam), 1963.

Orne, Martin T. "On the Social Psychology of the Psychological Experiment: With Particular Reference to Demand Characteristics and Their Implications." *American Psychologist,* 1962, **17,** 776–783.

Orne, Martin T. "Demand Characteristics and the Concept of Quasi-Controls." In Robert Rosenthal and Ralph Rosnow (Eds.), *Artifact in Behavioral Research.* New York: Academic Press, 1969.

Orne, Martin T. "Communication by the Total Experimental Situation: Why It Is Important, How It Is Evaluated, and Its Significance for the Ecological Validity of Findings." In P. Pilner, L. Kramer, and T. Alloway (Eds.), *Communication and Affect.* New York: Academic Press, 1973, pp. 157–191.

Otto, Rudolf. *The Idea of the Holy: An Inquiry into the Non-Rational Factor in the Idea of the Divine and Its Relation to the Rational.* New York: Oxford University Press, 1923.

Ovsiankina, M. "Die wiederaufnahme unter-brochener handlungen." *Psychologische Forschung,* 1928, **11**, 302–379.

Papez, James W. "A Proposed Mechanism of Emotion." *Archives of Neurology and Psychiatry,* 1937, **38**, 725–744.

Parsons, T. "Family Structure and the Socialization of the Child." In T. Parsons and B. F. Bales (Eds.), *Family, Socialization and Interaction Process.* New York: Macmillan (Free Press), 1955.

Pavlov, Ivan P. *Conditioned Reflexes: An Investigation into the Physiological Activity of the Cortex.* G. V. Anrep (Trans.). New York: Dover, 1927.

Pavlov, Ivan P. *Lectures on Conditioned Reflexes,* Vol. 1. W. Horsley Gantt (Trans.). New York: International Publishers, 1928.

Piaget, Jean. *The Origins of Intelligence in Children.* New York: International Universities Press, 1952.

Piaget, Jean. *The Construction of Reality in the Child.* Margaret Cook (Trans.). New York: Basic Books, 1954.

Piaget, Jean, and Bärbel Inhelder. *The Psychology of the Child.* New York: Basic Books, 1969.

Popper, Karl. *The Logic of Scientific Discovery.* New York: Basic Books, 1959.

Popper, Karl. *Conjectures and Refutations.* New York: Basic Books, 1963.

Rachman, Stanley (Ed.). *Critical Essays on Psychoanalysis.* New York: Macmillan, 1963.

Rapaport, David. "A Historical Survey of Psychoanalytic Ego Psychology." *Psychological Issues,* Monograph No. 1, Vol. 1. New York: International Universities Press, 1959.

Rapaport, David. *Emotions and Memory.* New York: International Universities Press, 1971.

Rank, Otto [1929]. *The Trauma of Birth.* New York: Harper & Row, 1973.

Rank, Otto [1932]. *The Myth of the Birth of the Hero.* New York: Vintage (Random House), 1959.

Rank, Otto. *Beyond Psychology.* New York: Dover, 1941.

Reider, N. "The Demonology of Modern Psychiatry." *American Journal of Psychiatry,* 1955, **111**, 851–856 (as cited by Bandura & Walters, 1963, p. 30).

Rogers, Carl R. *Counseling and Psychotherapy.* Boston: Houghton Mifflin, 1942.

Rogers, Carl R. *Client-Centered Therapy.* Boston: Houghton Mifflin, 1951.

Rogers, Carl R. "The Case of Mrs. Oak: A Research Analysis." In Carl R. Rogers and Rosalind F. Dymond (Eds.), *Psychotherapy and Personality Change.* Chicago: University of Chicago Press, 1954, pp. 259–348.

Rogers, Carl R. "The Necessary and Sufficient Conditions of Therapeutic Personality Change." *Journal of Consulting Psychology,* 1957, **21**, 95–103.

Rogers, Carl R. [1958]. "A Tentative Scale for the Measurement of Process in Psychotherapy." In Eli A. Rubenstein and Morris B. Parloff (Eds.), *Research in Psychotherapy,* Vol. 1. Washington, D. C.: American Psychological Association, 1962.

Rogers, Carl R. "A Theory of Therapy, Personality and Inter-personal Relationships as Developed in the Client-Centered Framework." In Sigmund Koch (Ed.), *Psychology: A Study of a Science,* Vol. III, *Formulations of the Person in the Social Context.* New York: McGraw-Hill, 1959.

Rogers, Carl R. *On Becoming a Person.* Boston: Houghton Mifflin, 1961.

Rogers, Carl R. (Ed.). *The Therapeutic Relationship and Its Impact: A Study of Psychotherapy with Schizophrenics.* Madison: University of Wisconsin Press, 1967.

Rogers, Carl R. *Freedom to Learn.* Columbus, Ohio: Charles E. Merrill, 1969, esp. Chap. 14.

Rogers, Carl R. [1974a]. "In Retrospect: Forty-Six Years." *American Psychologist,* 1974, **29,** No. 2, 115–123.

Rogers, Carl R. [1974b]. "The Emerging Person: A New Revolution." Mimeograph paper for private circulation. La Jolla, Calif.: Center for Studies of the Person (also published: Richard I. Evans, *Carl Rogers: The Man and His Ideas: A Dialogue.* New York: Dutton, 1975.).

Rogers, Carl R. [1974c]. "Remarks on the Future of Client-Centered Therapy." In David A. Wexler and Laura North Rice (Eds.), *Innovations in Client-Centered Therapy.* New York: John Wiley, 1974.

Rogers, Carl R., and Rosalind F. Dymond. *Psychotherapy and Personality Change.* Chicago: University of Chicago Press, 1954.

Rokeach, Milton. *The Open and Closed Mind.* New York: Basic Books, 1960.

Rokeach, Milton. *The Nature of Human Values.* New York: Macmillan (Free Press), 1973.

Rosenhan, David L. "On Being Sane in Insane Places." *Science,* January 1973, **179,** 250–258.

Rosenthal, Robert, and Lenore F. Jacobson [1968a]. *Pygmalion in the Classroom: Teacher Expectations and Pupils' Intellectual Development.* New York: Holt, Rinehart & Winston, 1968.

Rosenthal, Robert, and Lenore F. Jacobson [1968b]. "Teacher Expectations for the Disadvantaged." *Scientific American,* April 1968.

Rosenthal, Robert, and Ralph L. Rosnow (Eds.). *Artifact in Behavioral Research.* New York: Academic Press, 1969.

Ruesch, Jurgen. *Therapeutic Communication.* New York: W. W. Norton, 1961.

Sargent, S. Stansfield. "Reaction to Frustration: A Critique and Hypothesis." *Psychological Review,* 1948, **55,** 108–114.

Schur, Max. *Freud, Living and Dying.* New York: International Universities Press, 1972.

Sears, Robert R. "Non-Aggressive Reactions to Frustration." *Psychological Review,* 1941, **48,** 343–346.

Sechrest, Lee. "The Psychology of Personal Constructs." In Joseph M. Wepmann and Ralph M. Heine (Eds.), *Concepts of Personality.* Chicago: Aldine, 1963.

Shagass, Charles, and Albert B. Kerenyi [1958]. "Neurophysiological Studies of Personality." In H. J. Eysenck (Ed.), *Readings in Extraversion-Intraversion,* Vol. 3: *Bearings on Basic Psychological Processes.* London: Staples, 1971 (paper originally published: *Journal of Nervous and Mental Diseases,* 1958, **126,** 141–147).

Sheffield, Fred. [1954]. "A Drive-Induction Theory of Reinforcement." In Ralph Haber (Ed.), *Current Research in Motivation.* New York: Holt, Rinehart & Winston, 1966 (paper originally read at Psychology Colloquium, Brown University, November 1954).

Sheffield, Fred [1960]. "New Evidence on the Drive-Induction Theory of Reinforcement." In Ralph Haber (Ed.), *Current Research in Motivation.* New York: Holt, Rinehart & Winston, 1966 (revised version of paper read at Stanford Psychology Colloquium, November 1960).

Sheffield, Fred, J. J. Wulff, and R. Backer. "Reward Value of Copulation without

Sex Drive Reduction." *Journal of Comparative and Physiological Psychology,* 1951, **44**, 3–8.

Shlien, John M. "Phenomenology and Personality." In Joseph W. Wepman and Ralph W. Heine (Eds.), *Concepts of Personality.* Chicago: Aldine, 1963.

Simmel, Georg. *Conflict and the Web of Group Affiliations.* K. H. Wolff and R. Bendix (Trans.). New York: Macmillan (Free Press), 1955.

Skinner, Burrhus F. *Science and Human Behavior.* New York: Macmillan (Free Press), 1953.

Skinner, B. F. "Critique of Psychoanalytic Concepts and Theories." In *Minnesota Studies in the Philosophy of Science,* Vol. 1. Minneapolis: University of Minneapolis Press, 1956.

Skinner, B. F. "Behaviorism at Fifty." *Science,* 1963, **140**, 951–958.

Skinner, B. F. *Beyond Freedom and Dignity.* New York: Knopf, 1971.

Skinner, B. F. *About Behaviorism.* New York: Knopf, 1974.

Skinner, B. F. "The Steep and Thorny Way to a Science of Behavior." *American Psychologist,* 1975, **30**, 42–49.

Speck, Ross V., and Carolyn Attneave. *Family Networks.* New York: Vintage (Random House), 1973.

Spielberger, Charles D., and L. Douglas DeNike. "Descriptive Behaviorism versus Cognitive Theory in Verbal Operant Conditioning." *Psychological Review,* 1966, **73**, 306–326.

Spielmann, J. [1963]. "The Relation between Personality and the Frequency and Duration of Involuntary Rest Pauses during Massed Practice" (unpublished doctoral dissertation, University of London; cited by H. J. Eysenck, 1953b).

Spitz, René. *The First Year of Life.* New York: International Universities Press, 1965.

Stephenson, William. *The Study of Behavior: Q-Technique and Its Methodology.* Chicago: University of Chicago Press, 1953.

Stern, Paul J. *C. G. Jung: The Haunted Prophet.* New York: Braziller, 1976.

Sullivan, Harry Stack [1953a]. *Conceptions of Modern Psychiatry.* New York: W. W. Norton, 1953.

Sullivan, Harry Stack [1953]. *The Interpersonal Theory of Psychiatry.* New York: W. W. Norton, 1953.

Sullivan, Harry Stack. *The Psychiatric Interview.* New York: W. W. Norton, 1954.

Sullivan, Harry Stack. *Clinical Studies in Psychiatry.* New York: W. W. Norton, 1956.

Sullivan, Harry Stack. *Schizophrenia as a Human Process.* New York: W. W. Norton, 1962.

Sullivan, Harry Stack. *The Fusion of Psychiatry and Social Science.* New York: W. W. Norton, 1964.

Sullivan, Harry Stack. *Personal Psychopathology.* New York: W. W. Norton, 1972.

Szasz, Thomas S. "The Myth of Mental Illness." *American Psychologist,* 1960, **15**, 113–118.

Szasz, Thomas S. *The Myth of Mental Illness: Foundations of a Theory of Personal Conduct.* New York: Harper & Row, 1961.

Szasz, Thomas S. *The Manufacture of Madness.* New York: Dell, 1970.

Teplov, B. M. "The Historical Development of Pavlov's Theory of Typological Differences in the Dog." In J. A. Gray (Ed. and Trans.), *Pavlov's Typology.* New York: Macmillan, 1964.

Thompson, Richard F. *Foundations of Physiological Psychology.* New York: Harper & Row, 1967.

Vaihinger, Hans [1911]. *The Philosophy of "As If."* New York: Harcourt, Brace and World, 1925.

Van der Post, Laurens. *Jung and the Story of Our Time.* New York: Pantheon (Random House), 1975.

Watson, John B. "Psychology as the Behaviorist Views It." *Psychological Review,* 1913, **20**, 158–177.

Watson, Robert I. *The Great Psychologists.* Philadelphia: Lippincott, 1963.

Weisstein, Naomi. "Psychology Constructs the Female, or the Fantasy Life of the Male Psychologist (with Some Attention to the Fantasies of His Friends, the Male Biologist and the Male Anthropologist)." In Ira Cohen (Ed.), *Perspectives on Psychology.* New York: Praeger, 1975 (paper originally published as "Kinder, Kuche, Kirche as Scientific Law: Psychology Constructs the Female," *New England Free Press,* 1971).

White, Robert W. "Competence and the Psychosexual Stages of Development." In M. R. Jones (Ed.), *Nebraska Symposium on Motivation.* Lincoln: University of Nebraska Press, 1960.

White, Robert R. *The Enterprise of Living: Growth and Organization in Personality.* New York: Holt, Rinehart & Winston, 1972, Chaps. 3–11.

Whiting, J. W. M. "Sorcery, Sin, and the Superego: A Cross-Cultural Study of Some Mechanisms of Social Control." In M. R. Jones (Ed.), *Nebraska Symposium on Motivation.* Lincoln: University of Nebraska Press, 1959.

Whiting, J. W. M. "Resource Mediation and Learning by Identification." In I. Iscoe and H. W. Stevenson (Eds.), *Personality Development in Children.* Austin: University of Texas Press, 1960, pp. 112–126.

Wilkinson, John. "How Good Is Current Behavior Theory?" In Harvey Wheeler (Ed.), *Beyond the Punitive Society.* San Francisco: W. H. Freeman, 1973.

Witkin, Herman A., R. B. Dyk, H. F. Faterson, D. R. Goodenough, and S. A. Karp. *Psychological Differentiation.* New York: John Wiley, 1962.

Wolpe, Joseph. *Psychotherapy by Reciprocal Inhibition.* Stanford, Calif.: Stanford University Press, 1958.

Wolpe, Joseph. *The Practice of Behavior Therapy* (2d ed.). New York: Pergamon Press, 1973.

Woodworth, Robert S., and Harold Schlosberg. *Experimental Psychology* (Rev. ed.). New York: Holt, Rinehart & Winston, 1954.

Yerkes, R. M., and J. D. Dodson. "The Relation of Strength of Stimulus to Rapidity of Habit Formation." *Journal of Comparative and Physiological Psychology,* 1908, **18**, 459–482.

Zeigarnik, Bluma [1927]. "On Finished and Unfinished Tasks." In Willis D. Ellis (Ed.), *A Source Book of Gestalt Psychology.* New York: Humanities Press, 1967 (paper originally published as "Uber das Behalten von erledigten und unerledigter Handlungen." *Psychologische Forschung,* 1927, **9**, 1–85).

Zilboorg, Gregory. *A History of Medical Psychology.* New York: W. W. Norton, 1941.

Sigmund Freud
National Library of Medicine,
Bethesda, Maryland

THE
THEORISTS

Carl G. Jung

Alfred Adler
Wide World Photos

Karen Horney
The Karen Horney
Psychoanalytic Institute and Center

Harry Stack Sullivan
The William Alanson White
Psychiatric Foundation, Inc.

R. D. Laing
Wide World Photos

George Kelly
Office of Public Affairs,
Brandeis University

Erik Erikson
Harvard University News Office

Erich Fromm
Pictorial Parade

Kurt Lewin
Wide World Photos

Gordon Allport
Harvard University News Office

Abraham Maslow
Office of Public Affairs,
Brandeis University

Carl Rogers
Channel 13—WNET

John Dollard

Neal Miller
American Psychological
Association Monitor

Albert Bandura

Hans Eysenck
The Times, London

INDEX

Eysenck, Hans J., 8, 14, 19, 54*n*, 199, 591–638
    dates, 27(*tab.*)
    introversion-extroversion study, 23–26,
        158, 159, 161, 593–602, 607–608, 609,
        610(*tab.*), 611(*tab.*), 612–13, 616–38
Eysenck, Sybil B. G., cited, 598, 634
Eysenck Personality Inventory, 634, 635
Eysenck Personality Questionnaire, 23, 634,
    635

factor analysis, 593, 595, 635
failure-success estimates, 400–13, 414, 416
Falk, John L., cited, 464
family, 212–13, 218, 230
    birth order in, 201, 203–205, 207
    coping strategies of, 305–308
    death fear and, 174, 305
    ethnicity and, 523
    experimental models, 583
    of Fromm, 383
    of Laing, 284–86, 309
    Role Construct Repertory Test, 312–19,
        320
    rules of, 302–305, 347, 510, 552, 553, 555
    schizophrenia and, 283, 302, 304–305, 309
    Sioux, 362, 364
    word association tests and, 132–33
    see also parents; siblings
fantasy; *see* dreaming; imagination
Faraday, Michael, 419
Farber, I. E., cited, 521
father relationships, 77–78, 129–30, 154, 155,
    212, 382
    of Adler, 173
    animus and, 151–52
    of "Anna O," 31, 32–33, 34–35
    competitive, 178, 190, 204, 206
    complementarity in, 306–307
    constructs of "Mildred Beal," 314, 316
        (*tab.*), 320
    of "Elisabeth von R.," 46, 48–49, 54
    of Erikson, 358, 359, 396
    of Freud, 62, 63–66, 82, 83, 84
    identification process, 71(*tab.*), 116, 117,
        118, 192, 203, 369, 582–83, 584
    of Jung, 142
    of Laing, 284–86
    maternal hostility and, 215
    seduction hypothesis and, 60–61, 69–70
fatigue, 614–15, 620
fear, 171–72, 279–82, 305–306, 376, 386
    illness and, 173, 361
    infancy and, 212–13, 249, 508–10, 552, 588
    in learning, 541–44, 545, 588, 605
    mob action and, 523, 525, 526, 528–29, 533
    modeling, in therapy, 585–87
    of self-knowledge, 495
    socioeconomic, 378–79, 523
    in warfare, 360–62
    see also anxiety
Fechner, Gustav, 107
Federn, Paul, 109

feeling, *see* emotion; sensation
Fehr, Elizabeth, 288
femininity, 231, 344–51; *see also* sexuality;
    women
feminist movement, 349–50
Fenichel, Otto, quoted, 9, 27
Feshbach, Seymour, cited, 540
Festinger, Leon, cited, 339, 402, 406, 407
fidelity, virtue of, 367, 373, 374, 398
field theory, of behavior, 400–43, 546
fixation of libido, 74–76, 78
fixed-role therapy, 323, 342
Fliess, Wilhelm, 60, 61, 63, 69, 76, 82
food; *see* hunger; nursing
force field theory, 400–43, 546
forgetting; *see* memory; repression
fragmentation of personality, 179, 180, 206
fragmentation of thought constructs, 324,
    330–31, 341
Frank, J. D., cited, 403
Franks, Cyril, cited, 619–20
Frazer, James George, 149
free association method, 41, 44, 55–56, 58, 77
    concentration and, 47–48
    dream elements and, 86
    self-analysis, 61–63
    word association studies and, 128–33, 167–
        68, 243–44
freedom
    alienation and, 377, 378–79, 382
    of choice, 320, 322–23, 328, 342, 377 (*see
        also* decision-making)
    mechanisms of escaping, 379–81, 393, 394,
        397
    sex differences and, 350
    in self-actualization, 496, 515, 516
French, J. D., cited, 625
Freud, Anna, 9–10, 112*n*, 352–53
    dream of, 80, 81, 124
    Erikson and, 351, 359, 360
Freud, Anna (sister of Sigmund Freud), 64,
    65
Freud, Philipp, 64, 65
Freud, Sigmund, 8–10, 17, 19, 20, 30–79, 137,
    172, 220, 527, 533, 542, 573
    Adler's break with, 176–81, 185, 205, 206,
        210
    Adlerian methods compared, by Jung,
        154–55
    Allport and, 444–45, 476
    on anal-sadistic personality, 393, 394
    Bandura and Walters on, 573, 575, 577,
        582, 584
    Breuer and, 30–36, 37, 40, 43, 44, 45, 76,
        99, 106–107
    dates, 27(*tab.*)
    on defense mechanisms, 227, 228, 230, 565
    on drive displacement, 185, 533, 534, 535,
        588
    ego concept changes of, 176–77, 351–52,
        353, 470

sympathetic magic, 149
Symposium, The (Plato), 110
synchronicity, 145, 163
syntaxic experience, 236, 240–41, 242(*tab.*), 263, 264, 265, 266(*tab.*)
systematic desensitization, 586–87
systematic "unconscious," 96
Szasz, Thomas S., 271, 272, 273, 308

taboo, 86–87, 388, 389
  family rules and metarules, 67, 75, 252, 284, 286, 287, 303, 309, 552, 553, 555, 558
"take for example this" (Cummings), 480
Tavistock Lectures (Jung), 158
technology, 384–85, 393, 394
  boredom and, 387–88
teething, 366
television, 493, 579–80
temperament theory, 199, 200(*tab.*), 598–602
  Pavlov and, 605–606, 607, 608, 610(*tab.*), 611 (*tab.*)
tension reduction, 106–107, 108
  Adler on, 179
  anxiety function in, 122, 541–42
  drive satisfaction and, 99, 522, 526–29, 530, 568, 613–14
  Fromm on, 111*n*
  mother-child empathy in, 249–50, 255, 265, 355
  by neurotic symptoms, 556–57, 558, 562, 565–67
  in task completion, 434–35, 436–39, 467, 474
  see also anxiety; catharsis
Teplov, B. M., 605, 606, 607, 608, 609–13, 620, 627
tests, 3, 8, 17–18, 446, 449, 466, 593–97, 602
  of aspiration levels, 400–403, 408–13, 596
  of auditory vigilance, 622–23, 635
  eye-blink, 618, 619–22
  of intelligence, 22, 596
  of interpersonal construct formation, 311–19, 342
  involuntary rest pauses, 622
  of language function in anxiety-mediation, 558–60
  memory, 434–35, 629–32
  of repression hypothesis, 54–55
  of self-perception, 323, 512–14
  of spatial organization, 344–47
thalamus, 623
Thanatos, 109, 111
"Theory and Experiment Relating Psychoanalytic Displacement to Stimulus-Response Generalization" (Miller), 575
therapist-client relationships
  of Breuer, 35–36, 39
  of Freud, 43, 44, 46, 47–48, 49, 52, 81, 444–45, 501–502
  at Mill Hill Hospital, 591–92
  of Rogers, 497–507, 512, 515–16

therapist-client relationships (*cont.*)
  transference, 105–106
"third force" psychology, 497
Thompson, Richard F., cited, 625
Thorndike, E. L., 521
thought, 94–95, 96, 151, 156, 168
  ARAS and, 625–26
  associative, 456
  Circumspection, Preemption, Control, 334–37
  development of, 236, 240–41, 242, 265, 329, 330–31, 468, 469
  dichotomous organizations of, 325–28, 336–37
  as ectopsychic function, 157, 158, 159–60, 161–62, 163
  fictional nature of, 191
  as human drive, 319–21, 329, 333, 334
  repression of, 556–62, 593, 594
  shared experience and, 331–33
thrift, 75–76
throne imagery, 144–45
thumb sucking, 66, 72, 76, 100
  selfhood and, 251–52
thwarting hypothesis of aggression, 529–30, 531–33
time
  awareness of, 157, 235, 376
  behavior and, 401(*fig.*), 413, 418(*tab.*), 421, 424, 441
  causality and, 149, 153, 163, 238–39, 242 (*tab.*) (*see also* causality)
  Christ and, 165
  chronology of personality theory, 27
  futurity, 147, 150, 276, 277, 308, 334, 337, 416, 449
  the *id* and, 113
  individual change in, 329, 449–50, 451, 477–78
  inner and external events and, 145
  life space and, 403, 414, 421, 423–24, 427, 428(*fig.*), 441
  memory and, 24–26, 63–64, 147
  peak experiences and, 493
  psychological laws and, 28
  similarities and recurrent themes in, 325, 326, 376
toilet training, 73, 74–75, 76, 78, 251–52, 254, 588
  autonomy and, 367–69
  frustration and, 552–53
Tomlinson, T. M., cited, 501
topology, 420
"totalism" of Murray, 17–18
traits, *see* characteristics
trait theory, 7–8, 9, 13(*tab.*), 14–15, 27, 448, 450–67, 476–77
transcendence need, 386, 389, 392
transcendent function, 163
transference phenomenon, 105–106, 482
transmarginal inhibition, 609, 612–13, 620, 627–28